Sarazm: A Site along the Proto-Silk Road at the Intersection of the Steppe and Oasis Cultures

# OXUS I

### STUDIES IN THE ARCHAEOLOGY & HISTORY OF CENTRAL ASIA, FROM THE CASPIAN SEA TO XINJIANG AND ALTAY

*General Editors*

Henri-Paul Francfort, *Académie des Inscriptions et Belle-Lettres, CNRS, Paris*
Marc Lebeau, *European Centre for Upper Mesopotamian Studies, Brussels*

*Advisory Board*

Nona Avanessova, *National University of Samarkand*
Raffaele Biscione, *Consiglio Nazionale delle Ricerche, Roma*
Saidmurad Bobomullaev, *Academy of Sciences of Tajikistan, Dushanbe*
Nikolaus Boroffka, *Deutsches Archäologisches Institut, Eurasia Department, Berlin*
Jean Bourgeois, *Universiteit Gent*
Frédérique Brunet, *CNRS, UMR 7041, Nanterre*
Corinne Debaine, *CNRS, UMR 7041, Nanterre*
Nadezhda Dubova, *Russian Academy of Sciences, Moscow*
Abdurasul Idriss, *Institute of Archaeology of the Autonomous Uighur Region, Urumqi, Xinjiang*
Lyubov Kircho, *Russian Academy of Sciences, Saint Petersburg*
Carl C. Lamberg-Karlovsky, *Harvard University, Cambridge MA*
Benjamin Mutin, *Sorbonne Université, UMR 8167 Orient & Méditerranée*
Marcel Otte, *Université de Liège*
Natalia Polosmak, *Russian Academy of Sciences, Novosibirsk*
Rauf Razzokov, *Historical and Culture Monument of Sarazm, Penjikent*
Rouhollah Shirazi, *University of Sistan and Baluchestan, Zahedan*
Ali Vahdati, *Provincial Office of Cultural Heritage, Handicrafts, and Tourism, Mashad*

OXUS is a part of the ARWA Collection

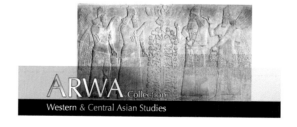

**Cover image:** Satellite image of the Zeravshan Valley between Tajikistan and Uzbekistan with location of Sarazm (basemap NASA), view of the architecture, and material culture from Excavation VII at Sarazm. The term 'Silk Road' is used here because it is convenient as it is a well-known term that designates past exchange networks between East Asia and Europe including more specifically throughout the Sogdian region where Sarazm lies, which was historically a key area within this exchange system. Yet, it is important to note here that the 'Silk Road', which was defined so by Ferdinand von Richthofen in the late nineteenth century, was neither a single route or road, nor based solely on silk.

# Sarazm: A Site along the Proto-Silk Road at the Intersection of the Steppe and Oasis Cultures

## Results from Excavation VII

by

Benjamin Mutin

BREPOLS

British Library Cataloguing in Publication Data

A catalogue record for this book is available from the British Library.

**Keywords:** Sarazm, Tajikistan, Central Asia, Middle Asia, Eurasian Steppe, Chalcolithic, Bronze Age, Archaeology, Intercultural Interaction.

The research and compilation of the manuscript for this final publication were made possible through a generous grant from The Shelby White and Leon Levy Program for Archaeological Publications.

Colour printing funded by the
UMR 8167 Orient & Méditerranée.

© 2023, Brepols Publishers n.v., Turnhout, Belgium

All rights reserved. No part of this publication may be reproduced, stored in a retrieval system, or transmitted, in any form or by any means, electronic, mechanical, photocopying, recording, or otherwise, without the prior permission of the publisher.

ISBN: 978-2-503-60294-3
e-ISBN: 978-2-503-60295-0
DOI: 10.1484/M.OXUS-EB.5.131848
D/2023/0095/145

Printed in the EU on acid-free paper

## Contents

List of Illustrations . . . . . . . . . . . . . . . . . . . . . . . . . . . . . . . . . . . . . . . . . . . . . . . . . . . . . . vii

List of Tables . . . . . . . . . . . . . . . . . . . . . . . . . . . . . . . . . . . . . . . . . . . . . . . . . . . . . . . . . . . xvii

Acknowledgements . . . . . . . . . . . . . . . . . . . . . . . . . . . . . . . . . . . . . . . . . . . . . . . . . . . . . xxi

Abbreviations . . . . . . . . . . . . . . . . . . . . . . . . . . . . . . . . . . . . . . . . . . . . . . . . . . . . . . . . . xxii

Preface . . . . . . . . . . . . . . . . . . . . . . . . . . . . . . . . . . . . . . . . . . . . . . . . . . . . . . . . . . . . . . . xxiii

**1. Contextualizing Sarazm and Excavation VII** . . . . . . . . . . . . . . . . . . . . . . . . . . . . . . . 1
    Sarazm as a 'Multicultural' Site . . . . . . . . . . . . . . . . . . . . . . . . . . . . . . . . . . . . . . . . 3
    Chronology . . . . . . . . . . . . . . . . . . . . . . . . . . . . . . . . . . . . . . . . . . . . . . . . . . . . . . . . 5
    Settlement Pattern, Function, and Society . . . . . . . . . . . . . . . . . . . . . . . . . . . . . . . 7
    Land, Minerals, and Metals: The *raison(s) d'être* of Sarazm . . . . . . . . . . . . . . . . . 9
    At the Intersection of the 'Middle Asian Interaction Sphere' and the Steppe Cultures . . 13
    Significance of Sarazm in the Understanding of the Origins of the Oxus Civilization . . . 16

**2. The Environmental Setting of Sarazm** . . . . . . . . . . . . . . . . . . . . . . . . . . . . . . . . . . . 17
    The Zeravshan River . . . . . . . . . . . . . . . . . . . . . . . . . . . . . . . . . . . . . . . . . . . . . . . . 17
    Mineral Resources . . . . . . . . . . . . . . . . . . . . . . . . . . . . . . . . . . . . . . . . . . . . . . . . . 17
    Climate . . . . . . . . . . . . . . . . . . . . . . . . . . . . . . . . . . . . . . . . . . . . . . . . . . . . . . . . . . . 23
    Topography, Geomorphology, and Micromorphology . . . . . . . . . . . . . . . . . . . . . 25
    Exploitation of Plant and Animal Resources . . . . . . . . . . . . . . . . . . . . . . . . . . . . . 27

**3. Archaeological Contexts** . . . . . . . . . . . . . . . . . . . . . . . . . . . . . . . . . . . . . . . . . . . . . . 33
    Digging the Archives . . . . . . . . . . . . . . . . . . . . . . . . . . . . . . . . . . . . . . . . . . . . . . . . 34
    Excavation Expanse, Stratigraphy, and Strategy . . . . . . . . . . . . . . . . . . . . . . . . . . 35
    Level I1 . . . . . . . . . . . . . . . . . . . . . . . . . . . . . . . . . . . . . . . . . . . . . . . . . . . . . . . . . . . 38
    Level I2 . . . . . . . . . . . . . . . . . . . . . . . . . . . . . . . . . . . . . . . . . . . . . . . . . . . . . . . . . . . 43
    Level I3 . . . . . . . . . . . . . . . . . . . . . . . . . . . . . . . . . . . . . . . . . . . . . . . . . . . . . . . . . . . 44
    Level I4 . . . . . . . . . . . . . . . . . . . . . . . . . . . . . . . . . . . . . . . . . . . . . . . . . . . . . . . . . . . 49
    Level I-North/East . . . . . . . . . . . . . . . . . . . . . . . . . . . . . . . . . . . . . . . . . . . . . . . . . . 50
    Level II1 . . . . . . . . . . . . . . . . . . . . . . . . . . . . . . . . . . . . . . . . . . . . . . . . . . . . . . . . . . . 51
    Level II2 . . . . . . . . . . . . . . . . . . . . . . . . . . . . . . . . . . . . . . . . . . . . . . . . . . . . . . . . . . . 55
    Level II-North/East . . . . . . . . . . . . . . . . . . . . . . . . . . . . . . . . . . . . . . . . . . . . . . . . . 56
    Level III1 . . . . . . . . . . . . . . . . . . . . . . . . . . . . . . . . . . . . . . . . . . . . . . . . . . . . . . . . . . 60
    Level III2 . . . . . . . . . . . . . . . . . . . . . . . . . . . . . . . . . . . . . . . . . . . . . . . . . . . . . . . . . . 61
    Level III2-North/East . . . . . . . . . . . . . . . . . . . . . . . . . . . . . . . . . . . . . . . . . . . . . . . . 65
    Level III3 . . . . . . . . . . . . . . . . . . . . . . . . . . . . . . . . . . . . . . . . . . . . . . . . . . . . . . . . . . 67
    Level III3-North/East . . . . . . . . . . . . . . . . . . . . . . . . . . . . . . . . . . . . . . . . . . . . . . . . 70
    Levels IV1–IV2 . . . . . . . . . . . . . . . . . . . . . . . . . . . . . . . . . . . . . . . . . . . . . . . . . . . . . 71
    'Antique Tomb' . . . . . . . . . . . . . . . . . . . . . . . . . . . . . . . . . . . . . . . . . . . . . . . . . . . . 77
    Unallocated Context Numbers . . . . . . . . . . . . . . . . . . . . . . . . . . . . . . . . . . . . . . . . 77
    Functions of the Areas Exposed in Excavation VII . . . . . . . . . . . . . . . . . . . . . . . . 78
    Features and Architectural Aspects of Excavation VII
        and their Parallels at Sarazm and Beyond . . . . . . . . . . . . . . . . . . . . . . . . . . . . 79

## 4. Radiocarbon Dates . . . . . . . . . . . . . . . . . . . . . . . . . . . . . . . . . . . . . . . . . . . . . . . . . . . . . . . . . . . 95

## 5. Ceramic Vessels . . . . . . . . . . . . . . . . . . . . . . . . . . . . . . . . . . . . . . . . . . . . . . . . . . . . . . . . . . . 101
Recording System . . . . . . . . . . . . . . . . . . . . . . . . . . . . . . . . . . . . . . . . . . . . . . . . . . . . 101
Classification . . . . . . . . . . . . . . . . . . . . . . . . . . . . . . . . . . . . . . . . . . . . . . . . . . . . . . . . 101
Quantities . . . . . . . . . . . . . . . . . . . . . . . . . . . . . . . . . . . . . . . . . . . . . . . . . . . . . . . . . . 104
Groups 1 and 2 . . . . . . . . . . . . . . . . . . . . . . . . . . . . . . . . . . . . . . . . . . . . . . . . . . . . . . 105
Group 3 . . . . . . . . . . . . . . . . . . . . . . . . . . . . . . . . . . . . . . . . . . . . . . . . . . . . . . . . . . . . 117
Group 4 . . . . . . . . . . . . . . . . . . . . . . . . . . . . . . . . . . . . . . . . . . . . . . . . . . . . . . . . . . . . 120
Group 5 . . . . . . . . . . . . . . . . . . . . . . . . . . . . . . . . . . . . . . . . . . . . . . . . . . . . . . . . . . . . 123
Group 6 . . . . . . . . . . . . . . . . . . . . . . . . . . . . . . . . . . . . . . . . . . . . . . . . . . . . . . . . . . . . 135
Group 7: Misfired Fragments . . . . . . . . . . . . . . . . . . . . . . . . . . . . . . . . . . . . . . . . . . 136
Evidence for Ceramic Production at Sarazm . . . . . . . . . . . . . . . . . . . . . . . . . . . . . 136
Function of the Vessels . . . . . . . . . . . . . . . . . . . . . . . . . . . . . . . . . . . . . . . . . . . . . . . 137
Stratigraphic Distribution of the Ceramics . . . . . . . . . . . . . . . . . . . . . . . . . . . . . . . 138
Spatial Distribution of the Ceramics . . . . . . . . . . . . . . . . . . . . . . . . . . . . . . . . . . . . 141
Chrono-cultural Relationships . . . . . . . . . . . . . . . . . . . . . . . . . . . . . . . . . . . . . . . . 147

## 6. Small Finds . . . . . . . . . . . . . . . . . . . . . . . . . . . . . . . . . . . . . . . . . . . . . . . . . . . . . . . . . . . . . 165
Classification . . . . . . . . . . . . . . . . . . . . . . . . . . . . . . . . . . . . . . . . . . . . . . . . . . . . . . . 165
Quantities . . . . . . . . . . . . . . . . . . . . . . . . . . . . . . . . . . . . . . . . . . . . . . . . . . . . . . . . . . 166
Analysis and Terminology . . . . . . . . . . . . . . . . . . . . . . . . . . . . . . . . . . . . . . . . . . . . 167
Bone Industry . . . . . . . . . . . . . . . . . . . . . . . . . . . . . . . . . . . . . . . . . . . . . . . . . . . . . . 168
Shell Industry . . . . . . . . . . . . . . . . . . . . . . . . . . . . . . . . . . . . . . . . . . . . . . . . . . . . . . 169
Terracotta Industry . . . . . . . . . . . . . . . . . . . . . . . . . . . . . . . . . . . . . . . . . . . . . . . . . . 169
Chalcedony, Flint, Quartz Sandstone Knapped Lithic Industry . . . . . . . . . . . . . . 175
Quartz (Rock Crystal) Knapped Lithic Industry and Bead Making . . . . . . . . . . . . 179
Carnelian Industry . . . . . . . . . . . . . . . . . . . . . . . . . . . . . . . . . . . . . . . . . . . . . . . . . . 181
Lapis Lazuli Industry . . . . . . . . . . . . . . . . . . . . . . . . . . . . . . . . . . . . . . . . . . . . . . . . 183
Turquoise Industry . . . . . . . . . . . . . . . . . . . . . . . . . . . . . . . . . . . . . . . . . . . . . . . . . . 185
Steatite and Frit Industries . . . . . . . . . . . . . . . . . . . . . . . . . . . . . . . . . . . . . . . . . . . 186
Stone Industry . . . . . . . . . . . . . . . . . . . . . . . . . . . . . . . . . . . . . . . . . . . . . . . . . . . . . . 188
Pigment and Remains Relating to Pigment Preparation . . . . . . . . . . . . . . . . . . . . 205
Copper Industry . . . . . . . . . . . . . . . . . . . . . . . . . . . . . . . . . . . . . . . . . . . . . . . . . . . . 208
Lead Industry . . . . . . . . . . . . . . . . . . . . . . . . . . . . . . . . . . . . . . . . . . . . . . . . . . . . . . 213
Iron Industry . . . . . . . . . . . . . . . . . . . . . . . . . . . . . . . . . . . . . . . . . . . . . . . . . . . . . . . 216
Stratigraphic and Spatial Distribution of the Small Finds . . . . . . . . . . . . . . . . . . . 216
Activities in the Areas Exposed in Excavation VII . . . . . . . . . . . . . . . . . . . . . . . . . 227
Raw Material Procurement and Cultural Relationships . . . . . . . . . . . . . . . . . . . . 230

## 7. Conclusion . . . . . . . . . . . . . . . . . . . . . . . . . . . . . . . . . . . . . . . . . . . . . . . . . . . . . . . . . . . . . 233
Chronology . . . . . . . . . . . . . . . . . . . . . . . . . . . . . . . . . . . . . . . . . . . . . . . . . . . . . . . . 233
Nature of the Occupations and Cultural Relationships . . . . . . . . . . . . . . . . . . . . 236

Works Cited . . . . . . . . . . . . . . . . . . . . . . . . . . . . . . . . . . . . . . . . . . . . . . . . . . . . . . . . . . . . . . . 239

# List of Illustrations

## 1. Contextualizing Sarazm and Excavation VII

Figure 1.1: Map of Middle Asia with location of Sarazm and additional archaeological sites mentioned in the text. ...................................................... 1

Figure 1.2: View of the protected archaeological area of Sarazm and villages and agricultural fields around. ...................................................... 2

Figure 1.3: Map of Sarazm with location of the main excavations (in grey) conducted until 2014. Map by J. Suire and R. Schwertdner (Mission Archéologique Française en Asie Centrale), modified by B. Mutin. .................. 2

Figure 1.4: View of Excavation VII within the south-eastern portion of the protected archaeological area of Sarazm. ...................................................... 3

Figure 1.5: View of Excavation VII at Sarazm in 1989. ...................................................... 3

Figure 1.6: View of Excavation VII at Sarazm in 1989. ...................................................... 3

## 2. The Environmental Setting of Sarazm

Figure 2.1: Map of the Zeravshan River in Tajikistan and Uzbekistan, with location of Sarazm and main current cities. ...................................................... 17

Figure 2.2: Map of the Zeravshan Valley and surrounding areas with location of the main geological and mineral resources. Adapted from the geological and mineral resource map of Tajikistan. ...................................................... 18

Figure 2.3: Map of the mineral resources available within a c. 350–450 km area around Sarazm. ...................................................... 18

Figure 2.4: Geomorphological map of the Zeravshan Valley around Sarazm. .................. 26

Figure 2.5: Alluvial terraces of the Zeravshan Valley near Sarazm. ........................... 26

Figure 2.6: Alluvial terraces of the Zeravshan Valley near Sarazm viewed in section. ....... 27

## 3. Archaeological Contexts

Plate 3.1: Sarazm, Excavation VII, architecture exposed in Levels I to IV, based on R. Besenval archives. ...................................................... 33

Plate 3.2: Sarazm, Excavation VII, north-west section in sq. L13–L14 and north-east section in sq. L15, based on R. Besenval archives. .......................... 34

Plate 3.3: Sarazm, Excavation VII, plan of Level I1, based on R. Besenval archives. .......... 42

| | | |
|---|---|---|
| Plate 3.4: | Sarazm, Excavation VII, plan of Level I2, based on R. Besenval archives. | 42 |
| Plate 3.5: | Sarazm, Excavation VII, plan of Level I3, based on R. Besenval archives. | 45 |
| Plate 3.6: | Sarazm, Excavation VII, plan of Level I4, based on R. Besenval archives. | 47 |
| Plate 3.7: | Sarazm, Excavation VII, sketch plan of Level I-North/East, based on R. Besenval archives. | 50 |
| Plate 3.8: | Sarazm, Excavation VII, plan of Level II1, based on R. Besenval archives. | 53 |
| Plate 3.9: | Sarazm, Excavation VII, plan of Level II2, based on R. Besenval archives. | 55 |
| Plate 3.10: | Sarazm, Excavation VII, sketch plan of Level II-North/East, based on R. Besenval archives. | 57 |
| Plate 3.11: | Sarazm, Excavation VII, plan of Level III1, based on R. Besenval archives. | 59 |
| Plate 3.12: | Sarazm, Excavation VII, plan of Level III2, based on R. Besenval archives. | 61 |
| Plate 3.13: | Sarazm, Excavation VII, sketch plan of Level III2-North/East, based on R. Besenval archives. | 64 |
| Plate 3.14: | Sarazm, Excavation VII, plan of Level III3, based on R. Besenval archives. | 66 |
| Plate 3.15: | Sarazm, Excavation VII, sketch plan of Level III3-North/East, based on R. Besenval archives. | 69 |
| Plate 3.16: | Sarazm, Excavation VII, plan of Levels IV1–IV2, based on R. Besenval archives. | 71 |
| Plate 3.17: | Sarazm, Excavation VII, sketch plan and section of the 'Antique tomb', based on R. Besenval archives. | 78 |
| Plate 3.18: | Sarazm, architecture exposed in Excavation VII, based on R. Besenval archives. | 86 |
| Plate 3.19: | Sarazm, architecture exposed in Excavations II, IV, V, IX, and XII. | 87 |
| Plate 3.20: | Sarazm, architecture exposed in Excavations III and XI. | 91 |
| Figure 3.1: | Sarazm, present-day surface of Excavation VII. South-westward view. | 36 |
| Figure 3.2: | Sarazm, Excavation VII, test trench opened in 1984 in sq. L13 and L14. South-westward view. | 36 |
| Figure 3.3: | Sarazm, Excavation VII, architectural levels identified within the 1984 test trench: Levels I3, II1, and III2. North-eastward view. | 36 |
| Figure 3.4: | Sarazm, Excavation VII, architectural levels identified within the 1984 test trench: Levels I1, I3, and II1. North-eastward view. | 36 |
| Figure 3.5: | Sarazm, Excavation VII, Level I1. South-eastward view. | 39 |
| Figure 3.6: | Sarazm, Excavation VII, Level I1. Northward view. | 39 |
| Figure 3.7: | Sarazm, Excavation VII, Level I1, Wall 6 with view of niche OF1 on the left. Southward view. | 39 |
| Figure 3.8: | Sarazm, Excavation VII, Level I1, Wall 6. Northward view. | 39 |

# LIST OF ILLUSTRATIONS

Figure 3.9: Sarazm, Excavation VII, Level I1, Hearth 1. .................................................. 39

Figure 3.10: Sarazm, Excavation VII, Level I1, stone accumulation (OF2) inside Room 2. North-westward view. ................................................ 39

Figure 3.11: Sarazm, Excavation VII, Level I1, stone accumulation (OF2) inside Room 2. South-eastward view. ................................................ 40

Figure 3.12: Sarazm, Excavation VII, Level I1, Room 3. South-eastward view. .................. 40

Figure 3.13: Sarazm, Excavation VII, Level I1, Room 3. Southward view. ....................... 40

Figure 3.14: Sarazm, Excavation VII, Level I1, Room 3, Hearth 2. Northward view. ............ 40

Figure 3.15: Sarazm, Excavation VII, Level I1, Room 3, postholes. Southward view. ........... 40

Figure 3.16: Sarazm, Excavation VII, Level I1, Room 4, Hearth 3. ............................ 40

Figure 3.17: Sarazm, Excavation VII, Level I1, Room 4 with view of the postholes in Room 3 on the left. South-eastward view. .................................................. 41

Figure 3.18: Sarazm, Excavation VII, Level I1, Room 4. North-westward view. ................ 41

Figure 3.19: Sarazm, Excavation VII, Level I1, Alleyway 1 south of Wall 6. Southward view. ... 41

Figure 3.20: Sarazm, Excavation VII, Level I1, Alleyway 1, layer or shallow pit containing animal bones and stones. ................................................ 43

Figure 3.21: Sarazm, Excavation VII, Level I2, postholes. North-westward view. .............. 43

Figure 3.22: Sarazm, Excavation VII, Level I3 with view of Alleyway 2 in the back. South-eastward view. ................................................................ 44

Figure 3.23: Sarazm, Excavation VII, Level I3, Room 5 with Hearth 4 and Room 9. Northward view. .................................................................... 46

Figure 3.24: Sarazm, Excavation VII, Level I3, Room 5, Wall 28. Southward view. .............. 46

Figure 3.25: Sarazm, Excavation VII, Level I3, Room 5, Wall 28 with red plaster fragments on and around it. Northward view. .......................................... 46

Figure 3.26: Sarazm, Excavation VII, Level I3, Room 5, Hearth 4. Northward view. ............ 46

Figure 3.27: Sarazm, Excavation VII, Level I3, Rooms 6 and 7, from left to right. North-eastward view. .............................................................. 46

Figure 3.28: Sarazm, Excavation VII, Level I3, Room 9 with Wall 28 in the middle ground and left side and Walls 30 and 31 on the right side. Level II1 Wall 8 and Level III2 Wall 6 are also visible. Southward view. ..................... 46

Figure 3.29: Sarazm, Excavation VII, Level I3, Room 9, Hearth 6. ............................ 48

Figure 3.30: Sarazm, Excavation VII, Level I3, Alleyway 2. Eastward view. .................... 48

Figure 3.31: Sarazm, Excavation VII, Level I3, detail of the surface of Alleyway 2. ............ 48

Figure 3.32: Sarazm, Excavation VII, Level I4, Hearths 7, 8, and 9. South-eastward view. ...... 48

Figure 3.33: Sarazm, Excavation VII, Level I4, postholes. ..................................... 49

Figure 3.34: Sarazm, Excavation VII, Level I4, postholes. ................................... 49

Figure 3.35: Sarazm, Excavation VII, Level II1, Rooms 1 and 2. South-westward view. ......... 52

Figure 3.36: Sarazm, Excavation VII, Level II1, Rooms 1 and 2. South-westward view. ......... 52

Figure 3.37: Sarazm, Excavation VII, Level II1, Room 2, Hearth 1. North-westward view. ...... 52

Figure 3.38: Sarazm, Excavation VII, Level II1, Walls 1 and 7 and Wall 8.
North-westward view. ................................................................. 53

Figure 3.39: Sarazm, Excavation VII, Level II1 Wall 8, Level III2 Wall 6, Level I3
Wall 31, and Level III2 Wall 12 from right to left. Northward view. ................ 53

Figure 3.40: Sarazm, Excavation VII, Level II1, Area 1, charred surface. ...................... 54

Figure 3.41: Sarazm, Excavation VII, Level II2, Area 3, postholes and Hearth 4.
South-eastward view. ................................................................. 54

Figure 3.42: Sarazm, Excavation VII, Level II2, Area 3, postholes. South-eastward view. ....... 54

Figure 3.43: Sarazm, Excavation VII, Level II2, Area 3, Hearth 5. South-westward view. ....... 56

Figure 3.44: Sarazm, Excavation VII, Level III1, Room 1, Hearth 1. ........................... 60

Figure 3.45: Sarazm, Excavation VII, Level III1, Pit 1. ....................................... 60

Figure 3.46: Sarazm, Excavation VII, Level III1, Pit 1. ....................................... 60

Figure 3.47: Sarazm, Excavation VII, Level III2, Room 4, Room 3, Rooms 7, 6, and 5.
South-eastward view. ................................................................. 60

Figure 3.48: Sarazm, Excavation VII, Level III2, Room 4. North-eastward view. ............... 63

Figure 3.49: Sarazm, Excavation VII, Level III2, Room 3, Hearth 3. ........................... 63

Figure 3.50: Sarazm, Excavation VII, Level III2, Room 3, Hearth 3. ........................... 63

Figure 3.51: Sarazm, Excavation VII, Level III2, Room 3, Pit 2. ............................... 63

Figure 3.52: Sarazm, Excavation VII, Level III2, Rooms 5, 6, and 7. North-westward view. ..... 64

Figure 3.53: Sarazm, Excavation VII, Level III2, Rooms 7, 6, and 5. South-eastward view. ..... 64

Figure 3.54: Sarazm, Excavation VII, Level III2, Room 5. South-eastward view. ............... 64

Figure 3.55: Sarazm, Excavation VII, Level III2, Room 5, Hearth 5. South-eastward view. ..... 66

Figure 3.56: Sarazm, Excavation VII, Level III3, Hearths 7 and 8. North-eastward view. ....... 66

Figure 3.57: Sarazm, Excavation VII, Level III3, Hearth 8. South-eastward view. .............. 68

Figure 3.58: Sarazm, Excavation VII, Level III3, Hearth 9. ................................... 68

Figure 3.59: Sarazm, Excavation VII, Level III3, Hearth 10. .................................. 68

Figure 3.60: Sarazm, Excavation VII, Level III3, Hearth 10. .................................. 68

Figure 3.61: Sarazm, Excavation VII, Level III3, Hearth 13. .................................. 68

# LIST OF ILLUSTRATIONS

Figure 3.62: Sarazm, Excavation VII, Level III3, Hearth 13. .................................................. 68

Figure 3.63: Sarazm, Excavation VII, Level III3, Pit 7,
with sherds of pottery and stones inside. ........................................................... 69

Figure 3.64: Sarazm, Excavation VII, Level IV1. North-eastward view. .................................. 73

Figure 3.65: Sarazm, Excavation VII, Level IV1, Room 4. North-eastward view. .................. 73

Figure 3.66: Sarazm, Excavation VII, Level IV1, Room 4, view of the clay lumps
with reed impressions. ....................................................................................... 73

Figure 3.67: Sarazm, Excavation VII, Level IV1, Room 4, ceramic fragments.
South-eastward view. ......................................................................................... 73

Figure 3.68: Sarazm, Excavation VII, Level IV1, Room 5, ceramic fragments. Westward view. .. 74

Figure 3.69: Sarazm, Excavation VII, Level IV1, Room 5, ceramic fragments. .................... 74

Figure 3.70: Sarazm, Excavation VII, Level IV1, Room 5. South-westward view. ................ 74

Figure 3.71: Sarazm, Excavation VII, Level IV1, Room 2. North-eastward view. ................ 74

Figure 3.72: Sarazm, Excavation VII, Level IV1, Room 2, ceramic fragments. .................... 74

Figure 3.73: Sarazm, Excavation VII, Level IV1, Room 2, postholes and stones.
South-westward view. ......................................................................................... 75

Figure 3.74: Sarazm, Excavation VII, Level IV1, Room 2, postholes and stones.
Westward view. ................................................................................................... 75

Figure 3.75: Sarazm, Excavation VII, Level IV1, Room 6, stones. South-westward view. ...... 75

Figure 3.76: Sarazm, Excavation VII, Level IV2, Hearth 1. South-westward view. .............. 75

Figure 3.77: Sarazm, Excavation VII, Levels IV1–IV2, architecture exposed in
Area 4. South-eastward view. ............................................................................. 76

Figure 3.78: Sarazm, Excavation VII, Levels IV1–IV2, architecture exposed in
Area 4. North-westward view. ............................................................................. 76

Figure 3.79: Sarazm, Excavation VII, Level IV2, Area 3, Hearth 2. Southward view. ............ 76

Figure 3.80: Sarazm, Excavation VII, Level IV2, Area 3, Hearth 2 (right). North-
westward view. ................................................................................................... 76

Figure 3.81: Sarazm, Excavation VII, Level IV2, Area 3, stones and ceramic
fragments. Eastward view. .................................................................................. 76

Figure 3.82: Sarazm, Excavation VII, plough tracks underneath the first natural
fill of the site. North-westward view. .................................................................. 76

Figure 3.83: Sarazm, Excavation VII, plough tracks underneath the first natural
fill of the site. ...................................................................................................... 77

Figure 3.84: Sarazm, Excavation VII, 'Antique tomb'. ......................................................... 79

Figure 3.85: Sarazm, Excavation VII, 'Antique tomb'. ......................................................... 79

Figure 3.86: Sarazm, Excavation VII, 'Antique tomb'. ... 79

Figure 3.87: Sarazm, Excavation VII, Level IV1, Room 3, clay lump with wood beam impressions. ... 86

Graph 3.1: Lengths, widths, and heights measured on the mud bricks from Sarazm. ... 82

Graph 3.2: Box and whisker plot showing the minimum, first quartile, median, third quartile, and maximum of the lengths, widths, and heights measured on the mud bricks from Sarazm. Graph based on the values and means in Table 3.18. ... 82

## 4. Radiocarbon Dates

Graph 4.1: Calibrated radiocarbon dates from Sarazm Excavation VII (95.4 per cent) presented unmodelled and after Bayesian model was applied to them (Multiple plot). ... 95

Graph 4.2: Calibrated radiocarbon dates from Sarazm Excavation VII (95.4 per cent) presented unmodelled and after Bayesian model was applied to them (Curve plot). ... 95

Graph 4.3: Calibrated radiocarbon dates from Sarazm (68.2 per cent, 95.4 per cent, 99.7 per cent). ... 97

## 5. Ceramic Vessels

Plate 5.1: Sections of ceramics from Sarazm photographed using a digital microscope, Groups 1, 2, and 3. ... 102

Plate 5.2: Sections of ceramics from Sarazm photographed using a digital microscope, Groups 4, 5, and 6. ... 103

Plate 5.3: Sarazm, Excavation VII, Group 1–2 bowls. ... 108

Plate 5.4: Sarazm, Excavation VII, Group 1–2 bowls. ... 109

Plate 5.5: Sarazm, Excavation VII, Group 1–2 bowls and pots. ... 110

Plate 5.6: Sarazm, Excavation VII, Group 1–2 bowls, deep bowls, and vats. ... 111

Plate 5.7: Sarazm, Excavation VII, Group 1–2 hole-mouth jars. ... 112

Plate 5.8: Sarazm, Excavation VII, Group 1–2 hole-mouth jars. ... 113

Plate 5.9: Sarazm, Excavation VII, Group 1–2 hole-mouth jars. ... 113

Plate 5.10: Sarazm, Excavation VII, Group 1–2 jars. ... 114

Plate 5.11: Sarazm, Excavation VII, Group 1–2 jars with out-flared rims and necked jars. ... 115

Plate 5.12: Sarazm, Excavation VII, Group 1 necked jar. ... 116

Plate 5.13: Sarazm, Excavation VII, Group 1–2 bases. ... 116

Plate 5.14: Sarazm, Excavation VII, Group 3 vats. ... 119

# LIST OF ILLUSTRATIONS

Plate 5.15: Sarazm, Excavation VII, Group 3 hole-mouth jars/bowls with incurving rims. ... 121

Plate 5.16: Sarazm, Excavation VII, Group 3 jars with out-flared rims and necked jars. ..... 122

Plate 5.17: Sarazm, Excavation VII, Group 3 rare forms. ..... 126

Plate 5.18: Sarazm, Excavation VII, Group 4 ceramics. ..... 126

Plate 5.19: Sarazm, Excavation VII, Group 5 bowls. ..... 126

Plate 5.20: Sarazm, Excavation VII, Group 5 bowls. ..... 127

Plate 5.21: Sarazm, Excavation VII, Group 5 deep bowls and goblets. ..... 129

Plate 5.22: Sarazm, Excavation VII, Group 5 jar. ..... 129

Plate 5.23: Sarazm, Excavation VII, Group 5 necked jars. ..... 131

Plate 5.24: Sarazm, Excavation VII, Group 6 necked jar. ..... 135

Plate 5.25: Sarazm, Excavation VII, Group 6 necked jar. ..... 135

Plate 5.26: Sarazm, Excavation VII, Group 6 sherds. ..... 135

Plate 5.27: Distribution of ceramic individuals in Sarazm Excavation VII Level I1. ..... 143

Plate 5.28: Distribution of ceramic individuals in Sarazm Excavation VII Level I3. ..... 144

Plate 5.29: Distribution of ceramic individuals in Sarazm Excavation VII Level II1. ..... 145

Plate 5.30: Distribution of ceramic individuals in Sarazm Excavation VII Level III2. ..... 146

Plate 5.31: Distribution of ceramic individuals in Sarazm Excavation VII Level III3. ..... 147

Plate 5.32: Distribution of ceramic individuals in Sarazm Excavation VII Levels IV1–IV2. ... 148

Figure 5.1: Sarazm, Excavation VII, Group 1 ceramics. ..... 106

Figure 5.2: Sarazm, Excavation VII, Group 1–2 ceramics. ..... 107

Figure 5.3: Sarazm, Excavation VII, Group 1 necked jar (SZM/86/VII/99/V). ..... 117

Figure 5.4: Sarazm, Excavation VII, Group 1 necked jar (SZM/86/VII/99/V), detail. ..... 117

Figure 5.5: Sarazm, Excavation VII, Group 3 ceramics. ..... 118

Figure 5.6: Sarazm, Excavation VII, Group 4 ceramics. ..... 124

Figure 5.7: Sarazm, Excavation VII, Group 5 ceramics. ..... 125

Figure 5.8: Sarazm, Excavation VII, Group 5 necked jar (SZM/86/VII/102/VIII). ..... 130

Figure 5.9: Sarazm, Excavation VII, Group 5 necked jar (SZM/86/VII/102/VIII). ..... 130

Figure 5.10: Sarazm, Excavation VII, Group 5 necked jar (SZM/86/VII/101/VII). ..... 132

Figure 5.11: Sarazm, Excavation VII, Group 5 necked jar (SZM/86/VII/89/II). ..... 132

Figure 5.12: Sarazm, Excavation VII, Group 5 necked jar (SZM/86/VII/90/III). ..... 132

Figure 5.13: Sarazm, Excavation VII, Group 6 necked jar (SZM/86/VII/91/IV). ..... 137

Figure 5.14: Sarazm, Excavation VII, Group 6 necked jar (SZM/86/VII/91/IV), detail. ....... 137

Figure 5.15: Sarazm, Excavation VII, Group 6 necked jar (SZM/86/VII/104/X). ............. 137

Figure 5.16: Sarazm, Excavation VII, misfired ceramic fragments. ........................ 137

Graph 5.1: Minimum Number of ceramic Individuals (MNI) from Sarazm Excavation VII and its distribution across the stylistic groups and archaeological levels identified within this excavation. ...................... 140

Graph 5.2: Number of sherds from Sarazm Excavation VII and its distribution across the archaeological levels identified within this excavation. ............. 141

Graph 5.3: Minimum Number of ceramic Individuals (MNI) from Sarazm Excavation VII and its distribution across the stylistic groups and archaeological levels identified within this excavation. ...................... 142

## 6. Small Finds

Plate 6.1: Distribution of small finds in Sarazm Excavation VII Level I1. ................. 218

Plate 6.2: Distribution of small finds in Sarazm Excavation VII Level I3. ................. 219

Plate 6.3: Distribution of small finds in Sarazm Excavation VII Level I4. ................. 220

Plate 6.4: Distribution of small finds in Sarazm Excavation VII Level I-North/East. ....... 221

Plate 6.5: Distribution of small finds in Sarazm Excavation VII Level II1. ................ 222

Plate 6.6: Distribution of small finds in Sarazm Excavation VII Level II2. ................ 223

Plate 6.7: Distribution of small finds in Sarazm Excavation VII Level II-North/East. ...... 224

Plate 6.8: Distribution of small finds in Sarazm Excavation VII Level III1. ............... 225

Plate 6.9: Distribution of small finds in Sarazm Excavation VII Level III2. ............... 225

Plate 6.10: Distribution of small finds in Sarazm Excavation VII Level III2-North/East. .... 226

Plate 6.11: Distribution of small finds in Sarazm Excavation VII Level III3. .............. 227

Plate 6.12: Distribution of small finds in Sarazm Excavation VII Levels IV1–IV2. .......... 228

Figure 6.1: Bone industry from Sarazm Excavation VII. ................................. 168

Figure 6.2: Shell industry from Sarazm Excavation VII. ................................ 169

Figure 6.3: Terracotta industry from Sarazm Excavation VII: perforated discs. ............ 171

Figure 6.4: Terracotta industry from Sarazm Excavation VII: discs. ..................... 172

Figure 6.5: Terracotta figurines from Sarazm: Excavation VII and Excavation IV. .......... 173

Figure 6.6: Chalcedony, flint, quartz sandstone knapped lithic industry from Sarazm Excavation VII. ........................................................ 175

Figure 6.7: Quartz (rock crystal) knapped lithic industry and bead making from Sarazm Excavation VII. ........................................................ 181

# LIST OF ILLUSTRATIONS

Figure 6.8: Beads, pendants, and raw mineral from Sarazm Excavation VII. ................184

Figure 6.9: Stone decorative tiles(?) from Sarazm Excavation VII: SF65 and SF331. .........189

Figure 6.10: Stone discs from Sarazm Excavation VII. ......................................190

Figure 6.11: Stone finials from Sarazm Excavation VII. ....................................191

Figure 6.12: Stone containers from Sarazm Excavation VII. ................................193

Figure 6.13: Ground stones from Sarazm Excavation VII. ..................................194

Figure 6.14: Hammer/grinding stones from Sarazm Excavation VII. .......................196

Figure 6.15: Stone pestles/sharpeners from Sarazm Excavation VII. ......................198

Figure 6.16: Stone sharpener from Sarazm Excavation VII (SF275). .......................199

Figure 6.17: Cobble flakes from Sarazm Excavation VII. ...................................201

Figure 6.18: Stone pebbles from Sarazm Excavation VII. ..................................202

Figure 6.19: Stone weight(?) from Sarazm Excavation VII (SF27). .........................203

Figure 6.20: Stone weight(?) from Sarazm Excavation VII (SF93). .........................203

Figure 6.21: Stone weight(?) from Sarazm Excavation VII (SF163). ........................203

Figure 6.22: Stone raw material from Sarazm Excavation VII. .............................204

Figure 6.23: Records of pigment and of remains relating to pigment preparation from Sarazm Excavation VII. ..................................................207

Figure 6.24: Flat stone used for pigment preparation from Sarazm Excavation VII (SF10). ...208

Figure 6.25: Flat stone used for pigment preparation from Sarazm Excavation VII (SF26). ...208

Figure 6.26: Goethite from Sarazm Excavation VII (SF211). ...............................208

Figure 6.27: Copper objects from Sarazm Excavation VII. .................................211

Figure 6.28: Copper ore (Chrysocolla) from Sarazm Excavation VII (SF313). ..............213

Figure 6.29: Lead objects from Sarazm Excavation VII. ...................................215

Figure 6.30: Lead ore (galena)(?) from Sarazm Excavation VII (SF208). ...................215

Figure 6.31: Iron object from Sarazm Excavation VII (SF205). .............................216

# List of Tables

## 1. Contextualizing Sarazm and Excavation VII

Table 1.1: Chronological chart for Sarazm and sites in the Steppe, Central Asia, Middle Asia, South Asia, and Mesopotamia. ..................................................4

Table 1.2: Distribution of the four periods of Sarazm (Periods I to IV) across some of the main excavations at this site. ..................................................8

## 2. The Environmental Setting of Sarazm

Table 2.1: Mineral resources within *c.* 350–450 km around the Zeravshan Valley recorded in the Mineral Resources Data System of the US Geological Survey. ......19

Table 2.2: Botanical remains from Excavation VII. ..................................................28

Table 2.3: Results of the zooarchaeological analysis conducted by J. Desse on bones from Excavations IV and VII. ..................................................31

## 3. Archaeological Contexts

Table 3.1: Sarazm, Excavation VII, list of features in Level I1. ..............................38

Table 3.2: Sarazm, Excavation VII, list of features in Level I2. ..............................43

Table 3.3: Sarazm, Excavation VII, list of features in Level I3. ..............................44

Table 3.4: Sarazm, Excavation VII, list of features in Level I4. ..............................48

Table 3.5: Sarazm, Excavation VII, list of features in Level I-North/East. ...............51

Table 3.6: Sarazm, Excavation VII, list of features in Level II1. .............................52

Table 3.7: Sarazm, Excavation VII, list of features in Level II2. .............................56

Table 3.8: Sarazm, Excavation VII, list of features in Level II-North/East. ..............58

Table 3.9: Sarazm, Excavation VII, list of features in Level III1. ............................59

Table 3.10: Sarazm, Excavation VII, list of features in Level III2. ..........................62

Table 3.11: Sarazm, Excavation VII, list of features in Level III2-North/East. .........65

Table 3.12: Sarazm, Excavation VII, list of features in Level III3. ..........................67

Table 3.13: Sarazm, Excavation VII, list of features in Level III3-North/East. .........69

Table 3.14: Sarazm, Excavation VII, list of features in Level IV1–IV2. ...................72

Table 3.15: Sarazm, Excavation VII, natural deposits on top of Levels IV1–IV2. ............... 77

Table 3.16: Sarazm, Excavation VII, 'Antique tomb'. ........................................... 78

Table 3.17: Mud-brick sizes from Sarazm. ........................................................ 81

Table 3.18: Mud-brick sizes from Sarazm rearranged for calculation. ...................... 82

Table 3.19: Wall thicknesses measured in Excavation VII at Sarazm. ...................... 82

Table 3.20: Thicknesses recorded on walls made with rammed earth at Sarazm. ............ 83

Table 3.21: Posthole diameters recorded in Sarazm Excavation VII. ...................... 85

Table 3.22: Room interior areas recorded in Sarazm Excavation VII. ..................... 88

Table 3.23: Lengths and widths of the pilasters from Sarazm illustrated on Plates 3.19 and 3.20 as well as lengths of the spaces in between. ................. 90

Table 3.24: Widths measured on doorways in Sarazm Excavation VII. ..................... 91

Table 3.25: Available dimensions of hearths and pits with pebbles from Sarazm Excavation VII. ........................................................................... 92

## 4. Radiocarbon Dates

Table 4.1: Uncalibrated radiocarbon dates from Sarazm Excavation VII. .................... 95

Table 4.2: Calibrated radiocarbon dates from Sarazm Excavation VII (95.4 per cent) presented unmodelled and after Bayesian model was applied to them. ........... 96

Table 4.3: Uncalibrated radiocarbon dates from Sarazm Excavations II, III, IV, V, VI, IX, XI, XII, XV, XVI, and TT5 and TT6. ........................................... 98

Table 4.4: Calibrated radiocarbon dates from Sarazm Excavations II, III, IV, V, VI, IX, XI, XII, XV, XVI, and TT5 and TT6. Calibrated using OxCal 4.3. .................... 99

## 5. Ceramic Vessels

Table 5.1: Minimum Number of ceramic Individuals (MNI) from Sarazm Excavation VII and its distribution across the stylistic groups identified within this excavation. ................................................ 104

Table 5.2: Minimum Number of ceramic Individuals (MNI) from Sarazm Excavation VII and its distribution across the functional categories identified within this excavation (NA = Not Available). ........................ 138

Table 5.3: Minimum Number of ceramic Individuals (MNI) from Sarazm Excavation VII and its distribution across the stylistic groups and functional categories identified within this excavation, classified by functions. ............ 139

Table 5.4: Sums of the quantities reported in Table 5.3. Minimum Number of ceramic Individuals (MNI) from Sarazm Excavation VII and its distribution across the stylistic groups and functional categories identified within this excavation, classified by functions. ...................... 139

| | | |
|---|---|---|
| Table 5.5: | Minimum Number of ceramic Individuals (MNI) from Sarazm Excavation VII and its distribution across the stylistic groups and archaeological levels identified within this excavation. | 140 |
| Table 5.6: | Number of sherds from Sarazm Excavation VII and its distribution across the archaeological levels identified within this excavation. | 141 |
| Table 5.7: | Minimum Number of ceramic Individuals (MNI) from Sarazm Excavation VII and its distribution across the stylistic groups and archaeological levels identified within this excavation. | 142 |
| Table 5.8: | List of ceramic individuals from Sarazm Excavation VII sorted by level and feature. | 150 |

## 6. Small Finds

| | | |
|---|---|---|
| Table/Graph 6.1: | Quantities of small finds from Sarazm Excavation VII classified by categories of raw material. | 166 |
| Table 6.2: | Quantities of small finds from Sarazm Excavation VII classified by functional categories. | 167 |
| Table 6.3: | Bone industry from Sarazm Excavation VII. | 168 |
| Table 6.4: | Shell industry from Sarazm Excavation VII. | 169 |
| Table 6.5: | Terracotta industry from Sarazm Excavation VII: perforated discs. | 170 |
| Table 6.6: | Terracotta industry from Sarazm Excavation VII discs. | 172 |
| Table 6.7: | Terracotta industry from Sarazm Excavation VII: finials. | 173 |
| Table 6.8: | Terracotta industry from Sarazm Excavation VII: figurine(?). | 173 |
| Table 6.9: | Terracotta industry from Sarazm Excavation VII: vessel(?). | 174 |
| Table 6.10: | Chalcedony, flint, quartz sandstone knapped lithic industry from Sarazm Excavation VII. | 176 |
| Table 6.11: | Quartz (rock crystal) knapped lithic industry and bead making from Sarazm Excavation VII. | 180 |
| Table 6.12: | Carnelian, lapis lazuli, turquoise, steatite, and frit industries from Sarazm Excavation VII. | 182 |
| Table 6.13: | Stone beads and pendants from Sarazm Excavation VII. | 188 |
| Table 6.14: | Stone drills from Sarazm Excavation VII. | 189 |
| Table 6.15: | Stone decorative tiles(?) from Sarazm Excavation VII. | 190 |
| Table 6.16: | Stone discs from Sarazm Excavation VII. | 190 |
| Table 6.17: | Stone finials from Sarazm Excavation VII. | 191 |
| Table 6.18: | Stone containers from Sarazm Excavation VII. | 192 |
| Table 6.19: | Stone mould from Sarazm Excavation VII. | 193 |

Table 6.20: Ground stones from Sarazm Excavation VII. ... 195

Table 6.21: Hammer/grinding stones from Sarazm Excavation VII. ... 197

Table 6.22: Stone pestles/sharpeners from Sarazm Excavation VII. ... 199

Table 6.23: Stone sharpener from Sarazm Excavation VII. ... 199

Table 6.24: Cobble flakes from Sarazm Excavation VII. ... 200

Table 6.25: Stone pebbles from Sarazm Excavation VII. ... 202

Table 6.26: Stone weights(?) from Sarazm Excavation VII. ... 204

Table 6.27: Records of stone raw material from Sarazm Excavation VII. ... 205

Table 6.28: Records of pigment and of remains relating to pigment preparation from Sarazm Excavation VII. ... 206

Table 6.29: Copper objects and records relating to copper metallurgy from Sarazm Excavation VII. ... 209

Table 6.30: Lead objects and records relating to lead metallurgy from Sarazm Excavation VII. ... 214

Table 6.31: Iron object from Sarazm Excavation VII. ... 216

Table/Graph 6.32: Quantities of small finds from Sarazm Excavation VII for which a provenience within Excavation VII could be determined, classified by levels. ... 217

# Acknowledgements

The first person I should thank is the late Roland Besenval (CNRS) who gave me the opportunity to study the archives and material assemblage from Excavation VII at Sarazm. He is also the one who, a little more than ten years ago, suggested that I contact Henri-Paul Francfort to inquire about the possibility to work at this site. I certainly regret that we have not been able to collaborate on this publication project and additional research projects, for he passed away before we had a chance to do so.

I would like to thank Henri-Paul Francfort (CNRS, Académie des Inscriptions et Belles-Lettres) for giving me the opportunity to work at Sarazm as part of the Mission Archéologique Française en Asie Centrale and for his encouragements as I was completing this volume. Our discussions have always helped me to put things into the right perspective.

Abdurauf Razzokov (Academy of Sciences of Tajikistan) did his best to provide me with access to the totality of the collection from Sarazm and to facilitate the study of the material assemblage from Excavation VII in the best possible conditions while I was excavating at this site. I also have very fond and fun memories of our collaboration in the field. I am also thankful to his team at the archaeological base of Penjikent as well as at Sarazm.

I would like to thank his son, Farhod Razzokov, for the invaluable exchanges we have had in the past years. His book, published in 2016, is the latest synthesis on Sarazm. A young, brilliant scholar, Farhod is sadly no longer with us as he passed away in 2022.

Saidmurod Bobomulloev (National Museum of Tajikistan in Dushanbe) has always been very welcoming. I am also grateful to him for giving me access to the material from Sarazm held by the National Museum of Tajikistan in Dushanbe.

Lastly, this volume was completed during the 2020–2021 pandemic. I am grateful to Sandra and Kip for supporting me during this endeavour, which was done mostly from home with them. For this reason, although this book is dedicated to the memory of Roland Besenval, it is also dedicated to them.

# Abbreviations

Aristob., *FGrH*  Aristobulus of Cassandreia, in F. Jacoby (ed.), *Die Fragmente der griechischen Historiker*, 1957–

Arr., *Anab.*  Arrian, *Anabasis*

Curt.  Curtius Rufus, *Historiae Alexandri Magni*

Ptol., *Geog.*  Ptolemy, *Geographia*

# Preface

This volume examines the archives and material assemblage from the archaeological excavation, Excavation VII, that Roland Besenval conducted between 1984 and 1994 at Sarazm in the Zeravshan Valley, Tajikistan. Sarazm is well known for being an archaeological site at the intersection of various cultural spheres located between southern Central Asia, the Iranian Plateau, the Indo-Iranian Borderlands, and the Eurasian Steppe from the Late Chalcolithic through the Early Bronze Age, *c.* 3500–2500 cal. BCE broadly speaking. Fieldwork at this site provided for the first time clear evidence for intercultural interaction between these spheres, along and across the Hindu Kush. With its well-documented stratigraphy, archaeological contexts, and unique material assemblage, Excavation VII is critical for the understanding of this site. Yet, save for three articles that present aspects of the results from this excavation (Besenval 1987; Besenval and Isakov 1989; Isakov et al. 2003), up to this day, no detailed and comprehensive presentation and analysis of the available data from Excavation VII had been offered. This volume examines this data, i.e. the archaeological contexts and material assemblage that were exposed as well as results from radiocarbon, archaeobotanical, and zooarchaeological analyses. This volume does not intend to re-examine all available data from Sarazm; yet, additional information gathered through the other digs at this site has been here recapitulated and sometimes updated when comparisons needed to be made and the discoveries made in Excavation VII needed to be contextualized.

## *Roland Besenval's Archaeological Investigations at Sarazm and in the Zeravshan Valley*

Roland Besenval's contributions to the cultural heritage of Tajikistan is multifold. His contributions to the archaeology of the Zeravshan Valley began in 1984 at Sarazm. Together with Henri-Paul Francfort (CNRS, Académie des Inscriptions et Belles-Lettres), he opened that year a test trench within the south-eastern portion of what is today the fenced, protected area of this archaeological site as registered on the UNESCO World Heritage List since 2010. Roland Besenval then took over the supervision of this fieldwork in 1985. This test trench was expanded that year and became Excavation VII, which he directed until 1991. Simultaneously, Roland Besenval began exploring the Zeravshan Valley and its surrounding. The main objective of this survey was to evaluate the mineral resources of this region within the Turkestan and Zeravshan Mountains and to locate mines, such as copper and tin mines, that were exploited at the time Sarazm was occupied, or more generally during the Late Chalcolithic and Bronze Age periods. The archives relating to this survey will be presented elsewhere. Although fieldwork in Excavation VII appears to have ended in 1991 and Roland Besenval seems then to have focused more on the survey aspect of his project, studies and documentation of the material assemblage from this excavation seem to have been carried out until 1994. That year, Roland Besenval organized with Abdullah I. Isakov an international conference at Penjikent, whose proceedings are currently in press per the efforts of Frédérique Brunet (CNRS), Henri-Paul Francfort, and Abdurauf Razzokov (Director of Penjikent archaeological base of the Institute of History, Archaeology, and Ethnography, A. Donish, Academy of Sciences of the Republic of Tajikistan) (Besenval et al. 2021). In the latter half of the 1990s and throughout the 2000s, he continued to maintain strong relationships with his Tajik colleagues, although he already had started working in Kech-Makran, Pakistan since 1987 and soon after created the Mission Archéologique Française au Makran (MAFM), which he directed for over twenty years. During that time, he helped prepare an application for Sarazm to be registered on the UNESCO World Heritage List (2010). Between 2011 and 2014, Roland Besenval also developed and conducted a new geomorphological project together with Eric Fouache (Sorbonne University, Paris) and Lucie Cez (PhD candidate at Panthéon-Sorbonne University, Paris) that focused on the study of ancient canals that he had identified north of the protected archaeological area of the site (Cez 2019; see **Chapter 2**).

## Publication Project

2011 was also the first field season of the renewed Tajik-French joint field research project at Sarazm. This revived fieldwork was prompted by Henri-Paul Francfort and has since then been conducted as part of the Mission Archéologique Française en Asie Centrale (MAFAC), which he was then directing and is now directed by Frédérique Brunet (CNRS). Between 2011 and 2014, I contributed to this renewed project as field director (see Mutin et al. 2020a for a recapitulation of this fieldwork). The idea of putting together with Roland Besenval a new volume about Excavation VII emerged from the realization that, save for three articles, the data from this excavation had never been entirely analysed and presented. I brought this fact and project up to Roland Besenval in 2011 at Sarazm, who thought that it was a good idea. Within the following few years, I secured funding from the Shelby White and Leon Levy Foundation for Archaeological Publications for this publication project and began studying and documenting the Excavation VII material assemblage at Sarazm and Penjikent as well as the archives relating to this fieldwork in Paris. The fact that I conducted this project at the same time as I was excavating at Sarazm was both greatly beneficial and complicated at times. It was beneficial in that I could easily access the totality of the material assemblage from this site available in Sarazm and Penjikent museums and archaeological bases, as well as in the National Museum of Tajikistan in Dushanbe. This certainly has helped me get both a broader and detailed view of this site and be prepared for the analysis of the Excavation VII material assemblage, with, for instance, a strategy as to how to approach and classify the ceramics (which also refers to the previous analysis done by Bertille Lyonnet (1996): see **Chapter 5**). First-hand knowledge of the terrain at Sarazm has helped me understand and interpret the field data reported in Roland Besenval archives. I mention this because, sadly, I ended up conducting this publication project by myself as Roland Besenval passed away on 29 September 2014. This project then got delayed because the archives relating to Sarazm are in Paris, while I was based in the United States until the completion of this volume, which did not make it easy for me to access these archives on a regular basis. Another reason is that, as is explained in **Chapter 3**, I have not been able to locate a significant part of Roland Besenval archives, which has made it extremely difficult to understand, reconstruct, and present his discoveries and homogenize the descriptions. A third reason is that I became increasingly committed to the preparation and development of a new field research project in Iran between 2014 and 2015. The first field season of this project eventually took place in 2016.

It is with great satisfaction that I am seeing this project coming to completion. At the same time as I wish I could have done more, I do not see how I could have done much more considering the missing archives. Certainly, new information will be gathered about Sarazm as new fieldwork is being conducted at this site and will most likely continue to be carried out in the future. The reconstructions and hypotheses I offer in this volume may then prove to be erroneous. Colleagues may already not agree with them. This volume has been put together precisely so that the raw data Roland Besenval collected in Excavation VII is made available and left open to interpretations and reinterpretations. Hopefully, it will be incorporated in new analyses and syntheses about Sarazm and the Zeravshan Valley, as well as broader reconstructions relating to the ancient Middle East and Central Asia. I also hope that it will help shape or refine new excavation strategies at this site.

## Funding and Support of the Publication Project

Analysis of the material assemblage from Excavation VII was done while I was conducting new fieldwork as part of the renewed joint project between the Academy of Sciences of Tajikistan and the MAFAC, then directed by Henri-Paul Francfort. Abdurauf Razzokov greatly facilitated access to this assemblage, which had been stored at the Archaeological Base of Penjikent since the 1980s and 1990s. Lastly, the analysis and preparation for publication of the assemblage and archives from Excavation VII was supported by a grant from the Shelby White and Leon Levy Program for Archaeological publications.[1] The colour printing was funded by the UMR 8167 Orient & Méditerranée.

---

[1] <https://whitelevy.fas.harvard.edu/people/benjamin-mutin> [accessed 10 April 2023].

## Outline of the Volume

The volume is divided into seven chapters. **Chapter 1** serves as an introduction that attempts to contextualize Sarazm and Excavation VII within the broader contexts of Middle Asia, Central Asia, and the Eurasian Steppe between the fourth and third millennia BCE. Aspects are discussed such as the 'multicultural' aspect of this site, its chronology, the spatial distribution of its material remains, the reason(s) for its foundation, its relationship with the rest of Middle Asia and Central Asia, and its significance in the understanding of the Oxus Civilization. **Chapter 2** presents the environmental setting of Sarazm. It compiles data relating to the Zeravshan River, the topography and geomorphology of the Sarazm region, as well as its climate. The mineral resources from the Zeravshan Valley and surrounding mountains are presented, as well as resources located up to *c.* 350–450 km distant from the site in Kazakhstan, Kyrgyzstan, Uzbekistan, and Afghanistan. Current and past fauna and plants are also discussed. The latter are described on the basis of the archaeobotanical and zooarchaeological assemblages from Excavation VII, which were studied by Georges Willcox and Jean Desse, respectively. **Chapter 3** describes the archaeological levels and areas exposed by Roland Besenval. It begins with a brief description of the issues I have had working with the archives and the strategy I have adopted to provide a consistent, albeit simplified, presentation of the archaeological contexts. A short section then discusses the function of these occupation levels and is followed by a comprehensive recapitulation of all the architectural aspects of Excavation VII and their parallels within Sarazm. Comparisons beyond Sarazm are then provided. **Chapter 4** offers recalibrations using OxCal 4.3 of the available radiocarbon dates from Excavation VII as well as from the other excavations at Sarazm. Results from these recalibrations are then discussed. **Chapter 5** is dedicated to the Excavation VII ceramic assemblage. Its different styles are presented. Quantitative data are provided. Sections then follow that look at the functions of the vessels, their distribution across the Excavation VII stratigraphic sequence, and their parallels. **Chapter 6** describes the small finds, which include all the other types of material remains. They are essentially classified according to their raw materials. The compositions of some of these objects were analysed by François Cesbron at the Laboratoire de Minéralogie-Cristallographie Pierre et Marie Curie (Paris VI), Paris, France (see Cesbron 1996). When available, results from these analyses are included in this chapter together with the descriptions of the objects. Sections are then provided that discuss the stratigraphic and spatial distribution of the small finds, the activities that were performed within Excavation VII, potential sources for raw material procurement, and the cultural relationships these objects suggest. A general **Conclusion** in **Chapter 7** then ends the volume.

# 1. Contextualizing Sarazm and Excavation VII

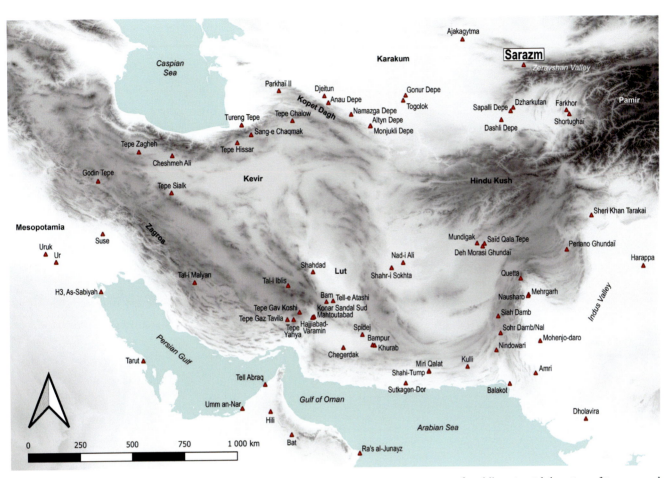

Figure 1.1: Map of Middle Asia with location of Sarazm and additional archaeological sites mentioned in the text. B. Mutin.

Sarazm is located in the Zeravshan Valley, north-western Tajikistan (Sughd Province), *c.* 13.5 km west of Penjikent and the fifth–eighth-century CE Sogdian 'Old Penjikent' city, and *c.* 45 km east of Samarkand in Uzbekistan (Lat. 39.508148°; Long. 67.459361°) (Figs 1.1–1.2 and 2.1). This site was discovered in 1976 when new cultivation lands were being extended over the archaeological area and farming engines began exposing archaeological deposits and artefacts. A. Tajlanov, who lived in a nearby village, was the one who brought these objects to the attention of A. I. Isakov, then director of the Archaeological Base of Penjikent (Academy of Sciences of Tajikistan). Isakov managed to stop the agricultural expansion over the site and began excavation in 1977 (Besenval and Isakov 1989, 7). Since then, Tajik investigations in the field or analysis of the material assemblages from Sarazm have never stopped. They have been led by A. Razzokov since the 1990s.

International joint projects have also been developed, including a Tajik-American cooperation in 1985 with C. C. Lamberg-Karlovsky and P. Kohl at Harvard University. In 1981, H.-P. Francfort visited Sarazm with A. A. Askarov and A. I. Isakov. In 1982, following the first Soviet-French symposium on the archaeology of Central Asia, which was held in Dushanbe and organized by V. Ranov and J.-C. Gardin, a cooperation agreement was signed between the French National Centre for Scientific Research (CNRS) and the Academy of Sciences of the USSR. This agreement included joint fieldwork at Sarazm, which began in 1984 in Excavation VII under the direction of H.-P. Francfort and then R. Besenval (CNRS, ER 315). This Tajik-French cooperation project

Figure 1.2: View of the protected archaeological area of Sarazm and villages and agricultural fields around. Google Earth.

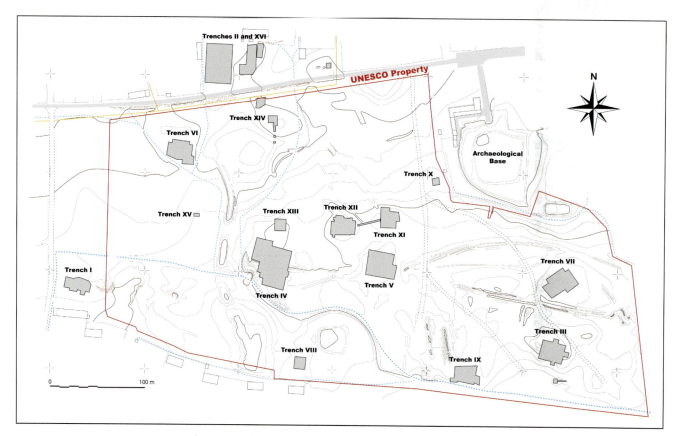

Figure 1.3: Map of Sarazm with location of the main excavations (in grey) conducted until 2014.
Map by J. Suire and R. Schwertdner (Mission Archéologique Française en Asie Centrale), modified by B. Mutin.

Figure 1.4: View of Excavation VII within the south-eastern portion of the protected archaeological area of Sarazm. Google Earth.

Figure 1.5: View of Excavation VII at Sarazm in 1989.
R. Besenval, edited by B. Mutin.

Figure 1.6: View of Excavation VII at Sarazm in 1989.
R. Besenval, edited by B. Mutin.

was renewed in 2011 as part of the Mission Archéologique Française en Asie Centrale (MAFAC), directed by H.-P. Francfort. Since 1977, eighteen excavations and additional test trenches have been opened at Sarazm (Isakov 1991; Razzokov 2008; Mutin et al. 2020a, 23 fig. 1; Figs 1.3–1.6). The archaeological site is believed to spread over 100 to 150 ha, although agricultural fields and three villages cover it today, which makes it difficult to delineate its actual expanse (Besenval and Isakov 1989, 7). In 2010, Sarazm became a UNESCO World Heritage site with a c. 15 ha fenced area that encloses most previous excavations.[1]

## Sarazm as a 'Multicultural' Site

Early on, Sarazm emerged as an exceptional site as Tajik and international specialists were quick to identify in the assemblages from its different excavations various styles of objects as well as different types of minerals and metals suggesting relationships to varied and, in many cases, distant cultural spheres. These remains essentially date the site to the Late Chalcolithic and Early Bronze Age periods, c. 3500–2500 cal. BCE, although it remains possible and certain radiocarbon dates and objects hint that the site was also occupied later than that too (see below and **Chapter 4**). To name but a few of these relationships, which have been abundantly discussed (e.g. Besenval 1987; Isakov and Lyonnet 1988; Besenval and Isakov 1989; Isakov 1991; 1994b; Lyonnet 1996; Kuzmina 2007), the ceramic assemblage from Sarazm illustrates evident connections to the Namazga plain and painted ceramic tradition known in Turkmenistan and north-eastern Iran, to grey burnished vessels typical of sites in north-eastern Iran such as Tepe Hissar south of Damghan as well as Tureng Tepe and Shah Tepe in the Gorgan Plain, and to painted ceramics essentially observed at sites between southern Afghanistan and Pakistan such as Mundigak (see Lyonnet 1996). Sarazm's lithic assemblage includes tools and technologies that relate to the Kel'teminar tradition in Uzbekistan as well as to the Eurasian Steppe

---

[1] <https://whc.unesco.org/en/list/1141/> [accessed 10 April 2023].

Table 1.1: Chronological chart for Sarazm and sites in the Steppe, Central Asia, Middle Asia, South Asia, and Mesopotamia. B. Mutin, partly adapted from Lyonnet and Dubova 2021, 8–9 tab. 1.1. The chronology of Sarazm is more specifically discussed in this volume.

| Dates cal. BCE | Sarazm | Kel'teminar | Steppe | Namazga/Anau | Tepe Hissar | Tureng Tepe | Shahr-i Sokhta | Tepe Yahya | Mundigak | Mehrgarh | Nausharo | Harappa | Mesopotamia |
|---|---|---|---|---|---|---|---|---|---|---|---|---|---|
| 2000 | | | | | IIIC | | | IVA | | VIII | IV | | Ur III |
| 2100 | | | Petrovka/ Sintashta Poltavka | VI | | IIIC | | | | | III | | |
| 2200 | | | | | | | | | | | | | |
| 2300 | | | Late | | | | | | | | | 3 | Akkad |
| 2400 | Late occupation? | | | V | IIIB | IIIB | IV | | | | II | | |
| 2500 | | | | | | | | IVB | | | | | Early Dynastic |
| 2600 | | | | | | | III | | | | | | |
| 2700 | | | | IV | IIIA | IIIA | | | IV | VII | I | 2 Kot Diji | |
| 2800 | | | Yamnaya | | | | II | | | | | | |
| 2900 | Main occupation | | | | | | | | | | | | Jemdet-Nasr |
| 3000 | | | | III | | | I | IVC | | VI | | | |
| 3100 | | | | | | | | | III | | | 1 | |
| 3200 | | | | | IIB | | | | | V | | | |
| 3300 | | Middle | | | | II | | | II | | | | |
| 3400 | | | | | | | | Hiatus (Aliabad) | | | | | |
| 3500 | Exc. IV Tombs? | | | II | | | | | | | | | Uruk |
| 3600 | | | Afanasievo | | | IIA | | | | IV | | | |
| 3700 | | | | | | | | | | | | | |
| 3800 | | | | | | | | | I | | | | |
| 3900 | | | | | I/II | | | VA | | III | | | |
| 4000 | | | | I | | | | | | | | | |

(Brunet and Razzokov 2016). A ceramic from Sarazm with a conical base and motifs incised on its surface is also often cited as a Kel'teminar-related item (Lyonnet 1996, 49, 59, 116 fig. 38 no. 1). Scholars have also seen in the funerary stone circle that surrounds the tomb of the famous 'Princess of Sarazm' a parallel with the burial mounds of the Afanasievo Steppe culture (Lyonnet 1996, 55, 57; Avanesova 2001; Francfort 2005, 259), although other scholars do not agree with this interpretation (Anthony, pers. comm. in 2013). Certain copper objects point at even more distant parallels. This is the case for one double-spiral headed pin found in Excavation VII, which has general equivalents between the Caucasus and Pakistan, including in Iran and Turkmenistan, and even as far west as south-eastern Europe (see **Chapter 6**). Parallels are also found in the Caucasus and adjacent regions for a stone 'beak' that was found at Sarazm (Kohl 2007, 61 fig. 3.3). An axe from this site compares perfectly with exemplars known in the Carpatho-Danubian region (Boroffka 2009, 250). It is also perhaps worth remembering that a golden rosette with a turquoise in its centre that was found within the burial of the 'Princess of Sarazm' parallels rosettes recorded in Mesopotamia, such as those found at Ur on a headdress in the tomb of Queen Puabi and on the statue of a rearing goat. However, both Mesopotamian objects date to the mid-third millennium BCE (Collins 2003, 110–11; Reade 2003, 121; see Isakov 1994b, 10), whereas the tomb at Sarazm is believed to be one millennium older. On the other hand, a more chronologically and stylistically compatible parallel may be found in Mesopotamia within the funerary deposits from Tepe Gawra dating to the first half of the fourth millennium BCE (Bache 1935). Another connection with Mesopotamia as well as with the Iranian Plateau is the single cylinder seal that has been recovered so far from Sarazm (Isakov 1994b, 11 fig. 10). The motif carved on this object, a bull, or a cow, has no exact equivalents, but the fact that it is carved on a cylinder seal brings to mind the Uruk, Jemdet-Nasr, Early Dynastic, and Proto-Elamite spheres of Mesopotamia and Iran where such objects are recorded (Mutin et al. 2022). Lastly, the presence at Sarazm of certain minerals in a raw form suggests connections to areas such as present-day Uzbekistan (turquoise), the Badakhshan Province of Afghanistan (lapis lazuli), and Pakistan or India (carnelian), where sources for these materials have been identified (see **Chapter 6**). Connections to the Arabian Sea are illustrated by the discovery of two bracelets within the tomb of the 'Princess of Sarazm', which are made from *Turbinella pyrum* seashells (see Besenval 2005, 4–6).

This inventory is certainly not comprehensive, and more details on the topic of the relationships of Sarazm may be found in the references listed in this volume as well as in **Chapters 3, 5, and 6** as far as the parallels for the archaeological features, ceramics, and small finds from Excavation VII are concerned. As is shown in these chapters, this excavation has considerably contributed to the picture of Sarazm as an exceptional, 'multicultural site'. Both ceramics relating to the Namazga ceramic tradition of Turkmenistan and to painted ceramics typical of southern Afghanistan and Pakistan during the Late Chalcolithic and Early Bronze Age periods were found in this excavation. The above-mentioned single double-spiral headed pin recorded at Sarazm comes from this excavation. Additionally, eight complete ceramic vessels relating to different stylistic traditions that were recovered from inside a building of Excavation VII Level IV1 are probably one of the best demonstrations of the apparent 'multiculturalism' of Sarazm. Explanations that have been provided to explicate the presence of elements from varied material cultures at Sarazm are recapitulated below. One parameter that needs to be kept in mind here is that the multicultural aspect of this site needs to be relativized and analysed against its duration. In other words, although there certainly are cases where materials from separate cultural spheres were found together within the same archaeological contexts, not all the intercultural interactions observed at Sarazm occurred with the same degree, or in the same amounts, at the same time.

## *Chronology*

Most scholars agree that Sarazm was founded around or slightly after 3500 cal. BCE. On the other hand, there is disagreement on the duration of this settlement. While some specialists see its end before or around 2500 cal. BCE, others would date it to around 2000 cal. BCE. This question is further complicated because the radiocarbon dates from Sarazm are at times contradictory in that they are not always consistent with the stratigraphy and material culture that have been exposed. As detailed in **Chapter 4**, these dates range from *c.* 4000 cal. BCE to *c.* 1250 cal. BCE. Although most available dates are earlier than *c.* 2500 cal. BCE, six to seven dates are later and include dates that are even later than *c.* 1600 BCE. In addition to divergences on the dating of the final occupation and the end of Sarazm, its periodization, which consists of four periods, Periods I to IV, has also been the topic of disagreements.

In the 1990s, Sarazm Period I, the foundation period, was dated to around the middle of the fourth millennium BCE (Lyonnet 1996, 57), or 3500–3300 cal. BCE according to Isakov (1991, 112). This period is known to be ceramically essentially connected to Turkmenistan during the end of the Namazga II Period (Isakov and Lyonnet 1988, 42; Lyonnet 1996, 55–57). The following Sarazm Period II was dated to the last third of the fourth millennium BCE (Lyonnet 1996, 58), 3300–3000 cal. BCE (Isakov 1991, 112). This period still mostly connects to Turkmenistan between the Late Namazga II and Namazga III Periods (Lyonnet 1996, 57–58). During both Sarazm Periods I and II, relationships with the Indo-Iranian Borderlands are observed through a limited number of pottery sherds. A disagreement is apparent in the dating of the next two periods of Sarazm, Periods III and IV. On the one hand, Lyonnet dated Period III to around 3000 cal. BCE. This period relates ceramically to the Namazga III Period in Turkmenistan, although, in contrast to Sarazm Periods I and II, ceramics with styles linked to the Indo-Iranian Borderlands appear to be more numerous than before (Lyonnet 1996, 58–59). She dated Sarazm Period IV to around 2800–2600 cal. BCE, although she pointed out the possibility that certain ceramic types found at this site may evince the existence of an occupation dating to around 2500 cal. BCE. This period sees even more material connected to the Indo-Iranian Borderlands, as well as a new type of grey ceramic that resembles vessels from north-eastern Iran (Lyonnet 1996, 59–61). On the other hand, Isakov dated Period III to 3000–2300 cal. BCE and Period IV to 2300–1900 cal. BCE (Isakov 1991, 112–13), although, elsewhere, he seemed to agree with Lyonnet as they wrote together (Isakov and Lyonnet 1988, 31):

> Il apparaît, après l'étude comparative [de la céramique], que la durée d'existence de l'ensemble du site n'est pas aussi considérable qu'il a été écrit et qu'elle n'excède sans doute pas 700 ou 800 ans. La fondation de Sarazm se situe vers le milieu du chalcolithique, probablement un peu avant 3500 avant J.-C, et sa phase finale au tout début de l'Âge du Bronze, vers 2700–2600 avant J.-C.

As Lyonnet (1996, 17–19) wrote, Sarazm's periodization may need to be considered with caution as it has been established on the basis of a portion, and not the totality, of the ceramic assemblage from this site. It indeed does not include data that have been excavated since the 1990s. She also mentioned issues that concern the stratigraphic position of certain ceramics that were used to build this periodization. Consequently, it is perhaps safer, considering the current state of knowledge and analysis, to discuss Sarazm's chronology in terms of the two phases that Isakov defined, one corresponding to Periods I–II and one to Periods III–IV (Isakov 1991; 1994b). For this reason and because there are disagreements about the chronology of certain excavations and how they relate to these periods, they do not appear in the chronological chart provided in Table 1.1. I nonetheless refer to them again in the **Conclusion** when I conclude on the chronology of Excavation VII. It is also important to note that Lyonnet, together with Dubova, recently revised this chronology, now proposing the following sequence (Lyonnet and Dubova 2021, 8 tab. 1.1): Period I: 3000–2900 cal. BCE; Period II: 2900–2700 cal. BCE; Period III: 2700–2500 cal. BCE; Period IV: 2500–2300 cal. BCE, leaving open the end of this period with a dashed line. As a matter of fact, working at Sarazm has made me question the mid-fourth millennium BCE date generally suggested for its foundation, while working on the Excavation VII archives and material assemblage has made me question the mid-third-millennium BCE date usually assigned to the end of this settlement.

On the date of Sarazm's foundation, I tend to agree more with Lyonnet and Dubova's more recent view. At a minimum, instead of around, or a little bit before, the middle of the fourth millennium BCE, it seems that most evidence from the main settlement points at the last third or quarter of the fourth millennium BCE, while that which suggests an earlier date is more questionable. This date appears to be in alignment with most parallels mentioned by Lyonnet and Isakov (e.g. Isakov and Lyonnet 1988, 42; Lyonnet 1996), most available radiocarbon dates from Sarazm (see **Chapter 4**), and Hiebert's (2002) and Kircho's (2021) views on the chronology of the Kopet Dagh region. The only exception known in the present state of knowledge that points at an earlier date are the burials found within a stone circle excavated underneath the first architectural layers of Excavation IV. These are thought to relate to the Afanasievo Steppe culture, which is earlier than c. 3300 BCE, while a recent radiocarbon analysis conducted on human remains that *may* belong to one of these burials gave a date of c. 3500 cal. BCE (see below). Additionally, as noted above, the gold rosette found within one of these burials parallels objects from Tepe Gawra dating to the first half of the fourth millennium BCE (Bache 1935). This would mean that this funerary monument predates by a minimum of two centuries the foundation of Sarazm main settlement. Incidentally, this hypothesis may explain why the groups who settled in the areas exposed in Excavation IV did not know that burials had been laid just below the houses they were about to build. Or else, if they knew, the meaning of their settling on top of these burials would need to be explained.

As for the end of Sarazm, I am in general agreement with Lyonnet's 1996 view given the fact that most ceramics from this site parallel materials that are generally not later than the mid-third millennium BCE. Most available radiocarbon dates also tend to fit this reconstruction (see **Chapter 4**). With regard to this, Isakov and Lyonnet (1988, 43) rightly observed:

> La continuité manifeste de la majeure partie des formes de la céramique, ainsi que les comparaisons faites pour chacune des quatre périodes du site, suggèrent que celles-ci se succèdent immédiatement les unes après les autres. Il semble donc difficile de supposer que Sarazm ait vécu très longtemps, d'autant que l'épaisseur des couches culturelles n'est pas très imposante.

As such, when considering the chronological ranges of most parallels, the main occupation of Sarazm may be placed within a period that lasted over half a millennium; yet, I tentatively would make it shorter and centre it around 3000 cal. BCE (see **Chapter 4**).

Lyonnet however also mentioned the possibility that Sarazm may have been occupied until around 2500 cal. BCE, but that this later occupation has been essentially removed by years of agricultural work (Lyonnet 1996, 60–61). She included in this phase a vessel that she dates to the Namazga IV Period (which Kircho dates to the Namazga V Period; Kircho 2021, 132) in addition to a few other ceramic types that stand out within Sarazm ceramic assemblage. Consistent with Lyonnet's past opinion that Sarazm did not continue to be occupied much longer after *c.* 2500 cal. BCE is the fact that more recent ceramics seem extremely rare at Sarazm. Also, there is no material relating to the Indus Civilization, which may seem rational considering the distance between Sarazm and the core of this civilization in Pakistan and India, but less so considering that earlier ceramics stylistically connected to the Indo-Iranian Borderlands are recorded at this site and that an Indus-related settlement was found at Shortughaï in northeastern Afghanistan (Francfort 1989). Furthermore, no material typical of the Oxus Civilization has been found either in the digs at Sarazm, although vestiges of this civilization are recorded over a large portion of southern Central Asia including in Tajikistan and including within the Zeravshan Valley at Zardcha-Halifa, *c.* 13 km east of Sarazm (see Lyonnet and Dubova 2021; Avanesova 2021). Yet, although a date to before or around 2500 cal. BCE for the end of Sarazm seems the most rational considering most evidence, it does not seem appropriate to discard the extremely limited evidence that may point at a later date. In that sense, I tend to agree more with Lyonnet and Dubova's recent contribution in which they push the end of Sarazm toward 2400/2300 cal. BCE, although I am still not certain what the right answer is. The evidence for a later date for the end of Sarazm includes a series of radiocarbon dates (see **Chapter 4**) as well as stone 'weights' or 'bags' and 'sceptres' or 'rods' that have been found on the surface of the site but usually not in the excavations, save for one stone 'weight' or 'bag' from Excavation II (Isakov 1991, fig. 13 no. 1, fig. 31; collection at the Sarazm and Penjikent museums). Although stone weights are recorded since the fourth millennium BCE in Turkmenistan, Iran, and Afghanistan (see Kircho 2021, 116–17), these types of objects and the rods are generally more common in the archaeological record between Central Asia, the Indo-Iranian Borderlands, and the Iranian Plateau beginning around the mid-late third millennium BCE, and usually associated with the Oxus Civilization (e.g. Vidale 2017b, 75–76; Mutin and Lamberg-Karlovsky 2021; Vinogradova 2021, 637 fig. 23.2). Chronological differences probably existed between the different types of weights observed from the fourth through the third millennia BCE, including perhaps between the bag-shaped (as in Excavation II) and disc-shaped weights, with the former being older than the latter. As is shown in this volume, additional types of objects from Excavation VII also seem to find their best parallels within assemblages dating to after the mid-third millennium BCE (see **Chapters 5 and 6**). The chronology of this excavation and of Sarazm is discussed again in the **Conclusion** of this volume, although current and future stratigraphic excavations at this site and ceramic chrono-typological reconstructions one may expect from this fieldwork will certainly be critical to help clarify these conundrums.

## *Settlement Pattern, Function, and Society*

It is perhaps not necessary to provide a detailed description of the totality of the ancient settlement of Sarazm as many aspects of this site have been presented and discussed on many occasions (e.g. Besenval and Isakov 1989; Isakov 1991; Razzokov 2008; F. Razzokov 2016; articles in the *Arkheologicheskie raboty v Tadzhikistane*; Mutin et al. 2020a regarding the recent Tajik-French excavations). Yet, it is probably important to recall a few key aspects of this site to contextualize Excavation VII.

An important characteristic of Sarazm is that excavations at this site have yielded relatively shallow archaeological sequences that are usually not more than 1.5 to 2 m thick. One reason for this is that the settlement shifted across the site over time resulting in a horizontal stratigraphy rather than a vertical one (Besenval and Isakov 1989, 8). In other words, not all the locations at the site appear to have been occupied simultaneously. F. Razzokov (2016, 87–100) recently re-examined this topic. His recent analysis does not contradict this general observation, although its results are slightly different at times from previous reconstructions (Isakov and Lyonnet 1988, 42–43; Lyonnet 1996, 61 tab. 10). A simplified version of his work is provided in Table 1.2. This table shows that: Period I has been identified in only three excavations; Periods II–III have been observed in all the excavations F. Razzokov considered in his analysis, which suggests that the settlement was more spread out during these periods than before; and Period IV is known only through three to four excavations, which suggests that the settlement expanse decreased at that time, or that its remains did not survive years of agricultural work or natural erosion. Excavation II emerges from F. Razzokov's analysis as the only excavation that has yielded Sarazm Period I to IV deposits, although Besenval and Isakov (1989, 8) wrote that deposits relating to Period IV were not found in this excavation. Excavation VII is one of the three or four excavations that have yielded vestiges relating to Period IV. Its earliest deposits are believed to be not earlier than Sarazm Period II.

Table 1.2: Distribution of the four periods of Sarazm (Periods I to IV) across some of the main excavations at this site. B. Mutin, adapted from F. Razzokov 2016, 89 tab. 3.

|            | Exc. I | Exc. II | Exc. III | Exc. IV | Exc. V | Exc. VI | Exc. VII | Exc. IX | Exc. XI | Exc. XII |
|------------|--------|---------|----------|---------|--------|---------|----------|---------|---------|----------|
| Sarazm I   |        | X       |          | X       | X      |         |          |         |         |          |
| Sarazm II  | X?     | X       | X        | X       | X      | X       | X        | X       | X       | X        |
| Sarazm III | X      | X       | X        | X       | X      | X       | X        | X       | X       | X        |
| Sarazm IV  |        | X       |          |         | X?     |         | X        |         |         | X        |

The first period, Period I, is known through a limited surface excavated within Excavation II and possibly Excavation V. Period I remains in Excavation II consist of mud-brick and rammed earth domestic architecture (F. Razzokov 2016, 180 fig. 5). The funerary stone circle containing the tomb of the 'Princess of Sarazm' found in Excavation IV is usually included in this period (e.g. Lyonnet 1996, 55), although, as noted above, it now seems increasingly apparent that most parallels for Periods I–II remains (Lyonnet 1996, 55–56) are not earlier than the late fourth millennium BCE, whereas this funerary monument points at the mid-fourth millennium BCE. Five burials were found inside this stone circle, including that of the famous 'Princess of Sarazm' (Besenval and Isakov 1989, 9; Isakov 1994a; 1994b). An additional burial was found in Excavation II, although it is more recent as it dates to Period III (Isakov 1991, figs 11, 18). More burials similar to the one in Excavation IV were recently located near the site (at 'Sarazm 2'; Bobomulloev et al. 2021).

Dwellings relating to Periods II and III are then observed in other areas of the site, including in Excavations I, II, VI, VII, and VIII (Isakov 1994b, 1), with Excavation II apparently being the densest dwelling area (Besenval and Isakov 1989, 8). Evidence for craft activities has also been recorded. In Excavation II,

> significant quantities of crucibles and slag were recovered [...] Though the architectural association and function remain somewhat unclear the crucibles and slag were recovered from surfaces of floors that were burned red. From this floor were recovered holes of hearths that were 18–25 cm in diameter and 20–30 cm in depth. It is not unlikely that these were 'pot-furnaces' for the smelting of ores. (Isakov et al. 1987, 101; see Isakov 1991, fig. 24; see also in Excavation XVI next to Excavation II: Mutin et al. 2020a, 31 fig. 9)

As is apparent in this description, these vestiges seem intermingled with those of residential areas. Furthermore, F. Razzokov (2016) noted that one room in Excavation II probably served as a workshop dedicated to copper metallurgical activities, which was at the same time directly connected to a dwelling, making it a 'home workshop'. Taken as whole, Sarazm is by some considered a large metallurgical centre and even 'the largest metallurgical centre of Central Asia engaged in export' (e.g. Kuzmina 2007, 212), although this interpretation probably needs to be re-examined (see below). Pottery kilns were also found, as well as evidence for the manufacture of items made from semi-precious stones such as lapis lazuli (Besenval and Isakov 1989, 18; see **Chapters 5 and 6**).

Alongside these remains were found more monumental constructions that do not resemble the above-mentioned most common types of dwellings and do not contain obvious remains of craft activities. One is a circular mud-brick structure associated with a rectangular, corridor-like construction that was exposed in Excavation V (Period II). This building is interpreted as a temple ('Temple of the Sun') (Isakov 1994b, 1; F. Razzokov 2016, 193 fig. 19). In Excavation III (Period III) was found what Isakov interpreted as a communal granary (Isakov 1994b, 1; F. Razzokov 2016, 183 fig. 8). The same author also wrote that part of the architecture exposed within Excavations IV and IX corresponds to religious complexes and that a palace and religious complex was built at the location of the Excavation V 'temple' (Isakov 1994b, 1, 7). Another distinctive construction was found in Excavation XI (Period II). It consists of a quadrangular room with a hearth in its centre, surrounded by a peripheral corridor (F. Razzokov 2016, 226 fig. 60, 231 fig. 66). With the discovery of these monumental constructions, Sarazm emerged as a site comparable to other Late Chalcolithic–Early Bronze Age sites such as Geoksyur, Altyn-Depe, Tepe Hissar, and Mundigak, where buildings interpreted as religious centres or palaces were uncovered. Isakov noted specific parallels for Sarazm's 'granary' and 'religious building' at Altyn-Depe and Geoksyur (Isakov 1994b, 7). Regardless of the interpretation one makes of these buildings, they may suggest the presence of individuals or groups with status higher, or different, than that of the rest of the population. The presence of elites at Sarazm is also inferred from a series of objects denoting 'high social status' (Isakov 1994b, 8–9), including a few objects from Excavation VII that may be interpreted along the same lines (see **Chapter 6**). With regard to this, it needs to be remembered that the impressive collection of grave goods found in the tomb of the 'Princess of Sarazm' (as well as in another burial nearby) is unique in the context of fourth-millennium BCE southern Central Asia and tends to agree with the view that the individuals buried with it enjoyed high social status (Besenval and Isakov 1989, 18; Isakov 1994a; 1994b, 5–6). Yet, for the reason explained above, this tomb might in fact be chronologically disconnected from the rest of the main settlement of Sarazm. Hopefully, current excavation of the above-mentioned graves found near this site (Sarazm 2) will shed a lot more light on the social structure of Sarazm society. In the present state of knowledge, since the elites of Sarazm remain rather elusive, one may only speculate on the potential role of such elites in the foundation of this site and control over activities relating to the exploitation and export of metals and minerals that some scholars have emphasized (see Mutin et al. 2022).

One last observation on Sarazm settlement regards the amount of material remains found at this site, which seems very low in comparison to those usually recorded at Middle Asian and Central Asian archaeological sites. This led Lyonnet to suggest that this site may have not been occupied all year round, although she acknowledged that J. Desse emphasized at the 1994 conference in Penjikent that the zooarchaeological data from Sarazm hints at a permanent occupation (Lyonnet 1996, 63 n. 66). Lyonnet's observation on the amount of material corroborates Besenval's comment on Excavation VII, who wrote in 1989 that most of the levels he had exposed until then appeared to have been carefully emptied before they were abandoned (Besenval and Isakov 1989, 14). Together with the fact that the archaeological deposits at Sarazm are generally not thick, these remarks tend to suggest rather short-lived occupations. This interpretation also agrees with the generally accepted view that mud-brick constructions and their architectural components in perishable matter cannot be repaired much after forty–fifty years of use, or even before, and need to be replaced. At the same time, one should admit that most of the site remains to be studied and that certain unexposed areas may contain greater concentrations of material remains. With regard to this, a large trash-pit recently excavated at Sarazm yielded unusual concentrations of animal bones and ceramics (Mutin et al. 2020a).

## Land, Minerals, and Metals: The raison(s) d'être of Sarazm

Four aspects of Sarazm need to be discussed within the broader contexts of Middle Asia, Central Asia, and the Eurasian Steppe: 1) the reason for its foundation; 2) its place or relationship within or with the cultural spheres this site seems to relate to the most; 3) its specific place at the intersection of the Eurasian Steppe and the Middle Asian Interaction Sphere; 4) its significance for the understanding of the origins of the Oxus Civilization.

Regarding the first aspect, putting aside the specific case of the burials in Excavation IV, there is little doubt that most of Sarazm settlement was founded by groups relating to the Namazga II–III tradition in Turkmenistan (Lyonnet 1996, 55–57; Kircho 2021, 117; Lyonnet and Dubova 2021, 20). No previous settlement has been identified in the Zeravshan Valley, and Sarazm material culture from Period I on is strongly connected to that of this tradition, which current data show developed within Turkmenistan, and not in Tajikistan. This implies that groups of people migrated from the west to the Zeravshan Valley toward the end of the fourth millennium BCE. On this topic, Isakov (1994b, 6) mentioned a study by T. K. Khodzhaiov, a physical anthropologist, who determined that the skeletons exposed within Excavation IV, which most scholars tend to think are culturally connected to the Steppe, were those of individuals that came from the southern regions of South-West Asia and Central Asia. He also wrote that (1994b, 6): 'Genetically, it seems that the community people of Sarazm are most closely connected to the Aeneolithic population of southern Turkmenistan, primarily Göksür and Qara-depe', although the basis for this claim is not indicated. A similar view that emphasizes a genetic connection to Turkmenistan is expressed in the following sentence (Lyonnet and Dubova 2021, 31):

> Specific craniometrics comparative research has been done by Hemphill (1999) to trace the origins of the northern Bactrian population: it points at a local origin with a possible gene flow from the previous Geoksjur component that the proximity with Sarazm could explain.

However, as C. C. Lamberg-Karlovsky (2002, 64) points out,

> [t]here is absolutely no evidence that genes are involved in determining the presence or absence of the cranial features studied; there are numerous non-genetic factors that account for cranial features and

their variation (for example, diet, infant cradling). To speak of 'gene flow' suggests a degree of understanding of the *genetic* structure of the architecture of the skull that we simply do not currently possess.

Recent DNA analysis was conducted on the human remains from two individuals from Sarazm. This analysis was part of a larger analysis programme conducted on 542 individuals dating to the Mesolithic through the Iron Age from Iran, Pakistan, Turkmenistan, Uzbekistan, Tajikistan, Afghanistan, Kyrgyzstan, Kazakhstan, and Russia (Narasimhan et al. 2019). Results from this analysis suggests 'low to almost no proportion of Anatolian farmer-related ancestry in Sarazm', an ancestry that is observed but increasingly declines from west to east through Iran into Turan.

> [S]ignificant West Siberian Hunter-Gatherer-related ancestry [is observed] in individuals from Iran and Turan during the early Neolithic period. That most extreme example of this are individuals from Sarazm in Tajikistan, dated to the mid-fourth millennium BCE, which can be modelled as having about ~20% of their ancestry attributable to this source [...] It is tempting to speculate that this ancestry is also characteristic of the hunter-gatherer Kelteminar culture that was spread over this region at this time.
>
> Taken together, these results imply that West Siberian Hunter-Gatherer-related ancestry was widespread in Kazakhstan and eastern Turan before the spread of the Yamnaya, and thus the Central Asian Steppe was a plausible conduit by which this ancestry might have arisen in these individuals from Turan. (Narasimhan et al. 2019, suppl. mat., 94–95, 199–200)

Unfortunately, there is no detailed information about the origin of the analysed human remains. One, identified genetically as a female, is noted as dating to 3700–3300 BCE (UZ-SZ-001, Sarazm 85 [1], burial 44–38 [I4290]). The second one (UZ-SZ-002 Sarazm 85 [2], burial 44–37 [I4910]), also a female, was radiocarbon dated to 3636–3521 cal. BCE (4765±20 BP, PSUAMS-2624). Although the possibility remains that one of these individuals is the one that was found in Excavation II, it seems more likely that both are from Excavation IV and that one might be the 'Princess of Sarazm'. Indeed, first, the year that is indicated on these samples (1985) is consistent with the field seasons the burials in this excavation were exposed (Besenval and Isakov 1989, 8); second, the 'UZ' label on these samples suggests an origin for this collection in Uzbekistan, and it is known that (part of?) these human remains were transferred at some point to Samarkand; third, considering that the burials

from Excavation IV are indeed linked to the Afanasievo Steppe culture, the above-mentioned radiocarbon date agrees with the chronology usually offered for this culture (e.g. 3800–3300 cal. BCE: Anthony 2007, 265–67, 275, 307–11).

In any case, considering the hypothesis that the burials in Excavation IV are earlier than the rest of Sarazm's settlement, this DNA analysis does not help clarifying much more than available material culture the origin of the groups that came to build houses and cultivate lands at this site and around it. Their remains show that they were farmers (see Chapter 2) that most likely were related to the Namazga tradition in Turkmenistan. They might have been pushed away and/or searched for new lands; yet, as stressed by Besenval and Isakov (1989, 18), 'Il est difficilement concevable que la capacité agricole de la région de Sarazm, capacité nullement supérieure à celle de nombreux autres secteurs en Asie centrale, soit à l'origine de telles relations.' Indeed, most scholars agree that Sarazm may have been founded for the reason that this site is located within a mineral-rich area. Kuzmina (2007, 211–12) writes that: 'It was founded by the former occupants of the Geoksyur oasis in the lower reaches of the Tedjen with a view to mining the rich deposits of polymetallic ores and turquoise' (see also Besenval and Isakov 1989, 18). Anthony (2007, 419) also emphasizes turquoise as a motive for the Sarazm settlement: 'Perhaps the lure that enticed Namazga farmers to venture north of the Kara Kum desert to Sarazm was the turquoise that outcropped in the desert near the lower Zeravshan River, a source they could have learned from Kelteminar foragers.' Francfort (2016, 474) draws attention to the abundance of gold in the sands of the Zeravshan River and the fact that this river 'becomes less turbulent where Sarazm is located', which must have facilitated its collection. Regardless of the fundamental reason for the foundation of Sarazm, its close and extended region is undeniably mineral-rich, and there is indeed evidence for craft activities at this site, including metallurgy as well as craft for semi-precious stones such as lapis lazuli (Besenval and Isakov 1989, 18; see **Chapter 6**). As noted above, some authors such as Kuzmina (2007, 212) believe that Sarazm was 'the largest metallurgical centre of Central Asia engaged in export' (see also Isakov 1991, 132–33; Razzokov 2008, 102). Similarly, Anthony (2007, 421) writes that: 'Sarazm exported both copper and turquoise southward during the Akkadian and Ur III periods.' The latter statement may not be wrong but is not well demonstrated archaeologically since most remains at this site predate these periods. Regarding the former statement, while there certainly is evidence for metallurgical activities at Sarazm, it is not that clear whether, or to what extent, these activities were directed to exportation and/or to local needs.

The metallic assemblage from Sarazm is described as 'unusually rich', consisting of 'numerous daggers, awls, chisels, a shaft-hole axe-adze, tweezers and wide variety of decorative rings, pendants, beads and pins' (Isakov et al. 1987, 90; see Isakov 1991 and Razzokov 2008; artefacts on display at the National Museum of Antiquities in Dushanbe as well as in the Penjikent and Sarazm museums; e.g. Mutin et al. 2020a, 30–31 fig. 9). The fact that this site is located within a mineral-rich region, that its material culture connects to distant cultural spheres, and that tools and waste relating to metal production, including crucibles, ingots, and moulds, have been found at this site are consistent with the view that sees Sarazm as a large, specialized centre for metallurgy and metalworking which attracted people over a very wide area. Yet, Isakov and some of his colleagues offered a nuanced view on this interpretation. They analysed the composition of a series of copper objects and concluded that 'very different objects were produced from a single smelt', which 'may argue against large scale production of a specialized nature' and 'is more indicative of [...] a production to fill immediate needs' (Isakov et al. 1987, 101). Furthermore, as noted above, available data shows that metal production at Sarazm appears to have taken place essentially within domestic contexts. These observations tend to show that Sarazm was different from contemporary major metallurgical centres such as Arisman and Tepe Hissar on the Iranian Plateau in that no 'industrial quarter' has been identified at this site. Arisman and Tepe Hissar 'have been considered major metal-producing centers, since both sites are covered with slag indicating large-scale production on the site' (Helwing 2007, 40). Specialized craft areas — 'industrial quarters' — that are separated from the domestic sphere are recorded at these sites, although metal processing is also recorded within domestic contexts (Helwing 2005, 174; 2007, 40–42; Thornton 2009, 189–98). Although it remains possible that specialized metallurgical areas and large amounts of slag will be identified at or near Sarazm in the future, metal production at this site seems at present to rather conform to the domestic workshops excavated at Arisman and Tepe Hissar. It may also be closer to configurations that have been noted within the Kura-Araxes sphere in the Caucasus. There, although a site exists (Dzedvebi) that

was occupied by a metallurgical community specializing in the extraction/production of gold [...] [this] extraordinary evidence [...] may not be fully representative of the more 'ordinary' and widespread copper metallurgy [...] Tedesco (2006) pointed out that evidence for copper-based metallurgical production is so common at Kura-Araxes sites that it could have been carried out on a small scale and possibly at the household-based level of production. (Palumbi 2016, 26)

In any case, current evidence does not seem enough to conclude on Sarazm being a major metallurgical centre dedicated to exportation. At a minimum, it does not seem to resemble major production centres known in Iran between the Late Chalcolithic and Bronze Age periods. Yet, many areas remain to be explored within the protected portion of this site, and many more archaeological deposits still lie below the villages and fields around it. Additionally, although Sarazm enjoys the special status of being unique within the context of Tajikistan and Uzbekistan, this site might perhaps be best understood if considered within a network of sites within the Zeravshan Valley and surrounding areas which we still know virtually nothing about. Avanesova mentions a number of 'settlements, short-time stations, places of ancient smelting works, manufacturing areas (Sarazm, Tugai, Ljavlkakan, Karnab, Aktashty, Tym, Madami, Beshbulak, Chakka, Navbag, etc.)' within the Zeravshan Valley extended region, with many of them being unpublished or whose reports are not easily accessible (Avanesova 2021, 667–68).[2] She emphasizes again the rich mineral resources available in this valley (including gold, silver, copper, lead, zinc, tin, arsenic, bismuth, and iron, as well as feldspar, talc, graphite, marble, granite, gypsum, turquoise, chalcedony, and onyx) and the fact that many of the places associated with these resources attest to ancient exploitation. It seems that most date to the Bronze Age and are posterior to Sarazm. Yet, more work probably needs to be done on this topic, even though many sites that may have been occupied at the same time as Sarazm may

---

[2] On a similar topic, N. Erb-Satulllo (2022, 10) writes about the metal crafting landscape in the Colchis region of the Caucasus between 1500–600 BCE that: 'Different production activities are spatially segregated but functionally linked through the *chaîne opératoire*. Ore was mined from the abundant copper deposits in the foothill and mountain zones. Smelting sites in the foothills are individually small, consisting of one or two furnaces and a working platform, possibly for roasting matte or ores [...] On a per site basis, [the] slag quantities pale in comparison with other Late Bronze and Early Iron Age smelting sites in the Near East [...] It is only in aggregate that the scale of the Colchian smelting industry, with its many sites, becomes apparent.'

today be buried under alluvium deposits or wiped out (see also **Chapter 2**).

With regard to this, the site of Tugai in Uzbekistan, *c.* 27 km west of Sarazm, yielded the remains of copper metallurgical activities as well as plain ceramic vessels (and a few additional types of objects) comparable to those from Sarazm (Avanesova 1996; 2021, 667–69, 674–76, 677 fig. 24.8, 679). Although caution should be exercised as this material might be more recent,[3] these ceramic connections with Tugai might be just the tip of the iceberg and bring to mind a question that Lyonnet (1997, 54) posed in these terms: 'Les sites chalcolithiques en Asie centrale orientale : simples comptoirs commerciaux[4] (A) ou traces résiduelles d'un véritable peuplement (B) ?' Sarazm has long appeared as an isolated site, far away from the cores of the cultural spheres it seems to relate to the most, i.e. in Turkmenistan and the Indo-Iranian Borderlands during the Late Chalcolithic and Early Bronze Age. This apparent situation together with the rich natural resources within its extended region make it rational to interpret this site as a trading post. Not necessarily contradictory with this hypothesis is also the possibility that Sarazm was part of (a) greater regional, or supraregional, settlement(s), that has(ve) mostly disappeared or has(ve) yet to be found. In addition to the potential case of Tugai, another site in the Zeravshan Valley, *c.* 50 km west of Sarazm, Zhukov, also yielded material remains connected to Sarazm as well as to the Kel'teminar, Afanasievo, and Yamnaya cultures. This site is interpreted as a ritual site (Avanesova 2013; Francfort 2020, 9, 22). Lyonnet also mentions a few sherds similar to Sarazm ceramic material that were found at Urgut, *c.* 40 km south-east of Samarkand (Lyonnet 1997, 55). Much further to the south-west, painted pottery fragments relating to the Geoksyur style (Namazga III) were found in the Murghab Delta, where they are interpreted as the remains of 'temporary settlements, possibly from groups on their way to the Zeravshan Valley' (Lyonnet and Dubova 2021, 20; see Vinogradova 2021, 635). This discovery suggests that the virtual absence of evidence between this region and the Samarkand region may be due to a lack of research in certain areas, or to the fact that Chalcolithic and Early Bronze Age sites are covered with alluvium deposits in others (Lyonnet 1997, 55). Besenval and Isakov also emphasized the latter possibility as well as the fact that archaeological sites may be underneath agricultural fields and may have been destroyed through the effect of plough tillage (Besenval and Isakov 1989, 7, 17–18). Other parameters need to be considered such as the one that Rante and Mirzaakhmedov mention in the case of the Bukhara Oasis. They note (Rante and Mirzaakhmedov 2019, 19) that the

> inner areas of the oasis were uninhabited because of its swampy and marshy ground. It is also possible that the main Zerafshan stream almost divided the oasis into two parts, of which the south-eastern one, where later Bukhara and other important sites were erected, might have developed later than the north-eastern one, probably because of the presence of branches of the Kashka Darya delta, which rendered the area unsuitable for settlement.

Similarly, to the south, Lyonnet identified six sites in the Taluqan Plain of north-eastern Afghanistan that yielded ceramic material dating to the Chalcolithic/Early Bronze Age periods, including sherds relating to both Sarazm and Mundigak in southern Afghanistan (Lyonnet 1981; Isakov and Lyonnet 1988; Lyonnet 1997). The observations she made in the Taluqan Plain led her to reckon that more Chalcolithic/Early Bronze Age sites probably existed in this plain as well as in other plains of north-eastern Afghanistan such as the Kunduz Plain and the Imam Sahib Plain, and that these sites may have been buried under alluvial deposits or wiped out (Lyonnet 1997, 55–56). Thus, the above-mentioned question that Lyonnet addressed cannot be answered in the present state of knowledge, but it certainly needs to be kept in mind that current evidence suggests that more sites likely existed that could have functioned together with Sarazm, be they stations, temporary settlements, or more permanent villages like this site.

## At the Intersection of the 'Middle Asian Interaction Sphere' and the Steppe Cultures

Sarazm currently remains unique within the context of eastern southern Central Asia for the expanse of material records relating to the Late Chalcolithic and Early Bronze Age periods it contains and the multicultural relationships these records exhibit. However, when considered within the broader context of Middle Asia and southern Central Asia, the multicultural aspect of Sarazm emerges as slightly less exceptional. In fact, Sarazm may also be seen as *merely* the north-easternmost site known at present of a broader sphere of intercultural interactions that characterized this vast region. In contrast to

---

[3] H.-P. Francfort, pers. comm.

[4] Although this term that refers to commerce may not be the most appropriate one for the case study and chronological periods that are of interest here.

most areas and sites of Middle Asia, however, Sarazm and the Zeravshan Valley intersect with Steppe cultural complexes, which are characterized by economic orientations and material remains generally different from those of the oasis cultures known further south.

The third millennium BCE in the regions between Mesopotamia, the Indus Valley, southern Central Asia, and the Persian Gulf is known as 'Middle Asian Interaction Sphere' (MAIS). This term defines the numerous interactions within this vast area that are documented by 'shared artifacts, including objects of trade and exchange as well as artifact styles and design motifs [...] [and] written documentation [...] for the maritime trade in the [Persian] Gulf' (Possehl 2002, 215; see Possehl 2002, 215–36; 2007). In the eastern part of Middle Asia, significant connections and parallels are observed between sites and assemblages in eastern Iran, southern Central Asia, and the Indian Subcontinent. Typical objects relating to the Indus Civilization (c. 2500–1900 BCE) such as seals, pottery, ivory sticks, and jewellery, are recorded in southern Central Asia including at Altyn-Depe and Gonur-Depe, as well as in Iran, Oman, and Mesopotamia. An Indus-related site, Shortughaï, was settled in north-eastern Afghanistan, far away from the core of the Indus Civilization, possibly 'to give the Harappans access to the lapis lazuli mines of Sar-i Sang, Badakhshan', additional mineral resources available in the region, and/or perhaps 'to procure Bactrian camels' (Possehl 2002, 229; see Francfort 1989; 2016; see below). Evident parallels for objects that characterize the Bactria-Margiana Archaeological Complex (BMAC), or Oxus Civilization (c. 2300–1700 BCE), are observed in Pakistan, eastern Iran, and as far as Susa in Khuzestan, such as metallic pins, seals, and adzes/axes; stone columns, disks, and containers; and pottery. Shahdad in south-eastern Iran and Mehrgarh in Pakistan are two well-known examples of sites containing Oxus-related materials (see Jarrige 1991; Hiebert 1994; Possehl 2002, 231–35; Mutin and Lamberg-Karlovsky 2021). This vast geographic distribution of Indus-related and Oxus-related objects, as well as objects with different cultural affiliations, is the result of various processes of intercultural interaction which are not fully understood. Trade, stylistic influences, migrations, and political expansions are all possible processes. As briefly discussed below, this intercultural interaction has been emphasized as an important contribution to the formation of the Oxus Civilization in addition to local dynamics.

It is also important to remember that the socio-political context of Middle Asia during the third millennium BCE, especially beginning around 2500 BCE, is commonly defined as an urban or proto-urban phase. While the earliest city-states emerged in Mesopotamia, 'complex polities or secondary states', civilizations such as the Indus Civilization and the Oxus Civilization, developed east of Sumer mostly from the mid-third millennium BCE onward broadly speaking, although it is important to also keep in mind that sites and regions that are defined as urban or proto-urban centres, such as Shahr-i Sokhta in Sistan and the Jiroft region in the Halil Rud Basin in Iran, already began to emerge during the first half of the third millennium BCE (Kohl 2007, 214–33). Besides the kingdoms and empires in Mesopotamia such as those of the Akkadian and Ur III dynasties and later rulers, Mesopotamian texts inform us about topics such as the trade, alliances, and conflicts between this area and political entities further east. Certain of them including Elam within western Iran, Dilmun centred on Bahrain in the Persian Gulf, and Meluhha thought to be the Indus Civilization between Pakistan and India have been located on maps. Francfort and Tremblay believe that the kingdom known in Mesopotamian texts as Marhashi corresponds to the Oxus Civilization, whereas Steinkeller thinks it was the Halil Rud culture in south-eastern Iran (Steinkeller 1982; Francfort and Tremblay 2010; Steinkeller 2014; Francfort 2016, 472).

On this topic, it is important to remember that Shortughaï and its broader region have been instrumental in suggesting that Marhashi was located in Central Asia and corresponded to the Oxus Civilization. In addition to other textual and archaeological evidence, two arguments are probably worth mentioning here, which are that this kingdom is thought to have had close ties with the Indus Civilization (Meluhha) and to have been located nearby the expanse of this civilization, and that its various types of resources must have attracted people. The above-mentioned lapis lazuli is one of them, while Francfort puts forth gold as an 'extremely desirable and abundant' mineral in eastern Bactria. This scholar points out that both must have been attractive, with the nuance that lapis lazuli was perhaps more so for the '"Western Bactrian" market and further West' than in the Indus (Francfort 2016, 473–74). As for the spatial proximity between the Indus (Meluhha) and Marhashi, he notes that (Francfort 2016, 472): 'We must keep in mind that Eastern Bactria, by the road of the Dorah Pass via Badakhshan, Chitral and Swât, is easily connected to Northern India/Pakistan.'

In any case, leading individuals or groups in the Bronze Age polities of Middle Asia made use of, and exchanged, specific items, symbols of power, and luxury goods, such as those mentioned above, and these objects and the raw materials to make them were sought after. Trade is documented in the Mesopotamian texts, and part of it,

> Many of the materials traded within the Middle Asian Interaction Sphere[,] appear to be luxury products, intended to satisfy the desires of elites and the needs of the Mesopotamian cult system. For the most part, the trade we see evidenced in the archaeological record involves semiprecious stones, metals, seals, jewellery, various forms of objets d'art, exotic animals, and the like. (Possehl 2002, 218)

Again, the lapis lazuli from Badakhshan, known to be the major source for this semi-precious stone in this part of the world (Herrmann 1968), is one of the materials that were exchanged. This source, as well as potentially that for gold in Samti, east of Shortughaï, was the one that provided sites in Mesopotamia with lapis lazuli, including for the making of the famous objects recovered from Ur in Iraq (Hansen 1998).[5] Chlorite carved containers in the 'Intercultural Style' are known to have been produced in south-eastern Iran and exchanged all the way to Mesopotamia (Kohl 2001). Tin emerged as an important traded material during the third millennium BCE and was used in Mesopotamian metallurgy. Sources for tin that may have fulfilled Mesopotamian needs are believed to be in Central Asia and/or southern and western Afghanistan (see Weeks 2004; 2012; Lyonnet 2005; Kaniuth 2007; see **Chapter 2**).[6] Certainly, the Mesopotamian market was not the only customer of the MAIS. The graveyards exposed at sites such as Gonur-Depe (Sarianidi 2007), Shahr-i Sokhta (Piperno and Salvatori 2007), Shahdad (Hakemi 1997), and the Halil Rud Valley (Madjidzadeh and Pittman 2008; Akbarzadeh and Piran 2013) show that demand was virtually everywhere.

At Sarazm, most, but perhaps not all, archaeological remains suggest that this site was not involved in these broad, interregional dynamics dating to the mid–late third through the mid-second millennia BCE, because they essentially are earlier, dating to before *c.* 2500 cal. BCE. These dynamics are nonetheless not a new phenomenon. In fact, substantial interregional interactions already existed in Middle Asia and Central Asia between the mid–late fourth and early–mid-third millennia BCE, around 3000 cal. BCE broadly speaking. Although the scale of these interactions is difficult to compare to that of the later periods, it does not seem irrational to characterize them as a sort of MAIS, or an early MAIS. This time roughly corresponds to the so-called Late Uruk and Proto-Elamite expansions in Iran, for which models have been put forth that emphasize the leading role of the Mesopotamian elites in the development of interregional exchanges across Middle Asia (Alden 1982; Algaze 1993). Yet, as also observed centuries later, many dynamics existed at that time independently of Mesopotamia. The identification of the same painted motifs on ceramics from sites in Turkmenistan, Shahr-i Sokhta, Mundigak, and in the Quetta Valley, where such material is named 'Quetta Ware', was one of the first evidence that led to the recognition of a vast interaction sphere between these sites and regions (Lamberg-Karlovsky and Tosi 1973, 25–26, 38), although the directions of the influences and most likely migrations that these similarities entail are still debated (see Mutin and Minc 2019 for a recapitulation and references). Additional interregional interactions dating to about the same time have since then been detected through the geographic distributions of other ceramic styles further south and west, between south-eastern Iran and Pakistan (see Wright 1984; 1989; Mutin 2012; 2013, 206–13). An additional interregional phenomenon is observed around 3000 cal. BCE, the Proto-Elamite phenomenon, which is thought to have developed in south-western Iran (at Susa or Tal-i Malyan; see Lamberg-Karlovsky 1978; Alden 1982; Mutin 2013; Petrie 2013) and spread eastward, including to Tepe Yahya and Shahr-i Sokhta in south-eastern Iran. Analogies between elements of the Proto-Elamite material culture and that in Central Asia[7] have led scholars to link the new developments observed around 3000 cal. BCE in eastern Middle Asia and southern Central Asia to the expansion of this phenomenon (see Lyonnet and Dubova 2021, 20, 41–42). This may not be wrong for a part of, or aspects of, these new dynamics but does not seem sufficient to explain the totality of them.

---

[5] <https://www.penn.museum/research/project.php?pid=49> [accessed 10 April 2023].

[6] The groups settled at Sarazm do not seem to have been involved in tin exploitation and exchange (Kraus 2021). The well-known copper and tin mines of Mushiston in the Zeravshan Mountains, *c.* 40 km south-east of Sarazm (*c.* 2830 m asl), and Karnab in Uzbekistan, *c.* 170 km west of Sarazm, both appear to have been exploited by Andronovo Steppe culture-related groups during the second millennium BCE (Boroffka et al. 2002; Parzinger and Boroffka 2003; see Garner 2021).

[7] The cylinder seal from Sarazm is, by default, best paralleled within the Uruk, Jemdet-Nasr, Early Dynastic and Proto-Elamite spheres of Mesopotamia and Iran, where cylinder seals and sealing impressions are common (Isakov 1994b, 11 fig. 10; Mutin et al. 2022). Also, parallels for the painted motifs of the Namazga III ceramics have been noted on wall paintings at Proto-Elamite (Banesh) Tal-i Malyan in Fars (see Kircho 2021, 116 for a recent recapitulation on this topic).

Lastly, the Kura-Araxes southward expansion from the Caucasus into Iran and additional regions further west deserves mention as it also occurred within the same chronological range (Kohl 2007, 216). Certainly, these interregional dynamics were not all strictly contemporaneous, nor did they all have similar natures and causes. As noted above, trade, stylistic influences, migrations, and political expansions are all possibilities that may explain the extensive and overlapping geographic distributions of materials with various cultural affiliations that characterize the archaeological record of this period in Middle Asia. In any case, the archaeological record at Sarazm clearly shows that this site was part of this vast sphere of interactions. Furthermore, elements of the vestiges from this site bring to mind the prestige items (and buildings) that were intended to satisfy the desires of elites which Possehl mentions for the MAIS centuries later.[8]

Sarazm, and more generally the Zeravshan Valley, appears to have also been linked to groups of seemingly very different 'worlds'. Although not all scholars agree on the interpretation that sees the funerary stone circle found at Sarazm Excavation IV as a Steppe-related, Afanasievo-like burial, many do believe so. Bonora (2021, 738) writes:

> [T]he rich Afanasievo-like burial from excavation 4 attributed to Sarazm period I and dated to the mid-fourth millennium (Lyonnet 1996, 33, 35 [type III.11], 47), although it raises several interpretative problems, is the earliest evidence of interactive processes east of the Caspian Sea between the cattle herders of the Eurasian steppe and the proto-urban communities of western Central Asia.

If not for this funerary structure, Steppe-related and Kel'teminar-related elements have been identified within Sarazm lithic industry (Brunet and Razzokov 2016; see **Chapter 6**). One pottery is often cited as Kel'teminar material (Lyonnet 1996, 49, 59, 116 fig. 38 no. 1). The turquoise from Sarazm may suggest some form of communication with Kel'teminar groups who lived and even controlled access to and exploitation of certain sources in Uzbekistan (as suggested by Anthony 2007, 419; see **Chapter 6**). In addition to Sarazm, the above-mentioned site of Zhukov also yielded materials relating to Sarazm, the Kel'teminar cultural complex, and the Steppe (Avanesova 2013). Intercultural interaction is observed at Tugai too, where Steppe-related, Sarazm-related, and southern Turkmenistan-related evidence was recorded (Avanesova 1996; 2021, 667–69, 674–76, 677 fig. 24.8, 679), although the dating of the evidence at this site may need clarification.

Avanesova (2021, 666–67) puts the situation in the Zeravshan Valley into perspective the following way:

> During the Paleometal period (Chalcolithic and Bronze Age), the Zeravshan area was one where cultural integration was the most intense in Central Asia, mixing different cultural traditions. The local basis for this process was the Sazagan-Kel'teminar substratum. Significant changes happened by the middle of the fourth millennium with the settlement of Geoksjur-type farming groups among the indigenous population at Sarazm [...] The local Neolithic hunter-fisherman population of the valley probably adopted the new and more productive methods of these newcomers. At about the same time and later on, other groups came from the steppes, from the Afanasievo and Jamnaj cultural horizons, and brought with them their own economic models.

She then inventories the groups present within the Zeravshan Valley between the mid-fourth and mid-second millennia BCE. Here should be remembered:

> 1. Sarazm, which developed on a complex farming and cattle breeding economy, combined with metal working. 2. Early mobile, small cattle breeders of the Afanas'evo-Jamnaja type (Zhukov cultic complex, Sarazm circular tomb(?), dispersed seasonal sites like Siab-2, Ljavljakan, and Ajakagitma) [...] 4. Kel'teminar groups continuing their traditional way of subsistence appropriation [...] 5. Specialized industrial complexes dedicated to mining and the metalworking production cycle [...] but also with elements of settled cattle breeding (Tugai, Medomi, Aktashi, etc.). (Avanesova 2021, 667)

---

[8] For instance, even before most of the settlement was founded, the 'Princess of Sarazm' was buried with: one copper bronze mirror, forty-nine gold beads and twenty-four silver beads, two clay figurines, three stone mace-heads, two shell bracelets similar to those recorded in Kech-Makran (Besenval 2005, 4–6 figs 9–12), one bone awl, as well as many lazurite, carnelian, turquoise, and chalk beads that are described as being 'in numbers ranging from thirty to one thousand' (Isakov 1994b, 5–6; see Isakov 1994a). In addition to this funerary material and the buildings seemingly of importance such as those that Isakov interpreted as a 'palace complex' in Excavation V and a 'religious building' in Excavation IV, objects interpreted as 'prestige' objects have been recorded at this site (Isakov 1994b; see **Chapter 6**).

## Significance of Sarazm in the Understanding of the Origins of the Oxus Civilization

These multiple intercultural interactions and the cultural integrations and formations that probably resulted from them that are evinced around 3000 BCE at Sarazm, along the Zeravshan Valley, and more broadly along, around, and across the Hindu Kush, between southern Central Asia, the Iranian Plateau, and the Indo-Iranian Borderlands, may easily be seen as a previous model, or background, for the development of the Oxus Civilization. As Francfort (2005, 260) puts it:

> C'est sur cette base complexe, dans laquelle interviennent aussi bien le phénomène de l'expansion urukéenne et proto-élamite que celle de l'Indus pré-harappéen, ainsi que l'interface avec le monde des steppes du moyen Oxus au Zeravshan Kel'teminar et Afanasevo, et non par un apport soudain que les deltas de la Bactriane et de la Margiane ont été peuplés au cours de la phase mûre de la Civilisation de l'Oxus. (See also Mutin and Francfort 2019; Lyonnet and Dubova 2021, 41–42)

Indeed, the Oxus Civilization certainly partly developed out of processes and earlier traditions local to southern Central Asia (Lyonnet and Dubova 2021, 20; see also the parallel between a monumental building from Sarazm and architecture from the Oxus Civilization: Muradov 2021, 162–63). Yet, it is currently generally admitted that this civilization emerged and grew as a result of various interactions between the archaeological complexes identified between southern Central Asia, the Iranian Plateau, the Indo-Iranian Borderlands (see Mutin and Lamberg-Karlovsky 2021, 567–70), and the Steppe. Kohl (2007, 237) writes:

> The origins of the Bactria-Margiana Archaeological Complex are not to be sought in a single place, but in southern Turkmenistan, eastern Iran, Baluchistan, the Indian subcontinent, and later, as this complex further developed — or, perhaps better — devolved, the Eurasian steppes. Like other cultural phenomena, it was a hybrid, the product of a unique convergence of different cultural traditions. The argument for cultural diversity is not based on political correctness, but on historical accuracy.

Although interactions between these areas probably existed before, it is beginning at the time Sarazm was founded that clear and numerous pieces of evidence appeared in the archaeological record.

On this topic, recent excavation and re-evaluation of Bronze Age cemeteries in south-western Tajikistan are probably worth mentioning (Francfort 2016; Vinogradova and Bobomulloev 2020; Vinogradova 2021). These sites include Farkhor, Gelot and Darnajchi cemeteries, dating to the third through the early second millennia BCE. Comparative analysis of the material assemblages at these sites as well as available radiocarbon dates suggest connections to sites in southern Central Asia (such as Altyn-Depe, Gonur-Depe, Sapalli Tepe, and Dzharkutan) and Iran (such as Tepe Hissar IIIC, Shahdad, and Tepe Chalow) as well as in Afghanistan including Shortughaï and Dashli Depe. In short, as Francfort (2016, 473) expresses it, this evidence

> completely and definitely invalidates the old model of a migration out of the Kopet Dagh piedmont by the cities people moving eastwards to 'colonize' Margiana, Bactria and reaching Eastern Bactria at the final phase of the Bronze Age [...] [W]e have to completely restate the question of the origin and evolution of the Oxus Civilization [...] In short, we may consider, as the best working hypothesis, that the Oxus Civilization proper appeared or 'emerged' somewhere in the Northern piedmonts of the Hindu Kuch in Afghanistan.

This scholar suggests renaming this material culture in eastern Bactria 'Panj culture' (Francfort 2016, 471). He notes that (Francfort 2020, 23): 'In Eastern Bactria, the Middle Bronze Age site of Farkhor (Tajikistan) on the North bank of the Panj coexisted with the neighbouring Indus site of Shortughai on the South bank of the Panj. It is even possible that at some point they coalesced into a "Panj culture."' Vinogradova (2021, 660) emphasizes the fact that 'this material culture results from the combination of a local Bactrian tradition with deep Mesopotamian and Elamite influences', including especially its toreutics and glyptic arts. We will see below that small finds uncovered at Sarazm also parallel objects from the Farkhor cemetery.

# 2. The Environmental Setting of Sarazm

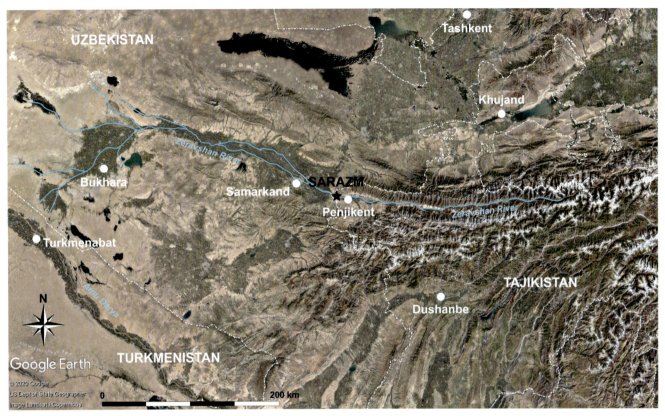

Figure 2.1: Map of the Zeravshan River in Tajikistan and Uzbekistan, with location of Sarazm (star) and main current cities (dots). Basemap Google Earth, modified by B. Mutin.

## The Zeravshan River

The Zeravshan River takes its source at *c.* 3000 m asl at the Zeravshan glacier within the northern Pamir Mountains, close to the border with Kyrgyzstan, within mountains topping at more than 4500 and 5000 m asl. It then flows west through a narrow valley parallel to the Turkestan and Zeravshan mountain ranges to the north and to the south, respectively, down to the village of Koshana (alt. *c.* 1150 m asl), *c.* 215 km west, where the Zeravshan Valley becomes wider. It is not until *c.* 15 km after Penjikent, at the border with Uzbekistan (alt. *c.* 880 m asl), *c.* 275 km distant from its source, that the Zeravshan is no more surrounded by mountains and opens to the vast Samarkand Plain (Samarkand is located *c.* 60 km west of Penjikent). From that point onward, this river keeps flowing in Uzbekistan for about 400 km through the Samarkand and Bukhara oases and then ends before it reaches the Amu Darya and the city of Turkmenabat in Turkmenistan (Fig. 2.1; see Besenval and Isakov 1989, 5–7; see also Rickmers 1913 and Bensidoun 1979).

## Mineral Resources

*Zeravshan* means gold purveyor in Persian and refers to the fact that gold has been observed in this river for millennia and is still actively exploited today in this region. This river was also named *Polytimetos* by the ancient Greek authors (Aristob., *FGrH* 139 F 28a; Arr., *Anab.* IV. 5. 6, IV. 6. 7; Ptol., *Geog.* VI. 14. 2; Curt. VII. 10. 1–3). Alongside gold, 'Tajikistan has more than 400 known mineral deposits including deposits of antimony, bismuth, crude petroleum, fluorspar […] lead, mercury, molybdenum, natural gas, tungsten, silver, and zinc' (Renaud 2019, 45.1). Today, plants are built in the portion of the Sughd Province that encompasses the Zeravshan Valley. These plants exploit local deposits, sometimes involving international cooperation such as with China. This is the case with the Konchoch and Skal'noye gold deposits in the Ayni District, *c.* 80 km east of Penjikent. The

18    2. THE ENVIRONMENTAL SETTING OF SARAZM

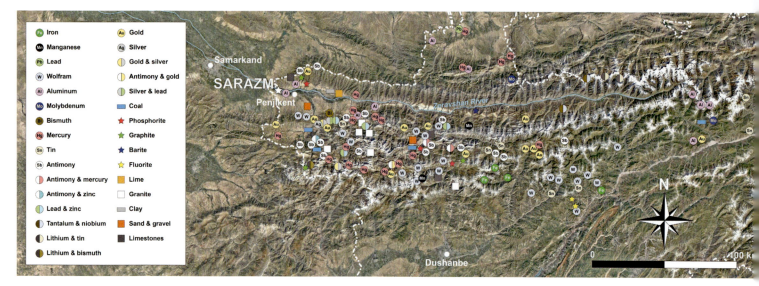

Figure 2.2: Map of the Zeravshan Valley and surrounding areas with location of the main geological and mineral resources. Adapted from the geological and mineral resource map of Tajikistan (<https://geoportal-tj.org/wp-content/uploads/deposits_map-scaled.jpg> [accessed 10 April 2023]. Basemap Google Earth, modified by B. Mutin.

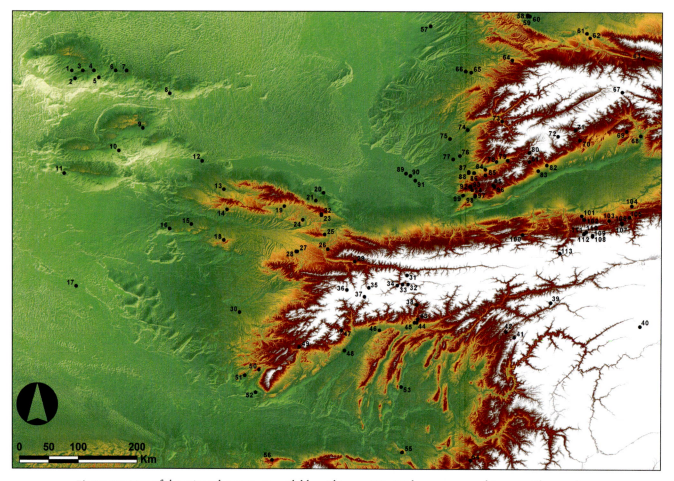

Figure 2.3: Map of the mineral resources available within a c. 350–450 km area around Sarazm. The numbers refer to those listed in Table 2.1. Sarazm is between nos 26 and 29. Adapted from the Mineral Resources Data System of the US Geological Survey (<https://mrdata.usgs.gov/mrds/> [accessed 10 April 2023]). B. Mutin.

Table 2.1: Mineral resources within *c.* 350–450 km around the Zeravshan Valley recorded in the Mineral Resources Data System of the US Geological Survey (<https://mrdata.usgs.gov/mrds/> [accessed 10 April 2023]). The numbers refer to those on Figure 2.3.

| Map | Site name | Country | Resources |
| --- | --- | --- | --- |
| 1 | Ak Dzhen | Uzbekistan | Gold; Palladium |
| 2 | Aytym | Uzbekistan | Gold |
| 3 | Bichanzor | Uzbekistan | Gold; Palladium |
| 4 | Gushsay | Uzbekistan | Palladium |
| 5 | Kok Patas | Uzbekistan | Gold; Palladium |
| 6 | Koch Bulak | Uzbekistan | Gold; Palladium |
| 7 | Kzyl Alma | Uzbekistan | Gold; Palladium; Platinum |
| 8 | Bauxite — Uzbekistan | Uzbekistan | Aluminium |
| 9 | Muruntau | Uzbekistan | Gold |
| 10A | Amantaytau | Uzbekistan | Gold |
| 10B | Daughystau | Uzbekistan | Gold |
| 11 | Taskazgan | Uzbekistan | Graphite; Nickel; Cobalt |
| 12 | Muruntau | Uzbekistan | Gold; Palladium |
| 13 | Lyangar | Uzbekistan | Tungsten; Molybdenum |
| 14 | Lyangar | Uzbekistan | Tungsten; Molybdenum |
| 15 | Kokand Phosacid Complex | Uzbekistan | Phosphorus-Phosphates |
| 16 | Sidzhak Area | Uzbekistan | Lead; Molybdenum; Vanadium |
| 17 | Chardzou Phosacid Complex | Uzbekistan | Phosphorus-Phosphates |
| 18A | Ingichka | Uzbekistan | Tungsten |
| 18B | Ingichke Mine | Uzbekistan | Copper; Tungsten |
| 19 | Charmitan | Uzbekistan | Gold |
| 20 | Uch-Kulach | Uzbekistan | Barium-Barite; Lead; Zinc |
| 21 | Uzbekistan Wollastonite | Uzbekistan | Wollastonite |
| 22 | Koytash Concentrator | Uzbekistan | Tungsten |
| 23 | Koytash | Uzbekistan | Molybdenum; Tungsten |
| 24 | Ugat | Uzbekistan | Tungsten |
| 25A | Karakutan | Uzbekistan | Gold |
| 25B | Mardzhanbulak | Uzbekistan | Gold |
| 26 | Takfon | Uzbekistan | Tungsten; Zinc |

| Map | Site name | Country | Resources |
| --- | --- | --- | --- |
| 27 | Uch Kulach | Uzbekistan | Lead; Zinc |
| 28 | Samarkand Phos — Acid Complex | Uzbekistan | Phosphorus-Phosphates |
| 29 | Dzhilav | Tajikistan | Tungsten |
| 30 | Kurgashin | Uzbekistan | Lead; Zinc |
| 31A | Jilau | Tajikistan | Gold |
| 31B | Taror | Tajikistan | Gold |
| 32 | Anzob | Tajikistan | Mercury; Antimony |
| 33 | Anzob | Tajikistan | Lead; Zinc; Silver |
| 34 | Maykhura | Tajikistan | Tungsten |
| 35 | Toror | Tajikistan | Gold |
| 36 | Karatyube | Tajikistan | Tungsten |
| 37 | Chokcharskoe Cadmium Deposit | Uzbekistan | Cadmium |
| 38 | Kabuty | Tajikistan | Tungsten |
| 39 | Lyanger Lake | Tajikistan | Boron-Borates; Sodium, Halite; Cobalt; Lithium; Sodium |
| 40 | Kommunarovo | Tajikistan | Gold |
| 41 | Safyet — Darya River | Tajikistan | Platinum |
| 42 | Yaksu | Tajikistan | Gold |
| 43 | Dzhizhikrut | Tajikistan | Antimony; Mercury |
| 44 | Takob | Tajikistan | Fluorine-Fluorite |
| 45 | Zeravshan | Tajikistan | Antimony |
| 46 | (Facility) Regar Smelter | Tajikistan | Aluminium, Contained or Metal |
| 47 | Khandiza | Uzbekistan | Lead; Zinc; Gold |
| 48 | (Facility) Karlyuk Smelter | Uzbekistan | Lead, Smelter |
| 49 | Gjumuslug | Uzbekistan | Lead; Zinc |
| 50 | Kugitang | Turkmenistan | Lead |
| 51A | Gaurdak Deposit Potash | Turkmenistan | Potassium; Sulphur |
| 51B | Gaurdak Deposit Sulfur | Turkmenistan | Potassium; Sulphur |
| 52 | Karlyuk Deposit — K2o Brines Plant | Turkmenistan | Potassium |
| 53 | Maykhura | Tajikistan | Tungsten; Tin |
| 54 | Taqcha Khana | Afghanistan | Sodium, Halite; Gypsum-Anhydrite |

| Map | Site name | Country | Resources |
|---|---|---|---|
| 55A | Kunduz | Afghanistan | Strontium |
| 55B | Kunduz | Afghanistan | Strontium |
| 56 | Alburz | Afghanistan | Sulphur |
| 57 | Suleiman-Sai Deposit S-Central Ussr | Kazakhstan | Vanadium; Lead; Zinc; Copper; Molybdenum |
| 58A | Aksuran | Kazakhstan | Lead; Zinc |
| 58B | Baizhan | Kazakhstan | Copper; Lead; Zinc |
| 58C | Baizhan Concentrator | Kazakhstan | Lead; Zinc |
| 58D | Chulak-Tau | Kazakhstan | Phosphorus-Phosphates |
| 58E | Molodezniy Mine | Kazakhstan | Phosphorus-Phosphates |
| 59 | Karatau District | Kazakhstan | Phosphorus-Phosphates |
| 60 | Kara Tau Deposits | Kazakhstan | Phosphorus-Phosphates |
| 61 | Rodnikovoe | Kazakhstan | Lead; Zinc; Silver |
| 62 | Dzhambul Phos-acid Complex | Kazakhstan | Phosphorus-Phosphates |
| 63 | Jerooy | Kyrgyzstan | Gold |
| 64 | Abail | Kazakhstan | Iron |
| 65 | Chimkent Phosphate Plant | Kazakhstan | Phosphorus-Phosphates |
| 66A | (Facility) Chimkent Lead Smelter | Kazakhstan | Lead, Smelter; Antimony; Bismuth; Copper; Gold; Silver; Tellurium |
| 66B | Chimkentzn | Kazakhstan | Zinc, Refiner |
| 67 | Balykty | Kyrgyzstan | Gold; Palladium |
| 68 | Sarybulak | Kyrgyzstan | Tin; Zirconium |
| 69 | Uchkoshkon | Kyrgyzstan | Tin |
| 70 | Sumsar | Kyrgyzstan | Lead; Zinc |
| 71 | Terek | Kyrgyzstan | Antimony |
| 72 | Chatkal River | Kyrgyzstan | Platinum; Gold |
| 73 | Ustarasai | Uzbekistan | Bismuth |
| 74 | (Facility) Chirchik Smelter and Alloy Plant | Uzbekistan | Tungsten; Molybdenum |
| 75 | Tashkent | Uzbekistan | Titanium, Pigment |
| 76 | Nakpai | Uzbekistan | Wollastonite |
| 77 | Toytepa | Uzbekistan | Fluorine-Fluorite |
| 78 | Kal'Makyr | Uzbekistan | Platinum |
| 79 | Angren | Uzbekistan | Aluminium |

| Map | Site name | Country | Resources |
|---|---|---|---|
| 80 | Kochbulak | Uzbekistan | Gold |
| 81 | Kochbulak Deposit | Tajikistan | Gold; Silver; Copper; Lead; Zinc; Iron; Antimony; Bismuth; Manganese; Tellurium |
| 82 | Altynkan | Uzbekistan | Gold |
| 83 | Kandzholo | Tajikistan | Silver |
| 84 | Kanimansur | Uzbekistan | Lead; Silver; Bismuth |
| 85 | South Yangikan | Uzbekistan | Molybdenum; Palladium |
| 86A | Almalyk Complex | Uzbekistan | Copper; Lead; Zinc; Molybdenum; Zinc |
| 86B | Almalyk Phos-Acid Complex | Uzbekistan | Phosphorus-Phosphates |
| 86C | Almalyklenin | Uzbekistan | Lead |
| 86D | Dalnee Deposit | Uzbekistan | Copper; Gold; Silver; Molybdenum |
| 86E | Kalmakir Mine | Uzbekistan | Copper; Gold; Silver; Molybdenum |
| 86F | Sary-Cheku Mine | Uzbekistan | Copper; Gold; Molybdenum |
| 87 | (Facility) Almalic Copper Smelter and Refinery | Uzbekistan | Copper |
| 88A | (Facility) Almalyk Zinc Smelter | Uzbekistan | Zinc, Refiner |
| 88B | Almalic Concentrator | Uzbekistan | Lead; Zinc; Copper; Molybdenum |
| 88C | Almalic Copper Concentrator | Uzbekistan | Copper; Lead; Molybdenum; Zinc |
| 89 | Almalyk Ore Field | Uzbekistan | Molybdenum; Copper; Zinc; Lead; Gold; Silver; Platinum; Palladium; Osmium |
| 90 | Dal'Neye | Uzbekistan | Molybdenum; Copper; Palladium; Platinum; Rhodium |
| 91 | Kal'Makyr | Uzbekistan | Molybdenum; Copper; Palladium; Platinum; Rhodium |
| 92 | Altyn-Topkan | Tajikistan | Lead; Zinc; Bismuth; Cadmium; Copper; Silver |
| 93 | Yubileynoe Mine | Tajikistan | Copper; Molybdenum; Tungsten |
| 94A | Choruk-Dairon Concentrator | Tajikistan | Molybdenum; Copper |
| 94B | Chorukh — Dairon Mine | Tajikistan | Tungsten; Molybdenum; Copper; Iron; Lead; Niobium; Tantalum; Zinc |

| Map | Site name | Country | Resources |
|---|---|---|---|
| 94C | Yashransk | Tajikistan | Molybdenum |
| 95 | Aprelevka | Tajikistan | Gold |
| 96A | Adrasman | Tajikistan | Bismuth |
| 96B | Adrasman | Tajikistan | Lead; Silver; Bismuth |
| 96C | Andrasman Concentrator | Tajikistan | Lead |
| 97 | Kansai Concentrator | Tajikistan | Gold |
| 98 | Bolshoi Kalimansur | Tajikistan | Silver; Lead |
| 99 | Yubileinoye | Tajikistan | Tungsten |
| 100 | Angren | Kyrgyzstan | Aluminium |
| 101 | Kan | Kyrgyzstan | Lead; Zinc |
| 102 | Kamil-Say | Kyrgyzstan | Antimony; Lead |
| 103 | (Facility) Kadamdzhay Smelter | Kyrgyzstan | Antimony |
| 104A | (Facility) Ulug-Tau Smelter | Kyrgyzstan | Mercury |
| 104B | Ulug-Tau | Kyrgyzstan | Mercury |
| 105 | Chauvay | Kyrgyzstan | Mercury; Antimony |
| 106 | Chonkoi Deposit | Kyrgyzstan | Mercury |
| 107 | Kadamdzhay | Kyrgyzstan | Antimony |
| 108 | Chanvay | Kyrgyzstan | Mercury |
| 109 | Novoye | Kyrgyzstan | Mercury; Antimony |
| 110A | Glubokaya | Kyrgyzstan | Mercury |
| 110B | Tsentral'Naya | Kyrgyzstan | Mercury |
| 111 | Khaydarkan | Kyrgyzstan | Mercury |
| 112A | Khaydarkan Concentrator | Kyrgyzstan | Antimony; Fluorine-Fluorite |
| 112B | (Facility) Khaydarkan Smelter | Kyrgyzstan | Mercury |
| 113 | Symap | Kyrgyzstan | Mercury |

Konchoch deposit also contains antimony, lead, silver, and other minerals (Renaud 2019, 45.2). The geological and mineral resource map of Tajikistan[1] shows a significant concentration and variety of mineral resources in the Sughd Province, along the Zeravshan Valley, in the Penjikent area, and in the Zeravshan Mountains south of the Zeravshan Valley (Fig. 2.2). These minerals include ferrous metals: iron and manganese; non-ferrous metals: aluminium, antimony, bismuth, lead, mercury, tin, and wolfram; rare earth metals: lithium, niobium, and tantalum; precious metals: gold and silver; energy minerals: coal; non-metallic minerals: barite, graphite, and phosphorite; and construction materials: clay, granite, limestones, lime, sand, and gravel. Besenval and Isakov (1989, 18) also mentioned turquoise. It is found in the areas of the Sughd Province located north of the Turkestan Mountains, near Adrasman in the Karamazar Mountains (Biruyakan deposit) and near Chorku. A deposit is also known near Samarkand in Uzbekistan in the Kara-Tyube Mountains (Agalyk U-V deposit). Another deposit is located in the Gorno-Badakhshan Region south of Khorog.[2] The Mineral Resources Data System of the US Geological Survey[3] has inventoried mineral resources in the Sughd Province, including some of those mentioned above, as well as resources within a c. 350–450 km area around the Zeravshan Valley in Kazakhstan, Kyrgyzstan, Uzbekistan, Tajikistan, and Afghanistan (Table 2.1, Fig. 2.3). These resources include aluminium, antimony, copper, gold, lead, silver, tin, and zinc.[4] Additional sources that are worth mentioning here are those for lapis lazuli. The most famous source for this mineral is at Sar-i Sang in the north-eastern Afghan Province of Badakhshan (Herrmann 1968; Wyart et al. 1981). It is c. 460 km as the crow flies south-east of

---

[1] <https://geoportal-tj.org/wp-content/uploads/deposits_map-scaled.jpg> [accessed 10 April 2023].

[2] <https://geoportal-tj.org/wp-content/uploads/deposits_map-scaled.jpg>; <https://www.mindat.org/loc-344841.html>; <https://www.mindat.org/loc-158385.html> [accessed 10 April 2023].

[3] <https://mrdata.usgs.gov/mrds/> [accessed 10 April 2023].

[4] <https://mrdata.usgs.gov/metadata/mrds.faq.html> [accessed 10 April 2023]. The USGS records are defined as 'Occurence' ('Ore mineralization in outcrop, shallow pit or pits, or isolated drill hole. Grade, tonnage, and extent of mineralization essentially unknown. No production has taken place and there has been no or little activity since discovery with the possible exception of routine claim maintenance.'); 'Prospect' ('A deposit that has gone beyond the occurrence stage. That is subsequent work such as surface trenching, adits, or shafts, drill holes, extensive geophysics, geochemistry, and/or geologic mapping has been carried out. Enough work has been done to at least estimate grade and tonnage. The deposits may or may not have undergone feasibility studies that would lead to a decision on going into production.'); 'Producer' ('A mine in production at the time the data was entered. An intermittent producer that produces on demand or seasonally with variable lengths of inactivity is considered a producer.'); 'Past Producer' ('A mine formerly operating that has closed, where the equipment or structures may have been removed or abandoned.'); 'Plant' ('A processing plant (smelter, refiner, beneficiation, etc.) that may or may not be currently producing at the time of data entry. A plant will have no geological information associated with it.'); 'Unknown' ('At the time of data entry, either the development status was unknown or the data source this record came from did not specify this value').

Sarazm. Additional sources for lapis lazuli are reported from the Pamir Mountains in southern Tajikistan, especially at Ladjevar-Dara (Casanova 2008). More distant sources are in the Lake Baikal region of Siberia (Herrmann 1968; Tosi 1974a; Barthélémy de Saizieu 2003, 27; see also Vidale and Lazzari 2017).

Various research programmes have focused on the ancient exploitation of these resources of southern Central Asia, in Uzbekistan and Tajikistan in particular. Considering the importance of turquoise and metal in the archaeological record and historical reconstructions of this area, it is worth recalling a few aspects of this research with a focus on these two materials (see also **Chapter 6**). Avanesova (2021, 668) reports that many investigations were done in Uzbekistan between 1961 and 1975 as part of the 'Ancient Mine Openings' project of the Uzbekistan Ministry of Geology. Results from these investigations are unfortunately not all published or are recorded within reports that are difficult to access. She notes that many of the places within the mountainous formation of the Zeravshan Valley, where mineral and ore resources have been identified, bear traces of ancient exploitation. These places include

> a great number of gold and turquoise deposits with earlier traces of exploitation [in the Nuratau Mountains]; ancient traces of mining of cinnabar, copper, and turquoise [...] in the Malguzar Mountains; tin and silver-arsenic ores in the Ziaetdin-Zirabulak Mountains; and copper and turquoise in the Karatube Mountains. (Avanesova 2021, 668)

The sites in question include sites with tunnels for mining, as well as scatter sites that suggest short-term occupations. The

> majority of these ancient mining works, slag heaps, remains of smelting furnaces, and mining settlements functioned during the Bronze Age and were operated by Catacomb-Srubno-Andronovo prospectors and metallurgists. (Avanesova 2021, 668)

Avanesova (2021, 668) adds that: 'According to geologists' reports, ancient smelting sites are attested all over the Zeravshan area', but most have not been studied save for Sarazm and Tugai.

Since these early investigations, international teams have worked on this topic, including in relation to the 'Tin Question'. As Kaniuth (2007, 23) phrases it:

> In essence, the debate centres on two main questions: First, what were the sources for the tin used as a routine ingredient in Mesopotamian metallurgy during the later third and second millennium BC and second, by which routes was the tin traded to Mesopotamia from its source region(s)?

Certainly, the origin of the copper and tin used in the objects relating to the Oxus Civilization has been of considerable interest too (see Garner 2021). Two source regions emerge as potential candidates: Central Asia as well as southern and western Afghanistan (Cleuziou and Berthoud 1982; Parzinger and Boroffka 2003; Weeks 2004, 188–89, 200; Lyonnet 2005; Kaniuth 2007, 24). As far as the former is concerned, the middle course of the Zeravshan Valley between Uzbekistan and Tajikistan is known as an important tin belt. Evidence for ancient mining was found in the copper and tin mines of Mushiston in the Zeravshan Mountains, *c.* 40 km south-east of Sarazm (*c.* 2830 m asl). This evidence was radiocarbon dated to *c.* 1500 cal. BCE, which does not preclude the possibility that these mines were used before. Another important massive evidence for tin mining is from Karnab in Uzbekistan, *c.* 170 km west of Sarazm. This site is radiocarbon dated to between *c.* 1900–1300 cal. BCE. Both sites are connected to the Andronovo Steppe culture (Boroffka et al. 2002; Parzinger and Boroffka 2003; Kaniuth 2007, 27 fig. 2; Anthony 2007, 420, 423 tab. 16.1; Weeks 2012, 304–05; see Garner 2021; Pigott 2021). The analysed copper objects from Sarazm show that they were not alloyed with tin, which may be explained by the fact that most, or the totality, of this settlement is essentially older than the period when tin bronze began being widely used (Kraus 2021). As for copper, recent compositional analysis of objects from Sarazm suggests that the communities settled at this site did not exploit the Mushiston deposits, while comparison with ores from central Iran, where well-known deposits are located, shows that the copper used at this site did not come from this area either. Consequently, the origin of the copper metal from Sarazm is not known (Kraus 2021, 784–85). Copper mines that are generally believed to have been exploited during the third millennium BCE at the earliest and to be later than most of Sarazm settlement are reported from the Pamir and Hissar Mountains, Kyzyl Kum Desert, Naukat Mountains, Karamazar Mountains, Talas-Alatau Mountains, and central Kazakhstan (Garner 2021, 804 fig. 28.1, 811–15). These are mines 'with archaeologically relevant finds [...], or that have been archaeologically investigated, or suggested as possible ore sources for the BMAC following geochemical analysis' (Garner 2021, 811). The single positive source determination that relates to Sarazm metallic assemblage seems to be that of the lead contained in a lead ingot from this site whose composition suggests that it comes from the Lashkerek deposits of the Karamazar Mountains (Kraus 2021, 783).[5]

Regarding turquoise, as noted above, sources are known in the Kyzyl Kum in Uzbekistan as well as in the Khujand region of northern Tajikistan. Although additional sources are mentioned in Afghanistan and Pakistan, there is no clear information about these sources, whereas some of those in Uzbekistan and Tajikistan are thought to have been exploited in antiquity. At a minimum, some mines were likely exploited by the third millennium BCE and workshops dedicated to this craft dating to that period were found in Uzbekistan (Barthélémy de Saizieu 2003, 27, 104–05 fig. 3; see also Tosi 1974b, 150 on the sources mentioned in Afghanistan and Iran).[6] These workshops, such as those at the Ljavljakan sites, Beshbulak, and Burli 3, which are in the Bukhantau Mountains, where turquoise mines have also been located, date to the mid-third through the early second millennia BCE, i.e. the mature or most recent phase of the Kel'teminar archaeological complex (Tosi 1974b; Brunet 2005, 93–95). Certainly, turquoise was used before that, as illustrated at Sarazm, and as observed at sites between the Indo-Iranian Borderlands, Central Asia, and the Iranian Plateau, including at Mehrgarh during the Neolithic period (Barthélémy de Saizieu 2003, 32–42; see **Chapter 6**). Another well-known source for turquoise is in the Neyshabur region, north-eastern Iran. Tosi wrote that the turquoise used between the Iranian Gorgan Plain and southern Turkmenistan, including at Tepe Hissar and Altyn-Depe, probably came from the Neyshabur area, the largest turquoise source of Iran (Tosi 1974b, 148). He however also wrote in the same article that (Tosi 1974b, 159): '[I]t is also quite conceivable that even the Hissar turquoise was of Central Asian origin and was imported through the neighbouring towns in Southern Turkmenia which were in constant communication with the Khorezm and the lower reaches of the Zeravshan.' Hiebert (2003, 23) writes that:

> Nishapur-P was probably, like tepe Yam, occupied by people related to those on the northern plain of the Kopet Dag. Nishapur-P is the prehistoric settlement approximately 12 km from the well-known medieval site of Nishapur [...] The settlement of this area, both during the medieval period and in prehistoric times, was in large part due to the proximity of the largest turquoise mines of Iran, in the nearby mountains. Nishapur-P's Anau II ceramics and small find assemblage suggest incorporation of this resource area into the Central Asian culture area during this time.

On the topic of turquoise, evidence from Shahr-i Sokhta, further south, deserves mention. Shahr-i Sokhta is an important site where turquoise items as well as evidence for turquoise working have been found. Tosi writes that (1974b, 160–61):

> Were it not for the Shahr-i Sokhta finds, turquoise would still be a material practically restricted to Central Asia and the object of sporadic trading between the proto-urban communities of southern Turkmenia and the semi-nomadic inhabitants of the Kel'teminar villages. Shahr-i Sokhta has thus become an exception to the rule [...] During the third millennium, turquoise was thus a product for which there was little demand and whose area of consumption moved along a north-south axis from Kyzyl Kum to Sistan [...] crossing, but never joining, the great lapis-lazuli route.

Foglini and Vidale (2017, 277–80) also agree with Tosi who believes in the existence of ideological connections, or shared tradition, between this site and Central Asia. In summary, turquoise has long been of considerable importance in Central Asia, where sources for this mineral were exploited since at least the third millennium BCE.

## *Climate*

Four climatic systems influence temperatures and precipitation regimes in Central Asia: Mid-Latitude Westerlies, Eastern Mediterranean cyclones, Siberian Highs, and Asian Monsoons (Fouache et al. 2016, 163). Climate in present-day Central Asia is generally defined as continental arid and semi-arid

with hot, cloudless, dry summers and moist, relatively warm winters in the south and cold winters with severe frosts in the north. Precipitation throughout most of the region has a spring maximum, which is associated with the northward migration of the Iranian branch of the Polar front. Most frequently rain is brought by the depressions which develop over the Mediterranean, migrate north-eastwards, and regenerate over the Caspian Sea. Westerly cyclones of the temperate zone change their trajectories in summer over the Aral Sea from a west-east to a north-south direction and

---

[5] On the topic of metallurgical analyses see also the publications by V. D. Ruzanov referenced in Avanesova 2021; Garner 2021; Kraus 2021; and Pigott 2021.

[6] On the topic of the archaeological evidence for the exploitation of turquoise, see the pioneering work by A. V. Vinogradov (1970; 1972a; 1972b; 1973; Vinogradov et al. 1965).

approach the zone affected by the Indian monsoon over the Zagros. (Lioubimtseva and Henebry 2009, 966)

Sarazm is located in a piedmont area at *c.* 915–25 m asl with annual rainfall usually between 250–400 mm. Most of the precipitation occurs between the end of the fall and the beginning of spring, with significant variation from one year to the next (Besenval and Isakov 1989, 5; Spengler and Willcox 2013, 215). Precipitation records (rain and snow) between 2015 and 2019 in Penjikent[7] are: *c.* 283 mm (2015), 187 mm (2016), 153 mm (2017), 191 mm (2018), 650 mm (2019). The lowest temperatures in the winter are: *c.* -4°C (2015), -1°C (2016), -5°C (2017), -1°C (2018), and -2°C (2019). The highest temperatures in the summer are: *c.* 29°C (2015), 27°C (2016), 29°C (2017), 30°C (2018), and 34°C (2019). The average annual temperatures are: *c.* 11°C (2015), 11.5°C (2016), 11.5°C (2017), 13°C (2018), and 15°C (2019). Average annual humidity ratios are: *c.* 43 per cent (2015), 46 per cent (2016), 43 per cent (2017), 42 per cent (2018), and 45 per cent (2019).

Research on ancient climate in Central Asia, between the Caspian Sea and Mongolia, has shown that climatic conditions have considerably varied over the past twelve millennia, since the beginning of the Holocene. In summary, climate may be characterized as warming and dry in the Early Holocene between 11,000–8000 BP, warm and more humid during the Mid-Holocene between 8000–5000 BP, and cooling and moderately wet in the Late Holocene since 5000 BP (Chen et al. 2008; Fouache et al. 2016, 163; Yang et al. 2019, 7; Fouache et al. 2021, 90–92; see also Walker et al. 2012). Although general trends are observed from the eastern Mediterranean to Central Asia, significant local and regional variations are noted, as is the considerable impact of the Indian Summer Monsoon (see Bar-Yosef 2014, 1411–12 about the eastern Mediterranean as well as Petrie and Weeks 2019 about the Iranian Plateau). Petrie and Weeks (2019, 298) point out two different situations in western and eastern Iran. Records from Lake Zeribar in the Zagros Mountains of western Iran show that temperatures and precipitation increased between *c.* 10,500–6500 BP, although 'this period was still drier than the later Holocene'. Climate became wetter between *c.* 6500–4500 BP, although a dry period is observed around 5400 BP. Spring precipitation then decreased in the Late Holocene (Stevens et al. 2001; 2006). Data from Lake Hamoun in the Sistan Province of south-eastern Iran, a region both under the influence of the Westerlies and the Indian Summer Monsoon, show that it was relatively wet during the Early Holocene. It became more arid and more prone to strong winds during the Mid-Holocene as the influence of the Indian Summer Monsoon decreased. Precipitation in this region during the Mid- and Late Holocene was now brought only by the Westerlies (Hamzeh et al. 2016a; 2016b). In addition to regional and local variations, a parameter that needs to be kept in mind is that abrupt events of cold and arid climate occurred during the Holocene between Western and Central Asia, including the *c.* 8.2, 5.2, 4.2, and 3.2 ky BP events (Courty and Weiss 1997; Bar-Matthews et al. 1998; Stevens et al. 2001; Mayewski et al. 2004; Madella and Fuller 2005; Petrie and Weeks 2019, 299–300; Yang et al. 2019, 7).

Luneau (2019) has recently provided a detailed and comprehensive synthesis on current paleoclimatic data for this period in southern Central Asia. Although she notes the general above-mentioned trends and reconstructions, she emphasizes 'the spatial variability and complexity of the climate system in Central Asia, as well as the sensitivity of the environment and the diversity of natural responses to climate change locally' (Luneau 2019, 284). Studies of lake records at the high-altitude Lake Issyk Kul in Kyrgyzstan (Ricketts et al. 2001) and Lake Karakul in Tajikistan (Heinecke et al. 2016) have concluded on an increasing dryness by *c.* 6900 BP and 6600 BP, respectively. These studies tend to impute this dryness to decreased influence from the Westerlies or the Indian Monsoon. Sedimentological, (bio)geochemical, isotopic, and palynological analyses at Lake Son Kol in Kyrgyzstan have identified relatively wet conditions until 4950 BP and then a dry phase between 4950–3900 BP. Climate then became wet again and then moderately drier again until today (Lauterbach et al. 2014). In contrast to the view that sees drier conditions beginning with the Late Holocene, Luneau (2019, 284) points out results from a study at the Lake Kichikol in Kyrgyzstan (Beer et al. 2007) that concludes on an increase in moisture brought by Westerlies at *c.* 5000 BP and 4000 BP. Similarly, a study in the south-eastern coastal area of the Caspian Sea (Kakroodi et al. 2012) does not conclude on an increasing dryness between *c.* 5000–2300 BP. On this topic, it is important to note that, although the Sistan region became more arid during part of the Mid-Holocene and Late Holocene, a more humid phase is noted during this period, which may have partly coincided with the rise of Shahr-i Sokhta and related Bronze Age settlements in this area from the late fourth through the third millennia BCE (Hamzeh et al. 2016b, 624).

---

[7] <https://www.worldweatheronline.com/panjakent-weather-averages/sughd/tj.aspx> [accessed 10 April 2023].

Considering the largest chronological window possible as defined by the cultural materials and available radiocarbon dates (see **Chapters 1 and 4**), Sarazm was occupied sometime between the early fourth and late second millennia BCE, i.e. *c.* 6000–3250 BP, a period encompassing parts of the Mid- and Late Holocene. Keeping in mind the above-mentioned regional and local variations, the key aspects of ancient climate in Central Asia during these periods that need to be remembered are probably best synthesized by Fouache et al. (2021, 92) who write that:

> After the prevalence of humid climatic conditions in Central Asia during the Mid-Holocene period, especially between 6 and 5 ky, the subsequent drying trend is a response to reducing summer insolation and the gradual reduction of the mid-latitude westerlies intensity [...] This moderately humid climate of the Late Holocene (it remained higher than during the Early Holocene) was interrupted by a pronounced dry interval between 4.9 and 3.9 ky in southeast Kyrgyzstan and northwest China. After 3.9 ky, a general cooling trend associated with more humid conditions is observed in overall western Central Asia [...] The rest of the Late Holocene period is characterized by a moderate and gradual drying of climate until the present and again interrupted by short-term warmer and drier spells, mainly from 4.8 to 4.4 ky, from 3.5 to 2.9 ky, and from 2.5 to 2.2 ky.

Analysis of settlement patterns over time combined with geomorphological studies offer additional insights into change in access to water and climate change. Luneau (2019, 285–86) notes a study in the Murghab Plain (Turkmenistan), where Cremaschi (1998) hypothesizes that water was more available than today until the second millennium BCE. Fouache et al. (2012) have observed significant variation in the Balkh River location in the Balkh Province of northern Afghanistan and have been able to correlate these changes with human occupation since the Bronze Age. Other observations have been made in eastern Iran, where, in the Sabzevar region (Khorasan Province), the Bam region (Kerman Province), and the Bampur Valley (Sistan-va-Balochistan Province), settlement location tends to change between the Chalcolithic and Bronze Age/Iron Age periods in an apparent relation to changing access to water (Fouache et al. 2013; Garazhian and Mutin, ongoing research in Bam; Mutin et al. 2017). Certainly, such observations cannot be made in the Penjikent region, where Sarazm remains the single Chalcolithic and Early Bronze Age site. The only observation that can be made is that this site appears to have been abandoned around, either slightly before or slightly after, the middle of the third millennium BCE, the later date being almost coincident with the above-mentioned cold and arid 4.2 ky BP event (see **Chapters 1 and 4** as well as the **Conclusion**). Additionally, recent geoarchaeological analysis has revealed an apparent change in hydro-agricultural strategies at this site during the third millennium BCE.

## *Topography, Geomorphology, and Micromorphology*

The Zeravshan Valley is a graben between the Turkestan and Zeravshan Mountains. More subsidence and erosion affected its southern side, where more colluviums accumulated and alluvial fans developed. Current location of the river toward the north, directly against the Turkestan Mountains, is the result of these dynamics (Cez 2019, 9, 10 fig. 6). The protected archaeological area of Sarazm lies *c.* 1.3 km south of the Zeravshan River. As noted above, it is between *c.* 915–25 m asl. It is currently surrounded by three small villages, Avazeli, Gourach, and Sohibnazar (Fig. 1.2; Isakov 1991, fig. 1), while the areas between these villages and the Zeravshan River to the north, as well as those south of these settlements up to the piedmonts of the Zeravshan Mountains, mostly consist of agricultural fields and areas for grazing and hunting. Sarazm and part of these villages are on a Pleistocene alluvial terrace made of large pebbles and covered with loess deposits dating to *c.* 55,000 BP (+/- 5000). This terrace (T3) is the highest and fourth of a four-terrace system (Figs 2.4–2.6). The most recent and first one (T0) corresponds to the current riverbed of the Zeravshan River. The second terrace (T2) is located just north of T3 at *c.* 899 m asl on average. It dates to *c.* 6800 BP (+/- 500) and is associated with a Mid-Holocene warm and humid period. The third terrace (T1) is at *c.* 897 m asl on average between T0 and T2 and corresponds to the drier Late Holocene period (Cez 2019, 5 fig. 3, 10 fig. 6). T0, the current riverbed of the Zeravshan River, is braided at Sarazm's longitude; it consists of many channels separated by braid bars (Cez 2019, 3). For the reason explained above, the three terraces T1, T2, and T3 are on the southern, left bank, of this river, whereas those in the northern side, against the Turkestan Mountains, have essentially disappeared.

In 2011 and 2012, R. Besenval, L. Cez, and E. Fouache made a number of geoarchaeological observations between the Zeravshan River and Sarazm and studied in detail sections of three ancient canals that had

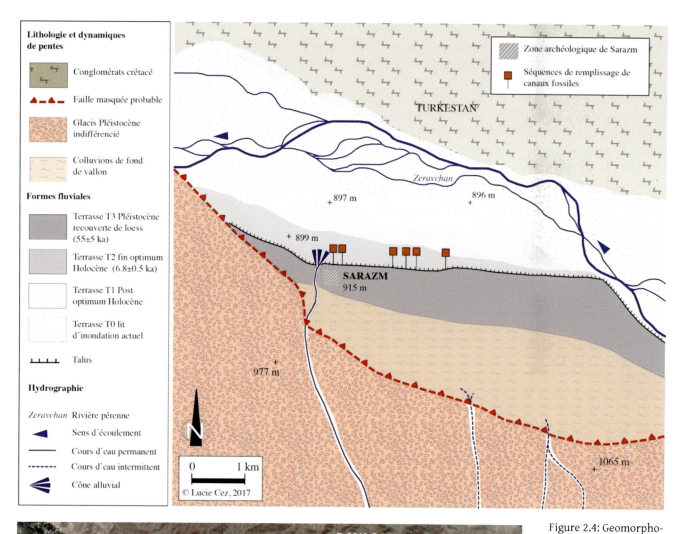

Figure 2.4: Geomorphological map of the Zeravshan Valley around Sarazm (Cez 2019, 10 fig. 6). Courtesy of L. Cez (2019).

Figure 2.5: Alluvial terraces of the Zeravshan Valley near Sarazm (Cez 2019, 5 fig. 3). Courtesy of L. Cez (2019).

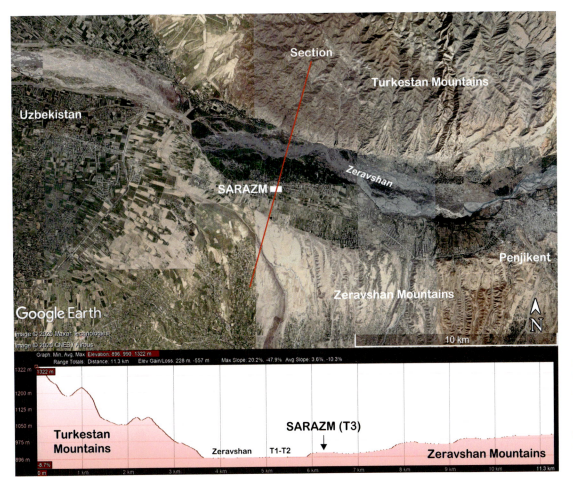

Figure 2.6: Alluvial terraces of the Zeravshan Valley near Sarazm viewed in section. Basemap and profile Google Earth, modified by B. Mutin.

been discovered by Besenval while he was working at Sarazm during the 1980–1990s. These canals are east–west oriented and located along the northern edge of T3, north of the protected archaeological area. The oldest one is *c.* 5.75 m wide and dates to *c.* 4500 BP (+/- 400), i.e. the middle of the third millennium cal. BCE. Cez reckons that this canal probably allowed for the irrigation of agricultural fields located west of the site on T3 as well as on T2 during the summer, with the water being derived from the Zeravshan River (Cez 2019, 7, 8 fig. 5, 11–12). Certainly, the fact that this canal was dug implies that the need arose to complement dry farming sometime after the site was founded. Although its date has a rather broad margin of error, it is chronologically not inconsistent with the above-mentioned dry interval observed between 4.9 and 3.9 ky in southeast Kyrgyzstan and north-west China, as well as with the above-mentioned cold and arid 4.2 ky BP event.

## Exploitation of Plant and Animal Resources

Today, the Zeravshan Valley around Sarazm combines dry farming and irrigated agriculture. Rice, clover, tobacco, and legumes are grown in the fields on the above-mentioned terraces between the protected archaeological area and the Zeravshan River. Fruits are also observed, including watermelon, while tobacco is grown further south near the site. Vegetation along the river consists of a tugai riparian forest, the Persian *jungle*, characterized by species such as poplar (*Populus* sp.), tamarisk (*Tamarix* sp.), Russian olive (*Elaeagnus angustifolia* L.), ash (*Fraxinus* sp.), and sea buckthorn (*Hippophae rhamnoides* L.). Willcox identified forest patches with maple (*Acer* sp.), wild almond (*Prunus* sp. subgenus *Amygdalus*), hackberry (*Celtis* sp.), and wild pistachio (*Pistacia vera* L.) at *c.* 1500 m asl in the Turkestan Mountains north of Sarazm. At about 2200 m asl, vegetation consists of shrubby mountain forest vegetation including barberry (*Berberis vulgaris* L.), cotoneaster (*Cotoneaster* sp.), walnut (*Juglans regia* L.), juniper (*Juniperus* sp.), wild apricots (*Prunus armeniaca* L.), gooseberries (*Ribes* sp.), mountain ash (*Sorbus* sp.), and elm (*Ulmus* sp.) (Spengler and

Table 2.2: Botanical remains from Excavation VII (after Spengler and Willcox 2013, 215 tab. 1).

| Flotation Sample no. | Litres | Archaeological context | Triticum aestivum/turgidum | Triticum sp. | Triticum cf. aestivum glume frag | Triticum cf. aestivum rachis | Hordeum vulgare var. nudum | Hordeum rachis | Hordeum vulgare var. vulgare | Hordeum cf. spontaneum | Hordeum murinum type | Avena sp. | Aegilops squarosa | Lolium sp. | Bromus sp. | Poaceae |
|---|---|---|---|---|---|---|---|---|---|---|---|---|---|---|---|---|
| | | | **DOMESTICATED** | | | | | | | **WILD GRASSES** | | | | | | |
| 14 | | Level I3 or I4, sq. L14, 'layer on floor' | 2 | | | | | | | | | | | | | |
| 32 | | Level III3, Area 6, sq. J14, charred soil | | | | | | | | | | | | | | |
| 45 | | Level III2, Area 4, Pits 4 and 5 | | | | | 100 | | | | | | | | | |
| 49 | | Level I3, unspecified floor of Level I3 building | 5 | | 3 | 2 | 2 | | 1 | | | 1 | | 1 | 1 | |
| 66 | | Level I1, Room 3, Hearth 2 | 1 | | | | | | 1 | | | | 2 | | | 1 |
| 90 | | Level I1, Room 1 | | | | | | | 1 | | | | | | | |
| 97 | | Level I1, Room 3 | | | | | | | | | | | | | | |
| 98 | | Level I1, Room 4, Hearth 3 | | | | | 3 | | | | | | | | | |
| 99 | | Level I1, Room 4, Hearth 3 | 1 | | | | | | 1 | | 1 | | 1 | | | 1 |
| 103 | | Level I1, Room 1 | | | | | | | | | | | | | | |
| 104 | | Level I1, Room 3 | | | | | | | 2 | | | | | | | |
| 106 | 20 | Level I1, Room 2, OF2 | | | | | 3 | | | | 1 | | | | | |
| 107 | 70 | Level I1, Room 2, OF2 | 2 | 1 | | | | | 3 | | 3 | | 1 | | | 1 |
| 122 | 60 | | 1 | | | | | | | | | | | | | |
| 125 | 10 | | | | | | | | | | | | | | | |
| 130 | 10 | | | | | | | | | | | | | | | |
| 131 | 10 | | | | | | 2 | | | | | | | | | |
| 134 | 10 | | 4 | | | 3 | 77 | 19 | | | | | 2 | | 1 | |
| 135 | 10 | | | | | | | | | | | | | | | |
| 138 | 40 | | 1 | | | | | | | | | | | | | |
| 142 | 50 | | 1 | | | | | | | | | | | | | |
| 143 | 40 | | | | | | 1 | | | | | | | | | |
| 145 | 50 | | | | | | 1 | | | | | | | | | |
| 147 | 40 | | | | | | | | | | | | | | | |
| 148 | 20 | | | | | 1 | | | | | | | | | | |
| 150 | 10 | | | | | | | | | | | 1 | | | | |
| | | **Totals** | 18 | 1 | 3 | 6 | 189 | 19 | 9 | 1 | 5 | 1 | 6 | 1 | 2 | 3 |

## EXPLOITATION OF PLANT AND ANIMAL RESOURCES

| Brassicaceae | Lamiceae | Lithospermum sp. | Heliotropium sp. | Echium sp. | Carex sp. | Scripus sp. | Fabaceae | Lens sp. | Apiaceae | Plantago sp. | Polygonaceae | Polygonum type | Galium sp. | Capparis sp. | Celtis sp. | Pistacia cf. vera | Elaeagnus sp. | Hippophae rhamnoides | Prunus sp. | cf. Rosa | Prunus (Amygdalus) | Totals |
|---|---|---|---|---|---|---|---|---|---|---|---|---|---|---|---|---|---|---|---|---|---|---|
| | | | | | | | | | | | | | | | | | | | | | | 2 |
| | | 38 | | | | 2 | | | | | | | | | | | | | | | | 40 |
| | | 23 | 4 | | | | | | | | | | | | | | | | | | | 127 |
| | | 100 | | | 3 | 2 | 2 | | 1 | 1 | | | | 1 | | | 1 | | | | | 129 |
| | | | | | | | | | | | | | 7 | | | | | | 1 | 1 | | 14 |
| | | 5 | | | 2 | | | | | | | | | | | | | | | | | 8 |
| | | 6 | | | | | | | | | | | | | 1 | | | | | | | 7 |
| | | | | | | | | | | | | | | | 2 | | 2 | | | | | 7 |
| | | | | | | | | | | | | | | | 1 | | | | | | | 6 |
| | | | | | | | | | | | | | | | 1 | | | | | | | 1 |
| | | 3 | | | | | | | | | | | | | | | | | | | | 5 |
| | | | | | | | | 1 | | | | | | | | | | | | | | 5 |
| | | | | | | | | | | | | | | | | | | | | | | 11 |
| | | | | | | | | | | | | | | | | | | | | | | 1 |
| | | 100 | | | | | | | | | | | | | | | | | | | | 100 |
| | | 100 | | | | | 1 | | | | | | | | | 1 | 1 | | | | | 103 |
| | | | | | 3 | | 4 | | | | | | | 1 | | | | | | | | 10 |
| 1 | | | | | | | 1 | | | 1 | | | | | | | | | | | | 109 |
| | | | | | | | | | | | | | | | 1 | | | | | | | 1 |
| | | | | | | | | | 2 | | | 2 | | | | | | | | | | 5 |
| | | | | | | | | | | | | | | | | | | | | | | 1 |
| | | | | | | | | | 1 | | | | | | | | | | | | | 2 |
| | | 2 | | | | | | | | | | | | | | | | | | | | 3 |
| | | 53 | | | | | | | | | | | | | | | | | | | | 53 |
| | | | | | | | | 1 | 1 | | | | | | | | | | | | | 3 |
| | | | | | | | | | | | | | | | | | | | | | | 1 |
| 1 | 0 | 430 | 4 | 0 | 8 | 4 | 8 | 1 | 2 | 5 | 0 | 1 | 9 | 1 | 7 | 0 | 2 | 3 | 1 | 1 | 0 | 754 |

Willcox 2013, 214–16; Cez 2019, 4; personal observations in 2011–2014). The First National Report on Biodiversity Conservation[8] also reports wormwood (*Artemisia absinthium*), wild relatives of barley (*Hordeum spontaneum*), vetch (*Vicia tenuifolia*), persimmon (*Diospyros lotus*), jujube (*Zizyphus jujuba*), pomegranate (*Punica granatum*), and grapes (*Vitis vinifera*) from mid-mountain xerophytic light forest ecosystems.

Cattle, sheep, goats, horses, donkeys, and chicken are raised. The tugai along the Zeravshan River today serves as a grazing area. Wild fauna in the mid-mountain xerophytic light forest ecosystem includes Persian gazelle (*Gazella subgutturosa*), urial (*Ovis vignei*), wolf (*Canis lupus*), fox (*Vulpes vulpes*), reptiles such as the Central Asian cobra (*Naja oxiana*) and the steppe tortoise (*Testudo horsfieldi*). Rare and endangered species are also reported in the juniper forests, including the brown bear (*Ursus arctos*), urial (*Ovis vignei*), Tajik markhur (*Capra falconeri*), *Vipera lebetina*, and ring dove (*Columba palumbus*).[9] Many species of birds are also present, including game birds such as the pheasant (*Phasianus colchicus*), which is currently hunted in the tugai near Sarazm. Wild boar (*Sus scrofa*) is today also hunted in this tugai, while tigers (*Felis tigris*) were present along the Zeravshan perhaps until the nineteenth century CE (Severtsov 1873).

Two main studies have so far determined the vegetal and animal species found in the ancient settlement at Sarazm, one by G. Willcox and one by J. Desse, respectively. The new archaeobotanical and zooarchaeological assemblages collected through the new excavations conducted since 2011 as part of the renewed Tajik-French fieldwork are respectively being analysed by M. Tengberg and S. Lepetz. Willcox conducted an archaeobotanical analysis in 1990 mostly on flotation samples collected in Excavation VII between 1988 and 1990 (forty-six samples). The rest of the samples he studied are from Excavations II, III, IV, V, and VI. Sample collection focused on archaeological deposits that 'appeared to be rich in carbonized organic material, such as hearths, house floors and middens' (Spengler and Willcox 2013, 213, 215 tab. 1, 216). As far as Excavation VII is concerned, I have been able to find in Besenval archives the archaeological contexts of half of the samples listed by Willcox: eleven are from Level I and two are from Level III (Table 2.2; Spengler and Willcox 2013, 215 tab. 1). A few plants listed in Table 2.2 have not been identified in Excavation VII, but in the botanical assemblages from one or more additional excavations at Sarazm that Willcox studied. In summary, Willcox (Spengler and Willcox 2013, 216–18) determined that wheat and barley were cultivated and processed near or on site, and that wild fruits were collected, including Russian olive, hackberry, sea buckthorn berry, and rosaceous relatives (*Prunus* and possibly *Rosa*), as well as wild pistachio (*Pistacia vera*) and capper (*Capparis* sp.). These trees as well as hackberry tree were also identified in the charcoal. Seeds of wild weeds were recorded too. Part of them such as *Galium*, *Plantago*, or *Chenopodium*, may come from the use of dung as fuel, whereas another part such as *Lithospermum* are weeds associated with cultivated fields. Spengler and Willcox (2013, 218) also emphasize the possibility that these wild seeds may have ended up in the archaeological deposits of Sarazm because they were foraged by the communities of this site, used in their architecture or for any other activity, or brought by the wind.

As for the wood charcoal assemblage, Spengler and Willcox note that it is unusually abundant at Sarazm in comparison with the seed assemblage. This suggests that wood was an important source for fuel, although dung is usually more common in Central Asia. Willcox determined eight main species at Sarazm from forty-four charcoal samples. They are listed in his original publication and in this volume with percentages that represent their presence across the assemblage (Spengler and Willcox 2013, 218, 219 tab. 2): willow/poplar (*Salicaceae*), 79.5 per cent; ash (*Fraxinus*), 27.3 per cent; Russian olive (*Elaeagnus*), 22.7 per cent; salt cedar (*Tamarix*), 22.7 per cent; reed grass (*Phragmites*), 9.1 per cent; hackberry (*Celtis*), 2.3 per cent; wild almond (*Prunus amygdalus*), 25 per cent; and wild pistachio (*Pistacia*), 4.5 per cent. Willow/poplar, salt cedar, and reed grass are 'characteristic river forest plants [...] [while t]he rest are from higher elevation forest wood' (Spengler and Willcox 2013, 218). Spengler and Willcox (2013, 214–16, 218) believe that the latter were probably closer to Sarazm at the time the site was occupied and later disappeared from this altitude through the effect of deforestation, although the possibility remains that they were also collected at higher altitudes. Additionally, Willcox identified the remains of carbonized beams made of willow/poplar (*Salix/Populus*) and almond tree (*Prunus amygdalus*). Reeds are known for being used in roof construction and are often found as impressions on clay lumps (see **Chapter 3**).

---

[8] <https://www.cbd.int/doc/world/tj/tj-nr-01-p02-en.pdf> [accessed 10 April 2023].

[9] <https://www.cbd.int/doc/world/tj/tj-nr-01-p02-en.pdf> [accessed 10 April 2023].

Table 2.3: Results of the zooarchaeological analysis conducted by J. Desse on bones from Excavations IV and VII.

| Wild animals (save for micromammals and birds) | Number of bones | % |
|---|---|---|
| *Ovis vignei* (mouflon) and *Capra aegagrus* (ibex) | 54 | 0.83 |
| *Gazella subgutturosa* (gazelle) | 7 | 0.11 |
| *Bos primigenius* (aurochs) | 2 | 0.03 |
| *Sus scrofa* (boar) | 2 | 0.03 |
| *Vulpes* sp. (fox) | 1 | 0.02 |
| *Lepus* sp. (hare) | 2 | 0.03 |
| *Hystrix* sp. (porcupine) | 1 | 0.02 |
| Total | 69 | 1.06 |

| Domesticated animals | Number of bones | % |
|---|---|---|
| *Ovis aries* (sheep) and *Capra hircus* (goat) | 6125 | 93.87 |
| *Bos taurus* (cattle) | 302 | 4.63 |
| *Canis familiaris* (dog) | 29 | 0.44 |
| Total | 6456 | 98.94 |
| Total wild and domesticated animals | 6525 | 100.00 |

Lastly apropos of the plant remains, it is important to note that the archaeobotanical assemblage from Sarazm has parallels with those from the Kopet Dag Mountains in Turkmenistan. Spengler and Willcox (2013, 218–19) note that pulses are lacking at this site as well as at Jeitun and Anau, and that barley is a mix of hulled and naked morphotypes at these three sites. As also seen below through the animal remains, likewise in Turkmenistan, the subsistence economy of Sarazm appears to have been based on typical Near Eastern domesticates. The same pattern has been observed too at other sites further east and north-east within the Inner Asian Mountain Corridor (IAMC) (Hermes et al. 2019; Hermes et al. 2021). However,

> isotopic research on archaeofauna from Dali [in the IAMC, *c.* 1000 km north-east of Sarazm,] documents substantial use of millet as part of a mobile herding subsistence economy by 2700 cal. B.C. High-resolution stable isotope analysis of domesticated sheep, goat, and cattle tooth enamel revealed winter foddering of livestock with millet, a crop which spread westward from farming communities in north-western China [...] in the early third millennium B.C. (Hermes et al. 2021, 357)

No millet appears to have been identified so far at Sarazm.

Desse analysed 6525 animal bones from Excavations IV and VII (Table 2.3), while A. K. Kasparov studied the fauna excavated by Isakov in other excavations. The only data on the fauna I have been able to gather in this volume is from a study by the former, in which he summarized and combined the identifications he made and the quantities of bones he recorded regardless of the excavation and archaeological levels and contexts the samples came from. New data have also been collected by Lepetz who has studied the zooarchaeological assemblage brought to light since 2011 by the new Tajik-French cooperative project. In his report, Desse emphasizes the fact that the bone assemblage he studied was generally poorly preserved and that he had issues determining certain species. Regardless, a clear fact that emerges from his analysis is the considerable discrepancy between the quantities of domesticates, *c.* 99 per cent, and those of wild animals, *c.* 1 per cent. Domesticates mostly consist of sheep and goats (*Ovis aries* and *Capra hircus*, *c.* 94 per cent), including over 60 per cent sheep. Cattle (*Bos taurus*) is less than 5 per cent, while dog bones (*Canis familiaris*) represent less than 0.5 per cent. Slaughter patterns on sheep and goats suggest a controlled, dual strategy focused both on meat production and acquisition of secondary products (milk and wool) (Desse 1997, 673 fig. 3). Cattle were slaughtered later and most likely used as draft animals (Desse 1997, 673). An additional, important observation Desse made is that these domesticated sheep, goats, and cattle are large animals, with sizes similar to those of their wild ancestors. As far as the sheep and goats are concerned, he suggests that they were domesticated locally and that they might have been regularly bred with wild animals (Desse 1997, 673, 674 fig. 4). As far as cattle are concerned, the sizes of certain individuals match those of aurochs (Desse 1997, 673 fig. 2). Desse recalls that domesticated cattle in Turkmenistan at Sar Tepe and Altyn-Depe are also of large sizes. He however hypothesizes that the largest cattle bones from Sarazm as well as those from Altyn-Depe may be aurochs' bones. Lastly on the domesticates, Desse surprisingly found no remains of equids (horse, donkey), camels, or pigs. He more specifically hypothesizes that eating pork might have been taboo considering the fact that wild boars must have been abundant in the tugai near the Zeravshan River and that the communities of Sarazm clearly had no issue domesticating even large animals (Desse 1997, 674–75; but see below).

With *c.* 1 per cent of this zooarchaeological assemblage, hunting seems to have been very marginal. It was also limited to very few species. Hunted animals mostly consist of mouflons and ibex. Gazelle, aurochs (see above), boar, fox, hare, and porcupine are also recorded, although it remains possible that some of them, such as fox, are intrusive. This result is quite surprising considering that game animals must have been present in large quantities near the site in the tugai along the Zeravshan River. Desse also observed no fish bone, including from archaeological layers that were entirely sieved. To him, this suggests that the communities at Sarazm did not fish, rather than the bones were not detected during excavation. Lastly, it is important to note that steppe animals such as wild equids and Saiga antelope are not recorded at Sarazm, whereas they are observed in the records from the major archaeological sites in Turkmenistan. Desse believes that this absence is simply due to the fact that the distribution of these animals did not extend much into the mountainous part of the Zeravshan Valley.

Results from recent analysis of an enormous zooarchaeological assemblage recovered at Sarazm deserves mention (see Brunet et al. 2019; Mutin et al. 2020a). This assemblage comes from a pit excavated in Trench XV over a *c.* 3 × 2 × 2 m area (*c.* two-thirds of this pit). This pit yielded about fifty-three thousand bones and teeth. Most of them are burnt and were found within charred and ashy layers. Lepetz has identified 80 per cent sheep and a few goat remains, 19 per cent cattle, and a small amount of dog, gazelle, and swine remains. Sheep include at the very least 170 individuals, and cattle, twenty-one individuals. The overwhelming quantities of sheep are consistent with Desse's observations. On the other hand, the presence of swine contrasts with what he observed in Excavations IV and VII. Another important result from the study of this pit is the substantial concentration of ceramic fragments recovered in it relative to the quantities that are usually recorded at Sarazm. They include fragments of bowls, pots, and jars with out-flared rims, used probably mostly for cooking and food presentation, as well as storage jars. There is little doubt that this pit, which first served to extract building material (loess; see **Chapter 3**), was then used as a trash pit. It was filled with a limited series of massive disposals of animal bones and charcoal, which agrees well with the hypothesis that sees these disposals as 'the remains of large collective meals or banquets' (Mutin et al. 2020a, 28). This structure has brought new knowledge about food social practice at Sarazm, while other observations suggest that additional pits filled with large quantities of bones are present at this site.

Lastly, it is probably important to recall here that these botanical and faunal remains from Sarazm have long represented the earliest evidence for plant and animal domestication east of the Kopet Dag Mountains in Turkmenistan. Indeed, east of the seventh-millennium BCE farming village of Jeitun, the question remains partly open as far as the seventh- to fourth-millennium BCE Kel'teminar communities in Uzbekistan are concerned. They are defined as hunters, fishermen, and herders (Brunet et al. 2013, 201), although it is unclear whether the faunal remains recorded at their sites were those of domesticated animals. The same may be said about the Neolithic Hissar culture of southern Tajikistan dated to between the sixth and second millennia BCE (see Taylor et al. 2021, 1169–70). However, recent analysis of bones from Obishir V in southern Kyrgyzstan has revealed the presence of domesticated sheep at this site *c.* 6000 BCE, suggesting sheep dispersal (and perhaps dispersal of additional animal and plant species) from western Asia earlier than previously thought (Taylor et al. 2021).

# 3. Archaeological Contexts

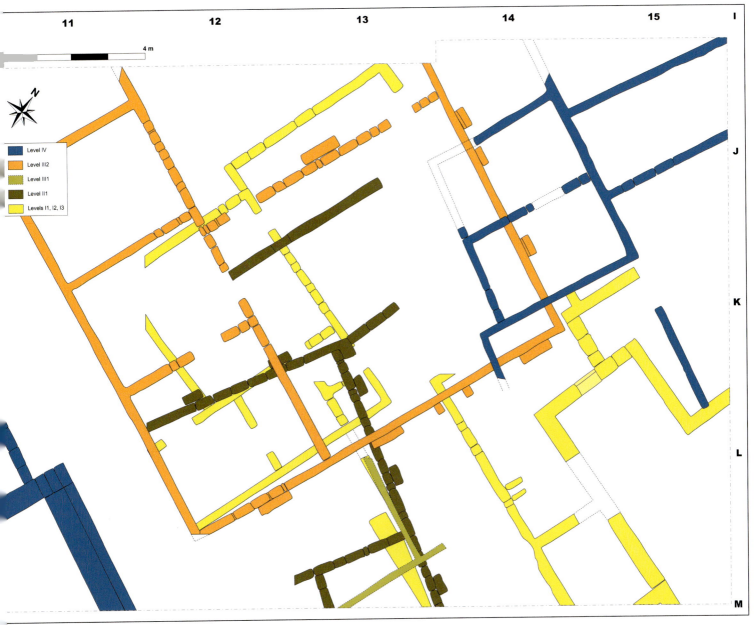

Plate 3.1: Sarazm, Excavation VII, architecture exposed in Levels I to IV. B. Mutin, based on R. Besenval archives.

The following description of the occupation levels and archaeological features that Besenval recorded and documented in Excavation VII is based on the field notebooks, lists, photographs, and architectural plans available in his archives, as well as the main article he wrote which synthesizes field seasons 1984–1989 in this excavation (Besenval and Isakov 1989).[1] Besenval defined four main archaeological levels, Levels I to IV, which he divided into separate phases. He labelled these phases Levels I1, I2, I3, I4, II1, II2, III1, III2, III3, IV1, and IV2 (Pl. 3.1). As is apparent in the description provided below, it would perhaps have been rational to reorganize a little bit this classification. It is indeed not clear why phases with no solid architecture, mostly consisting of postholes and hearths and seemingly of transient occupation (Levels I4, II2, and III3) were lumped together within the same levels as phases with mudbrick architecture (Levels I1, I2, I3, II1, III1, and III2). However, I purposely have kept this classification the way Besenval established it because it does not hin-

---

[1] Some of the plans of Excavation VII in this article appear to have been warped when they were formatted for publication.

der an understanding of Excavation VII's deposits and stratigraphy. Additionally, keeping the same classification has the benefit of not creating any confusion between the present publication, Besenval and Isakov's 1989 article, and available archival records.

## Digging the Archives

At the outset of this publication project, one of my objectives was to present Besenval's data as closely as possible to the way he recorded and interpreted it in his archives, refraining from intervening too much in both his recording system and interpretations. I however have had no other choice than to intervene more than I wished in many cases where key data was lacking. This has happened more specifically with data from field seasons 1986, 1990, and 1991. Regarding field season 1986, I have not been able to find in the archives any detailed plans with locations of the archaeological features and architectural remains exposed that year in Level III2. Furthermore, the descriptions I have found for this field season are very succinct. This was also the case for the archaeological remains excavated during field seasons 1990–1991 in the north-eastern part (sq. J16–17 to N16–17) and in the south-western part (sq. I10–M10) of Excavation VII. I have found virtually no archive for field season 1990. And, although I have been able to use records from the field season 1991 notebook, I have not located any final plan of the archaeological remains Besenval exposed that year, but only sketches of the architecture in the north-eastern part that he drew. The plans of this part of Excavation VII presented in this volume are reconstructions based on these sketch plans. As such, unlike most features exposed between 1984 and 1989, these reconstructions should be considered rough approximations and not be used for any detailed, comparative architectural analysis. In addition to lacking information about these remains, I am lacking data about their relationship to the other remains excavated further south and west. I have been able to generally connect them to one of the major levels defined in Excavation VII (Levels I to IV), but not necessarily to the phases. While it certainly is possible to hypothesize on their stratigraphic relationships with the phases, I have found it more prudent to present and discuss these remains within separate sections labelled 'Level I (II, III2, III3)-North/East' and to use separate plans.

Since a number of records and labels relating to the features and layers excavated within Excavation VII are missing in the archives, for the sake of consistency, I have relabelled the totality of the features and layers I have been able to find in these archives. Besenval's labels correspond to the initials of French words associated with numbers: M (*Mur*: wall); T (*Trou*: hearth, pit, and posthole); P (*Pièce*: room and court); S (*Sol*: floor and surface); C (*Couche*: fill/layer); and UF (*Unité de Fouille*: excavation unit, a label that includes various types of records including fills, floors, and hearths). His labels are mostly continuously numbered from 1984 to 1991, although some labels like 'C' and 'S' seem to have fallen out of use after field season 1985. The labels I have

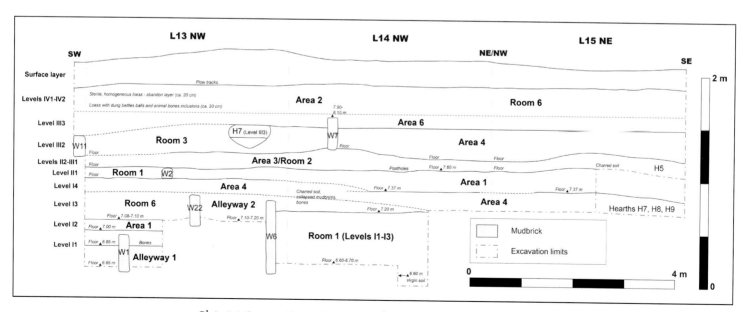

Plate 3.2: Sarazm, Excavation VII, north-west section in sq. L13–L14 and north-east section in sq. L15. B. Mutin, based on R. Besenval archives.

used in this volume (Feature Number) are: Room, Area, Alleyway, Wall, Posthole, Hearth, Pit, and Other Feature. Room, Area, and Alleyway comprise both fills and floors and consist of Besenval's UF, C, and S labels. I have had to establish this simplified system for the reason that a number of records are missing or are not detailed in the archives. For instance, fills and floors, or surfaces, are sometimes recorded together with the same number. Wall, Posthole, Hearth, and Pit are straightforward designations. I have used the label Other Feature to designate one feature that may be a hearth, one that is a niche, as well as two records that seem to correspond to specific layers or surfaces identified within one square. Each of these separate series of labels are numbered from #1 at each new major level. Tables are provided that list the totality of the records that I have found or created and relabelled for each phase. These tables also list Besenval's original labels (Archive Number) when I have been able to identify them in the archives. However, although I have done my best to locate and relabel as many of Besenval's records as possible, I have not been able to find the descriptions and planimetric and stratigraphic locations of a number of them. These problematic records are in the archives merely numbered with no additional information. However, since many features I have created new labels for are features I have identified on plans and in his notebooks, I am positive that at least a part of these records that Besenval did not detail corresponds to labels I have created.

These issues certainly do not mean that Besenval did not record enough data. In fact, in the complete archives that I have been able to study, detailed information on the architecture, features, stratigraphic relationships, and specific objects are usually noted. Large series of altitudes are also reported, although I have seen no mention of the altitude of the datum he used. It seems likely that this datum is the same as the one I used during field seasons 2011–2014, which is at 914.97 m asl. This is consistent with the fact that Besenval reached the virgin soil at $c.$ 6.60 m and recorded the surface of the site at $c.$ 8.40–8.60 m (see Pl. 3.2), since current surface of the site around Excavation VII is between $c.$ 922–24 m. Keeping this possibility in mind, I have found it more cautious to mention here the altitudes I have found in his archives the way Besenval reported them, i.e. not converted to metres asl. These altitudes are reported in the tables that list the features from each phase. When a single altitude or a short range of altitudes is reported for the Room, Area, and Alleyway categories, these altitudes are usually those recorded at the bases of these spaces, except when mentioned.

Despite these issues, which are essentially due to missing archives, and, although for this reason the descriptions provided here may appear at times incomplete or inconsistent, the quality of the records I have found in Besenval's archives have made it possible to reconstruct and make available here both the most essential and specific data from Excavation VII. Most of his excavation strategy as well as the stratigraphy and most parts of the plans of each level could be reconstructed.

## Excavation Expanse, Stratigraphy, and Strategy

Fieldwork in Excavation VII took place between 1984 and 1991. This excavation is oriented SW–NE/NW–SE. Available field notebooks and plans suggest that it ended up being at least as large as 454 m² at the end of field season 1991, considering the area between sq. J11 and N17 (Pls 3.1, 3.3–3.16). However, Besenval apparently extended its limits south-westward over an area of perhaps $c.$ 56 m² between sq. J10–M10, beginning in 1989, which would bring the surface of Excavation VII to $c.$ 510 m². Unfortunately, I cannot confirm this figure as I have found no detailed information about this extension, only one record relating to deposits he excavated in these squares as well as photographs of architectural structures he exposed. In any case, it seems that Excavation VII ended up being even much larger than $c.$ 510 m². Indeed, its limits were recorded again in 2011 as part of the renewed Tajik-French collaborative fieldwork at Sarazm. The surface then calculated was $c.$ 640 m², a result similar to the one I obtained by measuring Excavation VII using Google Earth. Available satellite image on Google Earth shows that the additional $c.$ 130 m² for which I have found no record mostly correspond to an extension along the north-west limit of Excavation VII, between sq. I12–I16, as well as possibly additional extensions along its south-west and southeast limits (Fig. 1.4). The same image tends to indicate that Besenval removed only the uppermost surface layers and did not reach any archaeological level in most of the north-west extension. No, or very little, architecture is indeed apparent in this area on this image, whereas architectural remains are clearly visible within most of the other areas exposed in Excavation VII. That he barely excavated in the north-west extensions seems corroborated by the fact that I have seen no photograph of any architecture in this location.

## 3. ARCHAEOLOGICAL CONTEXTS

Figure 3.1: Sarazm, present-day surface of Excavation VII. South-westward view. B. Mutin.

Figure 3.2: Sarazm, Excavation VII, test trench opened in 1984 in sq. L13 and L14. South-westward view. R. Besenval, edited by B. Mutin.

Figure 3.3: Sarazm, Excavation VII, architectural levels identified within the 1984 test trench: Levels I3, II1, and III2. North-eastward view. R. Besenval, edited by B. Mutin.

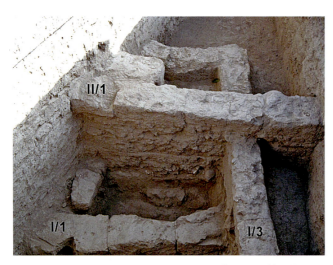

Figure 3.4: Sarazm, Excavation VII, architectural levels identified within the 1984 test trench: Levels I1, I3, and II1. North-eastward view. R. Besenval, edited by B. Mutin.

Excavation VII's stratigraphic sequence consists of deposits that are not thicker than about two metres between the virgin soil and the surface of the site (Pl. 3.2). Of the four archaeological levels Besenval defined, Levels I to IV, Level I is the oldest one and rests directly on top of the virgin soil, while Level IV is the most recent one and is underneath the site's surface layers. These levels include levels with solid, mud-brick, and/or rammed earth (*pakhsa*) architecture (Levels I1, I2, I3, II1, III1, III2, and IV1–IV2) as well as levels with no apparent architecture and just postholes and/or features that are settled on top of each major architectural level (Levels I4, II2, and III3). Unfortunately, Besenval could not study these four levels over extensive surfaces because he was required to keep all architectural remains and some of the other features intact as he was excavating downward. This obligation certainly had the benefit that the totality of the architecture in Excavation VII is now preserved, underneath a protective layer of soil, as is the architecture exposed in the other excavations at Sarazm (Fig. 3.1). However, this requirement made it very complicated to understand the lowest occupation levels in this excavation. Besenval mentioned this issue in many instances in his reports and field notes. Plate 3.1, which shows just the architecture exposed in Levels I1, I2, I3, II1, III1, III2, and IV, between sq. I11–M15, illustrates how difficult it must have been to study certain areas where walls were found on top of each other. For this reason, Besenval could not excavate certain deposits and was not able to determine certain stratigraphic relationships. Another parameter that needs to be kept in mind is that not all the levels he defined were preserved over the totality of Excavation VII's surface. As a result of these two factors, as is evident in the plans provided in this volume, while some occupation levels were studied over relatively large expanses, such as Level III2, others are known through much more limited surfaces.

In 1984, Besenval together with Francfort began fieldwork in Excavation VII by opening a 2 × 4 m test trench in the north-western half of sq. L13, along with a 4 × 4 m test trench in sq. L14 (Fig. 3.2). They identified in these test trenches three of the above-mentioned main four occupation levels that characterize Excavation VII (Levels I–III; Figs 3.3–3.4). In 1985, Besenval extended Excavation VII north-westward and south-eastward to include the rest of sq. L13, the north-western halves of sq. M13 and M14, and sq. K13. With the new data he collected during this field season he reinterpreted the stratigraphy of Excavation VII and relabelled the floors he and Francfort had observed in 1984. These floors were labelled S1 to S7 from bottom to top in 1984 and became S1 to S7 from top to bottom in 1985 (Pl. 3.2: sq. L13 NW). This change is reflected in the tables provided in this chapter.

While 1984 and 1985 field seasons had focused on establishing Excavation VII's stratigraphy, in 1986 Besenval expanded the surface of this excavation to get a better understanding of the spatial organization and function of the archaeological structures and areas he had studied thus far. He opened sq. J12, K12, and L12 south-west and west of the previous limits, as well as sq. J13 to the north-west. He also opened sq. J14–15, K14–15, and L14–15 to the north-west, north, and north-east. With these extensions, Besenval discovered an additional level, Level IV, just underneath the surface layers. This level yielded some of the most significant discoveries of this excavation, which include a group of complete ceramics with stylistic relationships with assemblages known in northern Iran, southern Afghanistan, and Pakistani Balochistan (see **Chapters 1, 5, and 6**). That year he focused on the latest levels of Excavation VII, Levels III and IV, leaving the study of the earliest levels for the next field seasons.

During 1987 field season, Besenval extended Excavation VII south-westward by opening sq. J11, K11, L11, and M11. He also studied more deposits in sq. J12–13, K12, L12, and M12, as well as in sq. J14–15, K14–15, L14–15, and M14–15. This work brought new data mostly about Levels I–III in the central, eastern, and north-eastern parts of Excavation VII, as well as on Level IV in its south-western part.

I assume that field season 1988 was dedicated to survey, or cancelled, as I have found no reference to any fieldwork in Excavation VII for that year.

In 1989, Besenval opened sq. J10, K10, L10, and M10 in the south-western part of Excavation VII. He uncovered in these squares Level IV-related architectural remains, which are in the archives documented only through photographs. He excavated between the walls of the Level III2 building in sq. J11, K11, and K13–14. He also extended the limits of Excavation VII onto sq. I15 and J15 to the north-east to study Level IV1 Room 1 and the deposits located underneath Level IV1 in the same area.

It seems that field seasons 1990 and 1991 were mostly focused on expanding Excavation VII northward and eastward. Records are lacking for field season 1990. However, the 1991 archives suggest that Besenval worked in sq. J16–17, K16–17, L16–17, M16–17, and half of N16–17 during both 1990–1991 field seasons.

He found in these squares a substantial amount of additional data relating to Levels I, II, and III, including large portions of buildings. It is unfortunate that I have not been able to locate any exploitable archives relating to 1990 field season and any plans of the archaeological remains he uncovered during both field seasons. These were the last two excavation-seasons in Excavation VII.

## Level I1

Level I1 is the earliest occupation level identified in Excavation VII (Pl. 3.3; Table 3.1). It rests directly on top of the virgin soil. It was identified between sq. K13–15 and M13–15 and could not be studied over an extensive area because the architecture belonging to the levels on top of it could not be removed.

Level I1 essentially consists of a building uncovered in sq. K14–15 to M14–15 over a *c.* 8.50 × 7.50 m surface (Figs 3.5–3.6). It is however apparent that this building was larger than this, since its walls seem to continue in all directions but south-west. It is WNW-ESE/NNE-SSW oriented. Its walls were preserved up to *c.* 60–70 cm in height. The lower sections of these walls are made of rammed earth, while their upper sections are built with mud bricks measuring 50–52 × 30–32 × 10 cm and aligned in a single row along their lengths. Available photographs however suggest that some of these walls are entirely built with rammed earth. I have been able to find more details only about Wall 6's construction. The rammed earth portion of this wall is *c.* 27 cm high. Three *c.* 24 cm wide gaps, filled up with compacted soil, were observed within this wall at the upper limit of its rammed earth segment (Figs 3.7–3.8). Wall 6 is plastered (*c.* 2–4 cm thick) on both its interior and exterior faces as well as on the faces of the gaps.

Three rooms that belong to this building were exposed in Excavation VII: Rooms 1, 2, and 3. They are distributed around a larger unit that may have been a courtyard: Room 4. Room 1, in the north-western part, has a L-shape. Its interior space is *c.* 4.80 × 3.80 m. Two floors were found inside this room, the

Table 3.1: Sarazm, Excavation VII, list of features in Level I1.

| Grid location | Feature number | Archive number | Category | Altitude (m) | On plan? |
|---|---|---|---|---|---|
| L13 | Wall 1 | M6 | Wall | *c.* 6.96 | Yes |
| L13 | Wall 2 | Not found | Wall | *c.* 6.96 | Yes |
| L13 | Wall 3 | Not found | Wall | Not found | Yes |
| L13 | Wall 4 | Not found | Wall | *c.* 6.93 | Yes |
| K13–14–L13–14 | Wall 5 | M18 | Wall | Not found | Yes |
| L13–14–M14 | Wall 6 | M5 | Wall | *c.* 7.28 | Yes |
| M14 | Wall 7 | Not found | Wall | *c.* 7.22 | Yes |
| L14–M14 | Wall 8 | M17 | Wall | *c.* 7.23–7.28 | Yes |
| L14 | Wall 9 | Not found | Wall | Not found | Yes |
| L15–M15 | Wall 10 | Not found | Wall | *c.* 7.02 | Yes |
| M15 | Wall 11 | Not found | Wall | *c.* 7.15 | Yes |
| M15 | Wall 12 | Not found | Wall | *c.* 7.15 | Yes |
| L14 | Wall 13 | Not found | Wall | Not found | Yes |
| K14 | Wall 14 | Not found | Wall | Not found | Yes |
| K14–15 | Wall 15 | Not found | Wall | *c.* 7.16–7.18 | Yes |
| K14–15 | Wall 16 | Not found | Wall | *c.* 7.16–7.18 | Yes |
| K15 | Wall 17 | Not found | Wall | *c.* 7.17–7.18 | Yes |
| K15–L15 | Wall 18 | Not found | Wall | *c.* 7.15–7.17 | Yes |
| L15 | Wall 19 | Not found | Wall | *c.* 7.15 | Yes |
| K15–L15 | Postholes 1–11 | Not found | Posthole | *c.* 6.58–6.66 (*c.* 6.40 inside) | Yes |
| K14–15–L14 | Room 1 | 84/S1a; 84/S1b; 85/S6; 85/S7; 85/UF111; 89/UF12; 89/UF18; 89/UF21 | Fill and floor | *c.* 6.54–7.28 | Yes |
| L14–15–M14–15 | Room 2 | 87/UF29 | Fill and floor | *c.* 6.61–6.66 | Yes |
| K14–15–L15 | Room 3 | 87/UF31; 89/UF17; 89/UF20 | Fill and floor | *c.* 6.58–6.66 | Yes |
| K15–L14–15–M15 | Room 4 | 87/UF30 | Fill and floor | *c.* 6.61–6.67 | Yes |
| L13–14–M13–14 | Alleyway 1 | 84/C8a; 84/C8b; 84/S2; 84/S1c; 85/S6; 89/UF24 | Fill and floor | *c.* 6.53 (virgin soil) –7.00 | Yes |
| L14 | Hearth 1 | T21 | Hearth | *c.* 6.40–6.54 | Yes |
| K15 | Hearth 2 | 87/T36; 87/UF32 | Hearth | *c.* 6.60 | Yes |
| L15 | Hearth 3 | T37 | Hearth | *c.* 6.60 | No |
| L14 | Other feature 1 | Not found | Niche | *c.* 7.03 | Yes |
| M14–15 | Other feature 2 | 89/UF19 | Hearth? | *c.* 6.80–6.92 | Yes |

LEVEL I1

Figure 3.5: Sarazm, Excavation VII, Level I1. South-eastward view. R. Besenval, edited by B. Mutin.

Figure 3.6: Sarazm, Excavation VII, Level I1. Northward view. R. Besenval, edited by B. Mutin.

Figure 3.7: Sarazm, Excavation VII, Level I1, Wall 6 with view of niche OF1 on the left. Southward view. R. Besenval, edited by B. Mutin.

Figure 3.8: Sarazm, Excavation VII, Level I1, Wall 6. Northward view. R. Besenval, edited by B. Mutin.

Figure 3.9: Sarazm, Excavation VII, Level I1, Hearth 1. R. Besenval, edited by B. Mutin.

Figure 3.10: Sarazm, Excavation VII, Level I1, stone accumulation (OF2) inside Room 2. North-westward view. R. Besenval, edited by B. Mutin.

Figure 3.11: Sarazm, Excavation VII, Level I1, stone accumulation (OF2) inside Room 2. South-eastward view. R. Besenval, edited by B. Mutin.

Figure 3.12: Sarazm, Excavation VII, Level I1, Room 3. South-eastward view. R. Besenval, edited by B. Mutin.

Figure 3.13: Sarazm, Excavation VII, Level I1, Room 3. Southward view. R. Besenval, edited by B. Mutin.

Figure 3.14: Sarazm, Excavation VII, Level I1, Room 3, Hearth 2. Northward view. R. Besenval, edited by B. Mutin.

Figure 3.15: Sarazm, Excavation VII, Level I1, Room 3, postholes. Southward view. R. Besenval, edited by B. Mutin.

Figure 3.16: Sarazm, Excavation VII, Level I1, Room 4, Hearth 3. R. Besenval, edited by B. Mutin.

Figure 3.17: Sarazm, Excavation VII, Level I1, Room 4 with view of the postholes in Room 3 on the left. South-eastward view. R. Besenval, edited by B. Mutin.

Figure 3.18: Sarazm, Excavation VII, Level I1, Room 4. North-westward view. R. Besenval, edited by B. Mutin.

Figure 3.19: Sarazm, Excavation VII, Level I1, Alleyway 1 south of Wall 6. Southward view. R. Besenval, edited by B. Mutin.

lower one (alt. *c.* 6.60 m) resting directly on top of the virgin soil, as well as one circular hearth (H1; Fig. 3.9). This hearth is *c.* 55 cm in diameter and has a crater in its centre that is *c.* 18 cm in diameter and *c.* 14 cm deep. Stones were recorded in this room, as well as a *c.* 50 × 50 cm niche against Wall 6 (OF1; Fig. 3.7). This niche is made of two vertical mud bricks. The interior space between the two mud bricks is *c.* 25 cm. This feature laid on the upper floor identified within Room 1.

Room 2 is east of Room 1 and Wall 8. This room is smaller, measuring *c.* 2.50 × 2.00 m. One feature consisting of an aggregate of stones was found against Wall 7 (OF2; Figs 3.10–3.11). It was interpreted as a hearth before it was excavated, but I do not know whether this interpretation was confirmed after it was excavated. In any case, photographs suggest that these stones were associated with a layer containing charcoal, ashes, animal bones, and more stones.

Room 3, in the north-eastern part, has a L-shape and is symmetrical to Room 1. The plan of this room on Plate 3.3 is not complete since photographs from field season 1989 clearly show that Room 3 was similar to Room 1, with Walls 15 and 19 connected to two additional east–west walls (Figs 3.12–3.13). Unfortunately, I have found no architectural plan, nor sketch, of this level with these additional walls. The available plan shows that the inside surface of this room is at least *c.* 3.80 × 1.90 m. It contains a floor as well as one square, *c.* 48 × 46 cm hearth (H2; Fig. 3.14). This hearth has a crater in its centre that is 15 cm in diameter and 7 cm deep. It contained carbonized seeds. Additionally, a series of eleven postholes were identified in Room 3 (PH1 to 11; Figs 3.15 and 3.17), dug into its floor. Five of them are parallel to Wall 18, while two series of two additional postholes are parallel to Walls 15 and 19. The architecture of this room in sq. K15 was later cut by a burial, which was defined as 'antique' (see below).

It is unclear whether Room 4 is a room or a courtyard (Figs 3.5–3.6, 3.12–3.13, 3.16–3.18). This area is accessible at a minimum from Room 1 through a doorway in Wall 13 (*c.* 65 cm wide). At least two floors were exposed inside, over a *c.* 6.90 × 4.10 m area. No feature is mapped on the plans of Room 4 available in the archives, although Besenval mentioned that a circular hearth with a cra-

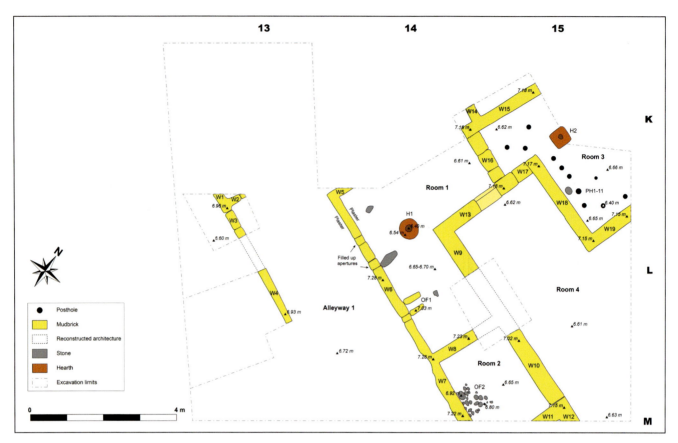

Plate 3.3: Sarazm, Excavation VII, plan of Level I1. B. Mutin, based on R. Besenval archives.

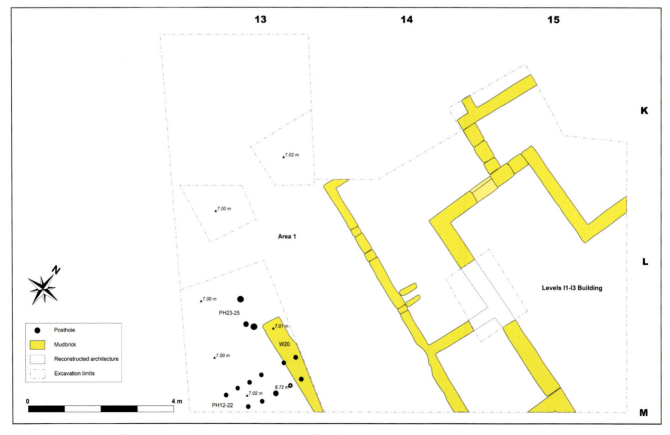

Plate 3.4: Sarazm, Excavation VII, plan of Level I2. B. Mutin, based on R. Besenval archives.

Figure 3.20: Sarazm, Excavation VII, Level I1, Alleyway 1, layer or shallow pit containing animal bones and stones. R. Besenval, edited by B. Mutin.

Table 3.2: Sarazm, Excavation VII, list of features in Level I2.

| Grid location | Feature number | Archive number | Category | Altitude (m) | On plan? |
|---|---|---|---|---|---|
| L13–M13 | Wall 20 | M19 | Wall | c. 7.01 | Yes |
| M13 | Postholes 12–22 | Not found | Posthole | c. 7.00–7.02 (c. 6.72 inside) | Yes |
| L13 | Postholes 23–25 | Not found | Posthole | c. 7.00 | Yes |
| K13–L13–M13 | Area 1 | 84/C7; 84/S3; 85/S5 | Fill and floor | c. 7.00–7.03 | Yes |

ter in its centre was present on one of the floors (H3, not mapped; Figs 3.5–3.6, and 3.16). This is confirmed by some photographs, which also show that an additional feature, perhaps a pit, was exposed on the same floor. I have found no detailed photograph that may inform us on the nature of this feature. The second floor yielded stones and a charred area (Figs 3.17–3.18). Since the Level I1 building continued to be used during Levels I2 and I3, it is possible that this second floor, as well as the additional floors observed in the other rooms of this building, functioned with Level I2 and/or Level I3.

About 2.50 m south-west of Wall 6, separated from this building by what appears to be an alleyway (Alleyway 1; Fig. 3.19), were found the portions of three to four walls with the same orientation as that of the above-described building (Walls 1, 2, 3, and 4). Two floors were found both north and south of Wall 3 (alt. c. 6.70 and c. 6.85 m). Squeezed in between these two floors was a layer of loose soil containing animal bones. Two features were identified in Alleyway 1: one is a layer, or a shallow pit, with numerous animal bones and stones (alt. c. 6.72 m; Fig. 3.20), and the other one is a black (probably burnt?) layer (alt. c. 6.89 m). Two hearths also appear to have been recorded in this area (alt. c. 6.87 m and c. 7.00 m), although I have found no other specific records than just a mention of these features. It is also possible that they belong to Level I2 instead of Level I1. The virgin soil was reached at alt. 6.53 m in this area.

## Level I2

Part, or the totality, of the Level I1 main building continued to be used during Level I2 (Pl. 3.4; Table 3.2). On the other hand, Walls 1, 2, 3, and 4, south of it, were now covered with a floor (alt. c. 7.00–7.03 m). This floor was observed in three locations in sq. K13, L13, and M13 and defined a new space on top of Level I1 Alleyway 1. I have labelled this space Area 1 for lack of a better term, since

Figure 3.21: Sarazm, Excavation VII, Level I2, postholes. North-westward view. R. Besenval, edited by B. Mutin.

it is unclear whether it is a room or a courtyard. With this floor is associated the portion of an architectural structure reported as either a mud-brick wall or a platform (Wall 20). Two parallel rows of postholes (PH12 to 22; Fig. 3.21), including three dug into Wall 20, were observed on this floor, as well as three additional postholes about one metre distant to the north-west (PH23 to 25). These features follow the same orientation as the Level I1 building. However, although it is clear that the Level I1 building was still being used when Level I2 features were set up, the exact stratigraphic relationship between the Level I2 floor and the Level I1 building was never established, for Besenval could not excavate this floor continuously all the way to this building.

## Level I3

Level I1 building continued to be used in Level I3 (Pl. 3.5; Table 3.3). However, in contrast to Levels I1 and I2, a large building as well as a surface made of small pebbles now laid west, south-west, and south of the Level

Figure 3.22: Sarazm, Excavation VII, Level I3 with view of Alleyway 2 in the back. South-eastward view. R. Besenval, edited by B. Mutin.

Table 3.3: Sarazm, Excavation VII, list of features in Level I3.

| Grid location | Feature number | Archive number | Category | Altitude (m) | On plan? |
|---|---|---|---|---|---|
| L12 | Wall 21 | Not found | Wall | Not found | Yes |
| L12–13 | Wall 22 | M4 | Wall | c. 7.34–7.37 | Yes |
| L12 | Wall 23 | Not found | Wall | Not found | Yes |
| K12–13–L12 | Wall 24 | M16 | Wall | c. 7.42 | Yes |
| L12 | Wall 25 | Not found | Wall | Not found | Yes |
| K13–L13 | Wall 26 | Not found | Wall | c. 7.38 | Yes |
| K12–L12 | Wall 27 | Not found | Wall | Not found | Yes |
| J12–K12–13 | Wall 28 | M15 | Wall | c. 7.44 | Yes |
| J12–K12 | Wall 29 | Not found | Wall | Not found | Yes |
| J12 | Wall 30 | Not found | Wall | Not found | Yes |
| I13–J12–13 | Wall 31 | Not found | Wall | c. 7.38 | Yes |
| I13–J13 | Wall 32 | Not found | Wall | Not found | Yes |
| L12 | Posthole 26 | Not found | Posthole | Not found | Yes |
| K12 | Posthole 27 | Not found | Posthole | Not found | Yes |
| J12–K12–13–L12 | Room 5 | 85/S4; 87/UF2 | Fill and floor | c. 7.13 | Yes |
| K12–13–L12–13 | Room 6 | 84/C5; 84/C6; 84–85/S4-S4a | Fill and floor | c. 7.10 | Yes |
| L12 | Room 7 | 87/UF9 | Fill and floor | c. 7.40 (top fill) | Yes |
| K12–L12 | Room 8 | 87/UF9 | Fill and floor | c. 7.40 (top fill) | Yes |
| J12–13–K12–14 | Room 9 | 85/S4; 87/UF1; 87/UF5; 87/UF8; 89/UF7 | Fill and floor | c. 7.11 | Yes |
| L13–14–M13–14 | Area 2 | 84/C5; 84–85/S4-S4b | Fill and floor | c. 7.05–7.07 | Yes |
| I14–15–J14–15–K14–15 | Area 3 | 89/UF22; 89/UF23 | Fill and floor | Not found | Yes |
| K13–L13–14–M13–14 | Alleyway 2 | 84/C5; 84/C6; 84–85/S4-S4b | Fill and floor | c. 7.11–7.12 | Yes |
| K12 | Hearth 4 | T28 | Hearth | c. 6.94–7.23 | Yes |
| K13 | Hearth 5 | T18 | Hearth | c. 7.11 | Yes |
| I13–K13 | Hearth 6 | T27 | Hearth | c. 7.10 | Yes |

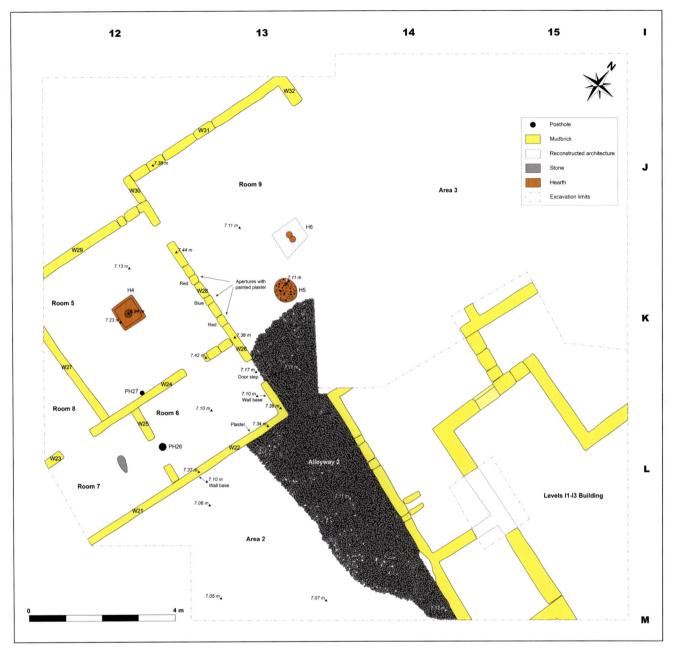

Plate 3.5: Sarazm, Excavation VII, plan of Level I3.
B. Mutin, based on R. Besenval archives.

I1 building (Alleyway 2; Fig. 3.22). This new building has the same WNW-ESE/NNE-SSW orientation as the Level I1 building. Its walls are made with mud bricks measuring 35–36 × 21 × 8 cm and are aligned in a single row. They are preserved mostly up to 15–20 cm in height. Besenval pointed out that the floors of the rooms inside this building were very well prepared; they are made with rammed earth, and their edges raise up against the bases of the walls. Also, both exterior and interior faces of the walls are plastered. Besenval reckoned that the overall construction did not seem to have been used for a long time.

Four rooms were identified, Rooms 5, 6, 7, and 8, as well as an additional space, Room 9, that is either a room or, more likely, a courtyard. I do not know the extent of this room to the north, and it is unclear whether its northern end in sq. J13–14–K13–14 is open, as is apparent on the plan, or the lack of architecture on this plan is due to the fact that this location was not fully excavated. In total, including Room 9, this construction was excavated over a c. 11.00 × 7.70 m area, but was larger than that since this area does not include its southern end, which was not exposed.

3. ARCHAEOLOGICAL CONTEXTS

Figure 3.23: Sarazm, Excavation VII, Level I3, Room 5 with Hearth 4 (foreground and middle ground) and Room 9 (background). Northward view. R. Besenval, edited by B. Mutin.

Figure 3.24: Sarazm, Excavation VII, Level I3, Room 5, Wall 28. Southward view. R. Besenval, edited by B. Mutin.

Figure 3.25: Sarazm, Excavation VII, Level I3, Room 5, Wall 28 with red plaster fragments on and around it. Northward view. R. Besenval, edited by B. Mutin.

Figure 3.26: Sarazm, Excavation VII, Level I3, Room 5, Hearth 4. Northward view. R. Besenval, edited by B. Mutin.

Figure 3.27: Sarazm, Excavation VII, Level I3, Rooms 6 and 7, from left to right. North-eastward view. R. Besenval, edited by B. Mutin.

Figure 3.28: Sarazm, Excavation VII, Level I3, Room 9 with Wall 28 in the middle ground and left side and Walls 30 and 31 on the right side (second wall starting from the right). Level II1 Wall 8 (left) and Level III2 Wall 6 (right) are on top in the centre of the photograph. Southward view. R. Besenval, edited by B. Mutin.

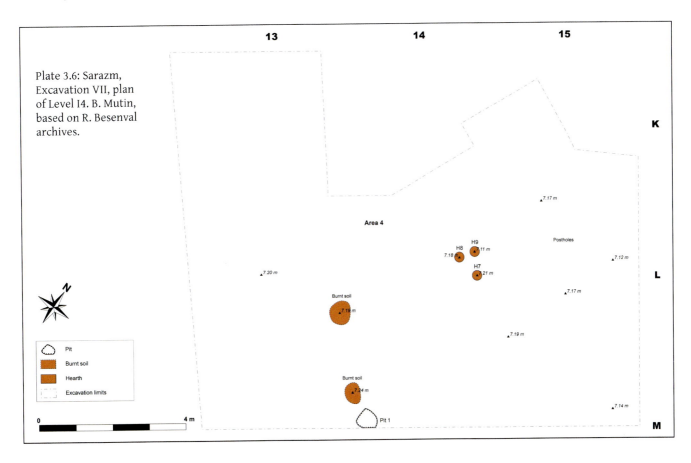

Plate 3.6: Sarazm, Excavation VII, plan of Level I4. B. Mutin, based on R. Besenval archives.

Room 5 has a *c.* 4.00 × 4.00 m interior area (Fig. 3.23). Its northern Wall 28 is preserved up to three courses of mud bricks. It has three gaps whose bases rest on top of the second course (Figs 3.24–3.25). These gaps are *c.* 25–27 cm wide and have traces of paint on their interior faces. Two of them have red paint (hematite) and one has blue paint (lapis lazuli) (see **Chapter 6**). This room has two doorways, one in Wall 28 (*c.* 55 cm), which gives access to Room 9, and one in its eastern Wall 24 (*c.* 60 cm), which connects to Room 6. Inside, the floor consists of a well-preserved surface made of rammed earth and plastered (alt. *c.* 7.13 m). The main feature in this room is a square, *c.* 72 × 72 cm hearth placed in its centre (H4; Figs 3.23 and 3.26). This hearth has a *c.* 10 cm high, 5 cm wide, raised edge and a central crater that is *c.* 19 cm deep and 22 cm in diameter. Additionally, a posthole (PH27) was found near Wall 24.

East of Room 5 is Room 6 (Fig. 3.27). This room is smaller, *c.* 3.00 × 2.20 m. In addition to the doorway that gives access to Room 5, Room 6 has one *c.* 70 cm wide doorway in Wall 26 and one *c.* 80 cm wide doorway in Wall 25. The former opens to Room 9 to the north while the latter connects to Room 7 to the south. A posthole (PH26) was found almost in the centre of the latter, and a doorstep was observed at the former. The floor inside Room 6 is the same as in Room 5 (alt. *c.* 7.10 m). Wall 22 is covered with plaster.

I have not found much information about Rooms 7 and 8. Room 7, south of Room 6, is 2.20 m wide and at least 2.80 m long; its southern end was not excavated (Fig. 3.27). Room 8 was excavated over a smaller surface. These two rooms are connected by a *c.* 95 cm wide doorway in Wall 23. Animal bones were apparently recorded on their floors, and one stone was mapped on the floor of Room 7.

Room 9, north of Rooms 5 to 8, is demarcated by Walls 31 and 32 on its west side and Walls 26, 28, and 30 on its south side (Fig. 3.28). On its east side is the Level I1 building. However, I do not know whether and how this building connects to Room 9, since the area where this could have been elucidated was covered with architecture that belongs to posterior levels and could not be excavated. Similarly, Room 9's northern end would have needed clarification as it is not known whether it is enclosed by a wall, blocked by the Level I1 building (which seems to extend upon this area), or open. Its western and southern sides suggest that this room may have been as large as *c.* 7.45 × 4.65 m. Two doorways provide access to it from Rooms 6 and 7. An access from outside the building is located in its south-eastern

Table 3.4: Sarazm, Excavation VII, list of features in Level I4.

| Grid location | Feature number | Archive number | Category | Altitude (m) | On plan? |
|---|---|---|---|---|---|
| K15–L15–M15 | Postholes 28-n | Not found | Posthole | c. 7.12–7.24 | No |
| K12–15–L12–15–M12–15 | Area 4 | 84/C5; 87/UF27; 87/UF28 | Fill and floor | c. 7.15–7.34 | Yes |
| M14–16–N14–16 | East of Area 4 | 90/UF51; 90/UF52 | Fill and floor | Not found | No |
| L14 | Hearth 7 | T4 | Hearth | c. 7.21 | Yes |
| L14 | Hearth 8 | T5 | Hearth | c. 7.18 | Yes |
| L14 | Hearth 9 | T6 | Hearth | c. 7.11 | Yes |
| M14 | Pit 1 | T20 | Pit | Not found | Yes |

Figure 3.29: Sarazm, Excavation VII, Level I3, Room 9, Hearth 6. R. Besenval, edited by B. Mutin.

Figure 3.30: Sarazm, Excavation VII, Level I3, Alleyway 2. Eastward view. R. Besenval, edited by B. Mutin.

Figure 3.31: Sarazm, Excavation VII, Level I3, detail of the surface of Alleyway 2. R. Besenval, edited by B. Mutin.

Figure 3.32: Sarazm, Excavation VII, Level I4, Hearths 7 (background), 8 (right), and 9 (left). South-eastward view. R. Besenval, edited by B. Mutin.

Figure 3.33: Sarazm, Excavation VII, Level I4, postholes. R. Besenval, edited by B. Mutin.

Figure 3.34: Sarazm, Excavation VII, Level I4, postholes. R. Besenval, edited by B. Mutin.

corner, through Alleyway 2 between the Level I1 and I3 buildings. It is *c.* 1.15 m wide. Inside, Room 9's floor (alt. *c.* 7.11 m) seems to have been built with rammed earth, as in the rest of the building, except in its south-eastern corner. In this area, including up to Room 6's doorstep, the floor consists of pebbles carefully incrusted within a layer of rammed earth. This floor continues outside of Room 9 into Alleyway 2. Two hearths were recorded inside Room 9. One is a *c.* 65 cm circular hearth located just west of the pebbles (H5). The second one is a *c.* 82 × 77 cm hearth with two heavily levelled central craters of *c.* 18 cm in diameter (H6; Fig. 3.29).

I have found virtually no information about Area 2, east of Level I3 building Rooms 6 and 7. The only information I have found is that its base is between *c.* 7.05–7.07 m in altitude. North of this area is Alleyway 2 with its floor made of rammed earth and incrusted pebbles (Figs 3.30–3.31). This floor (alt. *c.* 7.11–7.12 m) was excavated over *c.* 9.00 m in length and 2.50 m at its largest width. Besenval mentioned that a row of postholes was present in this floor, although I have not been able to locate any record relating to these postholes in the Level I archives. A possibility is that they belong to and were mapped with Level II2 features, as many postholes were recorded in this level just above this floor.

Lastly, I have found no information about Area 3, north of Room 9, although layers that appear to belong to Level I3 and perhaps to Level II too were excavated in this area. It seems that nothing remarkable, apparently no feature, was present between the northern half of Room 9 and Area 3.

## Level I4

In comparison with previous levels, Level I4 appears much more transient and was identified on a more limited surface (Pl. 3.6; Table 3.4). This level consists of features recorded on top of Level I3 destruction and abandon layers and underneath the Level II1 base. These layers contain mud bricks from collapsed architecture, burnt soil, animal bones, and very few artefacts. These include blue plaster fragments as well as burnt plaster fragments in the deposits on top of Level I3 Room 6 and Alleyway 2. Similar layers were noted in various parts of Excavation VII (Fig. 3.25), and it seems that most features that belong to Level I4 were observed in one area within sq. K12–15, L12–15, and M12–15, which I have labelled Area 4. Besenval excavated a few additional fill deposits just east of Area 4, in sq. M14–16 and N14–16. He wrote that these layers were underneath the Level II1 floor, which implies that they probably belong to Level I4. Unfortunately, I have found no additional information about them; at a minimum, it seems that no feature was recorded in these deposits.

Besenval emphasized that he found no floor *stricto sensu* in Level I4. However, he defined this level based on the stratigraphic position and relatively consistent altitudes (between *c.* 7.10–7.30 m) of a series of features he identified between Levels I3 and II1. These features consist of three hearths (*tannoor*), H7, H8, and H9, measuring respectively 25 cm, 25 cm, and 20 cm in diameter (Fig. 3.32), as well as a pit (Pit 1), *c.* 55 cm in diameter,

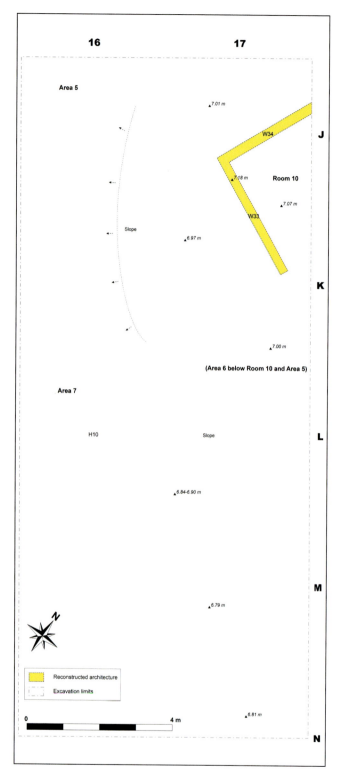

Plate 3.7: Sarazm, Excavation VII, sketch plan of Level I-North/East. B. Mutin, based on R. Besenval archives.

which contained animal bones and ashes. Associated with these features are small areas with patches of red-fired soil. Additionally, Besenval observed a series of postholes somewhere between sq. K15 and M15 that he assigned to Level I4. I have found no plan of these postholes, just photographs and a series of altitudes between *c.* 7.12–7.24 m. These photographs show that many of them appear to align and may have formed partition walls parallel to Level I1 Wall 18. Some were dug into this wall (Figs 3.33–3.34). Lastly, a hearth (H10) was recovered in sq. L16. It is discussed in the following section, because, like a number of other features found further north and east, its stratigraphic relationship to Levels I1–I4 is not entirely clear. However, it seems rational to hypothesize that this hearth functioned with Level I4 H7, H8, and H9, because it was apparently exposed directly underneath Level II.

## Level I-North/East

During 1990–1991 field seasons, Besenval found a series of features that belong to Level I between sq. J16–17 and N16–17, north and east of the areas he had studied so far (Pl. 3.7; Table 3.5). Since I am missing part of the archives from these field seasons, I have found no stratigraphic information that could have permitted me to establish a relationship between these remains and those of Levels I1, I2, I3, and I4 further south and west. Consequently, I have found it more prudent to present them separately. The main features of Level I-North/East are located within sq. J16–17 and K16–17. They consist of two mud brick walls (Walls 33 and 34) forming a room (Room 10) with an orientation similar or comparable to that of the architecture recorded in Levels I1–I3.[2] A floor was observed inside this room (alt. *c.* 7.07 m).

Outside of Room 10, in sq. J16–17 and K16–17, Besenval excavated layers underneath a floor that belongs to Level II (alt. *c.* 6.96–7.18 m, *c.* 6.97 m, *c.* 7.00–7.19 m, *c.* 7.01 m, *c.* 7.36 m). For lack of a better term, I have labelled this area, Area 5. A floor was observed in this area, with an altitude comparable to that of Room 10's floor (alt. *c.* 6.97 m in sq. J16–K16; alt. *c.* 7.00 m in sq. K17). At about the same altitude (alt. *c.* 7.01–7.03 m), a

---

[2] As previously noted, the map of Level I-North/East architecture presented here has been reconstructed based on sketch plans. The general orientation, thickness, and location of this architecture were not reported exactly the same way across these sketch plans. As such, the way this architecture is represented here combines and synthesizes all available information in the archives. It is not wrong but should be considered an approximation.

Table 3.5: Sarazm, Excavation VII, list of features in Level I-North/East.

| Grid location | Feature number | Archive number | Category | Altitude (m) | On plan? |
|---|---|---|---|---|---|
| J17–K17 | Wall 33 | Not found | Wall | c. 7.18 | Yes |
| J17 | Wall 34 | Not found | Wall | Not found | Yes |
| J17–K17 | Room 10 | 91/UF100 | Fill and floor | c. 7.02–7.07 | Yes |
| J16-17–K17 | Area 5 | 91/UF85; 91/UF89; 91/UF93; 91/UF94; 91/UF95; 91/UF96; 91/UF97; 91/UF99; 91/UF101; 91/UF106 | Fill and floor | c. 6.96–7.36 | Yes |
| J17–K17 | Area 6 | 91/UF101; 91/UF102A-B; 91/UF105; 91/UF108 | Fill and floor | c. 6.63–7.06 | Yes |
| L16-17–M16-17–N16-17 | Area 7 | 90/UF50; 91/UF83; 91/UF86; 91/UF87; 91/UF88; 91/UF92; 91/UF98; 91/UF103; 91/UF104; 91/UF107 | Fill and floor | c. 6.69–7.34 | Yes |
| L16 | Hearth 10 | T52 | Hearth | Not found | No |

floor with pebbles was noted in sq. J17, although it is unclear whether this floor is the continuation of the one I just mentioned, or a different one. Architectural remains were also noted in Area 5, although I do not know whether these remains are those of standing constructions or the remains of collapsed architecture; I have found no plan of this area. Additionally, a slope with black and yellow soil was observed in the southern part of sq. J16–K16.

Besenval excavated underneath Room 10 and Area 5. He found two concentrations of animal bones as well as a soft soil with bones, pebbles, and a few ceramic fragments, all between alt. c. 6.63/6.73–7.06 m. I have labelled these remains Area 6. Besenval then dug in this area down to the virgin soil at alt. c. 6.41 m.

Further east, in sq. L16-17, M16-17, and N16-17, he excavated various layers that were most likely connected to Area 5 or Area 6, and with altitudes compatible with those recorded in these areas (e.g. alt. c. 6.69–6.99 m, c. 6.71 m, c. 6.81–7.07 m, c. 6.84–6.99 m, c. 7.05–7.19 m, c. 7.34 m). Since I have found no detailed information about these layers, I have put them together under the label Area 7. A floor was noted in Area 7, with altitudes relatively consistent with those of Area 5's floor (alt. c. 6.84–6.90 m in sq. L17–M17; alt. c. 6.79 m in sq. M17–N17). In sq. N16-17, this floor (alt. c. 6.81–6.84 m) is covered with a layer of pebbles (alt. c. 6.83–6.91 m) in which a ceramic and a bone awl were recovered. Additionally, a slope going southward, like the one in Area 5, was recorded in sq. L17–M17. A circular hearth (Hearth 10) was also noted in sq. L16 but was not mapped. Sparse, unorganized mud bricks were found in sq. L17–M17, and an additional floor was recorded inside sq. M17 at alt. c. 7.19 m. Close to the south-eastern edge of Excavation VII, in sq. N16-17, a sherd of Geoksyur style pottery was found at about 20 cm above the virgin soil (alt. c. 6.73 m). Besenval recorded the virgin soil in sq. L17–M17–N17 at alt. c. 6.53 m, 6.56 m, and 6.59 m.

## *Level II1*

Level II1 is characterized by a new mud-brick building located in sq. K12-13, L12-13, and M13 (Pl. 3.8; Table 3.6). Like Level I constructions, this building is WNW–ESE/NNE–SSW oriented, although it is about 12 degrees more to the east. It was uncovered over a c. 7.50 m × 6.00 m area. It is preserved up to 10–15 cm in height. Its walls are made of mud bricks aligned in a single row, an arrangement observed in the previous levels. The mud bricks are 53–54 × 27 × 10–12 cm, which are dimensions closer to those recorded in Level I1 than in Level I3. The two outer walls of this building (Walls 1 and 2) have five pilasters on their exterior faces (Figs 3.35–3.36). The pilasters are c. 2.00 or 2.60 m distant from each other, and each of them consists of a single mud brick. Inside the building, one large room (Room 1) and what appears to be two smaller rooms (Rooms 2 and 3) were partly uncovered. Room 1's interior surface is at least 5.50 × 5.10 m; its south-west end was not excavated. The only feature that was noted in this room is a floor (alt. c. 7.43 m). This room yielded no other feature and no doorway. No doorway was found in Room 2 either. This room has a floor at about the same altitude as in Room 1 (alt. c. 7.39–7.44 m), as well as a circular hearth (H1; Fig. 3.37). This hearth is c. 45 cm in diameter and has a crater in its centre that is about 20 cm in diameter and 14 cm deep. I have found no information about the deposits in Room 3, which were excavated over a limited surface.

Table 3.6: Sarazm, Excavation VII, list of features in Level II1.

| Grid location | Feature number | Archive number | Category | Altitude (m) | On plan? |
|---|---|---|---|---|---|
| L12–K12–13 | Wall 1 | M8 | Wall | c. 7.63 | Yes |
| K13–L13 | Wall 2 | M3 | Wall | c. 7.53–7.55 | Yes |
| M13 | Wall 3 | M12 | Wall | c. 7.54 | Yes |
| M13 | Wall 4 | M11 | Wall | Not found | Yes |
| M13 | Wall 5 | Not found | Wall | Not found | Yes |
| M13 | Wall 6 | M13 | Wall | c. 7.53 | Yes |
| K13 | Wall 7 | Not found | Wall | c. 7.65 | Yes |
| J13–K12–13 | Wall 8 | M14 | Wall | c. 7.66 | Yes |
| L14–M14 | Postholes 1–9 | Not found | Posthole | c. 7.42 | Yes |
| K12-13–L12-13–M13 | Room 1 | 84-85/C4-C4b; 84-85/S5-S3; 87/UF7 | Fill and floor | c. 7.43 | Yes |
| M13 | Room 2 | 85/C4b; 85/S3 | Fill and floor | c. 7.39–7.44 | Yes |
| M13 | Room 3 | Not found | Fill and floor | Not found | Yes |
| K12-13–J13 | Alleyway 1 | 85/C4b; 85/S5 | Fill and floor | Not found | Yes |
| K13-15–L13-15–M13-15 | Area 1 | 84-85/C4-C4b; 84-85/S5-S3; 87/UF24; 87/UF25; 89/UF6; 89/UF10; 89/UF13; 89/UF16 | Fill and floor | c. 7.21–7.45 | Yes |
| J12-13–K12 | Area 2 | 87/UF4 | Fill and floor | c. 7.40–7.65 | Yes |
| M13 | Hearth 1 | T19 | Hearth | c. 7.23–7.37 | Yes |
| M14 | Hearth 2 | T17 | Hearth | c. 7.33 | Yes |

Figure 3.35: Sarazm, Excavation VII, Level II1, Rooms 1 and 2. South-westward view. R. Besenval, edited by B. Mutin.

Figure 3.37: Sarazm, Excavation VII, Level II1, Room 2, Hearth 1. North-westward view. R. Besenval, edited by B. Mutin.

Figure 3.36: Sarazm, Excavation VII, Level II1, Rooms 1 and 2. South-westward view. R. Besenval, edited by B. Mutin.

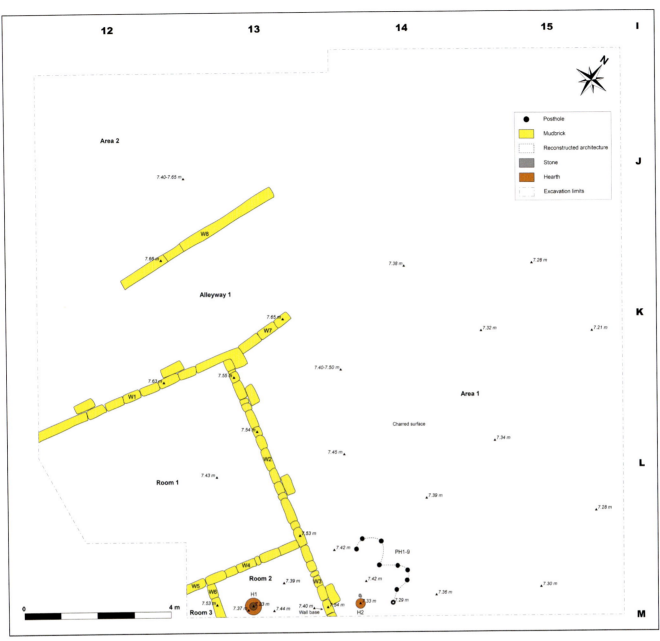

Plate 3.8: Sarazm, Excavation VII, plan of Level II1. B. Mutin, based on R. Besenval archives.

Figure 3.38: Sarazm, Excavation VII, Level II1, Walls 1 and 7 (foreground, wall across the photograph from left to right) and Wall 8 (wall parallel to them in the background). North-westward view. R. Besenval, edited by B. Mutin.

Figure 3.39: Sarazm, Excavation VII, Level II1 Wall 8, Level III2 Wall 6, Level I3 Wall 31, and Level III2 Wall 12 from right to left. Northward view. R. Besenval, edited by B. Mutin.

Figure 3.40: Sarazm, Excavation VII, Level II1, Area 1, charred surface. R. Besenval, edited by B. Mutin.

Figure 3.41: Sarazm, Excavation VII, Level II2, Area 3, postholes and Hearth 4. South-eastward view. R. Besenval, edited by B. Mutin.

Figure 3.42: Sarazm, Excavation VII, Level II2, Area 3, postholes. South-eastward view. R. Besenval, edited by B. Mutin.

A short wall (Wall 7) appears to be a later addition to the north-east end of Wall 1. Walls 1 and 7 are together roughly parallel to an additional wall, Wall 8, about 2.50–2.90 m distant to the north-west (Figs 3.28 and 3.38–3.39). These three walls delineate what appears to be an alleyway (Alleyway 1). I have found no information about this area, and no feature was mapped. The same observation applies to the deposits located north-west of Wall 8 in sq. J12–13 and K12 (Area 2). On the other hand, a surface and a few features were identified in the area located north-east of the building, Area 1 (alt. *c.* 7.36–7.45 m in sq. K13–14, L13–14, and M13–14). A red-fired surface was noted in sq. L14 (Fig. 3.40), as well as a series of nine postholes in sq. L14–M14, close to the building (PH1–9; alt. *c.* 7.42 m). These postholes appear to delineate a partition, and it seems rational to think that this partition functioned with a circular hearth located nearby, close to Wall 3 (H2; 26 cm in diameter).

Fragments of galena were found in it. No feature was recorded further to the north-east in sq. K15, L15, and M15. The altitude of Level II1's base in these squares is consistent with, yet slightly lower than, that recorded closer to the building (alt. *c.* 7.21–7.34 m). A destruction layer including mud-brick fragments and a blue painted plaster fragment was observed within sq. K15, L15, and M15 in the layer on top of the Level II1 base. The same type of layer was noted further to the south-west, where clay lumps with reed impressions were also recorded. These fragments probably come from a ceiling, or a partition wall, made of wattle and daub that collapsed. It is unclear whether similar impressions were found inside the building. A laminated deposit corresponding to an abandon layer was noted on top of this destruction layer. Lastly, I do not know whether Besenval found anything relating to Level II1 in sq. J14–15, north-west of Area 1.

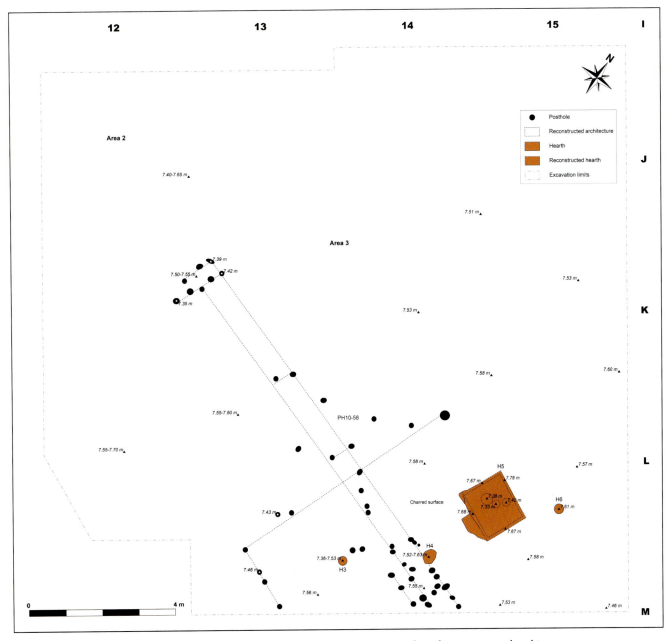

Plate 3.9: Sarazm, Excavation VII, plan of Level II2. B. Mutin, based on R. Besenval archives.

## Level II2

Level II2 consists of forty-eight postholes (PH10–58), c. 40 cm deep to the maximum, and four hearths (H3–6) recorded on a surface between c. 7.50–7.60 m in altitude (Pl. 3.9; Table 3.7). I have labelled Area 3 the area where most features seem to have been recorded, mostly between sq. K12–15, L13–15, and M13–15. Although a part of the postholes seems to have no specific arrangement, nine groups of them appear to be WNW–ESE/NNE–SSW oriented, in a way similar to Level I buildings (Figs 3.41–3.42). I have tentatively materialized these alignments with dashed lines on Plate 3.9, although I acknowledge that some of them may appear less convincing than others. In total, from one end to the other, these postholes were found within an area of about 11.50 × 6.50 m. Close to one alignment, in sq. L14–15, Besenval exposed a charred surface as well as one hearth (H5) a little bit over 1.50 m distant from the alignment. I have found no map of this hearth, so it is reconstructed on Plate 3.9 based on photographs and fieldnotes (Fig. 3.43). It is quadrangular and probably about 1.40 × 1.30 m. It was built with one row of mud bricks; this was observed at a minimum in the part

Table 3.7: Sarazm, Excavation VII, list of features in Level II2.

| Grid location | Feature number | Archive number | Category | Altitude (m) | On plan? |
|---|---|---|---|---|---|
| K12-13-L13-14-M13-14 | Postholes 10-58 | Not found | Posthole | c. 7.50–7.60 | Yes |
| J12-13-K12 | Area 2 | 87/UF4 | Fill and floor | c. 7.40–7.65 | Yes |
| K12-15-L13-15-M13-15 | Area 3 | 84-85/S6-S2bis; 84-85/C3-C4a; 85/UF103; 85/UF109; 87/UF6; 87/UF19; 87/UF23; 89/UF15; 89/UF16 | Fill and floor | c. 7.50–7.70 | Yes |
| M14 | Hearth 3 | T14 | Hearth | c. 7.36–7.53 | Yes |
| M14 | Hearth 4 | T13 | Hearth | c. 7.52–7.63 | Yes |
| L14-15 | Hearth 5 | M7; T33; 87/UF20 | Hearth | c. 7.67–7.78 | Yes |
| L15 | Hearth 6 | Not found | Hearth | c. 7.61 | Yes |

Figure 3.43: Sarazm, Excavation VII, Level II2, Area 3, Hearth 5. South-westward view. R. Besenval, edited by B. Mutin.

exposed in sq. L14 in 1985. In 1987, three small circular pits, between c. 25–35 cm deep, were found in it, in sq. L15. This hearth is clearly connected to the charred area that was identified south-west of it. They together functioned with the postholes discovered west and south-west of them. Furthermore, Hearth 5 seems to be oriented the same way as the main alignments of postholes I have reconstructed in Area 3. Two additional hearths were found around the postholes in sq. M14, including one within a row of postholes (H3 and H4; Fig. 3.41). Hearth 3 and Hearth 4 are two circular hearths measuring respectively 24 cm and 42 cm in diameter. Besenval mapped a fourth hearth, Hearth 6, just east of Hearth 5. It is c. 25 cm in diameter. In sq. K13-L13-14, he observed that the Level II2 surface was covered with a c. 10 cm thick, laminated layer, on top of which he noted a destruction layer with ash, animal bones, and mud-brick fragments. He found a similar laminated layer in sq. L12, upon which he recorded a quartz flake.

Lastly, the deposits recorded in Area 2 (in sq. J12-13 and part of K12), between altitudes c. 7.40–7.65, probably belong to both the end of Level II1 and to Level II2. I have found no information about this area, and I also do not know if anything was recovered north-west of Area 3 in sq. J14-15.

## Level II-North/East

Besenval found additional remains relating to Level II between sq. J16-17 and N16-17 during field seasons 1990–1991 (Pl. 3.10; Table 3.8). These remains mostly consist of a large mud-brick building, which suggests that these remains connect to Level II1 rather than to Level II2 in which no architecture was recorded. However, I have not been able to confirm this with the limited number of archives I have found for these field seasons, and it also remains possible that this building functioned with both levels. Additionally, the plan I have provided here for Level II-North/East's architecture should be taken with great caution, for I have elaborated it on the basis of a series of sketch plans Besenval drew in his 1991 field notebook. It is probably not entirely inaccurate, but it likely does not exactly correspond to the architecture recorded in the field. Indeed, the various sketch plans I have found do not show the exact same orientation and wall thickness. As a consequence, I have had no other choice than to produce a plan that seemed consistent with most of them, but I do not know which sketch plan is the closest to reality. Despite these imprecisions, there is no doubt that the Level II-North/East building has an orientation similar or comparable to those of Level I and II buildings described above, as well as to those of Level III and IV buildings described below, i.e. WNW–ESE/NNE–SSW.

# LEVEL II-NORTH/EAST

This building expands upon most of the area exposed between sq. J16–17 and N16–17 (*c.* 18 × 8 m). It is divided into eleven rooms (Rooms 4 to 14). None of these rooms was entirely excavated. A first series of rooms is located north-east of Walls 9, 10, and 11: Rooms 4, 5, and 6. In the continuity of these rooms, east of Room 6 and Wall 18, Room 10 was barely exposed. The interior space of Room 4 is *c.* 3.50 m wide and at least 4.50 m long. Room 3 is at least 3.90 × 2.20 m, while Room 6 is *c.* 2.80 m wide and at least 2.50 m long. I have found very limited information about these rooms, while only two context numbers, one in sq. J17 and one in sq. K17, were used to record the deposits excavated inside them as well as in Room 7, south-west of Wall 11. The altitude of the fill excavated in sq. J17 is between *c.* 7.37/7.40–7.59 m in Room 4. The single feature that was observed in this square is a hearth with a central crater (H7), also in Room 4. This hearth is *c.* 65 × 65 cm, its peripheral rim is 6 cm wide, and its central crater is *c.* 17 cm in diameter. The location and orientation of this structure on the plan provided here are an approximate reconstruction based on short descriptions in Besenval's 1991 field notebook. No doorway was observed in this building, although I have noticed a *c.* 1.00 m gap in Wall 19, between Rooms 6 and 9, on a couple of sketch plans in the 1991 field notebook. This may indicate that a doorway existed at some point in this location, although I have found no mention of it.

The fill excavated in sq. K17 has similar altitudes, between *c.* 7.37/7.40–7.65 m in Room 7, although one floor was observed at alt. *c.* 7.32 m. Room 7 is smaller than Rooms 4, 5, and 6; it is *c.* 2.00 m wide and at least 2.90 m long. This room seems to have a counterpart of about the same size immediately south-west of Wall 16: Room 8. Both rooms were not fully excavated, and I do not know whether their walls continue into Area 4 further west. Area 4 corresponds to the deposits excavated in sq. J16–K16. The only information I have found about this area is a series of altitudes between *c.* 7.38–7.71/7.74 m and that a bronze awl was recorded at alt. *c.* 7.28 m. I have labelled these deposits Area 4, because I have found no mention of any architecture in this location. The possibility however remains that this space is enclosed by walls, or that Rooms 7 and 8 continue into it.

Further east, Room 9 in sq. K17, L16–17, and M17 was almost entirely exposed. A floor was found at alt. *c.* 6.96 m, 7.01 m, and 7.19 m. The fill in this room was up to alt. *c.* 7.43 m, and the single altitude recorded on the architecture is *c.* 7.65 m at the top of Wall 20.

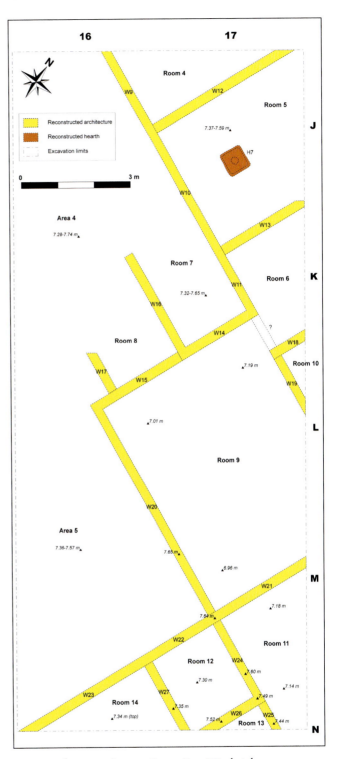

Plate 3.10: Sarazm, Excavation VII, sketch plan of Level II-North/East. B. Mutin, based on R. Besenval archives.

Table 3.8: Sarazm, Excavation VII, list of features in Level II-North/East.

| Grid location | Feature number | Archive number | Category | Altitude (m) | On plan? |
|---|---|---|---|---|---|
| J16 | Wall 9 | Not found | Wall | Not found | Yes |
| J16–17–K17 | Wall 10 | Not found | Wall | Not found | Yes |
| K17 | Wall 11 | Not found | Wall | Not found | Yes |
| J16–17 | Wall 12 | Not found | Wall | Not found | Yes |
| K17 | Wall 13 | Not found | Wall | Not found | Yes |
| K17–L17 | Wall 14 | Not found | Wall | Not found | Yes |
| L16–17 | Wall 15 | Not found | Wall | Not found | Yes |
| K16–17 | Wall 16 | Not found | Wall | Not found | Yes |
| L16 | Wall 17 | Not found | Wall | Not found | Yes |
| K17 | Wall 18 | Not found | Wall | Not found | Yes |
| L17 | Wall 19 | Not found | Wall | Not found | Yes |
| L16–M16–17 | Wall 20 | Not found | Wall | c. 7.65 | Yes |
| M17 | Wall 21 | Not found | Wall | c. 7.64 | Yes |
| M16–17–N16 | Wall 22 | Not found | Wall | c. 7.64 | Yes |
| N16 | Wall 23 | Not found | Wall | Not found | Yes |
| M17–N17 | Wall 24 | Not found | Wall | c. 7.49–7.60 | Yes |
| N17 | Wall 25 | Not found | Wall | c. 7.44 | Yes |
| N17 | Wall 26 | Not found | Wall | c. 7.52 | Yes |
| N16–17 | Wall 27 | Not found | Wall | c. 7.35 | Yes |
| J16–17 | Room 4 | 91/UF78 | Fill and floor | Not found | Yes |
| J17–K17 | Room 5 | 91/UF77; 91/UF78 | Fill and floor | c. 7.37–7.59 | Yes |
| K17 | Room 6 | 91/UF77 | Fill and floor | Not found | Yes |
| K16–17 | Room 7 | 91/UF77 | Fill and floor | c. 7.32–7.65 | Yes |
| K16–17–L16–17 | Room 8 | Not found | Fill and floor | Not found | Yes |
| K17–L16–17–M17 | Room 9 | 91/UF79 | Fill and floor | c. 6.96–7.43 | Yes |
| K17–L17 | Room 10 | Not found | Fill and floor | Not found | Yes |
| M17–N17 | Room 11 | 91/UF80 | Fill and floor | c. 7.14–7.45 | Yes |
| M17–N16–17 | Room 12 | 91/UF81 | Fill and floor | c. 7.30–7.35 | Yes |
| N17 | Room 13 | Not found | Fill and floor | Not found | Yes |
| N16–17 | Room 14 | 91/UF83 | Fill and floor | c. 7.34 (top fill) | Yes |
| J16–K16 | Area 4 | 91/UF84; 91/UF91 | Fill and floor | c. 7.28–7.74 | Yes |
| L16–M14–16–N14–16 | Area 5 | 90/UF46; 90/UF47; 90/UF48; 90/UF49; T51 | Fill and floor | c. 7.36–7.57 | Yes |
| J17 | Hearth 7 | Not found | Hearth | Not found | Yes |

No feature other than this floor was apparently observed in this room. Besenval uncovered parts of four additional rooms east of Room 9 in sq. M17 and N16–17: Rooms 11, 12, 13, and 14. Room 11 is at least 2.70 × 3.35 m. A floor as well as many animal bones were found in this room. Room 12 is a smaller unit of c. 2.20 × 1.95 m whose fill was excavated below alt. c. 7.35 m. Room 13 was barely exposed. Room 14 is larger as it is at least 3.40 × 1.95 m. The deposits excavated in this room are below alt. c. 7.34 m. No feature and no doorway were recorded in these four rooms. Their walls are between c. 7.35–7.64 m in altitude, and a floor, or a surface, was noted on top of them. This floor is reminiscent of the one observed on top of Levels II1–II2 further to the south and south-west.

I have found very limited information about the deposits located outside of the Level II-North/East building, in sq. L16, M16, and N16, as well as about those in sq. M14–15 and N14–15. I have labelled these deposits Area 5. Altitudes in this area are between c. 7.36–7.57 m, and the only feature that Besenval noted is a small expanse of charred soil with ashes that he identified on top of a floor at alt. c. 7.39 m in sq. N15. This floor is perhaps the same as the above-mentioned one recorded on top of Rooms 11 to 14. The altitude recorded on this floor in sq. N15 is consistent with this hypothesis and is consistent with the altitudes of Area 1's base in Level II1. Despite this link, I have no clear understanding as to how Area 5 connects to Levels II1 and II2, and the archives do not mention any postholes in this area, although many were recorded just nearby in Level II2.

# LEVEL II-NORTH/EAST

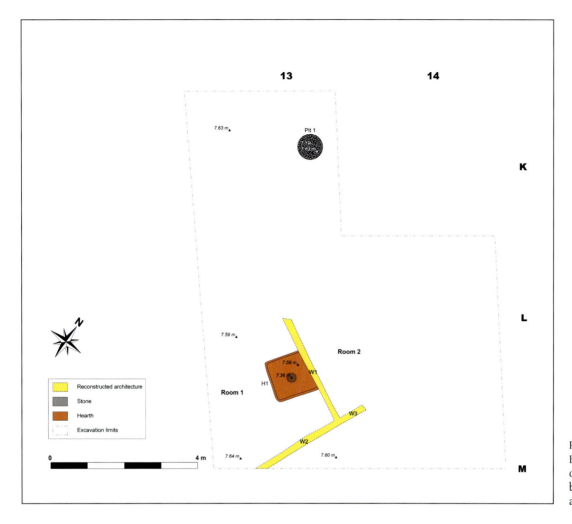

Plate 3.11: Sarazm, Excavation VII, plan of Level III1. B. Mutin, based on R. Besenval archives.

Table 3.9: Sarazm, Excavation VII, list of features in Level III1.

| Grid location | Feature number | Archive number | Category | Altitude (m) | On plan? |
|---|---|---|---|---|---|
| L13–M13 | Wall 1 | M9 | Wall | Not found | Yes |
| M13 | Wall 2 | M10 | Wall | Not found | Yes |
| M13–14 | Wall 3 | Not found | Wall | Not found | Yes |
| L13–M13 | Room 1 | 85/S2 | Fill and floor | *c.* 7.59–7.64 | Yes |
| L13–M13–14 | Room 2 | Not found | Fill and floor | Not found | Yes |
| J11, J14–15, K13–15, L12, L15–M15 | Area 1 | 87/UF6; 87/UF19; 87/UF23; 89/UF25 | Fill and floor | *c.* 7.45–7.70 | No |
| L17–M17–N17 | Area 2 | 91/UF74; 91/UF75 | Fill and floor | *c.* 7.29–7.78 | No |
| L13–M13 | Hearth 1 | T15 | Hearth | *c.* 7.36–7.58 | Yes |
| J11–12–K11 | Hearth 2 | T38 | Hearth | Not found | No |
| K13 | Pit 1 | T16 | Pit | *c.* 7.19–7.63 | Yes |

Figure 3.44: Sarazm, Excavation VII, Level III1, Room 1, Hearth 1. R. Besenval, edited by B. Mutin.

Figure 3.45: Sarazm, Excavation VII, Level III1, Pit 1. R. Besenval, edited by B. Mutin.

Figure 3.46: Sarazm, Excavation VII, Level III1, Pit 1. R. Besenval, edited by B. Mutin.

Figure 3.47: Sarazm, Excavation VII, Level III2, Room 4 (foreground), Room 3 (middle ground, left), Rooms 7, 6, and 5 (right side). South-eastward view. R. Besenval, edited by B. Mutin.

## Level III1

Virtually nothing was left of Level III1 when Besenval studied this level (Pl. 3.11; Table 3.9). It appears to have been heavily levelled before Level III2 was built. Most remaining features in Level III1 are in sq. K13, L13, and M13, while fills assigned to this level are recorded around. Level III1 features consist of three walls (Walls 1, 2, and 3), one hearth (H1) on a floor, and a pit (Pit 1). All features but Pit 1 are located in sq. L13–M13. The walls delineate parts of two WNW–ESE/NNE–SSW oriented rooms: Rooms 1 and 2. Room 1 extends over at least 3.00 × 2.50 m. A floor was found inside (alt. c. 7.59–7.64 m) and was not observed beyond this area. Hearth 1 was found in this room, positioned against Wall 1 (Fig. 3.44). It is square, c. 1.14 × 1.14 m, and has a central crater that is c. 25 cm in diameter and 22 cm deep. As for Room 2, it is materialized by just a small portion of Wall 3.

Pit 1 is located about six metres to the north-west in sq. K13 (Figs 3.45–3.46). Besenval reckoned that it belonged to the same level, and its altitude (c. 7.63 m) is consistent with this reconstruction. This pit is c. 68 cm in diameter and c. 44 cm deep. A large stone was found at its bottom. This stone was probably used for pigment preparation since its upper side is flat and covered with red colour (see **Chapter 6**). The rest of this pit's fill, on top of this stone, consists of pebbles.

Besenval excavated a series of fills around these features, within sq. J11, J14–15, K13–15, L12, and L15–M15, that he recorded as Level III1. Some were noted as

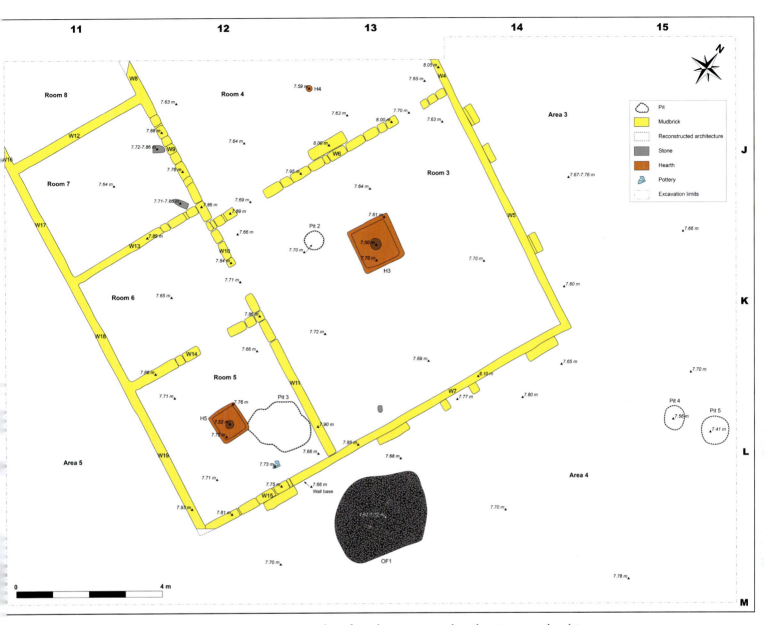

Plate 3.12: Sarazm, Excavation VII, plan of Level III2. B. Mutin, based on R. Besenval archives.

Level III and potentially Level III1 deposits, while some most likely include both Level II2 and Level III1 deposits (Area 1). Altogether, these fills are between c. 7.45–7.70 m in altitude. No feature appears to have been noted in these squares, save for a hearth (H2), observed somewhere within sq. J11–12 and K11. It was not mapped but only described as a square hearth with a central crater. Also, Besenval specifically mentioned three sherds that he found in a Level III1 context in sq. J11. Further to the northeast, in sq. L17–M17–N17, he assigned to Level III1 additional fills between c. 7.29–7.78 m in altitude (Area 2). He recorded no feature in this area, just one small find in sq. M17 (alt. c. 7.76 m).

## Level III2

In contrast to Level III1, Level III2 is defined by one of the largest buildings exposed in Excavation VII (Pl. 3.12; Table 3.10; Fig. 3.47). This building is WNW-ESE/NNE-SSW oriented, like Level I–II constructions. It is c. 12.00 × 11.70 m and preserved up to 25–30 cm in height. It is built with rammed earth and mud bricks aligned in a single row. The bricks are 52–54 × 21–24 × 12 cm. This building has pilasters on the exterior faces of two of its outer walls as well as one pilaster placed against Wall 6 inside (Figs 3.28 and 3.39). Three pilasters are along the north face of the building, against Walls 4 and 5. They all three consist of one mud brick. Two are about 60 cm distant from each other, and the third one is about 2.15 m apart. Three pilasters are along the east face of the building, against Walls 7 and 15. These pilasters are

Table 3.10: Sarazm, Excavation VII, list of features in Level III2.

| Grid location | Feature number | Archive number | Category | Altitude (m) | On plan? |
|---|---|---|---|---|---|
| I13–J13–14 | Wall 4 | Not found | Wall | c. 8.05 | Yes |
| J14–K14 | Wall 5 | Not found | Wall | Not found | Yes |
| J12–13 | Wall 6 | Not found | Wall | c. 7.89–8.00 | Yes |
| K14–L13–14 | Wall 7 | M2 | Wall | c. 7.88–8.10 | Yes |
| I11–J11 | Wall 8 | Not found | Wall | Not found | Yes |
| J11–12 | Wall 9 | Not found | Wall | c. 7.76–7.88 | Yes |
| K12 | Wall 10 | Not found | Wall | c. 7.84 | Yes |
| K12–L12–13 | Wall 11 | M1 | Wall | c. 7.86–790 | Yes |
| J11 | Wall 12 | Not found | Wall | Not found | Yes |
| J12–K11–12 | Wall 13 | Not found | Wall | c. 7.89 | Yes |
| K11–12–L11–12 | Wall 14 | Not found | Wall | c. 7.86 | Yes |
| L12–13 | Wall 15 | M7 | Wall | c. 7.75–7.81 | Yes |
| J11 | Wall 16 | Not found | Wall | Not found | Yes |
| J11–K11 | Wall 17 | Not found | Wall | Not found | Yes |
| K11–L11 | Wall 18 | Not found | Wall | Not found | Yes |
| L11–12 | Wall 19 | Not found | Wall | c. 7.93 | Yes |
| J13–14–K12–14–L13–14 | Room 3 | 84/S7a; 85/C3; 85/S1; 87/UF12; 87/UF21 | Fill and floor | c. 7.63–8.00 | Yes |
| J12–13 | Room 4 | Not found | Fill and floor | c. 7.63–7.65 | Yes |
| K12–L11–13 | Room 5 | 87/UF3 | Fill and floor | c. 7.66–7.73 | Yes |
| K11–12 | Room 6 | Not found | Fill and floor | c. 7.65–7.71 | Yes |
| J11–12–K11 | Room 7 | Not found | Fill and floor | c. 7.64–7.86 | Yes |
| I11–J11 | Room 8 | Not found | Fill and floor | Not found | Yes |
| I14–15–J14–15–K14–15 | Area 3 | 87/UF22; 89/UF11 | Fill and floor | c. 7.60–7.76 | Yes |
| K14–15–L12–15–M12–15 | Area 4 | 84/C2; 84/S7b; 85/C3; 85/S1; 87/UF14; 87/UF16 | Fill and floor | c. 7.65–7.80 | Yes |
| J11–K11–L11–12–M11–12 | Area 5 | Not found | Fill and floor | Not found | Yes |
| J13–K13 | Hearth 3 | T8; 85/UF110 | Hearth | c. 7.50–7.81 | Yes |
| J13 | Hearth 4 | T26 | Hearth | c. 7.59 | Yes |
| L12 | Hearth 5 | Not found | Hearth | c. 7.52–7.76 | Yes |
| K13 | Pit 2 | T12 | Pit | c. 7.70 | Yes |
| L12–13 | Pit 3 | T10?; 85/UF113 | Pit | Not found | Yes |
| L15 | Pit 4 | T32; 87/UF18 | Pit | c. 7.56–7.70 | Yes |
| L15 | Pit 5 | T31; 87/UF17 | Pit | c. 7.41–7.70 | Yes |
| L13–M13 | Other feature 1 | Not found | Layer | c. 7.67–7.72 | Yes |

Figure 3.48: Sarazm, Excavation VII, Level III2, Room 4. North-eastward view. R. Besenval, edited by B. Mutin.

Figure 3.49: Sarazm, Excavation VII, Level III2, Room 3, Hearth 3. R. Besenval, edited by B. Mutin.

Figure 3.50: Sarazm, Excavation VII, Level III2, Room 3, Hearth 3. R. Besenval, edited by B. Mutin.

Figure 3.51: Sarazm, Excavation VII, Level III2, Room 3, Pit 2. R. Besenval, edited by B. Mutin.

longer, measuring *c.* 95 cm. Two are about 3.70 m distant from each other, although the portions of two mud bricks (*c.* 20–23 cm) were placed in between. The third pilaster is about 2.55 m distant. The single pilaster that was observed inside the building is against the west face of Wall 6. It is *c.* 1.10 m long.

Six rooms were exposed inside this building, including four that were fully excavated: Rooms 3, 5, 6, and 7 (Figs 3.47–3.48 and 3.52). Two are larger than the others: Rooms 3 and 4. Besenval hypothesized that Room 3 may have been a courtyard. Its interior space is *c.* 7.15 × 6.80 m and is floored (alt. *c.* 7.63–7.72 m). This floor is covered with a layer containing ashes, animal bones, dung, and mud-brick fragments. One hearth was found on it (H3; Figs 3.49–3.50). This hearth is *c.* 1.25 × 1.20 m. It has a crater in its centre that is *c.* 30 cm in diameter and *c.* 20 cm deep. Near this hearth was found a pit (Pit 2; Fig. 3.51) which is *c.* 51 cm in diameter. A broken jar, fragments of quartz debitage and fragments of a type of copper ore, chrysobella, were found in it. Two doorways in Wall 6 (*c.* 75 and 90 cm wide) provide access to Room 4 to the west. This room has a floor (alt. *c.* 7.63–7.65 m) and a small, circular hearth (H4). This hearth is 17 cm in diameter and 12 cm deep.

The other four rooms of the Level III2 building lay in a row within its southern half (Figs 3.52–3.53). Rooms 5, 6, and 7 yielded a floor with the same altitude as in Rooms 3 and 4 (altogether between *c.* 7.64–7.73 m). I assume that the same is true for Room 8, which was partly excavated, although I have found no information about this room. Room 5 is the largest of them, measuring *c.* 4.00 × 3.80 m (Fig. 3.54). A *c.* 87 × 85 cm hearth (H5) was found in its centre (Fig. 3.55), as well as a pit (Pit 3) located nearby. The hearth has a crater in its centre and a rim that is slightly higher (*c.* 4 cm) than the rest of the structure. The crater is *c.* 20 cm in diameter and *c.* 20 cm deep. I have found no description about Pit 3 save for the fact that it is a *c.* 1.75 × 1.35 m structure, and I do

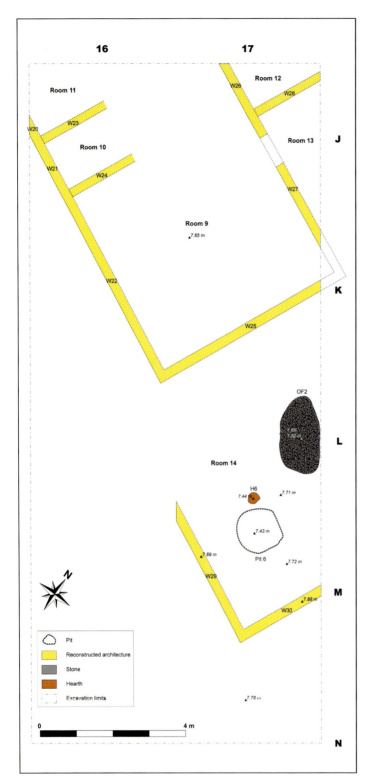

Plate 3.13: Sarazm, Excavation VII, sketch plan of Level III2-North/East. B. Mutin, based on R. Besenval archives.

Figure 3.52: Sarazm, Excavation VII, Level III2, Rooms 5, 6, and 7 (left side). North-westward view. R. Besenval, edited by B. Mutin.

Figure 3.53: Sarazm, Excavation VII, Level III2, Rooms 7, 6, and 5. South-eastward view. R. Besenval, edited by B. Mutin.

Figure 3.54: Sarazm, Excavation VII, Level III2, Room 5. South-eastward view. R. Besenval, edited by B. Mutin.

Table 3.11: Sarazm, Excavation VII, list of features in Level III2-North/East.

| Grid location | Feature number | Archive number | Category | Altitude (m) | On plan? |
|---|---|---|---|---|---|
| J16 | Wall 20 | Not found | Wall | Not found | Yes |
| J16 | Wall 21 | Not found | Wall | Not found | Yes |
| J16–L16 | Wall 22 | Not found | Wall | Not found | Yes |
| J16 | Wall 23 | Not found | Wall | Not found | Yes |
| J16 | Wall 24 | Not found | Wall | Not found | Yes |
| K16-17–L16-17 | Wall 25 | Not found | Wall | Not found | Yes |
| J16 | Wall 26 | Not found | Wall | Not found | Yes |
| J16–K16 | Wall 27 | Not found | Wall | Not found | Yes |
| J16 | Wall 28 | Not found | Wall | Not found | Yes |
| L17–M17 | Wall 29 | Not found | Wall | c. 7.89 | Yes |
| M17 | Wall 30 | Not found | Wall | c. 7.88 | Yes |
| J16-17–K16-17–L16 | Room 9 | 91/UF76; 91/UF90 | Fill and floor | c. 7.65 | Yes |
| J16 | Room 10 | 91/UF90 | Fill and floor | c. 7.74 | Yes |
| J16 | Room 11 | 91/UF90 | Fill and floor | c. 7.74 | Yes |
| J17 | Room 12 | Not found | Fill and floor | Not found | Yes |
| J17–K17 | Room 13 | Not found | Fill and floor | Not found | Yes |
| L17–M17 | Room 14 | 91/UF73 | Fill and floor | c. 7.71–7.72 | Yes |
| L17 | Hearth 6 | T64 | Hearth | c. 7.44–7.71 | Yes |
| L17–M17 | Pit 6 | T65 | Pit | c. 7.43–7.72 | Yes |
| L17 | Other feature 2 | Not found | Layer | c. 7.65–7.82 | Yes |

not know what its stratigraphic relationship with the hearth is. Room 5 connects to Room 6 through a c. 90 cm doorway in Wall 14. Room 6 is also connected to Room 3 through a c. 85 cm doorway in Wall 10. Its interior area is 3.80 × 3.00 m. Besides a floor, no feature was observed in this room. I have not been able to determine whether Room 7 has doorways that give access to Rooms 4, 6, and/or 8, although this seems likely. This room is about the same size as that of Room 6. Two stones were found in it on top of its floor.

I have divided the fills and features excavated outside of the Level III2 building into three areas: Area 3, north of the building; Area 4, east of it; and Area 5, south of it. The altitudes recorded at the base of Level III2 in Areas 3 and 4 are similar to those recorded inside the building, between c. 7.60–7.80 m. (I have found no data and no altitude relating to Area 5.) No feature was found in Area 3, save for a floor (alt. c. 7.67 m). This floor is probably the same as the one observed in Area 4 (alt. c. 7.65–7.80 m), which was described as being of the same type as the one exposed inside Room 3. Melted lead was found on this floor. The only feature that Besenval recorded directly east of the building, between sq. L12–14 and M12–14, is a c. 2.60 × 2.10 m pocket of grey sand and small pebbles in sq. L13–M13 (OF1; alt. c. 7.67–7.72 m). He also mapped two shallow pits (Pits 4 and 5), respectively c. 65 and 75 cm in diameter, a little over three metres apart from the building, in sq. L15. Willcox thinks that these pits served as small 'cache[s] of naked barley' as he identified a relatively large number of barley fragments in these pits (Spengler and Willcox 2013, 217; see Table 2.1). The layer Besenval excavated on top of these features in Area 4, between the floors and the top of Level III2 architecture, comprise collapsed mud-brick fragments as well as painted plaster fragments.

## Level III2-North/East

Besenval assigned to Level III2 the portions of two mud-brick buildings and additional deposits he exposed in 1990–1991 between sq. J16–17 and N16–17, north and east of the above-described remains (Pl. 3.13; Table 3.11). As explained above, I have found no final plan of the remains uncovered in this area, and the plan provided here is based on sketch plans available in Besenval's 1991 field notebook. It should therefore be considered an approximate reconstruction. One fact that is clear,

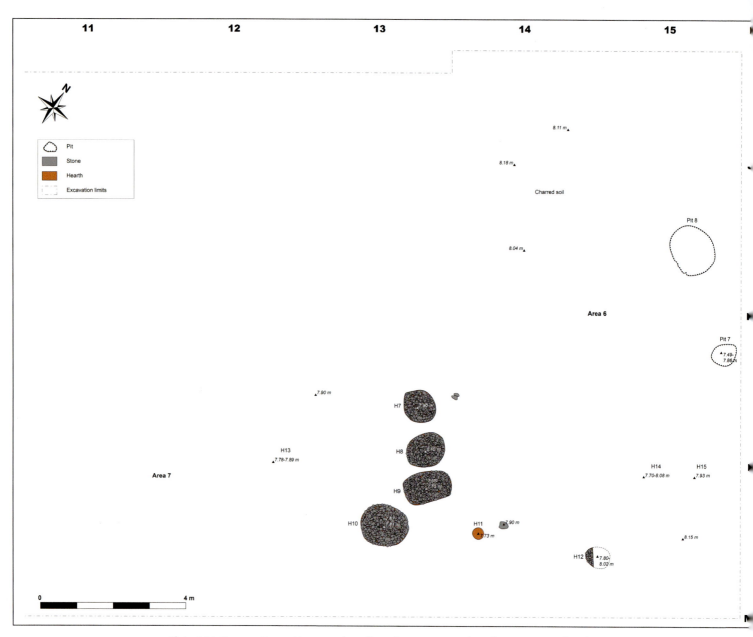

Plate 3.14: Sarazm, Excavation VII, plan of Level III3. B. Mutin, based on R. Besenval archives.

Figure 3.55: Sarazm, Excavation VII, Level III2, Room 5, Hearth 5. South-eastward view. R. Besenval, edited by B. Mutin.

Figure 3.56: Sarazm, Excavation VII, Level III3, Hearths 7 (left) and 8 (right). North-eastward view. R. Besenval, edited by B. Mutin.

LEVEL III3

Table 3.12: Sarazm, Excavation VII, list of features in Level III3.

| Grid location | Feature number | Archive number | Category | Altitude (m) | On plan? |
|---|---|---|---|---|---|
| J14–L14–J15–L15 | Area 6 | T29; 86/C3; 87/UF10; 87/UF11; 87/UF15; 89/UF8 | Fill and floor | c. 7.76–8.18 | Yes |
| L11-12–M11-12 | Area 7 | 89/UF2; 89/UF3; 89/UF4 | Fill and floor | Not found | Yes |
| L13 | Hearth 7 | T2 | Hearth | c. 7.90 | Yes |
| L13 | Hearth 8 | T1 | Hearth | c. 8.10 | Yes |
| L13 | Hearth 9 | T9; 85/UF112 | Hearth | c. 7.66–7.75 | Yes |
| L13–M13 | Hearth 10 | T7; 85/UF104 | Hearth | c. 7.67–7.81 | Yes |
| L14 | Hearth 11 | T3 | Hearth | c. 7.73–7.86 | Yes |
| M14-15 | Hearth 12 | T11 | Hearth | c. 7.80–8.02 | Yes |
| L12 | Hearth 13 | T24 | Hearth | c. 7.78–7.89 | No |
| L15 | Hearth 14 | T30 | Hearth | c. 7.70–8.08 | No |
| L15 | Hearth 15 | Not found | Hearth | c. 7.93 | No |
| K15 | Pit 7 | T35; 87/UF26 | Pit | c. 7.49–7.86 | Yes |
| J15–K15 | Pit 8 | Not found | Pit | Not found | Yes |

however, from these sketch plans, is that these constructions have an orientation comparable or identical to that of the Level III2 building excavated further to the south-west. One of them, located between sq. J16–17 and K16–17, is about six metres distant from that building. It extends over a c. 9.00 × 8.00 m surface and appears to be divided into five rooms, Rooms 9, 10, 11, 12, and 13, although substantial parts of Room 10 and 11 were not excavated and I do not know exactly how these rooms were arranged and connected to the rest of the building. The single room that was fully excavated is Room 9. It is a square room measuring c. 5.20 × 5.20 m. A floor was identified inside (alt. c. 7.65 m), while no other feature seems to have been recorded in this room. I have no information about Rooms 10 and 11, save for the fact that Room 10 is smaller (c. 1.40 wide) than Room 9. Also, a fill was recorded in sq. J16 and K16 with a bottom altitude of c. 7.74 m corresponding to that of a floor, or a surface. This fill most likely corresponds to the fill of both Rooms 10 and 11, as well as part of the fill of Room 9. I have found no data about Rooms 12 and 13. The latter is connected to Room 9 through a c. 85 cm doorway in Wall 27 and is possibly as large as this room.

Further east, the second mud-brick construction is represented by just one room: Room 14. This room was excavated over c. 3.85 × 2.45 m. It was certainly larger than this, but the archives do not clearly mention whether the rest of this room was completely levelled or could not be reached, and whether additional architecture existed that connected to Room 14. A floor was found inside this room (alt. c. 7.71–7.72 m), on which Besenval recorded a hearth (H6), a pit (Pit 6), and a pocket of pebbles (OF2). The hearth consists of a circular structure which may have been the crater of a larger hearth. It is c. 30 cm in diameter and 27 cm deep. The pit is c. 1.20 m in diameter and 29 cm deep. Its sides are vertical, and it contains soil and ashes. The third feature is c. 2.00 × 1.00 m and 17 cm deep.

*Level III3*

Besenval recorded no architecture and no floor in Level III3 (Pl. 3.14; Table 3.12). This level is characterized by a series of hearths and pits dug into Level III2. Four of them are located inside sq. L13 (H7, H8, H9, and H10). These hearths consist of pits filled with black ashes and burnt pebbles. They were found between altitudes c. 7.75–8.10 m. They are c. 1.00 m in diameter (H7; Fig. 3.56); c. 1.05 m in diameter (H8; Figs 3.56–3.57); c. 1.30 × 0.80 m (H9; Fig. 3.58); and c. 1.30 m in diameter (H10; Figs 3.59–3.60). They were described as c. 20–30 cm deep structures, although two of them seem shallower (c. 9 cm in H9; c. 14 cm in H10). A portion of what appears to be the same type of hearth was also exposed in sq. M14 (H12). It is c. 22 cm deep and at least 50 cm in diameter or length. Besenval listed an additional one (H13; Figs 3.61–3.62) in sq. L12, about three metres south-west of the first series of four hearths. I have found no plan relating to this feature; data about this feature I have been able to locate consists of two photographs, records

Figure 3.57: Sarazm, Excavation VII, Level III3, Hearth 8. Southeastward view. R. Besenval, edited by B. Mutin.

Figure 3.58: Sarazm, Excavation VII, Level III3, Hearth 9. R. Besenval, edited by B. Mutin.

Figure 3.59: Sarazm, Excavation VII, Level III3, Hearth 10. R. Besenval, edited by B. Mutin.

Figure 3.60: Sarazm, Excavation VII, Level III3, Hearth 10. R. Besenval, edited by B. Mutin.

Figure 3.61: Sarazm, Excavation VII, Level III3, Hearth 13. R. Besenval, edited by B. Mutin.

Figure 3.62: Sarazm, Excavation VII, Level III3, Hearth 13. R. Besenval, edited by B. Mutin.

LEVEL III3

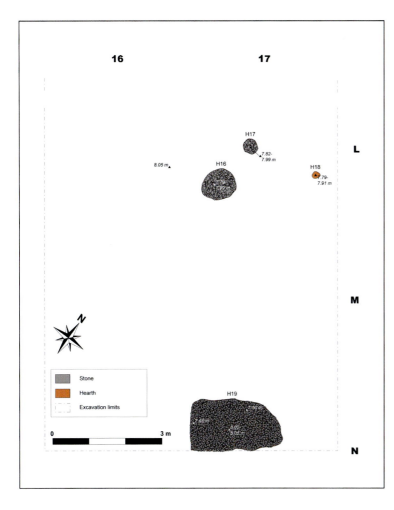

Plate 3.15: Sarazm, Excavation VII, sketch plan of Level III3-North/East. B. Mutin, based on R. Besenval archives.

Table 3.13: Sarazm, Excavation VII, list of features in Level III3-North/East.

| Grid location | Feature number | Archive number | Category | Altitude (m) | On plan? |
|---|---|---|---|---|---|
| L17 | Hearth 16 | T60 | Hearth | c. 7.79–7.99 | Yes |
| L17 | Hearth 17 | T61 | Hearth | c. 7.82–7.99 | Yes |
| L17 | Hearth 18 | T62 | Hearth | c. 7.79–7.91 | Yes |
| N17 | Hearth 19 | T63 | Hearth | c. 7.48–8.05 | Yes |

Figure 3.63: Sarazm, Excavation VII, Level III3, Pit 7, with sherds of pottery and stones inside. R. Besenval, edited by B. Mutin.

of its bottom and top altitudes (c. 7.78 m and 7.89 m), a dimension (c. 75 cm in diameter), and a mention that a fragment of a Turkmen-related black-on-red painted jar was found in it. On this note, Besenval also wrote that he found fragments of ceramics relating to Pakistani Balochistan near these hearths (Besenval and Isakov 1989, 13; see **Chapter 5**). Lastly, he recorded another hearth with pebbles in sq. L15 (H14), although I have found no details about this structure save for its altitude (c. 7.70–8.08 m).

Other types of hearths were found in Level III3. One is in sq. L14 (H11). It is a circular hearth, c. 32 cm in diameter and c. 13 cm deep. It is filled with ash. Another one was recorded in sq. L15, near H14 (H15). I have found no information about this feature, save for the fact that it is a circular hearth, probably of the same type as H14. Pebbles were noted just east of H14 and H15 in sq. M15. Further west, two pits were discovered in sq. J15–K15. One (Pit 7) is c. 65 cm in diameter and 37 cm deep. It contains sherds of pottery and stones at its bottom (Fig. 3.63). The second one (Pit 8) is larger, c. 1.35 × 1.15 m. I have found no description of this pit.

Around these features, Besenval recorded layers of soil that he assigned to Level III3, or that most likely belong to this level. I have labelled Area 6 these fills in sq. J14–L14 and J15–L15. They include one pocket of charred soil in sq. J14–K14, which Besenval thought could correspond to the remains of a hearth. I have labelled Area 7 another series of fills that he recorded in sq. L11–12 and M11–12 and that appear to belong to Level III3. He does not seem to have identified any features in this area. Lastly, I should note that I cannot entirely exclude the possibility that some of the fills recorded in the open areas of Level III2 include deposits that belong to Level III3 (such as the fills recorded as 87/UF12, 87/UF14, 87/UF16, 87/UF22, 89/UF2, 89/UF3, and 89/UF4).

## *Level III3-North/East*

Level III3 remains in the North/East extension of Excavation VII are limited to sq. L17 and N17 (Pl. 3.15; Table 3.13). They consist of four hearths (H16, H17, H18, and H19) at about the same altitude as the other Level III3 hearths identified further south. Three are of the above-described type filled with pebbles (H16, H17, and H19). H16 is round, c. 90 cm in diameter and

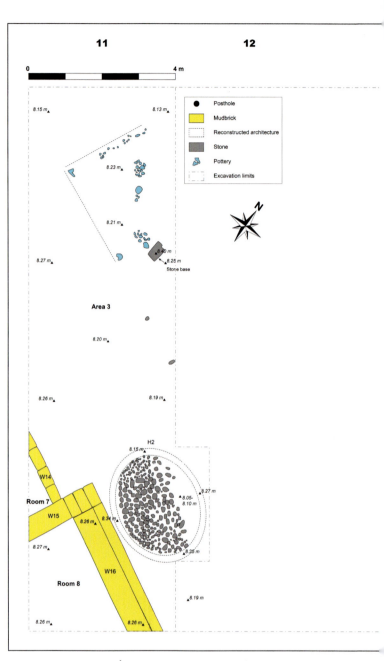

Plate 3.16: Sarazm, Excavation VII, plan of Levels IV1–IV2. B. Mutin, based on R. Besenval archives.

c. 20 cm deep. Its bottom is described as mostly flat. It is full of pebbles and ashes. H17 is round, c. 40 cm in diameter and c. 17 cm deep. H19 is oblong, c. 2.50 × 1.40 m and c. 57 cm deep. It contains pebbles, charred soil, ashes, and sherds of pottery. Besenval interpreted the fourth hearth (H18) as the bottom of a crater that may have belonged to a larger hearth similar to those observed for instance inside the Level III2 building (H3 and H5). It is c. 22 cm in diameter and c. 12 cm deep.

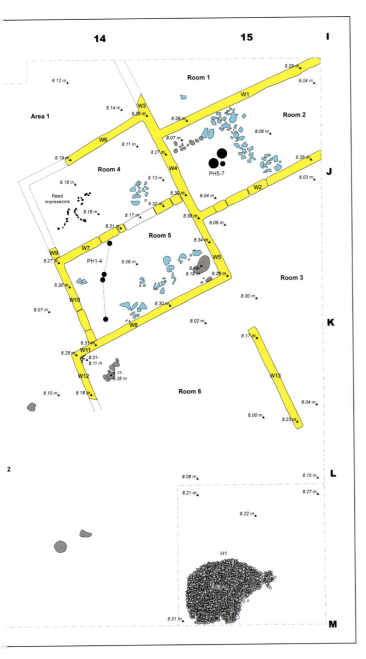

## Levels IV1–IV2

Levels IV1 and IV2 are the latest occupation levels in Excavation VII (Pl. 3.16; Table 3.14). The bases of these levels were found *c.* 40 cm below the surface of the site. Level IV1 was originally defined by one building in the northern corner of Excavation VII, while Level IV2 included all the remains found underneath the surface between sq. J11–M11 as well as between the eastern half of sq. L15 and the western half of sq. M15 (Besenval and Isakov 1989, 14). Level IV2 is thought to be more recent than Level IV1, and some elements are consistent with this distinction. However, as stated by Besenval (Besenval and Isakov 1989, 14), it is not always clear whether the totality of Level IV2 was more recent than Level IV1 or features of it could have functioned partly at the same time as those of Level IV1. He could not determine the stratigraphic relationship between all Levels IV1–IV2 features because these levels had been considerably damaged by modern ploughing engines. Dung beetles had also significantly affected Levels IV1–IV2; this issue is common at Sarazm.

Besenval emphasized that the Level IV1 building in the northern corner of Excavation VII did not strike him as a well-built construction compared to the previous Level III2 building (Fig. 3.64). Also, in contrast to previous levels, which appear to have been emptied before they were abandoned, Level IV1 produced eight complete or near complete ceramic vessels with styles relating to northern Iran and Pakistani Balochistan, in addition to distinctive objects described in **Chapter 6** (Besenval and Isakov 1989, 14–16). The Level IV1 building is WNW-ESE/NNE-SSW oriented, in a similar manner to the constructions in the earlier levels. It is preserved up to 15–20 cm in height. It is built with rammed earth and mud bricks. The size of the mud bricks could not be accurately recorded; they are noted as being 48–52(?) cm long and 22 cm wide. This building extends over *c.* 9.80 × 9.25 cm and continues beyond the limits of Excavation VII. It is divided into six rooms, Rooms 1, 2, 3, 4, 5, and 6. Two of them, Rooms 4 and 5, were fully excavated, and one, Room 2, was almost entirely excavated save for its northern end. Rooms 4 and 5 are about the same size: *c.* 3.70/3.70 × 2.10/2.20 m. They are connected through a *c.* 95 cm doorway in Wall 7. Many burnt clay lumps with reed impressions were found in Room 4 (Figs 3.65–3.66). They most likely correspond to the remains of a roof that burnt and collapsed inside this room (alt. *c.* 8.06–8.13 m). A concentration of sherds that belong to a jar were found on its floor (bottom alt.

Table 3.14: Sarazm, Excavation VII, list of features in Level IV1–IV2.

| Level | Grid location | Feature number | Archive number | Category | Altitude (m) | On plan? |
|---|---|---|---|---|---|---|
| IV1 | I15–J14–15 | Wall 1 | Not found | Wall | c. 8.28–8.29 | Yes |
| IV1 | J15 | Wall 2 | Not found | Wall | c. 8.26–8.30 | Yes |
| IV1 | J14 | Wall 3 | Not found | Wall | c. 8.26 | Yes |
| IV1 | J14–15 | Wall 4 | Not found | Wall | c. 8.27–8.30 | Yes |
| IV1 | J15–K15 | Wall 5 | Not found | Wall | c. 8.38–8.34 | Yes |
| IV1 | J14 | Wall 6 | Not found | Wall | c. 8.19–8.26 | Yes |
| IV1 | J14–15–K14 | Wall 7 | Not found | Wall | c. 8.31–8.32 | Yes |
| IV1 | K14–15 | Wall 8 | Not found | Wall | c. 8.28–8.31 | Yes |
| IV1 | J14–K14 | Wall 9 | Not found | Wall | c. 8.27 | Yes |
| IV1 | K14 | Wall 10 | Not found | Wall | c. 8.30 | Yes |
| IV1 | K14 | Wall 11 | Not found | Wall | c. 8.28–8.31 | Yes |
| IV1 | K14 | Wall 12 | Not found | Wall | c. 8.18–8.28 | Yes |
| IV1 | K15–L15 | Wall 13 | Not found | Wall | c. 8.17–8.23 | Yes |
| IV1 | L11 | Wall 14 | Not found | Wall | Not found | Yes |
| IV1 | L11 | Wall 15 | Not found | Wall | Not found | Yes |
| IV1 | L11–M11–12 | Wall 16 | Not found | Wall | c. 8.26 | Yes |
| IV1 | J14–K14 | Postholes 1–4 | Not found | Posthole | c. 8.06 | Yes |
| IV1 | J15 | Postholes 5–7 | Not found | Posthole | c. 8.04 | Yes |
| IV1 | I14–15–J14–15 | Room 1 | 89/UF5; P404 | Fill and floor | c. 8.00 | Yes |
| IV1 | I15–J14–15 | Room 2 | 89/UF5; P404 | Fill and floor | c. 7.99–8.24 | Yes |
| IV1 | J15–K15–L15 | Room 3 | P406 | Fill and floor | c. 8.00–8.04 | Yes |
| IV1 | J14–K14 | Room 4 | P403 | Fill and floor | c. 8.06–8.17 | Yes |
| IV1 | J14–15–K14–15 | Room 5 | P402 | Fill and floor | c. 8.05–7.16 | Yes |
| IV1 | K14–15–L14–15 | Room 6 | P401 | Fill and floor | c. 8.00–8.26 | Yes |
| IV2 | L11 | Room 7 | Not found | Fill and floor | Not found | Yes |
| IV2 | L11–M11 | Room 8 | 89/UF14 | Fill and floor | Not found | Yes |
| IV1 | I14–J13–14 | Area 1 | P405 | Fill and floor | c. 8.12–8.28 | Yes |
| IV1 | K13–14–L13–14–M13–14 | Area 2 | 84/C1b; 85/C2; 85/UF102; 85/UF106; 85/UF108; 87/UF13 | Fill and floor | c. 8.00–8.40 | Yes |
| IV2 | J11–K11–L11–12–M11–12 | Area 3 | 85/C2 | Fill and floor | c. 8.13–8.40 | Yes |
| IV1–IV2 | J10, K10, L10, M10 | Area 4 | 89/UF1 | Fill and floor | Not found | No |
| IV2 | M15 | Hearth 1 | T23 | Hearth | c. 8.22–8.25 | Yes |
| IV2 | L11–12 | Hearth 2 | T22 | Hearth | c. 8.05–8.34 | Yes |

Figure 3.64: Sarazm, Excavation VII, Level IV1 (background). North-eastward view. R. Besenval, edited by B. Mutin.

Figure 3.65: Sarazm, Excavation VII, Level IV1, Room 4 (foreground). North-eastward view. R. Besenval, edited by B. Mutin.

Figure 3.66: Sarazm, Excavation VII, Level IV1, Room 4, view of the clay lumps with reed impressions. R. Besenval, edited by B. Mutin.

Figure 3.67: Sarazm, Excavation VII, Level IV1, Room 4, ceramic fragments. South-eastward view. R. Besenval, edited by B. Mutin.

*c.* 8.07–8.15 m; Fig. 3.67; see **Chapter 5**). The floor inside Room 5 is also partly burnt. It yielded a few stones and numerous pottery fragments (bottom alt. *c.* 8.05–8.16 m; Figs 3.68–3.70). An additional layer was identified underneath this floor that contained ashes and charcoals. Four postholes were found within the southern half of this room (PH1–4). They may be the remains of a partition wall that existed at this placement. North of Room 4 is a space that seems more open and which I have labelled Area 1, although it may have been a room too. A ceramic as well as a lead seal (alt. *c.* 8.15 m) and a copper dagger (alt. *c.* 8.17 m) were found in this area within a loess deposit (see **Chapter 6**).

North of Area 1 and Rooms 4 and 5 are Rooms 1, 2, and 3. Room 1's interior space is at least *c.* 4.50 × 2.00 m. This room yielded less material than Rooms 2, 4, and 5, although pottery fragments were recovered too. Its floor is probably at about 8.00 m in altitude. More pottery was found on Room 2's floor, east of Room 1 (Figs 3.71–3.72). Room 2 is *c.* 2.20 wide and at least 4.70 m long. In addition to pottery fragments, three postholes (PH5–8) and a few stones were uncovered on its floor (alt. *c.* 7.99–8.03 m), all within its southern half (Figs 3.73–3.74). Two of the postholes have diameters large enough to hypothesize that beams were used in this location to help support the roof of this room. Room 3, east of Room 2, is a much larger space, possibly a courtyard of at least 7.30 × 3.60 m. Its floor was identified between *c.* 8.00–8.03 m in altitude. I have found no mentions of any features inside this room. It connects to the south to Room 6 through a *c.* 1.40 m doorway. An additional doorway may have existed at the eastern end of Wall 13, since this wall seems to be interrupted at this

Figure 3.68: Sarazm, Excavation VII, Level IV1, Room 5, ceramic fragments. Westward view. R. Besenval, edited by B. Mutin.

Figure 3.69: Sarazm, Excavation VII, Level IV1, Room 5, ceramic fragments. R. Besenval, edited by B. Mutin.

Figure 3.70: Sarazm, Excavation VII, Level IV1, Room 5. South-westward view. R. Besenval, edited by B. Mutin.

Figure 3.71: Sarazm, Excavation VII, Level IV1, Room 2. Northeastward view. R. Besenval, edited by B. Mutin.

Figure 3.72: Sarazm, Excavation VII, Level IV1, Room 2, ceramic fragments. R. Besenval, edited by B. Mutin.

location. The southern wall of Room 6, Wall 12, was not fully exposed. As it is, Room 6 must have enclosed an area of at least 6.00 × 4.50 m. A floor was found inside (alt. *c.* 8.00–8.02 m), as well as pebbles and stones clustered in the corner between Walls 11 and 12 (Fig. 3.75).

It is unclear whether Level IV1-related remains outside of this building, in sq. K13, L13–14, and M13–M14, as well as in sq. J12–M12, could not be excavated or were not preserved. This is the case for the eastern end of Wall 12, for instance. In any case, no features are reported in the archives. Besenval described the fills in these squares as a transitional layer between the sterile loess layer found just below the uppermost ploughed layer of the site and Level IV1 archaeological features underneath. This layer is between *c.* 8.00–8.30 m in altitude and contains dung beetles' balls, animal bones, pottery sherds, and pebbles. I have labelled this area, Area 2, although it is important to note that the same

Figure 3.73: Sarazm, Excavation VII, Level IV1, Room 2, postholes and stones (background). South-westward view. R. Besenval, edited by B. Mutin.

Figure 3.74: Sarazm, Excavation VII, Level IV1, Room 2, postholes and stones. Westward view. R. Besenval, edited by B. Mutin.

Figure 3.75: Sarazm, Excavation VII, Level IV1, Room 6, stones. South-westward view. R. Besenval, edited by B. Mutin.

Figure 3.76: Sarazm, Excavation VII, Level IV2, Hearth 1. South-westward view. R. Besenval, edited by B. Mutin.

type of layer was observed beyond these squares, for instance in sq. I12–15 as well as in Area 3. In contrast to Area 2, a floor (alt. c. 8.21–8.27 m) and a hearth (H1; Fig. 3.76) were found in sq. L15–M15, just east of the building. These squares were not excavated down to the same altitude as the floors inside the building, and these features are higher in altitude than these floors and roughly correspond to the top of the walls of this building. They also are higher than the fill observed within Area 2. For this reason, they have been assigned to Level IV2. The hearth is c. 2.50 × 1.70 m and filled with pebbles, an arrangement similar to that of hearths identified in the previous levels.

Further south, Besenval reported virtually no feature relating to Level IV between sq. I12–M12. He recorded more data between sq. J11–M11. As noted above, the archaeological remains found in this area were originally assigned to Level IV2, although they (or a part of them) may have been contemporary with the Level IV1 building further north. In sq. L11–M11, he identified a portion of a WNW–ESE/NNE–SSW oriented mud-brick construction which encloses two rooms: Rooms 7 and 8. I have found no information about this construction, although it is apparent on available plans that it has the same orientation as the above-described building of Level IV1. One of its walls, Wall 16, is unusually wide (c. 90 cm). Two altitudes were recorded on what appears to be a floor inside Room 8 (alt. c. 8.26 m and 8.27 m). Besenval wrote that he exposed more walls that connect to Levels IV1–IV2 in sq. J10, K10, L10, and M10 during field season 1989 (Area 4). Unfortunately, I have found no further information relating to this statement, although a series of photographs in the archives shows that he indeed excavated in this area more WNW–ESE/NNE–SSW oriented architecture as well as deposits that directly connect to Walls 14, 15, and 16. The building

Figure 3.77: Sarazm, Excavation VII, Levels IV1–IV2, architecture exposed in Area 4. South-eastward view. R. Besenval, edited by B. Mutin.

Figure 3.78: Sarazm, Excavation VII, Levels IV1–IV2, architecture exposed in Area 4. North-westward view. R. Besenval, edited by B. Mutin.

Figure 3.79: Sarazm, Excavation VII, Level IV2, Area 3, Hearth 2. Southward view. R. Besenval, edited by B. Mutin.

Figure 3.80: Sarazm, Excavation VII, Level IV2, Area 3, Hearth 2 (right). North-westward view. R. Besenval, edited by B. Mutin.

Figure 3.81: Sarazm, Excavation VII, Level IV2, Area 3, stones and ceramic fragments. Eastward view. R. Besenval, edited by B. Mutin.

Figure 3.82: Sarazm, Excavation VII, plough tracks underneath the first natural fill of the site. North-westward view. R. Besenval, edited by B. Mutin.

Table 3.15: Sarazm, Excavation VII, natural deposits on top of Levels IV1–IV2.

| Grid location | Feature number | Archive number | Category | Altitude (m) | On plan? |
|---|---|---|---|---|---|
| All over Excavation VII | Natural fill 1 | 84/C1a; 85/C1; 86/C1; 87/C1 | Natural fill | c. 8.14–8.60 | No |
| All over Excavation VII | Natural fill 2 | 84/C0; 85/UF101; 85/UF105; 85/UF107 | Natural fill | 8.40–8.60 (top) | No |

Figure 3.83: Sarazm, Excavation VII, plough tracks underneath the first natural fill of the site. R. Besenval, edited by B. Mutin.

he exposed consists of at least three more rooms and a series of seven parallel, narrow compartments, including Room 7 (Figs 3.77–3.78). These compartments have no equivalents within the rest of Excavation VII but are reminiscent of structures recorded within Excavation III (see below).

I have labelled Area 3 the areas Besenval excavated in sq. J11, K11, L11–12, and M11–12, including the deposits outside of Rooms 7 and 8 in sq. L11–12 and M11–12. He found a hearth (H2) in sq. L11–12, just north of Room 8 (Figs 3.79–3.80). This structure is oval-shaped and c. 3.10 × 2.50 m. Its base is covered with pebbles. It is unclear whether this hearth functioned with, or was posterior to, Rooms 7 and 8. Additional elements were recorded in sq. J11 and K11: a surface with a few stones in sq. K11 (alt. c. 8.19–8.27 m) and a concentration of pottery sherds in sq. J11 (Fig. 3.81). Tentatively, the distribution of these stones and sherds suggests that two partition walls that have now disintegrated existed in this location. They would have had the same orientation as that of the Level IV1–IV2 mud-brick buildings. Walls with similar orientation were apparently exposed in the same area (Fig. 3.78 and Fig. 3.80 background), although

I have found no plan nor information about this architecture, and it is not clear whether they belong to Level III2 or Levels IV1–IV2. Lastly, I have found no record relating to Levels IV1–IV2 in sq. J16–N16 and J17–N17 at the opposite end of Excavation VII.

The Level IV1–IV2 remains were then covered with a c. 20 cm thick sterile, homogeneous loess deposit, corresponding to a natural fill (Natural fill 1) on top of the above-mentioned fill with inclusion of animal bones, pottery sherds, pebbles, and dung beetles' balls in Areas 2 and 3 (Table 3.15). This layer was then covered with an additional c. 20–35 cm thick layer corresponding to the surface layer of the site in which agricultural activities took place up until the site was discovered in the 1970s (Natural fill 2). Its top altitude is between c. 8.40–8.60 m. This layer is coarser and less compact than the loess deposit underneath it. Besenval identified a series of parallel ridges corresponding to plough tracks at its bottom (Figs 3.82–3.83).

## 'Antique Tomb'

Besenval excavated a tomb he designated as 'antique tomb' within sq. J15–K15 (Table 3.16). He detected this tomb at alt. c. 7.76 m. A sketch section of it shows that it was c. 2.65 wide and 2.00 m high and was shaped as a catacomb with a step and a side chamber (Pl. 3.17). The step is at the level of a Level I1 floor. I have found no additional information about this tomb save for a few photographs (Figs 3.84–3.86).

## Unallocated Context Numbers

Since a substantial part of the archives from Excavation VII are missing, especially those from field season 1990, I have not been able to locate on a plan nor in one of the levels identified in this excavation certain context numbers that Besenval listed. In most cases, these context numbers are merely listed with no description as to what they correspond to, or, at best, I am lacking the minimum of information necessary to determine their spatial and stratigraphic position. Some, or all, of these context numbers may correspond to features for which I have created new labels. Also, Besenval sometimes labelled a single feature with more than one context number, so I assume that the context numbers I have been able to allocate and create cover most, if not all, the archaeological remains he excavated. For the sake of thoroughness, and in case one day someone finds the missing archives, I am listing these context numbers here: 1987/T25; 1987/T34; 1989/T39; 1990/UF53; 1990/UF54; 1990/T40; 1990/T41; 1990/T42; 1990/T43; 1990/T44; 1990/T45; 1990/T46; 1990/T47; 1990/T48; 1990/T49; 1990/T50; 1990/T53; 1990/T54; 1990/T55; 1990/T56; 1990/T57; 1990/T58; 1990/P308; 1990/P309; 1990/P310; 1990/P311; 1990/P312; 1990/P313; 1990/P314; and 1991/UF82.

## Functions of the Areas Exposed in Excavation VII

The architecture and features identified within Excavation VII virtually all suggest that the areas exposed in this excavation served as dwelling units including indoor and outdoor living spaces. The remains include building complexes with rooms with interior floors and courtyards. Hearths and pits are recorded both inside and outside of the buildings. The animal bones and plant remains (**Chapter 2**) as well as the material assemblage also essentially relate to domestic activities (pottery, lithics, and other types of objects; see **Chapters 5 and 6**). Some records do, however, relate to craft production (see **Chapters 5 and 6**), but there is no massive evidence suggesting that most, or a major part, of the activities conducted within Excavation VII were dedicated to the fabrication of artefacts. At a minimum, it can be said that such activities were integrated within the domestic sphere and that Excavation VII does not correspond to an industrial area. This question remains slightly more open, however, as far as the occupations of Levels I4, II2, and III3 are concerned. Postholes, hearths, pits, and pockets of charred soil characterize these levels. Still, although it is possible that the areas exposed within these levels held specific activities, the objects that were recorded do not suggest the presence of intensive craft activities and do not help define the nature of the occupations in these levels in terms more specific than dwellings with minimal craft production. Additionally, although these levels look like transient occupations within the limits of Excavation VII, the possibility remains that they correspond to outdoor areas, courtyards, associated with houses that are located outside of Excavation VII limits.

There is also no evidence that the areas exposed in Excavation VII served for specific rituals. In other words, the architectural structures from Excavation VII may hardly be interpreted as 'temples' in a way simi-

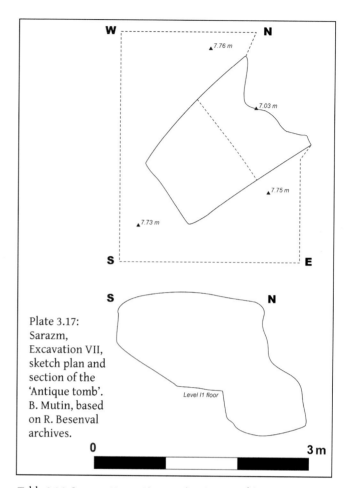

Plate 3.17: Sarazm, Excavation VII, sketch plan and section of the 'Antique tomb'. B. Mutin, based on R. Besenval archives.

Table 3.16: Sarazm, Excavation VII, 'Antique tomb'.

| Grid location | Feature number | Archive number | Category | Altitude (m) | On plan? |
|---|---|---|---|---|---|
| J15–K15 | Burial 1 | 89/UF9 | Burial | 7.76 | No |

lar to the circular mud-brick structure associated with a rectangular, corridor-like construction in Excavation V (Isakov 1994b, 1; F. Razzokov 2016, 193 fig. 19), or to the distinctive building with a peripheral corridor and walls with pilasters in Excavation XI (F. Razzokov 2016, 229 fig. 63). Nothing contradicts the possibility, however, that rituals were incorporated into the domestic spaces exposed in Excavation VII.

The only architecture that stands out in Excavation VII is the building with the parallel compartments found in Levels IV1–IV2 Area 4 (sq. J10, K10, L10, and M10). These compartments are too narrow to have served as living spaces. I have found no information in the archives that could help interpret the function of this compartmented building and may merely hypothesize that this structure either corresponds to the foundation of a building, or a granary as suggested too for

# FEATURES AND ARCHITECTURAL ASPECTS OF EXCAVATION VII

Figure 3.84: Sarazm, Excavation VII, 'Antique tomb'.
R. Besenval, edited by B. Mutin.

Figure 3.86: Sarazm, Excavation VII, 'Antique tomb'.
R. Besenval, edited by B. Mutin.

Figure 3.85: Sarazm, Excavation VII, 'Antique tomb'.
R. Besenval, edited by B. Mutin.

a construction exposed in Excavation III (Besenval and Isakov 1989, 9).

Lastly, it is worth noting that Besenval repeatedly observed that, save for Level IV1, he did not find much material in Excavation VII. To him, most of the levels he excavated appear to have been carefully emptied before they were abandoned (Besenval and Isakov 1989, 14). He also noted at times that these levels do not seem to have been occupied for prolonged periods of time. Furthermore, I have found no mention in the archives that any of the architecture exposed in Excavation VII was repaired or that the plan of one or more of its levels was modified. Thus, considering that rammed earth and mud-brick architecture needs to be redone or repaired after about forty–fifty years at most, the occupations found within this excavation indeed seem rather short-lived.

## Features and Architectural Aspects of Excavation VII and their Parallels at Sarazm and Beyond

As noted in **Chapter 1**, the remains Besenval brought to light in Excavation VII are part of a much larger settlement which has been studied through not less than eighteen excavations. Equivalents for aspects of the architecture and features exposed in Excavation VII have been observed elsewhere at Sarazm. Parallels have also been noted well beyond this site between Central Asia, the Iranian Plateau, and South Asia. This section explores and recapitulates these features and architectural aspects and their parallels.

Besenval recorded a number of observations on the architecture and additional features exposed in the other excavations that were being conducted at Sarazm at the time he was working in Excavation VII. Certainly, Isakov (1991), Razzokov (2008), and F. Razzokov (2016) also have made numerous comparisons between the various excavations opened at this site. Isakov (1991) established the four-period chronology of Sarazm precisely by comparing finds from all excavations at this site. More recently, F. Razzokov (2016) conducted a comparative analysis of the architecture from Sarazm that considers all excavations, save for Excavations XIV, XV, and XVI conducted as part of the renewed Tajik-French field research project at this site. It is not the place to completely reassess these analyses; it nonetheless seems useful to combine here the data I have found in Besenval's archives with that available in F. Razzokov 2016, discuss aspects of construction planning that had not been considered previously, and add my own observations with a focus on Excavation VII, as well as a little bit of calculation. The goal of this endeavour is to help situate Excavation VII within the chronological and spatial realms of Sarazm. The different types of vestiges and aspects of them that deserve comparative analysis may be divided into three main categories: those relating to building material (mud bricks and rammed earth, wall plaster and paint, floors, vegetal impressions on clay lumps, and postholes); those relating to the layout (orientation, space planning, pilasters, doorways, and apertures in walls); and the hearths/pits (circular hearths, quadrangular hearths, and hearths with pebbles).

**Mud Brick and Rammed Earth**

The Excavation VII architectural levels are similar to the rest of the occupations exposed at Sarazm in that the building material is the same: loess. Loess is available everywhere on and near Sarazm (see **Chapter 2**). It was mixed with straw and water and then shaped into mud bricks, or directly rammed, to build walls and other features such as hearths. Loess is not as suitable a building material as clay. This probably explains why many structures at Sarazm, once abandoned, are very much ruined, including in Excavation VII where walls are in some levels preserved only up to 15–20 cm in height. This also explains why it is sometimes quite difficult to identify and excavate the walls of Sarazm and to measure their bricks, an issue Besenval encountered in Excavation VII Level IV. Loess is still used today as building material in the villages settled on top and around the archaeological site. Like today, it was most likely extracted directly on-site five thousand years ago. Loess extraction might explain for instance part of the apparent depression in the relief of the site between Excavations VI, XIII, and XIV (Mutin et al. 2020a, 23 fig. 1). F. Razzokov believes that the remaining pits or depressions resulting from these extractions may then have served as reservoirs for water (F. Razzokov 2016, 101). Although this possibility remains valid, study of an extraction-pit in Excavation XV shows that this structure then served as a trash-pit. Additional evidence at the site suggests that more structures of this type were probably used the same way (Mutin et al. 2020a, 28).

F. Razzokov notes that mud bricks and rammed earth were both used from the beginning of the settlement at Sarazm and that the former is most common in the later periods. Another important piece of information is that the building complexes in Excavations II and VI were built using rammed earth only, whereas the rest of the buildings in the other excavations were mostly built with bricks (F. Razzokov 2016, 101–04 tabs 5–6; Tables 3.17 and 3.20). F. Razzokov also writes that the combination of rammed earth and mud brick has been observed only in Excavation I (F. Razzokov 2016, 102). As is apparent in the parallels noted below, most constructions in Excavation VII compare with those studied in the other excavations within the southern half of the site in their wall thicknesses and the fact that they were built using bricks. However, Besenval observed the combination of mud-brick and rammed earth techniques in Excavation VII, and some photographs suggest that some of the walls of Level I1 construction were built with rammed earth. This hypothesis is consistent with the fact that these walls have thicknesses similar to those of the rammed earth walls recorded in Excavations II and VI, within the northern half of Sarazm.

The mud bricks of Sarazm have various sizes. Tables 3.17 and 3.18 report all the mud-brick sizes recorded in Excavations I, III, IV, V, VII, IX, XI, XII, and XVI. These tables and Graphs 3.1 and 3.2 show that, except for a few records (six out of thirty-three), mud-brick heights are consistently between 10–12 cm across the various excavations and levels where they were recorded. Mud-brick lengths and widths are on the other hand more variable, with values respectively ranging between 26–60 cm (mostly 46–52 cm) and 15–37 cm (mostly 24.5–30 cm). No apparent correlation has been observed between brick size and chronological period (F. Razzokov 2016, 105). The mud bricks from Excavation VII Level I1 (50–52 × 30–32 × 10 cm) are comparable in size to bricks recorded in Excavation IV Level 3 and Excavation XII Level 1–2. The mud bricks from Excavation VII Level I3 (35–36 × 21 × 8 cm) emerge as relatively isolated. Their length has no close parallel, the closest being 26 cm and 40–43 cm. Their height is shorter than that of most mud bricks (all save for one record). Only their width matches that of mud bricks from Excavation XI, although it is shorter than that of most mud bricks (all save for one record). Excavation VII Level II1 mud bricks (53–54 × 27 × 10–12 cm) have sizes similar to those from Excavation V Level 1 and close to those from

Table 3.17: Mud-brick sizes from Sarazm.

| Excavation | Level | Brick size (cm) | References |
|---|---|---|---|
| I | 2 | 49–50 × 24–25 × 11–12.5 | F. Razzokov 2016, 104 tab. 6 |
| I | 2 | 50 × 25 × 11 | Besenval's archives; F. Razzokov 2016, 104 tab. 6 |
| III | 2 | 57–60 × 26–30 × 10–12 | F. Razzokov 2016, 104 tab. 6 |
| III | 3 | 50 × 25 × 11 | F. Razzokov 2016, 104 tab. 6 |
| III | ? | 58–59 × 26–27 × 11–12 | Besenval's archives |
| IV | 'B' (3?) | 50 × 37 × 12 | Besenval's archives |
| IV | 'B' (3?) | 50 × 32–33 × 12 | Besenval's archives |
| IV | 'C' (4?) | 49–50 × 24–25 × 11–12 | Besenval's archives |
| IV | 2 | 47 × 25–27 × 10 | F. Razzokov 2016, 104 tab. 6 |
| IV | 2 | 48–50 × 24–25 × 10–11 | F. Razzokov 2016, 104 tab. 6 |
| IV | 3 | 47–50 × 24–27 × 12–13; 52 × 32 × 12 | F. Razzokov 2016, 104 tab. 6 |
| IV | 4 | 50–51 × 24–25 × 10–15 | F. Razzokov 2016, 104 tab. 6 |
| V | 1 | 54 × 27–28 × 10–11 | F. Razzokov 2016, 104 tab. 6 |
| V | 2 | 50–52 × 25 × 10–11 | F. Razzokov 2016, 104 tab. 6 |
| V | 3 | 50–52 × 25 × 10–11 | F. Razzokov 2016, 104 tab. 6 |
| V | 3 | 50 × 29 × 14 | F. Razzokov 2016, 104 tab. 6 |
| VII | I1 | 50–52 × 30–32 × 10 | Besenval's archives |
| VII | I3 | 35–36 × 21 × 8 | Besenval's archives |
| VII | II1 | 53–54 × 27 × 10–12 | Besenval's archives |
| VII | III2 | 52–54 × 21–24 × 12 | Besenval's archives |
| VII | IV | 48–52(?) × 22 × ? | Besenval's archives |
| VII | IV | 59–60 × 29–31 × ? | Pl. 3.16 |
| IX | 1 | 45 × 30 × 12 | F. Razzokov 2016, 104 tab. 6 |
| IX | 1 | 45 × 30 × 10–12 | F. Razzokov 2016, 104 tab. 6 |
| IX | 2 | 26 × 15 × 10; 45 × 30 × 12 | F. Razzokov 2016, 104 tab. 6 |
| IX | 3 | 52 × 24 × 11 | F. Razzokov 2016, 104 tab. 6 |
| XI | 2 | 40–43 × 20–22 × 10–13 | F. Razzokov 2016, 104 tab. 6 |
| XI | 3 | 48 × 25 × 9–10 | F. Razzokov 2016, 104 tab. 6 |
| XII | 1–2 | 43 × 27 × 12; 50–51 × 33–34 × 10–11 | F. Razzokov 2016, 104 tab. 6 |
| XII | 2 | 52–54 × 33–34 × 7–7.5 | F. Razzokov 2016, 104 tab. 6 |
| XII | 3 | 43–45 × 27–28 × 10 | F. Razzokov 2016, 104 tab. 6 |
| XVI | 5 | 58 × 24–25 × 11 | Mutin's archives |

Excavation V Levels 2 and 3. Excavation VII Level III2 mud bricks (52–54 × 21–24 × 12 cm) are consistent with those from Excavation IX Level 3. As for Excavation VII Level IV mud bricks, I am missing information and may only say that the length of those in the northern building (48–52(?) × 22 × ? cm) is comparable to those of almost half of the mud-brick lengths recorded at Sarazm (fifteen records), while their width is at the lower end of available measurements. The bricks in the southern building (59–60 × 29–31 × ?, measured based on Level IV plan) are close in length and width to those in Excavation III Level 2 and in length to bricks recorded in Excavation XVI.

Besenval was not able to record much information about the way the bricks were arranged in Excavation VII architectural levels, because most constructions were not sufficiently preserved. Only Level I1 yielded walls as high as 60–70 cm. A photograph of Wall 6's north facade in this level shows that the bricks were bound by a mortar that was probably not more than four centimetres thick (Fig. 3.8). A general observation can be made about Excavation VII that most walls in this excavation consist of single rows of bricks aligned along their lengths, their thickness corresponding to the bricks' widths plus the plaster's thickness. For most of these walls the recorded thicknesses range from *c.* 22 to 28 cm (Table 3.19). Then are walls with thicknesses between *c.* 30–35 cm, as well as walls with thicknesses between *c.* 36–45 cm, which include both walls built with mud brick and walls built with rammed earth. It is however not always clear on the plans available in the archives whether some of the rammed earth walls could in fact be mud-brick walls for which the bricks were not delineated. Two much larger walls contrast with the rest of the architecture exposed inside Excavation VII: Walls 15 and 16 in Levels IV1–IV2 (Pl. 3.16). They are respectively *c.* 59–60 cm and *c.* 88.5 cm thick. Wall 15 is made of bricks that are aligned side by side instead of being aligned along their lengths only. Wall 16 consists of three parallel rows of bricks aligned along their lengths (Figs 3.77–3.78). Save for these two Level IV1–IV2 walls and the rest of the building they are connected to in the south-western part of Excavation VII, there is no apparent chronological correlation for the wall thicknesses recorded in this excavation. Indeed, Level I1 yielded various wall thicknesses, and sim-

Table 3.18: Mud-brick sizes from Sarazm rearranged for calculation.

| Excavation | Level | L (cm)* | W (cm)* | H (cm)* |
|---|---|---|---|---|
| I | 2 | 49.5 | 24.5 | 11.75 |
| I | 2 | 50 | 25 | 11 |
| III | 2 | 58.5 | 28 | 11 |
| III | 3 | 50 | 25 | 11 |
| III | ? | 58.5 | 26.5 | 11.5 |
| IV | 2 | 47 | 26 | 10 |
| IV | 2 | 49 | 24.5 | 10.5 |
| IV | 3 | 48.5 | 25.5 | 12.5 |
| IV | 3 | 52 | 32 | 12 |
| IV | 4 | 50.5 | 24.5 | 12.5 |
| IV | 'B' (3?) | 50 | 32.5 | 12 |
| IV | 'B' (3?) | 50 | 37 | 12 |
| IV | 'C' (4?) | 49.5 | 24.5 | 11.5 |
| V | 1 | 54 | 27.5 | 10.5 |
| V | 2 | 51 | 25 | 10.5 |
| V | 3 | 50 | 29 | 14 |
| V | 3 | 51 | 25 | 10.5 |
| VII | I1 | 51 | 31 | 10 |
| VII | I3 | 35.5 | 21 | 8 |
| VII | II1 | 53.5 | 27 | 11 |
| VII | III2 | 53 | 22.5 | 12 |
| IX | 1 | 45 | 30 | 11 |
| IX | 1 | 45 | 30 | 12 |
| IX | 2 | 26 | 15 | 10 |
| IX | 2 | 45 | 30 | 12 |
| IX | 3 | 52 | 24 | 11 |
| XI | 2 | 41.5 | 21 | 11.5 |
| XI | 3 | 48 | 25 | 9.5 |
| XII | 2 | 53 | 33.5 | 7.25 |
| XII | 3 | 44 | 27.5 | 10 |
| XII | 1–2 | 43 | 27 | 12 |
| XII | 1–2 | 50.5 | 33.5 | 10.5 |
| XVI | 5 | 58 | 24.5 | 11 |

\* Mean when a range was provided

## 3. ARCHAEOLOGICAL CONTEXTS

Table 3.19: Wall thicknesses measured in Excavation VII at Sarazm.

| Exca-vation | Level | Wall | Wall thickness (cm) | References |
|---|---|---|---|---|
| VII | I1 | W16, W19 | 36–38 | Pl. 3.3 |
| VII | I1 | W19, W10 | 45 | Pl. 3.3 |
| VII | I1 | W3, W6 | 24.5–28 | Pl. 3.3 |
| VII | I1 | W7, W8, W15, W18 | 30–34.5 | Pl. 3.3 |
| VII | I3 | W22, W24, W28 | 22–22.5 | Pl. 3.5 |
| VII | I3 | W29, W31 | 26 | Pl. 3.5 |
| VII | II1 | W1, W2, W3, W4, W8 | 22.5–27.5 | Pl. 3.8 |
| VII | III2 | W14 | 28 | Pl. 3.12 |
| VII | III2 | W5, W6, W7, W11, W12, W19 | 23–25 | Pl. 3.12 |
| VII | IV | W14 | 29–30 | Pl. 3.16 |
| VII | IV | W15 | 59–60 | Pl. 3.16 |
| VII | IV | W16 | 88.5 | Pl. 3.16 |
| VII | IV | W2, W8, W13 | 22 | Pl. 3.16 |

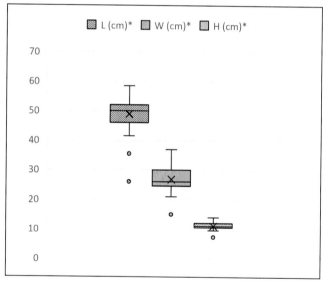

Graph 3.2: Box and whisker plot showing the minimum, first quartile, median, third quartile, and maximum of the lengths, widths, and heights measured on the mud bricks from Sarazm. Graph based on the values and means in Table 3.18. B. Mutin.

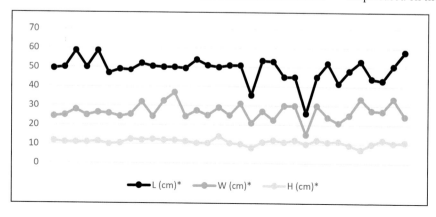

Graph 3.1: Lengths, widths, and heights measured on the mud bricks from Sarazm. Graph based on the values and means in Table 3.18. B. Mutin.

Table 3.20: Thicknesses recorded on walls made with rammed earth at Sarazm.

| Excavation | Level | Building complex | Wall thickness (cm) | References |
|---|---|---|---|---|
| II | 1 | Building complex I | 45–50 | F. Razzokov 2016, 103 tab. 5 |
| II | 1 | Building complex II | 45–50 | F. Razzokov 2016, 103 tab. 5 |
| II | 2 | Building complex I | 45–50 | F. Razzokov 2016, 103 tab. 5 |
| II | 2 | Building complex II | 40–50 | F. Razzokov 2016, 103 tab. 5 |
| II | 2 | Building complex III | 40–45 | F. Razzokov 2016, 103 tab. 5 |
| II | 2 | Building complex IV | 40–45 | F. Razzokov 2016, 103 tab. 5 |
| II | 2 | Building complex IX | 35–40 | F. Razzokov 2016, 103 tab. 5 |
| II | 2 | Building complex V | 40–50 | F. Razzokov 2016, 103 tab. 5 |
| II | 2 | Building complex VIв | 35–50 | F. Razzokov 2016, 103 tab. 5 |
| II | 2 | Building complex VIн | 35–50 | F. Razzokov 2016, 103 tab. 5 |
| II | 3 | Building complex I | 45–55 | F. Razzokov 2016, 103 tab. 5 |
| II | 3 | Building complex II | 40–50 | F. Razzokov 2016, 103 tab. 5 |
| II | 3 | Building complex III | 50 | F. Razzokov 2016, 103 tab. 5 |
| II | 3 | Building complex IV | 40–45 | F. Razzokov 2016, 103 tab. 5 |
| IV | 2 | Building complex III | 50 | F. Razzokov 2016, 103 tab. 5 |
| VI | 2 | Building complex I | 22–25 | F. Razzokov 2016, 103 tab. 5 |
| VI | 2 | Building complex III | 45–55 | F. Razzokov 2016, 103 tab. 5 |
| VI | 3 | Building complex II | 40–50 | F. Razzokov 2016, 103 tab. 5 |

ilar thicknesses are recorded in Levels I1, I3, II1, III2, and IV1–IV2.

Both in thickness and arrangement, most mud-brick walls from Excavation VII have parallels in other areas of Sarazm. Mud-brick walls at Sarazm were generally built with single rows of bricks aligned along their lengths (see F. Razzokov 2016, 108). Also, as noted above, except for Level I3, the brick sizes recorded in Excavation VII are generally similar to those recorded across the site and have specific equivalents in certain excavations. The walls with greater thicknesses (c. 30–45 cm) in Excavation VII apparently include mud-brick walls and mostly rammed earth walls. These thicknesses are comparable to those of the seemingly less common mud-brick walls with the widest bricks recorded at Sarazm (see above) as well as those of the rammed earth walls which are noted as being usually between c. 35–50 cm thick in F. Razzokov's analysis (Table 3.20). As for the thickest walls exposed in Excavation VII Levels IV1–IV2, parallels for Wall 15 (c. 59–60 cm thick), with bricks laid side by side, are in Excavations VIII, IX, XI, and XII (F. Razzokov 2016, 211 fig. 42, 212 fig. 43, 221 fig. 53, 226 fig. 60, 234 fig. 69, 239 fig. 75). Parallels for three-row mud-brick Wall 16 (c. 88.5 cm thick) are in Excavation V (F. Razzokov 2016, 193 fig. 19, 196 fig. 23, 198 fig. 25) and apparently in Excavation XII too (F. Razzokov 2016, 108). The three-row mud-brick wall in Excavation V is about 90 cm thick. Two-row mud-brick walls were found in Excavations V, XI, and XII (F. Razzokov 2016, 193 fig. 19, 231 fig. 66, 239 fig. 75). These thicker walls are usually found within more complex and larger buildings (F. Razzokov 2016, 108) and include types of arrangements different from those observed in Excavation VII. This is at least true for the massive building exposed in Excavation III and the circular building in Excavation IV (F. Razzokov 2016, 109, 183 fig. 8, 193 fig. 19).

**Wall Plaster and Paint**

Besenval observed plaster on walls in all levels of Excavation VII, either directly on walls, or as plaster fragments recovered from destruction and abandon layers. Plaster is usually a less than five centimetres thick layer of loess/clay mixed with straw and water and applied on the surfaces of the walls. Besenval recorded black, blue, and red coloured plaster in Excavation VII (see **Chapter 6**). Plaster has been observed in other excavations at Sarazm, including in Excavation IX where fragments with black/brown, white, red, and yellow colours were found. The motifs on these fragments include crosses and crenelated motifs in a fashion similar to the designs painted on Namazga III pottery. More broadly speaking, walls with red colour (ochre) are not uncommon at Sarazm. Traces of red paint have been observed on walls or floors in Excavation II Levels 2 and 3, Excavation IV Levels 2 and 3, Excavation V Level 2, and Excavation IX Level 3 (F. Razzokov 2016, 114–15, 225 fig. 59).

## Floors

Most floors in Excavation VII also appear to have been plastered. Although Besenval did not specifically state this, he did mention floors in each architectural level. He also pointed out that Level I3 building floors were particularly well-prepared floors consisting of rammed earth and having their edges raised up against the bases of the walls. This description tends to indicate that the floors in Excavation VII, at least in this level, were plastered at the same time as the walls. Such a practice seems to be common at Sarazm (see F. Razzokov 2016, 113). The surface made of small pebbles found in Level I3 Alleyway 2 also has equivalents elsewhere at Sarazm. Similar surfaces have been observed in an outdoor context in Excavation IX as well as inside rooms in Excavations IX and XI. In the latter examples they served as foundations for plaster to be applied (F. Razzokov 2016, 106, 113, 221 fig. 53).

## Vegetal Impressions on Clay Lumps

Reeds and wood beams impressions on clay fragments were recorded in Excavation VII (Figs 3.65–3.66 and 3.87). These fragments were most likely originally part of roofs that collapsed. Such impressions are observed at least between the Mediterranean Sea and Central Asia since the Neolithic period. The roofs they were part of are flat and made with beams upon which were laid parallel reeds creating a lattice which was then covered with a layer of clay (or loess) mixed with straw. Similar impressions were recorded in Excavation XII (F. Razzokov 2016, 110) and Excavation II (Isakov 1991, fig. 28).

## Postholes

Besenval identified postholes in Excavation VII Levels I1, I2, II1, II2, and IV1–IV2. Although I have found no systematic, detailed records about the diameter and depth of these postholes, their arrangements, placement, and available measurements taken from available plans[3] make it likely that the beams corresponding to these postholes did not all serve the same function. Their diameters range from *c.* 7.5 to 28 cm and more than half of them are *c.* 12.5 or *c.* 13.5 cm (Table 3.21).

Some, large enough and found inside rooms as a single posthole or groups of two to three postholes, appear to have served as roof supports. This must have been the case with Level I2 Area 1 PH23–25 (Pl. 3.4), Level I3 Room 6 PH26 (Pl. 3.5), and Level IV1 Room 2 PH5–7 (Pl. 3.16). Other ones with smaller diameters seem rather to have served to hold small partition walls made of perishable material, such as Level II1 Area 1 PH1–9 (Pl. 3.8). Larger series of postholes, aligned and close to each other, may have supported larger and heavier structures made of perishable material, such as tents and canopies. This may be especially true for Level II2 in which numerous postholes were identified, including many that seem to align in a coherent fashion and to delineate different compartmented areas (PH10–58 (Pl. 3.9); see also Level I1 Room 3 PH1–11 (Pl. 3.3) and Level I2 Area 2 PH12–25 (Pl. 3.4)). Besenval mentioned that the postholes in this level were a maximum of 40 cm deep.

These postholes are not unique at Sarazm. Postholes are reported from other excavations where they have measurements consistent with those from Excavation VII, i.e. between *c.* 15–30 cm in diameter and 35 cm deep (F. Razzokov 2016, 105, 110–11). They were recorded in Excavations I (F. Razzokov 2016, 178 fig. 2), IV (F. Razzokov 2016, 186 fig. 11, 190 fig. 16), VI (F. Razzokov 2016, 202 fig. 31), IX (F. Razzokov 2016, 212 fig. 43, 214 fig. 45), XI (F. Razzokov 2016, 229 fig. 63), XII (F. Razzokov 2016, 241 fig. 79), and XVI (Mutin et al. 2020a). Stones have often been observed inside them; they were most likely used to wedge the posts.

## Orientation

All Excavation VII buildings as well as most posthole alignments have orientations close to WNW–ESE/NNE–SSW, with minor differences in orientation between levels. Similar orientations are observed in the other building complexes excavated at Sarazm, although more variation is noted.[4] In Excavation I, one building is between N–S/W–E and WNW–ESE/NNE–SSW oriented, while the other architectural structures in this excavation are WNW–ESE/NNE–SSW oriented. Similarly, Excavation II architecture mostly includes buildings that have orientations between N–S/W–E and WNW–ESE/NNE–SSW. Yet, a few are WNW–ESE/

---

[3] It is important to note that part of these postholes was seemingly mapped in a standardized fashion. Consequently, although the measurements taken on the postholes on available plans are not wrong, they should be taken with caution and considered approximations with margins of error of a few centimetres.

[4] Caution should be exercised at times as to the orientation of the illustrated architecture from Sarazm. Although most plans are certainly accurate, minor discrepancies are observed between illustrations of some of them (e.g. compare F. Razzokov 2016, 238 fig. 74, 239 fig. 75, 242 fig. 80, 243 fig. 82).

Table 3.21: Posthole diameters recorded in Sarazm Excavation VII.

| Excavation | Level | Posthole # | Diameter (cm) |
|---|---|---|---|
| VII | I1 | PH1 | 12.5 |
| VII | I1 | PH2 | 12.5 |
| VII | I1 | PH3 | 12.5 |
| VII | I1 | PH4 | 15.5 |
| VII | I1 | PH5 | 9 |
| VII | I1 | PH6 | 12.5 |
| VII | I1 | PH7 | 12.5 |
| VII | I1 | PH8 | 12.5 |
| VII | I1 | PH9 | 12.5 |
| VII | I1 | PH10 | 12.5 |
| VII | I1 | PH11 | 12.5 |
| VII | I2 | PH12 | 12.5 |
| VII | I2 | PH13 | 12.5 |
| VII | I2 | PH14 | 15 |
| VII | I2 | PH15 | 12.5 |
| VII | I2 | PH16 | 12.5 |
| VII | I2 | PH17 | 12.5 |
| VII | I2 | PH18 | 12.5 |
| VII | I2 | PH19 | 12.5 |
| VII | I2 | PH20 | 12.5 |
| VII | I2 | PH21 | 12.5 |
| VII | I2 | PH22 | 12.5 |
| VII | I2 | PH23 | 18.5 |
| VII | I2 | PH24 | 15 |
| VII | I2 | PH25 | 18.5 |
| VII | I3 | PH26 | 20.5 |
| VII | I3 | PH27 | 12.5 |
| VII | II1 | PH1 | 12.5 |
| VII | II1 | PH2 | 12.5 |
| VII | II1 | PH3 | 12.5 |
| VII | II1 | PH4 | 12.5 |
| VII | II1 | PH5 | 12.5 |
| VII | II1 | PH6 | 12.5 |
| VII | II1 | PH7 | 12.5 |
| VII | II1 | PH8 | 12.5 |
| VII | II1 | PH9 | 12.5 |
| VII | II2 | PH10 | 13.5 |
| VII | II2 | PH11 | 13.5 |
| VII | II2 | PH12 | 13.5 |
| VII | II2 | PH13 | 13.5 |
| VII | II2 | PH14 | 13.5 |
| VII | II2 | PH15 | 13.5 |
| VII | II2 | PH16 | 15.5 |
| VII | II2 | PH17 | 18 |
| VII | II2 | PH18 | 18.5 |
| VII | II2 | PH19 | 16 |

| Excavation | Level | Posthole # | Diameter (cm) |
|---|---|---|---|
| VII | II2 | PH20 | 16 |
| VII | II2 | PH21 | 20.5 |
| VII | II2 | PH22 | 21 |
| VII | II2 | PH23 | 16.5 |
| VII | II2 | PH24 | 18 |
| VII | II2 | PH25 | 14 |
| VII | II2 | PH26 | 15.5 |
| VII | II2 | PH27 | 14 |
| VII | II2 | PH28 | 13.5 |
| VII | II2 | PH29 | 13.5 |
| VII | II2 | PH30 | 13.5 |
| VII | II2 | PH31 | 14.5 |
| VII | II2 | PH32 | 16 |
| VII | II2 | PH33 | 14.5 |
| VII | II2 | PH34 | 17.5 |
| VII | II2 | PH35 | 24.5 |
| VII | II2 | PH36 | 16.5 |
| VII | II2 | PH37 | 18 |
| VII | II2 | PH38 | 7.5 |
| VII | II2 | PH39 | 13.5 |
| VII | II2 | PH40 | 16.5 |
| VII | II2 | PH41 | 18.5 |
| VII | II2 | PH42 | 28 |
| VII | II2 | PH43 | 17.5 |
| VII | II2 | PH44 | 14 |
| VII | II2 | PH45 | 17.5 |
| VII | II2 | PH46 | 13.5 |
| VII | II2 | PH47 | 13.5 |
| VII | II2 | PH48 | 17.5 |
| VII | II2 | PH49 | 13.5 |
| VII | II2 | PH50 | 17.5 |
| VII | II2 | PH51 | 18.5 |
| VII | II2 | PH52 | 18.5 |
| VII | II2 | PH53 | 14 |
| VII | II2 | PH54 | 18.5 |
| VII | II2 | PH55 | 13.5 |
| VII | II2 | PH56 | 14 |
| VII | II2 | PH57 | 20 |
| VII | II2 | PH58 | 25.5 |
| VII | IV1 | PH1 | 13.5 |
| VII | IV1 | PH2 | 13.5 |
| VII | IV1 | PH3 | 13.5 |
| VII | IV1 | PH4 | 13.5 |
| VII | IV1 | PH5 | 13.5 |
| VII | IV1 | PH6 | 27.5 |
| VII | IV1 | PH7 | 27.5 |
| **Average** | | | **15.2** |

3. ARCHAEOLOGICAL CONTEXTS

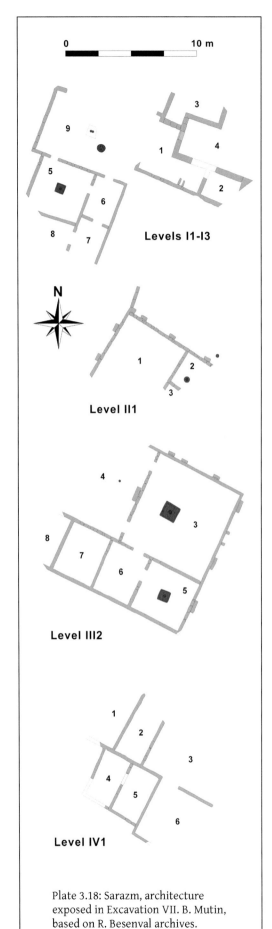

Plate 3.18: Sarazm, architecture exposed in Excavation VII. B. Mutin, based on R. Besenval archives.

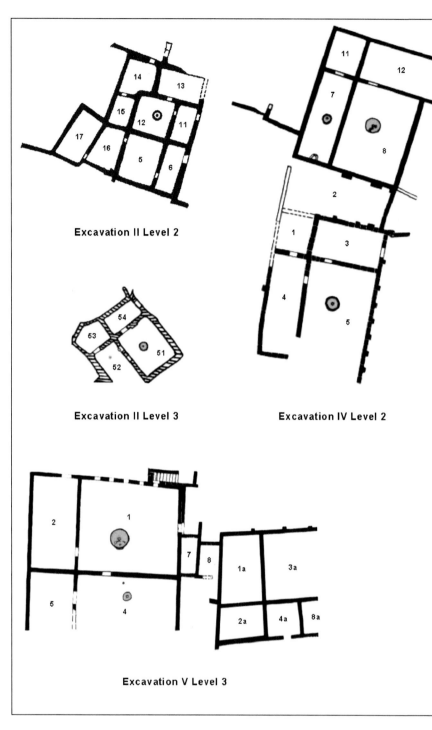

Figure 3.87: Sarazm, Excavation VII, Level IV1, Room 3, clay lump with wood beam impressions. R. Besenval, edited by B. Mutin.

Plate 3.19: Sarazm, architecture exposed in Excavations II, IV, V, IX, and XII. Adapted after F. Razzokov 2016.

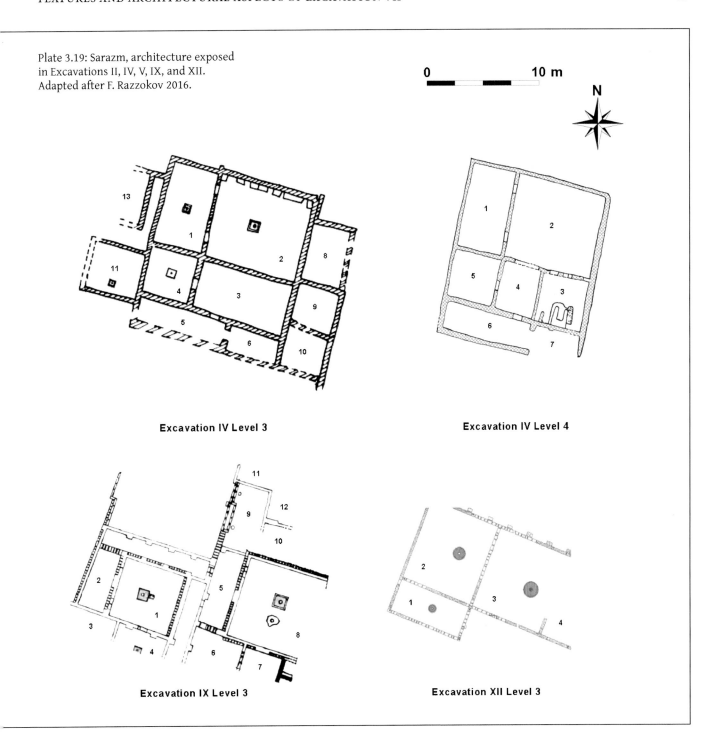

NNE–SSW and between WNW–ESE/NNE–SSW and NW–SE/NE–SW oriented. The eastern extension of Excavation II is slightly different as one building is N–S/W–E oriented, two are NNW–SSE/WSW–ENE oriented, and one is near NW–SE/NE–SW oriented. The Excavation III massive building is between N–S/W–E and WNW–ESE/NNE–SSW oriented. Excavation IV architectural structures have orientations around WNW–ESE/NNE–SSW and between N–S/W–E and WNW–ESE/NNE–SSW. Excavation V architecture is virtually N–S/E–W oriented. Excavation VI architecture is essentially organized on a WNW–ESE/NNE–SSW grid. The few walls found in Excavation VIII have N–S/W–E orientations. Excavation IX and XI buildings are between N–S/W–E and WNW–ESE/NNE–SSW oriented. Lastly, Excavation XII architectural structures essentially have orientations around WNW–ESE/NNE–SSW.

## Space Planning

I have found no evident parallels in available plans at Sarazm for the L-shaped Rooms 1 and 3 observed in the Excavation VII Level I1 building (Pl. 3.18).[5] Tentatively, Rooms 14 and 45 in Excavation II Level 2 may be mentioned as comparisons as these rooms have L shapes (F. Razzokov 2016, 180 fig. 5, 181 fig. 6; Pl. 3.19). Also, Room 4 in the Excavation VII Level I1 building, which was incompletely excavated, is somewhat reminiscent of Excavation I Level 2 Room 3 (F. Razzokov 2016, 178 fig. 2) and Excavation IX Level 3 Rooms 11 and 12 (F. Razzokov 2016, 221 fig. 53; Pl. 3.19). Excavation VII Levels I3, II1, and III2 buildings (Pl. 3.18) have plans that consist of one to two large rooms associated with smaller rooms aligned in a row within one side of these buildings. Such a configuration is not the most common one observed in Excavations I, II, and VI as well as part of Excavation IV Level 2, where building complexes are mostly characterized by two to five rooms placed in a row. Also, the way the buildings in Excavations I, II, and VI are laid out, where it seems that certain rooms were added afterward and where certain spaces are not strictly quadrangular nor orthonormal, tends to contrast with that of Excavation VII architectural levels and other excavations, where construction seems to have been more planned ahead of its realization. Two buildings in Excavation II however deserve mention, although they cannot be considered strict equivalents of those observed in Excavation VII. A building in the north-eastern corner of Excavation II Level 2 has eight to nine rooms (F. Razzokov 2016, 181 fig. 6; Pl. 3.19), and the configuration of four of its rooms (Rooms 5, 6, 11, and 12) is somewhat reminiscent of the Excavation VII Level I3 building, although their surfaces are smaller. Another building in the southern part of Excavation II (extension) Level 3 is divided into four rooms, with one room bigger than the others (F. Razzokov 2016, 180 fig. 5; Pl. 3.19). This configuration resembles that of the Level I3 building, although this building was not completely excavated.

More layouts closer to those of Excavation VII Levels I3, II1, and III2 are in Excavation IV Levels 2, 3, and 4; Excavation V Level 3; Excavation IX Level 3; and Excavation XII Level 3 (F. Razzokov 2016, 190 fig. 16, 191 fig. 17, 192 fig. 18, 193 fig. 19, 197 fig. 24, 221 fig. 53, 243 fig. 82; Pl. 3.19). At a minimum, like

Table 3.22: Room interior areas recorded in Sarazm Excavation VII.

| Level | Room | Length (m) | Width (m) | Area (m²) | Comments |
|---|---|---|---|---|---|
| I1 | 1 | 4.80 | 3.80 | 18.25 | L-shaped |
| I1 | 2 | 2.50 | 2.00 | 5.00 | |
| I1 | 3 | 3.80 | 1.90* | At least 8.00 | L-shaped, partially excavated |
| I1 | 4 | 6.90* | 4.10* | At least 19.60 | L-shaped, partially excavated |
| I3 | 5 | 4.00 | 4.00 | 16.00 | |
| I3 | 6 | 3.00 | 2.20 | 6.60 | |
| I3 | 7 | 2.80* | 2.20 | At least 6.00 | Partially excavated |
| I3 | 8 | 2.65* | 1.90* | At least 5.00 | Partially excavated |
| I3 | 9 | 7.45 | 4.65 | 34.65 | |
| II1 | 1 | 5.50* | 5.10 | At least 28.00 | Partially excavated |
| II1 | 2 | 1.95* | 2.50 | At least 4.80 | Partially excavated |
| II1 | 3 | 0.85* | 0.60* | At least 0.50 | Partially excavated |
| III2 | 3 | 7.15 | 6.80 | 48.60 | |
| III2 | 4 | 7.15 | 4.75* | At least 34.00 | Partially excavated |
| III2 | 5 | 4.00 | 3.80 | 15.20 | |
| III2 | 6 | 3.80 | 3.00 | 11.40 | |
| III2 | 7 | 3.80 | 3.15 | 12.00 | |
| III2 | 8 | 3.80 | 2.50* | At least 9.50 | Partially excavated |
| IV | 1 | 4.50* | 2.00* | At least 9.00 | Partially excavated |
| IV | 2 | 4.70* | 2.20 | At least 10.30 | Partially excavated |
| IV | 3 | 7.30* | 3.60* | At least 26.20 | Partially excavated |
| IV | 4 | 3.70 | 2.10 | 7.75 | |
| IV | 5 | 3.70 | 2.20 | 8.15 | |
| IV | 6 | 6.00* | 4.50* | At least 27.00 | Partially excavated |
| IV | 7 | 1.45* | 0.70* | At least 0.50 | Partially excavated |
| IV | 8 | 3.35* | 1.35* | At least 4.50 | Partially excavated |
| * Maximum excavated | | | | | |

Excavation VII, these levels include layouts more complex than just layouts based on rooms *à l'enfilade*. One may note that Excavation IV Level 2 Room 3 has a slightly oblique, short wall attached to its northeastern corner, which resembles Excavation VII Level II1 Room 1 Wall 7. Most importantly, Excavation VII Level III2, which yielded the most complete architectural plan in this excavation, seems more specifically very similar to Excavation IV Levels 3 and 4. Identical is in particular the fact that two larger rooms (Rooms

---

[5] I have not taken into account here the plans of the architecture exposed in the Excavation VII North/East extension, as these have been reconstructed based on sketches.

3 and 4 in Excavation VII Level III2 and Rooms 1 and 2 in both Excavation IV Levels 3 and 4) are connected by two doorways. Associated with these larger rooms are smaller ones, and both the larger and smaller rooms have about the same sizes in these three levels (Table 3.22). Their orientations also are similar. The only apparent difference is that Excavation IV Level 3 and 4 buildings have no pilaster, whereas Excavation VII Level II1 and III2 buildings do.

The only parallel in layout for the Excavation VII Level IV1–IV2 compartmented building (Figs 3.77 and 3.78) is the monumental construction exposed in Excavation III (F. Razzokov 2016, 183 fig. 8; Pl. 3.20). Furthermore, as noted above, these two buildings have bricks of similar sizes. The Excavation III building is a 14 × 15 m construction erected on a 75 high cm terrace and interpreted as a public warehouse (Besenval and Isakov 1989, 8–9) or a communal granary (Isakov 1994b, 1, 7). Nothing from Excavation VII compares to the circular construction excavated in Excavation V Level 2 (Besenval and Isakov 1989, 9 fig. 9), or to the unique quadrangular construction with a peripheral corridor exposed in Excavation XI Level 2 (F. Razzokov 2016, 231 fig. 66; Pl. 3.20). These two architectural structures probably have functions different from those of the buildings in Excavation VII and their parallels in the other excavations, which most likely served as dwellings.

**Pilasters**

Pilasters are in Excavation VII recorded in Levels II1 and III2. Five pilasters are placed on the exterior facade of the Level II1 building. They consist of bricks (56 × 24 cm and 62 × 24 cm along Wall 1; 54 × 26 cm and 53 × 25 cm along Wall 2; and 53 × 24 cm along Wall 3) and are *c.* 2.00 m (Walls 1 and 2) and 2.60 m (Wall 3) distant from each other. The Level III2 building has seven exterior pilasters and one inside. Three are along its north facade (Wall 5), each consisting of a brick (54 × 27 cm; 51 × 19 cm; 55 × 26 cm) about *c.* 60 cm and 2.15 m apart from each other. The four other pilasters are along the east facade (Walls 7 and 15). Three are *c.* 95 × 26 cm, 95 × 21 cm, and 95 × 24 cm, while one (*c.* 1.10 m long) consists of two 23 × 26 cm and 20 × 28 cm brick fragments separated by an empty space. These pilasters are *c.* 1.55 m, 1.05 m, and 2.55 m apart. The single interior pilaster is *c.* 1.10 × 0.30 m and placed in the middle of Wall 6, with two doorways on both sides.

Interior and exterior pilasters are common at Sarazm. Pilasters are recorded in Excavation I Level 2; Excavation II Levels 1 and 2; Excavation IV Level 2; Excavation V Level 3; Excavation VI Level 2; Excavation IX Levels 1 and 3; Excavation XI Levels 2 and 3; and Excavation XII Levels 2 and 3. They appear more common, however, in excavations spatially closer to Excavation VII than in Excavations I, II, and VI. The sizes of the pilasters and distances between them I have been able to record on just the available plans on Plates 3.19 and 3.20 (Table 3.23) are consistent with those recorded in Excavation VII.[6] The pilasters are between 35–130 cm long and on average 56 cm long. They are between 15–35 cm wide and on average 27 cm wide. The spaces in between them are between 65–350 cm and on average 165 cm.

**Doorways**

Not considering the remains exposed in its North/East extension, twelve doorways were recorded in Excavation VII and could be measured based on available plans (Table 3.24). Save for one in Level IV1 Wall 13, which is larger (*c.* 140 cm) and might not be a doorway, their widths range from 55 to 95 cm and are 78 cm on average. These widths agree with F. Razzokov's records from all other excavations. He writes that doorways are usually between 50–70 cm wide and sometimes up to 80–1.10 m wide. He also notes that entrances to buildings always have doorsteps, a feature recorded in Excavation VII Level I3 (see F. Razzokov 2016, 109–10).

**Apertures in Walls**

Besenval identified apertures in two walls in Levels I1 (Wall 6) and I3 (Wall 28). These apertures are too narrow and are placed at too low heights in these walls to be considered windows *per se*, although they certainly gave light and facilitated ventilation inside these buildings. Since these walls were not preserved over significant heights, one cannot discard the possibility, however, that these apertures were longer and continued upward across a larger portion of the walls in a fashion similar to *meurtrières*. The bases of the three apertures in Level I1 are *c.* 27 cm higher than the base of Wall 6 and are *c.* 24 cm wide (Figs 3.7–3.8). The three apertures in Level I3 are very low too, as they were identified on top of the second course of bricks in Wall 28. They have about the same sizes as those in Level I1: *c.* 25–27 cm (Fig. 3.24). Traces of paint were observed on their inte-

---

[6] These measurements should be considered approximations.

Table 3.23: Lengths and widths of the pilasters from Sarazm illustrated on Plates 3.19 and 3.20 as well as lengths of the spaces in between.

| Excavation | Level | Room | Length (cm) | Width (cm) | Space when applicable (cm) | References |
|---|---|---|---|---|---|---|
| IV | 2 | 8 | 100 | 35 | | Pl. 3.19 |
| IV | 2 | 8 | 105 | 30 | 165 | Pl. 3.19 |
| IV | 2 | 3 | 40 | 20 | | Pl. 3.19 |
| IV | 2 | 3 | 40 | 20 | 165 | Pl. 3.19 |
| IV | 2 | 3 | 65 | 20 | 65 | Pl. 3.19 |
| IV | 2 | 5 | 40 | 20 | | Pl. 3.19 |
| IV | 2 | 5 | 40 | 20 | 190 | Pl. 3.19 |
| IV | 2 | 5 | 40 | 25 | 105 | Pl. 3.19 |
| IV | 2 | 5 | 40 | 20 | 95 | Pl. 3.19 |
| IV | 2 | 5 | 40 | 20 | 95 | Pl. 3.19 |
| IV | 2 | 5 | 45 | 25 | 95 | Pl. 3.19 |
| IV | 2 | 5 | 45 | 20 | 95 | Pl. 3.19 |
| IV | 2 | 4 | 50 | 30 | | Pl. 3.19 |
| V | 3 | 1a | 35 | 25 | | Pl. 3.19 |
| V | 3 | 3a | 35 | 20 | 245 | Pl. 3.19 |
| V | 3 | 3a | 35 | 15 | 190 | Pl. 3.19 |
| IX | 3 | North corridor | 55 | 25 | | Pl. 3.19 |
| IX | 3 | North corridor | 55 | 25 | 120 | Pl. 3.19 |
| IX | 3 | North corridor | 55 | 30 | 155 | Pl. 3.19 |
| IX | 3 | North corridor | 60 | 30 | 145 | Pl. 3.19 |
| IX | 3 | North corridor | 45 | 25 | | Pl. 3.19 |
| IX | 3 | North corridor | 50 | 25 | 130 | Pl. 3.19 |
| IX | 3 | North corridor | 50 | 25 | 150 | Pl. 3.19 |
| IX | 3 | North corridor | 50 | 25 | 160 | Pl. 3.19 |
| IX | 3 | 2 | 120 | 30 | | Pl. 3.19 |
| IX | 3 | 2 | 40 | 30 | 170 | Pl. 3.19 |
| IX | 3 | 2 | 40 | 30 | 185 | Pl. 3.19 |
| IX | 3 | 4 | 65 | 25 | | Pl. 3.19 |
| IX | 3 | 4 | 55 | 25 | 165 | Pl. 3.19 |
| IX | 3 | 5 | 50 | 30 | | Pl. 3.19 |
| IX | 3 | 5 | 105 | 30 | | Pl. 3.19 |
| IX | 3 | 6 | 60 | 25 | | Pl. 3.19 |
| IX | 3 | 7 | 125 | 25 | | Pl. 3.19 |

| Excavation | Level | Room | Length (cm) | Width (cm) | Space when applicable (cm) | References |
|---|---|---|---|---|---|---|
| XI | 2 | North wall | 60 | 30 | | Pl. 3.20 |
| XI | 2 | North wall | 50 | 30 | 350 | Pl. 3.20 |
| XI | 2 | North wall | 55 | 25 | 230 | Pl. 3.20 |
| XI | 2 | North wall | 50 | 25 | 290 | Pl. 3.20 |
| XI | 2 | West wall | 70 | 35 | | Pl. 3.20 |
| XI | 2 | West wall | 50 | 30 | | Pl. 3.20 |
| XI | 2 | West wall | 50 | 30 | | Pl. 3.20 |
| XI | 2 | West wall | 50 | 30 | | Pl. 3.20 |
| XI | 2 | West wall | 45 | 30 | | Pl. 3.20 |
| XI | 2 | East wall | 130 | 30 | | Pl. 3.20 |
| XI | 2 | East wall | 50 | 30 | 185 | Pl. 3.20 |
| XI | 2 | East wall | 50 | 30 | 250 | Pl. 3.20 |
| XI | 2 | East wall | 50 | 30 | 250 | Pl. 3.20 |
| XI | 2 | East wall | 50 | 30 | 125 | Pl. 3.20 |
| XI | 2 | North corridor | 55 | 30 | | Pl. 3.20 |
| XI | 2 | North corridor | 50 | 30 | | Pl. 3.20 |
| XI | 2 | North corridor | 50 | 35 | | Pl. 3.20 |
| XI | 2 | North corridor | 55 | 25 | | Pl. 3.20 |
| XI | 2 | West corridor | 55 | 30 | | Pl. 3.20 |
| XI | 2 | West corridor | 50 | 30 | | Pl. 3.20 |
| XI | 2 | East corridor | 50 | 25 | | Pl. 3.20 |
| XI | 2 | Central room | 50 | 30 | | Pl. 3.20 |
| XI | 2 | Central room | 55 | 25 | | Pl. 3.20 |
| XII | 3 | 2 | 45 | 30 | | Pl. 3.19 |
| XII | 3 | 2 | 45 | 25 | 155 | Pl. 3.19 |
| XII | 3 | 3 | 45 | 20 | 140 | Pl. 3.19 |
| XII | 3 | 3 | 55 | 35 | 140 | Pl. 3.19 |
| XII | 3 | 3 | 60 | 30 | 140 | Pl. 3.19 |
| XII | 3 | 3 | 55 | 30 | 130 | Pl. 3.19 |
| | | Minimum | 35 | 15 | 65 | |
| | | Maximum | 130 | 35 | 350 | |
| | | Average | 56 | 27 | 165 | |

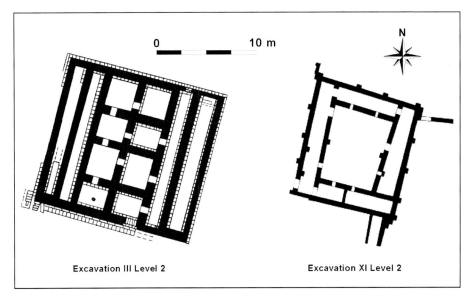

Plate 3.20: Sarazm, architecture exposed in Excavations III and XI. Adapted after F. Razzokov 2016.

Table 3.24: Widths measured on doorways in Sarazm Excavation VII.

| Level | Wall # | Width (cm) |
|---|---|---|
| I1 | 13 | 65 |
| I3 | 28 | 55 |
| I3 | 26 | 70 |
| I3 | 24 | 60 |
| I3 | 25 | 80 |
| I3 | 23 | 95 |
| III2 | 6 | 75 |
| III2 | 6 | 90 |
| III2 | 10 | 85 |
| III2 | 14 | 90 |
| IV1 | 7 | 95 |
| IV1 | 13 | 140 |

rior faces; two have red paint (hematite) and one has blue paint (lapis lazuli; see **Chapter 6**). Painted apertures are not reported from any of the other excavations at Sarazm, although, as noted above, painted floors and walls are recorded. On the other hand, apertures have been found, such as in Excavation XI Level 2 Room 1, where they have about the same width (25–30 cm) and are 50 cm high. These apertures are placed higher in the walls than in Excavation VII. One, 35 cm wide, is reported from Excavation IX Level 3 Room 1, while five were observed in Excavation V Level 3 Room 1. They measure 40–45 × 50 cm (F. Razzokov 2016, 113–14, 195 fig. 21, 197 fig. 24, 221 fig. 53, 232 fig. 66).

**Hearths and Pits with Pebbles**

Various types of structures that appear to have been used for fire-related activities, such as heating, cooking, lighting, and/or rituals, were found in Excavation VII. These structures include circular hearths consisting of just a hole (which Besenval reported as *tannoor*); circular hearths with a crater in their centres; quadrangular hearths with a crater in their centres and usually raised edges; and pits filled with pebbles. Those for which I have been able to find measurements are listed in Table 3.25. These measurements show that the holes have diameters between 17–42 cm and 27 cm on average. Their depths are between 9–27 cm and 15 cm on average. The two circular hearths with craters from Excavation VII have diameters measuring 45 cm and 55 cm, and their craters are 18 cm and 20 cm in diameter and 14 cm deep. The single circular hearth with no crater is 65 cm in diameter. The two quadrangular hearths with craters and no raised edge are 48 × 46 cm and 82 × 77 cm. Their craters are 15 cm and 18 cm in diameter respectively, and the depth of the former is 7 cm. The quadrangular hearths with craters and raised edges have lengths between 65–140 cm, 101 cm on average, and widths between 65–130 cm, 98 cm on average. Their craters have diameters between 17–30 cm and 21 cm on average. They are between 19–35 cm deep and 18 cm deep on average. The pits with pebbles have either circular or oblong shapes. In the former case, their diameters are between 40–130 cm and are 84 cm on average. In the latter case, their lengths are between 130–310 cm and 233 cm on average, while their widths are between 80–250 cm and 158 cm on average. The depths of these pits vary between 9 and 57 cm and are 22 cm on average.

A simpler type of hearth that consists of a shallow pit with stones and charcoal was observed in Level I3 Room 9 (H5). OF2 in Level I1 Room 2, with stones, charcoal, ashes, and animal bones, was also probably a simpler type of hearth which was most likely connected to cooking activities. Such simple hearths or cooking areas have parallels elsewhere at Sarazm as do the above-listed more sophisticated structures (F. Razzokov 2016, 115). Circular hearths and quadrangular hearths with craters in their centres have many parallels including in Excavations II, IV, V, VI, IX, XI, and XII, and including inside the above-noted buildings with layouts similar to that of the Excavation VII Level III2 building (F. Razzokov

Table 3.25: Available dimensions of hearths and pits with pebbles from Sarazm Excavation VII.

| Level | Room/Area | Feature number | Type | Length (cm) | Width (cm) | Diameter (cm) | Depth (cm) | Crater diameter (cm) | Crater depth (cm) |
|---|---|---|---|---|---|---|---|---|---|
| I1 | Room 1 | H1 | Circular hearth with crater | | | 55 | | 18 | 14 |
| I1 | Room 3 | H2 | Quadrangular hearth with crater | 48 | 46 | | | 15 | 7 |
| I3 | Room 5 | H4 | Quadrangular hearth with crater and raised edge | 72 | 72 | | | 22 | 19 |
| I3 | Room 9 | H5 | Circular hearth | | | 65 | | | |
| I3 | Room 9 | H6 | Quadrangular hearth with crater | 82 | 77 | | | 18 | |
| I4 | Area 4 | H7 | Hole | | | 25 | | | |
| I4 | Area 4 | H8 | Hole | | | 25 | | | |
| I4 | Area 4 | H9 | Hole | | | 20 | | | |
| II1 | Room 2 | H1 | Circular hearth with crater | | | 45 | | 20 | 14 |
| II1 | Area 1 | H2 | Hole | | | 26 | 9 | | |
| II2 | Area 3 | H3 | Hole | | | 24 | 17 | | |
| II2 | Area 3 | H4 | Hole | | | 42 | 11 | | |
| II2 | Area 3 | H5 | Quadrangular hearth with crater and raised edge | 140 | 130 | | | 15–30 | 25–35 |
| II2 | Area 3 | H6 | Hole | | | 25 | | | |
| II–N/E | Room 5 | H7 | Quadrangular hearth with crater and raised edge | 65 | 65 | | | 17 | |
| III1 | Room 1 | H1 | Quadrangular hearth with crater and raised edge | 114 | 114 | | | 25 | 22 |
| III2 | Room 3 | H3 | Quadrangular hearth with crater and raised edge | 125 | 120 | | | 30 | 20 |
| III2 | Room 4 | H4 | Hole | | | 17 | 12 | | |
| III2 | Room 5 | H5 | Quadrangular hearth with crater and raised edge | 87 | 85 | | | 20 | 20 |
| III2 | Area 4 | OF1 | Pit with pebbles | 260 | 210 | | | | |
| III2–N/E | Room 14 | H6 | Hole | | | 30 | 27 | | |
| III2–N/E | Room 14 | OF2 | Pit with pebbles | 200 | 100 | | 17 | | |
| III3 | Area 6 | H7 | Pit with pebbles | | | 100 | 20–30 | | |
| III3 | Area 6 | H8 | Pit with pebbles | | | 105 | 20–30 | | |
| III3 | Area 6 | H9 | Pit with pebbles | 130 | 80 | | 9 | | |
| III3 | Area 6 | H10 | Pit with pebbles | | | 130 | 14 | | |
| III3 | Area 6 | H11 | Hole | | | 32 | 13 | | |
| III3 | Area 6 | H12 | Pit with pebbles | | | 50 | 22 | | |
| III3 | Area 6 | H13 | Pit with pebbles | | | 75 | 11 | | |
| III3–N/E | Sq. L17 | H16 | Pit with pebbles | | | 90 | 20 | | |
| III3–N/E | Sq. L17 | H17 | Pit with pebbles | | | 40 | 17 | | |
| III3–N/E | Sq. N17 | H19 | Pit with pebbles | 250 | 140 | | 57 | | |
| IV2 | Sq. L15–M15 | H1 | Pit with pebbles | 250 | 170 | | | | |
| IV2 | Area 3 | H2 | Pit with pebbles | 310 | 250 | | 30 | | |

2016, 180 fig. 5, 186 fig. 11, 190 fig. 16, 191 fig. 17, 192 fig. 18, 193 fig. 19, 197 fig. 24, 198 fig. 25, 202 fig. 31, 212 fig. 43, 214 fig. 45, 221 fig. 53, 223 fig. 56, 224 figs 57–58, 226 fig. 60, 234 fig. 69, 238 fig. 74, 243 figs 82–83, 244 fig. 84). These hearths are commonly termed altars and interpreted as ritual hearths (F. Razzokov 2016, 116), although there is usually little evidence that may confirm this hypothesis. The sizes reported from the other excavations (F. Razzokov 2016, 118 tab. 7, 119 tab. 8) agree with those recorded in Excavation VII, although no circular hearth as large as those recovered for instance in Excavations V and XII (F. Razzokov 2016, 195 fig. 22, 243 figs 82–83) was found in Excavation VII. Available data suggest that the circular type of hearth is observed in virtually all periods at Sarazm, whereas the quadrangular type tends to be more common in the later periods (F. Razzokov 2016, 121).

The pits filled with pebbles are in Excavation VII found in Levels III and IV. In most available records I have found about these pits, mention is made of ashes or burnt pebbles, evidence relating to fire-related activities. This is apparent also in the photographic archives, including photographs of Level IV2 H2 which has a thick layer of burnt soil on top of the pebbles (Fig. 3.79; see also Figs 3.57–3.60). Pits filled with pebbles are not rare at Sarazm, where they are usually considered typical of its last period, Period IV. The sizes recorded in Excavation VII do not disagree with those recorded in the other excavations (F. Razzokov 2016, 106). Yet, an issue remains with these pits, which is that it is unclear whether all of them were indeed used for fire-related activities. Some certainly were, and the above-mentioned Excavation VII Level IV2 H2 is reminiscent of a large structure with pebbles found in Excavation II Level 3 (F. Razzokov 2016, 182 fig. 7). This structure is interpreted as a pottery kiln, although I do not agree with the reconstruction and interpretation that have been offered for this structure (see **Chapter 5**). Regardless, not all the pits with pebbles at Sarazm appear to bear evidence for firing activities. F. Razzokov (2016, 106) studied ten pits of this type and did not observe any traces of burning. Only sometimes did he record some bone fragments underneath the pebbles. I have made the same observation on some of these pits between 2011 and 2014. The function of part of these structures thus still remains unclear.

**Parallels beyond Sarazm**

The topic of the architecture and hearths from Sarazm and their parallels have been studied and presented on several occasions (e.g. Besenval and Isakov 1989; Isakov 1991; F. Razzokov 2016). Results from these comparative analyses are valid for Excavation VII too, since the architecture and hearths exposed within this excavation conform to those recorded elsewhere at Sarazm. Although it is probably not worth repeating here the totality of these analyses, it seems necessary to mention again that the best parallels are in Turkmenistan and southern Afghanistan during the fourth and third millennia BCE. Close equivalents for the architecture from Sarazm are reported in Turkmenistan at sites such as Altyn-Depe, Geoksyur, Ilgynly-Depe, and Yalangach-Depe as well as at Mundigak in Afghanistan (Isakov 1991; 1994b, 7; F. Razzokov 2016, 137–58). As for the quadrangular and circular hearths with craters, Besenval and Isakov noted parallels at Kara-Depe, Geoksyur, Altyn-Depe, Mundigak, Shahr-i Sokhta, and Tepe Hissar (Besenval and Isakov 1989, 8 n. 24).

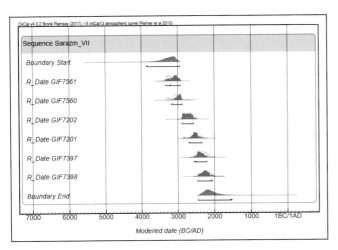

Graph 4.1: Calibrated radiocarbon dates from Sarazm Excavation VII (95.4 per cent) presented unmodelled and after Bayesian model was applied to them (Multiple plot). Calibrated and modelled using OxCal 4.3. Graph created using OxCal 4.3. B. Mutin.

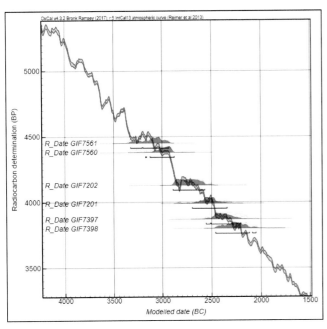

Graph 4.2: Calibrated radiocarbon dates from Sarazm Excavation VII (95.4 per cent) presented unmodelled and after Bayesian model was applied to them (Curve plot). Calibrated and modelled using OxCal 4.3. Graph created using OxCal 4.3. B. Mutin.

Six charcoal samples from Excavation VII were radiocarbon dated: two from Level I1, one from Level II1, one from Level III3, and two from Level IV1. The archaeological contexts of these samples are detailed in Table 4.1. I have recalibrated these dates using OxCal 4.3 software and applied a Bayesian model to this series (Table 4.2).[1] As a result, the ranges of three dates are now narrower when modelled in comparison to their ranges obtained when unmodelled and in comparison to the ranges of the other dates: GIF7560, GIF7201,

---

[1] <https://c14.arch.ox.ac.uk/oxcal.html> [accessed 10 April 2023].

# 4. Radiocarbon Dates

Table 4.1: Uncalibrated radiocarbon dates from Sarazm Excavation VII.

| Lab. # | BP | Interval | Material | Context |
|---|---|---|---|---|
| GIF7561 | 4450 | 60 | Charcoal | Level I1 (beginning), Room 3, Hearth 2 (Sample no. 46) |
| GIF7560 | 4380 | 70 | Charcoal | Level I1 (end), Room 2 (Sample no. 35) |
| GIF7202 | 4130 | 70 | Charcoal | Level II1, Area 1, Hearth 2 (Sample no. 6) |
| GIF7201 | 3990 | 70 | Charcoal | Level III3, Hearth 9 (Sample no. 2) |
| GIF7397 | 3870 | 90 | Charcoal | Level IV1, Room 5 floor (Sample no. 30) |
| GIF7398 | 3800 | 70 | Charcoal | Level IV1, Room 2 floor (Sample no. 31) |

and GIF7397. Although six radiocarbon dates are certainly not enough to establish a solid chronology of Excavation VII, and regardless of whether these dates are acceptable in absolute terms, which is discussed in the **Conclusion**, they are consistent with the stratigraphy, both when modelled and unmodelled. The overall range of this series is c. 3350–2000 cal. BCE. The two dates from Level I1 are between the late fourth and early third millennia BCE. The one conducted on a sample collected in the early deposits of Level I1 is earlier than the one conducted on a sample collected in deposits relating to the end of this level. The date from Level II1 is in the first half of the third millennium BCE. The date from Level III3 is centred on the middle of the third millennium BCE. The two dates from Level IV1 are placed within the second half of the third millennium BCE (Graphs 4.1–4.2).

Thirty-five additional radiocarbon dates are currently available from Sarazm Excavations II, III, IV, V, VI, IX, XI, XII, XV, and XVI, as well as from two test trenches (Table 4.3). These dates were also recalibrated using OxCal 4.3. At two sigmas (95.4 per cent), they range between c. 4000–1250 cal. BCE (Table 4.4; Graph 4.3).

– Four are between c. 4000–3350 cal. BCE. Two of them are within the first half of the fourth millennium

Table 4.2: Calibrated radiocarbon dates from Sarazm Excavation VII (95.4 per cent) presented unmodelled and after Bayesian model was applied to them.

| Name | Unmodelled (BCE/CE) from | to | % | Modelled (BCE/CE) from | to | % | Indices Amodel 122.5 Aoverall 121.7 Acomb | A | L | P | C |
|---|---|---|---|---|---|---|---|---|---|---|---|
| Sequence Sarazm_VII | | | | | | | | | | | |
| Boundary Start | | | | -3852 | -2937 | 95.4 | | | | | 96.8 |
| R_Date GIF7561 | -3341 | -2929 | 95.4 | -3326 | -2932 | 95.4 | | 100.8 | | | 99.7 |
| R_Date GIF7560 | -3333 | -2889 | 95.4 | -3172 | -2878 | 95.4 | | 117.1 | | | 99.8 |
| Interval Phases I–II | | | | 38 | 485 | 95.4 | | | | | 99.8 |
| R_Date GIF7202 | -2889 | -2496 | 95.4 | -2891 | -2568 | 95.4 | | 103.3 | | | 99.8 |
| Interval Phases II–III | | | | 0 | 396 | 95.4 | | | | | 99.9 |
| R_Date GIF7201 | -2855 | -2291 | 95.4 | -2696 | -2342 | 95.4 | | 115.3 | | | 99.8 |
| Interval Phases III–IV | | | | 0 | 343 | 95.4 | | | | | 99.9 |
| R_Date GIF7397 | -2576 | -2043 | 95.4 | -2555 | -2206 | 95.4 | | 113 | | | 99.9 |
| R_Date GIF7398 | -2464 | -2037 | 95.4 | -2460 | -2052 | 95.4 | | 104.8 | | | 99.7 |
| Boundary End | | | | -2453 | -1530 | 95.4 | | | | | 96.7 |

BCE, LE2172 (Excavation IV Level 1 or 2) and LE2174 (Excavation II Level 1), while two are between the first half and second third of the fourth millennium BCE, LE2173 (Excavation IV Level 1 or 2) and BLN556 (Excavation V Level 2).

- There is then a series of twenty-two dates between c. 3350–2900 cal. BCE (twenty-four including GIF7560 and GIF7561 from Excavation VII Level I1) from Excavations III, VII, IX, XI, XII, XV, and XVI, as well as TT5 and TT6: BETA368883 (Excavation XVI UF 206), BETA356255 (Excavation XV Level 1a), UGAMS6860 (Excavation IX Level 1), BETA368882 (Excavation XVI UF 212), BETA356257 (Excavation XV Pit B), UGAMS6861 (Excavation IX Level 1), BETA368886 (Excavation XVI UF 141), BETA368884 (Excavation XVI UF 129), BETA368885 (Excavation XVI UF 134), GIF7560 (Excavation VII Level I1), BETA356498 (Excavation XV Level 1c), BETA356259 (Excavation XV Level 1a), BETA368887 (Excavation XVI UF 200), BETA311525 (TT6), BETA356499 (Excavation XVI UF 33), BETA356497 (Excavation XV Pit A), GIF7561 (Excavation VII Level I1), LE1806 (Excavation III Level 2), UGAMS6858 (Excavation XII Level 1), BETA311524 (TT5), UGAMS6862 (Excavation XI Level 2), BETA311526 (TT6), BETA356258 (Excavation XV Pit A), and UGAMS6859 (Excavation XII Level 1). As also noted in **Chapter 1**, this series appears to be coincident with a period during which the site was occupied over a greater surface, around 3000 cal. BCE broadly speaking, which is likely to have been the peak occupation period at this site.

- A third cluster of radiocarbon dates may be defined by three dates that are between c. 2900–2450 cal. BCE (four including GIF7202 from Excavation VII Level II1), save for one whose upper limit lies in the mid–late fourth millennium BCE: LE3124 (Excavation IV), LE1808 (Excavation III Level 2), GIF7202 (Excavation VII Level II1), and LE3262 (Excavation VI).

- One date, GIF7201 (Excavation VII Level III3) emerges as relatively isolated as it is centred on the middle of the third millennium BCE. The following series consists of three dates between c. 2550–1950 cal. BCE (five including GIF7397 and GIF7398 from Excavation VII Level IV1): GIF7397 (Excavation VII Level IV1), LE1807 (Excavation II Level 3), GIF7398 (Excavation VII Level IV1), LE1420 (Excavation III Level 2), and LE 2477 (Excavation VI Level 2). Three last radiocarbon dates cluster between c. 1600–1250 cal. BCE: LE2478 (Excavation VI Level 3), LE2475 (Excavation V Level 3), and LE2476 (Excavation VI Level 3).

As is apparent from the data listed above, the two radiocarbon dates from the oldest level in Excavation VII (GIF7561 and GIF7560, Level I1) are consistent with the numerous available radiocarbon dates from Sarazm that are around 3000 cal. BCE, an apparent period of

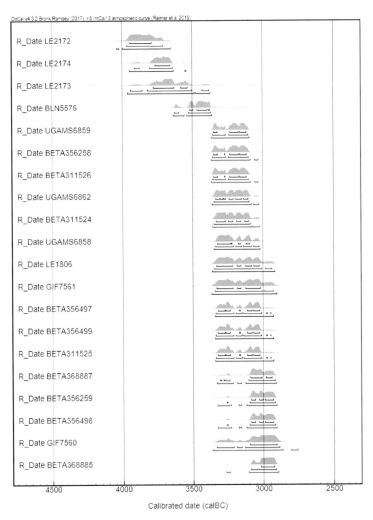
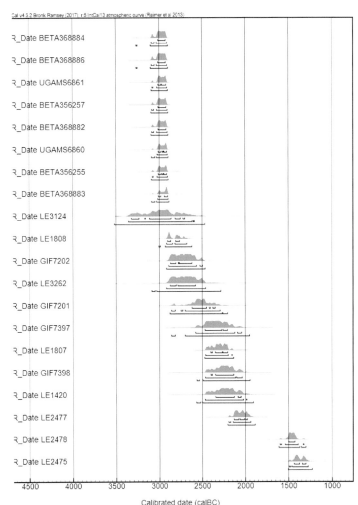

Graph 4.3: Calibrated radiocarbon dates from Sarazm (68.2 per cent, 95.4 per cent, 99.7 per cent). Calibrated using OxCal 4.3. Graphs created using OxCal 4.3.

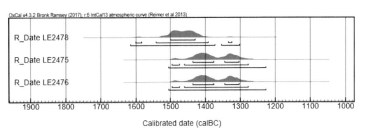

peak occupation at this site. This suggests that the area of Excavation VII was not settled at the very beginning of the settlement, but at the time of this peak occupation. Indeed, Besenval and Isakov (1989, 17) noted that Excavation VII earliest occupations did not correspond to Sarazm foundation period. Similarly, F. Razzokov recently assigned the beginning of Excavation VII to Sarazm Period II (F. Razzokov 2016, 89 tab. 3). However, considering that these statements are true, how long after the beginning of Sarazm settlement the area of Excavation VII was settled is not very clear. Indeed, as noted in **Chapter 1** and above, only four radiocarbon dates from Sarazm are earlier than c. 3350 cal. BCE. Two of them, within the first half of the fourth millennium BCE, are from Excavation IV Level 1 or 2 and Excavation II Level 1, while two dates, between the first half and second third of the fourth millennium BCE, are from Excavation IV Level 1 or 2 and Excavation V Level 2.

Although it would not be appropriate to completely reject these dates, one should point out that they raise several issues. One issue is that they do not seem to fit with the chronology as established through the material culture and its parallels. Regarding the date from Excavation II, it is probably also worth noting that all dates from nearby Excavation XVI are consistently clustered within a c. 3350–2900 cal. BCE range. This excavation is located just east of Excavation II, and the radiocarbon dated deposits from this excavation are continuous with those exposed in Excavation II. The radiocarbon dates from Excavation XVI tend to confirm the inclusion of Excavation II levels, or a part of them, within the above-mentioned c. 3000 cal. BCE peak occupation period. They also challenge the date from Excavation II that gave a result within the first half of the fourth millennium BCE, although it remains possible that deposits were exposed in nearby Excavation II that are older than those from Excavation XVI.

Table 4.3: Uncalibrated radiocarbon dates from Sarazm Excavations II, III, IV, V, VI, IX, XI, XII, XV, XVI, and TT5 and TT6.

| Excavation | Lab. # | BP | Interval | Material | Context |
|---|---|---|---|---|---|
| II | LE2174 | 4940 | 50 | Charcoal? | Level 1 (F. Razzokov 2016, 88 tab. 1; Isakov et al. 1987, 91 tab. 1) |
| II | LE1807 | 3840 | 40 | Charcoal? | Level 3 (F. Razzokov 2016, 88 tab. 1; Isakov et al. 1987, 91 tab. 1) |
| III | LE1806 | 4460 | 50 | Charcoal? | Level 2 (F. Razzokov 2016, 88 tab. 1); Level 1 (Isakov et al. 1987, 91 tab. 1) |
| III | LE1808 | 4230 | 40 | Charcoal? | Level 2, hearth (F. Razzokov 2016, 88 tab. 1; Isakov et al. 1987, 91 tab. 1) |
| III | LE1420 | 3790 | 80 | Charcoal? | Level 2, House 2, floor (F. Razzokov 2016, 88 tab. 1; Isakov et al. 1987, 91 tab. 1) |
| IV | LE2172 | 5050 | 60 | Charcoal? | Level 2, bottom layer of a pit (F. Razzokov 2016, 88 tab.1); Level 1 (Isakov et al. 1987, 91 tab. 1) |
| IV | LE2173 | 4880 | 90 | Charcoal? | Level 2, pit (F. Razzokov 2016, 88 tab. 1); Level 1 (Isakov et al. 1987, 91 tab. 1) |
| IV | LE3124 | 4320 | 130 | Charcoal? | Sample no. 72, posterior to tomb (Archives R. Besenval; erroneously attributed to Excavation VII in F. Razzokov 2016, 88 tab. 1) |
| V | BLN5576 | 4682 | 35 | Charcoal? | Level 2, near the circular building (F. Razzokov 2016, 90 tab. 2) |
| V | LE2475 | 3120 | 40 | Charcoal? | Level 3, top (F. Razzokov 2016, 88 tab. 1) |
| VI | LE3262 | 4120 | 100 | Charcoal? | Pit (F. Razzokov 2016, 88 tab. 1) |
| VI | LE2477 | 3670 | 40 | Charcoal? | Level 2, bottom (F. Razzokov 2016, 88 tab. 1) |
| VI | LE2476 | 3120 | 40 | Charcoal? | Level 3, top (F. Razzokov 2016, 88 tab. 1) |
| VI | LE2478 | 3190 | 40 | Charcoal? | Level 3, top of first floor (F. Razzokov 2016, 88 tab. 1) |
| IX | UGAMS6861 | 4360 | 25 | Charcoal? | Level 1, House 2 (F. Razzokov 2016, 90 tab. 2) |
| IX | UGAMS6860 | 4350 | 25 | Charcoal? | Level 1, House 2 (F. Razzokov 2016, 90 tab. 2) |
| XI | UGAMS6862 | 4500 | 30 | Charcoal? | Level 2, House 1, hearth (F. Razzokov 2016, 90 tab. 2) |
| XII | UGAMS6858 | 4470 | 25 | Charcoal? | Level 1, Corridor 1 (F. Razzokov 2016, 90 tab. 2) |
| XII | UGAMS6859 | 4520 | 25 | Charcoal? | Level 1, Corridor 2 (F. Razzokov 2016, 90 tab. 2) |
| XV | BETA356255 | 4350 | 30 | Charcoal | Level 1a, uppermost (Mutin et al. 2020, 24 tab. 1) |
| XV | BETA356259 | 4400 | 30 | Charcoal | Level 1a, uppermost (Mutin et al. 2020, 24 tab. 1) |
| XV | BETA356498 | 4400 | 30 | Charcoal | Level 1c, lowest (Mutin et al. 2020, 24 tab. 1) |
| XV | BETA356497 | 4450 | 30 | Charcoal | Pit A (Mutin et al. 2020, 24 tab. 1) |
| XV | BETA356258 | 4520 | 30 | Charcoal | Pit A (Mutin et al. 2020, 24 tab. 1) |
| XV | BETA356257 | 4360 | 30 | Charcoal | Pit B (Mutin et al. 2020, 24 tab. 1) |
| XVI | BETA368882 | 4360 | 30 | Charcoal | UF 212 (Mutin et al. 2020, 24 tab. 1) |
| XVI | BETA368883 | 4330 | 30 | Charcoal | UF 206 (Mutin et al. 2020, 24 tab. 1) |
| XVI | BETA368884 | 4370 | 30 | Charcoal | UF 129 (Mutin et al. 2020, 24 tab. 1) |
| XVI | BETA368885 | 4380 | 30 | Charcoal | UF 134 (Mutin et al. 2020, 24 tab. 1) |
| XVI | BETA368886 | 4370 | 30 | Charcoal | UF 141 (Mutin et al. 2020, 24 tab. 1) |
| XVI | BETA368887 | 4410 | 30 | Charcoal | UF 200 (Mutin et al. 2020, 24 tab. 1) |
| XVI | BETA356499 | 4450 | 30 | Bone | UF 33 (Mutin et al. 2020, 24 tab. 1) |
| TT5 | BETA311524 | 4490 | 30 | Charcoal | Mutin et al. 2020, 24 tab. 1 |
| TT6 | BETA311526 | 4520 | 30 | Charcoal | Mutin et al. 2020, 24 tab. 1 |
| TT6 | BETA311525 | 4450 | 30 | Charcoal | Mutin et al. 2020, 24 tab. 1 |

Table 4.4: Calibrated radiocarbon dates from Sarazm Excavations II, III, IV, V, VI, IX, XI, XII, XV, XVI, and TT5 and TT6. Calibrated using OxCal 4.3.

| Name | Unmodelled (BCE/CE) |||||||||
|---|---|---|---|---|---|---|---|---|---|
| | from | to | % | from | to | % | from | to | % |
| R_Date LE2476 | -1436 | -1304 | 68.2 | -1496 | -1278 | 95.4 | -1505 | -1227 | 99.7 |
| R_Date LE2475 | -1436 | -1304 | 68.2 | -1496 | -1278 | 95.4 | -1505 | -1227 | 99.7 |
| R_Date LE2478 | -1500 | -1430 | 68.2 | -1601 | -1325 | 95.5 | -1616 | -1302 | 99.7 |
| R_Date LE2477 | -2134 | -1979 | 68.2 | -2195 | -1939 | 95.4 | -2206 | -1890 | 99.7 |
| R_Date LE1420 | -2346 | -2050 | 68.2 | -2468 | -1985 | 95.4 | -2567 | -1907 | 99.7 |
| R_Date GIF7398 | -2399 | -2136 | 68.2 | -2464 | -2037 | 95.4 | -2562 | -1947 | 99.7 |
| R_Date LE1807 | -2401 | -2206 | 68.2 | -2461 | -2154 | 95.4 | -2472 | -2136 | 99.7 |
| R_Date GIF7397 | -2468 | -2208 | 68.2 | -2576 | -2043 | 95.4 | -2855 | -1951 | 99.7 |
| R_Date GIF7201 | -2621 | -2350 | 68.3 | -2855 | -2291 | 95.4 | -2873 | -2206 | 99.7 |
| R_Date LE3262 | -2871 | -2578 | 68.2 | -2916 | -2461 | 95.4 | -3089 | -2282 | 99.7 |
| R_Date GIF7202 | -2866 | -2620 | 68.3 | -2889 | -2496 | 95.4 | -2916 | -2466 | 99.7 |
| R_Date LE1808 | -2902 | -2760 | 68.2 | -2913 | -2678 | 95.4 | -3007 | -2621 | 99.7 |
| R_Date LE3124 | -3321 | -2701 | 68.3 | -3354 | -2589 | 95.5 | -3519 | -2468 | 99.7 |
| R_Date BETA368883 | -3010 | -2899 | 68.2 | -3019 | -2894 | 95.4 | -3090 | -2882 | 99.7 |
| R_Date BETA356255 | -3011 | -2911 | 68.2 | -3081 | -2901 | 95.4 | -3091 | -2892 | 99.7 |
| R_Date UGAMS6860 | -3011 | -2911 | 68.2 | -3023 | -2904 | 95.4 | -3090 | -2893 | 99.7 |
| R_Date BETA368882 | -3011 | -2918 | 68.2 | -3085 | -2904 | 95.4 | -3095 | -2895 | 99.7 |
| R_Date BETA356257 | -3011 | -2918 | 68.2 | -3085 | -2904 | 95.4 | -3095 | -2895 | 99.7 |
| R_Date UGAMS6861 | -3011 | -2918 | 68.2 | -3081 | -2907 | 95.4 | -3091 | -2899 | 99.7 |
| R_Date BETA368886 | -3012 | -2924 | 68.2 | -3089 | -2907 | 95.4 | -3263 | -2896 | 99.7 |
| R_Date BETA368884 | -3012 | -2924 | 68.2 | -3089 | -2907 | 95.4 | -3263 | -2896 | 99.7 |
| R_Date BETA368885 | -3020 | -2926 | 68.2 | -3090 | -2913 | 95.4 | -3266 | -2897 | 99.7 |
| R_Date GIF7560 | -3096 | -2906 | 68.2 | -3333 | -2889 | 95.4 | -3364 | -2761 | 99.7 |
| R_Date BETA356498 | -3087 | -2930 | 68.2 | -3262 | -2917 | 95.4 | -3327 | -2906 | 99.7 |
| R_Date BETA356259 | -3087 | -2930 | 68.2 | -3262 | -2917 | 95.4 | -3327 | -2906 | 99.7 |
| R_Date BETA368887 | -3092 | -2940 | 68.2 | -3309 | -2917 | 95.5 | -3330 | -2908 | 99.7 |
| R_Date BETA311525 | -3320 | -3025 | 68.2 | -3336 | -2945 | 95.5 | -3341 | -2927 | 99.7 |
| R_Date BETA356499 | -3320 | -3025 | 68.2 | -3336 | -2945 | 95.5 | -3341 | -2927 | 99.7 |
| R_Date BETA356497 | -3320 | -3025 | 68.2 | -3336 | -2945 | 95.5 | -3341 | -2927 | 99.7 |
| R_Date GIF7561 | -3330 | -3020 | 68.2 | -3341 | -2929 | 95.4 | -3366 | -2904 | 99.7 |
| R_Date LE1806 | -3330 | -3027 | 68.1 | -3348 | -2938 | 95.4 | -3361 | -2917 | 99.7 |
| R_Date UGAMS6858 | -3326 | -3093 | 68.2 | -3336 | -3028 | 95.4 | -3348 | -3020 | 99.7 |
| R_Date BETA311524 | -3332 | -3101 | 68.2 | -3348 | -3090 | 95.4 | -3358 | -3024 | 99.7 |
| R_Date UGAMS6862 | -3336 | -3106 | 68.2 | -3347 | -3097 | 95.4 | -3361 | -3027 | 99.7 |
| R_Date BETA311526 | -3350 | -3116 | 68.1 | -3356 | -3101 | 95.4 | -3366 | -3032 | 99.7 |
| R_Date BETA356258 | -3350 | -3116 | 68.1 | -3356 | -3101 | 95.4 | -3366 | -3032 | 99.7 |
| R_Date UGAMS6859 | -3349 | -3117 | 68.2 | -3354 | -3103 | 95.4 | -3362 | -3095 | 99.7 |
| R_Date BLN5576 | -3517 | -3376 | 68.3 | -3627 | -3368 | 95.4 | -3634 | -3361 | 99.7 |
| R_Date LE2173 | -3779 | -3533 | 68.2 | -3941 | -3381 | 95.4 | -3962 | -3371 | 99.7 |
| R_Date LE2174 | -3766 | -3659 | 68.2 | -3913 | -3639 | 95.4 | -3947 | -3542 | 99.7 |
| R_Date LE2172 | -3944 | -3791 | 68.2 | -3965 | -3709 | 95.4 | -4037 | -3653 | 99.7 |

Another issue concerns the radiocarbon dates from Excavation IV, perhaps more specifically one that gave a date within the first half of the fourth millennium BCE. These radiocarbon dates were conducted on samples from architectural levels posterior to the funerary stone circle that contains the 'Princess of Sarazm'. Yet, as noted in **Chapter 1**, recent radiocarbon analysis conducted on human remains that *may* come from one of the burials in this stone circle gave a date of 3636–3521 cal. BCE (4765±20 BP, PSUAMS-2624) (Narasimhan et al. 2019, suppl. mat., 95). The main issue with this recent date is that the exact origin of the analysed human remains is not known, although there is a reasonable possibility that they come from this funerary stone circle. This date is also consistent with the parallels noted for this structure with the Afanasievo Steppe culture.

Lastly, the radiocarbon date from Excavation V is from Level 2 in this excavation, which is believed to be on the same chronological horizon as Excavation VII Levels I1 and I3, Excavation IX Level 1, Excavation XI Levels 1 and 2, and Excavation XII Levels 1 and 2, to name more recent fieldwork with recent radiocarbon analyses (F. Razzokov 2016, 89 tab. 3). The five available radiocarbon dates from contexts assigned to this horizon in Excavations IX, XI, and XII gave dates altogether set between the late fourth and early third millennia cal. BCE (Tables 4.3–4.4). As seen above, the same is true for the two radiocarbon dates from Excavation VII Level I1.

It is probably important to recall that the archaeological deposits that have been defined as Sarazm Period I have been exposed over limited surfaces. Consequently, this period will be better defined when more of these deposits are studied. This was precisely one of the objectives of Excavation XVI, near Excavation II, and yet, this excavation failed to find deposits older than the late fourth and early third millennia BCE, although it reached the virgin soil. In the present state of knowledge, most evidence thus points at this chronological bracket for the beginning of Sarazm settlement, while an earlier occupation period remains elusive. The only exception is the funerary stone circle in Excavation IV, which may date to around the middle of the fourth millennium BCE, although an updated re-examination of the objects associated with the burials in this circle would probably be helpful to confirm this statement. In any case, as noted in **Chapter 1**, currently available data seems consistent and suggests a chronological gap between these burials and the main settlement of Sarazm. In summary, one should certainly keep in mind the three to four older radiocarbon dates as well as the fact that they are marginal and not consistent with most data. A possibility would be that they represent a case of 'old wood effect'. Regardless, the fact remains that it is unclear how long after the beginning of Sarazm settlement the area of Excavation VII was settled (see **Conclusion**).

The single date from Excavation VII Level II1 (GIF7202) clusters with a few other dates from Excavations III, IV, and VI within the first half of the third millennium BCE. The single date from Excavation VII Level III3 (GIF7201), centred around the middle of the third millennium BCE, is slightly posterior. It is between the cluster of dates relating to the date from Excavation VII Level II1 (GIF7202) and a cluster of dates placed within the second half of the third millennium BCE. Although a single date is not enough, this radiocarbon date from Level III3 suggests that Level III2 architecture dates to the first half of the third millennium BCE, together with Level II1.

The two dates from Level IV1 (GIF7397 and GIF7398) are both within the second half of the third millennium BCE. They also match dates from Excavations II, III, and VI and are not as low as some from Excavations V and VI which are reported as being as low as c. 1250 cal. BCE. As discussed in **Chapter 1**, these low dates from Excavation VII are in agreement with Isakov's view on Sarazm's chronology, who dates Sarazm Period III to 3000–2300 cal. BCE and Period IV to 2300–1900 cal. BCE (Isakov 1991, 112–13), whereas most available evidence suggests that the settlement ended around the mid-third millennium BCE. Although the very low dates from Excavations V and VI do not seem consistent with Sarazm material assemblage, the two dates from Excavation VII Level IV1 deserve further discussion together with the objects recovered from this level, which do not all necessarily appear to contradict these dates (see **Chapters 5 and 6**).

I wrote above that parallels for the architecture and archaeological features identified in Excavation VII Levels I3, II1, and III2 are in: Excavation IV Levels 2, 3, and 4; Excavation V Level 3; Excavation IX Level 3; and Excavation XII Level 3. Excavation VII Level III2 seems more specifically very similar to Excavation IV Levels 3 and 4. As noted above, the radiocarbon dates from Excavation VII show that Levels I3, II1, and III2 date to between the last third of the fourth and the middle of the third millennia BCE. There are unfortunately no available radiocarbon dates from Excavation IV Levels 3 and 4. The only three radiocarbon dates from this excavation are two dates from Level 1 or 2 and one from deposits posterior to Level 1. They do not help much refining the dating of Excavation VII architecture, as the two former are between 3965–3709 cal. BCE (LE2172, 95.4 per cent) and 3941–3381 cal. BCE (LE2173, 95.4 per cent), and the latter is between 3354–2589 (LE3124, 95.5 per cent). They just do not contradict a dating of Excavation VII Levels I–III to sometime between c. 3350–2450 cal. BCE, corresponding to the above-mentioned two clusters of dates across Sarazm the radiocarbon dates from these levels belong to. The two radiocarbon dates from Excavation V are from Levels 2 and 3. The former is between 3627–3368 cal. BCE (BLN5576, 95.4 per cent), which again just corroborates the fact that Excavation VII architecture and its parallels in Excavation V Level 3 are later than c. 3350 cal. BCE. The latter, from Excavation V Level 3, is between 1496–1278 cal. BCE (LE2475, 95.4 per cent), which does not make a lot of sense and seems to be too late considering the parallels for its vestiges and the dates of these parallels. As for the radiocarbon dates from Excavations IX and XII, all four are from the first levels in these excavations, Level 1. In Excavation IX, they are between 3023–2904 cal. BCE (UGAMS6860, 95.4 per cent) and 3081–2907 cal. BCE (UGAMS6861, 95.4 per cent), while in Excavation XII they are between 3354–3103 cal. BCE (UGAMS6859, 95.4 per cent) and 3336–3028 cal. BCE (UGAMS6858, 95.4 per cent). In absolute terms, these dates agree with the fact that the third levels in these excavations, Level 3, and their parallels in Excavation VII are most likely posterior to 3350 cal. BCE.

# 5. Ceramic Vessels

Lyonnet studied part of the ceramic assemblage from Sarazm (Lyonnet 1996). Her study focused on material excavated between 1977 and 1985, *c.* 1500 sherds, including part of the ceramic assemblage from Excavation VII (Lyonnet 1996, 9). Although the present analysis concerns the totality of the ceramic assemblage from this excavation, it also refers to this previous work, including the parallels Lyonnet found for the ceramics from Sarazm, in addition to my own observations on this assemblage and the whole collection from this site. Lyonnet had first-hand knowledge of many ceramic types collected throughout Central Asia, so I trust the parallels she mentioned. Additionally, although the present chapter presents many more vessels from Excavation VII and a more detailed analysis of this assemblage than what was published before, the ceramics found after 1985 in this excavation have not radically changed the general picture of the ceramic assemblage from Sarazm that Lyonnet established using material excavated between 1977 and 1985.

## Recording System

Besenval recorded the ceramics from Excavation VII by batches (*lots*) which were numbered continuously from 1984 to 1991. I have found in his archives a list of these batches with information about the archaeological contexts the ceramics come from, either a feature number or a grid location, for most of those recorded between 1984 and 1989. Unfortunately, such information was not reported for the 1991 assemblage and is available for only a few of the ceramics collected in 1990.

## Classification

The approach I have used in this volume to characterize and classify the ceramics from Excavation VII follows and combines common principles of ceramic analysis including reconstruction of the *chaîne opératoire* and typological (morphometrical and morphological) analysis (e.g. Balfet et al. 1983; Balfet 1991; Méry 2000). I sorted out the material with the naked eye with, first, a focus on the manufacturing aspects of the vessels, including the kind, size,[1] and amount of inclusions/tempering agents in their fabrics, their surface colours, texture, hardness, and any other macrotraces relating to their fabrication, from building macrotraces to surface treatment and firing. Although no actual petrographic analysis has been conducted on the Excavation VII material, I examined a group of sherds from Sarazm using a digital microscope. Examples of sections of ceramics from this site photographed using this microscope are presented on Plates 5.1 and 5.2 and give an idea of the fabric variety that was present there.

Although more analysis certainly needs to be done on the ceramic material from Sarazm,[2] these observations and review of the totality of the ceramic collection from this site available in Penjikent led me to distinguish six main stylistic groups, Groups 1 to 6. The fabric of each of them generally corresponds to a specific inventory of forms and profiles, types of surface treatments (such as burnishing and wash/slip), and/or decoration techniques (such as painting, incision, and appliqué) and motifs.

Groups 1 to 3 are plain, sand- to granule-tempered ceramics. Although Group 2 is usually coarser than Group 1, it is difficult in some cases to distinguish between these two groups, as some Group 1 vessels appear to represent a sort of transitional fabric category between the two groups, with more mineral inclusions than in the rest of Group 1 vessels. Distinction between Groups 1 and 2 is rendered more complicated by the fact that variations are observed in the amounts of inclusions depending on the portions of the vessels that are examined. It appears, as a general rule, that inclusions are usually more numerous within bases. This implies

---

[1] Inclusion size classification refers to Wentworth's scale (1922).
[2] Composition analyses were conducted on thirty-five sherds from Excavation VII as part of a broader analytical research project called ROXIANA (Archaeological Research on Metal and Pottery Assemblages from the Oxus Basin to the Indus Valley during Protohistory; <https://anr.fr/Project-ANR-11-FRAL-0016> [accessed 10 April 2023]). This project included additional material from other excavations at Sarazm as well as materials from other sites between Uzbekistan and Pakistan. Results from the analysis on the ceramics from Sarazm will be presented elsewhere.

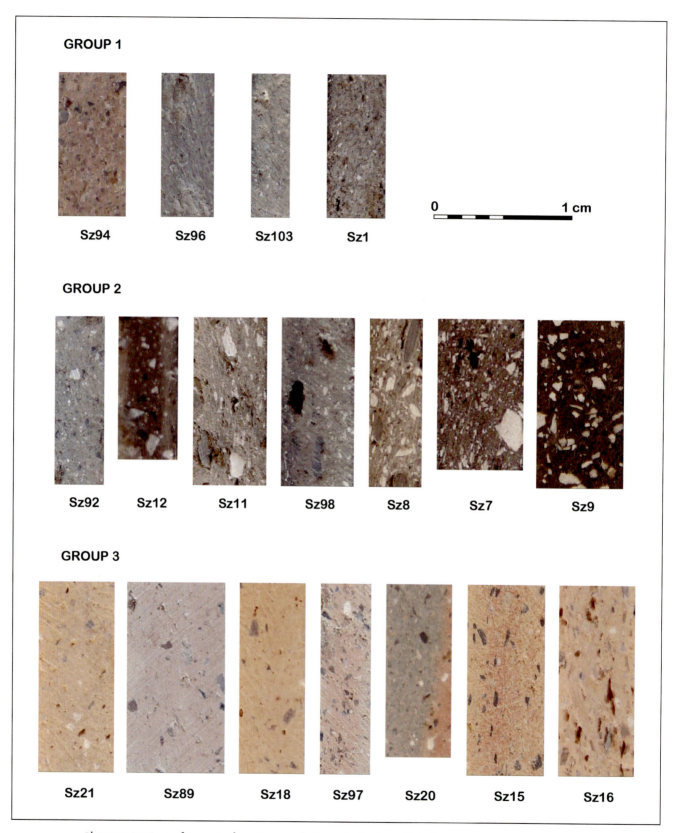

Plate 5.1: Sections of ceramics from Sarazm photographed using a digital microscope, Groups 1, 2, and 3. Photos and plates by B. Mutin.

CLASSIFICATION

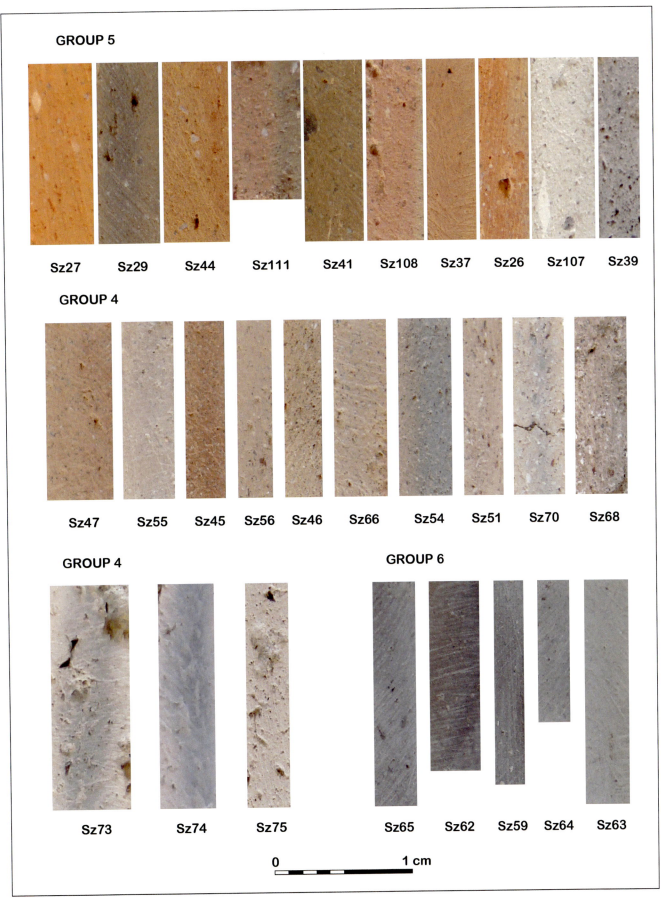

Plate 5.2: Sections of ceramics from Sarazm photographed using a digital microscope, Groups 4, 5, and 6.

that, in this case, inclusions were deliberately added and served as tempering agents. Furthermore, although certain forms are typical of Group 1, other forms were made with both Group 1 and 2 fabrics, having in both groups the exact same profiles. Lyonnet made the same observation and wrote in her description of what I have termed here Group 2 that (Lyonnet 1996, 22–23):

> Nous avons toutefois joint à ce groupe une série non négligeable de vases dont l'aspect extérieur est beaucoup plus soigné, entièrement polissé, généralement noir avec des taches brunes et dont la pâte est du même type que celle de la vaisselle de table polissée [Group 1] [...] La facture de ces derniers peut, dans certains cas, être extrêmement régulière et l'on observe alors sur leur face interne, non polissée, des stries parallèles très fines. Nous les avons classés ici et non dans le groupe précédent dans la mesure où leurs formes sont d'exactes répliques des vases de cuisine de facture grossière [(Group 2)], même dans leurs variantes. En fait, on constate souvent sur la céramique grossière de cuisine des traces de lissage, parfois très discret n'occasionnant qu'un contact doux au toucher, mais parfois plus net, voire très dense.

Groups 4 and 5 are finer materials with painted decorations. Group 6 consists of very fine, grey burnished ceramics. Group 7, which is mentioned in some of the tables and graphs relating to this chapter, is not a stylistic group but includes all misfired fragments found in Excavation VII.

I classified the vessel forms from each of these groups using metric measurements commonly employed to record vessel sizes, as well as metric ratios including the ratio RimD/MaxD, which distinguishes between open (RimD ≥ MaxD) and close (RimD < MaxD) forms and the ratio H/MaxD (or H/RimD in the case of open forms), which distinguishes between deep and shallow forms.

Below are presented the six stylistic groups and misfired fragments recovered from Excavation VII, their quantities, forms, and other attributes, as well as their parallels. Evidence for ceramic production at Sarazm and the functions of the ceramics from Excavation VII are then discussed in separate sections, as are their stratigraphic and spatial distributions as well as the cultural spheres they relate to.

## Quantities

The ceramic assemblage from Excavation VII includes 4991 sherds. This number includes 512 rims fragments, ninety-four base fragments, and nine vessels with complete profiles. To this number must be added eight complete vessels.[3] Rim fragments are usually used in ceramic analysis to provide an estimate of the Minimum Number of Individuals (MNI), i.e. the smallest possible number of vessels in a ceramic assemblage. In the present case, the MNI is equivalent to 529, corresponding to 512 rim fragments, eight complete vessels, and nine vessels with complete profiles. It however became apparent that by just considering these individuals certain types would be underrepresented or even not represented. This is particularly true for materials in Groups 4, 5, and 6. I therefore added to these 529 records forty-six diagnostic sherds (forty body fragments and six bases) that did not reassemble with any of the above-mentioned 529 records.[4] This brought the MNI to 575 records (Tables 5.1 and 5.8).

Out of these 575 vessels and vessel fragments, plain Group 1, 2, and 3 ceramics are together the most represented group (66.1 per cent), with Group 1 amounting to 40.9 per cent. Painted Group 5 is quite frequent, since it totals 28.3 per cent, whereas painted Group 4 and plain Group 6 represent 4 per cent and 0.7 per cent, respectively. Five misfired sherds were found in Excavation VII; they represent less than 1 per cent.

Table 5.1: Minimum Number of ceramic Individuals (MNI) from Sarazm Excavation VII and its distribution across the stylistic groups identified within this excavation.

| Stylistic group | Quantity | % |
| --- | --- | --- |
| Group 1 | 235 | 40.9 |
| Group 2 | 73 | 12.7 |
| Group 3 | 72 | 12.5 |
| Group 4 | 23 | 4.0 |
| Group 5 | 163 | 28.3 |
| Group 6 | 4 | 0.7 |
| Group 7 | 5 | 0.9 |
| **Total** | **575** | **100.0** |

---

[3] Although these complete vessels are today almost all in the Penjikent museum, I found in the archaeological base of Penjikent sherds that belong to them. These sherds amount to 183 fragments and are not included in the above-mentioned 4991 sherds.

[4] Although they could not be reassembled, the fabrics and painted decorations of five of these additional records, in Group 4, suggest that they might be part of the same ceramic individual.

## Groups 1 and 2

Groups 1 and 2 (Figs 5.1–5.2) are here described together for the reasons explained above that similar forms and manufacturing marks are observed between both groups and that the fabrics of some vessels appear to be transitional between these two groups. It is however important to remember that a clear distinction can generally be made between Groups 1 and 2, hence the definition of two separate groups of vessels.

Group 1 are ceramics with sand-tempered fabrics, with mineral inclusions usually less than 1 mm, mostly equivalent to fine to medium sand. These ceramics are black, grey, brown, buff, or red. Their surfaces are usually burnished (interior, exterior, or both surfaces). As Lyonnet pointed out, it seems that these ceramics were either burnished directly, or were slipped before they were burnished. The difference between the two is not always easy to make with the naked eye. Another observation she made is that the colours of the surfaces and sections of Group 1 material are highly variable, a variation which probably results from heterogenous firing conditions. Indeed, red vessels with black and buff patches on their surfaces, buff vessels with red and black patches, and black vessels with red and beige patches are observed (Lyonnet 1996, 20). Group 1 corresponds to Lyonnet's 'céramique de table polissée' as well as part of the types she defined as 'céramique de cuisine' (Lyonnet 1996, 80–81 figs 2–3, 83–85 figs 5–7, 101 fig. 23). It is the most common ceramic style at Sarazm. It is reported from all excavations and all periods. Parallels for these ceramics are mentioned at Tugai and Zhukov, two sites located west of Sarazm in Uzbekistan (Avanesova 1996; 2013; see **Chapter 1**). Vessels with burnished surfaces are well attested across Middle Asia during the Late Chalcolithic and Early Bronze Age periods, particularly in northern Iran and in the Caucasus, and were also recorded in south-eastern Iran (see Mutin 2013, 113–15 for a recapitulation). Closer to Sarazm, in addition to the material excavated at Tugai and Zhukov, Lyonnet found more specific parallels for vessels similar to Excavation VII Group 1 ceramics essentially in Turkmenistan between the mid-fourth and early third millennia BCE broadly speaking (Lyonnet 1996, 40–41). While these ceramics may be defined as local to Sarazm for the reason that they appear to be the most common types of vessels at this site, the parallels that Lyonnet noted and my own observation of the ceramic collection from Anau available at the Peabody Museum of Archaeology and Ethnology, Harvard University, have made it quite clear to me that they are connected to the Turkmen ceramic tradition between the Chalcolithic and Early Bronze Age periods.

Compared to Group 1, Group 2 is a coarser grey-to-black, and more rarely brown, ware. The mineral inclusions in its fabric are quite numerous and mostly of medium to very coarse sand/granule size, which means that some measure less than 1 mm and others are bigger than that. Also, in contrast to Group 1, white, angular (shell-like?) inclusions seem more common in Group 2 fabric. However, I recorded finer sherds in this style, which makes it difficult in some cases to distinguish Group 2 from Group 1. Furthermore, as noted above, the exterior surfaces of these vessels are sometimes burnished, like Group 1 material. Group 2 ceramics are often burnt and interpreted for this reason as kitchen ware, 'céramiques de cuisine' in Lyonnet's classification (Lyonnet 1996, 91–101 figs 13–23). These ceramics are well attested at Sarazm and are reported from all periods. As with Group 1, it seems that most parallels for Group 2 are in Turkmenistan (Lyonnet 1996, 44–45). The shell-like, or simply put, white, inclusions observed in some Group 2 vessels is reminiscent of Andronovo material as described at Tugai (Avanesova 1996, 122) and material relating to the Kel'teminar culture including material found at Sarazm (Lyonnet 1996, 27), as well as Early Bronze Age ceramics from Dali, Kazakhstan, in the IAMC (see the fabrics of the ceramics in Hermes et al. 2021, 359 fig. 8 c, d, e).

In Excavation VII, Group 1 is represented by 230 rim sherds, one complete jar, two vessels with complete profiles, and two bases, totalling 235 records (Table 5.1). Setting aside thirty-three fragments whose forms could not be determined, these records divided into seventy-six bowls, sixteen bowls or pots, six pots, forty hole-mouth jars, forty-four jars, eleven jars with out-flared rims, and nine necked jars. Group 2 consists of sixty-nine rim fragments and four bases, for a total of seventy-three records (Table 5.1). These records represent six bowls, sixteen bowls or pots, six pots, twenty-four hole-mouth jars, nine jars, and one necked jar, as well as eleven fragments whose forms are unknown. Each of these functional categories includes vessels with various profiles.

**Bowls, Pots, and Vats**

In this category is a series of bowls with everted walls and rims with essentially rounded or tapered lips (Pl. 5.3), save for one with a flattened lip (Pl. 5.3: no. 7). Another series consists of bowls with flattened lips

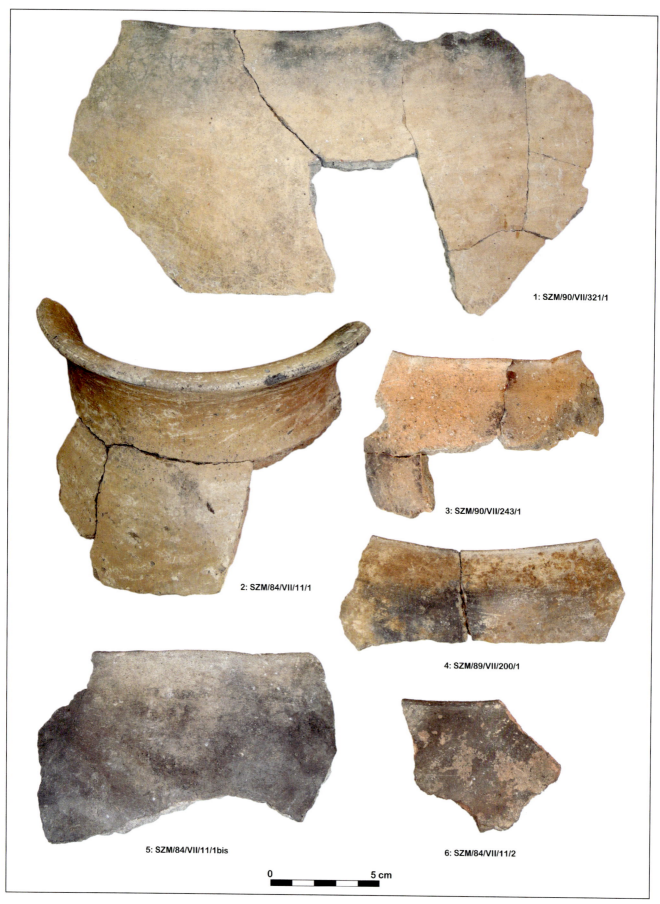

Figure 5.1: Sarazm, Excavation VII, Group 1 ceramics. Photographs and plate by B. Mutin.

Figure 5.2: Sarazm, Excavation VII, Group 1–2 ceramics.
Photographs and plate by B. Mutin.

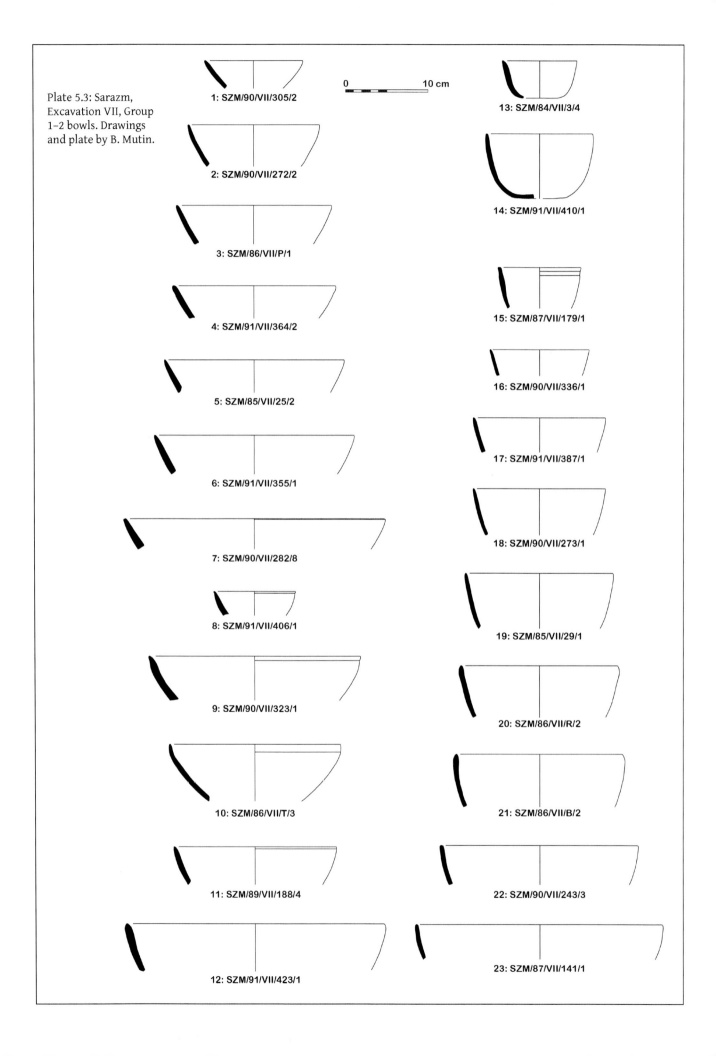

Plate 5.3: Sarazm, Excavation VII, Group 1–2 bowls. Drawings and plate by B. Mutin.

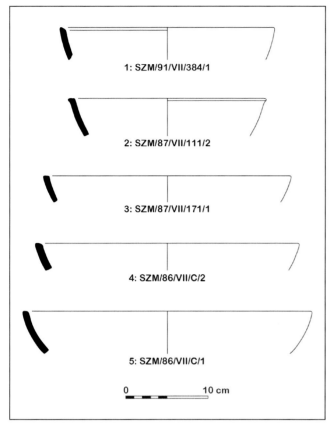

Plate 5.4: Sarazm, Excavation VII, Group 1–2 bowls. Drawings and plate by B. Mutin.

including horizontal lips, horizontal and slightly protruding lips, and oblique lips (Pl. 5.4). They have thicker walls on average than the vessels of the first series. Forms from both series vary as to the orientation of their walls and rims, with vessels being more everted than others and vessels with rims that are almost vertical (Pl. 5.3: no. 10). Differences are also observed regarding the morphologies of the walls and rims, with vessels that have straight walls and rims, whereas other have slightly more concave walls and rims. Altogether these ceramics have rim diameters ranging from 9 to 32 cm, although those with flattened lips and thicker walls are larger, with rim diameters between 25 and 35 cm.

The second major series includes bowls and pots with vertical, or near vertical, walls and rims. Since most fragments in this series consist of rim sherds, it is not always possible to tell whether these ceramics are bowls or pots. However, the profiles and smaller rim diameters of vessels such as Plate 5.5: nos 1–2 tend to show that they belong to bowls, whereas larger and thicker vessels with rim diameters of 35 cm and higher (and possibly those that are smaller too), such as Plate 5.5: nos 11–13, appear to be pots rather than bowls with lower H/RimD ratios. Altogether, these bowls and pots with vertical walls and rims have rim diameters ranging from 21.5 to 40 cm. Different types of lip profiles are observed, with lips that are rounded or slightly tapered (Pl. 5.5: nos 1–4), flattened lips (Pl. 5.5: nos 8–13), and flattened and slightly protruding lips (Pl. 5.5: nos 5–7).

The third series of forms consists of bowls and deep bowls with inverted rims, save for one vessel with a much larger rim diameter that is probably best defined as a vat (Pl. 5.6: no. 5). They are essentially open forms, although their rims are inverted. In this series are vessels with plain flat lips (Pl. 5.6: no. 5) and vessels with flattened lips that slightly protrude inward (Pl. 5.6: nos 2–4). One bowl is different in that its lip slightly protrudes outward (Pl. 5.6: no. 1). The walls of these vessels are concave. In this series are also vessels with rounded or tapered lips (Pl. 5.6: nos 6–9). Their walls can be concave (Pl. 5.6: nos 6–7), or, as is apparent on some exemplars, their lower portions can be straight and their profiles marked by a sharper inflexion, or even a carination, where the wall orientation changes (Pl. 5.6: nos 8–9). The rim diameters of these bowls and deep bowls with inverted rims are between 12 and 28 cm. The above-mentioned vat has a rim diameter measuring 44 cm.

**Jars and Hole-Mouth Jars**

In this category are closed forms with inverted upper walls (or shoulders) and rims. There is a thin line between some of the open forms with inverted rims described above and some of the jars presented in this section. Although these jars are generally closer forms, some profiles and types of lips are indeed similar to those observed in the above-described vessel category. Consequently, it is difficult to classify small rim fragments and tell whether they belong to one or the other categories. Group 1 and 2 jars include hole-mouth jars with lips that are rounded (Pl. 5.7: nos 6–10); tapered (Pl. 5.7: nos 1–5); flattened and oblique (Pl. 5.8); and flattened and protruding inward (Pl. 5.9); as well as jars with lips that are flattened (Pl. 5.10: no. 1); flattened and protruding outward (Pl. 5.10: nos 2–15); flattened, oblique, and protruding outward (Pl. 5.10: nos 16–21). Their profiles also vary regarding their walls, which can be straight or concave (e.g. Pl. 5.8: nos 1–5 vs nos 6–8). Their rim diameters range from 13 to 46 cm; most of them are larger than 25 cm.

110

5. CERAMIC VESSELS

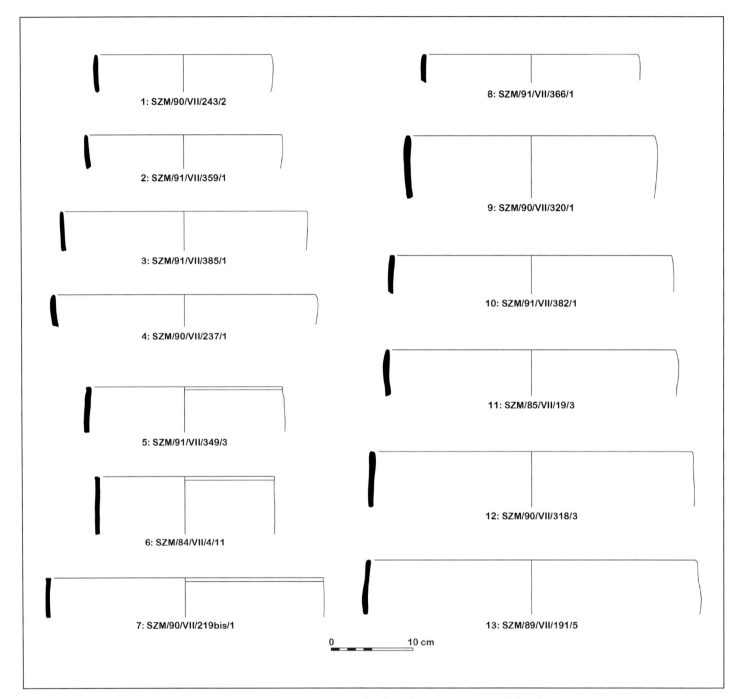

Plate 5.5: Sarazm, Excavation VII, Group 1–2 bowls and pots. Drawings and plate by B. Mutin.

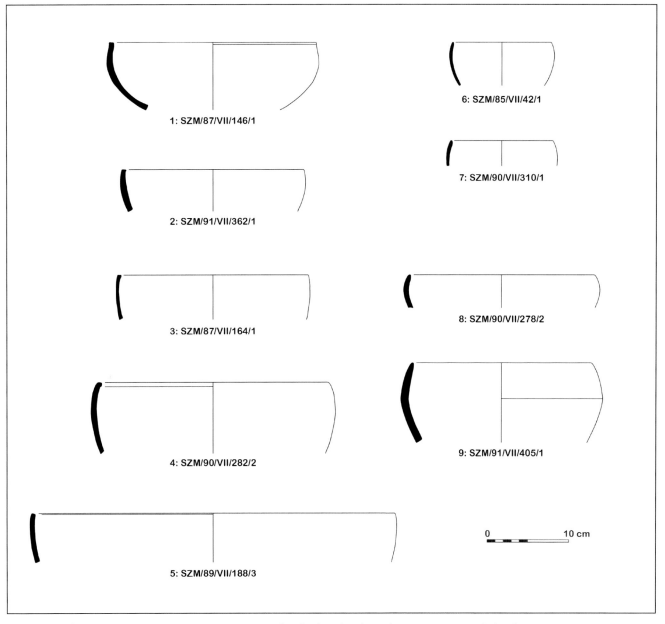

Plate 5.6: Sarazm, Excavation VII, Group 1–2 bowls, deep bowls, and vats. Drawings and plate by B. Mutin.

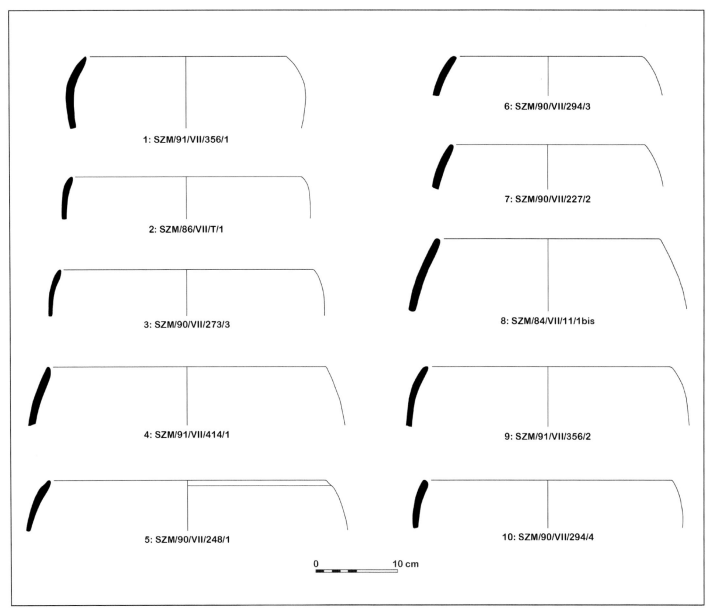

Plate 5.7: Sarazm, Excavation VII, Group 1–2 hole-mouth jars.
Drawings and plate by B. Mutin.

GROUPS 1 AND 2

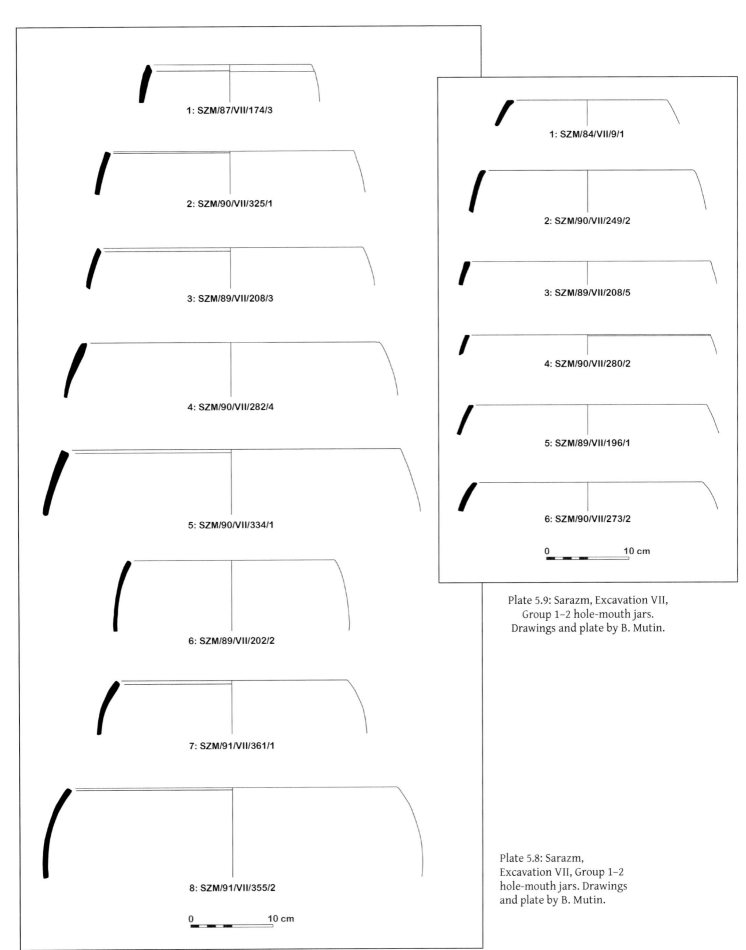

Plate 5.9: Sarazm, Excavation VII, Group 1–2 hole-mouth jars. Drawings and plate by B. Mutin.

Plate 5.8: Sarazm, Excavation VII, Group 1–2 hole-mouth jars. Drawings and plate by B. Mutin.

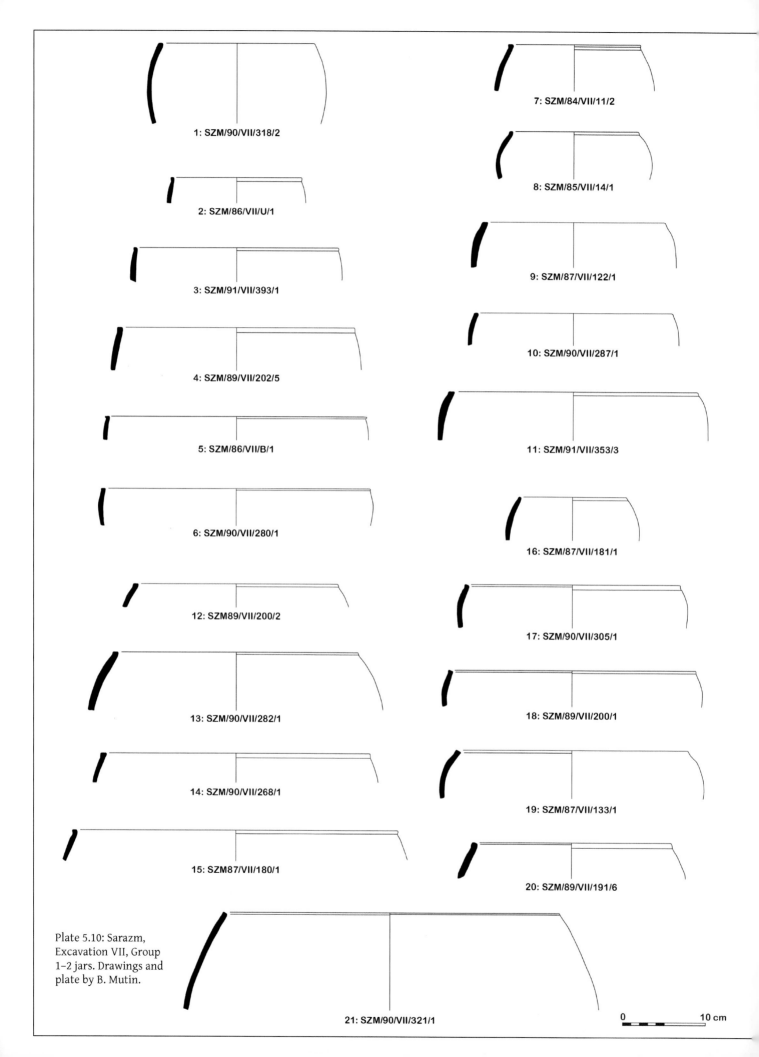

Plate 5.10: Sarazm, Excavation VII, Group 1–2 jars. Drawings and plate by B. Mutin.

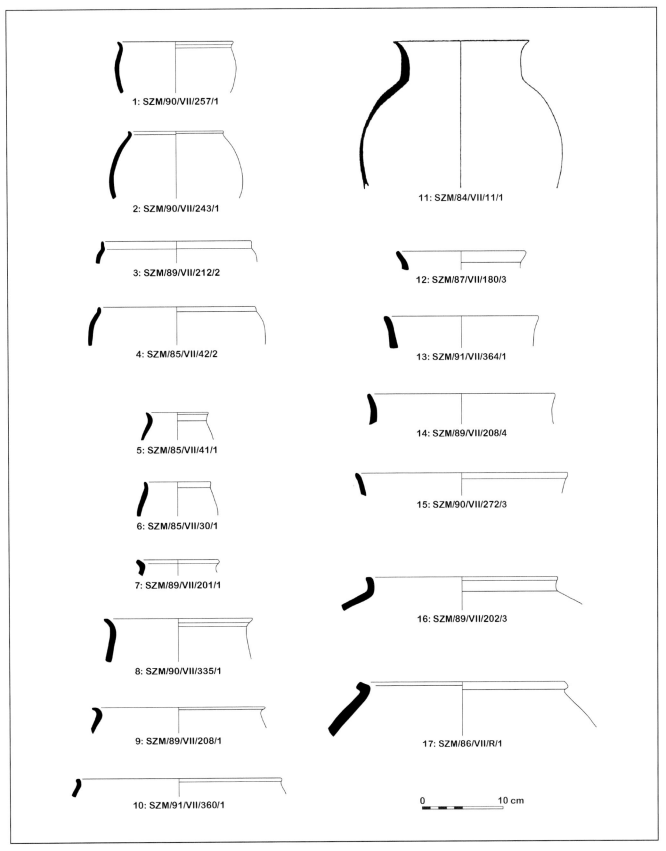

Plate 5.11: Sarazm, Excavation VII, Group 1–2 jars with out-flared rims and necked jars. Drawings and plate by B. Mutin, save for no. 11 by B. Lyonnet (R. Besenval archives).

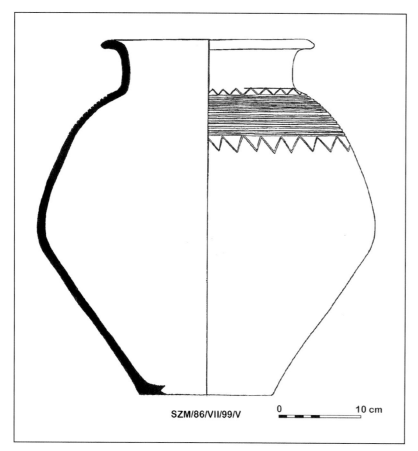

Plate 5.12: Sarazm, Excavation VII, Group 1 necked jar. Drawing by B. Lyonnet (R. Besenval archives).

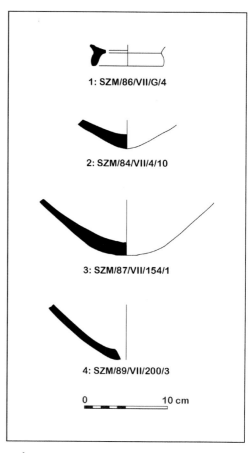

Plate 5.13: Sarazm, Excavation VII, Group 1–2 bases. Drawings and plate by B. Mutin.

### Jars with Out-Flared Rims and Necked jars

This category includes closed forms with out-flared rims or necks. The distinction between these two general types, which seems to be reliable in most cases, is based on the length of the portion added to the shoulder of the vessels. It is less than 1 cm and corresponds to an out-flared rim for the jars with out-flared rims, whereas it is more than 1 cm and may be defined as a neck for the necked jars. The latter are also usually closer forms. The rim diameters of these closed forms are between 7.5 and 26 cm, and different profiles are observed, with some vessels being closer than others. Also, some rims are more out-flared than others, while some are almost vertical (Pl. 5.11: nos 3–4). Lips are tapered, rounded, or flattened, and both vessels with concave walls and vessels with straight walls are observed.

One complete ceramic stands out as it is one of the few complete ceramics found in Excavation VII (Pl. 5.12; Figs 5.3–5.4). Its fabric is of Group 1 type. It is a necked jar, c. 42 cm tall and 41 cm wide, and with a rim diameter measuring 26 cm. In addition to being complete, this jar has the particularity that it bears an incised decoration on the exterior surface of its shoulder. This decoration consists of a series of horizontal, parallel, straight lines framed by two zigzag lines above and underneath it.

### Bases

Group 1 and 2 bases include three rounded bases and one pedestal base (Pl. 5.13). However, ceramics that are illustrated in previous publications such as in Isakov 1991 and Lyonnet 1996, as well as those that were excavated more recently (e.g. Mutin et al. 2020a, 25 fig. 3), suggest that Group 1 and 2 bases are usually flat.

### Parallels

As noted above, Group 1 corresponds to Lyonnet's 'céramique de table polissée' as well as part of the types she defined as 'céramique de cuisine' (Lyonnet 1996, 80–81 figs 2–3, 83–85 figs 5–7, 101 fig. 23), while Group 2

Figure 5.3: Sarazm, Excavation VII, Group 1 necked jar (SZM/86/VII/99/V). R. Besenval, edited by B. Mutin.

Figure 5.4: Sarazm, Excavation VII, Group 1 necked jar (SZM/86/VII/99/V), detail. R. Besenval, edited by B. Mutin.

ceramics are Lyonnet's 'céramiques de cuisine' (Lyonnet 1996, 91–101 figs 13–23). Groups 1 and 2 generally relate to Lyonnet's Types I,1–I,2; I,4–I,6; II,1–II,4; II,6–II,12; III,10–III,11; and III,13–III,17.

It is probably not necessary to detail all the results of the in-depth research Lyonnet conducted on the parallels for these ceramic types (Lyonnet 1996, 40–41, 44–45, 47). What is important to remember here is that most parallels for Groups 1 and 2 are in Turkmenistan where they seem to generally appear during the Namazga II Period and to be found during the Namazga III Period (Yalangach and Geoksyur periods). Lyonnet also found an exact parallel for the single complete Group 1 necked jar (#99/V). She writes (Lyonnet 1996, 49): 'Une forme exactement semblable, en céramique grise, provient de Kara-Depe, niveau IA [...] Elle ne porte pas de décor mais d'autres vases trouvés dans le même niveau ont un décor de lignes incisées horizontales droites ou en zig-zag.' This would date this necked jar to around 2900 cal. BCE according to Hiebert's chronology (Hiebert 2002, 28 fig. 2). Relationships are also noted for Groups 1 and 2 with Pakistan and Afghanistan for certain techniques and forms such as the slips observed on Group 1 material from Sarazm. They are generally consistent chronologically with the parallels noted with Turkmenistan (e.g. Mundigak III and Mehrgarh VI–VII). However, it is important to remember that some of the forms and fabrication techniques recorded on Group 1 and 2 ceramics from Sarazm are generic enough that they find equivalents over a very wide area and time across Middle Asia and probably beyond. In that sense, there is probably a risk of 'overdoing it', and it seems reasonable to perhaps limit the comparisons to materials that are chronologically consistent and culturally relevant in Turkmenistan. Nonetheless, the above-mentioned parallels with material described as Andronovo-related from Tugai, material relating to the Kel'teminar culture, and the Early Bronze Age ceramics from Dali in Kazakhstan probably need to be remembered.

## Group 3

Group 3 consists of ceramics with relatively coarse fabrics (Fig. 5.5). Mineral inclusions in their fabrics are quite numerous, although they are more sparsely distributed than in Group 1 material. They are essentially fine-medium to very coarse sand, which means that some are less than 1 mm while some are bigger. In contrast to Group 2 ceramics, white inclusions do not appear common in Group 3. The surfaces of these vessels are usually white-slipped or beige-slipped, while their sections are of cream or reddish yellow to pink colour. Vessels of this group have also been observed that are red and have a red slip. Group 3 material mostly consists of jars and large vats, corresponding to some of Lyonnet's 'céramiques de stockage' (Lyonnet 1996, 102–04 figs 24–26, 112–13 figs 34–35). However, it also includes additional, rarer types of forms, as is observed in Excavation VII and detailed below. Most of these ceramics are thicker than the rest of the ceramics from Sarazm; only a few Group 3 vessels that belong to these additional, unusual types of forms have thicknesses comparable to those of the rest of the production at Sarazm. Group 3 seems less abundant than Groups 1 and 2 but is not rare at Sarazm. Parallels for this type of ceramic product are in Turkmenistan, essentially consistent chronologically with those for Groups 1 and

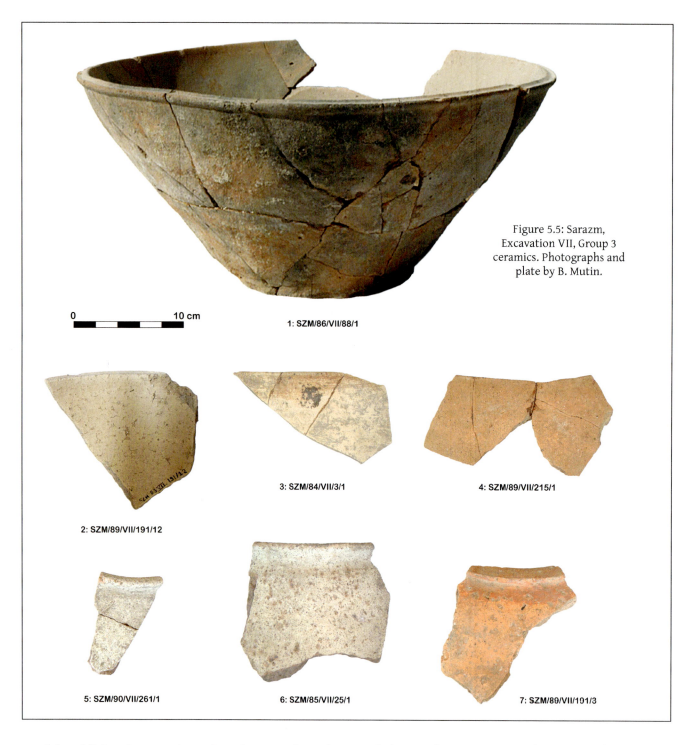

Figure 5.5: Sarazm, Excavation VII, Group 3 ceramics. Photographs and plate by B. Mutin.

2, while additional comparisons have been made with material in Afghanistan including at Taluqan in the north-east and further south at Mundigak and Said Qala Tepe (Lyonnet 1996, 45, 47).

In Excavation VII, the seventy-two Group 3 records consist of one complete vessel and seventy-one rim fragments (Table 5.1). With only one vessel fragment whose form could not be determined, these records divide into twenty-six vats, two bowls, one bowl or pot, six hole-mouth jars, nine jars, four jars with out-flared rims, and twenty-three necked jars.

**Vats**

Group 3 vats are among the largest ceramic types recovered from Excavation VII and more generally Sarazm (Pl. 5.14). Their rim diameters range from 28 to 48 cm. Their profiles are typically 'V' shaped with everted walls

GROUP 3

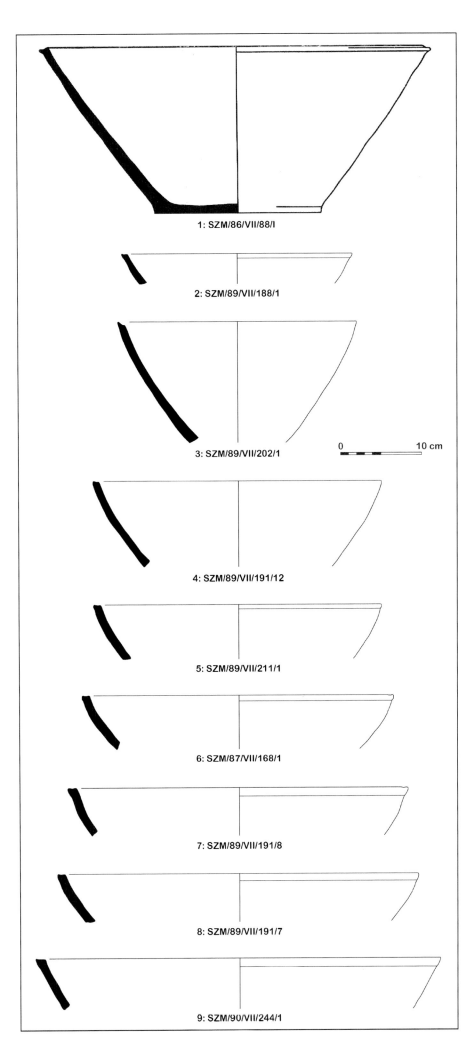

Plate 5.14: Sarazm, Excavation VII, Group 3 vats. Drawings and plate by B. Mutin, save for no. 1 by B. Lyonnet (R. Besenval archives).

119

and rims, which are straight or slightly concave. Their lips are flat with a groove in their centre that is parallel to the rim circumference. Their bases are flat; this is at a minimum what the single complete vessel of this type found at Sarazm shows (Pl. 5.14: no. 1).

### Hole-Mouth Jars/Bowls with Incurving Rims

These vessels have rim diameters between 21 and 43 cm (Pl. 5.15). The smallest one (Pl. 5.15: no. 1) may correspond to a bowl rather than a jar, whereas the opposite seems true for the other ones. They are characterized by incurving rims and flattened lips, although variation exists between vessels with slightly incurved rims and those with very incurved rims. The lips are oblique, with the exception of one ceramic whose lip is horizontal and has a groove in its centre, like the above-described vats (Pl. 5.15: no. 6). This ceramic is slightly different than most Group 3 hole-mouth jars/bowls with incurving rims also for the reason that its rim is less incurved and bears a horizontal red painted band. A single hole-mouth jar (Pl. 5.15: no. 7) may be considered a separate type of hole-mouth jar because it is much thicker than the rest of them and its wide, *c.* 1.55 cm lip is both flat along its exterior circumference and oblique along its interior circumference.

### Jars with Out-Flared Rims and Necked jars

This category groups different types of closed shapes with rim diameters between 17 and 40 cm (Pl. 5.16). They include vessels with various profiles, rims, and lips, as well as various RimD/MaxD ratios, which means that some are more open (Pl. 5.16: nos 1–3) than others. Some have necks (e.g. Pl. 5.16: nos 4–6), whereas others have what seems to be best defined as out-flared rims (e.g. Pl. 5.16: nos 1, 10). The rims are usually everted, although examples with inverted rims are observed (Pl. 5.16: nos 4, 6). The lips are either rounded, flattened, or tapered. A single ceramic bears a painted decoration, which consists of two horizontal, red bands, one applied over the exterior surface of its neck and upper part of its wall, and one applied over the interior surface of its neck (Pl. 5.16: no. 4).

### Rare Forms

Group 3 rare forms consist of one bowl (Pl. 5.17: no. 1; RimD = 22 cm) and three jars including two jars with out-flared rims (Pl. 5.17: no. 2; RimD = 15 cm; Pl. 5.17: no. 3; RimD = 12.5 cm) and one jar with a long neck (Pl. 5.17: no. 4; RimD = 16 cm).

### Parallels

Save perhaps for the vats, since Group 3 ceramics are plain material with relatively generic profiles and most of them consist of rim fragments, it is rather difficult to find precise parallels for them. Another issue that Lyonnet pointed out is that, in contrast to painted ceramics, such types of vessels often do not make it into archaeological publications. Yet, Lyonnet wrote important observations that are worth mentioning here again. She found parallels for the vats in Turkmenistan at Kara-Depe, although these parallels are not illustrated and are described as larger, with 60 cm rim diameters. She also mentioned parallels at Tureng Tepe Periods IIIB–IIIC2 (Deshayes 1969, 143 fig. 8) as well as in Afghanistan, at Mundigak and Said Qala Tepe in the south and Taluqan in the north-east (Lyonnet 1981, 63 fig. 5 a). She emphasized that this type of form is present between Afghanistan and Pakistan but is usually not illustrated (Lyonnet 1996, 47, Type V,1). Lyonnet reported parallels in Turkmenistan for vessels that are classified here as Group 3 hole-mouth jars, although these parallels are painted material with a fine fabric (Lyonnet 1996, 47, Type IV). Perhaps more convincing are plain sherds from Taluqan. Their profiles are indeed similar, and their lips are flattened and oblique, like those of the hole-mouth jars described here (Lyonnet 1981, 63 fig. 5 d–g). Lastly, Sarazm Excavation VII Group 3 necked jars and jars with out-flared rims are included in Lyonnet's Types III,1 to III,3. She found equivalents for these types in Turkmenistan in contexts dating to between Namazga Periods II and IV, including material from Ilgynly-Depe and Geoksyur that she observed in collections. The comparisons she mentioned for these vessels with material in Afghanistan and Pakistan seem vaguer (Lyonnet 1996, 45, Types III,1, III,2, III,4).

## *Group 4*

Group 4 ceramics are fine, mineral-tempered vessels. No inclusions are usually visible; when they are, they measure less than 1 mm and are sparsely distributed. These vessels are buff to red. Their surfaces are well smoothed and are burnished in some cases. Their forms essentially include bowls that are painted black and red, and sometimes yellow, on their exterior surfaces. Their decorations include typical stepped motifs, metopes, and

GROUP 4

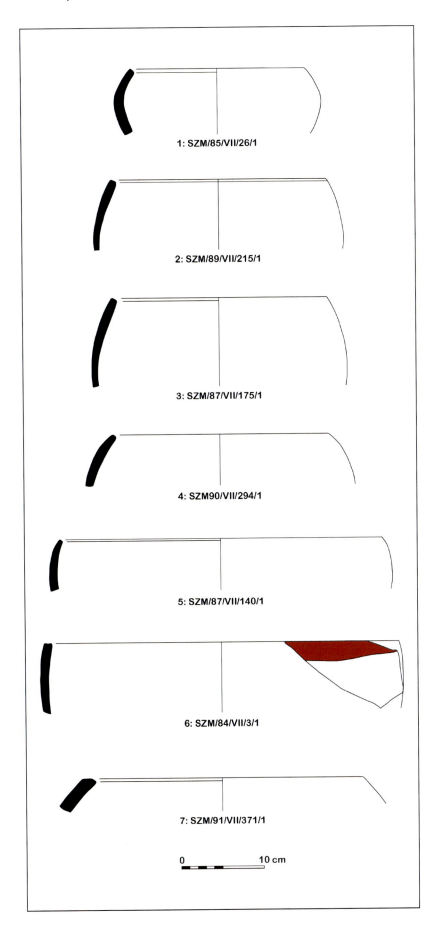

Plate 5.15: Sarazm, Excavation VII, Group 3 hole-mouth jars/bowls with incurving rims. Drawings and plate by B. Mutin.

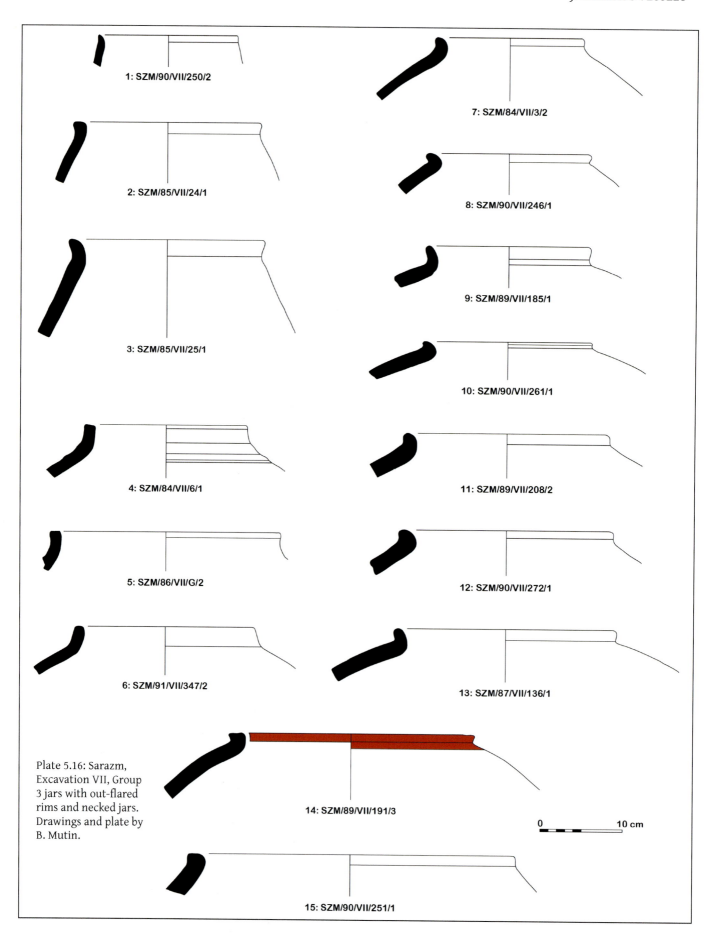

Plate 5.16: Sarazm, Excavation VII, Group 3 jars with out-flared rims and necked jars. Drawings and plate by B. Mutin.

gridded patterns. Group 4 vessels correspond to types included within Lyonnet's 'céramiques de table polissées' and 'céramiques de table non polissées' (Lyonnet 1996, 82 fig. 4, 85 fig. 7 no. 7, 90 fig. 12 nos 3–4). This material seems less frequent than Groups 1, 2, 3, and 5 at Sarazm, where it seems to characterize Sarazm Periods II and III (Lyonnet 1996, 57–58). Group 4 painted ceramics have evident parallels in Turkmenistan between the mid–late fourth and early third millennia BCE, as well as in Iran, southern Afghanistan, and Pakistan where vessels with similar motifs have been recorded (Lyonnet 1996, 41–42).

In Excavation VII, the twenty-three Group 4 ceramics are limited to eight to ten vessels whose shapes could be reconstructed: three bowls, two goblets or deep bowls, one to three jars, and two necked jars (Pl. 5.18; Fig. 5.6; Table 5.1). The thirteen remaining sherds counted as ceramic individuals mostly consist of small-size fragments.[5] These ceramics are virtually all black and red painted. A cream to buff colour slip is observed on some of them. The two goblets or deep bowls have vertical walls and rims as well as tapered lips. One of them (Pl. 5.18: no. 5) has a 13 cm rim diameter. They also are both bichrome, black and red painted. The bowls have everted rims and tapered lips (Pl. 5.18: nos 1–3). Two are black and red painted, while the fragment of the third one (Pl. 5.18: no. 2) has red paint over both its interior and exterior surfaces. Its rim diameter as well as that of one of the other two that could be measured (Pl. 5.18: no. 1) are 18 cm. The jar (Pl. 5.18: no. 6) appears to be globular in shape. Its diameter is about 14 cm at what seems to be its neck, or the part of its shoulder that connects to its rim. It is painted black and red over a pinkish cream to buff colour slip on its exterior surface. Two additional body fragments (Fig. 5.6: nos 10–11) may belong to this jar or to very similar jars. The best-preserved exemplar of the two necked jars (Pl. 5.18: no. 4) has a 28 cm rim diameter. It is painted black over a red painted background. The second necked jar (Fig. 5.6: no. 9) is also black and red painted.

The most common and clearly recognizable painted motif on Group 4 ceramics is a crenelated or stepped motif that consists of a triangle with black painted crenelated sides (Fig. 5.6: nos 1, 3–4, 8–11). What seems to be a chevron motif was observed in one instance (Fig. 5.6: no. 6), while another motif consists of a solid red Maltese cross with a black contour (Fig. 5.6: no. 7), also observed on a single fragment. This cross is framed within a larger one. These painted decorations clearly relate to the Namazga ceramic tradition in Turkmenistan. The crenelated motif finds exact equivalents within Namazga III Period assemblages (e.g. Kircho 1981, 103 fig. 1: Altyn 10, Geoksyur 1; Dupont-Delaleuf 2016, 93 fig. 3 at Ulug-Depe), dating to between the mid–late fourth and early third millennia BCE and probably more to after 3100 BCE according to Hiebert (2002, 28 fig. 2; 2003, 7 tab. 1.1, 21).[6] A bowl with a similar motif was also found in the foundation period of Shahr-i Sokhta, Period I (Bonora et al. 2000, 506 fig. 8; Salvatori and Tosi 2005, 282 fig. 2 no. 5), dating to 3150–2750 cal. BCE (Salvatori and Tosi 2005, 289–90 figs 12–13). A bowl with the same type of decoration is reported from Mundigak Period III6, and a sherd with a crenelated motif that resembles this decoration was found in Period III4 at the same site (Casal 1961, fig. 55 no. 81, fig. 59 no. 117). South of the Hindu Kush, this type of decoration is part of the ceramic style known as Quetta Ware, more specifically its solid variant. This style has been identified between southern Afghanistan (including at Mundigak) and Anjira in Pakistan (see de Cardi 1983, 44 fig. 6; Petrie and Shaffer 2019, 199). The cross motif painted on one ceramic from Excavation VII (Fig. 5.6: no. 7) is also part of the decorative repertoire known in Turkmenistan during the Namazga Period, including within Namazga Period III assemblages (Kircho 1981, 103 fig. 1).

## Group 5

Group 5 ceramics are fine, mineral-tempered material (Fig. 5.7). No inclusions are usually visible; when they are, they most often measure less than 1 mm and are sparsely distributed in comparison to the above-described Groups 1 and 2. Their fabrics are in this regard similar to those of Group 4 material. They also do not always appear very different from those of Group 3; with the naked eye, the coarser Group 5 individuals are even almost comparable, or close, to the finest Group 3 examples. Group 5 ceramics are essentially of buff to red colours, although a few grey sherds are observed. Their surfaces are usually well smoothed, and some specific parallel marks which result from smoothing/shaping the vessel using a tool while the vessel was rotating, are

---

[5] The fabrics and decorations of four sherds suggest that they may be part of the same vessel as one of the above-mentioned necked jars.

[6] Different dates have been provided for Namazga III Period: e.g. 3500–3000 cal. BCE (Dupont-Delaleuf 2016, 92 fig. 2); 3200–2800 cal. BCE (Vidale 2017b, 9 tab. 1); 3200–2700 cal. BCE (Olson 2020, 102 tab. 3); see **Chapter 1**.

Figure 5.6: Sarazm, Excavation VII, Group 4 ceramics. Photographs and plate by B. Mutin.

GROUP 5

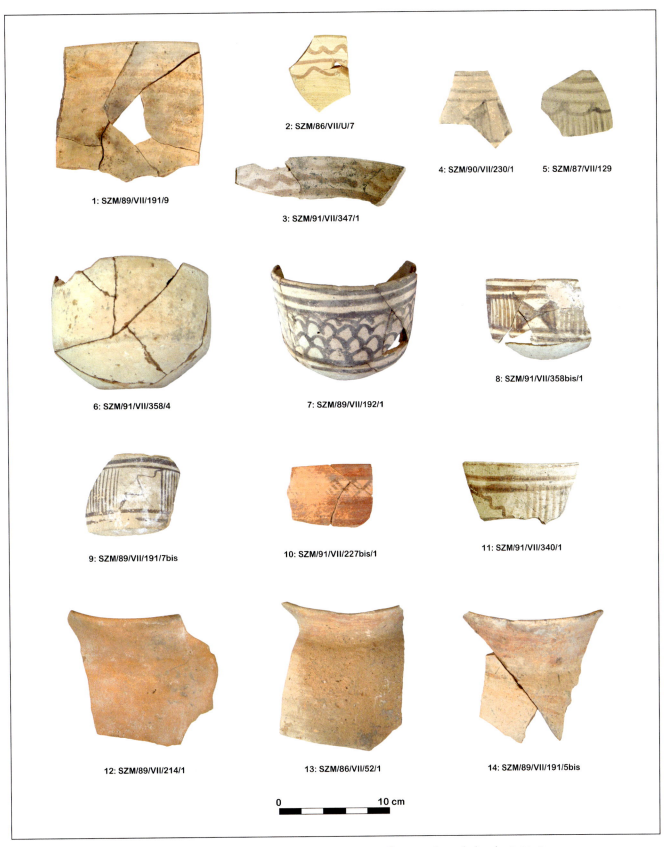

Figure 5.7: Sarazm, Excavation VII, Group 5 ceramics. Photographs and plate by B. Mutin.

5. CERAMIC VESSELS

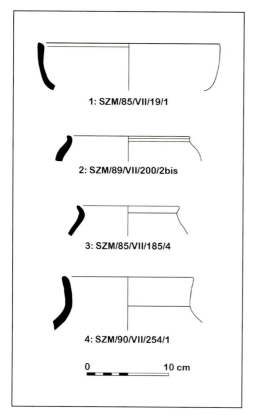

Plate 5.17: Sarazm, Excavation VII, Group 3 rare forms. Drawings and plate by B. Mutin.

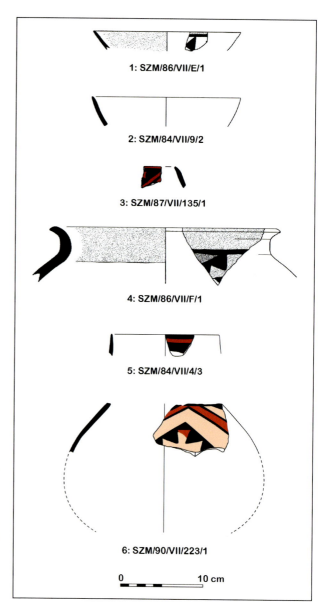

Plate 5.18: Sarazm, Excavation VII, Group 4 ceramics. Drawings and plate by B. Mutin, save for nos 1 and 4 by B. Lyonnet (R. Besenval archives).

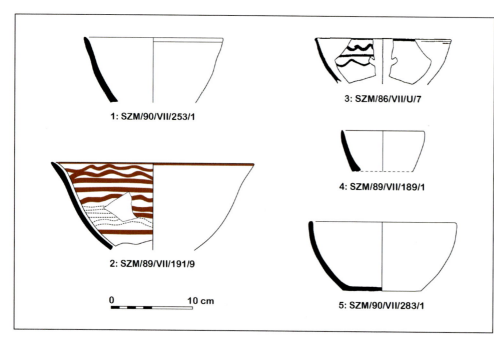

Plate 5.19: Sarazm, Excavation VII, Group 5 bowls. Drawings and plate by B. Mutin, save for no. 3 by B. Lyonnet (R. Besenval archives).

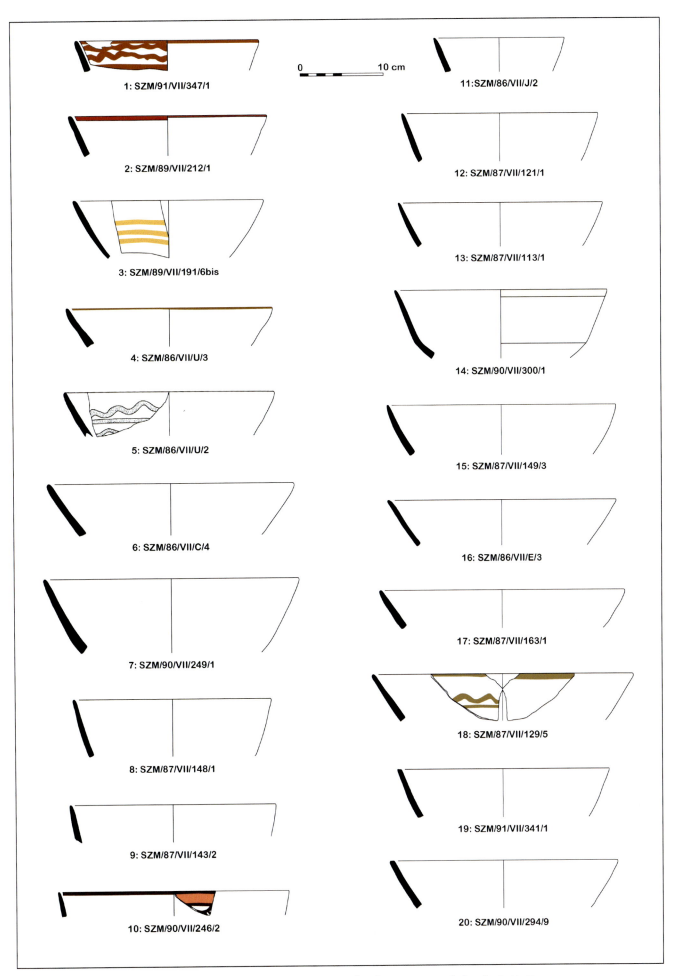

Plate 5.20: Sarazm, Excavation VII, Group 5 bowls. Drawings and plate by B. Mutin, save for no. 5 by B. Lyonnet (R. Besenval archives).

often observed on their exterior surfaces (Mutin and Razzokov 2014, 130 fig. 7).[7] Their forms include bowls, carinated bowls, carinated deep bowls/goblets, jars, and necked jars. They are painted red, brown, or black. Their decorations essentially consist of metopes, parallel straight and/or wavy lines, and festooned hatched bands on bowls and deep bowls/goblets, as well as bands and vegetal motifs on necked jars. In many cases, the paint has partly or almost completely disappeared from the surfaces of these vessels, which makes it likely that many of the Group 5 plain sherds with a fine fabric of buff to red colour found in Excavation VII were originally part of painted vessels. Group 5 corresponds to ceramics included in Lyonnet's 'céramiques de table non polissées' and 'céramiques de stockage' (Lyonnet 1996, 86–89 figs 8–11, 105–06 figs 27–28). They are relatively common at Sarazm, although they have not been recovered in quantities comparable to those of Groups 1 and 2. Lyonnet concluded that they appeared at this site essentially during Period III and were found in greater amounts during Period IV (Lyonnet 1996, 57–60).[8] Most parallels for these ceramics are between southern Afghanistan and Pakistan prior to the Indus Civilization, dating from the mid–late fourth to the mid-third millennia BCE, although some parallels are noted in Turkmenistan too (Lyonnet 1996, 42–44, 46). For instance, parallels for some of the painted motifs and forms of Group 5 ceramics are at Mundigak Periods III and IV. The necked jars resemble Kot-Dijian jars, which are typical of Pakistan during the first half of the third millennium BCE (see Mutin and Razzokov 2014; Jarrige et al. 2011a).

In Excavation VII, the 163 Group 5 ceramic individuals consist of four complete vessels, seven with complete profiles, 133 rim fragments, and nineteen body sherds (Table 5.1). Save for eleven sherds that could not be assigned a form, Group 5 divides into fifty-seven bowls, thirty-eight deep bowls or goblets, one jar, and fifty-six necked jars. These ceramics are painted. The decorative themes and their location on the vessels are usually specific to each functional category. Plain vessels are also observed. However, as mentioned above, although it remains possible that plain vessels with fabric and forms similar to those of the painted ones were made, I suspect that this plain material corresponds to painted vessels whose decorations disintegrated.

## Bowls

Group 5 bowls in Excavation VII usually have rim diameters ranging from 20 to 32 cm (Pl. 5.20). Most have a 'V' profile with everted walls and rims that are straight or slightly concave. Variation is observed regarding the lips, which are tapered, rounded, or flattened. Only one carinated bowl was observed (Pl. 5.20: no. 14), although it is certainly possible that carinated bowls were more numerous and that the carinated portions of these vessels ended up not being part of the ceramic fragments found in Excavation VII. Five vessels deserve specific mention as they are slightly different from most Group 5 bowls. One (Pl. 5.19: no. 2) is a bowl with an inflexion on the upper part of its wall, below its rim, making this part slightly convex and the whole profile of this vessel look like a 'tulip'. Another bowl (Pl. 5.19: no. 1), of smaller rim diameter than the above-described ceramics (17 cm), also has an inflexion on its upper wall, although, in this case, the wall and rim are less everted and its rim less out-flaring. It has an incised line just below the lip, parallel to the rim. A third bowl (Pl. 5.19: no. 4) is also different in that it is much smaller (10 cm in rim diameter) and its wall and rim are slightly less everted than most Group 5 bowls. The fourth bowl (Pl. 5.19: no. 5) has a different profile, closer to a 'U' profile, in that its rim is vertical and its upper wall is less everted than other Group 5 bowls. Its rim diameter is 18 cm.

As for the decorations of Group 5 bowls, they chiefly consist of series of straight and wavy lines parallel to the rim, painted on their interior surfaces. A line is usually also painted over the lip down onto the interior and/or exterior surface. It is perhaps worth mentioning that the decoration is generally not very well executed.[9] The colours as they appear today on the vessels include black, red, brown, and orange. One vessel (Pl. 5.20: no. 14) has a whitish band painted over the exterior surface of its rim, and in only one case did I observe an exterior decoration. It consists of a festooned hatched band (Pl. 5.20: no. 10). As noted above, this type of material has many parallels at Sarazm, more specifically in Soundings 11–11A, where many bowls were found (Mutin and Razzokov 2014, 128 fig. 6). In these soundings, however, many vessels of this type bear a painted decoration on their exterior surfaces, whereas only one such bowl (Pl. 5.20: no. 10) was recorded in Excavation VII. Yet,

---

[7] Such marks are often observed on ceramics in the regions located south of the Hindu-Kush.

[8] Rare examples are noted in the previous Period II.

[9] This observation brings to mind examples of ceramics from Mundigak Period IV1 (Casal 1961, fig. 75 no. 252a) and Shahr-i Sokhta (Vidale et al. 2014).

GROUP 5

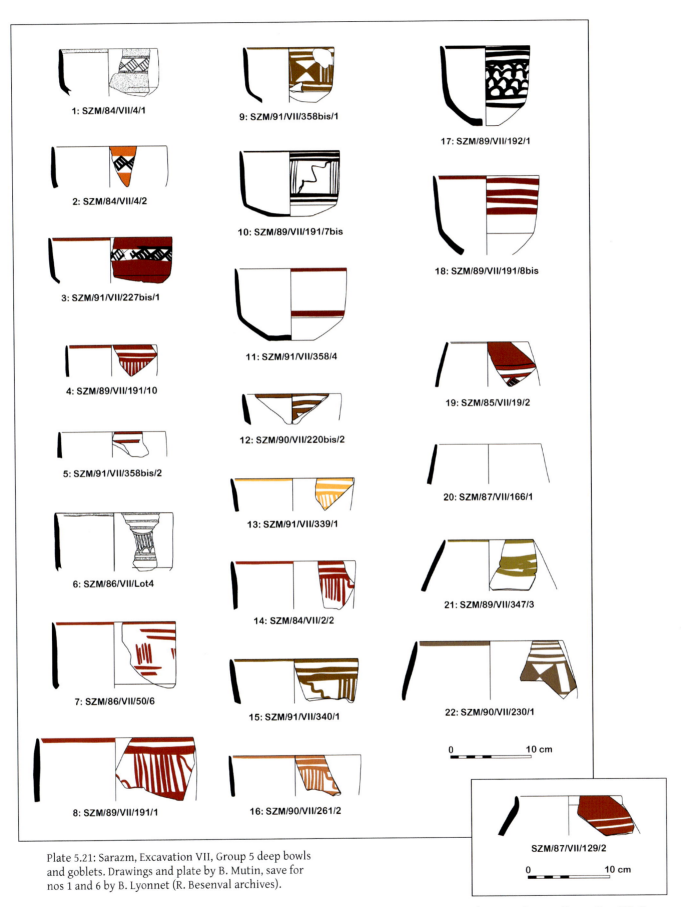

Plate 5.21: Sarazm, Excavation VII, Group 5 deep bowls and goblets. Drawings and plate by B. Mutin, save for nos 1 and 6 by B. Lyonnet (R. Besenval archives).

Plate 5.22: Sarazm, Excavation VII, Group 5 jar. Drawing and plate by B. Mutin.

Figure 5.8: Sarazm, Excavation VII, Group 5 necked jar (SZM/86/VII/102/VIII). R. Besenval, edited by B. Mutin.

again, considering the profiles of Group 5 bowls in this excavation, I suspect that part of them are bowls with exterior decorations whose paint disintegrated.

### Deep Bowls/Goblets

The deep bowls or goblets have rim diameters between 11 and 19 cm (Pl. 5.21; Fig. 5.6). The most complete vessels show that some are deeper than others and that at least three ranges of H/RimD ratios exist: 0.85 (Pl. 5.21: no. 17), 0.63–0.64 (Pl. 5.21: nos 10–11), and less than 0.60 (based on Pl. 5.21: no. 3). Most vessels have vertical and straight walls and rims and a carination located below mid-height of the vessels that connects to the base through an everted lower wall. The walls are in some cases slightly concave. They may also be slightly everted instead of vertical, while a few ceramics have inverted walls and rims (Pl. 5.21: nos 19–22). The lips are tapered, save for a few examples with flattened lips (Pl. 5.21: nos 16, 19–20). The bases of the complete exemplars are flat.

The decorations of these deep bowls or goblets consist of friezes or panels painted on their exterior surfaces, with a line painted over the lip down onto the interior surface. The paint colours are black, brown, red, and orange. Bichrome black and red ceramics are observed. The motifs used to fill these friezes and panels are: hatched diamonds; parallel, horizontal thick lines; metopes filled with parallel vertical lines or one oblique wavy line; festooned hatched bands; scales; and solid hourglasses.

Figure 5.9: Sarazm, Excavation VII, Group 5 necked jar (SZM/86/VII/102/VIII). R. Besenval, edited by B. Mutin.

### Jar

One ceramic stands out as a single type of jar (Pl. 5.22). It is different from the vessels described above as it is a close shape and is different from the necked jars described below in that it has a shorter neck and is not as close a form as these necked jars. The exterior surface of its neck and upper wall is decorated with a red painted horizontal band, while two red lines, or one line and one band, are painted below.

### Necked jars

The necked jars are ceramics with rims diameters between 11.5 and 21 cm (Pl. 5.23). The four complete vessels of this type found in Excavation VII have the following measurements: #101/VII (Pl. 5.23: no. 1; Fig. 5.10): RimD = 11.6 cm; H = 17.9 cm; MaxD = 21.8 cm; #102/VIII (Pl. 5.23: no. 8; Figs 5.8–5.9): RimD = 15.2 cm; H = 26.3 cm; MaxD = 38 cm; #89/II (Pl. 5.23: no. 7; Fig. 5.11): RimD = 12.4 cm; H = 18 cm; MaxD = 25.9 cm; and #90/III (Pl. 5.23: no. 2; Fig. 5.12): RimD = 16.4 cm; H = 30.6 cm; MaxD = 34.5 cm. Many of the other necked jar fragments from Excavation VII fall within the same ranges of dimensions, although vessels with smaller and larger sizes are present. These four complete vessels delineate two main categories of necked jars, with one deeper than the other; their H/MaxD ratios are: 0.88 (#90/III), 0.82 (#101/VII), 0.69 (#102/VIII), and 0.69 (#89/II). Their profiles essentially consist in each case of an everted,

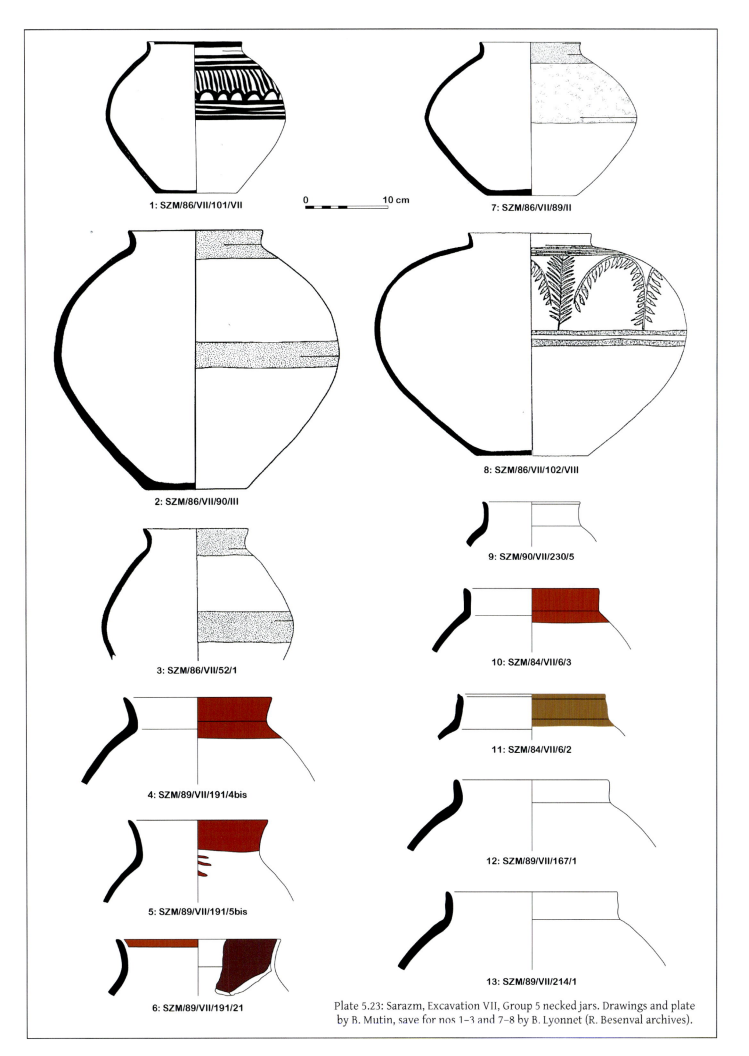

Plate 5.23: Sarazm, Excavation VII, Group 5 necked jars. Drawings and plate by B. Mutin, save for nos 1–3 and 7–8 by B. Lyonnet (R. Besenval archives).

5. CERAMIC VESSELS

Figure 5.10: Sarazm, Excavation VII, Group 5 necked jar (SZM/86/VII/101/VII). R. Besenval, edited by B. Mutin.

Figure 5.11: Sarazm, Excavation VII, Group 5 necked jar (SZM/86/VII/89/II). R. Besenval, edited by B. Mutin.

straight lower wall joining an inverted, concave upper wall at about mid-height of the vessel. The upper wall is attached to a short neck with an everted rim. The lip is usually tapered. Rounded and flattened lips are however also observed. The bases of these vessels are flat. Certainly, variations exist with, for instance, a change in the orientation of the wall placed lower than at its mid-height (e.g. Pl. 5.23: no. 3), and necks being higher than usual (e.g. Pl. 5.23: nos 4–6) and vertical instead of being everted (e.g. Pl. 5.23: nos 9–10, 13), or even inverted (Pl. 5.23: no. 11). Also, necked jar #89/II (Pl. 5.23: no. 7) shows that some of these vessels can be almost biconical, with a carination, or a sharper angle, at the junction between the lower and upper walls.

These necked jars are painted. The most frequent decoration consists of a wide horizontal band, painted over the rim, neck, and upper part of the upper wall as well as one wide horizontal band painted at the junction between the lower and upper walls. A band or line is also observed on the interior surface of some vessels. It usually covers just the lip but may also extend onto the neck. There is usually no motif between the two bands on the exterior surface, and it seems that the lower band is not always present (e.g. #89/II: Pl. 5.23: no. 7). In one case, however, a few parallel, short lines, which are part of a motif that is not possible to determine,[10]

Figure 5.12: Sarazm, Excavation VII, Group 5 necked jar (SZM/86/VII/90/III). R. Besenval, edited by B. Mutin.

were painted below the upper band (Pl. 5.23: no. 5). Two ceramics have different decorations. One (#102/VIII: Pl. 5.23: no. 8) has parallel, horizontal lines instead of bands on its neck and body, and the space in between is filled with vegetal motifs that look like fern. The second one (#101/VII: Pl. 5.23: no. 1) also has lines instead of bands. The space in between is filled with a festooned hatched band, a motif similar to that observed on deep bowls or goblets from Excavation VII (see above) as well

---

[10] Perhaps a vegetal motif similar to the one painted on ceramic #102/VIII (Fig. 5.23: no. 8) as well as on sherds from Soundings 11–11A (Mutin and Razzokov 2014, 125 fig. 3 nos 24–28)?

as on deep bowls or goblets and bowls from Soundings 11–11A (Mutin and Razzokov 2014, 128 fig. 6). The colour of these decorations is typically red or red-to-brown, while black seems less frequent.

**Parallels**

Lyonnet found a number of parallels for Group 5 ceramics, which correspond to Types I,11–I,14 and III,5–III,6 in her classification. I am repeating here some of the comparisons she mentioned (Lyonnet 1996, 42–43, 46) and adding some observations that more specifically relate to the Excavation VII material as well as parallels that I noted when I studied the ceramic assemblage from Soundings 11–11A. What needs to be remembered is that, although certain forms and decorations of Group 5 material find parallels in Turkmenistan, as Lyonnet pointed out, this group seems mostly connected to the regions south of Sarazm, including between southern Afghanistan and Pakistan, where Mundigak is a prominent reference. It is probably important to mention, however, that not all Group 5 vessels find exact equivalents beyond Sarazm. This remark is true for certain profiles such as those of the carinated bowls, as well as for certain motifs in the way they are represented and laid out (see Mutin and Razzokov 2014).

Keeping this in mind, the decorations made of parallel, straight and/or wavy lines on Sarazm Excavation VII Group 5 bowls have parallels at Mundigak Periods II and III (Casal 1961, fig. 51 no. 37, fig. 52 nos 43, 47). The painted straight lines are reminiscent of those observed in the Quetta Valley on ceramics such as Kechi Beg Red Paint (Fairservis 1956, 262 fig. 54B), Faiz Mohammad Grayware, and Quetta Red-brown-on-Dark Slip (Fairservis 1956, 264 fig. 55A–B). Decorations with straight lines were also recorded in the Loralai Valley on Kili Ghul Mohammad Black-on-Red Slip (Fairservis 1959, 366 fig. 64a, 287 no. 19, 408 nos 254–58) and in Shahr-i Sokhta Period I (Amiet and Tosi 1978, fig. 13; Biscione 1984, 77 fig. 10.14). At the latter site were also found decorations made of straight and wavy lines (Amiet and Tosi 1978, fig. 13), combinations that are observed in the Quetta Valley on Quetta Ware (Fairservis 1956, 281 and particularly 284 no. 145), at Dabar Kot in the Loralai Valley on Faiz Mohammed Ware (Fairservis 1959, 312 fig. 20k), and at Periano Ghundai in the Zhob Valley on Periano Painted ceramics (Fairservis 1959, 340 fig. 45).

Motifs comparable to the festooned hatched bands observed on one bowl, deep bowls/goblets, and one necked jar from Excavation VII were reported from Mundigak Periods III and IV1–2 (Casal 1961, fig. 54 no. 67, 58 no. 111, 67 no. 201–201a, 70 no. 214, 74 no. 246, 89 no. 393), as well as Period IV3 (Casal 1961, fig. 96 no. 441), Said Qala Tepe on Quetta Black-on-red Surface and Quetta Black-on-buff Surface (Shaffer 1978, fig. 24 nos 2–3, 25 no. 3), and Deh Morasi Ghundai on Morasi Black-on-buff Surface (Dupree 1963, 91 nos 91–92). Parallels are also present in the Quetta Valley on a black-on-red slip ware (Fairservis 1956, 314 no. 508), Quetta Ware (Fairservis 1956, 283 nos 134–38, 301 no. 350), and Kechi Beg Ware (Fairservis 1956, 275 no. 46); at Periano Ghundai in the Zhob Valley on Periano Painted (Fairservis 1959, 338 fig. 43b, 410 no. 281); at Togau on a creamed-slipped red ware which was compared to Nal-type material of Anjira Period IV (de Cardi 1983, 60 fig. 13 no. 17); at Barra Kapoto on a cream-slipped red ware (de Cardi 1983, 64 fig. 15 no. 6); at Siah Damb Period II, phase III, including on a carinated bowl (de Cardi 1965, 148 fig. 15 nos 52, 56); at Zari Damb on a cream-slipped ware assigned to Anjira Late Period III–Early Period IV (de Cardi 1983, 70 fig. 18 no. 21); at Singen Kalat on an orange-red slipped red ware assigned to Anjira Period III (de Cardi 1983, 78 fig. 22 no. 12), and even at Amri, c. 1500 km south of Sarazm (Casal 1964, fig. 55 no. 149, fig. 56 no. 156, fig. 61 no. 179, fig. 65 no. 225).

The metopes that characterize Group 5 deep bowls/goblets bring to mind decorations on ceramics from Mundigak Periods III–IV2 (Casal 1961, fig. 53 no. 59, fig. 56 no. 89, fig. 58 nos 108, 113, fig. 60 no. 133, fig. 66 no. 192, fig. 67 nos 198–198a, fig. 89 nos 383–383a), on Quetta Ware from the Quetta Valley (Fairservis 1956, 283 no. 142, 303 no. 371, 315 nos 515, 523, 254 fig. 48), Periano Painted from Periano Ghundai in the Zhob Valley (Fairservis 1959, 338, fig. 43 g, j–l, n), a Red-on-Red Slip ceramic from Rana Ghundai in the Loralai Valley (Fairservis 1959, 401 nos 398–410), ceramics from Nausharo Period IC (Jarrige et al. 2011b, 221 fig. 2 no. 22), ceramics from Mehrgarh Periods IV/V (C. Jarrige et al. 1995, 443 fig. 9.13 b), Periods V/VI (C. Jarrige et al. 1995, 497 fig. 10.29 a), and Period VI (C. Jarrige et al. 1995, 122 fig. 1.11 a, 123 fig. 1.12 k, 158 fig. 2.20 c, d, f, 161 fig. 2.23 n), as well as a goblet from Amri Period ID (Casal 1964, fig. 62, 206).

The scale pattern on ceramic #192/1 (Pl. 5.21: no. 17) is reminiscent of decorations from Amri Period ID (Jarrige et al. 2011b, 263 fig. 22 nos 7, 9), although the scales, or loops, are upside down on the examples from this site and the shapes of the vessels bearing them are not the same. Scale or loop motifs are observed on ceramics recorded between southern Afghanistan and

Pakistan dating to between the late fourth and mid-third millennia BCE. They are often combined with lines (e.g. from Mundigak Periods III and IV1: Casal 1961, fig. 57 no. 102, fig. 59 no. 123, fig. 83 no. 306a; from Pakistan: de Cardi 1983, 54 fig. 10 no. 18, 70 fig. 18 no. 6, 72 fig. 19 nos 7–8; from Mehrgarh Period VII: C. Jarrige et al. 1995, 129 fig. 1.18 j). However, I have found no exact equivalent for ceramic #192/1.

As far as the profiles of Group 5 open forms are concerned, the profiles of the vessels outside of Sarazm that bear decorations similar or comparable to those of Group 5 material are not always exactly the same. Parallels for the bowls are most often within the range of generic resemblances. Deep bowls/goblets generally comparable to those from Excavation VII Group 5 are widely observed between Afghanistan and Pakistan between the mid-late fourth and mid-third millennia BCE, including carinated vessels. Examples from Mundigak are worth mentioning, where the exemplars from Period III include ceramics with profiles apparently closer to those from Sarazm than those of Period IV1 (Casal 1961, fig. 53 nos 50–57, fig. 56 no. 89, fig. 58 no. 113, fig. 59 nos 124, 126–28, fig. 82 nos 295, 303, fig. 87 no. 363, fig. 89 nos 383–87). This type of form was also reported from Pakistan including from Mehrgarh Periods IV/V to VII (C. Jarrige et al. 1995, 122 fig. 1.11 a, 123 fig. 1.12 k, 127 fig. 1.16 l, m, n, 130 fig. 1.19 d, 158 fig. 2.20 c, d, f, 161 fig. 2.23 l, m, n, 171 fig. 2.33 b, 443 fig. 9.13 b, e, f, 497 fig. 10.29 a, b, c) and Zari Damb (de Cardi 1983, 70 fig. 18 nos 24–30). Many deep bowls/goblets from plundered sites in Pakistan were recently published by Franke and Cortesi (2015). This material includes forms similar to those recorded at Sarazm, including vessels with flat bases, as well as analogous decorations such as friezes filled with hatched diamonds, scale patterns, and metopes (although the motifs in the metopes are not the same as those observed at Sarazm). These vessels are monochrome and polychrome. Franke and Cortesi date most of them to 3300–3100 cal. BCE and ascribe the brackets of 3500–3200 cal. BCE, 3300–2900 cal. BCE, and 3100–2800/2700 cal. BCE to a part of them. Although the same type of form continued into the 3100–2800/2700 cal. BCE period, the main style seems in this period mostly different and now corresponded to the Nal horizon style (see Franke and Cortesi 2015). It is probably worth mentioning that these recently published deep bowls/goblets from Pakistan have flat bases, like Group 5 open forms from Sarazm Excavation VII, whereas, at Mundigak, ring-bases were recorded on bowls and deep bowls/goblets. Similarly, Excavation VII, and to a greater extent, Sarazm, is missing clear diagnostics from Mundigak Periods III-IV such as those illustrated in Casal 1961, plates XXIXB, XXXB, and XXXI-XXXIII, including typical pedestal vessels, as well as the typical pear-shaped beakers which are characteristic of the first half of the third millennium BCE at this site and at Shahr-i Sokhta (Salvatori and Vidale 1997, 89–90 figs 92–93, 109 fig. 130, 120 fig. 153, 136–37 figs 181–82).

As for Group 5 necked jars, their best parallels seem to be between southern Afghanistan and Pakistan too, including at Mundigak Periods III-IV2, Mehrgarh Period VII, in the Quetta Valley (Quetta Ware), and at Anjira Periods III-IV. The comparisons Lyonnet pointed out for this type of material include a jar from Mundigak, decorated with a painted band over its neck and upper wall, a type that was recorded from Period III5 to Period IV2 (Casal 1961, fig. 75 no. 249; Lyonnet 1996, 46). Yet, one should admit that the profile of this jar is slightly different from those of the necked jars from Sarazm Excavation VII Group 5. Jars with painted bands were also found in the Quetta Valley (Mian Ghundai Dark Rim: Fairservis 1956, 267 fig. 57) and are reminiscent of the early Harappan Kot Diji jars or related types that were recorded in the first period of this site, as well as at sites such as Mehrgarh Period VII, Nausharo Period I, Mundigak Period IV, Harappa Periods I-II, and Shahr-i Sokhta Period II (Lyonnet 1996, 46; see J.-F. Jarrige et al. 2011a, 17 fig. 9; Salvatori and Tosi 2005, 285; Cortesi et al. 2008, 14–15). Additional examples were reported from the northern valleys of Pakistan at Ghalagai in the Swat Valley, Sarai Khola Periods IA-II in the Taxila Valley, and Rehman Dheri and Gumla further to the south (Stacul 1969, 53; Mughal and Halim 1972, 38–39, 48 figs 18–22; Durrani et al. 1995, 83). However, as I expressed elsewhere (Mutin and Razzokov 2014, 130),

> although the painted bands of the jars from Sarazm bond these vessels to the Kot Diji-type jars, their forms and decorations are usually not exactly the same as those of the southern vessels. Some profiles are comparable to some of the Kot Diji-type jars, but not to all of them, and, most importantly, the surface treatments and decorations of the latter are in most cases different and not represented at Sarazm. For example, the closest comparanda at Sarai Khola are mostly red-slipped and black painted while the other Kot Dijian jars from this site include features (profiles, painted designs, slips, and mud-coating) [Mughal and Halim 1972, figs 17–22; 84–88] not observed at Sarazm. There are however examples of jars at Lewan in the Bannu Basin, with red bands and no slip, that tend to better resemble those from Sarazm [Allchin et al. 1986, sheet

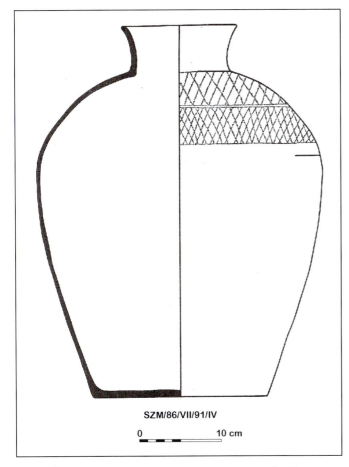

Plate 5.24: Sarazm, Excavation VII, Group 6 necked jar. Drawing by B. Lyonnet (R. Besenval archives), plate by B. Mutin.

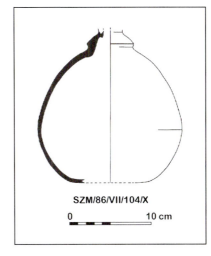

Plate 5.25: Sarazm, Excavation VII, Group 6 necked jar. Drawing by B. Lyonnet (R. Besenval archives), plate by B. Mutin.

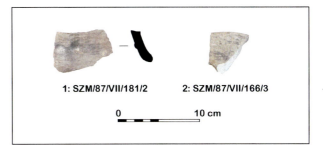

Plate 5.26: Sarazm, Excavation VII, Group 6 sherds. Photographs and plate by B. Mutin.

1 no. 5, sheet 12 no. 11], although we have not seen the sherds in original. According to the investigators of the site, the contexts of these materials are connected to the second period at Rehman Dheri [Allchin et al. 1986, 110; Durrani et al. 1995, 83].

It is perhaps also worth mentioning that certain vegetal motifs painted on Mundigak ceramics from Periods III–IV2 (Casal 1961, fig. 53 no. 52, fig. 56 no. 83, fig. 65 no. 185, fig. 69 no. 209, fig. 93 nos 413, 417) bring to mind the painted decoration of necked jar #102/VIII (Pl. 5.23 no. 8), although they are not designed the same way. The same remark seems valid for the vegetal motifs that are reported from the Quetta Valley on Quetta Ware (Fairservis 1956, 306 nos 414–15, 307 no. 422), in the Loralai Valley at Dabar Kot on sherds of Kechi Beg Polychrome (Fairservis 1959, 352 fig. 57 l), in the Zhob Valley at Periano Ghundai on a black-on-brown ware (Fairservis 1959, 336 fig. 41 n), and on a canister from Shahr-i Sokhta Period I (Cortesi et al. 2008, 12 fig. 4 no. 4).

Lastly, it is important to recall here ceramics that were collected on the surface of six sites in the Taluqan Plain of north-eastern Afghanistan. Lyonnet, who studied this material, determined that part of this material resembles vessels that I have included here in Group 5 and their parallels dating to between the mid-fourth and mid-third millennia BCE in southern Afghanistan and Pakistan including at Mundigak and Said Qala Tepe (Lyonnet 1981; 1997). The profiles of some of the bowls and necked jars from this region indeed look similar to those recorded in Group 5 (Lyonnet 1981, 63 fig. 4).

## Group 6

This group consists of four very fine, grey ceramics that are unusual within the context of Excavation VII and very rare at Sarazm (Table 5.1). They include one complete vessel, one almost complete vessel, and two sherds. They are briefly presented individually here. The first one (Pl. 5.24; Figs 5.13–5.14) is a fine necked jar that has a 14 cm rim diameter and is *c.* 44 cm high and 35 cm wide. This ceramic is essentially grey with a few buff to pink patches on its surface. It has a streak-burnished decoration on its shoulder that consists of two horizontal cross-hatched bands (Lyonnet 1996, 114 fig. 36 no. 4). The second one (Pl. 5.25; Fig. 5.15) is a fine necked jar that is missing its neck. It is *c.* 18 cm high without the neck and 18 cm wide. It is grey with a few patches of buff-pink colour on its surface. Its exterior surface is burnished (Lyonnet 1996, 114 fig. 36 no. 5). Additional sherds were found in Excavation VII that may belong to this jar. The third Group 6 record (Pl. 5.26: no. 1) is a body sherd that belongs to a fine, grey ware. Its exterior surface is burnished and has knobs. The fourth one (Pl. 5.26: no. 2) is a rim fragment of a fine grey necked jar. Its interior and exterior surfaces appear to be burnished, although both are worn out.

A few grey vessels that generally compare to this material are reported from Excavations II and IV at Sarazm. Parallels for these vessels have been established with material in Turkmenistan which are chronologically consistent with those found for the above-described other stylistic groups from Excavation VII (Namazga III Period), whereas other parallels with ceramics in Iran point at more recent periods (Lyonnet 1996, 48–49, Types VI,1, VI,2, VI,6, 114 fig. 36 nos 1–3, 115 fig. 37 no. 1). These ceramics in Iran are fine grey burnished material from sites such as Tureng Tepe, Tepe Hissar, and Shah Tepe (Lyonnet 1996, 48–49; Besenval and Isakov 1989, 14). The streak-burnishing decoration on #91/IV (Pl. 5.24) has equivalents at Tureng Tepe Periods IIIB through IIIC2 (e.g. Deshayes 1969, 145 figs 19–20), Tepe Hissar Periods IIIB–IIIC (Schmidt 1937, 179 H3820, 180, 182) and Shah Tepe Periods IIb–IIa (Arne 1945, 185, 188 figs 364–65, 189 figs 367–68, 190–92 figs 370–74, 193 fig. 378, 194 fig. 380, 195 figs 382–83, 197 fig. 390, 199 fig. 394, 200 fig. 398, 201 figs 400–02, 204 fig. 408, 207 figs 413–14; Gürsan-Salzmann 2016, 287 fig. 6.15). The neck of #91/IV also has parallels at Tureng Tepe (Deshayes 1969, 148 fig. 38). Similarly, the form of #104/X (Pl. 5.25) is comparable to jars found at Tepe Hissar (Schmidt 1937, 179 fig. 105) and Tureng Tepe (Besenval archives). At Tepe Hissar, they are characteristic of Period IIIB, although they were recorded in Period IIIA too. Interestingly, Lyonnet noticed that a comparable type of form was found at Mundigak Period IV1, although the vessels in question are at this site painted and not burnished grey material (Casal 1961, fig. 71 nos 217–19). Lastly, the above-mentioned knobbed fragment (Pl. 5.26: no. 1) is also faintly reminiscent of ceramics from Shah Tepe (Arne 1945, pls XLIII, XLV, and LXIII).

These parallels with Tepe Hissar and Tureng Tepe would generally place these ceramics between Early Namazga V and Early or Late Namazga VI Periods, between the mid-third and mid-second (or possibly later) millennia BCE (see Olson 2020, 158 tabs 3.6–3.7).

The parallels with Shah Tepe IIb–IIa are consistent with this dating, although Period IIb began before (Olson 2020, 277 tabs 5.1a–5.1b, 278 tab. 5.2; Gürsan-Salzmann 2016, 268–69 tab. 6.1).

## Group 7: Misfired Fragments

Five misfired ceramic fragments were found in Excavation VII (Table 5.1). All five are overfired and warped body sherds (Fig. 5.16). One (#156/1) belongs to Group 3. The four others (#192/4bis, #228/3, #234/3, and #348/2) belong to Group 5.

## Evidence for Ceramic Production at Sarazm

The five misfired fragments from Excavation VII suggest that ceramic making was taking place in or not very far from the areas exposed within this excavation, although no pottery kiln or any other vestiges were found in or nearby Excavation VII that suggest pottery making. I have been able to find the original location of only two of these five fragments. One is from Level IV1 Room 2 and the second one is from Level IV2 Room 8. It is probably worth mentioning that a large hearth paved with stones (H2) was identified right outside of Room 8, although this structure yielded no clue that may suggest that it may have been used for firing pottery. One kiln was found in Excavation IX, c. 100 m south-west of Excavation VII. The ceramics collected in this excavation, including apparently inside this structure, include material similar to Excavation VII Groups 4 and 5. Two additional pottery kilns were documented in Excavations III and VI, and one is mentioned in Excavation IV (Besenval and Isakov 1989, 9; Razzokov 2005; 2008, fig. 36, pl. 1; F. Razzokov 2016, 125–26, 185 fig. 10, 204 figs 34–35, 217–20 figs 48–52). A large firing structure found in Excavation II was also interpreted as a pottery kiln (see F. Razzokov 2016, 182 fig. 7). Having cleared this structure again while I was excavating Excavation XVI, located nearby, I now find this interpretation more dubious in this case; it seems to me that what was interpreted as the chamber entrance may be just one of the numerous pits that were dug into the level this structure belongs to.

# FUNCTIONS OF THE VESSELS

Figure 5.14: Sarazm, Excavation VII, Group 6 necked jar (SZM/86/VII/91/IV), detail. R. Besenval, edited by B. Mutin.

Figure 5.13: Sarazm, Excavation VII, Group 6 necked jar (SZM/86/VII/91/IV). R. Besenval, edited by B. Mutin.

Figure 5.15: Sarazm, Excavation VII, Group 6 necked jar (SZM/86/VII/104/X). R. Besenval, edited by B. Mutin.

## Functions of the Vessels

Considering the above-mentioned ceramic MNI (less the misfired fragments) and putting together generally coarser Group 1 to 3 ceramics on the one hand and the finer, painted vessels of Groups 4 and 5 on the other hand, one observes that the former groups total twice as many records (380) as the latter (190). A functional distinction is apparent between the different stylistic groups from Excavation VII, with groups that include various vessel forms and groups that are limited to specific forms and functions. Groups 1 and 2 include vessels that seemingly were used to cook, serve, and present food and probably also store and perhaps transport foodstuff or other things. Functionally, Group 2 may be distinguished from Group 1 in that it contains more cooking vessels, whereas Group 1 contains more service vessels. Goblets or drinking vessels are however missing in both these two groups. Group 3 seems more clearly more dedicated to storage and/or transport. The function of Group 4 vessels is difficult to assess considering the limited number of fragments relating to this group

Figure 5.16: Sarazm, Excavation VII, misfired ceramic fragments. Photographs and plate by B. Mutin.

Table 5.2: Minimum Number of ceramic Individuals (MNI) from Sarazm Excavation VII and its distribution across the functional categories identified within this excavation (NA = Not Available).

| Form | Quantity | % | % (- NA) |
|---|---|---|---|
| Bowl | 144 | 25.0 | 28.5 |
| Deep bowl/goblet | 40 | 7.0 | 7.9 |
| Bowl/pot | 33 | 5.7 | 6.5 |
| Pot | 12 | 2.1 | 2.4 |
| Vat | 26 | 4.5 | 5.1 |
| Hole-mouth jar | 70 | 12.2 | 13.9 |
| Jar | 66 | 11.5 | 13.1 |
| Jar with out-flared rim | 15 | 2.6 | 3.0 |
| Necked jar | 94 | 16.3 | 18.6 |
| Misfired | 5 | 0.9 | 1.0 |
| NA | 70 | 12.2 | |
| Total | 575 | 100 | 100 |

found inside Excavation VII. One may just note that food and beverages were probably presented in vessels of this group, while the jar fragments suggest storage and/or transport. Group 5 is restricted to very limited types of vessels that served for food and beverage presentation as well as storage and/or transport. Group 6 appears to be associated only with storage and/or transport.

Tables 5.2, 5.3, and 5.4 show classifications of Excavation VII stylistic groups and forms according to their functional categories and purported functions. These classifications are in Tables 5.2 and 5.3 established on the basis of the 575 records corresponding to Excavation VII ceramic MNI, less seventy fragments whose form could not be reconstructed and five misfired fragments. This classification should be considered an approximation since, for instance, it remains possible that a part of Group 1 and 2 hole-mouth jars or Group 1 jars with out-flared rims were used to store stuff, and not for cooking, that Group 1 to 3 bowls/pots were rather used to store and transport things than for food service, or that Group 1 jars with out-flaring rims were used to serve stews and soups. Additionally, Group 3 vats may have had a function different from transport and/or storage. Keeping this in mind, this classification suggests that 43.4 per cent of the vessels were used to serve food and beverages, 28.2 per cent to 32.6 per cent were used for cooking, and 24 per cent to 28.4 per cent were used to store and/or transport foodstuff, liquids, or other things. One parameter that needs to be remembered to appreciate these percentages is that, as a rule, more fragile and more mobile vessels tend to be renewed more often than thicker and less mobile ceramics. For this reason, it seems logical to expect in archaeological assemblages retrieved from habitat deposits that vessel fragments such as bowl and goblet fragments will be more numerous than sherds from storage jars (see Mayor 1994).[11] Another parameter is that repeated exposure to fire fragilizes vessels (see Arnold 1985, 153). With regard to this, Groups 1 and 2 include ceramics with walls that appear to be prone to cracks or breaks. This fragility is even more remarkable in the cases of large Group 1 and 2 vessels that have walls very thin relative to their sizes. These cases, which are not uncommon, are so remarkable that I wondered in many instances how some of these large size containers with such thin walls could have lasted or could even have been carried without breaking.

Lastly, it is probably important to recall the unique collection of eight complete ceramics recovered from Level IV1. They were found inside the rooms of the building located between sq. I14–15 and K14–15 (Besenval and Isakov 1989, 14–16). This exceptional discovery was made because this building burnt for some unknown reason and was abandoned when this happened or soon after. Its occupants left behind them their stuff or a part of it, including these ceramics. All eight vessels appear to be storage and/or transport vessels.

## Stratigraphic Distribution of the Ceramics

In this section, I present and discuss elements of the stratigraphic and spatial distribution of Excavation VII ceramics. Great caution should be exercised since, as already mentioned in **Chapter 3**, I have not found certain archives where the locations and descriptions of many archaeological contexts must have been reported. Furthermore, information relative to the archaeological contexts of many ceramics is missing in available archives. Consequently, I have been able to pinpoint on a plan or against the stratigraphic sequence of Excavation VII only 310 records, which is a little more than half of the 575 records corresponding to the ceramic MNI used in this ceramic study. Similarly, of the 4991 sherds that comprise the Excavation VII assemblage I have been able to locate 3029 sherds, to which should be added the complete vessels. However, most

---

[11] This would also explain why ceramics such as storage vessels would not evolve stylistically as fast as vessels that are more mobile.

of the missing data is from field seasons 1990–1991.[12] As such, if my interpretation of the archives is correct, which is that Besenval mainly worked in sq. J16–17, K16–17, L16–17, M16–17, and half of N16–17 during these field seasons, this would mean that these 310 records essentially correspond to the totality of the material that was exposed within the main excavated area, that is between sq. I11 and M15. Although this certainly is good news considering the difficulties I have experienced with the archives, the data and results presented in this section should probably be considered trends rather than absolute results. Furthermore, it also remains possible that materials from separate archaeological layers were bagged together during the excavation. Such a mishap is mentioned in one instance. Most importantly, finding the original archaeological contexts of the ceramics from Excavation VII has required me to look at and interpret in some cases two types of records and numbering systems, one relating to the archaeological contexts and one relating to the ceramics, as well as the association between the two. This certainly has left some room for error.

Keeping these cautions in mind, Graphs 5.1 and 5.2 show a sharp contrast between the quantities recorded in Levels I1 to II2 and those recorded in Levels III2 to IV2, the latter amounting to about two-thirds of the above-mentioned 310 records (66.5 per cent) and of the 3029 sherds (66.4 per cent). Graph 5.2 also shows that Level III1 yielded only one (or possibly four) sherd, which seems possible considering the low amounts of ceramic material reported from the previous levels and the fact that Level III1 was poorly preserved and excavated over a very thin layer and small area. This is also generally consistent with a note by Besenval who reported that he found three sherds in this level.

A closer look at the distribution of the stylistic groups (Graphs 5.1 and 5.3) shows that Groups 1, 2, and 3 were found from Levels I to IV, save for Level I2 which contains only Group 1 material. Group 4 was recorded in Level I3, possibly in Level I4, Level III2, Level III3, and Level IV1. Similarly, Group 5 was found from Level I3. It was then recorded across all levels, save perhaps for Level II1. Group 6 was present in Levels I1, III2, and IV1. As noted above, two of the misfired fragments (Group 7) could be located, one in Level IV1, and the second one in Level IV2. Available quantitative data tend to delin-

---

[12] Save for three ceramic batch numbers from field seasons 1984 and 1989 for the MNI records and five from the same field seasons for the batch records.

Table 5.3: Minimum Number of ceramic Individuals (MNI) from Sarazm Excavation VII and its distribution across the stylistic groups and functional categories identified within this excavation, classified by functions.

| Function | Groups and forms | Total |
|---|---|---|
| Food/beverages service | Groups 1, 2, 3, 4, 5 bowls | 144 |
| Food/beverages service | Groups 1, 2, 3 bowls/pots | 33 |
| Food/beverages service | Groups 4, 5 deep bowls/goblets | 40 |
| Cooking | Groups 1, 2 hole-mouth jars | 64 |
| Cooking | Groups 1, 2, 3, 4, 5 jars | 66 |
| Cooking | Group 1 jars with out-flared rims | 11 |
| Cooking and/or storage/transport | Groups 1, 2 necked jars | 10 |
| Cooking and/or storage/transport | Groups 1, 2 pots | 12 |
| Storage/transport | Group 3 vats | 26 |
| Storage/transport | Group 3 hole-mouth jars | 6 |
| Storage/transport | Group 3 jars with out-flared rims | 4 |
| Storage/transport | Groups 3, 4, 5, 6 necked jars | 84 |
| Total | | 500 |

Table 5.4: Sums of the quantities reported in Table 5.3: Minimum Number of ceramic Individuals (MNI) from Sarazm Excavation VII and its distribution across the stylistic groups and functional categories identified within this excavation, classified by functions.

| Function | Quantity | Percentage |
|---|---|---|
| Food/beverages service | 217 | 43.4 |
| Cooking | 141 | 28.2 |
| Cooking and/or storage/transport | 22 | 4.4 |
| Storage/transport | 120 | 24 |
| Total | 500 | 100 |

eate a significant trend, which is that not only Group 5 appears later on in the Excavation VII sequence, but also the amount of Group 5 ceramics increases across this sequence. It is rational to think that since more vessels were found in the later levels, more Group 5 material is expected to be found in these levels. Yet, Graph 5.3, which shows the contribution of each stylistic group relative to the total amount of records in each level, clearly illustrates that Group 5 emerges as a dominant ceramic component in Level III3 through Levels IV1–IV2. At the same time, Group 1 contributes less than before. This observation is in general agreement with Lyonnet and Isakov's conclusion that a shift in ceramic stylistic composition occurred between the

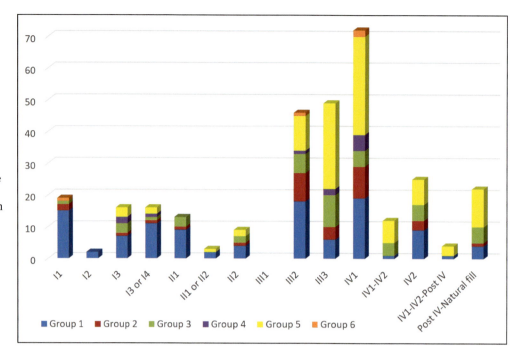

Graph 5.1: Minimum Number of ceramic Individuals (MNI) from Sarazm Excavation VII and its distribution across the stylistic groups and archaeological levels identified within this excavation. Distribution based on 310 records for which a provenience could be determined. B. Mutin.

Table 5.5: Minimum Number of ceramic Individuals (MNI) from Sarazm Excavation VII and its distribution across the stylistic groups and archaeological levels identified within this excavation. Distribution based on 310 records for which a provenience within Excavation VII could be determined.

| Level | Group 1 | Group 2 | Group 3 | Group 4 | Group 5 | Group 6 | Group 7 | Total |
|---|---|---|---|---|---|---|---|---|
| I1 | 15 | 2 | 1 | | | 1 | | 19 |
| I2 | 2 | | | | | | | 2 |
| I3 | 7 | 1 | 3 | 2 | 3 | | | 16 |
| I3 or I4 | 11 | 1 | 1 | 1 | 2 | | | 16 |
| II1 | 9 | 1 | 3 | | | | | 13 |
| II1 or II2 | 2 | | | | 1 | | | 3 |
| II2 | 4 | 1 | 2 | | 2 | | | 9 |
| III1 | | | | | | | | 0 |
| III2 | 18 | 9 | 6 | 1 | 11 | 1 | | 46 |
| III3 | 6 | 4 | 10 | 2 | 27 | | | 49 |
| IV1 | 19 | 10 | 5 | 5 | 31 | 2 | 1 | 73 |
| IV1–IV2 | 1 | | 4 | | 7 | | | 12 |
| IV2 | 9 | 3 | 5 | | 8 | | 1 | 26 |
| IV1–IV2–Post IV | 1 | | | | 3 | | | 4 |
| Post IV–Natural fill | 4 | 1 | 5 | | 12 | | | 22 |
| Total | 108 | 33 | 45 | 11 | 107 | 4 | 2 | 310 |

early and later periods of Sarazm, by which more Group 5-related vessels are recorded in the later periods (Isakov and Lyonnet 1988, 43; see **Chapter 1**).

Certainly, this result may also reflect a change in the functions of the areas exposed, which would have made Group 1 vessels less needed and Group 5 vessels more needed from Level III3 on (see below). On the other hand, there is no significant difference in the distribution of Group 4. Lyonnet and Isakov concluded that this ceramic style became slightly less frequent during Sarazm Periods III and IV (Isakov and Lyonnet 1988, 42). Nothing suggests a decrease in Excavation VII, and Group 4 was recorded in low amounts in this excavation beginning with its earliest level, Level I. This tends to corroborate the observation noted in **Chapter 1** that Excavation VII relates more to the later periods of Sarazm than to its first periods. This would

Table 5.6: Number of sherds from Sarazm Excavation VII and its distribution across the archaeological levels identified within this excavation. Distribution based on 3029 records for which a provenience could be determined.

| Level | Quantity | % |
|---|---|---|
| I1 | 132 | 4.4 |
| I2 | 36 | 1.2 |
| I3 | 114 | 3.8 |
| I3 or I4 | 112 | 3.7 |
| I4 | 11 | 0.4 |
| II1 | 133 | 4.4 |
| II1 or II2 | 22 | 0.7 |
| II2 | 149 | 4.9 |
| II2 or III1 | 3 | 0.1 |
| III1 | 1 | 0.0 |
| III2 | 562 | 18.6 |
| III3 | 411 | 13.6 |
| IV1 | 790 | 26.1 |
| IV1–IV2 | 91 | 3.0 |
| IV2 | 157 | 5.2 |
| IV1–IV2–Post IV | 32 | 1.1 |
| Post IV–Natural fill | 273 | 9.0 |
| Total | 3029 | 100 |

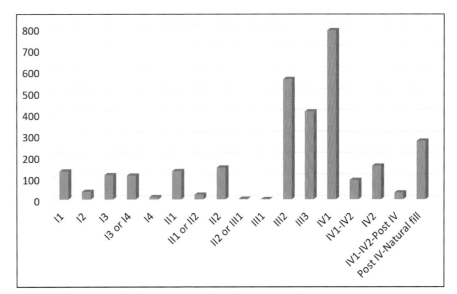

Graph 5.2: Number of sherds from Sarazm Excavation VII and its distribution across the archaeological levels identified within this excavation. Distribution based on 3029 records for which a provenience could be determined. B. Mutin.

mean that this excavation does not contain levels as early as those observed elsewhere at Sarazm. However, Excavation VII's early levels are early enough that a shift in the composition of its ceramic assemblage is observed across its sequence that seems to correspond to the general shift observed at the site level between its early and late periods. As for Group 6, three of the four ceramic individuals of this group were found in Levels III2 and IV1. The fourth one was recovered from Level I1. These very low quantities do not allow us to interpret much further this distribution.

No significant patterns emerge when plotting the forms against Levels I to IV. One observation is however probably worth mentioning: save for one record in Level I3 or I4, the Group 3 vats were found only from Level III2 on. Similarly, save for one record in Level I3, Group 5 necked jars were found only from Level III2 on.

## *Spatial Distribution of the Ceramics*

In this section I provide short descriptions of the ceramic distribution in each level exposed in Excavation VII. These descriptions are based on the above-mentioned 310 records that I have been able to map. They are marked on Plates 5.27–5.32 using their batch and individual numbers (e.g. 180.6), preceded by a number and one or more letter(s). The number corresponds to the ceramic stylistic group number (i.e. Groups 1 to 7), and the letter(s) correspond(s) to the form category: B (bowl), DB/G (deep bowl/goblet), B/P (bowl/pot), P (pot), V (vat), J (jar), HMJ (hole-mouth jar), JOF (jar with out-flared rim), NJ (necked jar), and NA (not available).

### Ceramics in Level I1

The few ceramic individuals recorded in Level I1 were all found inside the main building of this level and essentially in Rooms 3 and 4 (Pl. 5.27). They mostly consist of Group 1 vessels, save for two Group 2, one Group 3, and one Group 6 vessels.

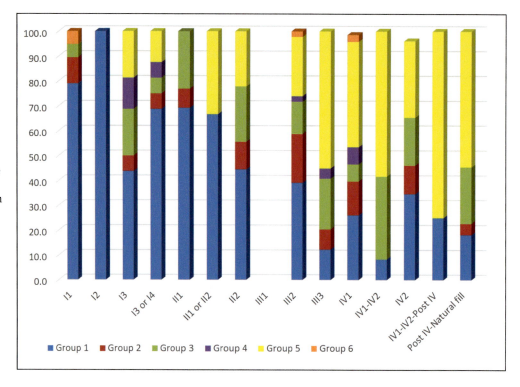

Graph 5.3: Minimum Number of ceramic Individuals (MNI) from Sarazm Excavation VII and its distribution across the stylistic groups and archaeological levels identified within this excavation. Distribution based on 310 records for which a provenience could be determined. Here, instead of quantities, the relative contribution of each group to each level is indicated. B. Mutin.

Table 5.7: Minimum Number of ceramic Individuals (MNI) from Sarazm Excavation VII and its distribution across the stylistic groups and archaeological levels identified within this excavation. Distribution based on 310 records for which a provenience could be determined. Here, instead of quantities, the relative contribution of each group to each level is indicated.

| Level | Group 1 | Group 2 | Group 3 | Group 4 | Group 5 | Group 6 | Group 7 | Total |
|---|---|---|---|---|---|---|---|---|
| I1 | 78.9 | 10.5 | 5.3 | | | 5.3 | | 100 |
| I2 | 100.0 | | | | | | | 100 |
| I3 | 43.8 | 6.3 | 18.8 | 12.5 | 18.8 | | | 100 |
| I3 or I4 | 68.8 | 6.3 | 6.3 | 6.3 | 12.5 | | | 100 |
| II1 | 69.2 | 7.7 | 23.1 | | | | | 100 |
| II1 or II2 | 66.7 | | | | 33.3 | | | 100 |
| II2 | 44.4 | 11.1 | 22.2 | | 22.2 | | | 100 |
| III1 | | | | | | | | 0 |
| III2 | 39.1 | 19.6 | 13.0 | 2.2 | 23.9 | 2.2 | | 100 |
| III3 | 12.2 | 8.2 | 20.4 | 4.1 | 55.1 | | | 100 |
| IV1 | 26.0 | 13.7 | 6.8 | 6.8 | 42.5 | 2.7 | 1.4 | 100 |
| IV1–IV2 | 8.3 | | 33.3 | | 58.3 | | | 100 |
| IV2 | 34.6 | 11.5 | 19.2 | | 30.8 | | 3.8 | 100 |
| IV1–IV2–Post IV | 25.0 | | | | 75.0 | | | 100 |
| Post IV–Natural fill | 18.2 | 4.5 | 22.7 | | 54.5 | | | 100 |

# SPATIAL DISTRIBUTION OF THE CERAMICS

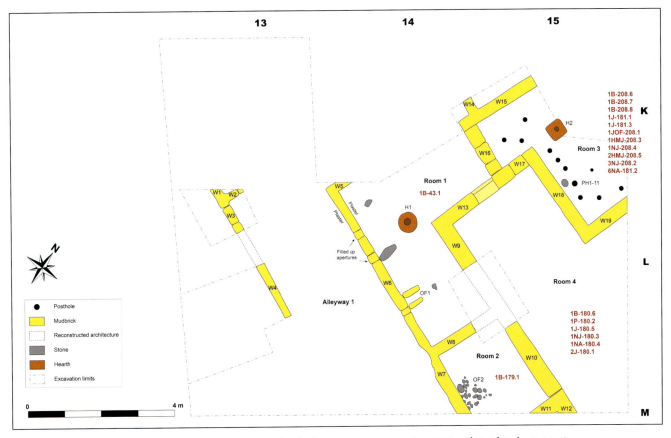

Plate 5.27: Distribution of ceramic individuals in Sarazm Excavation VII Level I1. Plate by B. Mutin.

## Ceramics in Level I2

The two ceramic individuals from Level I2 were both found in Area 1. They are Group 1 material.

## Ceramics in Levels I3 and I4

The ceramic individuals from Level I3 were found in about the same quantities in Rooms 5, 6, 7–8 and Alleyway 2 on the one hand and in Room 9 and Area 3 on the other hand (Pl. 5.28). Ceramics of Groups 1, 2, 3, 4, and 5 were recorded together in Room 9. Furthermore, it is possible that an additional sixteen ceramic individuals belong to Level I3. These ceramics are Group 1, 2, 3, 4, 5 vessels that belong to either Level I3 (Room 6, Area 2, or Alleyway 2), or Level I4 Area 4.

## Ceramics in Level II1

The ceramic individuals from Level II1 were essentially recovered from Room 1 and Area 1 (Pl. 5.29). Group 1, 2, and 3 materials were found together in these contexts, while one Group 5 bowl rim was recorded in Area 2, although this bowl may belong to Level II2 too.

## Ceramics in Level II2

Save for one problematic sherd that may belong to either Level II1 or Level II2, all ceramic individuals from Level II2 were found in Area 3. They consist of four Group 1, one Group 2, two Group 3, and two Group 5 vessels, showing again the association within the same context of ceramics with different styles.

## Ceramics in Level III1

Level III1 did not yield any ceramic individuals.

## Ceramics in Level III2

Most ceramic individuals in Level III2 are in Area 4, Room 7, and Room 3 (Pl. 5.30). Group 1 to 5 vessels were found together in Area 4. Additional associations of different ceramic styles are observed in this level such as in Room 4 (Groups 1, 5, 6, and possibly 3) and Room 7 (Groups 1, 2, 3, and possibly 5).

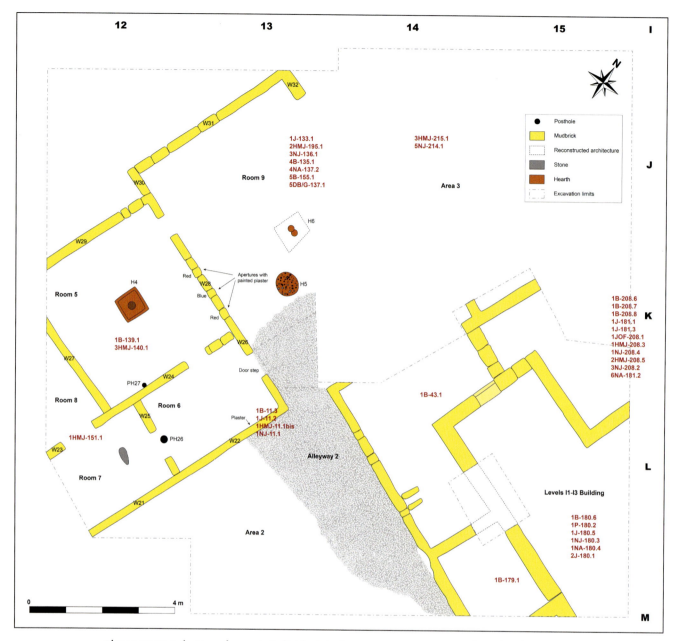

Plate 5.28: Distribution of ceramic individuals in Sarazm Excavation VII Level I3. Plate by B. Mutin.

## Ceramics in Level III3

Ceramic individuals were found in the deposits around the structures that characterize Level III3 in Areas 6 and 7, with more material in Area 7 (Pl. 5.31). One rim of a Group 4 necked jar was recorded in Hearth 3. All styles are represented, save for Group 6. Group 5 is dominant, consisting of c. 55 per cent of the assemblage from this level. Group 3 comes next with c. 20 per cent. As noted above, Group 5 material is recorded in earlier levels of Excavation VII; yet, it seems that this ceramic group became a major component of this excavation's assemblage beginning with Level III3. It is probably also worth noting that, considering just Group 3 vats, jars, and necked jars, Group 4 single necked jars, and Group 5 necked jars, transport and/or storage vessels amount to twenty-two individuals, which is slightly less than half of the individuals from Level III3 whose forms could be determined (forty-nine less four individuals). This c. 49 per cent is about twice the above-mentioned 24 per cent to 28.4 per cent that correspond to the total percentage of vessels in Excavation VII that were allegedly used to store and/or transport foodstuff, liquids, or other things. This may suggest that the activities conducted in this level required these types of vessels more than in the other levels.

# SPATIAL DISTRIBUTION OF THE CERAMICS

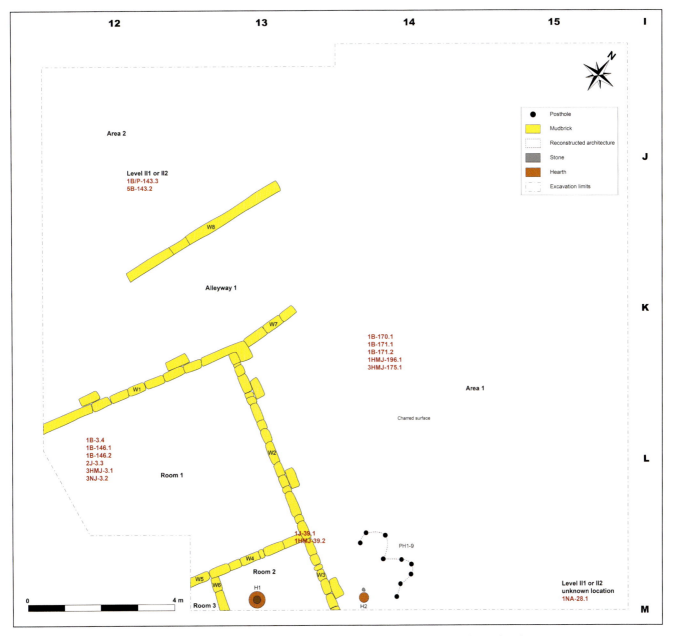

Plate 5.29: Distribution of ceramic individuals in Sarazm Excavation VII Level II1. Plate by B. Mutin.

## Ceramics in Levels IV1–IV2

In contrast to the other levels, Level IV1 yielded eight complete or virtually complete vessels. These ceramics were found inside the building that characterizes this level. They are: Group 6 necked jar 104.X in Area 1; Group 6 necked jar 91.IV in Room 4; Group 3 vat 88.I, Group 5 necked jar 89.II, and Group 5 necked jar 90.III in Room 5; Group 1 necked jar 99.V, Group 5 necked jar 101.VII, and Group 5 necked jar 102.VIII in Room 2 (Pl. 5.32). These vessels clearly suggest storage and/or transport of food-stuff, liquids, or other things. The other ceramic individuals recorded inside and around this building include necked jars, jars, and vats too, although additional types of forms are observed, including cooking and service vessels, which hint at other types of activities than just those suggested by the complete ceramics. As noted in **Chapter 1**, the fact that the above-mentioned complete vat and seven necked jars found in this building have different styles symbolizes Sarazm as a multicultural site. The rest of the assemblage from Level IV1 illustrates this too since Groups 1, 2, 3, 4, 5, and 6 vessels were found together in this level, although it is important to remember that Group 5 now represented about 42.5 per cent of this assemblage. When classifying this assemblage using the

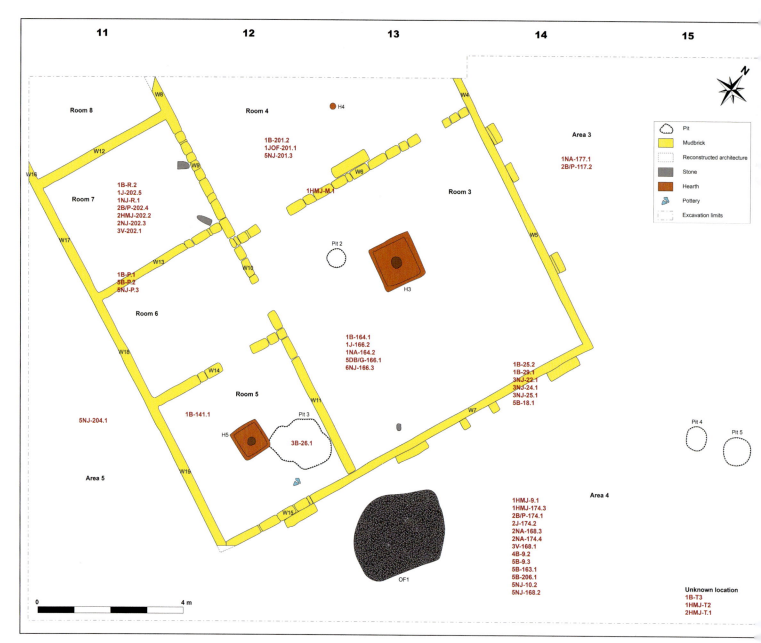

Plate 5.30: Distribution of ceramic individuals in Sarazm Excavation VII Level III2. Plate by B. Mutin.

functional categories defined above,[13] one observes that 41.9 per cent of the vessels were used to serve food and beverages, 22.6 per cent to 27.4 per cent were used for cooking, and 30.6 per cent to 35.5 per cent were used to store and/or transport foodstuff, liquids, or other things. These percentages suggest a slightly greater emphasis on storage/transport vessels and a slightly less emphasis on cooking vessels than observed on average across the Excavation VII assemblage.

[13] Based on the sixty-two ceramic individuals (out of the seventy-three that comprise the Level IV1 assemblage) whose forms could be reconstructed.

The Level IV2 ceramic assemblage essentially comes from Room 8 inside the compartmented building that was exposed in this level, as well as from Area 3, outside of this building. One ceramic individual was found in Hearth 1, south-east of it. The ceramic styles recorded in this more limited assemblage consist of Group 1, 2, 3, and 5 material. Its composition is slightly different than that of the Level IV1 assemblage in that there are no Group 4 and 6 vessels, and that Group 5 is less dominant whereas Groups 1 and 3 are proportionally more represented.

# CHRONO-CULTURAL RELATIONSHIPS

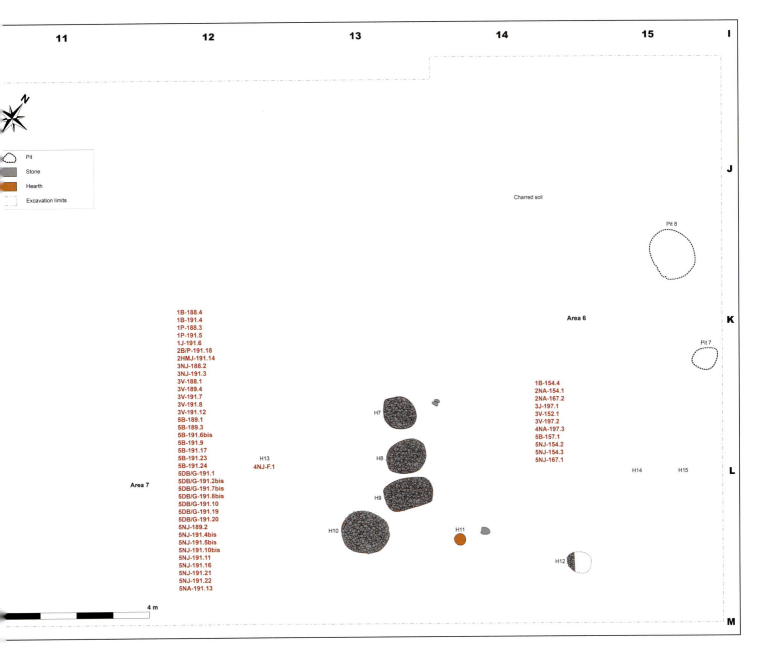

Plate 5.31: Distribution of ceramic individuals in Sarazm Excavation VII Level III3. Plate by B. Mutin.

### Ceramics in the Natural Fills

The material collected in the layers above Levels IV1 and IV2 probably originally belonged to these levels, or to levels on top of them, and were removed and mixed through the effect of ploughing. This material consists of twenty-six ceramic individuals. As expected, their styles are the same as those from Levels IV1–IV2. They consist of Group 1, 2, 3, and 5 vessels, and Group 5 is the most common style.

## Chrono-cultural Relationships

The ceramic assemblage from Excavation VII is stylistically similar to the rest of the material excavated at Sarazm. An important part of it, Groups 1 and 2, seem to point at Turkmenistan during the Namazga II and III Periods, according to Lyonnet's in-depth comparative analysis of ceramics of these styles.[14] Most scholars agree that the Namazga III Period dates to around 3200/3100–2800/2700 cal. BCE (e.g. Hiebert 2002, 28

---

[14] However, again, the above-mentioned parallels with material described as Andronovo-related from Tugai, material relating to the Kel'teminar culture, and the Early Bronze Age ceramics from Dali in Kazakhstan probably need to be remembered.

fig. 2; 2003, 7 tab. 1.1; Vidale 2017b, 9 tab. 1; Olson 2020, 102 tab. 3). The connections with Namazga II material would push these ceramics closer to the mid-fourth millennium BCE, *c.* 3400/3300 cal. BCE. Group 4 is consistent with these relationships as it also parallels Namazga III material. More specifically, equivalents for Group 4 painted motifs are at Altyn-Depe 10 and Geoksyur 1, which Hiebert appears to date to around 2900 cal. BCE (Hiebert 2002, 28 fig. 2). Group 4 also resembles ceramics found at Shahr-i Sokhta and between southern Afghanistan and Pakistan, including at Mundigak. However, these parallels are not as tight as those observed with the assemblages from Turkmenistan since at Shahr-i Sokhta, Mundigak, and in Pakistan the ceramics in question appear to be mostly black-on-buff (pinkish at times) painted material. These parallels seem to rather suggest in this case that Sarazm was indirectly connected to these sites and areas as part of a shared, broader sphere of stylistic diffusion. In any case, these stylistic links with Shahr-i Sokhta are chronologically consistent with those noted in Turkmenistan as they point at the foundation period at this site, Period I, dating to 3150–2750 cal. BCE (Salvatori and Tosi 2005, 289–90 figs 12–13).

In contrast to Groups 1, 2, and 4, Group 5 ceramics stylistically mostly connect to Afghanistan and Pakistan. The dating of this material is however a little bit tricky for the reason that part of the parallels for this group date to the second half of the fourth millennium BCE, whereas another part seems more 'at home' within the first half of the third millennium BCE. This conclusion indeed emerges when considering all the comparisons with assemblages from sites such as Mundigak (Periods II to IV) and Mehrgarh (Periods IV to VII) (see Franke 2008, 669 fig. 31 for a chronological chart with alignment of the regional sequences of southern Afghanistan and Pakistan). A shorter *c.* 3300–2700 cal. BCE period may tentatively be suggested that would correspond to the period during which most parallels tend to overlap. This is true for the bowls and the deep bowls/goblets. This chronological bracket, and perhaps a dating even closer to and centred around *c.* 3000 cal. BCE, is consistent with the date of Namazga III-related Group 4 ceramics and the fact that both Group 4 and 5 ceramics were found together in the same levels in Excavation VII. Yet, one should keep in mind that Group 5 necked jars tend to also include parallels closer to the mid-third millennium BCE than to 3000 BCE, although

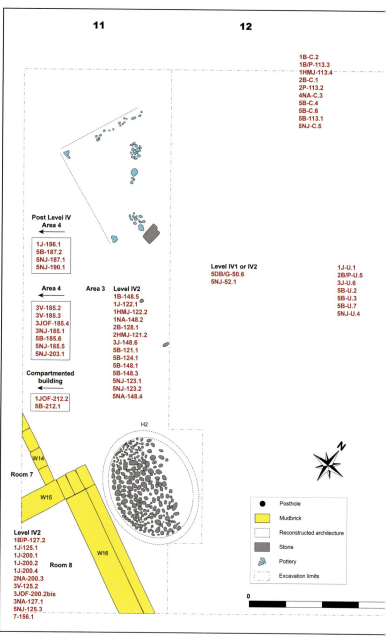

Plate 5.32: Distribution of ceramic individuals in Sarazm Excavation VII Levels IV1–IV2. Plate by B. Mutin.

these parallels are in most cases not as precise as those identified for the deep bowls/goblets.

On this topic, another observation that needs to be remembered is that while Group 4 appears to have exact equivalents within the Namazga II–III cultural sphere in Turkmenistan, exact parallels seem to be lacking for a part of Group 5 ceramics. This brings to mind the question recapitulated in **Chapter 1** that concerns the status of Sarazm vis-à-vis this Namazga-related cultural sphere of Central Asia and vis-à-vis the sphere defined between Afghanistan and Pakistan by sites such as Mundigak and

# CHRONO-CULTURAL RELATIONSHIPS

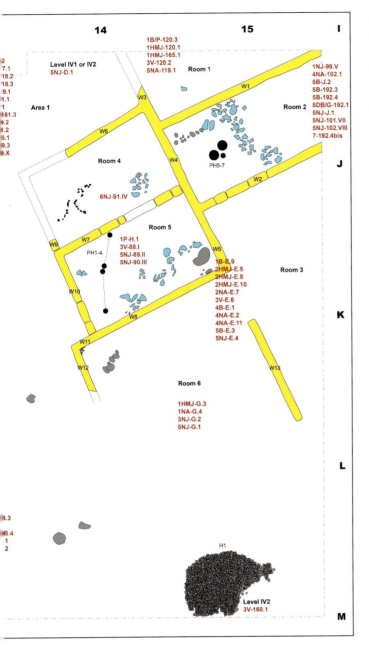

Hindu Kush, there is certainly a lot of room for stylistic innovation and variation within their numerous valleys. Taking this into account, that part of Group 5 ceramics do not always find exact parallels beyond Sarazm is not very surprising. In fact, it is perhaps even more rational to expect more stylistic variation than strict equivalents. What may need to be more emphasized, instead, is the development of similar practices during the Late Chalcolithic and Early Bronze Age between the regions north and south of the Hindu Kush, as reflected for instance by the emergence of comparable types of goblets.

Lastly, although most of the parallels for the Excavation VII ceramic assemblage point at the period between *c.* 3500–2500 cal. BCE broadly speaking, those for Group 6 ceramics appear to essentially relate to material from northern Iran dating to *c.* 2500–1500 cal. BCE broadly speaking. This period generally corresponds to the Early Namazga V and Early or Late Namazga VI Periods in Turkmenistan (see Olson 2020, 158 tabs 3.6–3.7).[15] Although these chronological relationships do not seem consistent with those observed for the rest of this ceramic assemblage, they should probably not be overlooked as they raise the question as to whether Sarazm was still occupied during the second half of the third millennium BCE (see Lyonnet 1996, 60–61). This question is addressed again below in the **Conclusion** with consideration of the small finds recovered from Excavation VII, which are examined in the next chapter.

Mehrgarh. Was Sarazm an isolated settlement, distant from, but connected to, the cores of these two spheres, or were these spheres greater than what most of their vestiges suggest, in which case Sarazm would have been incorporated in them? In both cases, limited discoveries such as at Tugai and Zhukov in Uzbekistan as well as Taluqan in Afghanistan tend to allude to the possibility that more settlements relating to Sarazm and sites such as Altyn-Depe on the one hand and Mundigak on the other hand may have existed in the areas in between these sites. Considering the southern sphere, although a large part of the *c.* 860 km of lands between Sarazm and Mundigak consist of the high mountains of the

---

[15] The parallels noted for Group 3 are chronologically consistent with those observed for Groups 1, 2, 4, and 5, although some also appear to be on the same chronological horizon as those of Group 6.

Table 5.8: List of ceramic individuals from Sarazm Excavation VII sorted by level and feature (NA = Not Available).

| Year | Level | Feature number | Batch # | Cer. # | Preservation | Group | Form |
|---|---|---|---|---|---|---|---|
| 1990 | I? | sq. K16 | 227bis | 1 | Rim | Group 5 | Deep bowl/goblet |
| 1990 | I? | sq. K16 | 227bis | 2 | Rim | Group 1 | Jar |
| 1990 | I? | sq. K16 | 227bis | 3 | Rim | Group 1 | Hole-mouth jar |
| 1990 | I? | sq. M16 | 249 | 1 | Rim | Group 5 | Bowl |
| 1990 | I? | sq. M16 | 249 | 2 | Rim | Group 1 | Hole-mouth jar |
| 1990 | I? | sq. M16 | 249 | 3 | Rim | Group 1 | NA |
| 1985 | I1 | Room 1 | 43 | 1 | Rim | Group 1 | Bowl |
| 1987 | I1 | Room 2 | 179 | 1 | Rim | Group 1 | Bowl |
| 1987 | I1 | Room 3 | 181 | 1 | Rim | Group 1 | Jar |
| 1987 | I1 | Room 3 | 181 | 2 | Body | Group 6 | NA |
| 1987 | I1 | Room 3 | 181 | 3 | Rim | Group 1 | Jar |
| 1989 | I1 | Room 3 | 208 | 1 | Rim | Group 1 | Jar with out-flared rim |
| 1989 | I1 | Room 3 | 208 | 2 | Rim | Group 3 | Necked jar |
| 1989 | I1 | Room 3 | 208 | 3 | Rim | Group 1 | Hole-mouth jar |
| 1989 | I1 | Room 3 | 208 | 4 | Rim | Group 1 | Necked jar |
| 1989 | I1 | Room 3 | 208 | 5 | Rim | Group 2 | Hole-mouth jar |
| 1989 | I1 | Room 3 | 208 | 6 | Rim | Group 1 | Bowl |
| 1989 | I1 | Room 3 | 208 | 7 | Rim | Group 1 | Bowl |
| 1989 | I1 | Room 3 | 208 | 8 | Rim | Group 1 | Bowl |
| 1987 | I1 | Room 4 | 180 | 1 | Rim | Group 2 | Jar |
| 1987 | I1 | Room 4 | 180 | 2 | Rim | Group 1 | Pot |
| 1987 | I1 | Room 4 | 180 | 3 | Rim | Group 1 | Necked jar |
| 1987 | I1 | Room 4 | 180 | 4 | Rim | Group 1 | NA |
| 1987 | I1 | Room 4 | 180 | 5 | Rim | Group 1 | Jar |
| 1987 | I1 | Room 4 | 180 | 6 | Rim | Group 1 | Bowl |
| 1985 | I2 | Area 1 | 41 | 1 | Rim | Group 1 | Jar with out-flared rim |
| 1985 | I2 | Area 1 | 44 | 1 | Rim | Group 1 | Hole-mouth jar |
| 1989 | I3 | Area 3 | 214 | 1 | Rim | Group 5 | Necked jar |
| 1989 | I3 | Area 3 | 215 | 1 | Rim | Group 3 | Hole-mouth jar |
| 1987 | I3 | Room 5 | 139 | 1 | Rim | Group 1 | Bowl |
| 1987 | I3 | Room 5 | 140 | 1 | Rim | Group 3 | Hole-mouth jar |
| 1984 | I3 | Room 6 or Alleyway 2 | 11 | 1 | Rim | Group 1 | Necked jar |
| 1984 | I3 | Room 6 or Alleyway 2 | 11 | 2 | Rim | Group 1 | Jar |
| 1984 | I3 | Room 6 or Alleyway 2 | 11 | 3 | Rim | Group 1 | Bowl |
| 1984 | I3 | Room 6 or Alleyway 2 | 11 | 1bis | Rim | Group 1 | Hole-mouth jar |
| 1987 | I3 | Room 7 or Room 8 | 151 | 1 | Rim | Group 1 | Hole-mouth jar |
| 1987 | I3 | Room 9 | 133 | 1 | Rim | Group 1 | Jar |
| 1987 | I3 | Room 9 | 135 | 1 | Rim | Group 4 | Bowl |
| 1987 | I3 | Room 9 | 136 | 1 | Rim | Group 3 | Necked jar |

| Year | Level | Feature number | Batch # | Cer. # | Preservation | Group | Form |
|---|---|---|---|---|---|---|---|
| 1987 | I3 | Room 9 | 137 | 1 | Body | Group 5 | Deep bowl/goblet |
| 1987 | I3 | Room 9 | 137 | 2 | Body | Group 4 | NA |
| 1987 | I3 | Room 9 | 155 | 1 | Rim | Group 5 | Bowl |
| 1989 | I3 | Room 9 | 195 | 1 | Rim | Group 2 | Hole-mouth jar |
| 1985 | I3 or I4 | Room 6, Area 2, Alleyway 2, or Area 4 | 30 | 1 | Rim | Group 1 | Jar with out-flared rim |
| 1984 | I3 or I4 | Room 6, Area 2, Alleyway 2, or Area 4 | 4 | 1 | Rim | Group 5 | Deep bowl/goblet |
| 1984 | I3 or I4 | Room 6, Area 2, Alleyway 2, or Area 4 | 4 | 2 | Rim | Group 5 | Deep bowl/goblet |
| 1984 | I3 or I4 | Room 6, Area 2, Alleyway 2, or Area 4 | 4 | 2 | Rim | Group 5 | Deep bowl/goblet |
| 1984 | I3 or I4 | Room 6, Area 2, Alleyway 2, or Area 4 | 4 | 3 | Rim | Group 4 | Deep bowl/goblet |
| 1984 | I3 or I4 | Room 6, Area 2, Alleyway 2, or Area 4 | 4 | 4 | Rim | Group 1 | Bowl/pot |
| 1984 | I3 or I4 | Room 6, Area 2, Alleyway 2, or Area 4 | 4 | 6 | Rim | Group 1 | Bowl |
| 1984 | I3 or I4 | Room 6, Area 2, Alleyway 2, or Area 4 | 4 | 7 | Rim | Group 1 | Bowl |
| 1984 | I3 or I4 | Room 6, Area 2, Alleyway 2, or Area 4 | 4 | 8 | Rim | Group 1 | Hole-mouth jar |
| 1986 | I3 or I4 | Room 6, Area 2, Alleyway 2, or Area 4 | 4 | 9 | Rim | Group 2 | Pot |
| 1984 | I3 or I4 | Room 6, Area 2, Alleyway 2, or Area 4 | 4 | 10 | Base | Group 1 | NA |
| 1984 | I3 or I4 | Room 6, Area 2, Alleyway 2, or Area 4 | 4 | 11 | Rim | Group 1 | Bowl/pot |
| 1984 | I3 or I4 | Room 6, Area 2, Alleyway 2, or Area 4 | 4 | 12 | Rim | Group 3 | Vat |
| 1984 | I3 or I4 | Room 6, Area 2, Alleyway 2, or Area 4 | 4 | 13 | Rim | Group 1 | NA |
| 1985 | I3 or I4 | Room 6, Area 2, Alleyway 2, or Area 4 | 42 | 1 | Rim | Group 1 | Bowl |
| 1985 | I3 or I4 | Room 6, Area 2, Alleyway 2, or Area 4 | 42 | 2 | Rim | Group 1 | Jar with out-flared rim |
| 1985 | I3 or I4 | Room 6, Area 2, Alleyway 2, or Area 4 | 42 | 3 | Rim | Group 1 | Bowl |
| 1987 | II1 | Area 1 | 170 | 1 | Rim | Group 1 | Bowl |
| 1987 | II1 | Area 1 | 171 | 1 | Rim | Group 1 | Bowl |
| 1987 | II1 | Area 1 | 171 | 2 | Rim | Group 1 | Bowl |
| 1987 | II1 | Area 1 | 175 | 1 | Rim | Group 3 | Hole-mouth jar |
| 1989 | II1 | Area 1 | 196 | 1 | Rim | Group 1 | Hole-mouth jar |
| 1987 | II1 | Room 1 | 146 | 1 | Rim | Group 1 | Bowl |
| 1987 | II1 | Room 1 | 146 | 2 | Rim | Group 1 | Bowl |
| 1984 | II1 | Room 1 | 3 | 1 | Rim | Group 3 | Hole-mouth jar |
| 1984 | II1 | Room 1 | 3 | 2 | Rim | Group 3 | Necked jar |
| 1984 | II1 | Room 1 | 3 | 3 | Rim | Group 2 | Jar |
| 1984 | II1 | Room 1 | 3 | 4 | Complete profile | Group 1 | Bowl |
| 1985 | II1 | Room 1, Room 2, or Area 1 | 39 | 1 | Rim | Group 1 | Jar |
| 1985 | II1 | Room 1, Room 2, or Area 1 | 39 | 2 | Rim | Group 1 | Hole-mouth jar |
| 1987 | II1 or II2 | Area 2 | 143 | 2 | Rim | Group 5 | Bowl |
| 1987 | II1 or II2 | Area 2 | 143 | 3 | Rim | Group 1 | Bowl/pot |
| 1985 | II1 or II2 | Room 2, Alleyway 1, Area 1, or Area 3 | 28 | 1 | Rim | Group 1 | NA |
| 1987 | II2 | Area 3 | 176 | 1 | Rim | Group 1 | Bowl |
| 1985 | II2 | Area 3 | 19 | 1 | Rim | Group 3 | Bowl |
| 1985 | II2 | Area 3 | 19 | 2 | Rim | Group 5 | Deep bowl/goblet |

| Year | Level | Feature number | Batch # | Cer. # | Preservation | Group | Form |
|---|---|---|---|---|---|---|---|
| 1985 | II2 | Area 3 | 19 | 3 | Rim | Group 2 | Pot |
| 1985 | II2 | Area 3 | 19 | 4 | Rim | Group 1 | Bowl/pot |
| 1985 | II2 | Area 3 | 19 | 5 | Rim | Group 1 | NA |
| 1985 | II2 | Area 3 | 19 | 6 | Rim | Group 1 | Hole-mouth jar |
| 1984 | II2 | Area 3 | 2 | 1 | Rim | Group 3 | Necked jar |
| 1984 | II2 | Area 3 | 2 | 2 | Rim | Group 5 | Deep bowl/goblet |
| 1987 | III2 | Area 3 | 177 | 1 | Rim | Group 1 | NA |
| 1987 | III2 | Area 3 | 177 | 2 | Rim | Group 2 | Bowl/pot |
| 1986 | III2 | Area 4 | 10 | 2 | Rim | Group 5 | Necked jar |
| 1987 | III2 | Area 4 | 163 | 1 | Rim | Group 5 | Bowl |
| 1987 | III2 | Area 4 | 168 | 1 | Rim | Group 3 | Vat |
| 1987 | III2 | Area 4 | 168 | 2 | Rim | Group 5 | Necked jar |
| 1987 | III2 | Area 4 | 168 | 3 | Base | Group 2 | NA |
| 1987 | III2 | Area 4 | 174 | 1 | Rim | Group 2 | Bowl/pot |
| 1987 | III2 | Area 4 | 174 | 2 | Rim | Group 2 | Jar |
| 1987 | III2 | Area 4 | 174 | 3 | Rim | Group 1 | Hole-mouth jar |
| 1987 | III2 | Area 4 | 174 | 4 | Rim | Group 2 | NA |
| 1989 | III2 | Area 4 | 206 | 1 | Rim | Group 5 | Bowl |
| 1984 | III2 | Area 4 | 9 | 1 | Rim | Group 1 | Hole-mouth jar |
| 1984 | III2 | Area 4 | 9 | 2 | Rim | Group 4 | Bowl |
| 1984 | III2 | Area 4 | 9 | 3 | Rim | Group 5 | Bowl |
| 1989 | III2 | Area 5 | 204 | 1 | Rim | Group 5 | Necked jar |
| 1986 | III2 | NA | T | 1 | Rim | Group 2 | Hole-mouth jar |
| 1986 | III2 | NA | T | 2 | Rim | Group 1 | Hole-mouth jar |
| 1986 | III2 | NA | T | 3 | Rim | Group 1 | Bowl |
| 1985 | III2 | Pit 3 | 26 | 1 | Rim | Group 3 | Bowl |
| 1987 | III2 | Room 3 | 164 | 1 | Rim | Group 1 | Bowl |
| 1987 | III2 | Room 3 | 164 | 2 | Rim | Group 1 | NA |
| 1987 | III2 | Room 3 | 166 | 1 | Rim | Group 5 | Deep bowl/goblet |
| 1987 | III2 | Room 3 | 166 | 2 | Rim | Group 1 | Jar |
| 1987 | III2 | Room 3 | 166 | 3 | Rim | Group 6 | Necked jar |
| 1985 | III2 | Room 3 or Area 4 | 18 | 1 | Rim | Group 5 | Bowl |
| 1985 | III2 | Room 3 or Area 4 | 22 | 1 | Rim | Group 3 | Necked jar |
| 1985 | III2 | Room 3 or Area 4 | 24 | 1 | Rim | Group 3 | Necked jar |
| 1985 | III2 | Room 3 or Area 4 | 25 | 1 | Rim | Group 3 | Necked jar |
| 1985 | III2 | Room 3 or Area 4 | 25 | 2 | Rim | Group 1 | Bowl |
| 1985 | III2 | Room 3 or Area 4 | 29 | 1 | Rim | Group 1 | Bowl |
| 1986 | III2 | Room 3 or Room 4 | M | 1 | Rim | Group 1 | Hole-mouth jar |
| 1989 | III2 | Room 4 | 201 | 1 | Rim | Group 1 | Jar with out-flared rim |
| 1989 | III2 | Room 4 | 201 | 2 | Rim | Group 1 | Bowl |

# CHRONO-CULTURAL RELATIONSHIPS

| Year | Level | Feature number | Batch # | Cer. # | Preservation | Group | Form |
|---|---|---|---|---|---|---|---|
| 1989 | III2 | Room 4 | 201 | 3 | Rim | Group 5 | Necked jar |
| 1987 | III2 | Room 5 | 141 | 1 | Rim | Group 1 | Bowl |
| 1989 | III2 | Room 7 | 202 | 1 | Rim | Group 3 | Vat |
| 1989 | III2 | Room 7 | 202 | 2 | Rim | Group 2 | Hole-mouth jar |
| 1989 | III2 | Room 7 | 202 | 3 | Rim | Group 2 | Necked jar |
| 1989 | III2 | Room 7 | 202 | 4 | Rim | Group 2 | Bowl/pot |
| 1989 | III2 | Room 7 | 202 | 5 | Rim | Group 1 | Jar |
| 1986 | III2 | Room 7 | R | 1 | Rim | Group 1 | Necked jar |
| 1986 | III2 | Room 7 | R | 2 | Rim | Group 1 | Bowl |
| 1986 | III2 | Rooms 6 and 7 | P | 1 | Rim | Group 1 | Bowl |
| 1986 | III2 | Rooms 6 and 7 | P | 2 | Rim | Group 5 | Bowl |
| 1986 | III2 | Rooms 6 and 7 | P | 3 | Rim | Group 5 | Necked jar |
| 1990 | III2? | sq. K15–16 | 225bis | 1 | Body | Group 5 | Deep bowl/goblet |
| 1990 | III2? | sq. K15–16 | 225bis | 2 | Rim | Group 2 | Bowl/pot |
| 1990 | III2? | sq. M16 | 229bis | 3 | Rim | Group 1 | Bowl |
| 1990 | III2? | sq. M16 | 229bis | 4 | Rim | Group 2 | Hole-mouth jar |
| 1987 | III3 | Area 6 | 152 | 1 | Rim | Group 3 | Vat |
| 1987 | III3 | Area 6 | 154 | 1 | Base | Group 2 | NA |
| 1987 | III3 | Area 6 | 154 | 2 | Rim | Group 5 | Necked jar |
| 1987 | III3 | Area 6 | 154 | 3 | Rim | Group 5 | Necked jar |
| 1987 | III3 | Area 6 | 154 | 4 | Rim | Group 1 | Bowl |
| 1987 | III3 | Area 6 | 157 | 1 | Rim | Group 5 | Bowl |
| 1987 | III3 | Area 6 | 167 | 1 | Rim | Group 5 | Necked jar |
| 1987 | III3 | Area 6 | 167 | 2 | Rim | Group 2 | NA |
| 1989 | III3 | Area 6 | 197 | 1 | Rim | Group 3 | Jar |
| 1989 | III3 | Area 6 | 197 | 2 | Rim | Group 3 | Vat |
| 1989 | III3 | Area 6 | 197 | 3 | Body | Group 4 | NA |
| 1989 | III3 | Area 7 | 188 | 1 | Rim | Group 3 | Vat |
| 1989 | III3 | Area 7 | 188 | 2 | Rim | Group 3 | Necked jar |
| 1989 | III3 | Area 7 | 188 | 3 | Rim | Group 1 | Pot |
| 1989 | III3 | Area 7 | 188 | 4 | Rim | Group 1 | Bowl |
| 1989 | III3 | Area 7 | 189 | 1 | Complete profile | Group 5 | Bowl |
| 1989 | III3 | Area 7 | 189 | 2 | Rim | Group 5 | Necked jar |
| 1989 | III3 | Area 7 | 189 | 3 | Rim | Group 5 | Bowl |
| 1989 | III3 | Area 7 | 189 | 4 | Rim | Group 3 | Vat |
| 1989 | III3 | Area 7 | 191 | 1 | Rim | Group 5 | Deep bowl/goblet |
| 1989 | III3 | Area 7 | 191 | 3 | Rim | Group 3 | Necked jar |
| 1989 | III3 | Area 7 | 191 | 4 | Rim | Group 1 | Bowl |
| 1989 | III3 | Area 7 | 191 | 5 | Rim | Group 1 | Pot |
| 1989 | III3 | Area 7 | 191 | 6 | Rim | Group 1 | Jar |

| Year | Level | Feature number | Batch # | Cer. # | Preservation | Group | Form |
|---|---|---|---|---|---|---|---|
| 1989 | III3 | Area 7 | 191 | 7 | Rim | Group 3 | Vat |
| 1989 | III3 | Area 7 | 191 | 8 | Rim | Group 3 | Vat |
| 1989 | III3 | Area 7 | 191 | 9 | Rim | Group 5 | Bowl |
| 1989 | III3 | Area 7 | 191 | 10 | Rim | Group 5 | Deep bowl/goblet |
| 1989 | III3 | Area 7 | 191 | 11 | Rim | Group 5 | Necked jar |
| 1989 | III3 | Area 7 | 191 | 12 | Rim | Group 3 | Vat |
| 1989 | III3 | Area 7 | 191 | 13 | Body | Group 5 | NA |
| 1989 | III3 | Area 7 | 191 | 14 | Rim | Group 2 | Hole-mouth jar |
| 1989 | III3 | Area 7 | 191 | 16 | Rim | Group 5 | Necked jar |
| 1989 | III3 | Area 7 | 191 | 17 | Rim | Group 5 | Bowl |
| 1989 | III3 | Area 7 | 191 | 18 | Rim | Group 2 | Bowl/pot |
| 1989 | III3 | Area 7 | 191 | 19 | Rim | Group 5 | Deep bowl/goblet |
| 1989 | III3 | Area 7 | 191 | 20 | Rim | Group 5 | Deep bowl/goblet |
| 1989 | III3 | Area 7 | 191 | 21 | Rim | Group 5 | Necked jar |
| 1989 | III3 | Area 7 | 191 | 22 | Rim | Group 5 | Necked jar |
| 1989 | III3 | Area 7 | 191 | 23 | Rim | Group 5 | Bowl |
| 1989 | III3 | Area 7 | 191 | 24 | Rim | Group 5 | Bowl |
| 1989 | III3 | Area 7 | 191 | 10bis | Rim | Group 5 | Necked jar |
| 1989 | III3 | Area 7 | 191 | 2bis | Rim | Group 5 | Deep bowl/goblet |
| 1989 | III3 | Area 7 | 191 | 4bis | Rim | Group 5 | Necked jar |
| 1989 | III3 | Area 7 | 191 | 5bis | Rim | Group 5 | Necked jar |
| 1989 | III3 | Area 7 | 191 | 6bis | Rim | Group 5 | Bowl |
| 1989 | III3 | Area 7 | 191 | 7bis | Complete profile | Group 5 | Deep bowl/goblet |
| 1989 | III3 | Area 7 | 191 | 8bis | Complete profile | Group 5 | Deep bowl/goblet |
| 1986 | III3 | Hearth 13 | F | 1 | Rim | Group 4 | Necked jar |
| 1986 | IV1 | Area 1 | 104 | X | Mostly complete | Group 6 | Necked jar |
| 1987 | IV1 | Area 1 | 115 | 1 | Rim | Group 5 | Bowl |
| 1987 | IV1 | Area 1 | 116 | 1 | Rim | Group 5 | NA |
| 1987 | IV1 | Area 1 | 116 | 2 | Rim | Group 1 | Bowl |
| 1987 | IV1 | Area 1 | 117 | 1 | Rim | Group 1 | Bowl/pot |
| 1987 | IV1 | Area 1 | 118 | 2 | Rim | Group 1 | Hole-mouth jar |
| 1987 | IV1 | Area 1 | 118 | 3 | Rim | Group 1 | Hole-mouth jar |
| 1987 | IV1 | Area 1 | 149 | 1 | Rim | Group 2 | Bowl/pot |
| 1987 | IV1 | Area 1 | 149 | 2 | Rim | Group 5 | Necked jar |
| 1987 | IV1 | Area 1 | 149 | 3 | Rim | Group 5 | NA |
| 1987 | IV1 | Area 1 | 161 | 1 | Rim | Group 2 | NA |
| 1987 | IV1 | Area 1 | 161 | 2 | Rim | Group 5 | Necked jar |
| 1987 | IV1 | Area 1 | 161 | 3 | Rim | Group 5 | Deep bowl/goblet |
| 1985 | IV1 | Area 2 | 14 | 1 | Rim | Group 1 | Jar |
| 1985 | IV1 | Area 2 | 15 | 1 | Rim | Group 5 | Necked jar |

# CHRONO-CULTURAL RELATIONSHIPS

| Year | Level | Feature number | Batch # | Cer. # | Preservation | Group | Form |
|---|---|---|---|---|---|---|---|
| 1984 | IV1 | Area 2 | 16 | 1 | Complete profile | Group 5 | Bowl |
| 1984 | IV1 | Area 2 | 16 | 2 | Rim | Group 5 | Necked jar |
| 1986 | IV1 | Area 2 | B | 1 | Rim | Group 1 | Jar |
| 1986 | IV1 | Area 2 | B | 2 | Rim | Group 1 | Bowl |
| 1986 | IV1 | Area 2 | B | 3 | Rim | Group 2 | Hole-mouth jar |
| 1986 | IV1 | Area 2 | B | 4 | Rim | Group 5 | Deep bowl/goblet |
| 1986 | IV1 | Areas 1–2 | U | 1 | Rim | Group 1 | Jar |
| 1986 | IV1 | Areas 1–2 | U | 2 | Rim | Group 5 | Bowl |
| 1986 | IV1 | Areas 1–2 | U | 3 | Rim | Group 5 | Bowl |
| 1986 | IV1 | Areas 1–2 | U | 4 | Rim | Group 5 | Necked jar |
| 1989 | IV1 | Areas 1–2 | U | 5 | Rim | Group 2 | Bowl/pot |
| 1986 | IV1 | Areas 1–2 | U | 6 | Rim | Group 3 | Jar |
| 1986 | IV1 | Areas 1–2 | U | 7 | Rim | Group 5 | Bowl |
| 1987 | IV1 | Room 1 | 119 | 1 | Body | Group 5 | NA |
| 1987 | IV1 | Room 1 | 120 | 1 | Rim | Group 1 | Hole-mouth jar |
| 1987 | IV1 | Room 1 | 120 | 2 | Rim | Group 3 | Vat |
| 1987 | IV1 | Room 1 | 120 | 3 | Rim | Group 1 | Bowl/pot |
| 1987 | IV1 | Room 1 | 165 | 1 | Rim | Group 1 | Hole-mouth jar |
| 1986 | IV1 | Room 2 | 99 | V | Complete | Group 1 | Necked jar |
| 1986 | IV1 | Room 2 | 102 | 1 | Body | Group 4 | NA |
| 1986 | IV1 | Room 2 | 101 | VII | Complete | Group 5 | Necked jar |
| 1986 | IV1 | Room 2 | 102 | VIII | Complete | Group 5 | Necked jar |
| 1989 | IV1 | Room 2 | 192 | 1 | Complete profile | Group 5 | Deep bowl/goblet |
| 1989 | IV1 | Room 2 | 192 | 3 | Rim | Group 5 | Bowl |
| 1989 | IV1 | Room 2 | 192 | 4 | Rim | Group 5 | Bowl |
| 1989 | IV1 | Room 2 | 192 | 4bis | Body | Group 7 | Misfired ceramic |
| 1986 | IV1 | Room 2 | J | 1 | Rim | Group 5 | Necked jar |
| 1986 | IV1 | Room 2 | J | 2 | Rim | Group 5 | Bowl |
| 1986 | IV1 | Room 3, Room 5, or Room 6 | E | 1 | Rim | Group 4 | Bowl |
| 1986 | IV1 | Room 3, Room 5, or Room 6 | E | 2 | Body | Group 4 | NA |
| 1986 | IV1 | Room 3, Room 5, or Room 6 | E | 3 | Rim | Group 5 | Bowl |
| 1986 | IV1 | Room 3, Room 5, or Room 6 | E | 4 | Rim | Group 5 | Necked jar |
| 1986 | IV1 | Room 3, Room 5, or Room 6 | E | 5 | Rim | Group 2 | Hole-mouth jar |
| 1986 | IV1 | Room 3, Room 5, or Room 6 | E | 6 | Rim | Group 3 | Vat |
| 1986 | IV1 | Room 3, Room 5, or Room 6 | E | 7 | Rim | Group 2 | NA |
| 1986 | IV1 | Room 3, Room 5, or Room 6 | E | 8 | Rim | Group 2 | Hole-mouth jar |
| 1986 | IV1 | Room 3, Room 5, or Room 6 | E | 9 | Rim | Group 1 | Bowl |
| 1986 | IV1 | Room 3, Room 5, or Room 6 | E | 10 | Rim | Group 2 | Hole-mouth jar |
| 1986 | IV1 | Room 3, Room 5, or Room 6 | E | 11 | Body | Group 4 | NA |
| 1986 | IV1 | Room 4 | 91 | IV | Complete | Group 6 | Necked jar |

| Year | Level | Feature number | Batch # | Cer. # | Preservation | Group | Form |
|---|---|---|---|---|---|---|---|
| 1986 | IV1 | Room 5 | 88 | I | Complete | Group 3 | Vat |
| 1986 | IV1 | Room 5 | 89 | II | Complete | Group 5 | Necked jar |
| 1986 | IV1 | Room 5 | 90 | III | Complete | Group 5 | Necked jar |
| 1986 | IV1 | Room 5 | H | 1 | Rim | Group 1 | Pot |
| 1986 | IV1 | Room 6 | G | 1 | Body | Group 5 | Necked jar |
| 1986 | IV1 | Room 6 | G | 2 | Rim | Group 3 | Necked jar |
| 1986 | IV1 | Room 6 | G | 3 | Rim | Group 1 | Hole-mouth jar |
| 1986 | IV1 | Room 6 | G | 4 | Base | Group 1 | NA |
| 1987 | IV1 | sq. I12–13 | 113 | 1 | Rim | Group 5 | Bowl |
| 1987 | IV1 | sq. I12–13 | 113 | 2 | Rim | Group 2 | Pot |
| 1987 | IV1 | sq. I12–13 | 113 | 3 | Rim | Group 1 | Bowl/pot |
| 1987 | IV1 | sq. I12–13 | 113 | 4 | Rim | Group 1 | Hole-mouth jar |
| 1986 | IV1 | sq. J12–13 | C | 1 | Rim | Group 2 | Bowl |
| 1986 | IV1 | sq. J12–13 | C | 2 | Rim | Group 1 | Bowl |
| 1986 | IV1 | sq. J12–13 | C | 3 | Body | Group 4 | NA |
| 1986 | IV1 | sq. J12–13 | C | 4 | Rim | Group 5 | Bowl |
| 1986 | IV1 | sq. J12–13 | C | 5 | Rim | Group 5 | Necked jar |
| 1986 | IV1 | sq. J12–13 | C | 6 | Rim | Group 5 | Bowl |
| 1986 | IV1–IV2 | Area 1 | D | 1 | Rim | Group 5 | Necked jar |
| 1986 | IV1–IV2 | Area 2 or Area 3 | 50 | 6 | Rim | Group 5 | Deep bowl/goblet |
| 1986 | IV1–IV2 | Area 2 or Area 3 | 52 | 1 | Rim | Group 5 | Necked jar |
| 1989 | IV1–IV2 | Area 4 | 185 | 1 | Rim | Group 3 | Necked jar |
| 1989 | IV1–IV2 | Area 4 | 185 | 2 | Rim | Group 3 | Vat |
| 1989 | IV1–IV2 | Area 4 | 185 | 3 | Rim | Group 3 | Vat |
| 1989 | IV1–IV2 | Area 4 | 185 | 4 | Rim | Group 3 | Jar with out-flared rim |
| 1989 | IV1–IV2 | Area 4 | 185 | 5 | Body | Group 5 | Necked jar |
| 1989 | IV1–IV2 | Area 4 | 185 | 6 | Rim | Group 5 | Bowl |
| 1989 | IV1–IV2 | Area 4 | 203 | 1 | Rim | Group 5 | Necked jar |
| 1989 | IV1–IV2 | Area 4 compartmented building | 212 | 1 | Rim | Group 5 | Bowl |
| 1989 | IV1–IV2 | Area 4 compartmented building | 212 | 2 | Rim | Group 1 | Jar with out-flared rim |
| 1990 | IV1–IV2? | sq. L16–M16 | 221bis | 1 | Rim | Group 1 | Bowl |
| 1990 | IV1–IV2? | sq. L16–M16 | 222bis | 1 | Rim | Group 5 | Necked jar |
| 1990 | IV1–IV2? | sq. L16–M16 | 222bis | 2 | Rim | Group 5 | Bowl |
| 1989 | IV1–IV2–Post IV | Area 4–Natural fill 1 | 186 | 1 | Rim | Group 1 | Jar |
| 1989 | IV1–IV2–Post IV | Area 4–Natural fill 1 | 187 | 1 | Rim | Group 5 | Necked jar |
| 1989 | IV1–IV2–Post IV | Area 4–Natural fill 1 | 187 | 2 | Rim | Group 5 | Bowl |
| 1989 | IV1–IV2–Post IV | Area 4–Natural fill 1 | 190 | 1 | Rim | Group 5 | Necked jar |

# CHRONO-CULTURAL RELATIONSHIPS

| Year | Level | Feature number | Batch # | Cer. # | Preservation | Group | Form |
|---|---|---|---|---|---|---|---|
| 1987 | IV2 | Area 3 | 121 | 1 | Rim | Group 5 | Bowl |
| 1987 | IV2 | Area 3 | 121 | 2 | Rim | Group 2 | Hole-mouth jar |
| 1987 | IV2 | Area 3 | 122 | 1 | Rim | Group 1 | Jar |
| 1987 | IV2 | Area 3 | 122 | 2 | Rim | Group 1 | Hole-mouth jar |
| 1987 | IV2 | Area 3 | 123 | 1 | Rim | Group 5 | Necked jar |
| 1987 | IV2 | Area 3 | 123 | 2 | Rim | Group 5 | Necked jar |
| 1987 | IV2 | Area 3 | 124 | 1 | Rim | Group 5 | Bowl |
| 1987 | IV2 | Area 3 | 128 | 1 | Rim | Group 2 | Bowl |
| 1987 | IV2 | Area 3 | 148 | 1 | Rim | Group 5 | Bowl |
| 1987 | IV2 | Area 3 | 148 | 2 | Rim | Group 1 | NA |
| 1987 | IV2 | Area 3 | 148 | 3 | Rim | Group 5 | Bowl |
| 1987 | IV2 | Area 3 | 148 | 4 | Rim | Group 5 | NA |
| 1987 | IV2 | Area 3 | 148 | 5 | Rim | Group 1 | Bowl |
| 1987 | IV2 | Area 3 | 148 | 6 | Rim | Group 3 | Jar |
| 1987 | IV2 | Hearth 1 | 160 | 1 | Rim | Group 3 | Vat |
| 1987 | IV2 | Room 8 | 125 | 1 | Rim | Group 1 | Jar |
| 1987 | IV2 | Room 8 | 125 | 2 | Rim | Group 3 | Vat |
| 1987 | IV2 | Room 8 | 125 | 3 | Rim | Group 5 | Necked jar |
| 1987 | IV2 | Room 8 | 127 | 1 | Rim | Group 3 | NA |
| 1987 | IV2 | Room 8 | 127 | 2 | Rim | Group 1 | Bowl/pot |
| 1987 | IV2 | Room 8 | 156 | 1 | Body | Group 7 | Misfired ceramic |
| 1989 | IV2 | Room 8 | 200 | 1 | Rim | Group 1 | Jar |
| 1989 | IV2 | Room 8 | 200 | 2 | Rim | Group 1 | Jar |
| 1989 | IV2 | Room 8 | 200 | 3 | Base | Group 2 | NA |
| 1989 | IV2 | Room 8 | 200 | 4 | Rim | Group 1 | Jar |
| 1989 | IV2 | Room 8 | 200 | 2bis | Rim | Group 3 | Jar with out-flared rim |
| 1991 | NA | NA | 367 | 2 | Rim | Group 4 | Deep bowl/goblet |
| 1991 | NA | NA | 424 | 1 | Rim | Group 4 | Necked jar |
| 1989 | NA | NA | 210 | 1 | Rim | Group 1 | NA |
| 1989 | NA | NA | 211 | 1 | Rim | Group 3 | Vat |
| 1990 | NA | NA | 220 | 1 | Rim | Group 5 | Bowl |
| 1990 | NA | NA | 221 | 1 | Rim | Group 1 | Jar |
| 1990 | NA | NA | 221 | 2 | Rim | Group 1 | Hole-mouth jar |
| 1990 | NA | NA | 222 | 1 | Body | Group 4 | NA |
| 1990 | NA | NA | 223 | 1 | Body | Group 4 | Jar |
| 1990 | NA | NA | 225 | 1 | Rim | Group 3 | Jar |
| 1990 | NA | NA | 226bis | 1 | Body | Group 4 | NA |
| 1990 | NA | NA | 227 | 1 | Body | Group 4 | NA |
| 1990 | NA | NA | 227 | 2 | Rim | Group 1 | Hole-mouth jar |
| 1990 | NA | NA | 228 | 2 | Rim | Group 2 | Bowl/pot |

| Year | Level | Feature number | Batch # | Cer. # | Preservation | Group | Form |
|---|---|---|---|---|---|---|---|
| 1990 | NA | NA | 228 | 3 | Rim | Group 7 | Misfired ceramic |
| 1990 | NA | NA | 229 | 1 | Rim | Group 1 | Jar |
| 1990 | NA | NA | 229 | 2 | Rim | Group 2 | NA |
| 1990 | NA | NA | 230 | 1 | Rim | Group 5 | Deep bowl/goblet |
| 1990 | NA | NA | 230 | 2 | Rim | Group 5 | Necked jar |
| 1990 | NA | NA | 230 | 3 | Rim | Group 5 | Bowl |
| 1990 | NA | NA | 230 | 4 | Rim | Group 5 | Bowl |
| 1990 | NA | NA | 230 | 5 | Rim | Group 5 | Necked jar |
| 1990 | NA | NA | 231 | 1 | Rim | Group 1 | NA |
| 1990 | NA | NA | 233 | 1 | Rim | Group 2 | Hole-mouth jar |
| 1990 | NA | NA | 233 | 2 | Rim | Group 3 | Vat |
| 1990 | NA | NA | 234 | 1 | Rim | Group 1 | Bowl |
| 1990 | NA | NA | 234 | 2 | Rim | Group 1 | Bowl |
| 1990 | NA | NA | 234 | 3 | Body | Group 7 | Misfired ceramic |
| 1990 | NA | NA | 234 | 4 | Rim | Group 5 | Necked jar |
| 1990 | NA | NA | 234 | 5 | Rim | Group 3 | Necked jar |
| 1990 | NA | NA | 234 | 6 | Rim | Group 5 | Necked jar |
| 1990 | NA | NA | 235 | 1 | Rim | Group 3 | Bowl/pot |
| 1990 | NA | NA | 235 | 2 | Rim | Group 1 | Hole-mouth jar |
| 1990 | NA | NA | 236 | 1 | Rim | Group 2 | Bowl/pot |
| 1990 | NA | NA | 237 | 1 | Rim | Group 1 | Bowl |
| 1990 | NA | NA | 241 | 1 | Body | Group 5 | Bowl |
| 1990 | NA | NA | 241 | 2 | Rim | Group 5 | NA |
| 1990 | NA | NA | 242 | 1 | Rim | Group 1 | NA |
| 1990 | NA | NA | 242 | 2 | Rim | Group 1 | NA |
| 1990 | NA | NA | 242 | 3 | Rim | Group 5 | Necked jar |
| 1990 | NA | NA | 243 | 1 | Rim | Group 1 | Jar with out-flared rim |
| 1990 | NA | NA | 243 | 2 | Rim | Group 1 | Bowl |
| 1990 | NA | NA | 243 | 3 | Rim | Group 2 | Bowl |
| 1990 | NA | NA | 243 | 4 | Rim | Group 2 | Bowl |
| 1990 | NA | NA | 244 | 1 | Rim | Group 3 | Vat |
| 1990 | NA | NA | 246 | 1 | Rim | Group 3 | Necked jar |
| 1990 | NA | NA | 246 | 2 | Rim | Group 5 | Bowl |
| 1990 | NA | NA | 246 | 3 | Body | Group 5 | Deep bowl/goblet |
| 1990 | NA | NA | 246 | 4 | Rim | Group 2 | Bowl/pot |
| 1990 | NA | NA | 246 | 5 | Rim | Group 1 | Jar |
| 1990 | NA | NA | 246 | 6 | Rim | Group 5 | Necked jar |
| 1990 | NA | NA | 246 | 7 | Rim | Group 5 | Necked jar |
| 1990 | NA | NA | 246 | 8 | Rim | Group 5 | Necked jar |
| 1990 | NA | NA | 248 | 1 | Rim | Group 1 | Hole-mouth jar |

| Year | Level | Feature number | Batch # | Cer. # | Preservation | Group | Form |
|---|---|---|---|---|---|---|---|
| 1990 | NA | NA | 248 | 2 | Rim | Group 2 | Bowl |
| 1990 | NA | NA | 250 | 1 | Body | Group 5 | Deep bowl/goblet |
| 1990 | NA | NA | 250 | 2 | Rim | Group 3 | Jar with out-flared rim |
| 1990 | NA | NA | 251 | 1 | Rim | Group 3 | Necked jar |
| 1990 | NA | NA | 253 | 1 | Rim | Group 5 | Bowl |
| 1990 | NA | NA | 254 | 1 | Rim | Group 3 | Necked jar |
| 1990 | NA | NA | 254 | 2 | Rim | Group 1 | Bowl |
| 1990 | NA | NA | 255 | 1 | Rim | Group 1 | Bowl |
| 1990 | NA | NA | 256 | 1 | Rim | Group 5 | Necked jar |
| 1990 | NA | NA | 257 | 1 | Rim | Group 1 | Jar with out-flared rim |
| 1990 | NA | NA | 257 | 2 | Body | Group 5 | Deep bowl/goblet |
| 1990 | NA | NA | 257 | 3 | Rim | Group 5 | Deep bowl/goblet |
| 1990 | NA | NA | 257 | 4 | Rim | Group 3 | Vat |
| 1990 | NA | NA | 258 | 1 | Rim | Group 2 | Hole-mouth jar |
| 1990 | NA | NA | 259 | 1 | Rim | Group 1 | Pot |
| 1990 | NA | NA | 260 | 1 | Rim | Group 5 | Necked jar |
| 1990 | NA | NA | 261 | 1 | Rim | Group 3 | Jar with out-flared rim |
| 1990 | NA | NA | 261 | 2 | Rim | Group 5 | Deep bowl/goblet |
| 1990 | NA | NA | 261 | 3 | Body | Group 5 | Deep bowl/goblet |
| 1990 | NA | NA | 263 | 1 | Rim | Group 1 | Hole-mouth jar |
| 1990 | NA | NA | 263 | 2 | Rim | Group 5 | Bowl |
| 1990 | NA | NA | 265 | 1 | Body | Group 5 | Deep bowl/goblet |
| 1990 | NA | NA | 266 | 1 | Body | Group 4 | Jar |
| 1990 | NA | NA | 268 | 1 | Rim | Group 1 | Jar |
| 1990 | NA | NA | 270 | 1 | Rim | Group 1 | Bowl |
| 1990 | NA | NA | 272 | 1 | Rim | Group 3 | Necked jar |
| 1990 | NA | NA | 272 | 2 | Rim | Group 1 | Bowl |
| 1990 | NA | NA | 272 | 3 | Rim | Group 1 | Necked jar |
| 1990 | NA | NA | 272 | 4 | Rim | Group 5 | Necked jar |
| 1990 | NA | NA | 273 | 1 | Rim | Group 1 | Bowl |
| 1990 | NA | NA | 273 | 2 | Rim | Group 1 | Hole-mouth jar |
| 1990 | NA | NA | 273 | 3 | Rim | Group 2 | Hole-mouth jar |
| 1990 | NA | NA | 273 | 4 | Rim | Group 1 | Bowl |
| 1990 | NA | NA | 274 | 1 | Body | Group 4 | NA |
| 1990 | NA | NA | 278 | 1 | Rim | Group 1 | Jar |
| 1990 | NA | NA | 278 | 2 | Rim | Group 1 | NA |
| 1990 | NA | NA | 278 | 3 | Rim | Group 3 | Jar |
| 1990 | NA | NA | 279 | 1 | Rim | Group 1 | Bowl |
| 1990 | NA | NA | 280 | 1 | Rim | Group 1 | Jar |
| 1990 | NA | NA | 280 | 2 | Rim | Group 1 | Hole-mouth jar |

| Year | Level | Feature number | Batch # | Cer. # | Preservation | Group | Form |
|---|---|---|---|---|---|---|---|
| 1990 | NA | NA | 280 | 3 | Rim | Group 2 | Bowl/pot |
| 1990 | NA | NA | 281 | 1 | Body | Group 4 | Jar |
| 1990 | NA | NA | 281 | 2 | Rim | Group 2 | Jar |
| 1990 | NA | NA | 281 | 3 | Rim | Group 2 | Hole-mouth jar |
| 1990 | NA | NA | 281 | 4 | Rim | Group 1 | Bowl |
| 1990 | NA | NA | 281 | 5 | Rim | Group 1 | Hole-mouth jar |
| 1990 | NA | NA | 281 | 6 | Rim | Group 1 | NA |
| 1990 | NA | NA | 281 | 7 | Rim | Group 1 | NA |
| 1990 | NA | NA | 281 | 8 | Rim | Group 1 | NA |
| 1990 | NA | NA | 282 | 1 | Rim | Group 1 | Jar |
| 1990 | NA | NA | 282 | 2 | Rim | Group 1 | Bowl |
| 1990 | NA | NA | 282 | 3 | Rim | Group 1 | Bowl |
| 1990 | NA | NA | 282 | 4 | Rim | Group 1 | Hole-mouth jar |
| 1990 | NA | NA | 282 | 5 | Body | Group 4 | NA |
| 1990 | NA | NA | 282 | 6 | Rim | Group 5 | Bowl |
| 1990 | NA | NA | 282 | 7 | Rim | Group 5 | Deep bowl/goblet |
| 1990 | NA | NA | 282 | 8 | Rim | Group 1 | Bowl |
| 1990 | NA | NA | 283 | 1 | Complete profile | Group 5 | Bowl |
| 1990 | NA | NA | 286 | 1 | Rim | Group 2 | Bowl/pot |
| 1990 | NA | NA | 286 | 2 | Rim | Group 1 | Hole-mouth jar |
| 1990 | NA | NA | 287 | 1 | Rim | Group 1 | Jar |
| 1990 | NA | NA | 289 | 1 | Rim | Group 1 | Bowl/pot |
| 1990 | NA | NA | 289 | 2 | Rim | Group 1 | Jar |
| 1990 | NA | NA | 292 | 1 | Rim | Group 2 | Bowl/pot |
| 1990 | NA | NA | 292 | 2 | Rim | Group 1 | Hole-mouth jar |
| 1990 | NA | NA | 292 | 3 | Rim | Group 2 | Hole-mouth jar |
| 1990 | NA | NA | 292 | 4 | Rim | Group 1 | Bowl/pot |
| 1990 | NA | NA | 293 | 1 | Rim | Group 1 | Hole-mouth jar |
| 1990 | NA | NA | 293 | 2 | Rim | Group 2 | Hole-mouth jar |
| 1990 | NA | NA | 294 | 1 | Rim | Group 3 | Hole-mouth jar |
| 1990 | NA | NA | 294 | 2 | Rim | Group 3 | Necked jar |
| 1990 | NA | NA | 294 | 3 | Rim | Group 1 | Hole-mouth jar |
| 1990 | NA | NA | 294 | 4 | Rim | Group 2 | Hole-mouth jar |
| 1990 | NA | NA | 294 | 5 | Rim | Group 2 | Jar |
| 1990 | NA | NA | 294 | 6 | Rim | Group 2 | Hole-mouth jar |
| 1990 | NA | NA | 294 | 7 | Rim | Group 1 | Jar |
| 1990 | NA | NA | 294 | 8 | Rim | Group 1 | NA |
| 1990 | NA | NA | 294 | 9 | Rim | Group 5 | Bowl |
| 1990 | NA | NA | 295 | 1 | Rim | Group 1 | Jar |
| 1990 | NA | NA | 296 | 1 | Rim | Group 2 | NA |

# CHRONO-CULTURAL RELATIONSHIPS

| Year | Level | Feature number | Batch # | Cer. # | Preservation | Group | Form |
|---|---|---|---|---|---|---|---|
| 1990 | NA | NA | 296 | 2 | Rim | Group 1 | NA |
| 1990 | NA | NA | 297 | 1 | Rim | Group 2 | Jar |
| 1990 | NA | NA | 297 | 2 | Rim | Group 3 | Necked jar |
| 1990 | NA | NA | 297 | 3 | Rim | Group 3 | Necked jar |
| 1990 | NA | NA | 297 | 4 | Rim | Group 1 | Bowl/pot |
| 1990 | NA | NA | 298 | 1 | Body | Group 5 | Bowl |
| 1990 | NA | NA | 300 | 1 | Rim | Group 5 | Bowl |
| 1990 | NA | NA | 302 | 1 | Rim | Group 1 | Hole-mouth jar |
| 1990 | NA | NA | 305 | 1 | Rim | Group 2 | Jar |
| 1990 | NA | NA | 305 | 2 | Rim | Group 1 | Bowl |
| 1990 | NA | NA | 305 | 3 | Rim | Group 1 | Bowl |
| 1990 | NA | NA | 310 | 1 | Rim | Group 1 | Bowl |
| 1990 | NA | NA | 316 | 1 | Rim | Group 1 | NA |
| 1990 | NA | NA | 318 | 1 | Rim | Group 3 | Necked jar |
| 1990 | NA | NA | 318 | 2 | Rim | Group 2 | Jar |
| 1990 | NA | NA | 318 | 3 | Rim | Group 2 | Pot |
| 1990 | NA | NA | 320 | 1 | Rim | Group 1 | Bowl |
| 1990 | NA | NA | 320 | 2 | Rim | Group 2 | Jar |
| 1990 | NA | NA | 321 | 1 | Rim | Group 1 | Jar |
| 1990 | NA | NA | 323 | 1 | Rim | Group 1 | Bowl |
| 1990 | NA | NA | 323 | 2 | Rim | Group 1 | Bowl/pot |
| 1990 | NA | NA | 324 | 1 | Rim | Group 1 | Bowl |
| 1990 | NA | NA | 325 | 1 | Rim | Group 2 | Hole-mouth jar |
| 1990 | NA | NA | 326 | 1 | Rim | Group 1 | NA |
| 1990 | NA | NA | 329 | 1 | Rim | Group 1 | Bowl |
| 1990 | NA | NA | 334 | 1 | Rim | Group 2 | Hole-mouth jar |
| 1990 | NA | NA | 335 | 1 | Rim | Group 1 | Jar with out-flared rim |
| 1990 | NA | NA | 336 | 1 | Rim | Group 1 | Bowl |
| 1990 | NA | NA | 338 | 1 | Base | Group 2 | NA |
| 1991 | NA | NA | 339 | 1 | Rim | Group 5 | Deep bowl/goblet |
| 1991 | NA | NA | 339 | 2 | Rim | Group 3 | Vat |
| 1991 | NA | NA | 339 | 3 | Rim | Group 3 | Vat |
| 1991 | NA | NA | 340 | 1 | Rim | Group 5 | Deep bowl/goblet |
| 1991 | NA | NA | 340 | 2 | Rim | Group 1 | Bowl/pot |
| 1991 | NA | NA | 341 | 1 | Rim | Group 5 | Bowl |
| 1990 | NA | NA | 342 | 1 | Rim | Group 2 | NA |
| 1991 | NA | NA | 344 | 1 | Rim | Group 5 | Necked jar |
| 1991 | NA | NA | 346 | 1 | Body | Group 5 | Bowl |
| 1991 | NA | NA | 347 | 1 | Rim | Group 5 | Bowl |
| 1991 | NA | NA | 347 | 2 | Rim | Group 3 | Necked jar |

| Year | Level | Feature number | Batch # | Cer. # | Preservation | Group | Form |
|---|---|---|---|---|---|---|---|
| 1991 | NA | NA | 347 | 3 | Rim | Group 5 | Deep bowl/goblet |
| 1991 | NA | NA | 348 | 1 | Rim | Group 1 | NA |
| 1991 | NA | NA | 348 | 2 | Body | Group 7 | Misfired ceramic |
| 1991 | NA | NA | 349 | 1 | Rim | Group 2 | Pot |
| 1991 | NA | NA | 349 | 2 | Rim | Group 1 | Jar |
| 1991 | NA | NA | 349 | 3 | Rim | Group 2 | Bowl/pot |
| 1991 | NA | NA | 349 | 4 | Rim | Group 2 | Hole-mouth jar |
| 1991 | NA | NA | 349 | 5 | Rim | Group 1 | NA |
| 1991 | NA | NA | 350 | 1 | Rim | Group 1 | Hole-mouth jar |
| 1991 | NA | NA | 351 | 1 | Body | Group 4 | NA |
| 1991 | NA | NA | 351 | 2 | Body | Group 4 | NA |
| 1991 | NA | NA | 352 | 1 | Rim | Group 1 | Jar |
| 1991 | NA | NA | 353 | 1 | Rim | Group 1 | Jar |
| 1991 | NA | NA | 353 | 2 | Rim | Group 1 | Jar |
| 1991 | NA | NA | 353 | 3 | Rim | Group 1 | Jar |
| 1991 | NA | NA | 353 | 4 | Rim | Group 1 | NA |
| 1991 | NA | NA | 355 | 1 | Rim | Group 1 | Bowl |
| 1991 | NA | NA | 355 | 2 | Rim | Group 1 | Hole-mouth jar |
| 1991 | NA | NA | 355 | 3 | Rim | Group 5 | NA |
| 1991 | NA | NA | 355 | 4 | Rim | Group 1 | Necked jar |
| 1991 | NA | NA | 356 | 1 | Rim | Group 1 | Hole-mouth jar |
| 1991 | NA | NA | 356 | 2 | Rim | Group 1 | Hole-mouth jar |
| 1991 | NA | NA | 357 | 1 | Rim | Group 1 | Jar |
| 1991 | NA | NA | 358 | 1 | Rim | Group 1 | Jar |
| 1991 | NA | NA | 358 | 2 | Rim | Group 1 | Jar |
| 1991 | NA | NA | 358 | 3 | Rim | Group 1 | Jar |
| 1991 | NA | NA | 358 | 4 | Complete profile | Group 5 | Deep bowl/goblet |
| 1991 | NA | NA | 358 | 5 | Rim | Group 5 | Bowl |
| 1991 | NA | NA | 358 | 6 | Rim | Group 5 | NA |
| 1991 | NA | NA | 358 | 7 | Rim | Group 3 | Jar |
| 1991 | NA | NA | 358bis | 1 | Rim | Group 5 | Deep bowl/goblet |
| 1991 | NA | NA | 358bis | 2 | Rim | Group 5 | Deep bowl/goblet |
| 1991 | NA | NA | 359 | 1 | Rim | Group 1 | Bowl |
| 1991 | NA | NA | 359 | 2 | Rim | Group 1 | NA |
| 1991 | NA | NA | 359 | 3 | Rim | Group 5 | NA |
| 1991 | NA | NA | 360 | 1 | Rim | Group 1 | Jar with out-flared rim |
| 1991 | NA | NA | 361 | 1 | Rim | Group 1 | Hole-mouth jar |
| 1991 | NA | NA | 362 | 1 | Rim | Group 1 | Bowl |
| 1991 | NA | NA | 362 | 2 | Rim | Group 5 | Bowl |
| 1991 | NA | NA | 362 | 3 | Rim | Group 1 | NA |

# CHRONO-CULTURAL RELATIONSHIPS

| Year | Level | Feature number | Batch # | Cer. # | Preservation | Group | Form |
|---|---|---|---|---|---|---|---|
| 1991 | NA | NA | 364 | 1 | Rim | Group 1 | Necked jar |
| 1991 | NA | NA | 364 | 2 | Rim | Group 1 | Bowl |
| 1991 | NA | NA | 366 | 1 | Rim | Group 1 | Bowl |
| 1991 | NA | NA | 366 | 2 | Rim | Group 3 | Jar |
| 1991 | NA | NA | 367 | 1 | Rim | Group 1 | Bowl |
| 1991 | NA | NA | 368 | 1 | Rim | Group 1 | Necked jar |
| 1991 | NA | NA | 370 | 1 | Rim | Group 3 | Jar |
| 1991 | NA | NA | 371 | 1 | Rim | Group 3 | Hole-mouth jar |
| 1991 | NA | NA | 381 | 1 | Rim | Group 1 | NA |
| 1991 | NA | NA | 382 | 1 | Rim | Group 2 | Pot |
| 1991 | NA | NA | 384 | 1 | Rim | Group 1 | Bowl |
| 1991 | NA | NA | 385 | 1 | Rim | Group 2 | Bowl |
| 1991 | NA | NA | 387 | 1 | Rim | Group 1 | Bowl |
| 1991 | NA | NA | 387 | 2 | Rim | Group 1 | NA |
| 1991 | NA | NA | 388 | 1 | Rim | Group 2 | Hole-mouth jar |
| 1991 | NA | NA | 388 | 2 | Rim | Group 1 | NA |
| 1991 | NA | NA | 389 | 1 | Rim | Group 1 | Jar |
| 1991 | NA | NA | 393 | 1 | Rim | Group 1 | Jar |
| 1991 | NA | NA | 393 | 2 | Rim | Group 1 | NA |
| 1991 | NA | NA | 400 | 2 | Rim | Group 1 | Bowl/pot |
| 1991 | NA | NA | 402 | 1 | Rim | Group 1 | Jar with out-flared rim |
| 1991 | NA | NA | 402 | 2 | Rim | Group 1 | NA |
| 1991 | NA | NA | 402 | 3 | Rim | Group 1 | NA |
| 1991 | NA | NA | 405 | 1 | Rim | Group 1 | Bowl |
| 1991 | NA | NA | 405 | 2 | Rim | Group 2 | Bowl/pot |
| 1991 | NA | NA | 406 | 1 | Rim | Group 1 | Bowl |
| 1991 | NA | NA | 409 | 1 | Rim | Group 1 | Bowl |
| 1991 | NA | NA | 410 | 1 | Complete profile | Group 1 | Bowl |
| 1991 | NA | NA | 414 | 1 | Rim | Group 2 | Hole-mouth jar |
| 1991 | NA | NA | 414 | 2 | Rim | Group 1 | Bowl |
| 1991 | NA | NA | 415 | 1 | Rim | Group 1 | Pot |
| 1991 | NA | NA | 423 | 1 | Rim | Group 1 | Bowl |
| 1991 | NA | NA | 432 | 1 | Rim | Group 1 | Bowl |
| 1984 | NA | NA | Am | 1 | Body | Group 5 | Deep bowl/goblet |
| 1990 | NA | sq. K16 | 220bis | 1 | Body | Group 5 | Deep bowl/goblet |
| 1990 | NA | sq. K16 | 220bis | 2 | Rim | Group 5 | Deep bowl/goblet |
| 1990 | NA | sq. L16 | 219bis | 1 | Rim | Group 1 | Bowl/pot |
| 1990 | NA | sq. L16 | 219bis | 2 | Rim | Group 3 | Jar |
| 1987 | Post IV | Natural fill 1 | 111 | 1 | Body | Group 5 | NA |
| 1987 | Post IV | Natural fill 1 | 111 | 2 | Rim | Group 1 | Bowl |

| Year | Level | Feature number | Batch # | Cer. # | Preservation | Group | Form |
|---|---|---|---|---|---|---|---|
| 1987 | Post IV | Natural fill 1 | 129 | 1 | Body | Group 5 | Deep bowl/goblet |
| 1987 | Post IV | Natural fill 1 | 129 | 2 | Rim | Group 5 | Jar |
| 1987 | Post IV | Natural fill 1 | 129 | 3 | Rim | Group 1 | Bowl/pot |
| 1987 | Post IV | Natural fill 1 | 129 | 4 | Rim | Group 5 | NA |
| 1987 | Post IV | Natural fill 1 | 129 | 5 | Rim | Group 5 | Bowl |
| 1987 | Post IV | Natural fill 1 | 130 | 1 | Rim | Group 3 | Vat |
| 1987 | Post IV | Natural fill 1 | 130 | 2 | Rim | Group 5 | Bowl |
| 1987 | Post IV | Natural fill 1 | 130 | 3 | Rim | Group 5 | Necked jar |
| 1987 | Post IV | Natural fill 1 | 130 | 4 | Rim | Group 2 | Bowl/pot |
| 1986 | Post IV | Natural fill 1 | A | 1 | Rim | Group 1 | Jar |
| 1986 | Post IV | Natural fill 1 | A | 2 | Body | Group 5 | Bowl |
| 1986 | Post IV | Natural fill 1 | A | 3 | Rim | Group 5 | Necked jar |
| 1986 | Post IV | Natural fill 1 | A | 4 | Rim | Group 3 | Vat |
| 1986 | Post IV | Natural fill 1 | A | 5 | Rim | Group 5 | Bowl |
| 1986 | Post IV | Natural fill 1 | A | 6 | Rim | Group 1 | Jar |
| 1985 | Post IV | Natural fill 1–2 | 17 | 1 | Rim | Group 3 | Vat |
| 1984 | Post IV | Natural fill 1–2 | 6 | 1 | Rim | Group 3 | Necked jar |
| 1984 | Post IV | Natural fill 1–2 | 6 | 2 | Rim | Group 5 | Necked jar |
| 1984 | Post IV | Natural fill 1–2 | 6 | 3 | Rim | Group 3 | Necked jar |
| 1985 | Post IV | Natural fill 1–2 | 6 | 4 | Rim | Group 5 | Necked jar |

# 6. Small Finds

The small finds from Excavation VII consist of 332 records. These records usually correspond to a single item, although Besenval sometimes recorded two to four and up to six items under the same small find number. In total, 358 items were recorded including one quartz (rock crystal) record that is listed as 'several flakes' (SF317). This total and the list provided in this volume are slightly different from the original list of small finds in Besenval archives. The original list contains 305 records. I have removed from this list a clay lump with a beam impression recovered from Level IV1 Room 3 that is presented in **Chapter 3** (SF28; Fig. 3.87), as well as a small find described as 'sand' collected on the ground of Level III2 Area 4 (SF316, sample 8), for which I have found no information. Furthermore, I have identified additional small finds in the archaeological storage room of Penjikent that did not have a small find number. I added them to this list, each with a new small find number.

Another important list in Besenval archives is the list of analytical samples. These samples total 274 records including samples from Excavation VII as well as samples from other excavations at Sarazm and from additional archaeological sites and surveyed areas in Tajikistan. The samples from Excavation VII amount to 143 records (not considering the ceramic samples). They include artefacts and raw material sampled for composition analysis, archaeobotanical samples including many obtained through flotation, and samples for C14 dating. Putting aside the archaeobotanical samples and samples for C14 dating, forty-nine records remain that are objects and raw material selected for composition analysis. More than half of these samples are each associated with a small find record; however, twenty of them correspond to items for which I have found no small find record. I have added small find numbers to these records, including to records of raw material, for the sake of consistency, since Besenval had already recorded samples of raw material as small finds.

## Classification

These small finds are primarily classified and presented in this volume according to the materials they are made from. I have defined fourteen main categories of materials, which are: bone industry; shell industry; terracotta industry; chalcedony, flint and quartz sandstone knapped lithic industry; quartz (rock crystal) knapped lithic industry and bead making; carnelian industry; lapis lazuli industry; turquoise industry; steatite and frit industries; stone industry; pigment and pigment preparation related remains; copper industry; lead industry; and iron industry. The materials of a number of items were not mentioned in Besenval archives, or only in very vague terms. This is especially true for many stone items that I have not been able to examine and that were vaguely described as beige stone, black stone, green stone, grey stone, pink stone, red stone, and white stone, as well as alabaster, gypsum, marble, onyx, and quartz(?). In the absence of more accurate determinations, I have grouped these ambiguous items together under the generic label 'stone industry' and classified them according to what I believe their functions may have been. Many of them correspond to river rocks rounded and polished by the action of moving water. Also, chalcedony, flint, and quartz sandstone items are presented together in the 'knapped lithic industry' category for the reason that a more detailed determination and analysis of this material will be presented elsewhere in collaboration with F. Brunet. This volume outlines only the main characteristics of the lithic industry from Excavation VII. Additionally, unlike the rest of the small finds, the 'pigment and remains relating to pigment preparation' category includes both raw material and tools because it is clear that the latter were used for this type of activity. Lastly, a discussion is provided regarding the actual presence of frit in Excavation VII; this is why the 'frit' items are grouped together with the single steatite item found in this excavation.

## Quantities

The 'chalcedony, flint, quartz sandstone knapped lithic industry' and 'stone industry' categories are the largest categories of small finds recorded in Excavation VII, representing together nearly 63 per cent (35.8 per cent and 27.1 per cent respectively) of the above-mentioned 358 items[1] (Table/Graph 6.1). The third largest category is the terracotta objects (8.4 per cent), which is followed by the records relating to pigment preparation (7.3 per cent), those relating to copper industry (5.9 per cent), the quartz (rock crystal) items (4.5 per cent), and the turquoise items (2.8 per cent). The other categories each represent less than 2 per cent and consist of six items or less. Certainly, it is not surprising that the 'stone industry' category is the second largest category, since it incorporates various types of stones, whereas most of the other small find categories have been defined according to the materials they are made from. Also, it is probably worth remembering that the 'chalcedony, flint, quartz sandstone knapped lithic industry' category mostly consists of fragments resulting from debitage activities, whereas most of the other categories are essentially composed of objects. Setting aside records that are not objects,[2] computation of the remaining 183 items classified according to what I believe their functions may have been, regardless of their materials, shows that ornaments (beads, bead-buttons, and pendants) and small discs (discs and perforated discs) are the two most common categories of objects found in Excavation VII (both categories amount to thirty-two items, 8.9 per cent) (Table 6.2). Then come the ground stones (thirteen items, 3.6 per cent), cobble flakes (eleven items, 3.1 per cent), hammer/grinding stones (eleven items, 3.1 per cent), pestles/sharpeners (eleven items, 3.1 per cent), and plaster (eleven items, 3.1 per cent). Awls follow (eight items, 2.2 per cent) and are followed by containers and vessels (seven items, 2 per cent), finials (seven items, 2 per cent), pebbles (seven items, 2 per cent), blades and daggers (six items, 1.7 per cent), pins (five items, 1.4 per cent), and weights(?) (five items, 1.4 per cent). The rest of the objects are found in three exemplars or less.

---

[1] Bearing in mind that the quartz (rock crystal) is represented by a few additional items not counted here.

[2] Most of those in the 'chalcedony, flint, quartz sandstone knapped lithic industry' category (save for four items: one bifacial blade (SF53), one drill (SF185), one disc (SF224), and one arrowhead? (SF57)), two records that are not clear whether they are objects, all records relating to raw materials, and those relating to debitage on quartz, as well as ores and slag, which amounts to 159 records and 175 items (48.9 per cent).

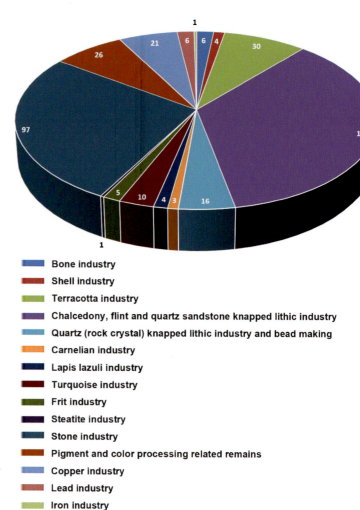

- ■ Bone industry
- ■ Shell industry
- ■ Terracotta industry
- ■ Chalcedony, flint and quartz sandstone knapped lithic industry
- ■ Quartz (rock crystal) knapped lithic industry and bead making
- ■ Carnelian industry
- ■ Lapis lazuli industry
- ■ Turquoise industry
- ■ Frit industry
- ■ Steatite industry
- ■ Stone industry
- ■ Pigment and color processing related remains
- ■ Copper industry
- ■ Lead industry
- ■ Iron industry

Table/Graph 6.1: Quantities of small finds from Sarazm Excavation VII classified by categories of raw material.

| Category | Records | Quantity | % |
|---|---|---|---|
| Bone industry | 6 | 6 | 1.7 |
| Shell industry | 3 | 4 | 1.1 |
| Terracotta industry | 30 | 30 | 8.4 |
| Chalcedony, flint and quartz sandstone knapped lithic industry | 116 | 128 | 35.8 |
| Quartz (rock crystal) knapped lithic industry and bead making | 11 | 16 | 4.5 |
| Carnelian industry | 2 | 3 | 0.8 |
| Lapis lazuli industry | 4 | 4 | 1.1 |
| Turquoise industry | 10 | 10 | 2.8 |
| Frit industry | 5 | 5 | 1.4 |
| Steatite industry | 1 | 1 | 0.3 |
| Stone industry | 96 | 97 | 27.1 |
| Pigment and colour processing related remains | 20 | 26 | 7.3 |
| Copper industry | 21 | 21 | 5.9 |
| Lead industry | 6 | 6 | 1.7 |
| Iron industry | 1 | 1 | 0.3 |
| Total | 332 | 358 | 100 |

Table 6.2: Quantities of small finds from Sarazm Excavation VII classified by functional categories.

| Category | Records | Quantity | % |
|---|---|---|---|
| Arrowhead? | 1 | 1 | 0.3 |
| Awl & awl? | 8 | 8 | 2.2 |
| Bead | 23 | 26 | 7.3 |
| Bead-button | 1 | 1 | 0.3 |
| Blade & dagger | 6 | 6 | 1.7 |
| Cobble flake | 11 | 11 | 3.1 |
| Container & vessel | 7 | 7 | 2.0 |
| Decorative tile? | 2 | 3 | 0.8 |
| Disc & perforated disc | 32 | 32 | 8.9 |
| Drill & drill? | 3 | 3 | 0.8 |
| Figurine? | 1 | 1 | 0.3 |
| Finial | 7 | 7 | 2.0 |
| Flat stone for pigment processing | 3 | 3 | 0.8 |
| Ground stone | 13 | 13 | 3.6 |
| Hammer/grinding stone | 11 | 11 | 3.1 |
| Hook? | 1 | 1 | 0.3 |
| Ingot? | 1 | 1 | 0.3 |
| Mould | 1 | 1 | 0.3 |
| Needle | 1 | 1 | 0.3 |
| Pebble | 7 | 7 | 2.0 |
| Pendant | 5 | 5 | 1.4 |
| Pestle/sharpener | 11 | 11 | 3.1 |
| Pin | 5 | 5 | 1.4 |
| Plaster | 5 | 11 | 3.1 |
| Seal | 1 | 1 | 0.3 |
| Sharpener | 1 | 1 | 0.3 |
| Weight? | 5 | 5 | 1.4 |
| Lithic | 112 | 124 | 34.6 |
| Raw material & other flakes/fragments | 35 | 39 | 10.9 |
| Ore & ore? | 7 | 7 | 2.0 |
| Slag, slag? & melted lead | 3 | 3 | 0.8 |
| Unknown | 2 | 2 | 0.6 |
| Total | 332 | 358 | 100 |

## Analysis and Terminology

Forty-six of these small finds have a sample number, which means that Besenval planned to have their compositions analysed. It seems, however, that not all the small finds with a sample number were eventually analysed since I have found results from composition analyses for only a limited number of them. The archives suggest that F. Cesbron conducted all the composition analyses at the Laboratoire de Minéralogie-Cristallographie Pierre et Marie Curie (Paris VI), Paris, France (see Cesbron 1996). Besenval and Isakov (1989, 19 n. 38) also specify that Ms Vachey and Sichère worked with him on the analyses. When available, results from these analyses are provided below together with the descriptions of the small finds.

Besenval measured some of these small finds, while most were not. Consequently, the dimensions of the small finds reported in this volume were measured either directly on the objects I was able to access, or from available photographs. In Tables 6.3–6.31, records that could not be documented have 'NA' (Not Available) marks in the columns 'preservation', 'dimensions', and/or 'observations'.

As for the terminology employed in this chapter, I have used different sources. My primary source is the information reported by Besenval and Cesbron. Publications by Barthélémy de Saizieu and Bouquillon have been extremely useful as far as the ornaments and various types of stones recorded in Excavation VII are concerned. Also, general morphological descriptions of the objects are inspired by previous works such as the study of the small finds from Tepe Yahya by Beale (1986) as well as that of the lapis lazuli assemblage from Shahr-i Sokhta by Vidale and Lazzari (2017).

Table 6.3: Bone industry from Sarazm Excavation VII.

| Year | SF no. | Sample no. | Material | Object category | Q. | Image | Preservation | Dimensions | Observations | Level | Context | Context category |
|---|---|---|---|---|---|---|---|---|---|---|---|---|
| 1987 | 47 | NA | Bone | Awl | 1 | Yes | Fragment | L = 3.2 cm; W (max) = 0.8 cm | / | II1 | Area 1 | Fill and floor |
| 1989 | 79 | NA | Bone | Awl | 1 | Yes | Incomplete | L = 10.5 cm; W (max) = 1 cm | / | I1 | Room 3 | Fill and floor |
| 1991 | 252 | NA | Bone | Awl? | 1 | No | NA | NA | / | NA | North/East area; likely between sq. J16-17-K16-17-L16-17-M16-17-N16-17 | NA |
| 1991 | 290 | NA | Bone | Needle | 1 | Yes | Fragment | L = 1.6 cm; D = 0.2 cm | / | III1 | North/East; Area 2 | Fill and floor |
| 1991 | 304 | NA | Bone | Tool? | 1 | Yes | Incomplete | L = 7.6 cm; W (max) = 1.8 cm | / | NA | North/East area; likely between sq. J16-17-K16-17-L16-17-M16-17-N16-17 | NA |
| 1991 | 305 | NA | Bone | Awl | 1 | Yes | Fragment | L = 4.3 cm; W (max) = 1 cm | / | NA | North/East area; likely between sq. J16-17-K16-17-L16-17-M16-17-N16-17 | NA |

## *Bone Industry*

Bone industry consists of six records (Table 6.3; Fig. 6.1). These records include fragments of three awls and an additional potential one that is undocumented. The best-preserved exemplar is 10.5 cm long (SF79). The two other bone items are a fragment of a needle and a fragment of a worked bone, although it is unclear whether the latter is an artefact. The awls and needle have parallels at Sarazm (Isakov 1991, figs 33, 40; Razzokov 2008, figs 25–26), and these types of objects are found at many Chalcolithic and Bronze Age sites between Central Asia and the Near East including at Mundigak (Casal 1961, fig. 132) and Anau (Hiebert 2003, 82 fig. 7.2, 90 fig. 7.10).

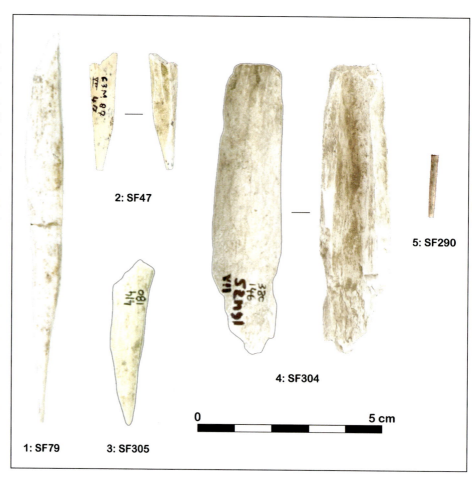

Figure 6.1: Bone industry from Sarazm Excavation VII.
Photographs by R. Besenval, plate by B. Mutin.

Table 6.4: Shell industry from Sarazm Excavation VII.

| Year | SF no. | Sample no. | Material | Object category | Q. | Image | Preservation | Dimensions | Observations | Level | Context | Context category |
|------|--------|------------|----------|-----------------|-----|-------|--------------|------------|--------------|-------|---------|------------------|
| 1987 | 34 | NA | Shell | Bead | 1 | Yes | Complete | L = 1.1 cm; W (max) = 0.9 cm | Gastropod | III2 | Area 4 | Fill and floor |
| 1987 | 49 | NA | Shell | Bead | 1 | Yes | Complete | L = 2.5 cm; W (max) = 0.6 cm | Tusk shell | I1 | Room 4 | Fill and floor |
| 1990 | 151 | NA | Shell | Bead | 2 | Yes | Complete | L = 1.3/1.1 cm; W (max) = 0.9/0.8 cm | Gastropod | NA | Possibly between sq. L16–17–M14–17–N14–17 | NA |

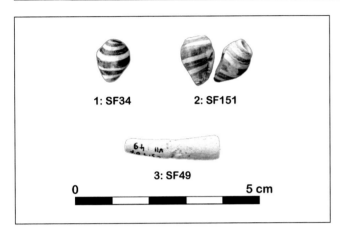

Figure 6.2: Shell industry from Sarazm Excavation VII. Photographs by R. Besenval, plate by B. Mutin.

## *Shell Industry*

Shell industry is represented by three records representing four beads (Table 6.4; Fig. 6.2). One (SF49) is a bead made from a tusk shell (order *dentaliida*; family *dentaliidae*), while the two other records are three beads made of gastropods (super family: *tonnoidea*; family *tonnidae*; species *tonna sulcosa* born). These shells are found in the Indian Ocean (Dance 2002, 90, 206).

Shells and shell ornaments have been recorded at Sarazm (e.g. Isakov 1991, fig. 40), although they do not seem to be very common or have not been much documented in general at this site. The most famous examples are two shell bracelets recorded inside the tomb of the 'Princess of Sarazm' (Besenval 2005, 5 figs 11–12). These bracelets have exact parallels in fourth-millennium BCE graves excavated at Shahi-Tump, in the Kech-Makran region of south-western Pakistani Balochistan (Besenval 2005, 4 figs 9–10, 6). Tusk shell beads such as the one found in Excavation VII were recorded in these graves, while Tosi (1974b, 152) also reports the use of tusk shell in the Khorezm (Vinogradov 1970; 1973).

## *Terracotta Industry*

Terracotta objects amount to thirty items which divide into perforated discs, discs, finials, one figurine(?), and one vessel.

### Perforated Discs

Twenty terracotta objects are perforated discs (Table 6.5; Fig. 6.3). They are made from recut ceramic sherds. For this reason, their colours and fabrics are similar to those of some of the ceramic groups described in **Chapter 5**: they are of buff, red, or grey colours; and discs with no visible inclusions and discs with sand-size mineral inclusions are observed. They usually are circular, although some were carelessly made and have irregular, almost squarish, outlines. Their diameters range from 2.3 to 4.5 cm, while their thicknesses equal those of the ceramics they were recut from. Discs of this type have parallels in other excavations at Sarazm, and examples have been observed where the hole in their centres was not finished (Isakov 1991, fig. 3 nos 1–2, 5–7, fig. 22 nos 1–3, 7–10, 15–15, fig. 53 nos 14–16, fig. 61 nos 4–6, 9–11, 15–16, fig. 74 nos 1–4; Razzokov 2008, fig. 29 no. 2). These objects are commonly interpreted as spindle-whorls, although they may also be viewed as clay beads, especially the thicker ones, or tokens. Stone versions of them are also recorded in Excavation VII (see below) and in other excavations at Sarazm (Razzokov 2008, fig. 29 nos 1, 6).

Table 6.5: Terracotta industry from Sarazm Excavation VII: perforated discs.

| Year | SF no. | Sample no. | Material | Object category | Q. | Image | Preservation | Dimensions | Observations | Level | Context | Context category |
|---|---|---|---|---|---|---|---|---|---|---|---|---|
| 1984 | 5 | NA | Terracotta | Perforated disc | 1 | Yes | Incomplete | D = 2.8 cm | Grey colour | I3 or I4 | Level I3 Room 6, Area 2, or Alleyway 2; or Level I4 Area 4 | Fill and floor |
| 1986 | 20 | NA | Terracotta | Perforated disc | 1 | No | Complete | NA | NA | IV1 | Area 1 | Fill and floor |
| 1987 | 31 | NA | Terracotta | Perforated disc | 1 | No | Complete | NA | NA | III2 | Area 4 | Fill and floor |
| 1987 | 32 | NA | Terracotta | Perforated disc | 1 | No | Complete | NA | NA | III2 | Area 4 | Fill and floor |
| 1987 | 60 | NA | Terracotta | Perforated disc | 1 | No | Complete | NA | NA | III3 | Area 6 | Fill and floor |
| 1987 | 61 | NA | Terracotta | Perforated disc | 1 | No | Complete | NA | NA | IV1 | Sq. I12–13 | Fill and floor |
| 1987 | 62 | NA | Terracotta | Perforated disc | 1 | No | Fragment | NA | Several holes | II1 | Room 1 | Fill and floor |
| 1989 | 70 | NA | Terracotta | Perforated disc | 1 | Yes | Complete | D = 2.6 cm | Buff colour | IV1–IV2 | Area 4 | Fill and floor |
| 1990 | 110 | NA | Terracotta | Perforated disc | 1 | Yes | Complete | D = 4.4 cm | Buff colour | IV1–IV2? | North/East area; sq. L16–M16 | NA |
| 1990 | 111 | NA | Terracotta | Perforated disc | 1 | Yes | Complete | D = 4.2 cm | Red colour | NA | Possibly between sq. L16–17–M14–17–N14–17 | NA |
| 1990 | 147 | NA | Terracotta | Perforated disc | 1 | Yes | Complete | D = 2.8 cm; T = 1.5 cm | Buff colour | NA | Possibly between sq. L16–17–M14–17–N14–17 | NA |
| 1990 | 148 | NA | Terracotta | Perforated disc | 1 | Yes | Complete | D = 4.5 cm | Grey colour | NA | Possibly between sq. L16–17–M14–17–N14–17 | NA |
| 1990 | 188 | NA | Terracotta | Perforated disc | 1 | Yes | Incomplete | D = 3.5 cm | Black colour | NA | Possibly between sq. L16–17–M14–17–N14–17 | NA |
| 1990 | 193 | NA | Terracotta | Perforated disc | 1 | Yes | Complete | D = 3.2 cm | Red colour | NA | Possibly between sq. L16–17–M14–17–N14–17 | NA |
| 1991 | 233 | NA | Terracotta | Perforated disc | 1 | Yes | Complete | D = 3.4 cm | Buff colour | NA | North/East area; likely between sq. J16–17–K16–17–L16–17–M16–17–N16–17 | NA |
| 1991 | 235 | NA | Terracotta | Perforated disc | 1 | Yes | Complete | D = 2.5 cm | Red colour | NA | North/East area; likely between sq. J16–17–K16–17–L16–17–M16–17–N16–17 | NA |
| 1991 | 236 | NA | Terracotta | Perforated disc | 1 | Yes | Complete | D = 3.3 cm | Buff colour | III1 | North/East; Area 2 | Fill and floor |
| 1991 | 237 | NA | Terracotta | Perforated disc | 1 | Yes | Complete | D = 3.3 cm | Red colour | III1 | North/East; Area 2 | Fill and floor |
| 1991 | 238 | NA | Terracotta | Perforated disc | 1 | Yes | Complete | D = 3.3 cm | Buff colour | III1 | North/East; Area 2 | Fill and floor |
| 1991 | 255 | NA | Terracotta | Perforated disc | 1 | Yes | Complete | D = 2.3 cm | Grey colour | NA | North/East area; likely between sq. J16–17–K16–17–L16–17–M16–17–N16–17 | NA |

TERRACOTTA INDUSTRY

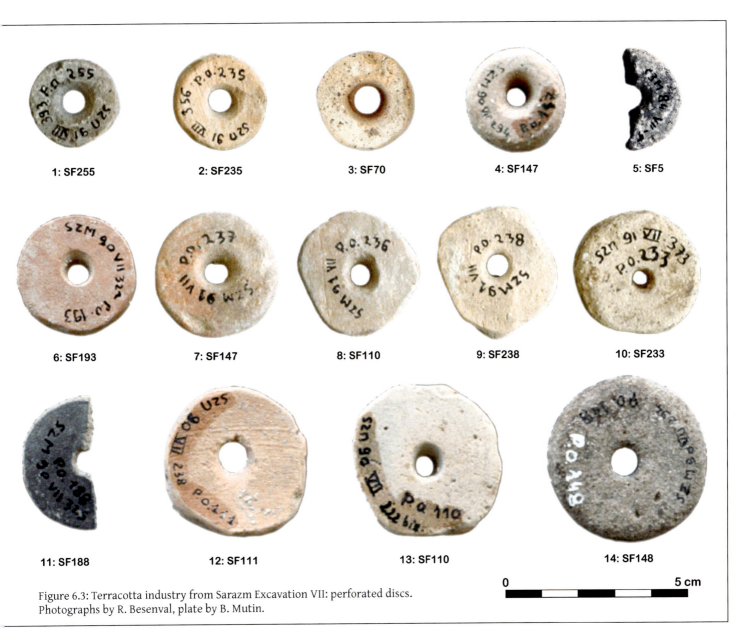

Figure 6.3: Terracotta industry from Sarazm Excavation VII: perforated discs. Photographs by R. Besenval, plate by B. Mutin.

## Discs

Six terracotta objects are discs that are not perforated (Table 6.6; Fig. 6.4). Like the above-described perforated items, these discs are made from recut ceramic sherds of buff or red colour. One has a sandy fabric and a cream slip on both surfaces (SF308) in a fashion similar to ceramic Group 3 (see **Chapter 5**). It remains unclear whether these discs are unfinished versions of perforated discs or had a different function. Consistent with the former hypothesis is the fact that none of them have regular contours, while two of them (SF307 and SF311) show what appear to be the beginning of perforations in their centres. Four have diameters between 2.8–4.4 cm, consistent with those of the perforated discs, while two have diameters over 6 cm (SF308 and SF310).

172                                                                                                                            6. SMALL FINDS

Figure 6.4: Terracotta industry from Sarazm Excavation VII: discs. Photographs by R. Besenval, plate by B. Mutin.

Table 6.6: Terracotta industry from Sarazm Excavation VII: discs.

| Year | SF no. | Sample no. | Material | Object category | Q. | Image | Preservation | Dimensions | Observations | Level | Context | Context category |
|------|--------|------------|-----------|-----------------|----|-------|--------------|------------|--------------|-------|---------|------------------|
| 1987 | 306 | NA | Terracotta | Disc | 1 | Yes | Complete | D = 4.4 cm | Red colour | IV2 | Area 3; sq. J11 | Fill and floor |
| 1990 | 307 | NA | Terracotta | Disc | 1 | Yes | Complete | D = 3.6 cm | Red colour | NA | North/East area; sq. L16 | Fill and floor |
| 1990 | 308 | NA | Terracotta | Disc | 1 | Yes | Complete | D = 6.6 cm | Buff colour | NA | Possibly between sq. L16–17–M14–17–N14–17 | NA |
| 1990 | 309 | NA | Terracotta | Disc | 1 | Yes | Complete | D = 4 cm | Buff colour | NA | North/East area; likely between sq. J16–17–K16–17–L16–17–M16–17–N16–17 | NA |
| 1991 | 310 | NA | Terracotta | Disc | 1 | Yes | Complete | D = 6.2 cm | Buff colour | NA | Possibly between sq. L16–17–M14–17–N14–17 | NA |
| 1990 | 311 | NA | Terracotta | Disc | 1 | Yes | Complete | D = 2.8 cm | Red colour | IV1–IV2? | North/East area; sq. L16–M16 | NA |

# TERRACOTTA INDUSTRY

Table 6.7: Terracotta industry from Sarazm Excavation VII: finials.

| Year | SF no. | Sample no. | Material | Object category | Q. | Image | Preservation | Dimensions | Observations | Level | Context | Context category |
|---|---|---|---|---|---|---|---|---|---|---|---|---|
| 1990 | 154 | NA | Terracotta | Finial | 1 | No | Complete | D = 2.2 cm | NA | NA | Possibly between sq. L16-17-M14-17-N14-17 | NA |
| 1990 | 155 | NA | Terracotta | Finial | 1 | No | Complete | D = 2.2 cm; T = 1.7 cm | NA | NA | Possibly between sq. L16-17-M14-17-N14-17 | NA |

Table 6.8: Terracotta industry from Sarazm Excavation VII: figurine(?).

| Year | SF no. | Sample no. | Material | Object category | Q. | Image | Preservation | Dimensions | Observations | Level | Context | Context category |
|---|---|---|---|---|---|---|---|---|---|---|---|---|
| 1990 | 175 | NA | Terracotta | Figurine? | 1 | Yes | Fragment | H = 2.2 cm; W (max) = 1.5 cm | Buff colour | NA | Possibly between sq. L16-17-M14-17-N14-17 | NA |

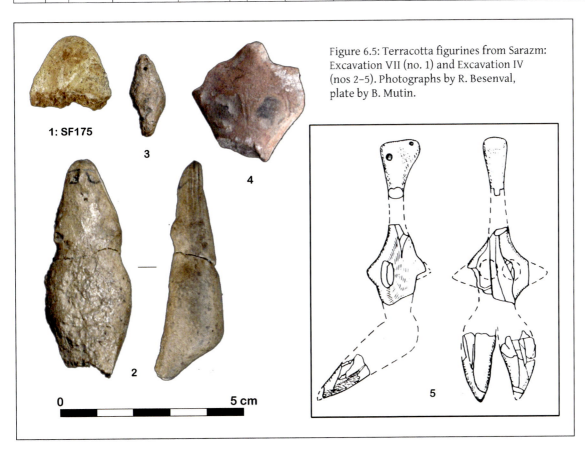

Figure 6.5: Terracotta figurines from Sarazm: Excavation VII (no. 1) and Excavation IV (nos 2-5). Photographs by R. Besenval, plate by B. Mutin.

## Finials

Two terracotta small finds are objects that are commonly characterized as finials (SF154 and SF155) (Table 6.7). These objects are both 2.2 cm in diameter. I have found no illustration for them, although I assume that they are not very different from those generally found at Sarazm, including types made of stone (see below; Isakov 1991, fig. 22 nos 5-6, 11-14, fig. 53 nos 12-13, fig. 61 nos 7-8, 12-14, fig. 74 nos 5-14).

## Figurine?

Besenval recorded one terracotta fragment that he thought might be part of a human figurine (SF175) (Table 6.8; Fig. 6.5). This hypothesis cannot be confirmed, but it remains possible that this fragment was part of the head or a limb of a human figurine. Human figurines at Sarazm were found in Excavation IV including in the funerary stone circle in Excavation IV that contained the tomb of the 'Princess of Sarazm' (Isakov 1991, fig. 68) (Fig. 6.5).

Table 6.9: Terracotta industry from Sarazm Excavation VII: vessel(?).

| Year | SF no. | Sample no. | Material | Object category | Q. | Image | Preservation | Dimensions | Observations | Level | Context | Context category |
|---|---|---|---|---|---|---|---|---|---|---|---|---|
| 1991 | 302 | NA | Terracotta | Vessel? | 1 | No | Fragment | NA | Rectangular vessel | NA | North/East area; likely between sq. J16-17-K16-17-L16-17-M16-17-N16-17 | NA |

**Vessel?**

Lastly, Besenval recorded a fragment of a terracotta vessel (SF302), which he described as a rectangular vessel. I have found no image of this object (Table 6.9). However, one may wonder whether this fragment could have been that of a terracotta house model, or a box with inner partitions, such as those observed at Shortughaï (Francfort 1989, pl. 62 nos 11-13) and Farkhor (Vinogradova 2021, 638, 639 fig. 23.4 nos 2-2a).

**Parallels**

Perforated and unperforated discs made from recut ceramic fragments are relatively common between Central Asia and Middle Asia. Unperforated discs are for instance generally observed on the surfaces of Indus Civilization sites. However, considering most parallels for the ceramics from Sarazm, it is probably more specifically worth noting that perforated discs were for instance recorded in fourth-millennium BCE contexts at Anau, where they are interpreted as whorls (Hiebert 2003, 88 fig. 7.8 nos 6-10). The same interpretation is offered for the most refined exemplars from Mundigak which were recorded at this site from Periods III5 to VI. Casal notes that he found at this site many ceramic sherds that were roughly recut and perforated in their centres, which may have been used as whorls or for other activities (Casal 1961, 232 fig. 133 no. 3). This description seems to conform to those from Sarazm. Additional parallels are at Sheri Khan Tarakai in Pakistan, where they are common and essentially date to the fourth millennium BCE (Knox et al. 2010, 217, 256 57). Fairservis also reported perforated and unperforated, roughly rounded ceramic sherds from Damb Sadaat Periods I to III in the Quetta Valley and Sur Jangal in the Loralai Valley, as well as from Periano Ghundai, Moghul Ghundai, and Kaudani in the Zhob Valley. He interprets these objects as 'clay stoppers' or 'gaming pieces' and qualifies them as being typical of northern Pakistani Balochistan (Fairservis 1956, 230; 1959, 299, 303 fig. 13 m, n, 353 fig. 58 t, u, 358, 359 fig. 60 g, 360 fig. 61 a). It is perhaps meaningful that none is illustrated further south. At a minimum, none is reported in the C. Jarrige et al. 1995 volume on Mehrgarh nor in the de Cardi 1965 report on her excavations in the Surab region. A possibility may be that such objects did not make the cut in these publications, although this possibility seems unlikely in the former which is quite thorough. Similarly, such discs seem rare and even possibly absent before the Indus Civilization further to the south-west in Kech-Makran. However, some are reported from Sohr Damb (Period II), where they are dated to between 3100-2800/2700 BCE (Franke 2015, pl. 18 g). Perforated discs made from recut ceramic sherds were also found at Shahr-i Sokhta, where they are interpreted as spindle-whorls (Tosi 1969, 371 fig. 41 h, i). Additionally, perforated and unperforated ceramic discs were recorded at Tepe Hissar in Period I and III levels (Schmidt 1937, 53 pl. XIVA H2666, H2286, 185 pl. XLIV H3127). This inventory is certainly not comprehensive but shows that Sarazm was part of a large area where the practice of cutting and grinding ceramic fragments into discs was shared, although it is unclear whether this practice was relating to gaming, weaving, closing containers, and/or counting. Lastly, it seems that this practice goes way back, as illustrated by the examples from the fifth millennium BCE at Tal-i Iblis (Chase et al. 1967, 155, 165, 166 fig. 34 no. 3, 168 fig. 36 no. 18; Evett 1967, 217-19, 218 fig. 8 nos 9, 11; Caldwell and Sarraf 1967, 300 fig. 14 no. 7) and from Neolithic and Chalcolithic Tepe Yahya in south-eastern Iran (Beale 1986, 192 fig. 7.18 h, 198).

Similarly, finials are also observed from at least Turkmenistan and northern Iran to Pakistan. They are recorded from the early fourth millennium BCE Chalcolithic period through the Bronze Age at Anau (Hiebert 2003, 84 fig. 7.3 no. 11, 87), Altyn-Depe in Namazga III levels (Masson 1988, pl. XXVII no. 11), Geoksyur (Sarianidi 1961, 316 pl. XIII), Dashliji-Depe (Khlopin 1961, 219 pl. XII), and Kara-Depe where some bear designs (Masson 1961, pl. 14 nos 10, 12). They are known to be 'commonly found at [...] Early Village settlements in Central Asia' (Hiebert 2003, 87). Such objects were observed in Periods IC through IIA at Tepe Hissar (Schmidt 1937, 53, 300, 304 pl. XIVA H2723), as well as at Shir-i Shian (Dyson and Thornton 2009, 15 fig. 10). Further to the south, I have found no records of finials in the publications from Shahr-i Sokhta, but Knox et al.

Figure 6.6: Chalcedony, flint, quartz sandstone knapped lithic industry from Sarazm Excavation VII. Photographs and plate by B. Mutin.

(2010, 216) cite a personal communication from M. Tosi who mentioned that such objects were found at this site. They were also used at Mundigak, where terracotta and stone exemplars were found. As far as the terracotta specimens are concerned, Casal writes that the oldest examples are from Period I3. They are then numerous in the following levels, especially in Period II2 and then virtually disappear from Period III2 onward. The stone examples consist of only seven items which were all recovered from Period I5 (Casal 1961, 226, fig. 130 nos 3, 3a). Additional terracotta objects from Mundigak are interpreted as spindle-whorls, although they are not entirely perforated and are in this regard reminiscent of finials. They seem common essentially in Period II (Casal 1961, 232 fig. 133 nos 2, 2a). Again, finials were also found in Pakistan. At a minimum, such objects with conical, biconical, and spherical shapes were recorded in large numbers at Sheri Khan Tarakai (Knox et al. 2010, 216, 252–55), although the specimens from that site include painted ones, whereas no painted finial has been recorded at Sarazm.

As for the terracotta vessel, without knowing what it looks like, I suggested that its description was reminiscent of terracotta house models or boxes from Shortughaï and Farkhor, while such an object also recalls examples in stone such as those from Shahdad (Hakemi 1997, 57 figs 34–35).

Lastly, the portion of the figurine that was found in Excavation VII is too small and inconclusive to be compared and to even ascertain it belonged to a figurine.

## Chalcedony, Flint, Quartz Sandstone Knapped Lithic Industry

One hundred and sixteen records are records of debitage on chalcedony and flint, representing 128 items (Table 6.10; Fig. 6.6). These records are not fully described here as they are the topic of a specific collaborative analysis with Brunet who has studied the totality of the lithic industry from Sarazm (see Brunet and Razzokov 2016).

Table 6.10: Chalcedony, flint, quartz sandstone knapped lithic industry from Sarazm Excavation VII.

| Year | SF no. | Material | Object category | Q. | Level | Context | Context category |
|---|---|---|---|---|---|---|---|
| 1984 | 1 | Lithic | Flake/Blade | 1 | III2 | Area 4 | Fill and floor |
| 1984 | 4 | Lithic | Flake/Blade | 1 | I3 or I4 | Level I3 Room 6, Area 2, or Alleyway 2; or Level I4 Area 4 | Fill and floor |
| 1984 | 7 | Lithic | Core | 1 | III2 | Area 4 | Fill and floor |
| 1984 | 8 | Lithic | Flake/Blade | 1 | III2 | Area 4 | Fill and floor |
| 1984 | 9 | Lithic | Flake/Blade | 1 | II2 | Area 3 | Fill and floor |
| 1984 | 13 | Lithic | Flake/Blade | 1 | I3 | Alleyway 2 | Fill and floor |
| 1985 | 15 | Lithic | Unknown | 1 | I1 | Alleyway 1 | Fill and floor |
| 1987 | 36 | Lithic | Flake/Blade | 1 | I3 | Room 9 | Fill and floor |
| 1987 | 40 | Lithic | Flake/Blade | 1 | IV1 | Sq. I14 | Fill and floor |
| 1987 | 43 | Lithic | Flake/Blade | 1 | III2 | Area 3 | Fill and floor |
| 1987 | 44 | Lithic | Flake/Blade | 1 | III2 | Area 3 | Fill and floor |
| 1987 | 46 | Lithic | Flake/Blade | 1 | III2 | Area 4 | Fill and floor |
| 1987 | 48 | Lithic | Flake/Blade | 3 | I1 | Room 4 | Fill and floor |
| 1987 | 50 | Lithic | Flake/Blade | 4 | I1 | Room 2 | Fill and floor |
| 1987 | 51 | Lithic | Flake/Blade | 2 | I4 | Area 4 | Fill and floor |
| 1987 | 53 | Lithic | Bifacial blade | 1 | I3 | Hearth 6 | Hearth |
| 1987 | 54 | Lithic | Flake/Blade | 4 | II1 | Area 2 | Fill and floor |
| 1987 | 55 | Lithic | Flake/Blade | 1 | Post-IV | Natural fill 1; sq. I14–15 | Natural fill |
| 1987 | 56 | Lithic | Flake/Blade | 1 | Post-IV | Natural fill 1; sq. I14–15 | Natural fill |
| 1987 | 57 | Lithic | Arrowhead? | 1 | I3 | Room 5 | Fill and floor |
| 1987 | 58 | Lithic | Flake/Blade | 1 | I3 | Room 9 | Fill and floor |
| 1987 | 59 | Lithic | Flake/Blade | 1 | III2 | Room 3 | Fill and floor |
| 1987 | 67 | Lithic | Flake/Blade | 2 | I1 | Room 3 | Fill and floor |
| 1987 | 68 | Lithic | Flake/Blade | 2 | II2 | Area 3 | Fill and floor |
| 1989 | 74 | Lithic | Flake/Blade | 1 | IV1–IV2 | Area 4 | Fill and floor |
| 1989 | 81 | Lithic | Flake/Blade | 1 | IV1 | Sq. M11 | Fill and floor |
| 1989 | 86 | Lithic | Flake/Blade | 1 | I3 | Room 9 | Fill and floor |
| 1989 | 87 | Lithic | Flake/Blade | 1 | I3 | Room 9 | Fill and floor |
| 1989 | 88 | Lithic | Flake/Blade | 1 | I3 | Room 9 | Fill and floor |
| 1989 | 89 | Lithic | Core | 1 | III2 | Area 5; sq. K11 | Fill and floor |
| 1989 | 90 | Lithic | Flake/Blade | 1 | III2 | Area 5; sq. K11 | Fill and floor |
| 1990 | 115 | Lithic | Flake/Blade | 1 | NA | Possibly between sq. L16–17–M14–17–N14–17 | NA |
| 1990 | 116 | Lithic | Flake/Blade | 1 | NA | Possibly between sq. L16–17–M14–17–N14–17 | NA |
| 1990 | 117 | Lithic | Flake/Blade | 1 | NA | Possibly between sq. L16–17–M14–17–N14–17 | NA |
| 1990 | 118 | Lithic | Unknown | 1 | NA | Possibly between sq. L16–17–M14–17–N14–17 | NA |
| 1990 | 119 | Lithic | Flake/Blade | 1 | NA | Possibly between sq. L16–17–M14–17–N14–17 | NA |
| 1990 | 120 | Lithic | Flake/Blade | 1 | NA | Possibly between sq. L16–17–M14–17–N14–17 | NA |

| Year | SF no. | Material | Object category | Q. | Level | Context | Context category |
|---|---|---|---|---|---|---|---|
| 1990 | 121 | Lithic | Flake/Blade | 1 | IV1–IV2? | North/East area; sq. L16–M16 | NA |
| 1990 | 122 | Lithic | Flake/Blade | 1 | NA | Possibly between sq. L16-17-M14-17-N14-17 | NA |
| 1990 | 123 | Lithic | Flake/Blade | 1 | NA | Possibly between sq. L16-17-M14-17-N14-17 | NA |
| 1990 | 124 | Lithic | Flake/Blade | 1 | NA | Possibly between sq. L16-17-M14-17-N14-17 | NA |
| 1990 | 125 | Lithic | Flake/Blade | 1 | NA | Possibly between sq. L16-17-M14-17-N14-17 | NA |
| 1990 | 126 | Lithic | Flake/Blade | 1 | NA | Possibly between sq. L16-17-M14-17-N14-17 | NA |
| 1990 | 127 | Lithic | Flake/Blade | 1 | II | North/East area; sq. M16 | NA |
| 1990 | 128 | Lithic | Flake/Blade | 1 | NA | Possibly between sq. L16-17-M14-17-N14-17 | NA |
| 1990 | 129 | Lithic | Flake/Blade | 1 | NA | Possibly between sq. L16-17-M14-17-N14-17 | NA |
| 1990 | 130 | Lithic | Flake/Blade | 1 | NA | Possibly between sq. L16-17-M14-17-N14-17 | NA |
| 1990 | 131 | Lithic | Flake/Blade | 1 | NA | Possibly between sq. L16-17-M14-17-N14-17 | NA |
| 1990 | 132 | Lithic | Flake/Blade | 1 | NA | Possibly between sq. L16-17-M14-17-N14-17 | NA |
| 1990 | 133 | Lithic | Flake/Blade | 1 | NA | Possibly between sq. L16-17-M14-17-N14-17 | NA |
| 1990 | 134 | Lithic | Flake/Blade | 1 | NA | Possibly between sq. L16-17-M14-17-N14-17 | NA |
| 1990 | 135 | Lithic | Flake/Blade | 1 | NA | Possibly between sq. L16-17-M14-17-N14-17 | NA |
| 1990 | 136 | Lithic | Flake/Blade | 1 | NA | Possibly between sq. L16-17-M14-17-N14-17 | NA |
| 1990 | 137 | Lithic | Flake/Blade | 1 | NA | Possibly between sq. L16-17-M14-17-N14-17 | NA |
| 1990 | 138 | Lithic | Flake/Blade | 1 | NA | Possibly between sq. L16-17-M14-17-N14-17 | NA |
| 1990 | 139 | Lithic | Flake/Blade | 1 | NA | Possibly between sq. L16-17-M14-17-N14-17 | NA |
| 1990 | 140 | Lithic | Flake/Blade | 1 | NA | Possibly between sq. L16-17-M14-17-N14-17 | NA |
| 1990 | 141 | Lithic | Flake/Blade | 1 | NA | Possibly between sq. L16-17-M14-17-N14-17 | NA |
| 1990 | 142 | Lithic | Flake/Blade | 1 | NA | Possibly between sq. L16-17-M14-17-N14-17 | NA |
| 1990 | 143 | Lithic | Flake/Blade | 1 | NA | Possibly between sq. L16-17-M14-17-N14-17 | NA |
| 1990 | 144 | Lithic | Flake/Blade | 1 | NA | Possibly between sq. L16-17-M14-17-N14-17 | NA |
| 1990 | 145 | Lithic | Flake/Blade | 1 | NA | Possibly between sq. L16-17-M14-17-N14-17 | NA |
| 1990 | 179 | Lithic | Flake/Blade | 2 | NA | Possibly between sq. L16-17-M14-17-N14-17 | NA |
| 1990 | 184 | Lithic | Unknown | 1 | NA | Possibly between sq. L16-17-M14-17-N14-17 | NA |
| 1990 | 185 | Lithic | Drill? | 1 | NA | Possibly between sq. L16-17-M14-17-N14-17 | NA |
| 1990 | 186 | Lithic | Flake/Blade | 1 | NA | Possibly between sq. L16-17-M14-17-N14-17 | NA |
| 1990 | 187 | Lithic | Flake/Blade | 1 | NA | Possibly between sq. L16-17-M14-17-N14-17 | NA |
| 1990 | 189 | Lithic | Flake/Blade | 1 | NA | Possibly between sq. L16-17-M14-17-N14-17 | NA |
| 1990 | 192 | Lithic | Flake/Blade | 1 | NA | Possibly between sq. L16-17-M14-17-N14-17 | NA |
| 1990 | 198 | Lithic | Flake/Blade | 1 | NA | Possibly between sq. L16-17-M14-17-N14-17 | NA |
| 1990 | 200 | Lithic | Flake/Blade | 1 | NA | Possibly between sq. L16-17-M14-17-N14-17 | NA |
| 1990 | 201 | Lithic | Flake/Blade | 1 | III2 | North/East area; sq. K16 | NA |
| 1990 | 202 | Lithic | Flake/Blade | 1 | III2 | North/East area; sq. K16 | NA |
| 1991 | 215 | Lithic | Flake/Blade | 1 | NA | North/East area; likely between sq. J16-17-K16-17-L16-17-M16-17-N16-17 | NA |
| 1991 | 216 | Lithic | Flake/Blade | 1 | NA | North/East area; likely between sq. J16-17-K16-17-L16-17-M16-17-N16-17 | NA |
| 1991 | 217 | Lithic | Flake/Blade | 1 | NA | North/East area; likely between sq. J16-17-K16-17-L16-17-M16-17-N16-17 | NA |

| Year | SF no. | Material | Object category | Q. | Level | Context | Context category |
|---|---|---|---|---|---|---|---|
| 1991 | 219 | Lithic | Flake/Blade | 1 | NA | North/East area; likely between sq. J16-17-K16-17-L16-17-M16-17-N16-17 | NA |
| 1991 | 220 | Lithic | Flake/Blade | 1 | NA | North/East area; likely between sq. J16-17-K16-17-L16-17-M16-17-N16-17 | NA |
| 1991 | 221 | Lithic | Flake/Blade | 1 | NA | North/East area; likely between sq. J16-17-K16-17-L16-17-M16-17-N16-17 | NA |
| 1991 | 222 | Lithic | Flake/Blade | 1 | NA | North/East area; likely between sq. J16-17-K16-17-L16-17-M16-17-N16-17 | NA |
| 1991 | 223 | Lithic | Flake/Blade | 1 | NA | North/East area; likely between sq. J16-17-K16-17-L16-17-M16-17-N16-17 | NA |
| 1991 | 224 | Lithic | Disc | 1 | NA | North/East area; likely between sq. J16-17-K16-17-L16-17-M16-17-N16-17 | NA |
| 1991 | 225 | Lithic | Flake/Blade | 1 | NA | North/East area; likely between sq. J16-17-K16-17-L16-17-M16-17-N16-17 | NA |
| 1991 | 226 | Lithic | Flake/Blade | 1 | NA | North/East area; likely between sq. J16-17-K16-17-L16-17-M16-17-N16-17 | NA |
| 1991 | 227 | Lithic | Flake/Blade | 1 | NA | North/East area; likely between sq. J16-17-K16-17-L16-17-M16-17-N16-17 | NA |
| 1991 | 228 | Lithic | Flake/Blade | 1 | NA | North/East area; likely between sq. J16-17-K16-17-L16-17-M16-17-N16-17 | NA |
| 1991 | 229 | Lithic | Flake/Blade | 1 | NA | North/East area; likely between sq. J16-17-K16-17-L16-17-M16-17-N16-17 | NA |
| 1991 | 230 | Lithic | Flake/Blade | 1 | NA | North/East area; likely between sq. J16-17-K16-17-L16-17-M16-17-N16-17 | NA |
| 1991 | 231 | Lithic | Flake/Blade | 1 | NA | North/East area; likely between sq. J16-17-K16-17-L16-17-M16-17-N16-17 | NA |
| 1991 | 232 | Lithic | Flake/Blade | 1 | NA | North/East area; likely between sq. J16-17-K16-17-L16-17-M16-17-N16-17 | NA |
| 1991 | 241 | Lithic | Flake/Blade | 1 | III1 | North/East; Area 2 | Fill and floor |
| 1991 | 242 | Lithic | Flake/Blade | 1 | NA | North/East area; likely between sq. J16-17-K16-17-L16-17-M16-17-N16-17 | NA |
| 1991 | 243 | Lithic | Flake/Blade | 1 | NA | North/East area; likely between sq. J16-17-K16-17-L16-17-M16-17-N16-17 | NA |
| 1991 | 244 | Lithic | Flake/Blade | 1 | NA | North/East area; likely between sq. J16-17-K16-17-L16-17-M16-17-N16-17 | NA |
| 1991 | 245 | Lithic | Flake/Blade | 1 | NA | North/East area; likely between sq. J16-17-K16-17-L16-17-M16-17-N16-17 | NA |
| 1991 | 246 | Lithic | Flake/Blade | 1 | NA | North/East area; likely between sq. J16-17-K16-17-L16-17-M16-17-N16-17 | NA |
| 1991 | 247 | Lithic | Flake/Blade | 1 | NA | North/East area; likely between sq. J16-17-K16-17-L16-17-M16-17-N16-17 | NA |
| 1991 | 248 | Lithic | Flake/Blade | 1 | NA | North/East area; likely between sq. J16-17-K16-17-L16-17-M16-17-N16-17 | NA |
| 1991 | 251 | Lithic | Flake/Blade | 1 | NA | North/East area; likely between sq. J16-17-K16-17-L16-17-M16-17-N16-17 | NA |
| 1991 | 253 | Lithic | Flake/Blade | 1 | NA | North/East area; likely between sq. J16-17-K16-17-L16-17-M16-17-N16-17 | NA |
| 1991 | 254 | Lithic | Flake/Blade | 1 | NA | North/East area; likely between sq. J16-17-K16-17-L16-17-M16-17-N16-17 | NA |
| 1991 | 258 | Lithic | Flake/Blade | 1 | NA | North/East area; likely between sq. J16-17-K16-17-L16-17-M16-17-N16-17 | NA |
| 1991 | 261 | Lithic | Flake/Blade | 1 | NA | North/East area; likely between sq. J16-17-K16-17-L16-17-M16-17-N16-17 | NA |
| 1991 | 262 | Lithic | Flake/Blade | 1 | NA | North/East area; likely between sq. J16-17-K16-17-L16-17-M16-17-N16-17 | NA |
| 1991 | 270 | Lithic | Flake/Blade | 1 | NA | North/East area; likely between sq. J16-17-K16-17-L16-17-M16-17-N16-17 | NA |
| 1991 | 271 | Lithic | Flake/Blade | 1 | NA | North/East area; likely between sq. J16-17-K16-17-L16-17-M16-17-N16-17 | NA |
| 1991 | 272 | Lithic | Flake/Blade | 1 | NA | North/East area; likely between sq. J16-17-K16-17-L16-17-M16-17-N16-17 | NA |
| 1991 | 273 | Lithic | Flake/Blade | 1 | NA | North/East area; likely between sq. J16-17-K16-17-L16-17-M16-17-N16-17 | NA |
| 1991 | 274 | Lithic | Flake/Blade | 1 | NA | North/East area; likely between sq. J16-17-K16-17-L16-17-M16-17-N16-17 | NA |
| 1991 | 283 | Lithic | Flake/Blade | 1 | NA | North/East area; likely between sq. J16-17-K16-17-L16-17-M16-17-N16-17 | NA |
| 1991 | 284 | Lithic | Flake/Blade | 1 | NA | North/East area; likely between sq. J16-17-K16-17-L16-17-M16-17-N16-17 | NA |
| 1991 | 287 | Lithic | Flake/Blade | 1 | NA | North/East area; likely between sq. J16-17-K16-17-L16-17-M16-17-N16-17 | NA |
| 1991 | 293 | Lithic | Flake/Blade | 1 | NA | North/East area; likely between sq. J16-17-K16-17-L16-17-M16-17-N16-17 | NA |
| 1991 | 296 | Lithic | Flake/Blade | 1 | NA | North/East area; likely between sq. J16-17-K16-17-L16-17-M16-17-N16-17 | NA |
| 1991 | 297 | Lithic | Flake/Blade | 1 | NA | North/East area; likely between sq. J16-17-K16-17-L16-17-M16-17-N16-17 | NA |

Virtually all the lithics from Excavation VII are made from a brown or grey homogeneous and fine-grained raw material. Two consist of a white, opaque material, and another one (SF 53, discussed below) appears to be a light grey quartzite sandstone according to descriptions of similar material from other excavations at Sarazm (Brunet and Razzokov 2016, 55, 62 fig. 4). Most of the records that I have been able to photograph and those described by Besenval include flakes and blades. It is important to note here that seventeen of these records are blades and flakes with cortex, and two are cores (SF7 and SF89). In addition to the flakes that have not been retouched, these records suggest that reduction activities including core preparation took place within or around the Excavation VII area, or at a minimum at the site. It is also important to note that even fragments with cortex appear to have been retouched and might have been used as tools, although this observation needs to be confirmed through detailed analysis of Excavation VII's lithic assemblage.

Four lithic records deserve specific mention. One is the above-mentioned lithic made from quartzite sandstone, which is a fragment of a bifacial blade (SF53). It was found inside Level I3 Hearth 6. This type of piece is relatively rare at Sarazm but has a few parallels elsewhere at this site (Isakov 1991, fig. 42 nos 12–15; Brunet and Razzokov 2016, 62 fig. 4), including two fragments that were found in a large trash-pit in Excavation XV (Mutin et al. 2016, 208 fig. 7). The second record is a drill (SF185), whose context of discovery inside Excavation VII is unfortunately not known. Two additional drills are listed below in the 'stone' section. The third piece is a retouched cortical flake shaped as a disc (SF224), whose context could not be determined. The fourth one is a retouched flake, possibly an arrowhead(?), found in Level I3 Room 5 (SF57).

The dominant raw material of the lithic assemblage from Excavation VII is consistent with what Brunet and Razzokov have observed across the site. These authors emphasize the difficulty in finding the sources for the materials knapped at Sarazm, although they mention that sources for chalcedony have been identified a few hundred kilometres away from this site and that quartz and sandstone may be coming from sources located near it. They also note that (Brunet and Razzokov 2016, 52):

> The presence on the site of tested nodules, and partially prepared cores, or pieces derived from the initial core preparation, indicates a local origin for the raw material considered; we can assume that it is also the case for the expedient debitages.

Certainly, the above-mentioned lithics with cortex from Excavation VII do not contradict this observation, and these authors' observations (Brunet and Razzokov 2016, 56) tend to suggest that virtually all the records that I have been able to photograph were probably processed locally. As for the functions of the lithics from Sarazm, it is probably worth mentioning that previous traceological analysis has shown that most of them were involved in activities relating to hunting and butchering as well as animal fur and leather preparation and bone working (Razzokov 2008, 104–18).

When compared to other sites, Sarazm's lithic industry tends to emerge as culturally ambiguous. Indeed, its flake, leaf-shaped points, and bifacial production is consistent with lithic assemblages typically observed within Central Asia between the Chalcolithic and Early Bronze Age periods. Yet, its blade and microblade production is more characteristic of the Neolithic and older technological traditions in Central Asia. There are also specific items that clearly evidence intercultural relationships. This is the case for instance of one white leaf-point, which is of Kel'teminar tradition, and of quartzite sandstone bifacial pieces, such as the above-mentioned exemplar from Excavation VII (SF53), which parallel materials from Kazakhstan and more generally the Eurasian Steppe. The leaf-shaped points also have morphological parallels at Chalcolithic and Early Bronze Age sites in Turkmenistan, Afghanistan, Pakistan, and Iran, although it is unclear whether those from Sarazm were made the same way (Brunet and Razzokov 2016, 56–58).

## *Quartz (Rock Crystal) Knapped Lithic Industry and Bead Making*

Eleven records are listed as 'quartz' and include two records that consist of beads (SF76 and SF152) with one record having two beads (Table 6.11; Fig. 6.7). The nine remaining records are listed as fragments or flakes amounting to at least twelve items of small sizes. Available documented records show that most of these quartz items are rock crystal, the colourless variety of quartz. Seven are registered as, or look like, rock crystal, while one record is described as a white quartz fragment. The remaining records are not specified.

The three beads are disc-shaped and are not more than 1 cm in diameter. Additional types of artefacts made from rock crystal have been found at Sarazm, including flakes, blades, bladelets, and leaf-shaped

Table 6.11: Quartz (rock crystal) knapped lithic industry and bead making from Sarazm Excavation VII.

| Year | SF no. | Sample no. | Material | Object category | Q. | Image | Preservation | Dimensions | Observations | Level | Context | Context category |
|---|---|---|---|---|---|---|---|---|---|---|---|---|
| 1986 | 22 | NA | Quartz | Flake/fragment | 1 | No | Fragment | NA | NA | III2 | Room 5 | Fill and floor |
| 1987 | 30 | NA | Quartz | Flake/fragment | 4 | Yes | Fragment | 3 × 2.3 cm; 2.1 × 1.9 cm; 1.4 × 0.75 cm; 0.4 × 0.3 cm | Rock crystal | II2 or III1 | Level II2 Area 3; or Level III1 Area 1 | Fill and floor |
| 1987 | 41 | NA | Quartz | Raw material | 1 | No | Fragment | NA | White quartz | III3 | Area 6 | Fill and floor |
| 1989 | 76 | NA | Quartz | Bead | 1 | Yes | Complete | D = 0.95 cm | Rock crystal | II1 or II2 | Level II1 Area 1; or Level II2 Area 3 | Fill and floor |
| 1989 | 77 | NA | Quartz | Flake/fragment | 2 | Yes | Fragment | 2.5 × 1.4 cm; 1.6 × 1.4 cm | Rock crystal | I3 | Area 3 | Fill and floor |
| 1989 | 78 | NA | Quartz | Flake/fragment | 1 | Yes | Fragment | 1.9 × 1.25 cm | Rock crystal | I1 | Room 1 | Fill and floor |
| 1989 | 85 | NA | Quartz? | Flake/fragment | 1 | No | Fragment | NA | NA | IV2 | Compartmented building | Fill and floor |
| 1990 | 152 | NA | Quartz | Bead | 2 | Yes | Complete | D = 1/0.8 cm; T = 0.4/0.3 cm | Rock crystal | NA | Possibly between sq. L16-17-M14-17-N14-17 | NA |
| 1990 | 162 | NA | Quartz | Flake/fragment | 1 | Yes | Fragment | 1.3 × 1 cm | Rock crystal | NA | Possibly between sq. L16-17-M14-17-N14-17 | NA |
| 1991 | 291 | NA | Quartz | Flake/fragment | 1 | No | Fragment | NA | NA | NA | North/East area; likely between sq. J16-17-K16-17-L16-17-M16-17-N16-17 | NA |
| 1985 | 317 | 9 | Quartz | Flake/fragment | 1 | No | Fragment | NA | Rock crystal | III2 | Pit 2 | Pit |

points. The fact that fragments and flakes were found inside Excavation VII suggests that rock crystal objects were made within the areas exposed in this excavation, or at least corroborate the fact that such objects were made somewhere at the site. As for the potential sources for this material, 'rock crystal outcrops [...] are known at a few hundred kilometres from Sarazm [...] It is also possible that quartz [...] come[s] from sources located around the site, although no source corresponding exactly to the rocks used at Sarazm has been found' (Brunet and Razzokov 2016, 52).

Rock crystal seems to have been used to make blades and other tools for a long time, at least since the Mesolithic or 'Proto-Neolithic' periods in Iran (Musche and Kröger 1993). Rock crystal is not uncommon between Central Asia, northern Iran, and South Asia. Rock crystal beads were found within a rich burial chamber at Altyn-Depe (Masson 1988, 51). In Iran, Schmidt recorded rock crystal beads and discs in Tepe Hissar Periods II and III (Schmidt 1937, 122–23, 135, 223, 229, 231, 305, 312). These artefacts include disc-shaped beads very similar to those from Sarazm Excavation VII (Schmidt 1937, 226 figs 136–37). Pendants and fragments were found at Shahr-i Sokhta (Tosi 1969, 372, 374 fig. 261). At Mundigak, Casal writes that rock crystal was used to make arrowheads from Period II2 onward (Casal 1961, 239 fig. 137). Further to the south, Barthélémy de Saizieu (2003, 28) reports one flake from Mehrgarh Period III, and Law (2011, 81) mentions beads from Harappa. Law (2001, 464) also writes that the Khirana Hills north of Harappa are a possible source for rock crystals, while Barthélémy de Saizieu (2003, 28) writes regarding quartz in general that:

L'origine des quartz microcristallins tels que les chalcédoines est en général liée à un environnement volcanique. La présence de roches volcaniques dans le Nord du Pakistan (Gilgit, Swat, Hazara) ainsi qu'à l'Ouest dans les monts Chagaï pourraient être des sources

Figure 6.7: Quartz (rock crystal) knapped lithic industry and bead making from Sarazm Excavation VII. Photographs and plate by B. Mutin.

potentielles mais aucun de ces minéraux, hormis les cristaux de quartz proprement dits [...], n'est mentionné au Pakistan sur les cartes et les ouvrages géologiques consultés.

## Carnelian Industry

Three carnelian beads (two records) were found in Excavation VII (Table 6.12; Fig. 6.8). I have been able to find only one bead (SF38) in the collection and archives. This bead is rounded cylindrical, or barrel-shaped, and measures 0.7 cm in diameter and 0.75 cm in length. These beads are not the only carnelian items recovered from Sarazm. On Figure 6.8 is an example from Excavation II. Besides, there is also 'an enormous collection of carnelian, lazurite, turquoise, and chalk beads (in numbers ranging from thirty to one thousand)' within the burial of the 'Princess of Sarazm' (Isakov 1994b, 6, 11 fig. 9; Besenval and Isakov 1989, 9).

The most evident sources for carnelian are sources in India, including those on the Deccan Plateau into the Gujarat region. Other Indian sources are reported from eastern Rajasthan in the beds of the Banas River and additional rivers (see Barthélemy de Saizieu 2003, 28; Law 2011, 36, 261, 279). Sources for carnelian are also mentioned in Waziristan, Pakistan (Durrani 1994–1995), as well as in Kashmir (During-Caspers 1972). Barthélemy de Saizieu (2003, 28) evokes the possibility that the Bolan Valley in Pakistan may have been a secondary source for chalcedony in general since small chalcedony pebbles are sometimes found in it. In this valley, the archaeological deposits at Mehrgarh contain carnelian ornaments since the Neolithic period. Sources are also reported from the region of Kandahar city in southern Afghanistan, as well as more generally speaking sources for agates in Uzbekistan, Tajikistan, and Kazakhstan. In Iran, carnelian sources are reported from the Shahr-i Sokhta area, the Dasht-e Lut, and the Bushehr Peninsula further south (see Law 2011, 282; Tosi 1969, 374; Prickett 1986, 390–99; Hakemi 1997, 15).

As for the archaeological evidence, carnelian beads and fragments were found at Shahr-i Sokhta, including within the graveyard that has been excavated at this site (Tosi 1969, 372–73 figs 251, 260; Piperno and Salvatori 2007; Vidale and Lazzari 2017). Carnelian artefacts were also recorded in Period I3 to IV deposits at Mundigak (Casal 1961, 242 fig. 138 nos 13, 23; Petrie and Shaffer 2019) as well as at Said Qala Tepe, where one photograph shows one biconical carnelian bead that looks similar to the one from Sarazm Excavation VII (Shaffer 1971, 95, 122 fig. 35 F, G). Further south, carnelian beads are a hallmark of the Indus Civilization and were also widely distributed among Middle Asian elites during the Bronze Age (Vidale 2000, 40; Frenez 2018, 391–92). Typical etched carnelian beads of that period were found at Shortughaï (Francfort 1989, 145 tab. 49) as well as in Iran including at Tepe Hissar, Shah Tepe, and Susa (see Heskel 1984, 341 for a recapitulation). As Law (2011, 252) puts it:

> The unmistakably Harappan-style 'etched' (bleached) carnelian beads recovered in Tepe Hissar IIIC levels (c. late third / early second millennium BC) and at several other late Bronze Age sites in Iran [...] demonstrate that some material goods made it to that distant region from South Asia during the Harappan Period.

Carnelian was also used in the Indo-Iranian Borderlands prior to the Indus Civilization, as seen through the above-mentioned examples from Afghanistan and Shahr-i Sokhta, and as illustrated at Mehrgarh since the Neolithic Period I (through the Oxus Civilization-related Period VIII) (Barthélemy de Saizieu 2003, 32–42) and in Tepe Yahya Neolithic and Chalcolithic Periods VIIB–VIIA and VIA–V (Beale 1986, 167, 170 tab. 7.1, 259).

Table 6.12: Carnelian, lapis lazuli, turquoise, steatite, and frit industries from Sarazm Excavation VII.

| Year | SF no. | Sample no. | Material | Object category | Q. | Image | Preservation | Dimensions | Observations | Level | Context | Context category |
|---|---|---|---|---|---|---|---|---|---|---|---|---|
| 1987 | 38 | NA | Carnelian | Bead | 1 | Yes | Complete | L = 0.75 cm; D = 0.7 cm | Rounded cylindrical | IV1 | Sq. I13/14 | Fill and floor |
| 1990 | 177 | NA | Carnelian | Bead | 2 | No | NA | NA | NA | NA | Possibly between sq. L16–17–M14–17–N14–17 | NA |
| 1984 | 11 | NA | Lapis lazuli | Bead | 1 | Yes | Half | L = 0.5; D = 0.3 cm | Rounded cylindrical | I3 | Alleyway 2 | Fill and floor |
| 1985 | 16 | NA | Lapis lazuli | Raw material | 1 | Yes | Fragment | 1.3 × 1.25 cm | / | I1 | Alleyway 1 | Fill and floor |
| 1990 | 160 | 154 | Lapis lazuli | Raw material | 1 | No | Fragment | NA | NA | NA | Possibly between sq. L16–17–M14–17–N14–17 | NA |
| 1990 | 174 | 160 | Lapis lazuli | Raw material | 1 | No | Fragment | NA | NA | NA | Possibly between sq. L16–17–M14–17–N14–17 | NA |
| 1986 | 21 | NA | Turquoise? | Pendant | 1 | Yes | Incomplete | D = 1.55 cm | Flower-shaped | IV1 | Room 6 | Fill and floor |
| 1986 | 23 | NA | Turquoise | Raw material | 1 | No | Fragment | NA | NA | IV1 | Room 2 | Fill and floor |
| 1987 | 37 | NA | Turquoise | Bead-button | 1 | Yes | Complete | D = 1.15 cm | Half-spherical, two holes | IV1 | Sq. I13/14 | Fill and floor |
| 1989 | 75 | 206 | Turquoise | Bead | 1 | Yes | Complete | L = 0.9 cm; D = 0.45 cm | Cylindrical | IV1–IV2 | Area 4 | Fill and floor |
| 1990 | 153 | NA | Turquoise | Bead | 1 | Yes | Complete | L = 0.8 cm; D = 0.6 cm | Rounded cylindrical | NA | Possibly between sq. L16–17–M14–17–N14–17 | NA |
| 1990 | 158 | NA | Turquoise | Raw material | 1 | No | Fragment | NA | NA | NA | Possibly between sq. L16–17–M14–17–N14–17 | NA |
| 1990 | 178 | NA | Turquoise | Bead | 1 | Yes | Complete | L = 0.6 cm; D = 0.4 cm | Cylindrical, slightly rounded, unpierced | NA | Possibly between sq. L16–17–M14–17–N14–17 | NA |
| 1990 | 199 | NA | Turquoise | Bead | 1 | Yes | Half | L = 0.7 cm; D = 0.6 cm | Cylindrical, slightly rounded | NA | Possibly between sq. L16–17–M14–17–N14–17 | NA |
| 1991 | 240 | NA | Turquoise | Bead | 1 | Yes | Complete | L = 1.6 cm; D = 1.55 cm | Half-rounded cylindrical | III1 | North/East; Area 2 | Fill and floor |
| 1991 | 212 | 175 | Turquoise | Raw material | 1 | No | Fragment | NA | NA | NA | North/East area; likely between sq. J16–17–K16–17–L16–17–M16–17–N16–17 | NA |
| 1991 | 213 | 176 | Steatite | Bead | 1 | No | Complete | NA | Fired steatite; square | III1 | North/East; Area 2 | Fill and floor |
| 1987 | 29 | NA | Frit | Bead | 1 | No | NA | NA | Green glaze | II1 or II2 | Area 2 | Fill and floor |
| 1989 | 80 | NA | Frit | Bead | 1 | Yes | Complete | L = 0.95 cm; D = 0.45 cm | Cylindrical; blue glaze | I1 | Room 1 | Fill and floor |
| 1990 | 156 | NA | Frit | Bead | 1 | Yes | Complete | L = 2.45 cm; W = 2.25 cm | Biconical; glazed | NA | Possibly between sq. L16–17–M14–17–N14–17 | NA |
| 1991 | 286 | 179 | Frit | Bead | 1 | No | NA | NA | Green glaze | NA | North/East area; likely between sq. J16–17–K16–17–L16–17–M16–17–N16–17 | NA |
| 1991 | 292 | 187 | Frit | Bead | 1 | Yes | Complete | L = 1.2 cm; D = 0.65 cm | Cylindrical; green glaze | NA | North/East area; likely between sq. J16–17–K16–17–L16–17–M16–17–N16–17 | NA |

Law (2011, 299) analysed samples of agates from Harappa, Mohenjo-daro, Chanhu-daro, Nagwada, Mehrgarh, Nausharo, and Shahr-i Sokhta, including carnelian items, and concluded that:

> The majority of the agate artifacts from Harappa and the five other Indus Tradition sites examined [...] appear to have come from sources in Gujarat. Residents of Harappa were acquiring material from that region by at least the Kot Diji Phase [prior to the Indus Civilization] [...] There are indications that Indus Tradition peoples sometimes utilized agate from regions outside of Gujarat. Four artifacts from Harappa (including a Period 3B bead fragment) as well as a few from Mehrgarh, Nausharo and Chanhu-daro are geochemically more analogous to artifacts from Shahr-i-Sokhta, which could mean that they may have come from the same sources (presumably in the Helmand region) used by residents of that site. Or it might simply indicate that they are from an as of yet unsampled deposit that happens to be more geochemically analogous to Iranian sources than to Gujarati ones.

Certainly, chemical composition analysis of the carnelian objects from Sarazm would help determine the origin of these objects or of the material they are made from. This question may probably be posed also for additional sites in Central Asia that yielded carnelian items. These items include carnelian beads from funerary contexts dating to the fourth millennium BCE at Anau (Periods IB2–IIA equivalent to Namazga I–II Periods; Hiebert 2003, 85 fig. 7.5 no. 8, 121 tab. B1; see page 15) and to the third millennium BCE at Parkhai II (Khlopin 1981, 27) and Altyn-Depe. These beads include the typical Indus-related etched types at the latter site (Masson 1988, 22, 36, 40–41, 43, 51, 63 fig. 20, 68).

## Lapis Lazuli Industry

Four lapis lazuli items were found in Excavation VII, consisting of one bead and three fragments/flakes (Table 6.12; Fig. 6.8). The bead (SF11) is rounded cylindrical, or barrel-shaped, and measures 0.5 cm in length and 0.3 cm in diameter to the maximum. One fragment I had access to is 1.3 × 1.25 cm, while the sizes of the two other fragments that Besenval listed are not specified. These two fragments were submitted for composition analysis (samples 154 and 160); I unfortunately have found no results relating to these analyses in Besenval archives. Alternatively, Cesbron studied the compositions of two lapis lazuli samples from different locations at Sarazm. One (SF1147/95, sample 229) is a fragment described as a large fragment of good quality with sparse pyrite crystals and a small white venule made of microcrystalline phlogopite mica ($KMg_3(AlSi_3O_{10})(F,OH)_2$). The second sample (SF1147/201, sample 230) corresponds to twenty-three barrel-shaped beads from the tomb of the 'Princess of Sarazm' in Excavation IV. Cesbron wrote that the lapis lazuli they are made from includes various qualities, with some having greyish blue surfaces. Pyrite is not abundant and has usually altered to give iron hydroxides.

As these two samples exemplify and as is well known, lapis lazuli is not rare at Sarazm. The most impressive assemblage was collected in the tomb of the 'Princess of Sarazm' and consists of 524 beads. About two hundred beads were recorded in another burial associated with this tomb (Besenval and Isakov 1989, 9; Isakov 1994b, 9; Barthélemy de Saizieu 2003, 102). In addition to ornaments, lapis lazuli was used to produce the blue colour on plaster recovered from Excavation VII (see below). Furthermore, in addition to the lapis lazuli fragments from Excavation VII, more evidence for the processing of this mineral was found during the 1987 and 1988 field seasons at Sarazm (Besenval and Isakov 1989, 18; e.g. Fig. 6.8: no. 5).

As noted in **Chapter 2**, the closest sources for lapis lazuli are in the Badakhshan Province of north-eastern Afghanistan, at Sar-i Sang in particular, as well as in the Pamir Mountains in southern Tajikistan, especially at Ladjevar-Dara (Casanova 2008). More distant sources are in the Lake Baikal region of Siberia (Herrmann 1968; Tosi 1974a; Barthélemy de Saizieu 2003, 27; Vidale and Lazzari 2017 for a comprehensive review of the question and detailed analysis of the lapis lazuli remains from Shahr-i Sokhta). In the archaeological record, lapis lazuli ornaments were found at Mehrgarh since the Neolithic Period I through Period VIII (Barthélemy de Saizieu 2003, 32–42). A workshop dating to the Chalcolithic Period III was studied at this site (Tosi and Vidale 1990). Lapis lazuli items were also recorded at Tepe Yahya Periods VB–VA (Beale 1986, 170 tab. 7.1, 177 fig. 7.8 e) as well as in the Bam region, south of the Lut Desert, on the surface of a Late Neolithic site (Mutin et al. 2020b). However, there is no doubt that this mineral became unprecedently more popular and widely distributed from Central Asia through the Iranian Plateau toward Mesopotamia, the Levant, and Egypt during the Bronze Age period, in the third and second millennia BCE (see Casanova 2019 for a recapitulation). Within this broader trading sphere, Sarazm is commonly conceived as an intermediary station. Casanova (2019, 305) put it this way:

Figure 6.8: Beads, pendants, and raw mineral from Sarazm Excavation VII (save for no. 2 from Excavation II and no. 5 from Excavation IX): nos 1–2, carnelian; nos 3–5, lapis lazuli; nos 6–12, turquoise; no. 13, grey stone; no. 14, white stone; no. 15, red stone; no. 16, white stone; nos 17–18, black stone; no. 19, green stone; nos 20–22, frit. Photographs by R. Besenval, save for nos 1, 6, 8, 10–14, 20, and 22 by B. Mutin, plate by B. Mutin.

Rather than assuming any kind of direct contacts between emissaries of Mesopotamian cities and the foreign lands of eastern Iran and Central Asia far to the east, the trade networks (and the markets with which they were linked) would thus appear to have formed a series of stations and thus intermediary markets between the different civilizations. In fact, third millennium sites such as Shahr-i Sokhta, Shahdad (Iran), Sarazm (Tajikistan), Mundigak (Afghanistan) are themselves at once major centers where lapis lazuli was imported from the deposits in Afghanistan, but they were also stations where the blue stone was transformed into prestige objects and exported to Susa in western Iran. (See also Barthélémy de Saizieu and Bouquillon 1993 on Mundigak)

However, a recent re-evaluation of this question regarding Shahr-i Sokhta concluded slightly differently on the end goal of this exchange network. It has made it more rational to think, as is apparent in the funerary deposits at this site and as other scholars have suggested, that lapis lazuli was mostly consumed locally. Many Lapis lazuli items have indeed been found inside the graveyard of this site, with the highest quantities recorded in Period I and then Period II graves, between the late fourth and mid-third millennia BCE. As phrased by Vidale,

> The lords of Shahr-i Sokhta [...] would appear less related to the imposing protohistorical figure of the Lord of Aratta, deeply involved in his trade and conflicts with Sumer, and more concerned with the use and consumption of precious ornaments to exhibit their own rank before their own community. (See Lazzari and Vidale 2017, 46–58; Vidale 2017a, 303 (quote), 303–21; see also Thornton 2012, 599–600)

As far as Sarazm is concerned, there is clear evidence that lapis lazuli was imported and transformed at this site. Yet, it remains unclear whether the quantities of lapis lazuli found at this site may support the view that it was a major centre and a station in the sense suggested by Casanova. Furthermore, most of the archaeological deposits that have been studied at Sarazm are earlier than the mid-third millennium BCE.

## *Turquoise Industry*

Turquoise finds in Excavation VII consist of ten items including one listed with a question mark (Table 6.12; Fig. 6.8). Three of them are fragments of raw material, which suggests that natural turquoise was transformed into artefacts, if not within or around the Excavation VII area, at Sarazm. Six are beads and one is a pendant, which are all documented. One bead (SF178) is not pierced, which, together with the above-mentioned fragments, suggests that turquoise was processed locally at Sarazm. Four of the beads are less than 1 cm in length and are cylindrical to rounded cylindrical (barrel-shaped) (SF75, SF153, SF178, and SF199). One is half-spherical and 1.15 cm in diameter (SF37). It has two holes, which makes it look like a button rather than a bead. The last one is 1.6 cm long and half-rounded cylindrical in shape (SF240). The pendant (SF21) is shaped as a flower and is 1.55 cm in diameter. Two of these turquoise items were sent for composition analysis. One is a fragment (SF212, sample 175), and one is a bead (SF75, sample 206). The only results I have found is that they were both determined to be turquoise, which has left me wonder whether these samples have ever been analysed or merely characterized with the naked eye.

On the same topic, it is probably worth mentioning that the colour of the turquoise from Excavation VII varies, with some being bluer and others being greener, and that some seem purer than the others. Such variations may suggest different origins. However, Barthélémy de Saizieu (2003, 26–27) writes that: 'Si ces variations peuvent se rattacher à des gisements différents, elles peuvent tout aussi bien s'expliquer par des degrés d'altération variables.' As noted in **Chapter 2**, sources for turquoise are known in the Kyzyl Kum in Uzbekistan as well as in the Khujand region of northern Tajikistan. Some sources are known to have been exploited during the Bronze Age, including some in Uzbekistan where mines and workshops dating to the third millennium BCE were found, such as those at the Ljavljakan sites, Beshbulak, and Burli 3 in the Bukhantau Mountains. The Neyshabur area of north-eastern Iran certainly also needs to be mentioned here as a potential source, as well as additional sources in Afghanistan and Pakistan, although there is no clear information about the latter sources (Tosi 1974b; Barthélémy de Saizieu 2003, 27, 104–05 fig. 3; Hiebert 2003, 22; Brunet 2005, 93–95).

The turquoise ornaments and fragments from Excavation VII are not the only turquoise items recovered from Sarazm. For instance, in addition to other finds, many turquoise beads were recorded inside the above-mentioned burial of the 'Princess of Sarazm' (Besenval and Isakov 1989, 9; Isakov 1994a; 1994b, 6). As far as the shape of the aforementioned turquoise pendant is concerned, additional pendants shaped as flowers, suns, or wheels, made from terracotta and red stone, were found at Sarazm. Beyond Sarazm, as noted in **Chapter 2**, turquoise has been recorded at sites between the Indo-Iranian Borderlands, Central Asia, and the Iranian Plateau. For instance, it was recorded from the Neolithic period and until Period VIII at Mehrgarh (Barthélémy de Saizieu 2003, 32–42), Sheri Khan Tarakai (Knox et al. 2010, 268–69), Mundigak, where there is evidence for its processing (Barthélémy de Saizieu and Bouquillon 1993), Anau (Period IB1 (Namazga I Period): Hiebert 2003, 84 fig. 7.3 nos 14–15, tab. 9.1, 120; see Tosi 1974b, 159 on Turkmenistan), and Tepe Hissar (Periods II–III: Schmidt 1937, 122–23, 223, 229, 231, 305, 312), although Tosi emphasizes that it is not very abundant at this site (Tosi 1974b, 159). Further south, turquoise beads with shapes similar to those of some exemplars from Sarazm Excavation VII were found at Shahr-i Sokhta (cylindrical and rounded cylindrical, the latter being termed 'truncated convex biconical' at Shahr-i Sokhta: Tosi 1974b, 157 fig. 9). Tosi (1974b, 157) writes that: '[T]he simplest and most common types (cylindrical, truncated convex biconical) account for almost the entire Kyzyl Kum production at Besbulak 1 towards the middle of the third millennium', although, conversely, Foglini and Vidale write that barrel-shaped beads are very rare (2017, 263, 270 tab. 14).

Turquoise is a topic of considerable importance in relation to the question of the foundation of Sarazm. As discussed in **Chapter 1**, Kuzmina and Anthony believe that this site was founded 'with a view to mining the rich deposits of polymetallic ores and turquoise' (Kuzmina 2007, 211–12; see Besenval and Isakov 1989, 18 and Anthony 2007, 419). Meanwhile, Tosi puts this view into a different perspective by writing that the turquoise trading sphere was essentially limited to Central Asia and expanded to Shahr-i Sokhta during the third millennium BCE (Tosi 1974b, 160–61). On the same topic, Barthélémy de Saizieu observes a dichotomy between the geographic distribution of glazed steatite beads on the one hand and turquoise beads on the other. Her view is that (Barthélémy de Saizieu 2003, 106):

> [S]i la faible demande de turquoise résulte de facteurs idéologiques, comme le souligne Tosi [...], ne serait-ce pas par ce qu'on avait précisément trouvé à la turquoise, un matériau de substitution qui en simulant sa couleur, en revêtait par ricochet son rôle ? Comme cet usage de glaçurer les perles en stéatite s'est répandu dans la plus grande partie du monde oriental, les perles en turquoise pourraient en effet avoir perdu leur raison d'être au sein de populations utilisant le matériau de substitution. Elles ne l'auraient conservé qu'au sein des populations du Séistan iranien et du bassin voisin du Kerman qui, apparemment, ne faisaient pas, ou seulement peu, usage de ce dernier pour des raisons encore difficiles à cerner, ou encore au sein des popu-

lations vivant non loin des gisements et des ateliers de Kyzyl Kum, peut-être en raison des règles d'échanges sous-tendant des modes de vie différents et complémentaires [...] Le choix et l'usage prépondérant de la stéatite glaçurée [...] furent probablement dus, aussi, aux extraordinaires propriétés physico-chimiques de la stéatite cuite (faible dureté et surtout réfractivité) qui permettait, grâce à l'usage du feu et à l'invention de la glaçure, de la transformer, ouvrant ainsi la voie aux possibilités de manipuler la matière, de la contrôler, voire, par la suite, d'en fabriquer avec la faïence.

## Steatite and Frit Industries

One bead from Excavation VII was formally determined by Cesbron as a fired steatite bead (SF213, sample 176) (Table 6.12; Fig. 6.8). It is unfortunately not illustrated but is described as a flat diamond-shaped plaque with two perforations parallel to the flat surfaces and to the longer diagonal line. This bead is far from being the single example of fired steatite at Sarazm; about forty thousand fired steatite beads were reportedly recovered from the tomb of the 'Princess of Sarazm' (Barthélémy de Saizieu 2003, 102). As noted above, Barthélémy de Saizieu (2003, 104) observes that, between Central Asia and the Indo-Iranian Borderlands,

> la présence abondante de la turquoise paraît s'opposer à celle de la stéatite cuite, et inversement la dominance de la stéatite cuite semble exclure l'usage fréquent de la turquoise. Cette relation d'opposition générale est moins forte, voire inexistante (?), dans les régions productrices de turquoise, ou du moins proches de ses sources, à savoir l'Asie centrale inclus l'Afghanistan (Mundigak).

Considering the discoveries made in the burial of the 'Princess of Sarazm', such opposition indeed does not seem to exist at Sarazm. Steatite might even be more present at Sarazm than has been reported, as it might be at Middle Asian sites where steatite objects are often erroneously identified as other types of materials (see below).

Five frit small finds are recorded in Excavation VII, all five corresponding to glazed beads, either green or blue when their colour is indicated (Table 6.12; Fig. 6.8). Two are cylindrical beads (SF80 and SF292) and one is biconical (SF156), while the shapes of the remaining two frit beads are not known. However, it is probably worth remembering that issues exist with the way the term 'frit' has been used and that there is no consensus as to what it is supposed to designate. Barthélémy de Saizieu and Bouquillon (2000, 94–95) write:

La fritte, au sens strict, ne définit aucun matériau mais le produit d'une opération, le frittage, destinée à faire un verre, une glaçure ou encore des pigments synthétiques (bleu égyptien par exemple). Le frittage consiste à chauffer une première fois, après broyage, les matériaux fournissant la silice, les fondants, la chaux et les colorants pour obtenir une masse homogène ; celle-ci est par la suite rebroyée et cuite de façon à obtenir un mélange amorphe (verre) ou semi-cristallin (pigments). En archéologie, le mot 'fritte' définit selon certains auteurs tous les corps polycristallins agglomérés qui, à la différence d'une faïence, n'ont pas été glaçurés. Cette distinction entre fritte (= faïence non glaçurée) et faïence (glaçurée) demeure toutefois ambiguë et contribue à perpétuer des erreurs concernant l'identification de matériaux vitrifiés anciens, aujourd'hui fortement altérés. Tite propose de définir la fritte comme un matériau aggloméré polycristallin, coloré dans la masse et non glaçuré. Ce matériau, obtenu par la chauffe d'un mélange intime de quartz, de chaux, d'oxyde colorant et d'alcalins, se différencie d'une faïence par la microstructure, par la composition chimique et minéralogique. Cette définition revenant cette fois à confondre partiellement frittes et pigments synthétiques (bleu égyptien notamment), nous n'y souscrirons pas ici, réservant l'usage de ce mot à la seule opération définie précédemment, le frittage.

Many glazed objects that have been recovered between the Nile and the Indus Valleys have been defined using vague terms and various labels (Barthélemy de Saizieu and Bouquillon 2000, 95 n. 13). In the present case, in the absence of detailed composition analysis, I cannot tell what kind of material the beads from Excavation VII labelled as 'frit' were made from. However, one fact remains is that they are all described as having a blue, green, or unspecified colour glaze. As such, they are part of a geographically and chronologically broader technological background. The first glazed objects appeared in the Mesopotamian-Egyptian area and the Indus Valley region during the fifth millennium BCE and are thought to have spread into Iran during the second half of the fourth millennium BCE (Barthélemy de Saizieu and Bouquillon 2000, 95–96). Most glazed objects until the third millennium BCE are beads with glazes of green or blue colours. So are the frit objects from Excavation VII, and their chronological context is consistent with the above-mentioned reconstruction.

It is probably important to recall here the specific role of steatite within the Indo-Iranian Borderlands since the end of the aceramic Neolithic period at Mehrgarh (Barthélemy de Saizieu 2003, 87). Steatite probably began being heated at that time, but it is only during the Chalcolithic period at this site (Period III between the mid-fifth and the mid-fourth millennia BCE) that it began to be truly fired (Barthélemy de Saizieu and Bouquillon 2000, 105; Barthélemy de Saizieu 2003, 88). I am emphasizing this material here because available photographs suggest that the powdery aspects of two frit beads from Excavation VII do not seem inconsistent with descriptions that have been made of fired steatite and the fact that this material may have been more common in the archaeological record than what has been reported. Indeed, Barthélemy de Saizieu and Bouquillon (2000, 97) write that:

> Au Chalcolithique, la glaçure ne subsiste plus dans le meilleur des cas que sous forme d'infimes et rares écailles bleu-vert; le plus souvent, elle a entièrement disparu de sorte que la plupart des perles présente une surface finement saccharoïde de couleur blanc-crème [...] typique de la stéatite noire naturelle chauffée à plus de 700°C.

Additionally, Barthélemy de Saizieu (2003, 90–105) suggests that many ornaments in many publications such as publications of sites in Turkmenistan, Iran, and Afghanistan, including sites such as Kara-Depe, Tepe Hissar, and Mundigak, that were vaguely defined as made from white stone, gypsum, or calcareous stone could in fact be fired steatite ornaments. In fact, glazed fired steatite appears to have been a dominant, or at least common, material for bead making between northern Iran and the Indus Valley in Pakistan, including Central Asia, Shahr-i Sokhta, and Kech-Makran in south-western Pakistan, but not so much within the rest of south-eastern Iran, until the third millennium BCE and the Indus Civilization (see also Francfort 1989, 136–37 for a recapitulation).

Lastly on this topic, items labelled as frit items are mentioned in the Mundigak and Tepe Hissar monographs. At the latter, however, Schmidt (1937, 55 n. 8) cautions that: 'The reader will, therefore, understand that throughout this publication the use of the words gypsum, frit, bitumen, grahamite and limestone, especially in connection with beads and seals, is not always positive identification.' This remark corroborates the above discussion. At the former, two frit objects are from contexts that are posterior to Sarazm settlement (Period V and Period VII or surface: Casal 1961, 229, 243, fig. 131 no. 18, fig. 138 no. 40), but two beads were found in contexts chronologically consistent with this site, one in Period I4 (Casal 1961, 240 fig. 138 no. 4) and one in Period III or Period IV (Casal 1961, 241 fig. 138 no. 10).

Table 6.13: Stone beads and pendants from Sarazm Excavation VII.

| Year | SF no. | Sample no. | Material | Object category | Q. | Image | Preservation | Dimensions | Observations | Level | Context | Context category |
|---|---|---|---|---|---|---|---|---|---|---|---|---|
| 1986 | 19 | NA | Grey stone | Bead | 1 | Yes | Complete | L = 1.6 cm; D = 0.6 cm | Cylindrical | Post-IV | Natural fill 1; sq. M15 or L15 | Natural fill |
| 1990 | 146 | NA | White stone | Bead | 1 | Yes | Complete | D = 2.5 cm; T = 0.8 cm | Disc-shaped | NA | Possibly between sq. L16-17–M14-17–N14-17 | NA |
| 1990 | 159 | NA | White stone | Pendant | 1 | No | Fragment | NA | Crenelated contour | NA | Possibly between sq. L16-17–M14-17–N14-17 | NA |
| 1990 | 190 | NA | Black stone | Pendant | 1 | Yes | Complete | D = 3.3 cm; T = 0.4 cm | Cross-shaped disc | NA | Possibly between sq. L16-17–M14-17–N14-17 | NA |
| 1990 | 203 | NA | Black stone | Pendant | 1 | Yes | Incomplete | L = 1.7 cm; W = 1.45 cm (at a minimum) | Quadrangular plaque, eight holes | NA | Possibly between sq. L16-17–M14-17–N14-17 | NA |
| 1990 | 204 | NA | White stone | Bead | 1 | Yes | Complete | L = 0.75 cm; D = 0.55 cm | Cylindrical | NA | Possibly between sq. L16-17–M14-17–N14-17 | NA |
| 1991 | 250 | NA | Red stone | Bead | 1 | Yes | Complete | D = 2.4 cm | Disc-shaped | NA | North/East area; likely between sq. J16-17–K16-17–L16-17–M16-17–N16-17 | NA |
| 1991 | 276 | NA | Green stone | Pendant | 1 | Yes | Complete | L = 2.6 cm; W = 1.6 cm | Pierced pebble | NA | North/East area; likely between sq. J16-17–K16-17–L16-17–M16-17–N16-17 | NA |

## *Stone Industry*

In this category are various types of stones that are not all precisely determined. Most of them seem to correspond to river rocks rounded and polished by the action of moving water, and some were defined as alabaster, gypsum, marble, onyx, and quartz(?), as well as beige stone, black stone, green stone, grey stone, pink stone, red stone, and white stone. Considering this lack of accurate determination and that I am not certain that those that were given are accurate, the stone records are here classified according to what I believe may have been their functions. These functional categories are: ornaments; drills; decorative tiles(?); discs; finials; containers; mould; ground stones; hammer stones, pestles/sharpeners, and grinding stones; sharpeners; cobble flakes; pebbles; weights(?); and raw material.

### Ornaments

Eight stone records are those of ornaments (Table 6.13; Fig. 6.8). They include four beads and four pendants made from black, green, grey, red, and white stones.

The beads consist of two large disc-shaped beads with diameters equal to *c.* 2.5 cm (SF146 and SF250) and two cylindrical beads that are *c.* 1.6 cm and 0.75 cm in length (SF19 and SF204). The pendants are: one pierced small pebble (SF276); one incomplete, 1.7 cm long, quadrangular plaque with eight holes in it (SF203); and one cross-shaped disc (SF190). I have found no details about the fourth pendant (SF159) save for the fact that Besenval described it as being made from a white stone and having a crenelated contour. Pendants have been found elsewhere at Sarazm. The above-described quadrangular one (SF203) is reminiscent of a pendant from Excavation IV, which is quadrangular and has holes, although it is made from a different type of stone. Additionally, one object in the Sarazm Museum, made from a black stone, resembles the above-described cross-shaped disc.

### Drills

Two drills are recorded (SF33 and SF63), with one described as a red stone (Table 6.14). Unfortunately, I have found no measurements nor illustrations relat-

Table 6.14: Stone drills from Sarazm Excavation VII.

| Year | SF no. | Sample no. | Material | Object category | Q. | Image | Preservation | Dimensions | Observations | Level | Context | Context category |
|---|---|---|---|---|---|---|---|---|---|---|---|---|
| 1987 | 33 | NA | Red stone | Drill | 1 | No | NA | NA | NA | III2 | Area 4 | Fill and floor |
| 1987 | 63 | NA | Stone | Drill | 1 | No | NA | NA | NA | Post-IV | Natural fill 1; sq. L11 | Natural fill |

Figure 6.9: Stone decorative tiles(?) from Sarazm Excavation VII: SF65 (left) and SF331 (right). Photographs by B. Mutin.

ing to these drills. One was discovered in a natural fill posterior to Level IV (SF63). The second one is from Level III2 Area 4. Together with additional drills found at Sarazm and the one mentioned above (SF185), as well as the unfinished beads and raw material recorded in Excavation VII, these stone drills suggest that bead making was taking place inside or near this excavation, or at a minimum at Sarazm.

### Decorative Tiles?

One record (SF65) is an 8 × 7.9 cm fragment of a beige, flat stone bearing incised decoration on one of its surfaces (Table 6.15; Fig. 6.9). The surfaces of this stone have a granulated texture. The decoration consists of three parallel incised lines which delimit three bands coloured in red, as well as a frieze of incised triangles alternatively coloured in red and yellow. The function of this object is unknown; it could be a sort of plaque or tile that perhaps was used to decorate Level III2 Room 5, where it was discovered. Although exact parallels are lacking for this object, it is probably worth noting that the motifs and colours are reminiscent of those observed on Sarazm Excavation VII Group 4 ceramics and their parallels in Turkmenistan.

Another record consists of two white, flat stone fragments (SF331), both made from the same material and both having one flat edge. One has two perpendicular grooves that meet at a right angle. They both look like tile or plaque fragments. They were sent for composition analysis (sample 186), but this analysis does not seem to have been conducted since I have found no results in Besenval archives.

### Discs

Five records are those of small stone discs including one with a hole in its centre and one with a hole that was left unfinished (SF195) (Table 6.16; Fig. 6.10). The latter was made from onyx(?). Another disc whose composition was analysed by Cesbron (SF280, sample 209) appears

Table 6.15: Stone decorative tiles(?) from Sarazm Excavation VII.

| Year | SF no. | Sample no. | Material | Object category | Q. | Image | Preservation | Dimensions | Observations | Level | Context | Context category |
|---|---|---|---|---|---|---|---|---|---|---|---|---|
| 1987 | 65 | NA | Beige stone | Decorative tile? | 1 | Yes | Fragment | 8 × 7.9 cm | Flat stone with incised decoration and red and yellow pigments | III2 | Room 5 | Fill and floor |
| 1991 | 331 | 186 | White stone | Decorative tile? | 2 | Yes | Fragment | 8 × 3.75 cm; 6.45 × 3.55 cm | Two flat stones with one flat-trimmed edge | NA | North/East area; likely between sq. J16–17–K16–17–L16–17–M16–17–N16–17 | NA |

Table 6.16: Stone discs from Sarazm Excavation VII.

| Year | SF no. | Sample no. | Material | Object category | Q. | Image | Preservation | Dimensions | Observations | Level | Context | Context category |
|---|---|---|---|---|---|---|---|---|---|---|---|---|
| 1987 | 45 | NA | Stone | Perforated disc | 1 | No | Complete | NA |  | III2 | Area 4 | Fill and floor |
| 1990 | 195 | NA | Onyx? | Disc | 1 | Yes | Complete | D = 4.75 cm | Beginning of perforation in the centre | III2 | North/East area | NA |
| 1991 | 218 | NA | Stone | Disc | 1 | Yes | Complete | D = 2.1 cm |  | NA | North/East area; likely between sq. J16–17–K16–17–L16–17–M16–17–N16–17 | NA |
| 1991 | 280 | 209 | Stone | Disc | 1 | Yes | Complete | D = 4.5 cm |  | NA | North/East area; likely between sq. J16–17–K16–17–L16–17–M16–17–N16–17 | NA |
| 1991 | 281 | NA | Stone | Disc | 1 | Yes | Complete | D = 3.5 cm |  | NA | North/East area; likely between sq. J16–17–K16–17–L16–17–M16–17–N16–17 | NA |

Figure 6.10: Stone discs from Sarazm Excavation VII. Photographs and plate by B. Mutin.

# STONE INDUSTRY

Table 6.17: Stone finials from Sarazm Excavation VII.

| Year | SF no. | Sample no. | Material | Object category | Q. | Image | Preservation | Dimensions | Observations | Level | Context | Context category |
|---|---|---|---|---|---|---|---|---|---|---|---|---|
| 1989 | 69 | NA | Black and white stone | Finial | 1 | Yes | Complete | D = 1.8 cm; T = 1.8 cm | Spherical | IV1 | Room 1 | Fill and floor |
| 1990 | 161 | NA | Stone | Finial | 1 | No | Complete | D = 2 cm; T = 1.5 cm | NA | NA | Possibly between sq. L16-17–M14-17–N14-17 | NA |
| 1990 | 196 | NA | Black stone | Finial | 1 | Yes | Complete | D = 2.25 cm; T = 1.8 cm | Truncated | III2 | North/East area | NA |
| 1991 | 234 | NA | Black and white stone | Finial | 1 | Yes | Complete | D = 2.1 cm; T = 1.8 cm (roughly) | Spherical | NA | North/East area; likely between sq. J16-17–K16-17–L16-17–M16-17–N16-17 | NA |
| 1991 | 303 | NA | Red stone | Finial | 1 | No | Fragment | D = 1.35 cm; T = 1.3 cm | Spherical | NA | North/East area; likely between sq. J16-17–K16-17–L16-17–M16-17–N16-17 | NA |

Figure 6.11: Stone finials from Sarazm Excavation VII. Photographs by R. Besenval, save for nos 1 and 3 by B. Mutin, plate by B. Mutin.

## Finials

Five finials were found in Excavation VII (Table 6.17; Fig. 6.11). I have been able to access four of them, while Besenval partly described the fifth one. Finials are decorative objects that were attached to one extremity of artefacts such as awls, pins, drills, and other small objects. One of the four exemplars from Excavation VII that I have been able to observe is truncated and is decorated with dots consisting of unfinished perforations (SF196). Two other finials (SF69 and SF234) are spherical. The diameters of these three objects are between 1.8 and 2.25 cm, and their thicknesses range from 1.5 and 1.8 cm. An additional spherical finial is smaller (SF303) with a diameter and a thickness equal to 1.35 and 1.3 cm, respectively. As noted above, two terracotta finials were also found in Excavation VII (SF154 and SF155), with diameters measuring 2.2 cm, while more finials have been recorded at Sarazm, including stone and terracotta finials. Such objects have parallels from the Iranian Plateau and Turkmenistan to Pakistan (see above).

to be made from dolomite (CaMg(CO$_3$)$_2$). The diameters of these stone discs range from 2.1 to 4.75 cm and are in this regard similar to the above-mentioned terracotta unperforated and perforated discs. Perforated and unperforated stone discs are reported from Namazga (Late III) IV/Early V Period burials at Farkhor in southern Tajikistan (c. 2800/2700–2300 BCE), where they are interpreted as lamp lids (Vinogradova 2021, 641 fig. 23.6 nos 6a–6c, 642 fig. 23.7 no. 5; Vinogradova and Bobomulloev 2020, 112).

Table 6.18: Stone containers from Sarazm Excavation VII.

| Year | SF no. | Sample no. | Material | Object category | Q. | Image | Preservation | Dimensions | Observations | Level | Context | Context category |
|---|---|---|---|---|---|---|---|---|---|---|---|---|
| 1984 | 6 | 218 | Onyx | Container | 1 | Yes | Fragment | Base D = 5.6 cm | Base fragment | I3 | Room 6 or Alleyway 2 | Fill and floor |
| 1987 | 42 | NA | White stone | Container | 1 | Yes | Fragment | 5.25 × 1.9 cm | Rim and neck fragment | III2 | Room 3 | Fill and floor |
| 1990 | 100 | 204 | Gypsum | Container | 1 | Yes | Fragment | 5.5 × 2.7 cm | Rim and neck fragment | NA | Possibly between sq. L16-17-M14-17-N14-17 | NA |
| 1990 | 149 | NA | Green stone | Container | 1 | Yes | Fragment | 5.4 × 2.5 cm | Base fragment | NA | Possibly between sq. L16-17-M14-17-N14-17 | NA |
| 1990 | 150 | NA | Black stone | Container | 1 | Yes | Complete | H = 4 cm; Rim D = 2.15 cm | Vial | NA | Possibly between sq. L16-17-M14-17-N14-17 | NA |
| 1990 | 197 | NA | Marble? | Container | 1 | Yes | Fragment | 5.3 × 2.8 cm | Body fragment | NA | Possibly between sq. L16-17-M14-17-N14-17 | NA |

## Containers

Stone containers are in Excavation VII represented by six records including one complete vial and five vessel fragments (Table 6.18; Fig. 6.12). The compositions of two of them were analysed: one is a gypsum ($CaSO_4$ $2H_2O$) jar rim and neck fragment (SF100, sample 204) and one is an onyx bowl base (SF6, sample 218). The rest are defined as black (SF150, vial), white (SF42, jar rim and neck), and green (SF149, vessel base) stones, as well as marble(?) (SF197, bowl fragment). The vial (SF150) is 4 cm high and has a rim diameter of 2.15 cm. The onyx bowl base's (SF6) diameter is 5.6 cm.

Additional stone containers have been found at Sarazm. Stone bowls, in particular, do not seem rare at this site (e.g. Isakov 1991, fig. 53 nos 1–11, fig. 61 no. 17, fig. 80 nos 1–9). Although the limited and fragmentary sample from Excavation VII does not allow for detailed comparison, it is perhaps worth remembering that stone bowls are ubiquitous between Central Asia, South Asia, and Middle Asia. Of specific interest are perhaps the two jar rim and neck fragments from Excavation VII (SF42 and SF100). Although stone vessels are recorded since the Neolithic Period, it seems that closed shapes and vessels with out-turned rims are more common beginning with the Bronze Age (e.g. Pottier 1984, 159–64 figs 25–30, 207–09 pls XXV–XXVII (Afghanistan); Masson 1988, pl. VII (Altyn-Depe); Akbarzadeh and Piran 2013 (Halil Rud Basin); see Casanova 1991 on the third and second millennia BCE in Iran and Central Asia). As for the vial from Excavation VII (SF150), at a minimum three additional ones with different shapes have been discovered at Sarazm (Isakov 1991, fig. 61 no. 1; Razzokov 2008, fig. 29 nos 7–8, fig. 31 no. 8; Razzokov and Kurbanov 2004, 188 fig. 4 no. 21). These vials are reminiscent of material found between south-eastern Iran and Central Asia at the time of the Oxus Civilization and prior to it during the Namazga IV/Early Namazga V Periods, such as vials from Afghanistan reported by Pottier (1984, 152–55 figs 18–21) and those from Farkhor cemetery in southern Tajikistan (Vinogradova 2021, 641 fig. 23.6 no. 6, 642 fig. 23.7 no. 5), as well as those from Shahdad (Hakemi 1997, 58 fig. 36, 618–20), although these parallels are usually decorated, whereas the exemplar from Excavation VII is not. These containers may have served as cosmetic jars, while Vinogradova (2021, 641 fig. 23.6 no. 6, 642 fig. 23.7 no. 5) suggests that those from Farkhor are stone lamps.

# STONE INDUSTRY

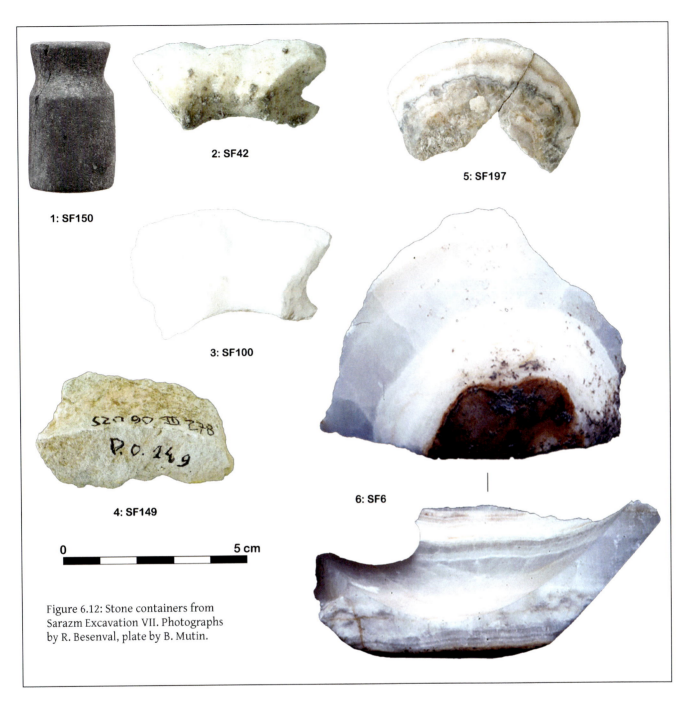

Figure 6.12: Stone containers from Sarazm Excavation VII. Photographs by R. Besenval, plate by B. Mutin.

Table 6.19: Stone mould from Sarazm Excavation VII.

| Year | SF no. | Sample no. | Material | Object category | Q. | Image | Preservation | Dimensions | Observations | Level | Context | Context category |
|---|---|---|---|---|---|---|---|---|---|---|---|---|
| 1990 | 94 | NA | Stone | Mould | 1 | No | NA | NA | NA | III2 | North/East area | Fill and floor |

## Mould

Besenval recorded one small stone mould in the Level III2 North/East area (SF94) (Table 6.19). I have found no information about this mould in his archives.

Figure 6.13: Ground stones from Sarazm Excavation VII. Photographs by R. Besenval, plate by B. Mutin.

Table 6.20: Ground stones from Sarazm Excavation VII.

| Year | SF no. | Sample no. | Material | Object category | Q. | Image | Preservation | Dimensions | Observations | Level | Context | Context category |
|---|---|---|---|---|---|---|---|---|---|---|---|---|
| 1984 | 12 | NA | Stone | Ground stone | 1 | No | NA | NA | NA | I3 | Alleyway 2 | Fill and floor |
| 1985 | 14 | NA | Stone | Ground stone | 1 | No | Fragment | NA | NA | III3 | Hearth 10 | Hearth |
| 1989 | 82 | NA | Stone | Ground stone | 1 | Yes | Fragment | 11 × 10 cm | Round or oval | IV1–IV2 | Unknown | Fill and floor |
| 1990 | 95 | NA | Stone | Ground stone | 1 | Yes | Incomplete | 35 × 27 cm | Round | III2 | North/East area | Fill and floor |
| 1990 | 101 | 159 | Green stone | Ground stone | 1 | Yes | Fragment | 21 × 9 cm | Triangular section | III | North/East area; sq. M17 | Fill and floor |
| 1990 | 102 | NA | Stone | Ground stone | 1 | No | NA | NA | NA | NA | Possibly between sq. L16-17–M14-17–N14-17 | NA |
| 1990 | 164 | NA | Stone | Ground stone | 1 | No | NA | NA | Round | IV1–IV2 | North/East area | NA |
| 1990 | 165 | NA | Stone | Ground stone | 1 | No | NA | NA | Oval | IV1–IV2 | North/East area | NA |
| 1990 | 166 | NA | Stone | Ground stone | 1 | No | NA | NA | Round | IV1–IV2 | North/East area | NA |
| 1990 | 167 | NA | Stone | Ground stone | 1 | No | NA | NA | Oval | IV1–IV2 | North/East area | NA |
| 1990 | 168 | NA | Stone | Ground stone | 1 | Yes | Incomplete | 47 × 32 cm | Oval | IV1 | North/East area | NA |
| 1990 | 169 | NA | Stone | Ground stone | 1 | Yes | Fragment | 37 × 27 cm | Oval | IV1–IV2 | North/East area; sq. M16-N16 | NA |
| 1991 | 301 | NA | Stone | Ground stone | 1 | Yes | Fragment | 11 × 6.5 cm | Round | NA | North/East area; likely between sq. J16-17–K16-17–L16-17–M16-17–N16-17 | NA |

## Ground Stones

Thirteen ground stones were recorded in Excavation VII (Table 6.20; Fig. 6.13). Only six are documented and could be measured based on photographs, while Besenval provided information about the shapes of four additional ones, i.e. that they are round or oval. Twelve of these ground stones are made from white-to-grey sandstones, and one is made from a green stone (SF101). The various sizes and morphologies of these artefacts suggest that they most likely did not all serve the same functions. At a minimum, it is safe to say that an object such as SF301 was probably not used the same way and for the same purpose as SF168. Two main groups of shapes may be distinguished from available data: four ground stones are round, while four are oval (and one is either round or oval). The above-mentioned fragment of green ground stone has a triangular section and is oblong. As for their sizes, large ground stones were recorded, with the largest being close to 50 cm in length (SF168), as well as small ground stones, with a diameter probably around 11 cm for one of the smallest ones (SF301).

Figure 6.14: Hammer/grinding stones from Sarazm Excavation VII.
Photographs by R. Besenval, plate by B. Mutin.

Table 6.21: Hammer/grinding stones from Sarazm Excavation VII.

| Year | SF no. | Sample no. | Material | Object category | Q. | Image | Preservation | Dimensions | Observations | Level | Context | Context category |
|---|---|---|---|---|---|---|---|---|---|---|---|---|
| 1989 | 91 | NA | Quartz? | Hammer/grinding stone | 1 | Yes | Complete | D = 7 cm | Spherical | II1 | Area 1 | Fill and floor |
| 1990 | 103 | NA | Stone | Hammer/grinding stone | 1 | Yes | Complete | D = 8 cm | Discoidal | NA | Possibly between sq. L16-17-M14-17-N14-17 | NA |
| 1990 | 104 | NA | Granite? | Hammer/grinding stone | 1 | Yes | Complete | L = 3.8 cm; D = 4.2 cm | Cylindrical | NA | Possibly between sq. L16-17-M14-17-N14-17 | NA |
| 1990 | 105 | NA | Stone | Hammer/grinding stone | 1 | Yes | Complete | D = 5.5 cm | Spherical | NA | Possibly between sq. L16-17-M14-17-N14-17 | NA |
| 1990 | 106 | NA | Stone | Hammer/grinding stone | 1 | Yes | Complete | D = 3.5 cm | Spherical | NA | Possibly between sq. L16-17-M14-17-N14-17 | NA |
| 1990 | 206 | NA | Quartz? | Hammer/grinding stone | 1 | Yes | Complete | D = 6.1–6.7 cm | Spherical | NA | Possibly between sq. L16-17-M14-17-N14-17 | NA |
| 1991 | 256 | NA | Quartz? | Hammer/grinding stone | 1 | Yes | Complete | D = 9 cm | Spherical | NA | North/East area; likely between sq. J16-17-K16-17-L16-17-M16-17-N16-17 | NA |
| 1991 | 257 | NA | Stone | Hammer/grinding stone | 1 | No | Complete | NA | Spherical | NA | North/East area; likely between sq. J16-17-K16-17-L16-17-M16-17-N16-17 | NA |
| 1991 | 263 | NA | Granite? | Hammer/grinding stone | 1 | Yes | Complete | D = 7.2 cm | Spherical | NA | North/East area; likely between sq. J16-17-K16-17-L16-17-M16-17-N16-17 | NA |
| 1991 | 267 | NA | Granite? | Hammer/grinding stone | 1 | Yes | Complete | D = 7.5–9 cm | Spherical | NA | North/East area; likely between sq. J16-17-K16-17-L16-17-M16-17-N16-17 | NA |
| 1987 | 333 | NA | Stone | Hammer/grinding stone | 1 | Yes | Complete | D = 10.2 cm | Discoidal | I1 | Room 2 | Fill and floor |

## Hammer Stones, Pestles/Sharpeners, and Grinding Stones

This category includes stone objects whose morphologies, aspects, and sizes suggest that they were used to strike as part of debitage activities (hammer stones) and objects that may have been used as part of activities such as food and pigment preparation (pestles and grinding stones) (Tables 6.21–6.22; Figs 6.14–6.15). These objects divide into four main groups of shapes: spherical, cylindrical, discoidal, and oblong. The objects in the three former groups appear to have been used as hammer and/or grinding stones. They consist of eleven items of sandstone, granite(?), and quartz(?), between 3.5 and 10.2 cm in diameter. The records in the latter group consist of eleven sandstone items ranging from 7.4 to 22 cm in length. They may have been used as pestles to hit, crush, and grind. With regard to this, peck marks are particularly evident on one end of SF66, while SF84 bears traces of green pigment inside its breakage. However, most of these pestles are not perfectly cylindrical; one of their faces tends to be flat. For this reason, Besenval suggested that they might have been used as sharpeners.

Figure 6.15: Stone pestles/sharpeners from Sarazm Excavation VII. Photographs by B. Mutin.

# STONE INDUSTRY

Table 6.22: Stone pestles/sharpeners from Sarazm Excavation VII.

| Year | SF no. | Sample no. | Material | Object category | Q. | Image | Preservation | Dimensions | Observations | Level | Context | Context category |
|---|---|---|---|---|---|---|---|---|---|---|---|---|
| 1987 | 66 | NA | Stone | Pestle/sharpener | 1 | Yes | Complete | L = 13.3; W = 3.2 cm | / | I3 | Room 5 | Fill and floor |
| 1989 | 83 | NA | Stone | Pestle/sharpener | 1 | Yes | Complete | L = 15.6 cm; W = 4.7 cm | / | IV1–IV2 | Unknown | Fill and floor |
| 1989 | 84 | NA | Stone | Pestle/sharpener | 1 | Yes | Fragment | L = 6.75 cm; W = 3.15 cm | Green pigment inside breakage | IV2 | Room 8 | Fill and floor |
| 1989 | 92 | NA | Stone | Pestle/sharpener | 1 | Yes | Complete | L = 19.9 cm; W = 5.5 cm | / | II1 | Area 1 | Fill and floor |
| 1990 | 172 | NA | Stone | Pestle/sharpener | 1 | No | Complete | L = 22 cm | / | III2 | North/East area; sq. K16; Room 9? | NA |
| 1991 | 259 | NA | Stone | Pestle/sharpener | 1 | Yes | Complete | L = 15.2 cm; W = 3.6 cm | / | NA | North/East area; likely between sq. J16-17–K16-17–L16-17–M16-17–N16-17 | NA |
| 1991 | 265 | NA | Stone | Pestle/sharpener | 1 | Yes | Complete | L = 22 cm; W = 4.7 cm | / | NA | North/East area; likely between sq. J16-17–K16-17–L16-17–M16-17–N16-17 | NA |
| 1991 | 269 | NA | Stone | Pestle/sharpener | 1 | Yes | Incomplete | L = 9.6; W = 3.6 cm | / | NA | North/East area; likely between sq. J16-17–K16-17–L16-17–M16-17–N16-17 | NA |
| 1991 | 295 | NA | Stone | Pestle/sharpener | 1 | No | Complete | NA | / | NA | North/East area; likely between sq. J16-17–K16-17–L16-17–M16-17–N16-17 | NA |
| 1991 | 298 | NA | Stone | Pestle/sharpener | 1 | Yes | Complete | L = 7.4 cm; W = 2.7 cm | / | NA | North/East area; likely between sq. J16-17–K16-17–L16-17–M16-17–N16-17 | NA |
| 1989 | 334 | NA | Stone | Pestle/sharpener | 1 | Yes | Complete | L = 9.9 cm; W = 2.5 cm | / | IV1–IV2 | Sq. J10; uppermost layer | Fill and floor |

Table 6.23: Stone sharpener from Sarazm Excavation VII.

| Year | SF no. | Sample no. | Material | Object category | Q. | Image | Preservation | Dimensions | Observations | Level | Context | Context category |
|---|---|---|---|---|---|---|---|---|---|---|---|---|
| 1991 | 275 | NA | Black stone | Sharpener | 1 | Yes | Fragment | L = 5.5 cm; W = 2 cm | / | NA | North/East area; likely between sq. J16-17–K16-17–L16-17–M16-17–N16-17 | NA |

## Sharpeners

In addition to some of, or all, the above pestles/sharpeners, one artefact from Excavation VII, a fragment of an oblong, flat, black stone is likely to have been used as a sharpener (SF275). This fragment is 5.5 cm long and 2 cm wide (Table 6.23; Fig. 6.16).

Figure 6.16: Stone sharpener from Sarazm Excavation VII (SF275). Photograph by B. Mutin.

Table 6.24: Cobble flakes from Sarazm Excavation VII.

| Year | SF no. | Sample no. | Material | Object category | Q. | Image | Preservation | Dimensions | Observations | Level | Context | Context category |
|---|---|---|---|---|---|---|---|---|---|---|---|---|
| 1985 | 18 | NA | Stone | Cobble flake | 1 | No | NA | NA | NA | I1 | Room 1 | Fill and floor |
| 1987 | 35 | NA | Stone | Cobble flake | 1 | Yes | Complete | L = 10.5 cm; W = 10.2 cm | Near round | II1 | Room 1 | Fill and floor |
| 1990 | 109 | NA | Stone | Cobble flake | 1 | Yes | Complete | L = 10.9 cm; W = 7.3 cm | Oval | II | North/East area; sq. L16 | NA |
| 1990 | 173 | NA | Stone | Cobble flake | 1 | Yes | Complete | L = 14.5 cm; W = 8.1 cm | Oval | NA | Possibly between sq. L16–17–M14–17–N14–17 | NA |
| 1990 | 180 | NA | Stone | Cobble flake | 1 | No | NA | NA | NA | NA | Possibly between sq. L16–17–M14–17–N14–17 | NA |
| 1990 | 181 | NA | Stone | Cobble flake | 1 | Yes | Complete | D = 9.8 cm | Round | NA | Possibly between sq. L16–17–M14–17–N14–17 | NA |
| 1990 | 182 | NA | Stone | Cobble flake | 1 | No | NA | NA | NA | NA | Possibly between sq. L16–17–M14–17–N14–17 | NA |
| 1990 | 183 | NA | Stone | Cobble flake | 1 | Yes | Complete | L = 14 cm; W = 7.5 cm | Oval | NA | Possibly between sq. L16–17–M14–17–N14–17 | NA |
| 1991 | 260 | NA | Stone | Cobble flake | 1 | Yes | Complete | D = 8 cm | Round | NA | North/East area; likely between sq. J16–17–K16–17–L16–17–M16–17–N16–17 | NA |
| 1991 | 264 | NA | Stone | Cobble flake | 1 | Yes | Complete | L = 11.15 cm; W = 8.8 cm | Oval | NA | North/East area; likely between sq. J16–17–K16–17–L16–17–M16–17–N16–17 | NA |
| 1991 | 266 | NA | Stone | Cobble flake | 1 | Yes | Complete | L = 10.3 cm; W = 5.8 cm | Oval | NA | North/East area; likely between sq. J16–17–K16–17–L16–17–M16–17–N16–17 | NA |

**Cobble Flakes**

Eleven small finds consist of large flakes of river cobbles (Table 6.24; Fig. 6.17). Such flakes are frequent at Sarazm (e.g. Razzokov 2008, fig. 4 no. 1, fig. 12 no. 1, figs 18, 21). They are usually retouched and may have been used for activities such as cutting or scraping, including scraping skins as suggested by Razzokov (2008, fig. 21). The exemplars from Excavation VII divide into two main groups of shapes: round or near round flakes with diameters or lengths between 8 and 10.5 cm, and oval flakes with lengths ranging from 10.3 to 14.5 cm.

# STONE INDUSTRY

Figure 6.17: Cobble flakes from Sarazm Excavation VII. Photographs by R. Besenval, plate by B. Mutin.

Figure 6.18: Stone pebbles from Sarazm Excavation VII. Photographs and plate by B. Mutin.

Table 6.25: Stone pebbles from Sarazm Excavation VII.

| Year | SF no. | Sample no. | Material | Object category | Q. | Image | Preservation | Dimensions | Observations | Level | Context | Context category |
|------|--------|------------|----------|-----------------|----|-------|--------------|------------|--------------|-------|---------|------------------|
| 1987 | 64 | NA | Red stone | Pebble | 1 | Yes | Complete | 1.8 cm | Spherical | IV1 | Sq. I14 | Fill and floor |
| 1991 | 268 | NA | Pink stone | Pebble | 1 | Yes | Complete | D = 4.8–5.3 cm | Spherical | NA | North/East area; likely between sq. J16–17-K16–17-L16–17-M16–17-N16–17 | NA |
| 1991 | 279 | NA | Stone | Pebble | 1 | No | Complete | NA | NA | NA | North/East area; likely between sq. J16–17-K16–17-L16–17-M16–17-N16–17 | NA |
| 1991 | 282 | NA | Green stone | Pebble | 1 | Yes | Complete | 2.3 × 2.3 cm | Flat, asymmetrical | NA | North/East area; likely between sq. J16–17-K16–17-L16–17-M16–17-N16–17 | NA |
| 1991 | 288 | NA | Stone | Pebble | 1 | No | Complete | NA | Flat | NA | North/East area; likely between sq. J16–17-K16–17-L16–17-M16–17-N16–17 | NA |
| 1991 | 299 | NA | White stone | Pebble | 1 | Yes | Complete | 2.4 × 1.35 cm | Oval | NA | North/East area; likely between sq. J16–17-K16–17-L16–17-M16–17-N16–17 | NA |
| 1991 | 300 | NA | White stone | Pebble | 1 | Yes | Complete | 2.55 × 2 cm | Oval | NA | North/East area; likely between sq. J16–17-K16–17-L16–17-M16–17-N16–17 | NA |

## Pebbles

Common findings in the archaeological deposits at Sarazm are natural pebbles. They appear to be just natural, unworked pebbles; yet the fact that they are quite frequent and that they sometimes are found in groups make it likely that they had some specific purpose(s) at this site. Seven were recorded in Excavation VII (Table 6.25; Fig. 6.18). They are of pink, red, green, and white colours and include spherical and oval stones, as well as one flat, asymmetrical stone. Their sizes range from 1.8 to c. 5 cm.

## Weights?

In this category are five large stones that I have tentatively labelled 'weights', although there is no crystal-clear indication that they were used as weights (Table 6.26; Figs 6.19–6.21). Only three are documented. One of these three stones (SF163) is oval-shaped and bears a groove carved out along its length. This object seems to be about 20 cm long, based on available photographs. The groove makes it likely that this stone was attached to a rope. Tentatively, although its shape is different, this object brings to mind the descriptions of stone

STONE INDUSTRY

Figure 6.19: Stone weight(?) from Sarazm Excavation VII (SF27). Photograph by R. Besenval, edited by B. Mutin.

Figure 6.20: Stone weight(?) from Sarazm Excavation VII (SF93). Photograph by R. Besenval, edited by B. Mutin.

Figure 6.21: Stone weight(?) from Sarazm Excavation VII (SF163). Photographs by R. Besenval, edited by B. Mutin.

Table 6.26: Stone weights(?) from Sarazm Excavation VII.

| Year | SF no. | Sample no. | Material | Object category | Q. | Image | Preservation | Dimensions | Observations | Level | Context | Context category |
|---|---|---|---|---|---|---|---|---|---|---|---|---|
| 1986 | 27 | NA | Stone | Weight? | 1 | Yes | Complete | L = 70 cm; T = 15 cm (very approximately) | One crest in the middle | III2 | Room 7 | Fill and floor |
| 1990 | 93 | NA | Stone | Weight? | 1 | Yes | Complete | L = 27 cm (approximately) | Four ridges perpendicular to its length | III2 | North/East area | Fill and floor |
| 1990 | 163 | NA | Stone | Weight? | 1 | Yes | Complete | L = 20 cm (very approximately) | One groove in the middle | III | North/East area | NA |
| 1990 | 170 | NA | Stone | Weight? | 1 | No | NA | NA | NA | IV1–IV2 | North/East area; sq. L16 | NA |
| 1990 | 171 | NA | Stone | Weight? | 1 | No | NA | NA | NA | IV1–IV2 | North/East area; sq. L16 | NA |

Figure 6.22: Stone raw material from Sarazm Excavation VII. Photographs and plate by B. Mutin.

hammers that were used in ancient mining activities to crack the rock: 'Many have a groove running around the middle of the stone to which a leather band or wooden handle could be attached' (Garner 2021, 811; see 806, 807 fig. 28.4). The second one (SF93) is a cylinder with four ridges perpendicular to its length. This stone seems to be c. 27 cm long, based on the available photograph. The ridges would make it easy to attach one or more ropes or strings around this stone. The third stone (SF27) is a quadrangular, c. 70 cm long stone. Its top part has a crest in its centre perpendicular to its length and is concave on each side of it. That this stone was attached to a rope to weigh down a mat, a canopy, or a tent, for instance, is not contradicted by its size, weight, and morphology. I however cannot ascertain that this was the case.

**Raw Material**

The last category of stone items consists of eight records of raw materials (Table 6.27; Fig. 6.22). I have been able to access and document only three of them. Four records are listed as marble (SF176), red stone (SF277), gypsum (SF327), and calcined stone (SF330). It is however unclear whether the items listed as marble and gypsum are truly made from these materials. Indeed, their compositions were supposed to be analysed (sample 153, sample 158), but I have found no indication that these analyses have ever been conducted. Similarly, the calcined stone was sent for analysis (sample 185), although I have found no record of this analysis in the archives. The items I had access to include two frag-

Table 6.27: Records of stone raw material from Sarazm Excavation VII.

| Year | SF no. | Sample no. | Material | Object category | Q. | Image | Preservation | Dimensions | Observations | Level | Context | Context category |
|---|---|---|---|---|---|---|---|---|---|---|---|---|
| 1990 | 107 | NA | Green stone | Raw material | 1 | Yes | Fragment | 6 × 4.5 cm | Asymmetrical | NA | Possibly between sq. L16-17-M14-17-N14-17 | NA |
| 1990 | 108 | NA | Green stone | Raw material | 1 | Yes | Fragment | 7.75 × 7 cm | Triangular | NA | North/East area; sq. K16 | NA |
| 1990 | 176 | 153 | Marble | Raw material | 1 | No | Fragment | NA | NA | Surf. | Possibly between sq. L16-17-M14-17-N14-17 | NA |
| 1991 | 239 | NA | Red-light brown stone | Raw material | 1 | Yes | Complete | 2.5 × 2.2 cm | Translucent stone, asymmetrical | III1 | North/East; Area 2 | Fill and floor |
| 1991 | 277 | NA | Red stone | Raw material | 1 | No | NA | NA | NA | NA | North/East area; likely between sq. J16-17-K16-17-L16-17-M16-17-N16-17 | NA |
| 1991 | 278 | NA | Stone | Raw material | 1 | No | NA | NA | NA | NA | North/East area; likely between sq. J16-17-K16-17-L16-17-M16-17-N16-17 | NA |
| 1990 | 327 | 158 | Gypsum | Raw material | 1 | No | NA | NA | NA | NA | Possibly between sq. L16-17-M14-17-N14-17 | NA |
| 1991 | 330 | 185 | Stone | Raw material | 1 | No | NA | NA | Calcined stone | NA | North/East area; likely between sq. J16-17-K16-17-L16-17-M16-17-N16-17 | NA |

ments of the same type of green stone, a stone that is similar to that of ground stone SF101 and to additional objects recovered elsewhere at Sarazm, including a vessel rim that was found in Excavation XIV. These fragments from Excavation VII are two flakes measuring 6 and 7.75 cm to the maximum. The third item I have been able to document is a 2.5 × 2.2 cm red-light brown, translucent stone (SF239).

## Pigment and Remains Relating to Pigment Preparation

Twenty records are pigments or remains relating to pigment preparation (Table 6.28; Figs 6.23–6.26). They consist of: ten ochre fragments, with six of them marked with a question mark; one fragment of a blue-green rock pigment; one fragment of goethite; fragments of red and blue plaster; one fragment of blue plaster; one fragment of red plaster; one blue powder and one red powder described as plaster in powder; and three stones with traces of colour that appear to have been used for pigment preparation. To this inventory must be added the above-mentioned SF84, a pestle/sharpener with traces of green pigment. Only eight of these records are documented and have descriptions. They include two yellow-light red, facetted mineral fragments defined as ochre(?). One is c. 5.4 × 2.5 cm (SF52), and the other one is c. 2.6 × 1.5 cm (SF285). One record is a c. 3 cm long goethite fragment (SF211). Three other records are plaster fragments of red and lapis lazuli blue colours (SF191, SF320, and SF332). Two are flat stones that were used to grind pigments on their surfaces. One is c. 26 × 26 cm and bears traces of red and blue pigments (SF10), and the second one is c. 18 × 8 cm and has traces of red and yellow pigments (SF26).

Thirteen records were submitted for composition analysis. Five of them were analysed by Cesbron (Besenval and Isakov 1989, 11). Two are plaster fragments. One is a blue plaster (SF318, sample 11) whose pigment consists of lapis lazuli (lazurite) powder mixed with calcite ($CaCO_3$). One is a red plaster (SF319, sample 12) whose pigment was made of hematite $Fe_2O_3$ (ochre) mixed with quartz. The third sample was described as a blue-green pigment that seems to consist of compacted powder (SF209, sample 173). It is composed of calcite ($CaCO_3$), zincite (ZnO), and a little bit of baryte ($BaSO_4$). The fourth sample was described as an ochre(?) fragment (SF285, sample 208). It consists of goethite (FeO(OH)). Another fragment listed as ochre (SF157, sample 222) is made of jarosite ($KFe_3(OH)_6(SO_4)_2$). Lastly,

Table 6.28: Records of pigment and of remains relating to pigment preparation from Sarazm Excavation VII.

| Year | SF no. | Sample no. | Material | Object category | Q. | Image | Preservation | Dimensions | Observations | Level | Context | Context category |
|---|---|---|---|---|---|---|---|---|---|---|---|---|
| 1984 | 2 | NA | Ochre? | Raw material | 1 | No | Fragment | NA | NA | II2 | Area 3 | Fill and floor |
| 1984 | 3 | NA | Ochre | Raw material | 1 | No | Fragment | NA | NA | I3 or I4 | Level I3 Room 6, Area 2, or Alleyway 2; or Level I4 Area 4 | Fill and floor |
| 1984 | 10 | NA | Stone | Flat stone for pigment processing | 1 | Yes | Complete | Flat; 26 × 26 cm | Stone with red and blue pigment | I3 | Alleyway 2 | Fill and floor |
| 1986 | 26 | NA | Stone | Flat stone for pigment processing | 1 | Yes | Complete | Flat schist; 18 × 8 cm | Stone with red and yellow pigment | IV1 | Room 2 | Fill and floor |
| 1987 | 52 | 44 | Ochre? | Raw material | 1 | Yes | Fragment | 5.4 × 2.5 cm | Used, faceted fragment | III2 | Area 4 | Fill and floor |
| 1990 | 113 | NA | Ochre | Raw material | 1 | No | Fragment | NA | NA | NA | Possibly between sq. L16–17–M14–17–N14–17 | NA |
| 1990 | 114 | NA | Ochre | Raw material | 1 | No | Fragment | NA | NA | NA | Possibly between sq. L16–17–M14–17–N14–17 | NA |
| 1990 | 157 | 222 | Ochre | Raw material | 1 | No | Fragment | NA | NA | NA | Possibly between sq. L16–17–M14–17–N14–17 | NA |
| 1990 | 191 | NA | Plaster | Raw material | 2 | Yes | Fragment | 7.65 × 5.3 cm; 4.6 × 3.4 cm | Red plaster | NA | Possibly between sq. L16–17–M14–17–N14–17 | NA |
| 1991 | 209 | 173 | Pigment rock | Raw material | 1 | No | Fragment | NA | Blue/green pigment rock | I | North/East area; Area 5 | Fill and floor |
| 1991 | 211 | 174 | Goethite | Raw material | 1 | Yes | Fragment | L = 3 cm | Goethite α-FeO(OH) | NA | North/East area; likely between sq. J16–17–K16–17–L16–17–M16–17–N16–17 | NA |
| 1991 | 285 | 208 | Ochre? | Raw material | 1 | Yes | Fragment | 2.6 × 1.5 cm | / | NA | North/East area; likely between sq. J16–17–K16–17–L16–17–M16–17–N16–17 | NA |
| 1985 | 314 | 4 | Stone | Flat stone for colour processing | 1 | No | Complete | NA | Stone with red pigment | III1 | Pit 1 | Pit |
| 1985 | 318 | 11 | Plaster | Raw material | 1 | No | Powder | NA | Blue plaster | III2 | Room 3 | Fill and floor |
| 1985 | 319 | 12 | Plaster | Raw material | 1 | No | Powder | NA | Red plaster | III2 | Room 3 | Fill and floor |
| 1985 | 320 | 13 | Plaster | Raw material | 6 | Yes | Fragment | 6.7 × 4.65 cm; 4.6 × 2.75 cm; 3.4 × 3.15 cm; 3.45 × 2.05 cm; 5.65 × 4.45 cm; 5 × 3.15 cm | Blue and red plaster | III2 | Room 3 | Fill and floor |
| 1986 | 322 | 28 | Ochre? | Raw material | 1 | No | Fragment | NA | NA | IV2 | Hearth 2 | Hearth |
| 1991 | 328 | 183 | Ochre? | Raw material | 1 | No | Fragment | NA | NA | NA | North/East area; likely between sq. J16–17–K16–17–L16–17–M16–17–N16–17 | NA |
| 1991 | 329 | 184 | Ochre? | Raw material | 1 | No | Fragment | NA | NA | NA | North/East area; likely between sq. J16–17–K16–17–L16–17–M16–17–N16–17 | NA |
| 1991 | 332 | 200 | Plaster | Raw material | 1 | Yes | Fragment | 6.2 × 5.15 cm | Black/dark blue plaster | NA | North/East area; likely between sq. J16–17–K16–17–L16–17–M16–17–N16–17 | NA |

PIGMENT AND REMAINS RELATING TO PIGMENT PREPARATION

Figure 6.23: Records of pigment and of remains relating to pigment preparation from Sarazm Excavation VII. Photographs and plate by B. Mutin.

Figure 6.24: Flat stone used for pigment preparation from Sarazm Excavation VII (SF10). Photograph by R. Besenval, edited by B. Mutin.

Figure 6.25: Flat stone used for pigment preparation from Sarazm Excavation VII (SF26). Photograph by R. Besenval, edited by B. Mutin.

Figure 6.26: Goethite from Sarazm Excavation VII (SF211). Photograph by R. Besenval, edited by B. Mutin.

the above-mentioned goethite fragment (SF211, sample 174; Fig. 6.26) was determined through composition analysis (α-FeO(OH)). Goethite is known to produce the red of hematite through heating at low temperatures (Bowles 2021).

## Copper Industry

The copper objects from Excavation VII consist of fifteen items: five pins (SF96, SF97, SF210, SF289, and SF294); four daggers (SF25, SF72, SF98, and SF207); three awls (SF71, SF73, and SF99); one item described as being the point of either an awl or a blade (SF17); what appears to be a hook (SF39); and one fragment that Besenval recorded as a copper item with a question mark (SF325). The compositions of three of these objects were analysed. Six additional records are findings relating to copper metallurgy (Table 6.29).

### Pins

The pins have long and thin stems and decorated heads (Table 6.29; Fig. 6.27). The four complete pins from Excavation VII are 7.3, 13.35, 15.5, and 21 cm long. Two of them have flat heads; one is diamond-shaped (SF210), and one is triangle-shaped (SF97). The head of the third complete pin consists of two spirals or coils joined together (SF96). Additional pins were found at Sarazm, including examples with stems with thickened extremities, as observed on SF97 and SF210 from Excavation VII. Diamond-shaped and triangle-shaped heads are observed on some of these parallels, although they are not exactly the same as those on the pins from Excavation VII. On the other hand, the single double-spiral headed pin from this excavation has no equivalent elsewhere at Sarazm (Isakov 1991, fig. 23 nos 1–4; 1994b, 4 fig. 5; metallic artefacts including pins, blades, awls, and hooks on display at the National Museum of Antiquities in Dushanbe, the Penjikent Museum, and the Museum at Sarazm). Beyond this site, headed-pins are recorded between the Iranian Plateau, Pakistan, and Central Asia from the Chalcolithic through the Middle Bronze Age periods, with the most sophisticated heads observed within assemblages dating to the mid–late third through the early second millennia BCE as part of the Oxus Civilization in Central Asia and at sites such as Shahdad and in the Halil Rud Basin in Iran (see Ligabue and Salvatori 1988; Masson 1988, pl. XXIX no. 4; Hakemi 1997, 61 fig. 38; see Ligabue and Rossi Osmida 2007; Helwing 2017, 113). Pins with simpler heads are observed before that, between the mid–late fourth and mid-third millennia BCE, at least from north-eastern Iran and Turkmenistan to Tajikistan and Pakistan, including pins similar to those found in Excavation VII and from other locations at Sarazm. Such objects are

Table 6.29: Copper objects and records relating to copper metallurgy from Sarazm Excavation VII.

| Year | SF no. | Sample no. | Material | Object category | Q. | Image | Preservation | Dimensions | Observations | Level | Context | Context category |
|---|---|---|---|---|---|---|---|---|---|---|---|---|
| 1990 | 96 | 168 | Copper | Pin | 1 | Yes | Complete | L = 13.35 cm; Stem D = 0.2–0.5 cm; Head = 3.75 × 1.75 cm | Double spiral-headed pin | IV1 | North/East area; sq. M16 | Fill and floor |
| 1990 | 97 | NA | Copper | Pin | 1 | Yes | Complete | L = 21 cm; Stem D = 0.2–0.6 cm; Head = 1.2 × 1.2 cm | Headed pin | II | North/East area; Area 5 or Room 14 | Fill and floor |
| 1991 | 210 | 177 | Copper | Pin | 1 | Yes | Complete | L = 15.5 cm; Stem D = 0.25–0.55 cm; Head = 1.65 × 1.15 cm | / | II | North/East area; Area 4 | Fill and floor |
| 1991 | 289 | NA | Copper | Pin | 1 | Yes | Complete | L = 7.3 cm; Stem D = 0.2–0.35 cm | / | NA | North/East area; likely between sq. J16-17-K16-17-L16-17-M16-17-N16-17 | NA |
| 1991 | 294 | NA | Copper | Pin | 1 | No | Fragment | L = 2.5 cm | / | NA | North/East area; likely between sq. J16-17-K16-17-L16-17-M16-17-N16-17 | NA |
| 1991 | 207 | 162 | Copper | Dagger | 1 | Yes | Complete | L = 26.45 cm; Blade W = 1.15–2.3; Point W = 0.5 cm; Tang W = 0.35–0.85 cm | / | NA | North/East area; likely between sq. J16-17-K16-17-L16-17-M16-17-N16-17 | NA |
| 1989 | 72 | 207 | Copper | Dagger | 1 | Yes | Fragment | L = 5.7 cm; Blade W = 0.7–1.25 cm | Paratacamite $(Cu_2(OH)_3Cl)$ | III3 | Area 7 | Fill and floor |
| 1990 | 98 | 169, 203 | Copper | Dagger | 1 | Yes | Complete | L = 16.95 cm; Blade W = 2.15–3 cm; Point W = 1 cm; Tang W = 0.3–1.25 cm | Mostly paratacamite $(Cu_2(OH)_3Cl)$, some cuprite $(Cu_2O)$, traces of azurite | IV1 | Sq. M15; c. 15 cm underneath Level IV2 Hearth 1 | Fill and floor |
| 1986 | 25 | NA | Copper | Dagger | 1 | Yes | Complete | L = 17.8 cm; Blade W = 0.7–3.6 cm; Point W = 0.6 cm; Tang W = 0.85–1.45 cm | / | IV1 | Area 1 | Fill and floor |
| 1989 | 71 | NA | Copper | Awl | 1 | Yes | Complete | L = 8.45 cm; D = 0.2–0.55 cm | / | III2 | Room 8 | Fill and floor |
| 1989 | 73 | NA | Copper | Awl | 1 | Yes | Fragment | L = 2.5 cm; D = 0.15–0.3 cm | Tip | III3 | Area 7 | Fill and floor |
| 1990 | 99 | NA | Copper | Awl | 1 | Yes | Complete | L = 8.25 cm; D = 0.2–0.6 cm | / | IV1 | North/East area; sq. M16 | Fill and floor |
| 1985 | 17 | NA | Copper | Awl or blade | 1 | No | Fragment | NA | NA | II1 | Hearth 2 | Hearth |
| 1987 | 39 | NA | Copper | Hook? | 1 | Yes | Fragment | L = 5.70 cm; D = 0.3–0.45 cm | / | I3 | Room 5 | Fill and floor |
| 1987 | 325 | 43 | Copper? | NA | 1 | No | Fragment | NA | NA | III2 | Room 3 | Fill and floor |
| 1985 | 313 | 3 | Ore | Fragment | 1 | Yes | Fragments | Fragments spread over a c. 1.8 × 1.5 cm area | Chrysocolla $(Cu,Al)_2H_2Si_2O_5(OH)_4 \cdot nH_2O)$ | III2 | Pit 2 | Pit |
| 1986 | 321 | 27 | Ore? | Fragment | 1 | No | Fragment | NA | NA | IV2 | Area 3 | Fill and floor |
| 1986 | 323 | 29 | Ore? | Fragment | 1 | No | Fragment | NA | NA | III3 | Area 6 | Fill and floor |
| 1987 | 326 | 64 | Ore? | Fragment | 1 | No | Fragment | NA | NA | III3 | Area 6 | Fill and floor |
| 1987 | 324 | 42 | Slag? | Fragment | 1 | No | Fragment | NA | NA | III2 | Room 3 | Fill and floor |
| 1990 | 112 | 205 | Slag | Fragment | 1 | No | Fragment | NA | Pyroxene (diopside-augite $Ca(Mg,Fe,Al)(Si,Al)_2O_6$) and quartz | NA | Possibly between sq. L16-17-M14-17-N14-17 | NA |

recorded for instance at Shah Tepe (Arne 1945, 298, 301–02), Tepe Hissar (Schmidt 1937, pl. XC.A), Altyn-Depe (Masson 1988, pl. XXVII no. 9), Geoksyur (Masson and Sarianidi 1972, 78 fig. 20 a–b), Farkhor (Vinogradova and Bobomulloev 2020, 202 pl. 5), Shahr-i Sokhta (Tosi 1968, fig. 113; Piperno and Salvatori 2007, 177 fig. 380 no. 7131, 192 fig. 418 no. 6272, 254 fig. 581 no. 7644, 279 fig. 644 no. 8284, 304 fig. 718 no. 8499, 317 fig. 754 no. 8516, 331 fig. 791 no. 7648, 339 fig. 809 no. 8172), Mundigak (Casal 1961, fig. 139 nos 5, 7, fig. 140 nos 19–20, 31), Said Qala Tepe (Shaffer 1971, 126 figs 43–44), and Sohr Damb (Franke 2015, pl. 8 no. Pl_19_f-Tr IX.jpg). The double-spiral headed pin from Excavation VII has many parallels within the same area including at Tepe Hissar (Schmidt 1933, pl. CIV.C; Schmidt 1937, pl. XXIX no. H4856), Parkhai II, Anau, Namazga-Depe (Khlopin 1981, 25 fig. 21 nos 1–2, 4–8, 25–26), Shahr-i Sokhta (Piperno and Salvatori 2007, 254 fig. 581 no. 7643, 271 fig. 627 no. 8016), Mundigak (Casal 1961, fig. 139 nos 4, 18), Said Qala Tepe (Shaffer 1971, 126 fig. 43), Mehrgarh (C. Jarrige et al. 1995, 202 fig. 3.15 a) and even further west such as at Tepe Sialk (Ghirshman 1938, pl. XCV a, e), within the Kura-Araxes sphere in the Caucasus and neighbouring regions, where the same motif is also observed on pottery (see Chataignier and Palumbi 2014), in Mesopotamia, and in south-eastern Europe (Kohl 2007, 30 fig. 2.5). This type of pin is also present within the Indus Civilization (Possehl 1996, 168–71; 2002, 226). Certainly, considerable variations are noted throughout this vast geographic and chronological expanse in the shapes and sizes of these double-spiral headed pins (e.g. Khlopin 1981, 25–26; Palumbi 2008, 128–30).

**Daggers**

The three complete daggers from Excavation VII have three different profiles (Table 6.29; Fig. 6.27). One (SF98) has a short tang, and part of its blade segment is thin. It is 17.8 cm long. The second one (SF25) has a short tang and a wider blade segment. It is 16.95 cm long. The third dagger (SF207) is 26.45 cm long. Its tang is longer too, and its tang end is folded. These three types of profiles have been observed elsewhere at Sarazm (Isakov 1991, figs 10, 75–77; 1994b, 4 fig. 4). Certainly, such objects were not unique to this site. Daggers are recorded at other sites contemporary with, or slightly more recent than, Sarazm, including Tepe Hissar (Schmidt 1933, pl. CIII), Tepe Chalow (Vahdati et al. 2019, 185 fig. 6 e), Altyn-Depe (Masson 1988, pl. XIV nos 1–2, pl. XXVII no. 10), Parkhai II (Khlopin 1981, 25 fig. 21 no. 12), Farkhor (Vinogradova and Bobomulloev 2020, 201 pl. 4 nos 12–16), Shahr-i Sokhta (Tosi 1968, fig. 114; Piperno and Salvatori 2007, 51 fig. 73 no. 6204, 279 fig. 645 no. 8295), Mundigak (Casal 1961, fig. 139 nos 6, 11, fig. 140 no. 30), as well as Hajjiabad-Varamin and Spidej in south-eastern Iran (Eskandari et al. 2020, 41 fig. 16 no. 25; Heydari et al. 2019, 55 pl. 22 no. 125/53). Daggers that generally parallel those from Sarazm have also been observed within Kura-Araxes assemblages, although many other daggers in the same assemblages are different (Kohl 2007, 92 fig. 3.15, 110 fig. 3.25). It should be noted that comparisons are at times difficult to make as available parallels are not always complete, such as at Mundigak. Perhaps from this brief survey some of the above-mentioned parallels from Altyn-Depe, Farkhor, Shahr-i Sokhta, and the Kura-Araxes sphere should be considered the closest equivalents for the daggers from Sarazm, with, tentatively in the present state of the analysis, certain specimens from the Caucasus looking quite close (see, in addition to the above-mentioned reference from Kohl 2007; Palumbi 2008, 126 fig. 4.15). A brief survey of daggers from the Chalcolithic and Bronze Age archaeological cultures in the Eurasian Steppe tends to show that these objects in these cultures appear to be mostly different (e.g. Anthony 2007, 357 fig. 14.4, 378 fig. 15.4, 392 fig. 15.10; Chernykh 2008, 73–93), although this preliminary observation needs to be confirmed through more thorough comparative typological analysis. Lastly, Isakov saw a parallel between the daggers from Sarazm and material in the Indus Civilization assemblage (Isakov 1991, tab. 15).

**Awls**

The two complete awls have virtually identical sizes and double-ogival profiles (SF71 and SF99) (Table 6.29; Fig. 6.27). Similar awls have been found elsewhere at Sarazm (Isakov 1991, fig. 23 nos 5–7; 1994b, 4 fig. 5). One was found in Excavation XVI where this object was still hafted in a bone haft (Mutin et al. 2020a, 31 fig. 9 no. 2), likewise one awl in a bone haft that was discovered at Mundigak (Casal 1961, pl. XXXIX.A). Copper awls with profiles similar to those from Sarazm were found at this site in all periods. Some of them still bear traces that show that they were hafted in wood hafts (Casal 1961, 247–48 fig. 139 no. 2). Awls with this type of profile are also recorded at Tepe Hissar (Schmidt 1933, pl. CIV.B no. H32; Schmidt 1937, pl. XVI H3707).

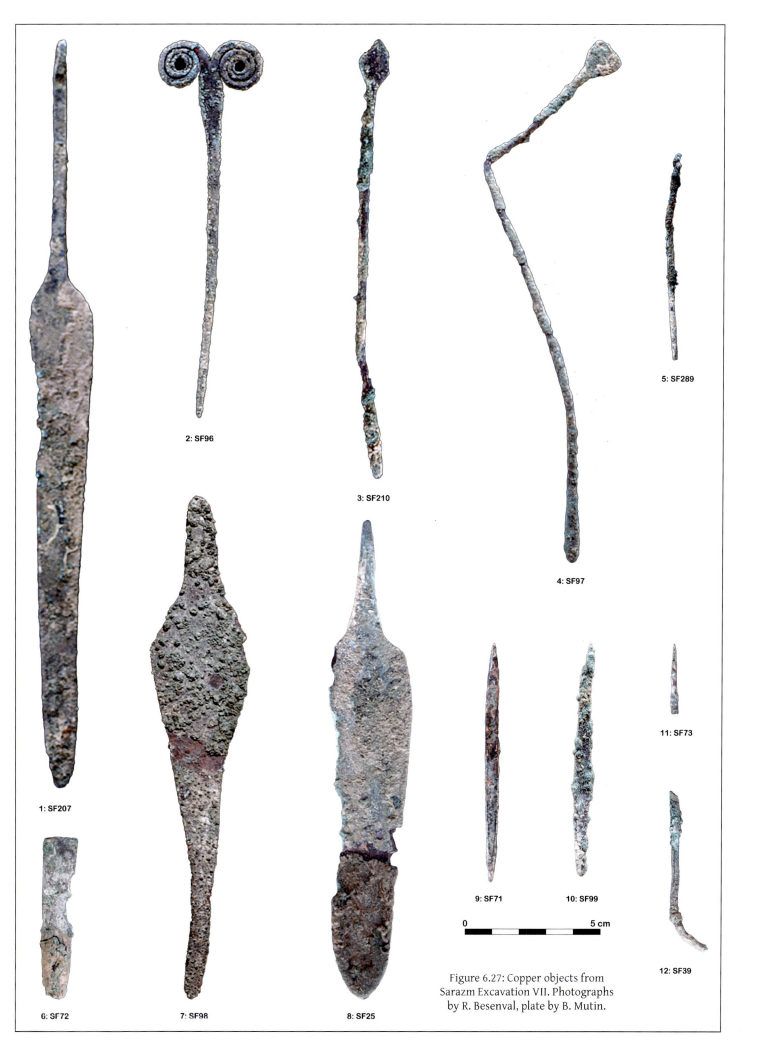

Figure 6.27: Copper objects from Sarazm Excavation VII. Photographs by R. Besenval, plate by B. Mutin.

**Hook?**

Although the possibility remains that the item recorded as a hook (SF39) is a hook (Table 6.29; Fig. 6.27), it may also be a pin or another type of oblong object that got bent. Indeed, copper hooks have been found at Sarazm (Isakov 1991, fig. 23 nos 8–9, 12; 1994b, 4 fig. 5), and the exemplar from Excavation VII is slightly different as it is thickened in two placements including one where the stem begins curving. Copper hooks were also found at Mundigak (Casal 1961, 249; fig. 139 no. 13).

**Compositional Analyses**

The compositions of three copper objects from Excavation VII were analysed: two daggers (SF72, sample 207a; SF98, sample 203) and one of the above-mentioned awls, although it is not clear which one it is (sample 207b). It is unfortunate that no information was found in Besenval archives about the type of analytical method that was used. Indeed, an important parameter that needs to be considered when interpreting results from compositional analysis is the analytical methods used, since some methods cannot detect certain elements. Available results show that all three copper objects are essentially composed of unalloyed copper, although it seems that only their corrosion products were observed, so potential alloying elements could not be detected (C. Thornton, pers. comm). For a long time, the only other compositional analyses that had been conducted on metal objects from Sarazm and published were those done by Isakov et al. (1987) as well as Isakov and Ruzanov (2008).[3] New compositional analyses were recently conducted by S. Kraus, T. Schifer, and E. Pernicka as part of the ROXIANA Project.[4]

> The chemical composition of the objects was determined by energy dispersive X-ray fluorescence spectrometry (ED-XRF) and neutron activation analysis (NAA). The determination of the lead isotope ratios was carried out using a multi-collector mass spectrometer with inductively coupled plasma (MCICP-MS). (Kraus 2021, 781)

These more recent analyses were conducted on objects from Sarazm such as daggers, arrowheads, spearheads, spatulas, and one axe. These analyses confirm the results from those conducted in the past including those conducted on the three objects from Excavation VII. They show that virtually all the analysed copper objects are unalloyed, save for two daggers with up to 2 per cent arsenic and one spatula with about 2 per cent lead. These analyses, however, have failed to identify the origin of the copper used at Sarazm, which remains unclear. One thing is certain is that the ores of the nearby Mushiston mines were not exploited (Kraus 2021, 784–85; see **Chapter 2**).

These results are of particular interest considering that a general shift is observed in ancient copper metallurgy between Anatolia and Central Asia, including in Iran, whereby coppersmiths in these regions largely replaced pure copper and leaded-copper with arsenical copper by the mid-fourth millennium BCE (Salvatori et al. 2009, 48; Thornton 2010, 31–32; Weeks 2013, 280, 282; see Palumbi 2016, 25). Therefore, the analysed copper objects from Sarazm, which probably mostly date to between c. 3500–2500 BCE and appear to be pure copper, do not fit this general picture. These results appear to conform more to what is observed in the mid-fourth millennium BCE Namazga II Period in Turkmenistan, such as at Ilgynli-Depe and contemporary sites, than in the Namazga III Period, in the late fourth/early third millennium BCE, during which 'a dramatic expansion in the use of arsenical copper' is noted (Weeks 2013, 282). At Ilgynli-Depe, Salvatori et al. analysed a large series of copper artefacts using EDXRF, with some submitted to metallographic and/or SEM. They found that

> the finished objects are composed of almost pure copper, lead being the second most important component. Lead irregularly varies from minimum traces in most specimens to the stronger peaks observed in few cases [...] Tin is absent, while arsenic, like silver, mainly occurs in trace amounts. (Salvatori et al. 2009, 53, 64)

Certainly, however, the apparent, spectacular expansion of arsenical copper use observed from around the mid-late fourth millennium BCE did not mean total replacement of previous practices everywhere. For instance, three copper items from Mundigak in Afghanistan (unspecified samples and tools from Periods I5, III6, and IV1, fourth and early third millennia BCE broadly speaking) were determined as pure copper objects (Casal 1961, 244–47).[5] On this topic, the case of Tepe Hissar also deserves mention. C. Thornton demonstrated that two

---

[3] Spectral analysis of fifty-nine metallic objects.

[4] Archaeological Research on Metal and Pottery Assemblages from the Oxus Basin to the Indus Valley during Protohistory; <https://anr.fr/Project-ANR-11-FRAL-0016> [accessed 10 April 2023].

[5] On the other hand, one axe from Mundigak Period III6 is a bronze object with 5 per cent tin. It was interpreted as an import.

Figure 6.28: Copper ore (Chrysocolla) from Sarazm Excavation VII (SF313). Photograph by R. Besenval, edited by B. Mutin.

different types of copper production existed simultaneously at this site: one that was mostly based on arsenical copper and practised in household courtyards on the Main Mound, and one that was based on pure copper and lead production and practised in what has been termed the 'industrial quarter' on the South Hill. Products from the former are believed to have been consumed locally, whereas products from the latter are thought to have been exported (Thornton 2009, 189–98). In summary, although Isakov et al. (1987, 100, 102) noted that 'Analyses of the metal artifacts indicate that the smiths of Sarazm produced metal objects in much the same fashion as contemporaneous coppersmiths in Mesopotamia, the Iranian Plateau and the Indus Valley', it will need to be explained why copper metallurgy at Sarazm is not very consistent with the general dramatic expansion of arsenical copper observed between the mid–late fourth and mid-third millennia BCE across Anatolia, Iran, Central Asia, and South Asia. Was it a deliberate choice, or could it be that this new technological trend took time to be spread to the Zeravshan Valley?

**Records Relating to Copper Metallurgy**

Besenval recorded ten items relating to metal processing. One includes fragments of copper ore (SF313, sample 3) and was determined as such through composition analysis, and one is a piece of slag (SF112, sample 205) which was also analysed (Table 6.29; Fig. 6.28). Four additional items were identified with the naked eye as three fragments of ore (SF321, SF323, and SF326) and one piece of slag (SF324). These four items have sample numbers, although it seems that they have never been analysed (sample 27, sample 29, sample 64, and sample 42). The remaining four records appear to relate more to lead metallurgy (see below).

The copper ore fragments (SF313) were found inside Level III2 Pit 2, together with fragments of quartz debitage. The exact provenience of the piece of slag (SF112) could not be determined in the archives. As for the items identified with the naked eye, four come from fills in open areas (SF323 and SF326 in Level III3; and SF321 in Level IV2) and one from Level III2 Room 3 (SF324).

## Lead Industry

The lead records from Excavation VII consist of two objects, one stamp-seal (SF24) and one disc (SF194), as well as four records relating to lead metallurgy (SF1, SF5, SF172, and SF178) (Table 6.30; Figs 6.29–6.30).

**Seal**

The seal (SF24) has a circular outline of 4 cm in diameter and two perforations placed at its centre. The motif on this seal is quadripartite, with each quarter being filled with two concentric triangles. Parallels for this seal are at Altyn-Depe and include: a circular bone seal with two perforations and a decoration similar to that of SF24 (Kircho 2009, 382 fig. 4 no. 14); a circular terracotta seal with no perforation but with an identical motif (Kircho 2009, 382 fig. 4 no. 12); and one seal in lazurite with two perforations and a similar motif, but rectangular in shape (Kircho 2009, 382 fig. 4 no. 8). A similar motif has also been recorded on a sealing impression found in the House of the Jars at Shahr-i Sokhta (Ameri 2020, 20 fig. 17 no. 5). Lastly, a comparable motif was engraved on a rectangular lapis lazuli seal with two perforations from Mundigak Period IV1 (Casal 1961, fig. 131 no. 16).

**Disc**

The disc (SF194) is an object of 16.6 cm in diameter interpreted as a weight or an ingot. It is half-preserved. Its decoration is openwork and appears to consist of two parallel rectangles in its centre surrounded by V-shaped, and possibly cross- and/or T-shaped, motifs along the edge. A similar lead, openwork disc was found on the surface of Sarazm. Although its diameter is big-

Table 6.30: Lead objects and records relating to lead metallurgy from Sarazm Excavation VII.

| Year | SF no. | Sample no. | Material | Object category | Q. | Image | Preservation | Dimensions | Observations | Level | Context | Context category |
|---|---|---|---|---|---|---|---|---|---|---|---|---|
| 1990 | 194 | 161, 171, 210 | Lead | Ingot? | 1 | Yes | Half | D = 16.6 cm | Openwork decoration; pure lead (Pb); oxidized surface: cerussite (PbCO$_3$), hydrocerussite Pb$_3$(CO$_3$)$_2$(OH)$_2$, lanarkite Pb$_2$(SO$_4$)O | NA | Possibly between sq. L16-17-M14-17-N14-17 | NA |
| 1986 | 24 | NA | Lead | Seal | 1 | Yes | Complete | D = 4 cm; T = 0.9 cm | Quadripartite decoration | IV1 | Area 1 | Fill and floor |
| 1991 | 208 | 172 | Ore | Fragment | 1 | Yes | Fragments | 0.65 × 0.45 cm; 0.45 × 0.35 cm; 0.35 × 0.25 cm | Galena? | I | North/East area; Area 7 | Fill and floor |
| 1991 | 214 | 178 | Ore | Fragment | 1 | No | Fragment | NA | Galena (PbS), lead ore, with traces of silver | III1 | North/East; Area 2 | Fill and floor |
| 1985 | 315 | 5 | Ore | Fragment | 1 | No | Fragment | NA | Galena (PbS), lead ore | II1 | Hearth 2 | Hearth |
| 1985 | 312 | 1 | Melted lead | Fragment | 1 | No | Fragment | NA | Melted lead covered with a layer of litharge (PbO) | III2 | Area 4 | Fill and floor |

ger and it does not have any motifs along its edge, this disc has two parallel rectangles in its centre that have the same size as the one preserved on the disc from Excavation VII. No similar lead objects appear to have been found so far beyond Sarazm. The closest parallels are stone objects. One is a stone disc from Altyn-Depe (Masson 1988, pl. XLIII no. 10). Although this object is not exactly the same as the lead discs from Sarazm, its shape and its openwork decoration, which appears to include T-shaped, crenelated, or cross motifs, are reminiscent of those of the disc from Excavation VII. Parallels in stone for the lead discs from Sarazm have been observed in southern Tajikistan at the Farkhor cemetery (Vinogradova and Bobomulloev 2020, 117 fig. 1 no. 1; Vinogradova 2021, 637 fig. 23.2 no. 1; with a crenelated cross motif in its centre), as well as in northern Afghanistan, where two circular discs with openwork cross and crenelated cross motifs are worth mentioning, in addition to discs with just a handle (Pottier 1984, 175 fig. 41 nos 291, 294, 217 pl. XXXV nos 290, 292). Additionally, circular openwork discs and discs with just a handle are recorded at Tepe Hissar (Schmidt 1937, pl. LXII). These parallels date to around the mid-third millennium BCE broadly speaking, c. 2800/2700–2300 BCE at Farkhor (Vinogradova and Bobomulloev 2020, 112). In the same general category of stone objects are items with different shapes, plain or with carved decorative motifs, known as 'weights' or 'bags'. These items have been found from Central Asia, including at Sarazm, to Iran (and even further west in Iraq and Syria) mostly from around the mid-third millennium BCE, although earlier examples have been recorded too (e.g. Altyn-Depe and Anau in Turkmenistan: Masson 1988, pl. XXXV nos 4, 6; Pumpelly 1908, 479 figs 506–08, 480 figs 509–10; Tepe Sialk, Tepe Chalow, Tepe Hissar, the Halil Rud Valley, and Tepe Yahya in Iran: Ghirshman 1938, pl. LXXXV nos 5, 22; Vahdati et al. 2019, 184 fig. 5; Schmidt 1937, pl. LXII; Akbarzadeh and Piran 2013, 34, 50, 65–68; Potts 2001, 141 fig. 4.40; Mundigak and Bactria in Afghanistan: Casal 1961, fig. 135 no. 4; Pottier 1984, 175 fig. 41 no. 293, 217 pl. XXXV no. 293; the Soch Valley in Uzbekistan: Kohl 2001, 227 fig. 9.14; Sarazm: Isakov 1991, fig. 31; Kyrgyzstan and Kazakhstan: Besenval and Isakov 1989, 17 fig. 30, 18; see also Kircho 2021, 116–17). These more distant parallels probably need to be remembered, although these objects are certainly not identical to the lead discs from Sarazm and their above-mentioned parallels in stone.

LEAD INDUSTRY

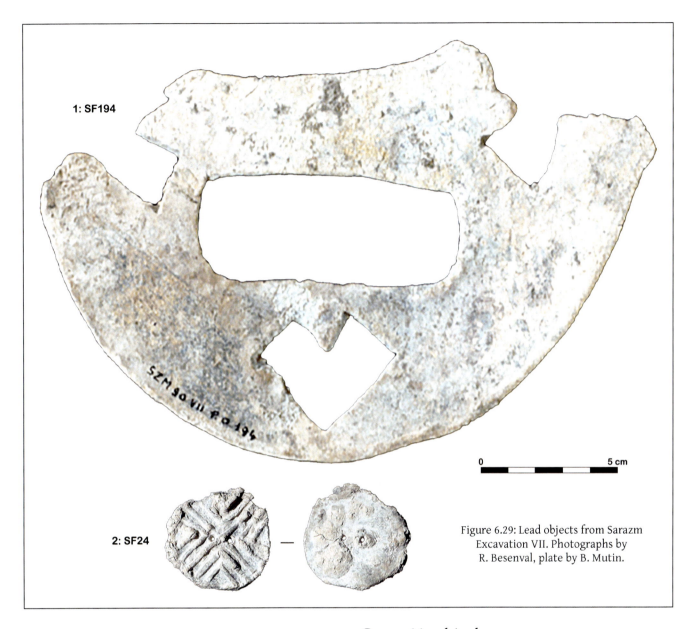

Figure 6.29: Lead objects from Sarazm Excavation VII. Photographs by R. Besenval, plate by B. Mutin.

Figure 6.30: Lead ore (galena)(?) from Sarazm Excavation VII (SF208). Photograph by R. Besenval, edited by B. Mutin.

## Compositional Analyses

The lead disc (SF194, sample 210) was analysed through Energy Dispersive Spectroscopy for Scanning Electron Microscope. This analysis concluded that this disc is a pure lead object (see also Cesbron 1996, 5–6), which also appears to be the case with the above-mentioned lead disc found on the surface of Sarazm, also analysed by Cesbron. Kraus and his colleagues analysed one ingot from Sarazm, which is likely one of these two discs. This analysis shows that this object is a pure lead object. These scholars also conducted lead isotope analysis on this ingot, which suggests that the lead comes from the Lashkerek deposits of the Karamazar Mountains (Kraus 2021, 783; see **Chapter 2**).

Table 6.31: Iron object from Sarazm Excavation VII.

| Year | SF no. | Sample no. | Material | Object category | Q. | Image | Preservation | Dimensions | Observations | Level | Context | Context category |
|---|---|---|---|---|---|---|---|---|---|---|---|---|
| 1990 | 205 | NA | Iron | Blade | 1 | Yes | Complete | L = 10.6 cm; D = 0.25–1.25 cm | / | NA | Possibly between sq. L16–17–M14–17–N14–17 | NA |

### Records Relating to Lead Metallurgy

Four items from Excavation VII relate to lead metallurgy. These items are three pieces of ore and one fragment of melted lead. Cesbron analysed two of the ores (SF214, sample 178 and SF315, sample 5). These analyses concluded that they were lead ore (galena). The third one was determined as galena with the naked eye only (SF208, sample 172). The melted lead fragment (SF312, sample 1) was analysed and characterized as melted lead covered with a layer of litharge (PbO). One of the pieces of ore (SF315) was found in Level II1 Hearth 2, while the other two ores and the melted lead fragment come from fills in open areas in Levels I, III1, and III2.

### *Iron Industry*

Besenval found a single iron object in Excavation VII (Table 6.31; Fig. 6.31). This object is a 10.6 cm long blade (SF205). The archaeological context of this iron blade is unfortunately not known; it may have been found somewhere between sq. L16–17–M14–17–N14–17.

### *Stratigraphic and Spatial Distribution of the Small Finds*

Unfortunately, for the reasons explained above, out of the 332 small find records (358 items) from Excavation VII, I have been able to locate on a plan, or assign to a level, only 149 records (167 items). These records consist of all the small finds recorded during field seasons 1984–1989 as well as thirty-nine from field seasons 1990 and 1991. I did not find in the archives any detailed contextual information for 183 small find records (191 items), all from field seasons 1990 and 1991. The best I have been able to do is to determine that these small finds were possibly found between sq. L16–17, M14–17, and N14–17, and that those collected in 1991 come from the North/East area, likely between sq. J16–17, K16–17, L16–17, M16–17, and half of sq. N16–17. Besenval's field-notebooks indeed suggest that he mostly focused on these areas located in the North/East extension of Excavation VII during these field seasons.

Figure 6.31: Iron object from Sarazm Excavation VII (SF205). Photograph by R. Besenval, edited by B. Mutin.

It also appears that he worked in 1990 in the south-eastern corner of Excavation VII in sq. M14–15 and N14–15. I have not seen any archives that show that he worked further west and south during the 1990 field season, although I am not in a position where I can guarantee that this did not happen. As for the archaeological levels he studied in 1990–1991, I have found evidence in his archives that he excavated contexts that belong to Levels I, II, and III in 1991 and to Levels I and II in 1990. It seems rational to think that he also dug Level IV deposits during these field seasons since he started from the surface of the site, although it is also possible that such deposits were not preserved in the areas he exposed at that time.

In this section are presented plans of the different archaeological levels defined in Excavation VII with placement of the 167 small finds for which I have found contextual information, i.e. the level, area or room, and sometimes feature in which they were found (Pls 6.1–6.12). As is apparent in the small find lists, nine of them could potentially belong to two different levels (SF3, SF4, SF5, SF29, SF30, SF76, SF110, SF121, and SF311). For the sake of consistency and in order to have all 167 small finds placed on a plan, I arbitrarily placed these small finds with ambiguous contextual data on one of the two plans they may belong to. Also, it should be noted that a number of records in the North/East area and western area (between sq. J10 and M10) of Excavation VII could not be assigned a specific archaeological phase; I have only been able to determine that they belong to one of the four main levels defined in Excavation VII: Levels I, II, III, or IV. Lastly, I have placed and indicated the small finds on the plans using their numbers. Codes that designate the small find categories

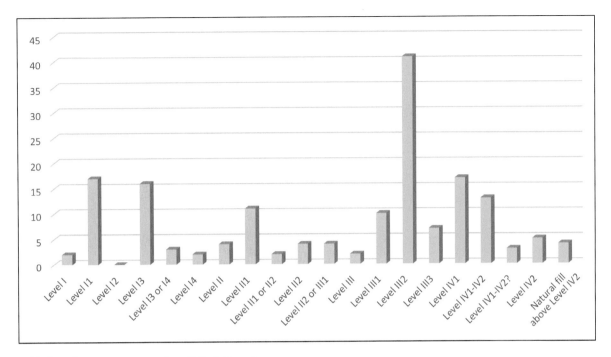

Table/Graph 6.32: Quantities of small finds from Sarazm Excavation VII for which a provenience within Excavation VII could be determined, classified by levels.

| Level | Quantity | % |
|---|---|---|
| Level I | 2 | 1.2 |
| Level I1 | 17 | 10.2 |
| Level I2 | 0 | 0.0 |
| Level I3 | 16 | 9.6 |
| Level I3 or I4 | 3 | 1.8 |
| Level I4 | 2 | 1.2 |
| Level II | 4 | 2.4 |
| Level II1 | 11 | 6.6 |
| Level II1 or II2 | 2 | 1.2 |
| Level II2 | 4 | 2.4 |
| Level II2 or III1 | 4 | 2.4 |
| Level III | 2 | 1.2 |
| Level III1 | 10 | 6.0 |
| Level III2 | 41 | 24.6 |
| Level III3 | 7 | 4.2 |
| Level IV1 | 17 | 10.2 |
| Level IV1–IV2 | 13 | 7.8 |
| Level IV1–IV2? | 3 | 1.8 |
| Level IV2 | 5 | 3.0 |
| Natural fill above Level IV2 | 4 | 2.4 |
| Total | 167 | 100 |

precede these numbers. These codes are the following: B (bone), Car (carnelian), CF (cobble flake), Co (copper), Ft (frit), GS (ground stone), H/GS (hammer/grinding stone), Lc (lithic), Ld (lead), LL (lapis lazuli), Pg (pigment and remains relating to pigment preparation), P/S (pestle/sharpener), Qz (Quartz), SC (stone container), Sh (shell), St (steatite), Sto (stone), TC (terracotta), Tq (turquoise), and W (weight).

The first observation that can be made about the distribution of the small finds in Excavation VII is that, if the small finds from 1990 and 1991 that could not be assigned precise contextual information truly come only from areas Besenval excavated between sq. J16–17, K16–17, L16–17, M14–17, and N14–17, then this means that the archaeological deposits in these areas are richer than those in the rest of this excavation considering that the surfaces exposed are smaller and the amounts of small finds are higher. Another observation is that certain levels of Excavation VII and areas within these levels yielded more small finds than others (Table/Graph 6.32; Pls 6.1–6.12). To give an idea, the above-mentioned 167 small finds divide into forty in Level I, twenty-five in Level II, sixty in Level III, thirty-eight in Level IV, and four in the natural fill above Level IV. The quantities recorded within these levels vary, with Level III2 being the richest as it contains almost 25 per cent of the recorded small finds. Below are discussed the small finds recovered from each level with an emphasis on distinctive objects and remains relating to craft activities.

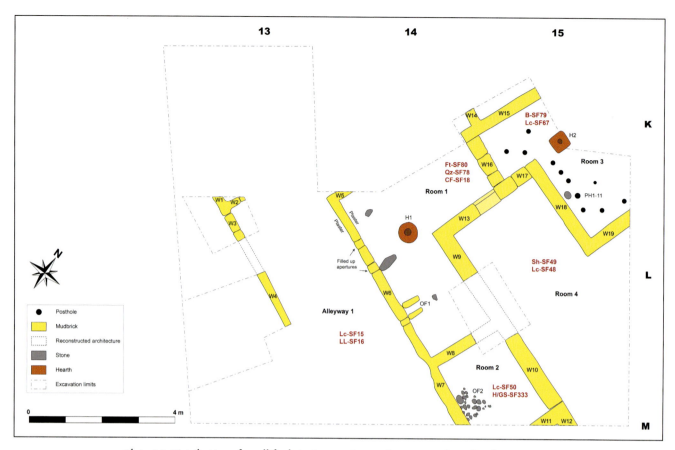

Plate 6.1: Distribution of small finds in Sarazm Excavation VII Level I1. Plate by B. Mutin.

## Small Finds in Level I1

Level I1 yielded seventeen items (eleven records) (Pl. 6.1). Eleven of these are lithics and quartz debitage remains. This number is too low to suggest that intensive lithic debitage activities took place in this level; far more lithic remains would have been observed and reported. It nonetheless remains possible that some of these types of items were occasionally retouched in or near the areas exposed in Level I1. Four of these items were found alongside a hammer/grinding stone inside Room 2. Additionally, a fragment of unworked lapis lazuli was recorded in Alleyway 1 and a bone awl in Room 3.

## Small Finds in Level I2

No small find was recorded in Level I2.

## Small Finds in Level I3

Sixteen small finds (fifteen records) were found in Level I3 (Pl. 6.2). Lithics including two remains of quartz debitage represent ten of these items. Five were found in Room 9 and the two quartz items are from nearby Area 3, hinting that occasional debitage activities may have happened, or were intended to happen, around these areas. An additional lithic, a distinctive broken bifacial blade (SF53) that parallels pieces from Kazakhstan, was also found in Room 9, inside Hearth 6. Another lithic, an arrowhead(?) (SF57), was found in Room 5, not far from Room 9. From Room 5 too were recovered one pestle/sharpener and one copper hook(?) (SF39). Lastly, a ground stone, a flat stone that appears to have served to prepare pigments, a lithic, a lapis lazuli bead, and possibly a stone vessel fragment (which may be from Room 6) were found in Alleyway 2. The flat stone may have been associated with an ochre fragment which was found around the same area, although it is not clear whether it is from Level I3 or I4 (see below).

## Small Finds in Level I4

Level I4 was excavated over a much smaller surface than Level I3 (Pl. 6.3). Only two small finds (one record) were found in this level, although three additional items may be from this level or from Level I3. These five small finds

# STRATIGRAPHIC AND SPATIAL DISTRIBUTION OF THE SMALL FINDS

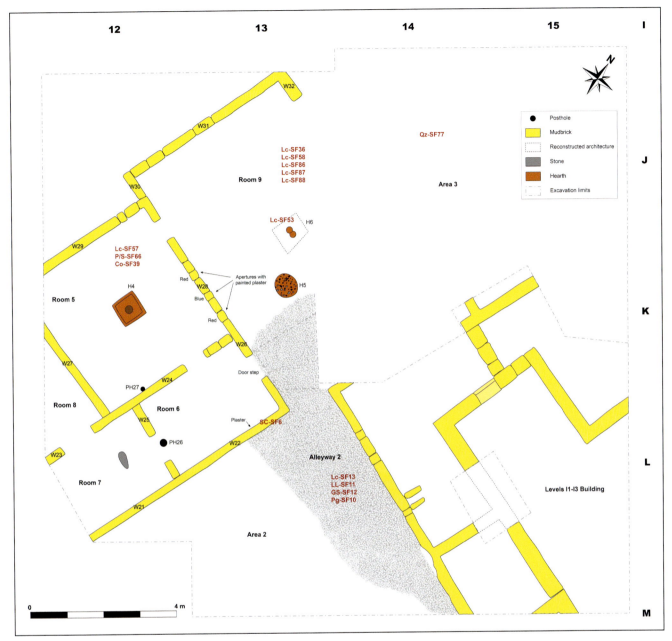

Plate 6.2: Distribution of small finds in Sarazm Excavation VII Level I3. Plate by B. Mutin.

are three lithics, one terracotta disc, and one ochre fragment that may have been used on the above-mentioned flat stone from Level I3.

## Small Finds in Level I-North/East

Two small find records were found in the Level I-North/East area, although more were probably collected but lost their contextual information (Pl. 6.4). They consist of one blue/green pigment rock fragment (SF209) and three fragments identified as galena (lead ore) that were probably originally part of the same ore fragment (SF208).

## Small Finds in Level II1

Level II1 yielded eleven small finds (eight records) (Pl. 6.5). Of special interest is the association of a copper awl or blade fragment (SF17) and a piece of lead ore (SF315) inside Hearth 2. These finds suggest that this hearth might have been used for small-scale metallurgical activities. It is located right outside of the main building of this level, between its wall W3 to the southwest and what appears to be the remains of a partition wall made of perishable material (PH1–9). The rest of the small finds in Level II1 include a perforated terra-

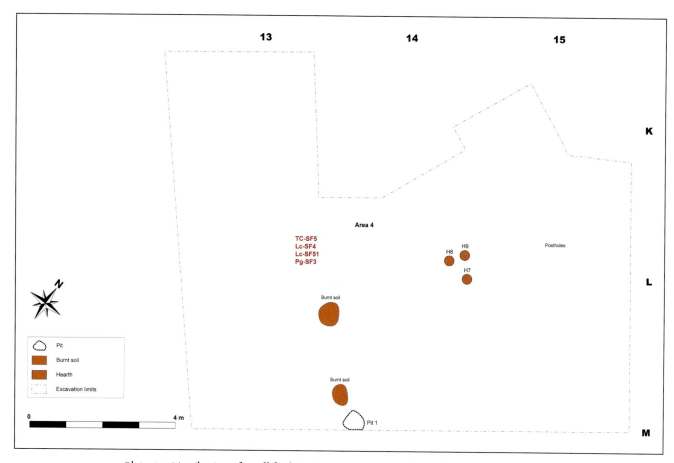

Plate 6.3: Distribution of small finds in Sarazm Excavation VII Level I4. Plate by B. Mutin.

cotta disc and a cobble flake in Room 1, inside the building, while nothing was found in Room 2. Outside, a bone awl, a hammer/grinding stone, and a pestle/sharpener were found in Area 1, while Area 2 yielded four lithics including two fragments with cortex.

### Small Finds in Level II2

Four small finds (three records) were recorded within Level II2, all four in Area 3 (Pl. 6.6). They consist of three lithics and one ochre fragment. One of the lithics bears cortex, while another one appears to be the distal portion of a blade. To these items may be added two small finds (two records) that may belong to this level or to Level II1, as well as four rock crystal fragments (one record) that are either Level II2 or Level III items. The former are two beads, one made from rock crystal (SF76) and one made from frit and glazed (SF29). The rock crystal fragments (SF30) were found in the same area as the bead made from the same material. This evidence is very limited, but still suggests that some quartz debitage-related activities must have been sporadically conducted somewhere in or around this area.

### Small Finds in Level II-North/East

Level II-North/East small finds consist of two complete copper pins, one cobble flake, and one lithic flake (Pl. 6.7). The two copper pins were found, one in Area 4 (SF177) and one in Area 5 or Room 14 (SF97).

### Small Finds in Level III1

Level III1 yielded ten small finds, with nine recorded within the North/East area of Excavation VII (Pl. 6.8). It is important to recall here that this level was excavated over a small expanse within the main area of Excavation VII. The single small find found within this area is a flat stone that appears to have been used for pigment preparation (SF314). It was found inside a pit (Pit 1). The small finds from the North/East area include one bone needle and three perforated terracotta discs. Although it is unclear whether they were all four found together, these items do not contradict the possibility that fabrics were weaved within or near this area, tentatively considering that the discs were used as spindle-whorls or weights. Two beads, one made from steatite

# STRATIGRAPHIC AND SPATIAL DISTRIBUTION OF THE SMALL FINDS

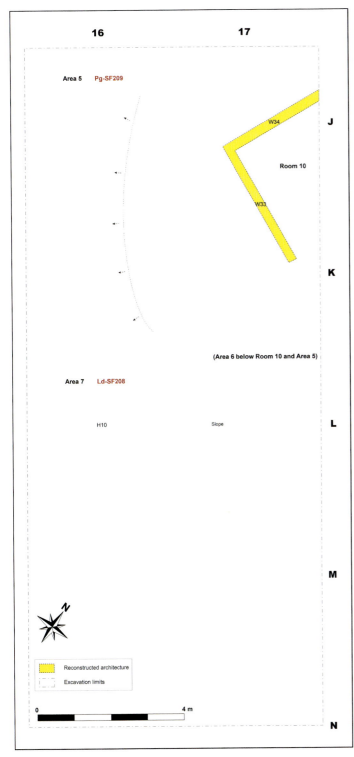

Plate 6.4: Distribution of small finds in Sarazm Excavation VII Level I-North/East. Plate by B. Mutin.

(SF213) and one made from turquoise (SF240), were also found, as well as a lithic and a stone. Lastly, a fragment of galena (lead ore) was also reported from Level III1 North/East area (SF214).

## Small Finds in Level III2

As noted above, Level III2 produced the largest number of small finds, with forty-one items (thirty-six records), including items from the North/East area that could be assigned to this level (Pl 6.9–6.10). These forty-one small finds were collected from inside and outside the building that characterizes this level. Inside, most of them come from Room 3. The walls of this room must have been decorated since eight fragments of red and blue plaster (three records) were found in it. The rest of the small finds in this room include one lithic and one stone vessel fragment. More interestingly, fragments of copper ore (SF313) and of quartz (SF317) were found inside a pit (Pit 2), also located in this room, while one piece of slag(?) (SF324) and a copper fragment (SF325) were recorded elsewhere in this room. Room 7 yielded one stone weight(?) (SF27), while a complete copper awl (SF71) was found in Room 8. Lastly, one quartz fragment as well as what might be a decorative tile (SF65) come from Room 5.

Outside of the building, most items come from Area 4 and the North/East area further to the northeast. Altogether, nineteen small finds were recorded in these two areas. They include six lithics including lithics with cortex. A ground stone, a pestle/sharpener and what may have served as a weight (SF93) were found in the North/East area. As far as metallurgy is concerned, a mould for which I have found no description (SF94) was reported from this area, while a fragment of melted lead (SF312) was collected in Area 4. Additional objects relating to craft activities were identified, including a drill (SF33) in Area 4 and a finial[6] (SF196) in the North/East area, as well as four perforated discs, two made from terracotta and two from stone (SF31, SF32, SF45, and SF195), from Area 4 and the North/East area. Lastly, a shell bead and some ochre were also reported from Area 4. Four additional small finds, all lithics, were found in Areas 3 and 5.

---

[6] Which may also be a decorative object.

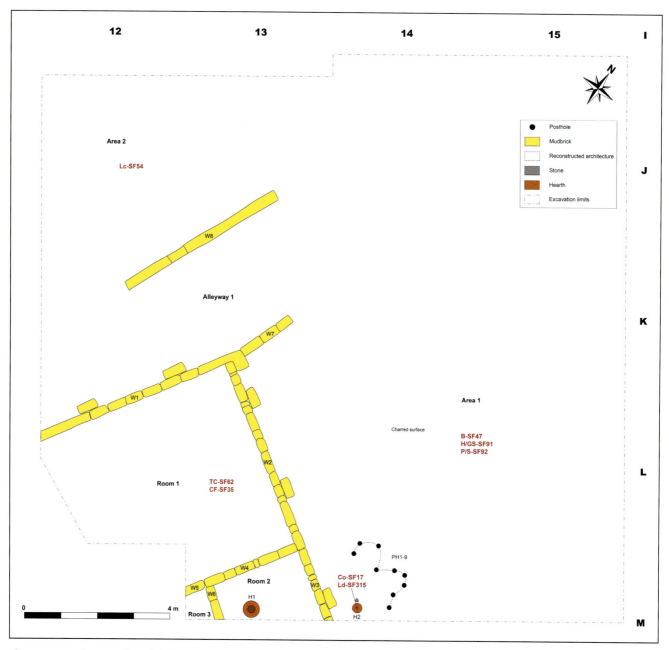

Plate 6.5: Distribution of small finds in Sarazm Excavation VII Level II1. Plate by B. Mutin.

## Small Finds in Level III3

Two incomplete copper objects, one dagger (SF72) and one awl (SF73), were found in Level III3, in addition to two fragments of ore(?) (SF323 and SF326) (Pl. 6.11). The rest of the small finds in this level consist of one ground stone (SF14), which was recovered from Hearth 10, one perforated terracotta disc, and one quartz fragment.

## Small Finds in Level III-North/East

The small finds in Level III-North/East area are one ground stone (SF101) and one object that may have served as a weight (SF163).

## Small Finds in Levels IV1–IV2

The small finds from Levels IV1–IV2 amount to thirty-eight items and essentially divide into four main groups: those found within and around the Level IV1 building located within the north-eastern half of Excavation VII; those found within the North/East area and assigned to Levels IV1–IV2; those from Level IV2 between sq. I11

# STRATIGRAPHIC AND SPATIAL DISTRIBUTION OF THE SMALL FINDS

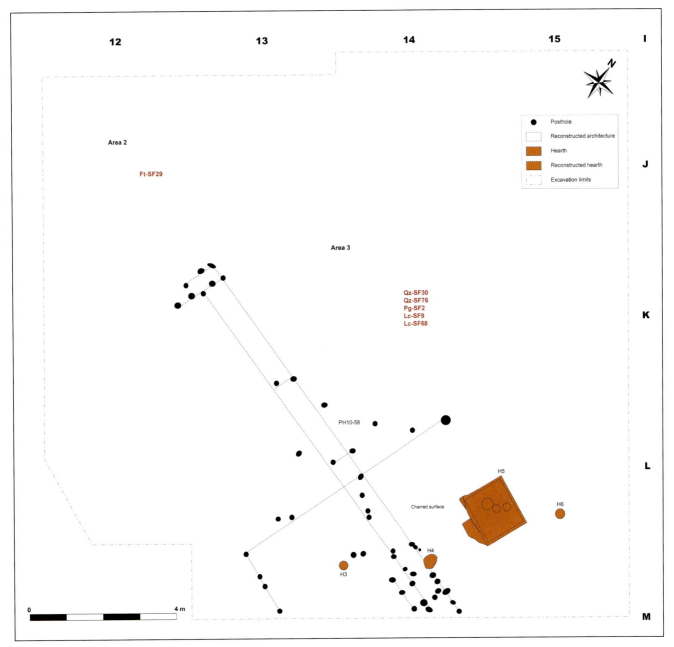

Plate 6.6: Distribution of small finds in Sarazm Excavation VII Level II2. Plate by B. Mutin.

and M11; and those assigned to Levels IV1–IV2 found further west within and around the compartmented building and Area 4 (Pl. 6.12).

In the first group are eleven small finds. Seven of them appear to have been collected within Area 1. They consist of: one lead stamp-seal (SF24), the single exemplar recorded at Sarazm; one copper dagger (SF25); one turquoise bead-button (SF37); one carnelian bead (SF38); and one red stone pebble (SF64). A lithic with cortex and a perforated terracotta disc must be added to this inventory. A few metres away to the south-west was found another perforated terracotta disc (SF61). Room 1 produced a stone finial (SF69), while Room 2 produced a flat stone that was probably used to prepare pigments (SF26), as well as a turquoise fragment (SF23). A turquoise(?) pendant (SF21) was recovered from Room 6. This inventory of distinctive, more sophisticated, or unusual, items, relative to the earlier levels, also includes a copper dagger which was found below Hearth 1 (SF98), south-east of the Level IV1 building. Two additional complete copper objects were reported nearby in sq. M16: one awl (SF99) and the single double-spiral headed pin (SF96) found at Sarazm.

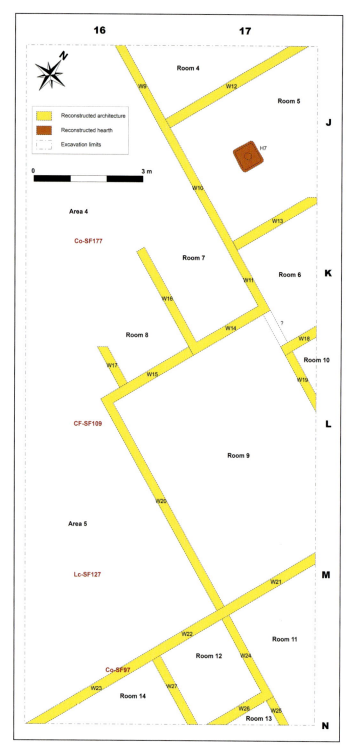

Plate 6.7: Distribution of small finds in Sarazm Excavation VII Level II-North/East. Plate by B. Mutin.

An unusual concentration of six ground stones is recorded within the North/East area, as well as two stones that might have been used as weights. These objects are labelled here Level IV1–IV2 objects, save for one that could be more specifically attributed to Level IV1. Three additional items were recovered from within the North/East area and might belong to either Level IV1 or Level IV2. These items are one perforated terracotta disc, one terracotta disc, and one lithic with cortex.

The small finds from Level IV2 between sq. I11 and M11 are: one fragment of copper ore (SF321) and one terracotta disc (SF306) in Area 3; one ochre fragment from Hearth 2 (SF322); and one pestle/sharpener bearing traces of green pigment inside Room 8 (SF84). In the same area was found a lithic that is thought to belong to Level IV1.

One quartz fragment was recovered from inside the compartmented building (SF85), while four additional objects were recorded also further to the southwest in Area 4. These objects are one pestle/sharpener, one perforated terracotta disc, one lithic, and one turquoise bead (SF75).

Lastly, one ground stone and one pestle/sharpener are listed as Level IV1–IV2 objects, although their proveniences are unclear (SF82 and SF83).

**Small Finds in Surface Deposits**

Four small finds were found within the surface deposits of Excavation VII, above the Level IV1–IV2 archaeological remains. They are two lithics, one stone drill, and one stone bead.

**Small Finds in sq. J16–17, K16–17, L16–17, M14–17, and N14–17**

As noted above, 191 small finds (183 records) could not be assigned a specific archaeological level. These small finds were collected during field seasons 1990 and 1991 and appear to be coming essentially from sq. J16–17, K16–17, L16–17, M14–17, and N14–17. Although the stratigraphic and spatial distribution of this material cannot be discussed, it is probably worth mentioning that a number of these small finds are distinctive objects which are reminiscent of the relatively unusual concentration of less common, perhaps 'prestige' items observed within and around the Level IV1 building. Indeed, half of the ornaments (beads and

225

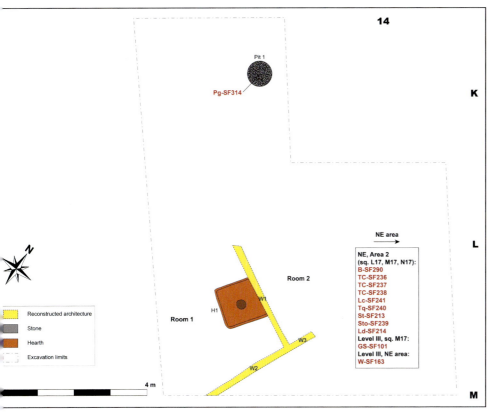

Plate 6.8: Distribution of small finds in Sarazm Excavation VII Level III1. Plate by B. Mutin.

Plate 6.9: Distribution of small finds in Sarazm Excavation VII Level III2. Plate by B. Mutin.

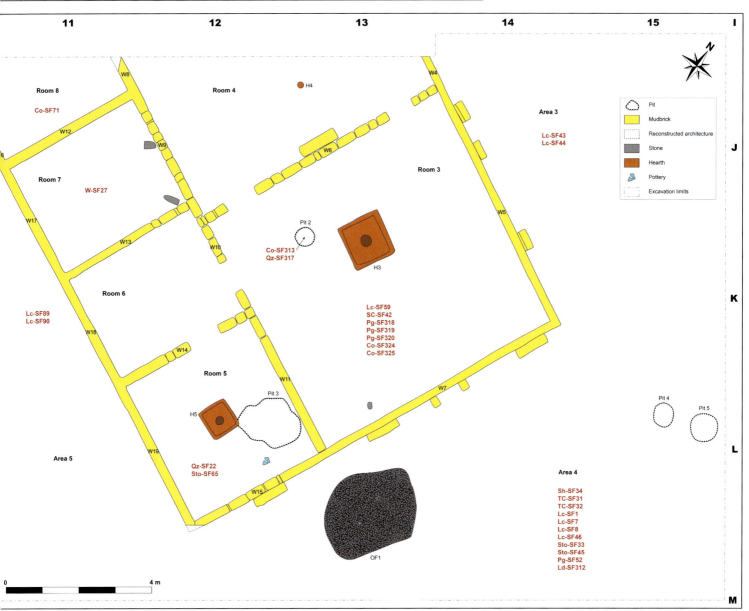

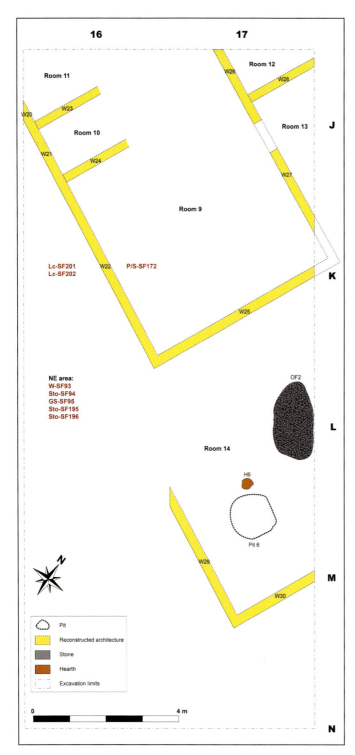

Plate 6.10: Distribution of small finds in Sarazm Excavation VII Level III2-North/East. Plate by B. Mutin.

pendants) from Excavation VII were recorded in these contexts, including: three turquoise beads (SF153, SF178, and SF199); two white stone beads (SF146 and SF204) and one pendant (SF159); three frit beads (SF156, SF286, and SF292); two black stone pendants (SF190 and SF203); one carnelian bead (SF177); one rock crystal bead (SF152); one red stone bead (SF250); one green stone bead (SF276); and one shell bead (SF151). Two turquoise fragments, two lapis lazuli fragments, and two quartz fragments were also found. The copper inventory consists of one dagger (SF207) and two pins (SF289 and SF294). The lead ingot SF194 was also found in these contexts, as well as the single complete stone vial (SF150). However, as noted above, I have found no evidence in the archives that Besenval excavated Level IV1–IV2 deposits in these areas, so I cannot establish that these less common types of small finds all come from these levels.

As for the rest, eighty lithics were reported, which represents the majority of the lithics recorded in Excavation VII. These lithics include a disc (SF224) and what appears to be a drill (SF185). With the above-mentioned stone vial, four out of the six stone containers collected in this excavation are from these contexts. Six out of the seven pebbles also come from these contexts. Various types of tools were found, including nine hammer/grinding stones (out of eleven recorded in total within Excavation VII); five pestles/sharpeners (out of eleven recorded in total within Excavation VII) and one sharpener (SF275); two ground stones; and eight cobble flakes (out of eleven recorded in total within Excavation VII). Additional records include: three bone tools (half of the total recorded within Excavation VII); seven stone fragments which were perhaps intended to be worked; five terracotta and stone finials (out of seven in total recorded within Excavation VII); seven terracotta and stone discs; eight terracotta perforated discs; one piece of slag (SF112); one iron blade (SF205); one terracotta figurine(?) fragment (SF175); one terracotta vessel (SF302); one decorative tile(?) (SF331). Lastly, three fragments of red and blue plaster show that some walls were decorated within sq. J16–17, K16–17, L16–17, M14–17, and N14–17, while six ochre fragments and one fragment of goethite suggest that pigments were prepared within these areas.

Again, the contexts of these finds are not clear. Besenval did not report that he excavated in these areas remains that could be connected to Level IV. The only information I have found in his archives is that

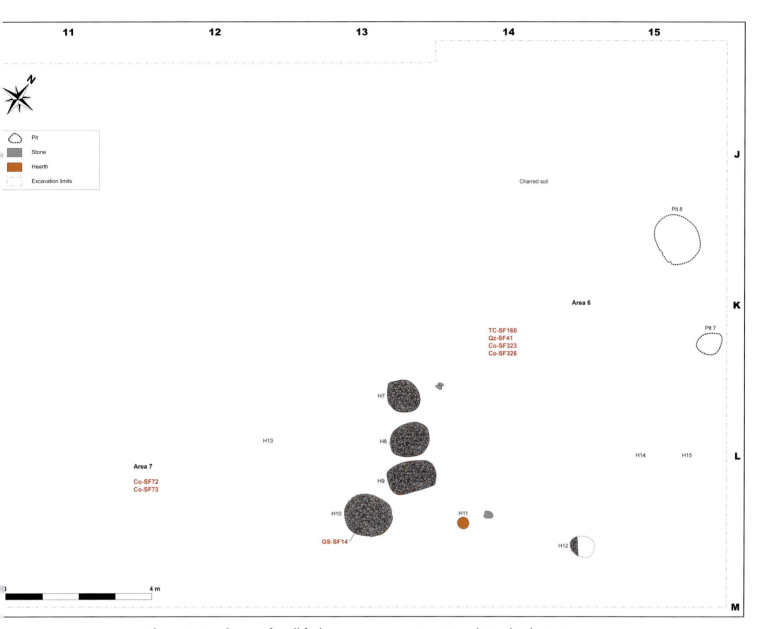

Plate 6.11: Distribution of small finds in Sarazm Excavation VII Level III3. Plate by B. Mutin.

he excavated contexts that belong to Levels I, II, and III in 1991 and to Levels I and II in 1990. As noted above, it seems rational to think that he also dug Level IV deposits during these field seasons since he began from the surface of the site, although it is also possible that such deposits were not preserved in the areas he exposed. What is evident on the other hand is that various types of activities must have taken place within sq. J16–17, K16–17, L16–17, M14–17, and N14–17, including food and pigment preparation, while rare objects relating to craft activities were also found in these areas, including bead making, possibly weaving, and metallurgy.

## Activities in the Areas Exposed in Excavation VII

Not all the rooms and open spaces exposed in Excavation VII yielded artefacts. In most cases, they are devoid of small finds or produced only a limited number of items. For this reason, Besenval and Isakov wrote that, save for Level IV1, all archaeological levels the former had studied in Excavation VII up until 1989 appear to have been carefully emptied before they were abandoned (Besenval and Isakov 1989, 14). It seems that Level IV1 stands out as an exception because a fire ended this occupation and, for some reason, the assemblage from this level, or a part of it, could not be saved before the place was abandoned. Except for Level IV1, the general lack of material observed within Excavation VII and the lack of contextual information for more than half of them make it difficult to recon-

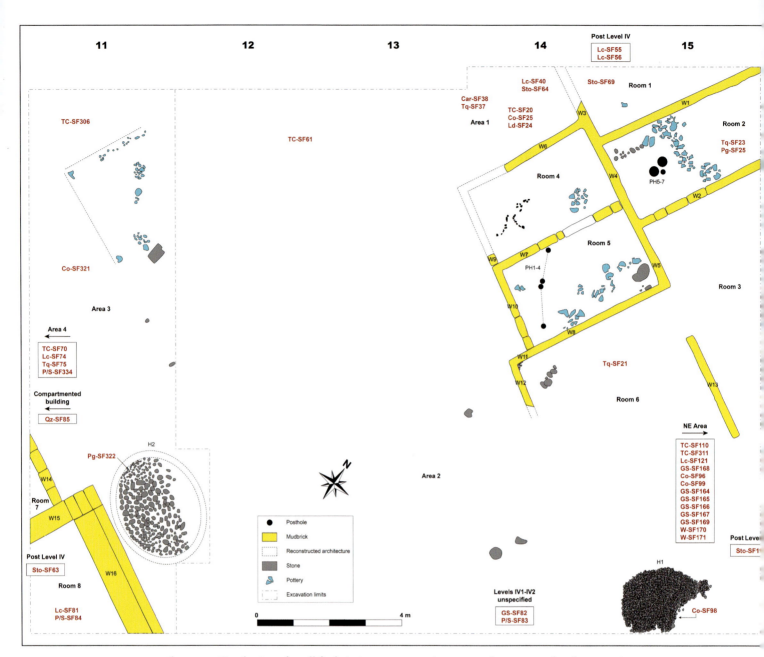

Plate 6.12: Distribution of small finds in Sarazm Excavation VII Levels IV1–IV2. Plate by B. Mutin.

struct the activities that took place within the areas exposed in this excavation.

As noted in **Chapter 5**, the ceramics recovered from Excavation VII include vessels that were used to cook, serve, and eat food, as well as vessels used to store and transport stuff. Part of the small finds hint at activities relating to food acquisition and preparation, such as lithics (including blades and the single arrowhead recorded in Excavation VII), ground stones, cobble flakes, and objects defined as hammer/grinding stones and pestle/sharpeners.

The small finds also include objects that were worn or displayed such as beads, pendants, copper pins, and daggers. Such objects were found in small amounts in virtually all levels, but a specific concentration rela-tive to the rest of the archaeological deposits studied within Excavation VII was observed in Level IV1, suggesting the presence in this level of some individuals and/or transactions of some importance. The single lead stamp-seal found in Excavation VII, also in Level IV1, may have served this purpose too, at the same time as it may have been used as a sealing object within the context of administrative activities. It is probably worth noting that the Level IV1 collection of distinctive small finds agrees well with the spectacular collection of complete ceramics discovered in this level.

Part of the above-mentioned and other categories of records appear to relate to craft activities. The main issue with identification of craft activities within Excavation VII, however, is that the evidence is not massive. No objects, tools, nor raw material were found in such amounts or concentration that could suggest that intensive craft activities were performed in any of the archaeological levels exposed within Excavation VII. Similarly, no specific structures or installations were found that could lead to such a conclusion. In this regard, this excavation is different from Excavation II and nearby Excavation XVI, where, for instance, much clearer evidence for metallurgical activities was uncovered. In Excavation II,

> significant quantities of crucibles and slag were recovered [...] Though the architectural association and function remain somewhat unclear the crucibles and slag were recovered from surfaces of floors that were burned red. From this floor were recovered holes of hearths that were 18–25 cm in diameter and 20–30 cm in depth. It is not unlikely that these were 'pot-furnaces' for the smelting of ores. (Isakov et al. 1987, 101; see Isakov 1991, fig. 24; Mutin et al. 2020a, 31 fig. 9)

Another example comes from Excavation IX, where a pottery oven was reported (Razzokov 2008). In Excavation VII, evidence relating to craft activities consists of sporadic and scattered artefacts, raw material, and residues, with only small concentrations and/or associations within a pit or hearth in certain cases. This evidence suggests that such activities were conducted within or near the areas exposed by Besenval but prevents us from being entirely positive in most cases. This evidence does exist, however, and we are left with an ambiguous impression and questions. Does this sporadic and scattered evidence represent the leftovers of more intensive craft activities whose most remains were carefully wiped out before the areas exposed within Excavation VII were abandoned, as Besenval and Isakov suggested apropos of the lack of material remains they observed in general within Excavation VII? Were certain ores and tools, such as awls, drills, and their finials, kept within the areas exposed in Excavation VII and used elsewhere at Sarazm? This certainly is possible. Why on the other hand would pieces of slag, flakes, and other types of craft residues have been kept as well? Although this seems unlikely, one may also wonder whether part of the evidence relating to craft activities was simply mistakenly removed during the excavation, or that important data are missing in the archives that I have been able to gather. On this note, the North/East area, which is unfortunately not well documented, appears to have yielded relatively significant amounts of materials. This might suggest that more craft activities might have been conducted within this area and around it and that the remains recovered inside the rest of Excavation VII are just peripheral remains of these activities. While this cannot be proven at the moment, a few observations may be offered about the small finds from Excavation VII and the craft activities they relate to.

Pigment preparation is attested by the presence of pigments in the form of powder or fragments as well as stone tools including pestle/sharpeners, ground stones, and other types of stones that may have served this function. Records that relate to pigment preparation were reported from Levels I3, I4, II2, III1, III2, IV1, and IV2.

Depending on how one interprets objects such as bone and copper awls, terracotta and stone finials, perforated discs, cobble flakes, certain types of lithics, it seems possible that activities such as weaving, sewing, and/or fur, leather, or bone working were conducted within some of the areas exposed within Excavation VII. The distribution of these objects suggests that this could have been the case in Levels I1, II1, III1, III2, III3, IV1, and IV2.

Evidence for bead making is extremely minimal and certainly not comparable to that recorded at a site such as Shahr-i Sokhta (Vidale and Lazzari 2017). It essentially consists of two drills and a limited number of scattered raw material fragments and flakes, as well as possibly the above-mentioned finials. These items were recorded in Levels I1, II2/III1, III2, III3, and IV1.

A lithic debitage area would have left unmissable remains. Such an area was probably not present within the deposits exposed within Excavation VII. It nonetheless remains possible that some flakes were sporadically retouched. Also, cores, fragments with cortex, and flakes that have not been retouched were found inside Excavation VII, which tends to suggest that reduction activities took place inside or around the Excavation VII area, or at a minimum at the site, which is also mentioned by Brunet and Razzokov (2016). Yet, regarding the fragments with cortex, it is also possible that their presence results from a strategy that would maximize available raw material, by which even flakes with cortex would have been retouched and used as tools. Again, a detailed analysis of the lithic assemblage from Excavation VII is needed to clarify this.

As far as metallurgy is concerned, the only fairly reasonable evidence that metallurgical activities were performed inside or near Excavation VII is the piece of slag and melted lead fragment from Level III2 as well as the copper awl or blade fragment and piece of lead ore found inside Level II1 Hearth 2. A mould was also found in Level III2, although I have found no description about this object. Additionally, Level III3 is essentially characterized by hearths and pits, while no architecture was recorded. This trait in addition to the specific concentration of vessels that were allegedly used to store and/or transport foodstuff, liquids, or other things that characterize the ceramic assemblage from Level III3 sets this level apart. It suggests that specific activities took place in this level that were not observed in the other occupations exposed in Excavation VII, which seem to correspond to dwellings. Yet, the two items recorded as ores found in Level III3 appear to be too rare evidence to conclude that this level served as a craft area. As for the other ores found in Levels I-North/East, III1, III2, and IV2, they were perhaps meant to be processed inside or near Excavation VII, although the possibility remains that they were just brought and stored in this location and were meant to be processed elsewhere at the site. As noted above, available evidence for metal processing in Excavation VII is in any case much less than that recovered from Excavation II. Yet, it is probably important to keep in mind that, even in Excavation II, the levels that yielded vestiges of metallurgical activities are best defined as dwellings, and not so much as specialized industrial areas (see Besenval and Isakov 1989; Isakov 1994b, 6–7; see **Chapter 1**). Besenval and Isakov even characterize Excavation II as the densest dwelling area of Sarazm (Besenval and Isakov 1989, 8). F. Razzokov (2016) noted that one room in this excavation probably served as a workshop dedicated to copper metallurgical activities, which was at the same time directly connected to a dwelling, making it a 'home workshop'. On the same note, it is important to remember that copper smelting does not require much equipment and would not necessarily leave many traces other than burnt areas if cleaned up and conducted within the framework of a small-scale activity.

## Raw Material Procurement and Cultural Relationships

The small finds recorded within Excavation VII, the styles of the objects, and the raw material recorded show that the groups that settled within the areas uncovered in this excavation were connected to and part of various networks of relationships, either directly or indirectly.

Certainly, they probably collected many of the raw materials they needed around or not very far from the site, including materials such as the various types of woods they must have needed to build posts and roofs, to heat and to cook, as well as other vegetal species to make baskets and mats that I assume must have been part of their material assemblage. There is also no doubt that the bones used to make tools were those of animals bred or hunted at or near the site, or within the Zeravshan Valley and the surrounding mountains. The same view may be suggested for part of the material that was knapped, pebbles and cobbles, as well as clay.

Excavation VII small find assemblage nonetheless also includes raw materials and objects that required more distant journeys, or connections to more distant groups that had access to, and/or distributed, these materials. Sources for copper and lead were recorded within the Zeravshan Mountains, but it is not proven that they were used at the time Sarazm was occupied while more distant sources within Tajikistan or in Uzbekistan may have been exploited. Lead is thought to have come from the Lashkerek deposits of the Karamazar Mountains further north. Turquoise suggests connections to known sources in the Kyzyl Kum in Uzbekistan as well as in the Khujand region of northern Tajikistan, in the Karamazar Mountains in particular. The closest sources for lapis lazuli are in the Badakhshan Province of north-eastern Afghanistan and in the Pamir Mountains in southern Tajikistan. Carnelian brings to mind sources in India as well as in Pakistan, although additional sources are noted in Central Asia, southern Afghanistan, and Iran.

As for the styles of the small finds recorded in Excavation VII, they generally parallel materials found within assemblages discovered in the regions around the Hindu Kush, between Central Asia, eastern Iran, southern Afghanistan, and Pakistan. There is no doubt that the groups that settled within the levels exposed inside Excavation VII were connected to other groups, or cultural spheres, within this vast area. The relationships seen through the small finds are consistent with those identified through the ceramics. However, precisely because similar types of objects are reported from many regions within this vast area, the parallels for the small finds from Excavation VII do not help determine more than the ceramics which one(s) of these groups, or cultural spheres, related the most to the communities settled in the areas exposed in Excavation VII. Similarly, they do not help determine the degree to which Excavation VII communities (and more broadly the communities settled at Sarazm) were connected to these groups. Were they part of the same families, or tribes, as one or more of these groups? Or could it be that, together with one or more of these groups, they shared similar standards in that they recognized the same values and practicalities in similar objects, but were different in many other aspects of their material lives and practices that are not preserved in the archaeological record? The double-spiral headed pin from Excavation VII, a type of object recorded from the Indus Valley to south-eastern Europe, is illustrative of the extensive geographic expanses of certain values, perhaps merely fashion in this case, that were shared during the Late Chalcolithic and Early Bronze Age periods across Eurasia. In this case, it seems more rational to think that the presence of this pin in Sarazm Excavation VII has something to do with some of its 'neighbours' in Central Asia, eastern Iran, or South Asia more than with groups settled further away in the Caucasus or Europe. Yet, the existence of direct connections and exchanges with groups from distant cultural spheres or regions should probably not be ruled out. The presence of certain types of materials such as lapis lazuli and certain types of objects such as the quartzite sandstone bifacial blade found in Excavation VII, as well as, much more tentatively, certain parallels with copper material from the Kura-Araxes area, may suggest such connections in addition to the fact that materials and fashions circulated through intermediaries.

Lastly, most parallels for the small finds from Excavation VII fall within a *c.* 3500–2500 BCE chronological range, which is consistent with most remains from Sarazm. Yet, a series of items seem to be best paralleled within assemblages that are posterior to the mid-third millennium BCE. As seen in **Chapter 5**, certain ceramic types suggest the same conclusion. These observations in both groups of objects shall now be discussed together in the **Conclusion**.

# 7. CONCLUSION

In this volume I have attempted to analyse and synthesize the totality of available data from Excavation VII at Sarazm. I have been able to cover many, probably most, aspects of this excavation on the basis of Besenval's previous publications and detailed information about the archaeological contexts that he recorded in his archives, and of the study of the assemblage he recovered, which was still carefully bagged and labelled in Tajikistan over twenty years after this fieldwork ended. As is apparent in this volume, however, significant parts of the archives are missing that relate to relatively large exposures of archaeological deposits and artefacts. While not much more can be said about this missing information than has been set out in this volume until these archives are found (if they are ever found), available data has allowed for the detailed analysis of most areas exposed in Excavation VII and a general reconstruction of various aspects of the communities that settled in these areas.

## Chronology

It emerges from the combined analysis of the architecture and stratigraphy (**Chapter 3**), radiocarbon dates (**Chapter 4**), and ceramic assemblage (**Chapter 5**) that perhaps one general way to look at Excavation VII's four main levels and eleven phases is to consider these occupations as a sequence of three main periods.[1] This three-period reconstruction happens to mirror chronological reconstructions that were offered before for Excavation VII (see below); however, as a matter of fact, it genuinely emerged as the result of systematic, quantitative analysis and synthesis of the totality of available data from this excavation.

The first period consists of Levels I1 to I3 or I4.[2] Two radiocarbon dates from Level I1 and one from Level II1 suggest that these levels date to sometime between c. 3350–2900 cal. BCE. Parallels for the material assemblage do not contradict this dating. Save for Level I4, there is no stratigraphic gap in this sequence as most Level I1 architecture continued to be used throughout Levels I2 and I3. The compositions of the ceramic assemblages in these levels are also generally similar. They essentially consist of plain ware (Groups 1 and 2), although a few painted ceramic individuals that connect to cultural spheres in Turkmenistan on the one hand (Group 4) and in Afghanistan and Pakistan on the other hand (Group 5) were recorded in Level I3.

The second period includes Levels II1 to III2. One radiocarbon date from Level II1 and one radiocarbon date from Level III3 suggest that these levels date to sometime between c. 2900–2500 cal. BCE. Most parallels for the ceramic assemblages in these levels seem more consistent with the beginning of this bracket than its end, although a date close to the mid-third millennium BCE is not entirely incompatible. In contrast to the first period, several structural changes are observed throughout this sequence, which are materialized by three architectural phases (Levels II1, III1, and III2) and one seemingly more transient, or less built, occupation (Level II2). However, both Level II1 and III2 buildings[3] are characterized by walls with pilasters built using mud bricks with similar lengths and heights, although their widths are slightly different between the two levels. Although Level III2 yielded more ceramics than the earlier levels, the general composition of its ceramic assemblage is not fundamentally different from that of Level II. Plain vessels still dominate, and the above-mentioned painted ceramic styles that connect to cultural spheres in Turkmenistan (Group 4) and Afghanistan and Pakistan (Group 5) continue to be observed.

The third period is defined by Levels IV1–IV2. The two available radiocarbon dates from Level IV1 suggest that this level dates to sometime between c. 2550–2200 cal. BCE or c. 2450–2050 cal. BCE. The architecture in this level and Level IV2 is different from that observed in the previous levels. Also, a dramatic change is noted in the composition of the Level IV1–IV2 ceramic

---

[1] The small finds do not appear to delineate clear differences between these levels and phases, although the stratigraphic distribution of certain small find categories and specific items deserves further discussion (see below).

[2] I am leaving here the question open for Level I4.

[3] Level III1 was too eroded to allow for any detailed observation.

assemblage by which the ceramic style that connects to cultural spheres in Afghanistan and Pakistan (Group 5) is now the most common, whereas it was not in the second and first periods. However, there are nonetheless important issues with the dating of this period because the parallels for most Level IV1–IV2 ceramics seem to essentially date to the first half of the third millennium BCE (see **Chapters 1 and 5**; see below).

In this reconstruction, Level III3 emerges as ambiguous. This level could be included in this third period alongside Levels IV1–IV2 because these levels are all three characterized by the same shift toward more southern style material in their ceramic assemblages. Yet, Level III3 is disconnected from Levels IV1–IV2 because it appears more transient, or less built, than these levels, which contain buildings. For the same reason, it is also disconnected from previous architectural Level III2. Furthermore, the single radiocarbon date from Level III3 gave a date of c. 2700–2350 cal. BCE, which is centred in between, and overlaps with, both Level IV1 dates and the single radiocarbon date from Level II1.

This three-period reconstruction is not very different from the previous chronological reconstructions that have been offered for Excavation VII, which have also been aligned with the general four-period chronology that has been established for Sarazm. Besenval and Isakov (1989, 17) noted that Levels I1 and I3 may belong to Sarazm Period II, Level III3 to Sarazm Period III, and Levels IV1–IV2 to Sarazm Period IV. More recently, F. Razzokov (2016, 89 tab. 3) similarly assigned Excavation VII Levels I1 and I3 to Sarazm Period II; Levels II1 and III3 to Sarazm Period III; and Levels IV1–IV2 to Sarazm Period IV. One issue that Besenval and Isakov did not address is the above-mentioned fact that the radiocarbon dates from Levels III3 to IV1–IV2, which date these levels to between c. 2700–2050 cal. BCE, are not in agreement with the parallels for part of the ceramic assemblage found in these levels. Indeed, these parallels appear to be not later than the middle of the third millennium BCE (see below). Similarly, questions remained as to how the occupations exposed in Excavation VII fit within the general chronology of Sarazm, including vis-à-vis its foundation period. This period, Sarazm Period I, was believed to date to the middle of the fourth millennium BCE at the time Besenval and Isakov made the above-mentioned correlations. They specifically mentioned that the radiocarbon dates from Excavation VII Level I1 implied that this level did not belong to Sarazm Period I since this period dates to the middle of the fourth millennium BCE (Besenval and Isakov 1989, 17). However, it now appears that most of the settlement may have been founded later, not before the late fourth millennium BCE. As a result, although the areas exposed in Excavation VII are thought to have been settled later than the earliest occupations at this site, it is unclear how long after they were settled.

The earliest level defined in this excavation, Level I, is probably more recent than the funerary stone circle found in Excavation IV, in which the tomb of the 'Princess of Sarazm' was excavated. Parallels for this structure and one radiocarbon date that was conducted on human remains that *may* have come from one of the burials found in it are consistent with a date around the mid-fourth millennium BCE, or within the first half of the fourth millennium BCE (see **Chapters 1 and 4**).[4] Besides this structure, the date of the foundation of Sarazm's main settlement remains elusive. Most evidence suggests a date of around the last third of the fourth and the beginning of the third millennia BCE, whereas there are inconsistencies with evidence collected in the past that points at an older date. Additionally, recent attempts to tackle this conundrum in the field have provided no elements that appear to be earlier than the late fourth millennium BCE (see Mutin et al. 2020a) (see **Chapters 1 and 4**). Yet, the question of the dating of Sarazm's foundation remains open, and the only way that this question can be clarified is probably through yet again more fieldwork focused on this topic. In the present state of knowledge, the fact remains that the radiocarbon dates and parallels for the material assemblage from the earliest occupations of Excavation VII date these occupations to between the late fourth and early third millennia BCE too. And, although it is not possible to state that these occupations were settled at the same time as the site was founded, current data tend to suggest that it may have been the case or that they appeared not long after.

Most parallels for the ceramic style observed in Excavation VII and elsewhere at Sarazm that relates to the regions south of the Hindu Kush (Group 5) point to the late fourth through the mid-third millennia BCE. This seems especially true for the deep

---

[4] Certainly, however, an updated and detailed re-examination of the structure of this funerary monument and of the material culture from these tombs would probably help specify its dating. It is perhaps worth noting here that the two shell bracelets that are recorded inside the tomb of the 'Princess of Sarazm' have exact parallels in graves from Shahi-Tump, south-western Pakistani Balochistan, dating to the mid-fourth millennium BCE (Besenval 2005, 4 figs 9–10, 5 figs 11–12, 6).

bowls/goblets which may hardly be dated to later than c. 2800/2700 cal. BCE in the south. The necked jars may push this low limit a little more toward the mid-third millennium BCE (see **Chapter 5**), but it seems unrealistic to think that this style continued to be produced for another five hundred years until the end of the third millennium BCE. This observation raises questions about the dating of Levels III3 and IV1–IV2 in Excavation VII, and more generally that of the later occupation phase of the site, Sarazm Periods III and IV, as defined by Isakov (see **Chapter 1**). Parallels for this material as well as for the few Turkmen-related Namazga III Period type sherds (Group 4) found in these levels date these levels to essentially before the mid-third millennium BCE, whereas the radiocarbon dates from Level III3 overlap with c. 2500 cal. BCE and those from Level IV1 are within the second half of the third millennium BCE. One view on this conundrum is to consider that these radiocarbon dates are inaccurate, and that the current dates of most parallels south of the Hindu Kush and in Turkmenistan should be trusted. Yet, it is important to remember that the chronologies of the Chalcolithic and Bronze Age sites and cultures south of the Hindu Kush are not all well established and are still debated (see on this topic Cortesi et al. 2008; Jarrige et al. 2011a; Helwing et al. 2019). Recent reappraisal of the chronology of Iranian Seistan during the Bronze Age shows that it has been a long work in progress (see Kavosh et al. 2019 vs Salvatori and Tosi 2005). Another parameter that should be taken into account is the fact that the vessels from Sarazm that relate to cultural spheres in Afghanistan and Pakistan are not all exactly identical to their parallels in the south. As such, the chronologies south of the Hindu Kush should perhaps not be directly used to date this material at Sarazm. On the same note,

> we can reasonably consider that the southern ceramic styles did not emerge and decline simultaneously in all the regions where they are found. In the present case, that short time-lapses existed to some extent between the emergences and declines of these styles in the regions located south and north of the Hindu Kush is possible. (Mutin and Razzokov 2014, 137)

In summary, a little bit of flexibility may perhaps need to be introduced in the comparisons with the southern assemblages. In the meantime, in addition to the radiocarbon dates, it does not seem right to discard the complete ceramics from Level IV1 that parallel material in Iran dating to the middle and second half of the third millennium BCE (Group 6; see **Chapter 5**). A number of distinctive small finds from Level IV1 (as well as Level III3) also do not disagree with this dating, such as the copper double-spiral headed pin (SF168), two copper daggers (SF25 and SF98), one copper awl (SF99), and one lead seal (SF24), as well as additional small finds from Excavation VII whose archaeological contexts could not be found in the archives, such as one lead ingot(?) (SF94) and one stone vial (SF150). To this inventory may be added another lead ingot collected on the surface of the site as well as surface finds such as stone rods and weights(?). These objects best parallel material dating to between c. 2500–1500 cal. BCE broadly speaking, including material from the Farkhor cemetery in southern Tajikistan, dated to c. 2800/2700–2300 BCE, although the weights are observed from the fourth millennium BCE (see also **Chapter 1**). Considering the view that Levels IV1–IV2 date to the second half of the third millennium BCE, one may even argue that the most 'problematic' ceramics, those that completely contradict this view, i.e. Group 4 vessels and Group 5 deep bowls/goblets, amount to only five and four ceramic individuals in these levels, respectively (Table 5.8; Pl. 5.32). They could be interpreted as intrusive.

Meanwhile, a view that sees Levels IV1–IV2 too close to the end of the third millennium BCE raises the issue that no material relating to the Oxus Civilization nor to the Indus Civilization was found in these levels. They are still essentially characterized by a material culture that emerged in the previous levels. Therefore, the most rational explanation for this absence of Oxus-related and Indus-related artefacts in Levels IV1–IV2 seems to be that these levels were occupied before elements of these civilizations appeared in Central Asia. The geographically closest Indus-related site, Shortughaï in Afghanistan, is dated to c. 2200–1700 cal. BCE (Francfort 1989, 241–42), and the Oxus Civilization is generally dated to c. (2300)2250–1700 cal. BCE (Lyonnet and Dubova 2021, 32) while the earliest Indus-related objects found in Central Asia were recorded at sites relating to this civilization (see Ratnagar 2021 for a review). Furthermore, again, considering that the southern ceramic styles appeared in contexts dating to around 3000 cal. BCE, it seems unrealistic to believe that they continued to be made until the end of the third millennium BCE. For these two reasons and those mentioned above, it seems that a date generally around 2400/2300 cal. BCE for the end of Levels IV1–IV2 (and additional above-noted objects from Excavation VII and the surface of Sarazm) would agree with the radiocarbon dates from these levels and most current material evidence and lack thereof. This date would also place the end of Excavation VII (and perhaps of Sarazm) just before, or generally at the same time as, the abrupt drought event that affected significant parts of the Eurasian, African, and American continents around 4200 BP, i.e. the two arid peaks that are noted between *c.* 2250–2150 cal. BCE and *c.* 2100–1900 cal. BCE (Courty and Weiss 1997; Bar-Matthews et al. 1998; Stevens et al. 2001; Madella and Fuller 2005; see Petrie and Weeks 2019, 300).

It is unfortunate that the 1990-1991 archives that relate to archaeological deposits excavated around the Level IV1–IV2 buildings are missing. More data would probably have helped clarify the dating of these levels. As noted in **Chapter 1**, the last period of Sarazm, Period IV, is known through limited exposures including the deposits exposed in Levels IV1–IV2 in Excavation VII, and it seems that most remains relating to this period may have been wiped out elsewhere. However, since we know that such levels were found in this excavation it would probably be useful to extend Excavation VII and/or study the areas around it.

## Nature of the Occupations and Cultural Relationships

Sarazm was settled during the fourth millennium BCE at a time when the climate in Central Asia is believed to have been humid and then transitioned to a drier climate with a more pronounced dry interval during the third millennium BCE. The communities in Excavation VII were farmers who cultivated wheat and barley and collected wild fruits as well as wood for fuel and construction. They barely hunted and mostly raised sheep and goats, as well as cattle to a very limited extent. These domesticated animals provided them with meat, milk, wool, and work force (cattle). Similarities are noted between the plant and animal assemblages from Sarazm, including from Excavation VII, and those from sites in Turkmenistan as well as, ultimately, South-West Asia. These similarities with Turkmenistan corroborate those observed through the architecture and specific features such as the hearths exposed at this site, in addition to the material assemblage. Relationships have also been noted for the architecture and material culture from Sarazm with sites in Iran and Afghanistan. However, among all the connections that have been observed in the vestiges exposed at this site, those relating to Turkmenistan appear to prevail since its earliest occupations. For this reason, Sarazm is generally believed to have been settled by groups relating to the Namazga tradition which characterizes Turkmenistan during the fourth and third millennia BCE. With regard

to the architecture, Excavation VII architecture conforms to that excavated elsewhere at Sarazm, consisting of rammed earth and mud-brick constructions. The buildings from Excavation VII parallel those from other excavations with regard to aspects such as brick sizes, general orientation, space planning, and the presence of pilasters. The hearths unearthed in this excavation are similar too.[5] Regarding the material assemblage, there are no typical Namazga III painted ceramics in the earliest layers of Excavation VII. This type of material appears in Level I3 and is then recorded in very low quantities throughout this excavation. Nonetheless, the parallels for the plain vessels found in these layers suggest that the Excavation VII ceramic assemblage was stylistically connected to those of sites in Turkmenistan from its earliest occupations on. Additional objects from this excavation corroborate the cultural relationships seen through these ceramics.

Ceramics that stylistically relate to cultural spheres in Afghanistan and Pakistan are in Excavation VII not observed before Level I3. As noted above, they then became dominant in Levels III3 and IV1–IV2. This shift in the composition of the ceramic assemblage mirrors a similar, general shift observed at the site level. It suggests that the relationships with, or the presence of, groups linked to these southern spheres increased at some point at Sarazm, including in the areas exposed in Excavation VII. This interpretation seems valid but may need to be nuanced by considering that this apparent increase may have resulted from various processes including transactions, movements of peoples, and/or perhaps the simple fact that the southern style became more in vogue at some point. Another parameter that needs to be kept in mind is that the amounts of ceramics recorded across the site are generally low relative to those recorded at sites in Turkmenistan and south of the Hindu Kush. Consequently, quantitative differences that are observed between archaeological levels in the composition of their ceramic assemblages are within the range of a few dozen sherds or ceramic individuals. This is the case in Excavation VII (**Chapter 5**) as well as in other excavations at Sarazm (Lyonnet 1996,

---

[5] I have observed no exact equivalent at Sarazm for any of Excavation VII architectural levels but close similarities in one or more of these aspects. This lack of exact parallel is probably partly due to the fact that segments of, and not entire, buildings were exposed in Excavation VII. On this note, it is probably worth remembering that the closest parallels I have found concern the most complete architectural plan of Excavation VII, Level III2, which seems more specifically very similar to Excavation IV Level 3 and 4 constructions, although the latter have no pilaster.

31–37). Certainly, these low quantitative data need to be carefully recorded and computed. However, as such, it is probably wise to remember that these data may considerably vary, and may even be highly distorted, depending on the types of areas that are excavated. This observation is suggested by the concentration of storage and/or transport vessels in Excavation VII Level III3 and the specific concentration of southern style ceramics (Group 5) in this level as well as in Soundings 11–11A (Mutin and Razzokov 2014).

On the topic of the relationships with the regions south of the Hindu Kush, most parallels are usually made with sites such as Mundigak in southern Afghanistan as well as Mehrgarh and sites in the Quetta Valley in Pakistani Balochistan. Although these connections are correct, additional parallels for certain ceramic types (Group 5 necked jars in particular) and small finds from Sarazm with sites in northern Pakistan probably deserve more attention, such as the parallels with sites in the Bannu Basin and Taxila Valley. Routes of communication exist between these Pakistani areas and Sarazm through the north-easternmost regions of Afghanistan, with, coincidentally, Sar-i Sang in the Badakhshan Province and the Taluquan Plain in the Takhar Province halfway in between. The former is known for its sources for lapis lazuli, while the latter yielded a few sites with ceramic vessels compatible with types recorded at Sarazm and at sites south of the Hindu Kush.

Excavation VII has been instrumental in characterizing Sarazm as a multicultural site. Available data shows that similar configurations have been observed at Middle Asian sites dating to around 3000 BCE, where objects and styles relating to various cultural spheres were found together within the same archaeological contexts (see **Chapter 1**). Shahr-i Sokhta (Period I) is one of them. It is interpreted as 'a sort of prehistoric caravanserai' (Thornton 2012, 600; see Mutin and Minc 2019 for a recent recapitulation and references), an interpretation that does not disagree with available data from Sarazm. Regardless, save perhaps for the time of its foundation (most likely due to Namazga groups) and specific materials, it is difficult to always pinpoint the origins of all material and architectural aspects of Sarazm precisely, because many of these aspects are observed in various regions around the Hindu Kush and even beyond. Furthermore, currently available low chronological resolution impedes such endeavour. Instead of only looking outside of Sarazm, however, one should also keep in mind that soon after it was founded the communities at this site probably evolved on the basis of both inputs from the founders and new dynamics related to the specific local and regional natural conditions and cultural connections that its location entailed, as well as additional inputs from new interregional relationships. As such, instead of being defined only through its spectacular, multicultural relationships, Sarazm needs also to be understood as a place where these various dynamics were incorporated into a form that became unique to this site (see Mutin, forthcoming on intercultural interaction and culture formation; Anthony 1990 on migrations).

Yet, while being unique, the above-mentioned specific dynamics and relationships that Sarazm was part of in the regions around the Hindu Kush, between eastern Iran, southern Central Asia, and the Indo-Iranian Borderlands, however probably need to be remembered as a distinctive entity that characterized these regions at the same time as it became a foundation of the rise of the later Oxus Civilization. The discoveries at Farkhor in southern Tajikistan have now added an important new piece to this puzzle in which the role of eastern Bactria and the processes involved there appear to have been prevalent in this culture formation (see Francfort 2016; 2020; see **Chapter 1**). On a related topic, more than 1000 km north-east of Sarazm, recent fieldwork at Dali in Kazakhstan illustrates the complex entanglement of the various dynamics involved in the formation of Bronze Age sites and societies along the Inner Asian Mountain Corridor (IAMC):

> Understanding the processes underlying the formation of social and cultural institutional domains at Dali, as elsewhere, is further muddled by evidence for diverse sources in terms of the formal, semiotic, and practical ways communities at Dali participated in cultural institutional domains such as subsistence economy, house building, and settlement organization, craft production, symbolic art, and burial ritual. The archaeological record at Dali ultimately illustrates a long history of community negotiation between deeply embedded socio-economic institutions and novel practices, likely stemming from a combination of social transmissions and population integrations that required active engagement in spheres of interregional connectivity. (Hermes et al. 2021, 376)

Sarazm was settled by farmers whose occupations appear to have been rather short-lived. It attracted people and materials from various cultural spheres, including raw materials from nearby and more distant sources that appear to have been worked locally. It is generally admitted that this site was a metallurgical centre, or a station involved in the manufacturing and export of metallic objects, as well as objects made from minerals such as lapis lazuli. In any case, the role of neighbouring or relatively close sources for raw materials such as gold and turquoise have been pointed out as motives for groups to come settle at Sarazm (see **Chapter 1**). Excavation VII does not contradict this general picture as it yielded remains of craft activities including raw materials, tools, and waste. The specific concentration of jars in Level III3 suggests a focus in this level on storage and/or transport of stuff. Yet, none of these remains are clearly suggestive of intensive manufacturing activities. This evidence seems too little (see **Chapter 6**), while the fact that it was essentially recorded within the context of dwellings (see **Chapter 3**) is not consistent with this view. More remains and structures relating to craft activities were found elsewhere at the site, including remains relating to metallurgy in Excavations II and XVI, as well as copper objects such as daggers in Excavation II and from the surface of the site. Certainly, these remains are more evocative than those from Excavation VII. Yet, the evidence at hand still leaves an ambiguous impression that does not help firmly conclude on the nature of the craft activities that took place at Sarazm and distinguish between activities that served local/regional needs and activities targeted for broader exchange networks. This evidence is not considerable; the vast quantities of waste one would expect to see on a manufacturing centre have not been found; and production seems to have taken place essentially within domestic contexts, not specialized areas.

While more evidence might be found in the future, current data bring to mind different hypotheses and parameters that probably need to be remembered. One is that most areas of the site have not been explored, including many areas that lie underneath the villages settled on the site, which may hold industrial quarters. Part of the evidence, such as tools, might have been taken away before the dwellings were abandoned. This possibility agrees with the general lack of material at Sarazm relative to other sites in Central Asia and Middle Asia as well as with Besenval and Isakov's (1989, 14) observation in Excavation VII who wrote that most levels in this excavation appear to have been emptied. Perhaps craft production and occupation at Sarazm may need to be conceived as an element of a greater network of sites in which Sarazm was associated with other sites including stations in the Zeravshan Valley and around where its artisans worked. Perhaps craft production may also need to be envisaged with greater consideration of the productive capacity of household-based production contexts (see **Chapter 1**).

These questions, as well as those that relate to the chronology of Sarazm, are beyond the topic of this volume because they need incorporation and re-evaluation of the totality of available data, as well as more fieldwork. After all, although the work conducted by Roland Besenval in Excavation VII has been of considerable importance, the areas exposed in this excavation remain one small component of a much larger site which still fully deserves much more investigation.

# Works Cited

**Akbarzadeh, D. & Piran, S.**
2013 *Objects from the Jiroft Treasury, Tehran: Soft Stone and Alabaster Objects (Recovered Collection) from the Halil River Basin; National Museum of Iran, with a Report by Dr Y. Madjidzadeh.* Pazineh Press, Tehran.

**Alden, J.**
1982 'Trade and Politics in Proto-Elamite Iran', *Current Anthropology* 23/6: 613–40.

**Algaze, G.**
1993 *The Uruk World System: The Dynamics of Expansion of Early Mesopotamian Civilization.* University of Chicago Press, Chicago.

**Allchin, F. R.; Allchin, B.; Durrani, F. A. & Farid Khan, M.**
1986 *Lewan and the Bannu Basin* (British Archaeological Reports, International Series 310). BAR, Cambridge.

**Ameri, M.**
2020 'Who Holds the Keys? Identifying Female Administrators at Shahr-i Sokhta', *Iran* 60/1: 1–38 <https://doi.org/10.1080/05786967.2020.1718542>.

**Amiet, P. & Tosi, M.**
1978 'Phase 10 at Shahr-i Sokhta. Excavations in Square XDV and the Late 4th Millennium B.C. Assemblage of Sistan', *East and West* 28/1–4: 9–31.

**Anthony, D.**
1990 'Migration in Archaeology: The Baby and the Water', *American Anthropologist* 92/4: 895–914.
2007 *The Horse, the Wheel, and Language: How Bronze-Age Riders from the Eurasian Steppes Shaped the Modern World.* Princeton University Press, Princeton.

**Arne, T. J.**
1945 *Excavations at Shah Tepe, Iran* (Reports from the Scientific Expedition to the North-Western Provinces of China under the Leadership of Dr Sven Hedin, The Sino-Swedish Expedition Publication 27/7, Archaeology 5). Elanders boktryckeri aktiebolag, Göteborg.

**Arnold, D. E.**
1985 *Ceramic Theory and Cultural Process* (New Studies in Archaeology). Cambridge University Press, Cambridge.

**Avanesova, N. A.**
1996 'Pasteurs et agriculteurs de la vallée du Zeravshan (Ouzbékistan) au début de l'âge du Bronze : relations et influences mutuelles', in B. Lyonnet (ed.), *Sarazm (Tadjikistan) Céramiques (Chalcolithique et Bronze Ancien)* (Mémoires de la Mission Archéologique française en Asie Centrale 7). De Boccard Édition – Diffusion, Paris: 117–31.
2001 'U istokov urbanisticheskogo Afrasiaba', *Istorija Material'noj Kul'tury Uzbekistana* 32: 57–68.
2013 'Zhukov, un "sanctuaire" énéolithique d'anciens nomades dans la vallée du Zeravshan (Ouzbékistan)', *Paléorient* 39/2: 85–108.
2021 'The Zeravshan Regional Variant of the Bactria-Margiana Archaeological Complex: Interaction between Two Cultural Worlds', in B. Lyonnet & N. A. Dubova (eds), *The World of the Oxus Civilization* (The Routledge Worlds). Routledge, New York: 665–97.

### Bache, C.
1935 'Burials of Tepe Gawra', *Scientific American* 153/6: 310–13.

### Balfet, H.
1991 'Chaîne opératoire et organisation sociale du travail : quatre exemples de façonnage de la poterie au Maghreb', in H. Balfet (ed.), *Observer l'action technique, des chaînes opératoires, pour quoi faire ?* Éditions du CNRS, Paris: 87–96.

### Balfet, H.; Fauvet-Berthelot, M.-F. & Monzon, S.
1983 *Pour la normalisation de la description des poteries.* Éditions du CNRS, Paris.

### Bar-Matthews, M.; Ayalon, A. & Kaufman, A.
1998 'Paleoclimate Evolution in the Eastern Mediterranean Region during the Last 58 000 Years as Derived from Stable Isotopes of Speleothems (Soreq Cave, Israel)', in *Isotope Techniques in the Study of Past and Current Environmental Change: Proceedings of an International Symposium on Isotope Techniques in the Study of Past and Current Environmental Changes in the Hydrosphere and the Atmosphere Organized by International Atomic Energy Agency and Held in Vienna, 14-18 April 1997.* International Atomic Energy Agency, Vienna: 673–82 (IAEA-SM-349/17).

### Barthélémy de Saizieu, B.
2003 *Les parures de Mehrgarh: perles et pendentifs du Néolithique précéramique à la période pré-Indus; fouilles 1974-1985.* Éditions Recherche sur les Civilisations, Paris.

### Barthélémy de Saizieu, B. & Bouquillon, A.
1993 'Les Parures en pierre de Mundigak, Afghanistan', *Paléorient* 19/2: 65–94.
2000 'Émergence et évolution des matériaux vitrifiés dans la région de l'Indus du 5$^e$ au 3$^e$ millénaire (Mehrgarh-Nausharo)', *Paléorient* 26/2: 93–111.

### Bar-Yosef, O.
2014 'The Origins of Sedentism and Agriculture in Western Asia', in Colin Renfrew & Paul Bahn (eds), *The Cambridge World Prehistory*, III: *West and Central Asia and Europe*. Cambridge University Press, Cambridge: 1408–38.

### Beale, T. W.
1986 *Excavations at Tepe Yahya, Iran 1967-1975: The Early Periods* (American School of Prehistoric Research Bulletin 38). Peabody Museum of Archaeology and Ethnology, Cambridge, MA.

### Beer, R.; Heiri, O. & Tinner, W.
2007 'Vegetation History, Fire History and Lake Development Recorded for 6300 Years by Pollen, Charcoal, Loss on Ignition and Chironomids at a Small Lake in Southern Kyrgyzstan (Alay Range, Central Asia)', *The Holocene* 17/7: 977–85.

### Bensidoun, S.
1979 *Samarcande et la vallée du Zerafshan: une civilisation de l'oasis en Ouzbékistan-URSS.* Éditions Anthropos, Paris.

### Besenval, R.
1987 'Découvertes récentes à Sarazm (R.S.S. du Tadjikistan) : attestation des relations au III$^e$ millénaire entre l'Asie centrale, l'Iran du Nord-Est et le Baluchistan', *Comptes-rendus des séances de l'Académie des Inscriptions et Belles-Lettres*, 131/2: 441–56.
2005 'Chronology of Protohistoric Kech-Makran', in C. Jarrige & V. Lefèvre (eds), *South Asian Archaeology 2001.* Éditions Recherche sur les Civilisations, Paris: 1–9.

# WORKS CITED

**Besenval, R.; Brunet, F.; Francfort, H.-P.; Isakov, A. I.; P'jankova, L. T. & Razzokov, A. (eds)**
2021 *Colloque franco-tadjike de Pendjikent (1994) et premières recherches de la MAFAC à Sarazm (1984-1994)*. Institut d'histoire, d'archéologie et d'ethnographie A. Donish de l'Académie des Sciences de la République du Tadjikistan, Douchanbé.

**Besenval, R. & Isakov, A. I.**
1989 'Sarazm et les débuts du peuplement agricole dans la région de Samarkand', *Arts asiatiques* 44: 5-20.

**Biscione, R.**
1984 'Baluchistan Presence in the Ceramic Assemblage of Period I at Shahr-i Sokhta', in B. Allchin (ed.), *South Asian Archaeology 1981*. Cambridge University Press, Cambridge: 69-80.

**Bobomulloev, S.; Vinogradova, N. M.; Bobomulloev, B.; Hudzhageldiev, T. U. & Navruzbekov, M.**
2021 'Preliminary Results of Investigations of Barrows in the Locality of Sarazm-2 in the Basin of the Zeravshan River in Summer and Autumn 2020' (in Russian), Археологические вести (Archaeological News) 3: 10-54.

**Bonora, G. L.**
2021 'The Oxus Civilization and the Northern Steppes', in B. Lyonnet & N. A. Dubova (eds), *The World of the Oxus Civilization* (The Routledge Worlds). Routledge, New York: 734-75.

**Bonora, G. L.; Domanin, C.; Salvatori, S.; Soldini, A. & De Marco, G.**
2000 'The Oldest Graves of the Shahr-i Sokhta Graveyard', in M. Taddei (ed.), *South Asian Archaeology 1997*. Istituto italiano per l'Africa e l'Oriente, Rome: 495-520.

**Boroffka, N.**
2009 'Simple Technology: Casting Moulds for Axe-Adzes', in T. L. Kienlin & B. Roberts (eds), *Metals and Society: Studies in Honour of Barbara S. Ottaway* (Universitätsforschungen zur Prähistorischen Archäologie 169). Habelt, Bonn: 246-57.

**Boroffka, N.; Cierny, J., & Lutz, J.**
2002 'Bronze Age Tin from Central Asia: Preliminary Notes', in K. Boyle, C. Renfrew & M. Levine (eds), *Ancient Interactions: East and West in Eurasia*. McDonald Institute for Archaeological Research, Cambridge: 136-60.

**Bowles, J. F. W.**
2021 'Hydroxides', in S. Elias & D. Alderton (eds), *Encyclopedia of Geology*, 2nd edn. Academic Press, Amsterdam: 442-51.

**Brunet, F.**
2005 'Pour une nouvelle étude de la culture néolithique de Kel'teminar, Ouzbékistan', *Paléorient* 31/2: 87-105.

**Brunet, F.; Francfort, H.-P.; Mutin, B.; Razzokov, A. & Besenval, R.**
2019 'Archaeological Study of Sarazm in 2014 by the Tajik-French Joint Expedition (MAFAC)' (in Russian), *Arkheologicheskie raboty v Tadzhikistane* 40: 64-80.

**Brunet, F.; Hudžanazarov, M. & Szymczak, K.**
2013 'Le site d'Ajakagytma et le complexe culturel de Kel'teminar au sein des processus de néolithisation en Asie centrale (travaux de la MAFANAC)', *Cahiers d'Asie centrale* 21-22: 191-205.

**Brunet, F. & Razzokov, A.**
2016 'Towards a New Characterisation of the Chalcolithic in Central Asia. The Lithic Industry of Sarazm (Tajikistan): The First Results of the Technological Analysis', in V. Lefèvre, A. Didier & B. Mutin (eds), *South Asian Archaeology and Art 2012*. Brepols, Turnhout: 49-62.

**Caldwell, J. R. & Sarraf, M.**

1967 'Exploration of Excavation Area B', in J. R. Caldwell (ed.), *Investigations at Tal-i Iblis* (Illinois State Museum Preliminary Reports 9). Illinois State Museum Society, Springfield: 272–308.

**de Cardi, B.**

1965 'Excavations and Reconnaissance in Kalat, West Pakistan: The Prehistoric Sequence in the Surab Region', *Pakistan Archaeology* 2: 85–182.

1983 *Archaeological Surveys in Baluchistan, 1948 and 1957* (Institute of Archaeology Occasional Publication 8). Institute of Archaeology, London.

**Casal, J.-M.**

1961 *Fouilles de Mundigak* (Mémoires de la Délégation Archéologique française en Afghanistan 17). Klincksieck, Paris.

1964 *Fouilles d'Amri* (Publication de la Commission des fouilles archéologiques. Fouilles du Pakistan). Klincksieck, Paris.

**Casanova, M.**

1991 *La vaisselle d'albâtre d'Iran et d'Asie centrale aux III$^e$ et II$^e$ millénaires av. J.-C.* Éditions Recherche sur les Civilisations.

2008 'Lapis lazuli from Tod Treasure, Egypt', in J. Aruz, K. Benzel & J. M. Evans (eds), *Beyond Babylon: Art, Trade and Diplomacy in the Second Millennium B.C.* Metropolitan Museum, New York: 102–03.

2019 'Exchanges and Trade during the Bronze Age in Iran', in J.-W. Meyer, E. Vila, M. Mashkour, M. Casanova & R. Vallet (dir.), *The Iranian Plateau during the Bronze Age: Development of Urbanisation, Production and Trade.* MOM Éditions, Lyon: 301–11.

**Cesbron, F.**

1996 'Les matériaux minéraux du site archéologique de Sarazm, Tadjikistan', *Bulletin de l'AMIS* 18: 3–8.

**Cez, L.**

2019 'Le paysage fluvial et irrigué de Sarazm dans la moyenne vallée du Zeravchan, Tadjikistan, Asie centrale. Étude des dynamiques et des temporalités d'un paysage de l'eau en milieu contraignant', *Projets de paysage* 20: 1–21.

**Chase, D. W.; Caldwell, J. R. & Fehervari, I.**

1967 'The Iblis Sequence and the Exploration of Excavation Areas A, C, and E', in J. R. Caldwell (ed.), *Investigations at Tal-i Iblis* (Illinois State Museum Preliminary Reports 9). Illinois State Museum Society, Springfield: 111–201.

**Chataignier, C. & Palumbi, G. (coord.).**

2014 'The Kura-Araxes Culture from the Caucasus to Iran, Anatolia and the Levant: Between Unity and Diversity', *Paléorient* 40/2: 247–60.

**Chen, F.; Yu, Z.; Yang, M.; Ito, E.; Wang, S.; Madsen, D. B.; Huang, X.; Zhao, Y.; Sato, T.; Birks, H. J. B.; Boomer, I.; Chen, J.; An, C. & Wünnemann, B.**

2008 'Holocene Moisture Evolution in Arid Central Asia and its Out-of-Phase Relationship with Asian Monsoon History', *Quaternary Science Reviews* 27: 351–64.

**Chernykh, E.**

2008 'The "Steppe Belt" of Stockbreeding Cultures in Eurasia during the Early Metal Age', *Trabajos de Prehistoria* 65/2: 73–93.

## Cleuziou, S. & Berthoud, T.
1982 'Early Tin in the Near East', *Expedition* 3: 14-19.

## Collins, P.
2003 'The Tomb of Puabi', in J. Aruz & R. Wallenfels (eds), *Art of the First Cities: The Third Millennium B.C. from the Mediterranean to the Indus*. Metropolitan Museum of Art, New York: 108-19.

## Cortesi, E.; Tosi, M.; Lazzari, A. & Vidale, M.
2008 'Cultural Relationships beyond the Iranian Plateau: The Helmand Civilization, Baluchistan and the Indus Valley in the 3rd Millennium BC', *Paléorient* 34/2: 5-35.

## Courty, M.-A. & Weiss, H.
1997 'The Scenario of Environmental Degradation in the Tell Leilan Region of NE Syria during the Late Third Millennium Abrupt Climate Change', in H. N. Dalfes, G. Kukla & H. Weiss (eds), *Third Millennium BC Climate Change and Old World Collapse*. Springer, Berlin: 107-47.

## Cremaschi, M.
1998 'Palaeohydrography and Middle Holocene Desertification in the Northern Fringe of the Murghab Delta', in A. Gubaev, G. A. Koshelenko & M. Tosi (eds), *The Archaeological Map of the Murghab Delta: Preliminary Reports 1990-1995*. Istituto Italiano per l'Africa e l'Oriente, Rome: 15-25.

## Dance, P.
2002 *Shells: The Photographic Recognition Guide to Seashells of the World* (Smithsonian Handbooks). Dorling Kindersley (Penguin Random House), New York.

## Deshayes, J.
1969 'Tureng-Tepe et la période Hissar IIIc', *Ugaritica* 7: 139-63.

## Desse, J.
1997 'Archéozoologie aux marges occidentales du Bélouchistan', *Anthropozoologica* 25-26: 671-76.

## Dupont-Delaleuf, A.
2016 'Ceramic Production at Ulug-Depe (Turkmenistan) from the Late Chalcolithic to the Early Bronze Age: Technical Traditions', in V. Lefèvre, A. Didier & B. Mutin (eds), *South Asian Archaeology and Art 2012*. Brepols, Turnhout: 81-97.

## Dupree, L.
1963 'Deh Morasi Ghundai: A Chalcolithic Site in South-Central Afghanistan', *Anthropological Papers of the American Museum of Natural History* 50/2: 57-136.

## During-Caspers, E.
1972 'Etched Carnelian Beads', *Bulletin of the Institute of Archaeology* 10: 83-98.

## Durrani, F. A.
1994-1995 *Excavations in the Gomal Valley: Rehman Dheri Report 2* (*Ancient Pakistan* 10, Special Issue). Department of Archaeology, University of Peshawar, Peshawar.

## Durrani, F. A.; Ali, I. & Erdosy, G.
1995 'New Perspectives on Indus Urbanism from Rehman Dheri', *East and West* 45/1-4: 81-96.

## Dyson, R. H. Jr. & Thornton, C. P.
2009 'Shir-i Shian and the Fifth-Millennium Sequence of Northern Iran', *Iran* 47: 1-22.

**Erb-Satullo, N. L.**
2022 'Towards a Spatial Archaeology of Crafting Landscapes', *Cambridge Archaeological Journal* 32/4: 1–17 <https://doi.org/10.1017/S095977432200004X>.

**Eskandari, N.; Desset, F.; Hessari, M.; Shahsavari, M.; Shafiee, M. & Vidale, M.**
2020 'A Late 4th to Early 3rd Millennium BC Grave in Hajjiabad-Varamin (Jiroft, South-Eastern Iran): Defining a New Period of the Halil Rud Archaeological Sequence', *Iranica Antiqua* 55: 1–48.

**Evett, D.**
1967 'Artifacts and Architecture of the Iblis I Period: Areas D, F, and G', in J. R. Caldwell (ed.), *Investigations at Tal-i Iblis* (Illinois State Museum Preliminary Reports 9). Illinois State Museum Society, Springfield: 202–55.

**Fairservis, W. A.**
1956 'Excavations in the Quetta Valley, West Pakistan', *Anthropological Papers of the American Museum of Natural History* 45/2: 165–402.
1959 'Archaeological Surveys in the Zhob and Loralaï Districts, West Pakistan', *Anthropological Papers of the American Museum of Natural History* 47/2: 277–448.

**Foglini, L. & Vidale, M.**
2017 'The Turquoise Industry', in M. Vidale & A. Lazzari (eds), *Lapis Lazuli Bead Making at Shahr-i Sokhta: Interpreting Craft Production in a Urban Community of the 3rd Millennium BC* (Associazione internazionale di studi sul Mediterraneo e l'Oriente, Serie orientale Roma n.s. 6). Associazione internazionale di studi sul Mediterraneo e l'Oriente, Rome: 263–80.

**Fouache, É.; Besenval, R.; Cosandey, C.; Coussot, C.; Ghilardi, M.; Huot, S. & Lamothe, M.**
2012 'Palaeochannels of the Balkh River (Northern Afghanistan) and Human Occupation since the Bronze Age Period', *Journal of Archaeological Science* 39: 3415–27.

**Fouache, É.; Cez, L.; Andrieu-Ponel, V. & Rante, R.**
2021 'Environmental Changes in Bactria and Sogdiana (Central Asia, Afghanistan, and Uzbekistan) from the Neolithic to the Late Bronze Age. Interaction with Human Occupation', in B. Lyonnet & N. A. Dubova (eds), *The World of the Oxus Civilization* (The Routledge Worlds). Routledge, New York: 82–109.

**Fouache, É.; Francfort, H.-P.; Cosandey, C.; Adle, C.; Bendezu-Sarmiento, J. & Vahdati, A. A.**
2013 'Les régions de Bam et de Sabzevar (Iran) : une évolution dans l'implantation des sites archéologiques et dans la gestion des ressources en eau compatible avec l'hypothèse d'une aridification croissante du climat entre 2500–1900 BC', in J. Bendezu-Sarmiento (ed.), *L'Archéologie française en Asie centrale post-soviétique: un enjeu sociopolitique et culturel* (Cahiers d'Asie Centrale 21–22). De Boccard, Paris: 559–72.

**Fouache, É.; Rante, R.; Mirzaakhmedov, D.; Ragala, R.; Dupays, M.; Vella, C.; Fleury, J.; Andrieu-Ponnel, V.; Zink, A.; Porto, E.; Brunet, F. & Cez, L.**
2016 'The Role of Catastrophic Floods Generated by Collapse of Natural Dams since the Neolithic in the Oases of Bukhara and Qaraqöl: Preliminary Results', *International Journal of Geohazards and Environment* 2/3: 150–65.

**Francfort, H.-P.**
1989 *Fouilles de Shortughaï: recherches sur l'Asie centrale protohistorique* (Mémoires de la Mission Archéologique française en Asie Centrale 2). De Boccard Édition - Diffusion, Paris.
2005 'La civilisation de l'Oxus et les Indo-Iraniens et Indo-Aryens', in G. Fussman, J. Kellens, H.-P. Francfort & X. Tremblay (eds), *Aryas, Aryens et Iraniens en Asie centrale* (Collège de France, Publications de l'Institut de Civilisation Indienne 72). De Boccard, Paris: 253–328.

2016 'How the Twins Met: Indus and Oxus Bronze Age Civilizations in Eastern Bactria. Shortughaï Revisited Forty Years Later', in N. A. Dubova, E. V. Antonova, P. M. Kožin, M. F. Kosarev, R. G. Muradov, R. M. Sataev & A. A. Tiškin (dir.), *To the Memory of Professor Victor Sarianidi* (Transactions of Margiana Archaeological Expedition). N. N. Miklukho-Maklay Institute of Ethnology and Anthropology of Russian Academy of Sciences, Altay State University, Moscow: 461–75.

2020 'Sarazm in Contemporary Scholarship. An Exceptional Long Distance Attractiveness in Late IVth Mid III mill. B.C.', in С.Г. Бобомуллоев & Б.Т. Кобилова (eds), *Sarazm 5500*. National Museum of Antiquities, Dushanbe: 5–24.

**Francfort, H.-P. & Tremblay, X.**
2010 'Marhaši et la Civilisation de l'Oxus', *Iranica Antiqua* 45: 51–224.

**Franke, U.**
2008 'Baluchistan and the Borderlands', in D. M. Pearsall (ed.), *Encyclopedia of Archaeology*, I. Academic Press, New York: 651–70.
2015 'Joint German-Pakistani Archaeological Mission to Kalat. Sohr Damb/Nal. Reconstruction of a Prehistoric Culture in Central Balochistan, Pakistan', *Pakistan Archaeology* 30: 31–144.

**Franke, U. & Cortesi, E.**
2015 *Lost and Found: Prehistoric Pottery Treasures from Baluchistan*. Museum of Islamic Art, Berlin.

**Frenez, D.**
2018 'The Indus Civilization Trade with the Oman Peninsula', in S. Cleuziou & M. Tosi, *In the Shadow of the Ancestors: The Prehistoric Foundations of the Early Arabian Civilization in Oman*, ed. D. Frenez & R. Garba, 2nd expanded edn. Ministry of Heritage and Culture, Muscat, Sultanate of Oman: 385–96.

**Garner, J.**
2021 'Metal Sources (Tin and Copper) and the BMAC', in B. Lyonnet & N. A. Dubova (eds), *The World of the Oxus Civilization* (The Routledge Worlds). Routledge, New York: 799–826.

**Ghirshman, R.**
1938 *Fouilles de Sialk près de Kashan 1933, 1934, 1937* (Musée du Louvre, Département des antiquités orientales et de la céramique antique, série archéologique). Geuthner, Paris.

**Gürsan-Salzmann, A.**
2016 *The New Chronology of the Bronze Age Settlement of Tepe Hissar, Iran* (University Museum Monographs 142). University of Pennsylvania Museum of Archaeology and Anthropology, Philadelphia.

**Hakemi, A.**
1997 *Shahdad: Archaeological Excavations of a Bronze Age Center in Iran* (Associazione internazionale di studi sul Mediterraneo e l'Oriente, Reports and Memoirs 27). Associazione internazionale di studi sul Mediterraneo e l'Oriente, Rome.

**Hamzeh, M. A.; Mahmudy-Gharaie, M. H.; Ketek Lahijani, H. A.; Djamali, M.; Moussavi Harami, R. & Naderi Beni, A.**
2016a 'Holocene Hydrological Changes in SE Iran, a Key Region between Indian Summer Monsoon and Mediterranean Winter Precipitation Zones, as Revealed from a Lacustrine Sequence from Lake Hamoun', *Quaternary International* 408: 25–39.

**Hamzeh, M. A.; Mahmudy-Gharaie, M. H.; Ketek Lahijani, H. A.; Moussavi Harami, R.; Djamali, M. & Naderi Beni, A.**
2016b 'Paleolimnology of Lake Hamoun (E Iran): Implication for Past Climate Changes and Possible Impacts on Human Settlements', *PALAIOS* 31: 616–29.

**Hansen, D. P.**

1998 'Art of the Royal Tombs of Ur: A Brief Interpretation', in R. L. Zettler & L. Horne (eds), *Treasures from the Royal Tombs of Ur*. University of Pennsylvania Museum of Archaeology and Anthropology, Philadelphia: 43–72.

**Heinecke, L.; Mischke, S.; Adler, K.; Barth, A.; Biskaborn, B. K.; Plessen, B.; Nitze, I.; Kuhn, G.; Rajabov, I. & Herzschuh, U.**

2016 'Late Pleistocene to Holocene Climate and Limnological Changes at Lake Karakul (Pamir Mountains, Tajikistan)', *Climate of the Past Discussions* <https://doi.org/10.5194/cp-2016-34>.

**Helwing, B.**

2005 'Long-Distance Relations of the Iranian Highland Sites during the Late Chalcolithic Period: New Evidence from the Joint Iranian-German Excavations at Arisman, Prov. Isfahan, Iran', in U. Franke-Vogt & H.-J. Weisshaar (eds), *South Asian Archaeology 2003*. Linden Soft, Aachen: 171–78.

2007 'The Rise and Fall of Bronze Age Centers around the Central Iranian Desert – A Comparison of Tappe Hesar II and Arisman', *Archäologische Mitteilungen aus Iran und Turan* 38: 35–48.

2017 'Die Frühe Bronzezeit im Hochland von Iran', in B. Helwing & S. Annen (eds), *Iran: Frühe Kulturen zwischen Wasser und Wüste, 13.4.2017–20.8.2017*. Kunsthalle der Bundesrepublik Deutschland, Bonn: 96–123.

**Helwing, B.; Vidale, M. & Fazeli Nashli, H.**

2019 'Radiocarbon Dates and Absolute Chronology', in H. A. Kavosh, M. Vidale & H. Fazeli Nashli (eds), *Prehistoric Sistan, II: Tappeh Graziani, Sistan, Iran: Stratigraphy, Formation Processes and Chronology of a Suburban Site of Shahr-i Sokhta* (Associazione internazionale di studi sul Mediterraneo e l'Oriente, Serie oriental Roma n.s. 18). Associazione internazionale di studi sul Mediterraneo e l'Oriente, Rome: 151–55.

**Hemphill, B. E.**

1999 'Biological Affinities and Adaptations of Bronze Age Bactrians: IV. A Craniometric Investigation of Bactrian Origins', *American Journal of Anthropology* 108: 173–92.

**Hermes, T. R.; Frachetti, M. D.; Doumani Dupuy, P. N.; Mar'yashev, A.; Nebel, A. & Makarewicz, C. A.**

2019 'Early Integration of Pastoralism and Millet Cultivation in Bronze Age Eurasia', *Proceedings of the Royal Society B: Biological Sciences* 286: 20191273 <http://dx.doi.org/10.1098/rspb.2019.1273>.

**Hermes, T. R.; Doumani Dupuy, P. N.; Henry, E. R.; Meyer, M.; Mar'yashev, A. N. & Frachetti, M. D.**

2021 'The Multi-period Settlement Dali in Southeastern Kazakhstan: Bronze Age Institutional Dynamics along the Inner Asian Mountain Corridor', *Asian Perspectives* 60/2: 345–81.

**Herrmann, G.**

1968 'Lapis-lazuli: The Early Phases of its Trade', *Iraq* 30: 21–57.

**Heskel, D. L.**

1984 'Iran-Indus Valley Connections: A Reevaluation', in B. B. Lal & S. P. Gupta (eds), *Frontiers of the Indus Civilization*. Books and Books, New Delhi: 333–46.

**Heydari, M.; Desset, F. & Vidale, M.**

2019 'A Late 4th – Early 3rd Millennium BC Grave at Spidej (Eastern Jazmurian, Iranian Baluchistan)', *Iranica Antiqua* 54: 17–57.

**Hiebert, F. T.**

1994 *Origins of the Bronze Age Oasis Civilization in Central Asia* (American School of Prehistoric Research Bulletin 42). Peabody Museum of Archaeology and Ethnology, Harvard University, Cambridge, MA.

2002 'The Kopet Dag Sequence of Early Villages in Central Asia', *Paléorient* 28/2: 25–41.

2003  *A Central Asian Village at the Dawn of Civilization, Excavations at Anau, Turkmenistan* (University Museum Monograph 116). University of Pennsylvania Museum of Archaeology and Anthropology, Philadelphia.

**Isakov, A. I.**

1991  *Sarazm*. Donish, Dushanbe.

1994a  'О работе международной археологической экспедиции на поселении саразм в 1985 г', *Arkheologicheskie raboty v Tadzhikistane* 25: 85–99.

1994b  'Sarazm: An Agricultural Center of Ancient Sogdiana', *Bulletin of the Asia Institute*, n.s. 8: 1–12.

**Isakov, A. I.; Besenval, R.; Razzokov, A. & Bobomulloev, C.**

2003  'Сработы советско-французской экспедиции в 1990 г.', *Arkheologicheskie raboty v Tadzhikistane* 28: 131–67.

**Isakov, A. I.; Kohl, P.; Lamberg-Karlovsky, C. C. & Maddin, R.**

1987  'Metallurgical Analysis from Sarazm, Tadjikistan SSR', *Archaeometry* 29: 90–102.

**Isakov, A. I. & Lyonnet, B.**

1988  'Céramiques de Sarazm (Tadjikistan, URSS): problèmes d'échanges et de peuplement à la fin du Chalcolithique et au début de l'Âge du Bronze', *Paléorient* 14/1: 31–47.

**Isakov, A. I. & Ruzanov, V. D.**

2008  'Rezul'taty spektral'nykh issledovanij metalla poselenija Sarazm' (Results from Spectral Analyses on the Metals of Sarazm), in V. I. Sarianidi (ed.), *Trudy Margianskoj arkheologicheskoj ekspeditsii*, II. Staryj Sad, Moscow: 225–33.

**Jarrige, C.; Jarrige, J.-F.; Meadow, R. H. & Quivron, G.**

1995  *Mehrgarh Field Reports 1974–1985: From Neolithic Times to the Indus Civilization*. The Department of Culture and Tourism, Government of Sindh, Pakistan, in Collaboration with the French Ministry of Foreign Affairs, Karachi.

**Jarrige, J.-F.**

1991  'The Cultural Complex of Mehrgarh (Period VIII) and Sibri. The Quetta Hoard', in M. Jansen, M. Mulloy & G. Urban (eds), *Forgotten Cities on the Indus: Early Civilization in Pakistan from the 8th to the End of the 2nd Millennium BC*. Von Zabern, Mainz: 94–103.

**Jarrige, J.-F.; Didier, A. & Quivron, G.**

2011a  'Shahr-i Sokhta and the Chronology of the Indo-Iranian Regions', *Paléorient* 37/2: 7–34.

**Jarrige, J.-F.; Jarrige, C. & Quivron, G.**

2011b  *Nindowari (Pakistan): The Kulli Culture, its Origin and its Relations with the Indus Civilisation*. Ginkgo, Paris.

**Kakroodi, A. A.; Kroonenberg, S. B.; Hoogendoorn, R. M.; Mohammad Khani, H.; Yamani, M.; Ghassemi, M. R. & Lahijani, H.**

2012  'Rapid Holocene Sea-Level Changes along the Iranian Caspian Coast', *Quaternary International* 263: 93–103.

**Kaniuth, K.**

2007  'The Metallurgy of the Late Bronze Age Sapalli Culture (Southern Uzbekistan) and its Implications for the "Tin Question"', *Iranica Antiqua* 42: 23–40.

**Kavosh, H. A.; Vidale, M. & Fazeli Nashli, H.**

2019  *Prehistoric Sistan*, II: *Tappeh Graziani, Sistan, Iran: Stratigraphy, Formation Processes and Chronology of a Suburban Site of Shahr-i Sokhta* (Associazione internazionale di studi sul Mediterraneo e l'Oriente, Serie orientale Roma n.s. 18). Associazione internazionale di studi sul Mediterraneo e l'Oriente, Rome.

**Khlopin, I. N.**

1961 'Dashlidzhi-depe i eneoliticheskie zemledel'tsy Juzhnogo Turkmenistana' (Dashlidji-depe and Chalcolithic Agropastoral Societies in Southern Turkmenistan), in V. M. Masson (ed.), *Juzhnoturkmenistanskij tsentr rannezemledel'cheskikh kul'tur (v svete rabot Juzhno-Turkmenskoj Arkheologicheskoj Kompleksnoj Ekspeditsii 1955-1958 gg.)* (The Early South Turkmenian Centre of Agropastoral Culture in the Light of Work of the Complex Archaeological Southern Turkmenistan Expedition in 1955-1958) (Trudy Ju.T.A.K.E. 10). AN TSSR, Ashgabat: 134-224.

1981 'The Early Bronze Age Cemetery of Parkhai II: The First Two Seasons of Excavations: 1977-78'. *Soviet Anthropology and Archaeology* 19/1-2: 3-34.

**Kircho, L. B.**

1981 'The Problem of the Origin of the Early Bronze Age Culture of Southern Turkmenia', *Soviet Anthropology and Archaeology* 19/1-2: 96-106.

2009 'Основные направления и характер культурных взаимодействий населения Южного Туркменистана в V–III тыс. до н. э.' (Main Directions and the Character of the Cultural Interactions of Southern Turkmenistan in Fifth-Third Millennium BC), *Stratum plus: Археология и культурная антропология (Stratum plus: Archaeology and Cultural Anthropology)* 2009/2: 374-92.

2021 'The Rise of the Early Urban Civilization in Southwestern Central Asia: From the Middle Chalcolithic to the Middle Bronze Age in Southern Turkmenistan', in B. Lyonnet & N. A. Dubova (eds), *The World of the Oxus Civilization* (The Routledge Worlds). Routledge, New York: 110-42.

**Knox, J. R.; Thomas, K. D.; Khan, F. & Petrie, C. A.**

2010 'Small Finds from Sheri Khan Tarakai', in F. Khan, J. R. Knox, K. D. Thomas, C. A. Petrie & J. C. Morris (eds), *Sheri Khan Tarakai and Early Village Life in the Borderlands of North-West Pakistan* (Bannu Archaeological Project Surveys and Excavations 1985-2001). Oxbow, Oxford: 211-303.

**Kohl, P.**

2001 'Reflections on the Production of Chlorite at Tepe Yahya: 25 Years Later', in D. T. Potts & C. C. Lamberg-Karlovsky (eds), *Excavations at Tepe Yahya, Iran 1967-1975: The Third Millennium* (American School of Prehistoric Research Bulletin 45). Peabody Museum Harvard University, Cambridge, MA: 209-30.

2007 *The Making of Bronze Age Eurasia* (Cambridge World Archaeology). Cambridge University Press, Cambridge.

**Kraus, S.**

2021 'Archaeometallurgical Studies on BMAC Artifacts', in B. Lyonnet & N. A. Dubova (eds), *The World of the Oxus Civilization* (The Routledge Worlds). Routledge, New York: 779-98.

**Kuzmina, E. E.**

2007 *The Origin of the Indo-Iranians*. Brill, Leiden.

**Lamberg-Karlovsky, C. C.**

1978 'The Proto-Elamites on the Iranian Plateau', *Antiquity* 52: 114-20.

2002 'Archaeology and Language. The Indo-Iranians', *Current Anthropology* 43/1: 63-88.

**Lamberg-Karlovsky, C. C. & Tosi, M.**

1973 'Shahr-i Sokhta and Tepe Yahya: Tracks on the Earliest History of the Iranian Plateau', *East and West* 23/1-2: 21-58.

**Lauterbach, S.; Witt, R.; Plessen, B.; Dulski, P.; Prasad, S.; Mingram, J.; Gleixner, G.; Hettler-Riedel, S.; Stebich, M.; Schnetger, B.; Schwalb, A. & Schwarz, A.**

2014 'Climatic Imprint of the Mid-latitude Westerlies in the Central Tian Shan of Kyrgyzstan and Teleconnections to North Atlantic Climate Variability during the Last 6000 Years', *The Holocene* 24/8: 970-84.

**Law, R. W.**
2011 *Inter-regional Interaction and Urbanism in the Ancient Indus Valley: A Geologic Provenience Study of Harappa's Rock and Mineral Assemblage* (Occasional Paper 11 Linguistics, Archaeology and the Human Past, Indus Project, Research Institute for Humanity and Nature). Nakanishi, Kyoto.

**Lazzari, A. & Vidale, M.**
2017 'Shahr-i Sokhta: Early Discoveries and Explorations', in M. Vidale & A. Lazzari (eds), *Lapis Lazuli Bead Making at Shahr-i Sokhta: Interpreting Craft Production in a Urban Community of the 3rd Millennium BC* (Associazione internazionale di studi sul Mediterraneo e l'Oriente, Serie orientale Roma n.s. 6). Associazione internazionale di studi sul Mediterraneo e l'Oriente, Rome: 17–59.

**Ligabue, G. & Rossi Osmida, G.**
2007 *Sulla via delle oasi: Tesori dell'Oriente Antico*. Il Punto, Trebaseleghe.

**Ligabue, G. & Salvatori, S. (eds)**
1988 *Battriana: una antica civiltà delle oasi dalle sabbie dell'Afghanistan*. Erizzo, Venice.

**Lioubimtseva, E. & Henebry, G. M.**
2009 'Climate and Environmental Change in Arid Central Asia: Impacts, Vulnerability, and Adaptations', *Journal of Arid Environments* 73: 963–77.

**Luneau, É.**
2019 'Climate Change and the Rise and Fall of the Oxus Civilization in Southern Central Asia', in L. E. Yang, H.-R. Bork, X. Fang & S. Mischke (eds), *Socio-Environmental Dynamics along the Historical Silk Road*. Springer, Cham: 275–98 <https://doi.org/10.1007/978-3-030-00728-7_14>.

**Lyonnet, B.**
1981 'Établissements chalcolithiques dans le Nord-Est de l'Afghanistan: leurs rapports avec les civilisations du bassin de l'Indus', *Paléorient* 7/2: 57–74.
1996 *Sarazm (Tadjikistan) Céramiques (Chalcolithique et Bronze Ancien)* (Mémoires de la Mission Archéologique française en Asie Centrale 7). De Boccard Édition – Diffusion, Paris.
1997 *Prospections archéologiques de la Bactriane orientale (1974-78), sous la direction de J.-C. Gardin*, II: *Étude de la céramique, essai sur l'histoire du peuplement (du Chalcolithique à la conquête arabe)* (Mémoires de la Mission Archéologique française en Asie Centrale 8). De Boccard Édition – Diffusion, Paris.
2005 'Another Possible Interpretation of the Bactro-Margiana Culture (BMAC) of Central Asia: The Tin Trade', in C. Jarrige & V. Lefèvre (eds), *South Asian Archaeology 2001*. Éditions Recherche sur les Civilisations, Paris: 191–200.

**Lyonnet, B. & Dubova, N. A.**
2021 'Questioning the Oxus Civilization or Bactria-Margiana Archaeological Culture (BMAC): An Overview', in B. Lyonnet & N. A. Dubova (eds), *The World of the Oxus Civilization* (The Routledge Worlds). Routledge, New York: 7–65.

**Madella, M. & Fuller, D. Q.**
2005 'Palaeoecology and the Harappan Civilisation of South Asia: A Reconsideration', *Quaternary Science Reviews* 25/11–12: 1283–1301.

**Madjidzadeh, Y. & Pittman, H.**
2008 'Excavations at Konar Sandal in the Region of Jiroft in the Halil Basin: First Preliminary Report (2002–2008)', *Iran* 46: 69–103.

**Masson, V. M.**

1961 'Kara-depe u Artyka' (Kara-depe in Artyk), in V. M. Masson (ed.), *Juzhnoturkmenistanskij tsentr rannezemledel'cheskikh kul'tur (v svete rabot Juzhno-Turkmenskoj Arkheologicheskoj Kompleksnoj Ekspeditsii 1955-1958 gg.)* (The Early South Turkmenian Center of Agropastoral Culture in the Light of Work of the Complex Archaeological Southern Turkmenistan Expedition in 1955-1958) (Trudy Ju.T.A.K.E. 10). AN TSSR, Ashgabat: 319-463.

1988 *Altyn-Depe*. University Museum. University of Pennsylvania, Philadelphia.

**Masson, V. M. & Sarianidi, V. I.**

1972 *Central Asia: Turkmenia before the Achaemenids* (Ancient Peoples and Places 79). Praeger, New York.

**Mayewski, P. A.; Rohling, E. E.; Stager, J. C.; Karlén, W.; Maasch, K. A.; Meeker, L. D.; Meyerson, E. A.; Gasse, F.; Kreveld, S. van; Holmgren, K.; Lee-Thorp, J.; Rosqvist, G.; Rack, F.; Staubwasser, M.; Schneider, R. R. & Steig, E. J.**

2004 'Holocene Climate Variability', *Quaternary Research* 62/3: 243-55.

**Mayor, A.**

1994 'Durées de vie des céramiques africaines : facteurs responsables et implications archéologiques', in F. Audouze & D. Binder (eds), *Terre cuite et société: la céramique, document technique, économique, culturel* (Actes des XIVe rencontres internationales d'archéologie et d'histoire d'Antibes). Association pour la promotion et la diffusion des connaissances archéologiques, Juan-les-Pins: 179-98.

**Méry, S.**

2000 *Les céramiques d'Oman et l'Asie moyenne: une archéologie des échanges à l'Âge du Bronze* (Monographie du Centre de Recherches Archéologiques 23). Éditions du CNRS, Paris.

**Mughal, M. R. & Halim, M. A.**

1972 'Excavations at Sarai Khola: The Pottery', *Pakistan Archaeology* 8: 33-110.

**Muradov, R. G.**

2021 'The Architecture of the Bactria-Margiana Archaeological Culture', in B. Lyonnet & N. A. Dubova (eds), *The World of the Oxus Civilization* (The Routledge Worlds). Routledge, New York: 145-77.

**Musche, B. & Kröger, J.**

1993 'Crystal, Rock', *Encyclopaedia Iranica* 6/4: 436-41.

**Mutin, B.**

2012 'Interactions céramiques en Asie moyenne autour de 3000 av. J.-C. : quel(s) modèle(s) ?', in V. Lefèvre (ed.), *Orientalismes: de l'archéologie au musée; mélanges offerts à Jean-François Jarrige* (Indicopleustoi 9). Brepols, Turnhout: 263-78.

2013 *The Proto-Elamite Settlement and its Neighbors: Tepe Yahya Period IVC* (American School of Prehistoric Research Monograph Series, Harvard University). Oxbow, Oxford.

forthcoming 'La place des échanges interculturels dans la formation des civilisations anciennes des mondes iranien, centrasiatique et indien (VIIe – IIe millénaires av. n. è.)', *Comptes rendus des séances de l'Académie des Inscriptions et Belles-Lettres (CRAI)*.

**Mutin, B. & Francfort, H.-P.**

2019 'Bronze Age Relationships between Central Asia and the Indus: Archaeology, Language, and Genetics', *Marg-A Magazine of the Arts* 70/4: *Gandhara: A Confluence of Cultures*: 14-25.

**Mutin, B.; Garazhian, O. & Shakooie, M.**

2020b 'The Neolithic Regional Settlement of Darestan, Southern Lut Desert, Iran', *Archaeological Research in Asia* 24: 100230 <https://doi.org/10.1016/j.ara.2020.100230>.

**Mutin, B. & Lamberg-Karlovsky, C. C.**
2021 'The Relationship between the Oxus Civilization and the Indo-Iranian Borderlands', in B. Lyonnet & N. A. Dubova (eds), *The World of the Oxus Civilization* (The Routledge Worlds). Routledge, New York: 551–89.

**Mutin, B. & Minc, L.**
2019 'The Formative Phase of the Helmand Civilization, Iran and Afghanistan: New Data from Compositional Analysis of Ceramics from Shahr-i Sokhta, Iran', *Journal of Archaeological Science: Reports* 23: 881–99.

**Mutin, B.; Moradi, H.; Sarhaddi-Dadian, H.; Fazeli Nashli, H. & Soltani, M.**
2017 'New Discoveries in the Bampur Valley (Southeastern Iran) and their Implications for the Understanding of Settlement Pattern in the Indo-Iranian Borderlands during the Chalcolithic Period', *Iran* 55/1: 1–21.

**Mutin, B. & Razzokov, A.**
2014 (2016) 'Contacts across the Hindu Kush in the Bronze Age. Additional Insights from Sarazm – Soundings 11–11A (Tajikistan)', *Archäologische Mitteilungen aus Iran und Turan* 46: 123–47.

**Mutin, B.; Razzokov, A.; Besenval, R. & Francfort, H.-P.**
2016 'Resuming Tajik-French Fieldwork at Sarazm, Tajikistan. Preliminary Activity Report on the 2011–2012 Field-Seasons', in V. Lefèvre, A. Didier & B. Mutin (eds), *South Asian Archaeology and Art 2012*. Brepols, Turnhout: 197–210.

**Mutin, B.; Razzokov, A.; Brunet, F. & Francfort, H.-P.**
2020a '2011–2014 Fieldwork of the Tajik-French Project at Sarazm', in L. Rose Greaves & A. Hardy (eds), *South Asian Archaeology and Art 2016*, I. Dev, New Delhi: 21–34.

**Mutin, B.; Razzokov, A. & Razzokov, F.**
2022 'One Cylinder-Seal and Four Stamp-Seals(?): Review of the Evidence for "Administrative Practices" at the Proto-Urban Site of Sarazm, Tajikistan', in A. Parpola & P. Koskikallio (eds), *Corpus of Indus Seals and Inscriptions* (Annales Academiae Scientiarum Fennicae / Memoirs of the Archaeological Survey of India). Suomalainen Tiedeakatemia, Helsinki: lx–lxx.

**Narasimhan, V.; Patterson, N.; Moorjani, P.; Rohland, N.; Bernados, R.; Mallick, S.; Lazaridis, I.; Nakatsuka, N.; Olalde, I.; Lipson, M.; Kim, A. M.; Olivieri, L. M.; Coppa, A.; Vidale, M.; Mallory, J.; Moiseyev, V.; Kitov, E.; Monge, J.; Adamski, N.; Alex, N.; Broomandkhoshbacht, N.; Candilio, F.; Callan, K.; Cheronet, O.; Culleton, B. J.; Ferry, M.; Fernandes, D.; Freilich, S.; Gamarra, B.; Gaudio, D.; Hajdinjak, M; Harney, E.; Harper, T. K.; Keating, D.; Lawson, A. M.; Mah, M.; Mandl, K.; Michel, M.; Novak, M.; Oppenheimer, J.; Rai, N.; Sirak, K.; Slon, V.; Stewardson, K.; Zalzala, F.; Zhang, Z.; Akhatov, G.; Bagashev, A. N.; Bagnera, A.; Baitanayev, B.; Bendezu-Sarmiento, J.; Bissembaev, A. A.; Bonora, G. L.; Chargynov, T. T.; Chikisheva, T.; Dashkovskiy, P. K.; Derevianko, A.; Dobeš, M.; Douka, K.; Dubova, N.; Duisengali, M. N.; Enshin, D.; Epimakhov, A.; Fribus, A. V.; Fuller, D.; Goryachev, A.; Gromov, A.; Grushin, S. P.; Hanks, B.; Judd, M.; Kazizov, E.; Khokhlov, A.; Krygin, A. P.; Kupriyanova, E.; Kuznetsov, P.; Luiselli, D.; Maksudov, F.; Mamedov, A. M.; Mamirov, T. B.; Meiklejohn, C.; Merrett, D. C.; Micheli, R.; Mochalov, O.; Mustafokulov, S.; Nayak, A.; Pettener, D.; Potts, R.; Razhev, D.; Rykun, M.; Sarno, S.; Savenkova, T. M.; Sikhymbaeva, K.; Slepchenko, S. M.; Soltobaev, O. A.; Stepanova, N.; Svyatko, S.; Tabaldiev, K.; Teschler-Nicola, M.; Tishkin, A. A.; Tkachev, V. V.; Vasilyev, S.; Velemínský, P.; Voyakin, D.; Yermolayeva, A.; Zahir, M.; Zubkov, V. S.; Zubova, A.; Shinde, V. S.; Lalueza-Fox, C.; Meyer, M.; Anthony, D.; Boivin, N.; Thangaraj, K.; Kennett, D. J.; Frachetti, M.; Pinhasi, R. & Reich, D.**
2019 'The Formation of Human Populations in South and Central Asia', *Science* 365, eaat7487: 1–15.

**Olson, K.**
2020 'Models of Trade and Polity Formation in Bronze Age Northeastern Iran, ca. 3200–1600 BCE' (unpublished doctoral dissertation, University of Pennsylvania).

**Palumbi, G.**

2008 *The Red and Black: Social and Cultural Interaction between the Upper Euphrates and the Southern Caucasus Communities in the Fourth and Third Millennium BC* (Studi di Preistoria Orientale 2). Studi di Preistoria Orientale, Rome.

2016 'The Early Bronze Age of the Southern Caucasus'. *Oxford Handbooks Online* <https://doi.org/10.1093/oxfordhb/9780199935413.013.14>.

**Parzinger, H. & Boroffka, N. (eds)**

2003 *Das Zinn in der Bronzezeit in Mittelasien*, I: *Die siedlungsarchäologischen Forschungen im Umfeld der Zinnlagerstätten* (Archäologie in Iran und Turan 5). Von Zabern, Mainz.

**Petrie, C. A. (ed.)**

2013 *Ancient Iran and its Neighbours: Local Developments and Long-Range Interactions in the 4th Millennium BC* (The British Institute of Persian Studies Archaeological Monographs Series 3). Oxbow, Oxford: 253–75.

**Petrie, C. A. & Shaffer, J. G.**

2019 'The Development of a "Helmand Civilisation" South of the Hindu Kush', in W. Ball & N. Hammond (eds), *The Archaeology of Afghanistan: from Earliest Times to the Timurid Period*, 2nd edn. Edinburgh University Press, Edinburgh: 161–259.

**Petrie, C. A. & Weeks, L. R.**

2019 'The Iranian Plateau and the Indus River Basin', in E. Chiotis (ed.), *Climate Changes in the Holocene: Impacts and Human Adaptation*. CRC Press, Boca Raton: 293–325.

**Pigott, V. C.**

2021 'The Acquisition of Tin in Bronze Age Southwest Asia', in B. Lyonnet & N. A. Dubova (eds), *The World of the Oxus Civilization* (The Routledge Worlds). Routledge, New York: 827–61.

**Piperno, M. & Salvatori, S.**

2007 *The Shahr-i Sokhta Graveyard (Sistan, Iran)* (IsIAO Reports and Memoirs, n.s. 6). Istituto italiano per l'Africa e l'Oriente, Rome.

**Possehl, G. L.**

1996 'Meluhha', in J. E. Reade (ed.), *The Indian Ocean in Antiquity*. Kegan Paul, London: 133–208.

2002 *The Indus Civilization: A Contemporary Perspective*. AltaMira, Walnut Creek.

2007 'The Middle Asian Interaction Sphere. Trade and Contact in the 3rd Millennium BC', *Expedition* 49/1: 40–42.

**Pottier, M.-H.**

1984 *Matériel funéraire de la Bactriane méridionale de l'Âge du Bronze*. Éditions Recherche sur les Civilisations, Paris.

**Potts, D. T.**

2001 *Excavations at Tepe Yahya, Iran 1967–1975: The Third Millennium* (American School of Prehistoric Research Bulletin 45). Peabody Museum Harvard University, Cambridge, MA.

**Prickett, M. E.**

1986 'Man, Land and Ware: Settlement Distribution and the Development of Irrigation Agriculture in the Upper Rud-i Gushk Drainage, Southeastern-Iran' (unpublished doctoral dissertation, Harvard University, Cambridge, MA).

**Pumpelly, R. (ed.)**

1908 *Explorations in Turkestan: Expedition of 1904; Prehistoric Civilizations of Anau; Origins, Growth, and Influence of Environment*, II. Carnegie Institution of Washington, Washington, DC.

**Rante, R. & Mirzaakhmedov, J.**
2019 *The Oasis of Bukhara*, I: *Population, Depopulation and Settlement Evolution* (Arts and Archaeology of the Islamic World 12). Brill, Leiden.

**Ratnagar, S.**
2021 'Interaction between the Worlds of South Asia and Central Asia', in B. Lyonnet & N. A. Dubova (eds), *The World of the Oxus Civilization* (The Routledge Worlds). Routledge, New York: 590–606.

**Razzokov, A.**
2005 'Работа саразмското отряда в 2002 г', *Arkheologicheskie raboty v Tadzhikistane* 30: 77–85.
2008 *Sarazm*. Ezod, Douchanbe.

**Razzokov, A. & Kurbanov, W. F.**
2004 'исследования саразмского отряда в 2003 г', *Arkheologicheskie raboty v Tadzhikistane* 29: 174–92.

**Razzokov, F.**
2016 *Строительные комплексы древнеземледельческого поселения Саразм в IV–III тыс. до н. э.* (Building Complexes of the Ancient Agricultural Settlement of Sarazm in the IVth–IIIrd Millennia BC). Horizon, St Petersburg.

**Reade, J.**
2003 'The Great Death Pit at Ur', in J. Aruz & R. Wallenfels (eds), *Art of the First Cities: The Third Millennium B.C. from the Mediterranean to the Indus*. Metropolitan Museum of Art, New York: 120–32.

**Renaud, K. M.**
2019 'The Mineral Industry of Tajikistan', *Tajikistan: US Geological Survey 2015 Minerals Yearbook*: 45.1–45.7.

**Ricketts, R. D.; Johnson, T. C.; Brown, E. T.; Rasmussen, K. A. & Romanovsky, V. V.**
2001 'The Holocene Paleolimnology of Lake Issyk-Kul, Kyrgyzstan: Trace Element and Stable Isotope Composition of Ostracodes', *Palaeogeography, Palaeoclimatology, Palaeoecology* 176/1: 207–27.

**Rickmers, W. R.**
1913 *The Duab of Turkestan*. Cambridge University Press, Cambridge.

**Salvatori, S. & Tosi, M.**
2005 'Shahr-i Sokhta Revised Sequence', in C. Jarrige & V. Lefèvre (eds), *South Asian Archaeology 2001*. Éditions Recherche sur les Civilisations, Paris: 281–92.

**Salvatori, S. & Vidale, M.**
1997 *Shahr-i Sokhta 1975–1978: Central Quarters Excavations. Preliminary Report* (IsIAO Reports and Memoirs, Series minor 1). Istituto italiano per l'Africa e l'Oriente, Rome.

**Salvatori, S.; Vidale, M.; Guida, G. & Masioli, E.**
2009 'Ilgynly-depe (Turkmenistan) and the 4th Millennium BC Metallurgy of Central Asia', *Paléorient* 35/1: 47–67.

**Sarianidi, V. I.**
1961 'Eneoliticheskoe poselenie Geoksijur' (The Chalcolithic Settlement of Geoksyur Oasis), in V. M. Masson (ed.), *Juzhnoturkmenistanskij tsentr rannezemledel'cheskikh kul'tur (v svete rabot Juzhno-Turkmenskoj Arkheologicheskoj Kompleksnoj Ekspeditsii 1955–1958 gg.)* (The Early South Turkmenian Center of Agropastoral Culture in the Light of Work of the Complex Archaeological Southern Turkmenistan Expedition in 1955–1958) (Trudy Ju.T.A.K.E. 10). AN TSSR, Ashgabat: 225–318.
2007 *Necropolis of Gonur*. Kapon editions, Athens.

**Schmidt, E.**

1933 *Tepe Hissar: Excavations of 1931* (The Museum Journal 23/4). University of Pennsylvania Museum, Philadelphia.

1937 *Excavations at Tepe Hissar, Damghan*. University Museum, University of Pennsylvania, Philadelphia.

**Severtsov, N.**

1873 *Vertical and Horizontal Distribution of Turkestan Wildlife*. Moscow.

**Shaffer, J. G.**

1971 'Preliminary Field Report on Excavations at Said Qala Tepe', *Afghanistan* 24/2: 89-127.

1978 *Prehistoric Baluchistan*. B.R. Publishing, Delhi.

**Spengler, R. N. & Willcox, G.**

2013 'Archaeobotanical Results from Sarazm, Tajikistan, an Early Bronze Age Settlement on the Edge: Agriculture and Exchange', *Journal of Environmental Archaeology* 18/3: 211-21.

**Stacul, G.**

1969 'Excavation near Ghaligai (1968) and Chronological Sequence of Protohistorical Cultures in the Swat Valley', *East and West* 19/1-2: 44-91.

**Steinkeller, P.**

1982 'The Question of Marhaši. A Contribution to the Historical Geography of Iran in the Third Millennium B.C.', *Zeitschrift für Assyriologie* 72: 237-65.

2014 'Marhaši and Beyond: The Jiroft Civilization in a Historical Perspective', in C. C. Lamberg-Karlovsky & B. Genito (eds), *My Life Is Like the Summer Rose: Maurizio Tosi e l'Archeologia come Modo di Vivere; Papers in Honour of Maurizio Tosi for his 70th Birthday* (British Archaeological Reports, International Series 2690). Archaeopress, Oxford: 691-707.

**Stevens, L. R.; Ito, E.; Schwalb, A. & Wright, H. E. Jr.**

2006 'Timing of Atmospheric Precipitation in the Zagros Mountains Inferred from a Multi-proxy Record from Lake Mirabad, Iran', *Quaternary Research* 66: 494-500.

**Stevens, L. R.; Wright, H. E. & Ito, E.**

2001 'Proposed Changes in Seasonality of Climate during the Late Glacial and Holocene at Lake Zeribar, Iran', *The Holocene* 11/6: 747-55.

**Taylor, W. T. T.; Pruvost, M.; Posth, C.; Rendu, W.; Krajcarz, M. T.; Abdykanova, A.; Brancaleoni, G.; Spengler, R.; Hermes, T.; Schiavinato, S.; Hodgins, G.; Stahl, R.; Min, J.; Alisher kyzy, S.; Fedorowicz, S.; Orlando, L.; Douka, K.; Krivoshapkin, A.; Jeong, C.; Warinner, C. & Shnaider, S.**

2021 'Evidence for Early Dispersal of Domestic Sheep into Central Asia', *Nature Human Behaviour* 5: 1169-79.

**Tedesco, L.**

2006 'Refining the Definition of Technology in the Southern Zone of the Circumpontic Metallurgical Province: Copper Alloy in Armenia during the Early and the Middle Bronze Age', in D. Peterson, M. Popova & A. Smith (eds), *Beyond the Steppe and the Sown: Proceedings of the 2002 University of Chicago Conference on Eurasian Archaeology*. Brill, Leiden: 310-21.

**Thornton, C. P.**

2009 'The Chalcolithic and Early Bronze Age Metallurgy of the Tepe Hissar, Northeast Iran: A Challenge to the "Levantine Paradigm"' (unpublished doctoral dissertation, University of Pennsylvania).

2010 'The Rise of Arsenical Copper in Southeastern Iran', *Iranica Antiqua* 45: 31-50.

2012 'Iran', in D. T. Potts (ed.), *A Companion to the Archaeology of the Ancient Near East*, I. Blackwell, Chichester: 596-606.

## Tosi, M.

1968 'Excavations at Shahr-i Sokhta, a Chalcolithic Settlement in the Iranian Sistan. Preliminary Report on the First Campaign, October-December 1967', *East and West* 18/1/2: 9–66.

1969 'Excavations at Shahr-i Sokhta Preliminary Report on the Second Campaign, September-December 1968', *East and West* 19/3–4: 283–386.

1974a 'The Lapis lazuli Trade across the Iranian Plateau in the 3rd Millennium B.C.', in *Gururājamañjarikā: Studi in onore di Giuseppe Tucci*. Istituto Universitario Orientale, Naples: 3–22.

1974b 'The Problem of Turquoise in Protohistoric Trade on the Iranian Plateau', *Studi di paletnologia, maleonatropolotia, paleontologia e geologia del quaternario*, II. Memorie dell'Istituto italiano di Paleontologia Umana, Rome: 147–62.

## Tosi, M. & Vidale, M.

1990 '4th Millennium BC Lapis Lazuli Working at Mehrgarh, Pakistan', *Paléorient* 16/2: 89–99.

## Vahdati, A. A.; Biscione, R.; La Farina, R.; Mashkour, M.; Tengberg, M.; Fathi, H. & Azadeh Mohaseb, F.

2019 'Preliminary Report on the First Season of Excavations at Tepe Chalow New GKC (BMAC) Finds in the Plain of Jajarm, NE Iran', in J.-W. Meyer, E. Vila, M. Mashkour, M. Casanova & R. Vallet (dir.), *The Iranian Plateau during the Bronze Age: Development of Urbanisation, Production and Trade*. MOM Éditions, Lyon: 179–200.

## Vidale, M.

2000 *The Archaeology of Indus Crafts: Indus Craftspeople and Why We Study Them* (IsIAO Reports and Memoirs, Series minor 4). Istituto italiano per l'Africa e l'Oriente, Rome.

2017a 'New Interpretations', in M. Vidale & A. Lazzari (eds), *Lapis Lazuli Bead Making at Shahr-i Sokhta: Interpreting Craft Production in a Urban Community of the 3rd Millennium BC* (Associazione internazionale di studi sul Mediterraneo e l'Oriente, Serie orientale Roma n.s. 6). Associazione internazionale di studi sul Mediterraneo e l'Oriente, Rome: 303–21.

2017b *Treasures from the Oxus*. I.B. Tauris, London.

## Vidale, M. & Lazzari, A. (eds)

2017 *Lapis Lazuli Bead Making at Shahr-i Sokhta: Interpreting Craft Production in a Urban Community of the 3rd Millennium BC* (Associazione internazionale di studi sul Mediterraneo e l'Oriente, Serie orientale Roma n.s. 6). Associazione internazionale di studi sul Mediterraneo e l'Oriente, Rome.

## Vidale, M.; Vendemi, D. & Loliva, E.

2014 (2016) 'Uncertainty and Errors in the Painted Buff Ware of Shahr-e Sukhte (Sistan, Iran)', *Archäologische Mitteilungen aus Iran und Turan* 46: 71–94.

## Vinogradov, A. V.

1970 'O lokal'nyh variantah neoliticeskoj kul'tury Kyzylkumov', *Kratkiye Soobshcheniya Instituta Arkheologii* 122: 31–36.

1972a 'Birjuza, pervobytnaja moda, etnogenez...', *Sovetskaja Etnografija* 5: 120–30.

1972b 'Kyzylkumskoie juveliry', *Uspehi Srednaziatskoj Arheologii* 2: 43–45.

1973 'Pervobytnye juveliry', *Nauka i Zizn* 3: 132–34.

## Vinogradov, A. V.; Lopatin, S. V. & Mamedov, E. D.

1965 'Kyzylkumskaja Birjuka', *Sovcrtskaja Etnografija* 2: 114–34.

## Vinogradova, N. M.

2021 'The Formation of the Oxus Civilization/BMAC in Southwestern Tajikistan', in B. Lyonnet & N. A. Dubova (eds), *The World of the Oxus Civilization* (The Routledge Worlds). Routledge, New York: 635–64.

**Vinogradova, N. M. & Bobomulloev, S.**
2020 Могильник Фархор: Памятник эпохи ранней и средней бронзы в Юго-Западном Таджикистане (Farkhor Burial Ground: A Monument of the Early and Middle Bronze Age in Southwestern Tajikistan) (Institute of Oriental Studies RAS). Institute of History, Archeology and Ethnography, A. Donish Tajik Academy of Sciences, Dushanbe.

**Walker, M. J. C.; Berkelhammer, M.; Björck, S.; Cwynar, L. C.; Fisher, D. A.; Long, A. J.; Lowe, J.; Newnham, R.; Rasmussen, S. O. & Weiss, H.**
2012 'Formal Subdivision of the Holocene Series/Epoch: A Discussion Paper by a Working Group of INTIMATE (Integration of Ice-Core, Marine and Terrestrial Records) and the Subcommission on Quaternary Stratigraphy (International Commission on Stratigraphy)', *Journal of Quaternary Science* 27/7: 649–59.

**Weeks, L. R.**
2004 *Early Metallurgy of the Persian Gulf: Technology, Trade, and the Bronze Age World* (American School of Prehistoric Research Monograph Series 2). Brill, Leiden.
2012 'Metallurgy', in D. T. Potts (ed.), *A Companion to the Archaeology of the Ancient Near East*. Blackwell, Oxford: 295–316.
2013 'Iranian Metallurgy of the Fourth Millennium BC in its Wider Technological and Cultural Contexts', in C. A. Petrie (ed.), *Ancient Iran and its Neighbours: Local Developments and Long-Range Interactions in the Fourth Millennium BC* (British Institute of Persian Studies Archaeological Monographs Series 3). Oxbow, Oxford: 277–91.

**Wentworth, C. K.**
1922 'A Scale of Grade and Class Terms for Clastic Sediments', *The Journal of Geology* 30/5: 377–92.

**Wright, R. P.**
1984 'Technology, Style and Craft Specialization: Spheres of Interaction and Exchange in the Indo-Iranian Borderlands, Third Millennium B.C.' (unpublished doctoral dissertation, Harvard University).
1989 'New Tracks on Ancient Frontiers: Ceramic Technology on the Indo-Iranian Borderlands', in C. C. Lamberg-Karlovsky (ed.), *Archaeological Thought in America*. Cambridge University Press, Cambridge: 268–79.

**Wyart, J.; Bariand, P. & Filippi, J.**
1981 'Lapis Lazuli from Sar-i Sang, Badakhshan, Afghanistan', *Gems and Gemmology* 17/4: 184–90.

**Yang, L. E.; Bork, H.-R.; Fang, X.; Mischke, S.; Weinelt, M. & Wiesehöfer, J.**
2019 'On the Paleo-climatic/Environmental Impacts and Socio-Cultural System Resilience along the Historical Silk Road', in L. E. Yang, H.-R. Bork, X. Fang & S. Mischke (eds), *Socio-Environmental Dynamics along the Historical Silk Road*. Springer, Cham: 3–22.

# OXUS

## Studies in the Archaeology & History of Central Asia, from the Caspian Sea to Xinjiang and Altay

All volumes in this series are evaluated by an Editorial Board, strictly on academic grounds, based on reports prepared by referees who have been commissioned by virtue of their specialism in the appropriate field. The Board ensures that the screening is done independently and without conflicts of interest. The definitive texts supplied by authors are also subject to review by the Board before being approved for publication. Further, the volumes are copyedited to conform to the publisher's stylebook and to the best international academic standards in the field.